OXFORD WORLD'S CLASSICS

——

FREDERICK DOUGLASS

# Life and Times of Frederick Douglass

——

*Edited with an Introduction, Appendix Note, and Chronology by*
CELESTE-MARIE BERNIER

*Edited with Note on the Text and Explanatory Notes by*
ANDREW TAYLOR

OXFORD
UNIVERSITY PRESS

## OXFORD
UNIVERSITY PRESS

Great Clarendon Street, Oxford, ox2 6DP,
United Kingdom

Oxford University Press is a department of the University of Oxford.
It furthers the University's objective of excellence in research, scholarship,
and education by publishing worldwide. Oxford is a registered trade mark of
Oxford University Press in the UK and in certain other countries

Introduction and Chronology © Celeste-Marie Bernier 2022
Note on the Texts and Explanatory Notes © Andrew Taylor 2022

The moral rights of the authors have been asserted

First published as an Oxford World's Classics paperback 2022

Impression: 1

Published in the United States of America by Oxford University Press
198 Madison Avenue, New York, NY 10016, United States of America

British Library Cataloguing in Publication Data

Data available

Library of Congress Control Number: 2022931933

ISBN 978-0-19-883532-5

Printed and bound in the UK by
Clays Ltd, Elcograf S.p.A.

# ACKNOWLEDGEMENTS

CELESTE-MARIE BERNIER: This new edition of *Life and Times of Frederick Douglass Written By Himself* would not have been possible without the inspirational support and exceptional generosity provided by the following individuals: Janet Black, Eddie Chambers, Maya Davis, Hannah Durkin, Dr Walter O. and Linda Evans, Christopher Haley, Kim F. Hall and the Hall family, Carla Hepburn, Lubaina Himid CBE RA, Michelle Houston, Katherine Inglis, Hannah Jeffery, Earnestine L. Jenkins, Carole Jones, Isaac Julien CBE RA, Michelle Keown, Bill E. Lawson, Robert S. Levine, Esther Lezra, George Lipsitz, Katherine Lymer, Marion Macpherson, John R. McKivigan, Dorothy Miell, Hannah-Rose Murray, Emily Owen, Diana Paton, Sir Geoff Palmer OBE, Dora Petherbridge, Ernest Quarles, Alan Rice, Jeremy Robbins, Fionnghuala Sweeney, Jane Taube, Alex Thomson, Parisa Urquhart, Robert K. Wallace, Jonathan Wild, Lisa Williams, and Jen Wood. I would also like to express my heartfelt gratitude to my graduate students for inspiring me every day: Lana Ajlani, Sequoia Barnes, Nick Batho, Katherine Burns, Zöe Charlery, Amy Cools, Eliza Cottingham, Christopher Counihan, Kiefer Holland, Carolina Palacios Guerra, Kiefer Holland, Aija Oksman, and Paul Young. I am profoundly indebted to the U.K. Leverhulme Trust Major Research Fellowship which made the completion of the research and writing of this new edition possible.

In the months I was working on this edition, I was deeply inspired by wonderful conversations with Isaac Julien CBE RA, world-renowned filmmaker and installation artist, Kenneth B. Morris, Jr, Anna Murray and Frederick Douglass' world-renowned great-great-great-grandson and President of Frederick Douglass Family Initiatives, Charles Randolph-Wright, world-renowned film, television, and theatre director, television producer, screenwriter, and playwright, all treasured friends: our life-giving collaborations are all the 'heart and hope', as Mr Frederick Douglass used to say, that I need to carry on.

I would like to dedicate this edition to all the wonderful members of the Frederick Douglass Honor Society and to my dearest friends in Easton, Talbot County, Maryland: Bennie Black, Childlene Brooks, Harriette Lowery, Priscilla B. Morris, Tenny Sener, Vickie Wilson, and Brenda Wooden.

This edition is in loving memory of Eric Lowery (1948–2020), an inspirational social justice campaigner and my beautiful 'whole-souled' friend, and Catherine Mary Nash (1977–2019), a visionary scholar and my sister-friend. As Frederick Douglass writes, 'my heart is with you' always.

# CONTENTS

# INTRODUCTION

FIRST published in 1892, Frederick Douglass' final autobiography, *Life and Times of Frederick Douglass Written By Himself*, is a work of antislavery radicalism, a human rights manifesto, a call to revolutionary arms, a philosophical meditation, a visionary political blueprint, a personal testimony, a literary protest, and a revisionist work of U.S. history. Frederick Douglass summarizes his last literary work by informing his readers, 'It will be seen in these pages that I have lived several lives in one: first, the life of slavery; secondly, the life of a fugitive from slavery; thirdly, the life of comparative freedom; fourthly, the life of conflict and battle; and, fifthly, the life of victory, if not complete, at least assured' (p. 399).

In a bold departure from his pre-war autobiographies, *Narrative of the Life of Frederick Douglass, An American Slave* (1845) and *My Bondage and My Freedom* (1855), *Life and Times* is Douglass' final literary work in which he remembers all his lives as lived in the freedom struggle in one place for the first time. In these pages, he recalls how he fought against the mental annihilations, bodily atrocities, and psychological traumas he experienced during his 'life of slavery' in the U.S. South, and of how he subsequently warred against the 'inveterate prejudice against color' (p. 211) he experienced in the northern states. Dedicating his 'voice and pen' (p. 318) to protesting against this 'inveterate prejudice' that worked to destroy his activist labours as 'a fugitive slave' (p. 173), he remembers how he resisted by every means necessary in order to defeat the white racist persecutions plaguing his new 'life of comparative freedom'.

While Douglass endorsed celebratory language to reassure readers of *Life and Times* that he had finally reached the 'life of victory', his emotional confessions regarding the pain he experienced in witnessing the unending 'wrongs of my people' (p. 317) in their 'battle of life' lays bare his conviction that not only was it the case that it was 'not complete' and far from 'assured', but also that he and millions more were still living lives of suffering and struggle. As an experimental and uncompromising literary work in which he shares his own experiences in fighting for all freedoms across pre- and post U.S. Civil War eras, *Life and Times* is a poignant memorial to the traumatizing reality that the physical and pyschological traumas Douglass experienced in his life were matched only by those he endured in the fight to publish his life story.

Even though Douglass was a world-renowned author by the 1880s and 1890s, *Life and Times* is accompanied by a complex, difficult, and painful publishing history, as Douglass encountered the racist prejudices of white U.S. editors and publishers.

## *Frederick Douglass' Fight against the 'Spirit of Slavery'*

'This day [is] . . . the anniversary of my escape from bondage. Fifty-six years ago to-day, it was my good fortune to cease to be a slave, a chattel personal, and to become a man.' With these powerful words, Frederick Douglass begins 'The Blessings of Liberty and Education', a dedicatory address he delivered before an audience of formerly enslaved women, children, and men and their descendants at the Manassas Industrial School for Colored Youth on 3 September 1894, just two years after he published his final edition of *Life and Times* and only months before his death on 20 February 1895.[1]

A pioneering educational institution, the Industrial School for Colored Youth had just been established in Manassas, Virginia, by Jane Serepta Dean, an inspirational educator and radical reformer who had also been born into slavery. For Douglass, the anniversary of the date of his 'escape from bondage' is the date not only of his self-liberation from slavery but of the start of his new life as a freedom-fighter and a social justice campaigner. However, the 'free' northern states to which he fled were dominated by prejudice, and on his arrival, Douglass' experiences were harrowing: 'I then found myself in a strange land, unknown, friendless, and pursued as if I were a fugitive from justice.'[2]

For Douglass, the anniversary was a terrible reminder for himself, and for his listeners, of their personal experiences of physical and psychological violence, and of the violations, persecutions, tortures, atrocities, and traumas experienced by enslaved women, children, and men of all ages over the centuries. Douglass was only too aware that his and their fight for survival was far from over. While he and his listeners may have secured their legal emancipation from slavery by the passing of the Thirteenth Amendment in 1865, he understood all too clearly that the 'malignant' and 'dangerous' 'spirit of caste' (p. 455) lived on in the

---

[1] Frederick Douglass, 'Blessings of Liberty and Education', 3 September 1894, reprinted in John W. Blassingame and John R. McKivigan (eds), *The Frederick Douglass Papers Series One: Speeches, Debates, and Interviews: Volume 5: 1881–95* (New Haven: Yale University Press, 1992). Also accessible online at 'Teaching American History': https://teachingamericanhistory.org/library/document/blessings-of-liberty-and-education/

[2] Ibid.

'infernal and barbarous spirit of slavery' (p. 252).[3] As his final autobiographical work, *Life and Times* is a memorial to his own life of 'conflict and battle' and a hard-hitting protest against the 'spirit of slavery' which continued to exert its persecutory hold over the lives of all Black people suffering from, and waging war against, the atrocities committed by the white supremacist U.S. nation.

In the same year Douglass published his final edition of *Life and Times*, he wrote a powerful letter to a friend dated 4 November 1892. Here he confides his overwhelming despair: 'My heart is sad and sore over the Dreadful things that are being done against the former slaves.'[4] Whether he was campaigning in the 1830s as an activist, or in the 1890s as a world-renowned author, Douglass' radical and revolutionary voice was the first and foremost weapon in his arsenal. For Douglass, a lifetime of activism was a life-time of oratory and authorship. The beliefs, thoughts, philosophies, and reforms he endorsed in the 'cause of the oppressed' for 'more than fifty years of conflict' survive in the 'more than fifty years' of literary works he produced as a renowned orator, inspirational essayist, and powerful letter-writer.[5] Laying claim to a determination to 'speak' and write 'just the word that seemed to *me* the word to be spoken' (p. 190) and written '*by* me' (p. 190), Douglass endorsed a psychologically powerful use of the written word. Recognizing the very real dangers presented by the widespread tendencies toward national forgetting when it came to the centuries-long history of inhumane bondage, Douglass relies on emotionally hard-hitting language to concede, 'The time is at hand when the last American slave and the last American slaveholder will disappear behind the curtain which separates the living from the dead and when neither master nor slave will be left to tell the story of their respective relations or what happened to either in those relations.' In these powerful words, he summarizes his life's purpose: 'My part has been to tell the story of the slave' (p. 399).

Living and labouring as a 'fugitive from justice', Douglass authored his first and second autobiographies, *Narrative of the Life of Frederick Douglass, An American Slave* in 1845 and *My Bondage and My Freedom*

---

[3] The Thirteenth Amendment was passed by U.S. Congress on 31 January 1865, and stipulated, 'Neither slavery nor involuntary servitude, except as a punishment for crime whereof the party shall have been duly convicted, shall exist within the United States, or any place subject to their jurisdiction.' The full text is available online: https://www.archives.gov/historical-docs/13th-amendment

[4] Frederick Douglass to Clarissa O. Keeler, 4 November 1892, General Correspondence Frederick Douglass Papers, Manuscripts Division, Library of Congress, Washington, D.C.

[5] Douglass, 'Blessings of Liberty and Education', 3 September 1894.

in 1855.[6] Immediate bestsellers, Douglass' early personal narratives played a transformative role in the service of the radical abolitionist movement by inspiring antislavery reform among his northern audiences in their thousands. *Narrative of the Life of Frederick Douglass, an American Slave* was written while he was undertaking gruelling lecturing tours sharing his first-hand experiences of the 'hell of slavery'.[7] It is a work that was heavily indebted to the oratorical power, moral denunciation, and emotional pain of his speeches. Summarizing the personal and political purpose of his autobiography for his readers, he writes, 'You have seen how a man was made a slave; you shall see how a slave was made a man.'[8]

A detailed literary work four times longer than his first narrative, in *My Bondage and My Freedom* Douglass is no less dedicated to using his life story as a weapon in the fight for Black liberation. Ultimately working to share his experiences in 'bondage' rather than in 'freedom' in the era of intensified antislavery campaigning during the decade leading up to the Civil War, Douglass' 'Part I—Life as a Slave' dominates this literary work by occupying over three hundred pages as compared to the one hundred pages he relies on for 'Part II—Life as a Freeman'. A work of literary protest in which he condemns the villainy of white U.S. enslavers, *My Bondage and My Freedom* is also Douglass' declaration of independence from white antislavery supporters who sought to control his voice and script his language. He indignantly remembers his rejection of their patronizing and disrespectful advice by recalling he was advised, ' "Better have a little of the plantation manner of speech than not; 'tis not best that you seem too learned." ' All too aware that by 1855 he was an established literary author and world-renowned political authority in his own right, he confirms, 'I could not always obey, for I was now reading and thinking.' 'New views of the subject were presented to my mind,' he concedes, admitting, 'It did not entirely satisfy me to narrate wrongs; I felt like denouncing them.'[9] For Douglass, the act of narrating his personal experiences was not only indivisible from

[6] Frederick Douglass, *Narrative of the Life of Frederick Douglass, An American Slave*, 1845, ed. Celeste-Marie Bernier (Peterborough, ON: Broadview Press, 2018); Frederick Douglass, *My Bondage and My Freedom*, 1855, ed. Celeste-Marie Bernier (Oxford: Oxford University Press, 2019).

[7] Douglass, *Narrative*, 96.

[8] Ibid., 133. For detailed analysis of Douglass' experimentation with literary form in his first autobiography, see Bernier, 'Introduction', 11–70, in this same volume.

[9] Douglass, *My Bondage and My Freedom*, 248. For an investigation into Douglass' experimentation with literary form in his second autobiography, see Bernier, 'Introduction', ix–xl, in this same volume.

the art of denunciation but from his accomplishments as a literary author and philosopher of human rights.

In the closing decades of Douglass' life he again turned to the story of his personal experiences by writing *Life and Times of Frederick Douglass Written By Himself*. *Life and Times* is more than one work.[10] Douglass initially authored and published the first and second parts of this autobiography as early as 1881, over ten years before he decided to add a third part to the final edition he published in 1892. As his final literary work consisting first of over five hundred, and finally, of over seven-hundred-and-fifty pages, Douglass effortlessly demonstrates his literary prowess and learning across literature, politics, history, and philosophy. Writing and rewriting his life story on an epic scale one last time across the two editions of *Life and Times*, Douglass pushed the formal boundaries of autobiography to their limits in his determination to narrate his personal memories while communicating his human rights philosophy.

Warring against the 'spirit of slavery' in his all-encompassing and multi-genre editions of his final work, Douglass refuses to rely on the powerful narration of his personal memories in isolation. Instead, he combines his autobiographical narrative with his oratorically inspired denunciations, historical analyses, philosophical meditations, and political commentaries. For Douglass, his final retelling not only of his 'life and times' but of the 'life and times' of the U.S. nation is a moral catalyst for inspiring individual and collective social and political change among his audiences. Nearing the end of his life, Douglass' *Life and Times* is an uncompromising work of radical protest. Writing out of a heartfelt determination to place 'a truthful impression of my slave-life' (p. 114) on official record one last time, he returned to his life story to rouse the conscience of the country to a realization that, 'Though slavery was abolished, the wrongs of my people were not ended' (p. 317). An emotionally unequivocal and politically revolutionary work, *Life and Times* is a hard-hitting denunciation of white supremacist legislation and racist acts of lynch law, murder, discrimination, disenfranchisement, and persecution as perpetuated against millions of enslaved, self-liberated, and free people and their descendants across the centuries.

---

[10] For a detailed analysis of Douglass' experimentation with literary genre in *Life and Times*, see Celeste-Marie Bernier, ' "His Complete History?": Revisioning, Recreating and Reimagining Multiple Lives in Frederick Douglass's *Life and Times* (1881, 1892)', *Slavery and Abolition*, 33.4 (2012): 595–610.

While Douglass lived with the painful realization that it was already far too late for the 'enslaved and battered millions' who had 'come, suffered, died and gone with all their moral and physical wounds into eternity', he was motivated to write *Life and Times* as a radical political manifesto in which he issued the 'demands of justice' for the benefit and betterment of the generations that were still living and that were still to come.[11] A philosophical treatise in which he advocates equal human rights, he retells his 'life and times' one last time out of a 'more than fifty year' determination to strike one last blow for 'human progress' (p. 451).

A powerful weapon in the fight for Black liberation that was and is needed more than ever, Douglass' final autobiography lives on as a definitive, experimental, and self-reflexive literary work and as a revolutionary call to arms. Ultimately, *Life and Times* is a powerful vindication of Douglass' lifelong prediction that 'nothing of justice, liberty, or humanity can come to us except through tears and blood' (p. 292).

## *Frederick Douglass as Author, Historian, and Educator*

'I am 74 years of age, and I think I have arrived at an age when I have a right to retire from all official duties,' so Frederick Douglass informs readers of the newspaper, the *Boston Journal*, on 19 September 1891.[12] While he was determined to extricate himself from his many public responsibilities which included his tenure as U.S. Marshal and Recorder of Deeds for the District of Columbia (1877–81; 1881–86) and Minister Resident and Consul General to Haiti (1889–91), he continued to hold himself accountable to the 'cause of the oppressed' in which he had been engaged for 'more than fifty years of conflict'. 'I certainly shall continue to take an ardent interest in, and do my part in shaping current events,' he confirms, admitting, 'I am unwilling to be an idler.' Instead, he expresses his ongoing 'hope to exert whatever influence I may possess so long as my life lasts'.

An indefatigable labourer in the freedom struggle over the decades, the government positions Douglass held in his later years came towards the end of a life he dedicated to activism. At just twenty-seven years of

[11] Douglass, 'Blessings of Liberty and Education', 3 September 1894.

[12] Anon., 'Frederick Douglass The Aged Leader of His Race Retires from Public Life. He Will Write a History of His Times and His Part Therein', *Boston Journal*, 19 September 1891. This newspaper clipping is held in Box 28-5, Frederick Douglass Collection, Manuscript Division, Moorland-Spingarn-Research Center, Washington, D.C.

age, he had gained world-renown by undertaking an eighteen-month lecturing tour campaigning for the end of slavery in Scotland, Ireland, Wales, and England. On his return to the U.S.A., he began editing his abolitionist and social justice newspapers, *The North Star* (1847–51), *Frederick Douglass' Paper* (1851–60), and *Douglass' Monthly* (1858–63) in Rochester, New York. All three newspapers were dedicated to the dissemination of his human rights philosophy: 'Right is of no sex—truth is of no color—God is the father of us all, and all we are brethren.'[13] For over twenty years, he and every member of his family— Anna Murray Douglass, a free born woman and Douglass' wife of over forty-four years, and their children—Rosetta, Annie, Lewis Henry, Frederick Jr, and Charles Remond Douglass—worked tirelessly as conductors on the Underground Railroad: the clandestine system of safe houses and transportation networks which made it possible for thousands of women, men, and children escaping from the southern enslaving states to make it to liberty. Writing in *Life and Times*, he remembers his work was accompanied by life-threatening risks: 'I could take no step in it without exposing myself to fine and imprisonment, for these were the penalties imposed by the fugitive-slave law for feeding, harboring, or otherwise assisting a slave to escape from his master' (p. 230). All these dangers notwithstanding, he declares, 'I never did more congenial, attractive, fascinating, and satisfactory work', triumphantly noting, 'the thought that there was one less slave, and one more freeman—having myself been a slave, and a fugitive slave— brought to my heart unspeakable joy' (p. 178). During the Civil War, he acted as a recruiting agent for Black combat soldiers while his sons, Lewis Henry and Charles Remond Douglass, served in segregated combat regiments. In the post-war era that followed, he campaigned for the rights of 'my people' to all legal, social, and political freedoms. During these later years, he again returned to journalism. Now living in Washington, D.C., he and his sons edited the activist newspaper *New National Era* (1870–4). In his final decades, Douglass continued to deliver speeches and write essays, philosophical tracts, and letters in which he protested against white racist persecution, segregation, murder, and lynchlaw at the same time that he continued his fight for women's equal rights, temperance reform, and education for all.

[13] This slogan first appeared on the masthead for the inaugural 3 December 1847 issue of *The North Star*. Available online: https://tile.loc.gov/storage-services/service/sgp/ sgpbatches/batch_dlc_bluebell_ver02/data/sn84026365/00222418240/1847120301/ 0003.pdf

At the time of writing this article in the *Boston Journal*, Douglass recognized the morally transformative power of his personal and public life which had exerted, and continued to exert, a social, political, and national 'influence' on the freedom struggle by 'shaping current events' in U.S. society. He was also only too aware of the political importance and historical value of authoring a written record of his decades of unceasing labour in the service of 'liberty, justice' and 'humanity'. 'I have determined to devote my future to literary work and prepare for publication reminiscences of my long life in connection with the stirring events of my times and relations thereto,' he declares. 'I shall do this for I feel it as a duty I owe to my children and my grandchildren, so that they may see what their father and grandfather has done, and that I may leave it as a monumental record of my life,' Douglass summarizes.[14]

The major 'literary work' and 'monumental record of my life' Douglass is referring to here is *Life and Times*. For the first time, he authored his 'reminiscences' not as a 'fugitive from justice' but as a veteran of the war for abolition and of the many wars generated by the 'stirring events' in which he had participated in the ongoing fight for equal rights over the decades. As he informs his readers, he had played a leading role not only in the abolitionist struggle but in the 'demands for justice' that followed on from the legal emancipation of slavery and which he rightly predicted were still to come in this institution's terrible aftermath. Writing as a self-appointed witness, Douglass' *Life and Times* is the definitive, final, and 'monumental record' of his life as lived in slavery and as a human rights campaigner. A pioneering account not solely of his personal and political life but of the public life of the U.S. nation, *Life and Times* is a painful work of powerful protest. Here he gives the lie to all white political leaders' pretensions to moral superiority by exposing their nefarious attempts to sanitize or obliterate the legal, political, and personal 'cruel wrongs' the U.S. nation had committed against 'my down-trodden and long-enslaved fellow-countrymen' (p. 211) over the centuries.

Warring against past, present, and future acts of murderous criminality and torturous cruelty, Douglass summarizes his lifetime of activism in *Life and Times*: 'My cause first, midst, last, and always, whether in office or out of office, was and is that of the black man; not because he is black, but because he is a man, and a man subjected in this country to

[14] Anon., 'Frederick Douglass The Aged Leader of His Race Retires from Public Life.'

peculiar wrongs and hardships' (p. 439). A memorial to the 'peculiar wrongs and hardships' endured not only by Black men but by 'my people' of all genders and ages across all generations, *Life and Times* is Douglass' condemnation of the 'conflict between the spirit of liberty and the spirit of slavery' (p. 451): a 'conflict' that was not only still raging but gaining momentum in the 1880s and 1890s. On these grounds, *Life and Times* is Douglass' last literary will and testament. Called 'upon the witness stand' one last time to 'give evidence', he named and shamed the injustices endured by 'myself and my emancipated brothers and sisters who, though free, are yet oppressed' (p. 427). In these pages, he lays bare his lifelong conviction that the fight for social justice must never die.

Part one and the opening chapters of part two of *Life and Times* betray Douglass' very real indebtedness to the narrations of his life as lived in slavery and as a 'fugitive from slavery' which he included in *Narrative of the Life of Frederick Douglass, an American Slave* and *My Bondage and My Freedom.* Across all his autobiographies, Douglass relates his first-hand experiences as one of nearly a thousand women, children, and men enduring the 'living death' (p. 153) that was life as lived on a labour camp of enslaved people in Talbot County, Maryland.[15] Writing in all his published narratives, Douglass bears witness to the defining role played by his immediate and extended kinship groups in securing his spiritual, psychological, and physical survival. 'My first experience of life, as I now remember it, and I remember it but hazily, began in the family of my grandmother and grandfather, Betsey and Isaac Bailey' (p. 29), he writes. He informs his readers, 'Living thus with my grandmother, whose kindness and love stood in place of my mother's, it was some time before I knew myself to be a slave' (p. 32). As he narrates in *Life and Times*, these mutually supportive relation-ships were not only with members of his biological family—including his grandparents, Betsey and Isaac Bailey, his mother, Harriet Bailey, his aunts, sisters, and brother—but with members of his extended kin-ships groups. Enslaved women and men who were not related to Douglass assume centre-stage in his autobiography by becoming his family. For Douglass, his 'first experience of life' was defined not by

---

[15] As regards our use of terminology, we refer to 'slaveholders' as 'enslavers' and to 'plantations' as 'labour camps' as per the terminology endorsed by Edward E. Baptist in his pioneering work, *The Half Has Never Been Told: Slavery and the Making of American Capitalism* (Philadelphia, PA: Perseus Books, 2014), xxvi. See also Michael Todd Landis, 'These Are Words Scholars Should No Longer Use to Describe Slavery and the Civil War', *History News Network*, available online: https://historynewsnetwork.org/article/160266

a consciousness of his identity as an enslaved person but by the sense of belonging and well-being he gained from the 'kindness and love', as well as the advice, knowledge, experience, understanding, empathy, cultural practices, and belief systems, that were powerfully shared with him by people living within his wider enslaved community.

As a point of origin, Douglass' relationships with his immediate family and wider enslaved kinship communities were at a social, political, and moral premium that had only gained in urgency by the 1880s and 1890s. For Douglass, *Life and Times* is a memorial to the life-giving power not only of his relationships with his extended kinship groups in southern slavery but of the emotional bonds within his own family: the family he had made for himself living in the northern states. These family members not only include Anna Murray Douglass, his wife, and their children—but also their children's daughters and sons: the many pioneering women and men who were the Douglass 'grandchildren'.[16] According to Douglass' social justice vision, the intergenerational trauma of his family ancestors living in slavery was to provide the emotional and political foundations for the intergenerational liberation of his family descendants fighting for survival against the 'spirit of slavery' in the twentieth and twenty-first centuries.

Douglass' memory of one family member in particular, his mother, Harriet Bailey, remained a lifelong source of personal and political trauma and triumph. Living all her life in slavery, Harriet Bailey endured years of back-breaking labour on a labour camp many miles distant from her son before she died. Following her premature death which occurred while he was still only a young child, Douglass confides that his grandmother's 'kindness and love stood in place of my mother's' (p. 32). Despite Betsey Bailey's determination to fulfill the 'place' of her daughter for her grandson, Harriet Bailey's loss left Douglass emotionally bereft and grief-stricken. 'To me it has ever been a grief that I knew my mother so little, and have so few of her words treasured in my remembrance' (p. 38). And yet, Douglass' painful memory of his emotional devastation in the early loss of his mother remained indivisible from his empowering remembrance of her self-sacrificial strength. As he recalled, Harriet Bailey 'walked twelve miles to see me, and had the same distance to travel over again before the morning sunrise' (p. 37).

---

[16] See Celeste-Marie Bernier, *The Anna Murray and Frederick Douglass Family Papers Collection Volumes 1–5* (Edinburgh: Edinburgh University Press, 2023) and *The Anna Murray and Frederick Douglass Family Reader and Douglass Family Lives: The Biography* (Edinburgh and Durham: Edinburgh University Press and Duke University Press, 2023).

Harriet Bailey's visits to her son were not only powerful statements of her maternal love but hard-hitting testaments to her personal acts of defiance. As an enslaved woman who lived a life of sacrifice, trauma, and pain and who was to suffer a premature death due to years of abuse at the hands of white persecutory enslavers, Douglass's mother's decision to undertake these journeys was nothing less than a declaration of war against the 'practice of separating mothers from their children and hiring them out at distances too great to admit of their meeting, save at long intervals' (p. 30): an inhumane and nefarious 'practice' which her son himself later diagnosed as 'a marked feature of the cruelty and barbarity of the slave system' (p. 30). Harriet Bailey's acts of heroism in making these visits to her son succeeded in teaching him a powerful life lesson: 'I learned as I had never learned before, that I was not only a child, but somebody's child' (p. 37). Harriet Bailey gave her son the emotional and psychological strength, as well as the belief in his own sense of selfhood and personal identity, that he needed to survive the dehumanizing influences of a 'ruthless bondage' (p. 189).

Douglass was insistent about his mother's definitive role not only in influencing but in making his intellectual life of liberation, as realized through his later life of letters, possible. Across his autobiographies, he writes, 'she was the only one of all the colored people of Tuckahoe who could read' (p. 38). Anxious to secure his readers' full comprehension of his mother's unprecedented and unparalleled literary accomplishments, he explains: 'That in any slave State a field-hand should learn to read is remarkable, but the achievement of my mother, considering the place and circumstances, was very extraordinary' (p. 38). As Douglass realized only too well, it was his mother's 'remarkable' literary prowess, as born of her determination to defy attempts to eradicate all trace of an enslaved person's intellectual life, that made his own 'extraordinary' achievements possible. 'I am happy to attribute any love of letters I may have, not to my presumed Anglo-Saxon paternity, but to the native genius of my sable, unprotected, and uncultivated mother—a woman who belonged to a race whose mental endowments are still disparaged and despised' (p. 38), he proclaims.

For Douglass, Black female intellectual self-liberation was the immediate genealogy for Black male intellectual prowess. As Douglass' words resonated in the 1840s and 1850s so they continued to live on in the 1880s and 1890s. No longer writing to end legal slavery but to end white racist acts of torture, discrimination, and murder, Douglass understood the social justice power of his narration of an enslaved mother and son's literary achievements for a Black readership. His message was clear. If Harriet Bailey, an 'unprotected' enslaved 'field-hand', could 'learn to read', so could the children, women, and men living in a post-slavery era in which the right not only to all freedoms but to access to the 'blessings of liberty' and even a basic 'education' was far from over.

In *Life and Times*, Harriet Bailey assumes the powerful status of Douglass' first educator. While her son does not state that his mother taught him to read—such a feat would have been impossible during those early all-too-brief and all-too-rare visits—there can be no doubt of her determination, while he was sitting 'upon my mother's knee' (p. 37), to communicate to her son a 'love of letters' by insisting on the urgency of his taking the first opportunity to learn to read whenever and wherever he would find it. Douglass' actions as a young child confirm her influence as shown when he made the decision 'to ask' Sophia Auld, his white enslaver, 'to teach me to read' (p. 73). As Harriet Bailey, a 'field-hand', made the courageous decision to 'learn to read' in fear of persecution, so too did her son. Years later Douglass, a young adult living the same 'life of living death' as a 'field-hand', gained renown as 'the only slave in that region who could read or write' (p. 122). A villainous object of hatred for his white enslavers and an inspirational subject for emulation among his enslaved friends, supporters, and family members, he readily admits, 'although I was hated' by 'my master', 'I was loved by the colored people, because they thought I was hated for my knowledge, and persecuted because I was feared' (p. 122).

While he was still living on a labour camp of enslaved people in Talbot County, Maryland, Douglass' assumption of a scholarly distinction previously held only by his mother proves he was his mother's son; as does his determination to undertake the revolutionary work of intellectual liberation among his 'brother slaves' (p. 122). Beginning a new life of educational activism in his mother's footsteps against all odds, Douglass informs his readers of his determination not only to obtain but to share his 'love of letters' by confirming, 'I was not long in bringing around me twenty or thirty young men, who enrolled themselves gladly in my Sabbath-school, and were willing to meet me regularly under the trees or elsewhere, for the purpose of learning to read' (p. 134). A pioneering enslaved educator risking everything 'to exercise my gifts and to impart to my brother-slaves the little knowledge I possessed' (p. 134), he recalls, 'I had at one time more than forty pupils, all of the right sort' (p. 135). He is at pains to inform his readers that his 'persecuted pupils' (p. 135) took as many risks as he did by attending his school 'with a liability of having forty stripes laid on their naked backs' (p. 135). Douglass understood his work as a teacher as among his first

activist labours. As he confides to his readers, 'I felt a delight in circumventing the tyrants and in blessing the victims of their curses' (p. 136).

In the long history of his life as narrated in *Life and Times*, Douglass'
early labours as an enslaved educator were not only the precursor to, but the
bedrock for, his more than 'fifty years of conflict' as a self-liberated freedom-
fighter and human rights philosopher. Adding to his life as a teacher,
Douglass confides that it was during this time, 'I here began my public
speaking' (p. 139). Lecturing his 'brother slaves' on 'the subject of slavery'
(p. 139), he 'dashed against it the condemning brand of God's eternal justice' (p. 139). Dedicating his early life to imparting the 'little knowledge' he
'possessed', Frederick Augustus Washington Bailey laid the foundations for
his lifetime of activism as Frederick Douglass. In so doing, he joined his
mother, Harriet Bailey, as an intellectual inspiration not only for their
immediate descendants but for generations of freedom-fighters working
within the centuries-long Black revolutionary and radical tradition.

For past, present, and future activists campaigning within the intergenerational Black liberation movement, the 'love of letters' of this
unknown enslaved mother and her world-renowned son survives as
a catalyst to their acts of resistance. As Douglass urged all his life,
'Education . . . means emancipation.'[17]

## The Civil War and Black Combat Heroism

Writing *Life and Times* against the backdrop of the late-nineteenth-
century fight for political and historical ownership of the national memory
of the Civil War, Frederick Douglass narrates the previously untold story
of his recruitment of Black combat soldiers for the Union army. Inspired
by a determination to rewrite the U.S. nation's wilfully inaccurate and
wholly erroneous depiction of the Civil War as a 'white man's war' (p. 288),
Douglass memorializes the distinguished military records of Black combat soldiers which had been obliterated from the official records.

Seminal among the many protest speeches Douglass wrote during
these years is the oration he decided to reprint in *Life and Times*, an
address he delivered in 1871, at the monument to the 'Unknown Loyal
Dead', a memorial erected on the sacred ground of Arlington National
Cemetery, Virginia.[18] Standing before this stone memorial less than

[17] Douglass, 'Blessings of Liberty and Education', 3 September, 1894.
[18] Widely recognized today as the Tomb of the Civil War Unknowns, the 'bones of two
thousand one hundred and eleven unknown soldiers' were interred in this monument.
See the 'Arlington National Cemetery' website: https://www.arlingtoncemetery.mil/
Explore/Monuments-and-Memorials/Civil-War-Unknowns

a decade after the Civil War, Douglass confronted the injustices that were then being generated by white national acts of forgetting and the deliberate perpetuation of the wrong kind of national memories. 'We are sometimes asked, in the name of patriotism, to forget the merits of this fearful struggle, and to remember with equal admiration those who struck at the nation's life and those who struck to save it, those who fought for slavery and those who fought for liberty and justice' (p. 346), he observes. While he expressed the profoundest respect for the lives of the 'unknown dead' of both armies, including the lives lost by those who 'fought for slavery' by declaring, 'I would not strike the fallen', he voices his powerful indignation by urging, 'may my "right hand forget her cunning and my tongue cleave to the roof of my mouth," if I forget the difference between the parties to that terrible, protracted, and bloody conflict' (p. 347).

According to Douglass' social justice philosophy, there was a moral, political, and, above all, human rights distinction between the white southern Confederate combatants who 'struck at the nation's life' and the Black and white Union soldiers who 'struck to save it' (p. 346). He urged there was no question that, 'if now we have a united country, no longer cursed by the hell-black system of human bondage', then 'we are indebted to the unselfish devotion of the noble army who rest in these honored graves all around us' (p. 347). Laying bare his determination only to remember the service records of soldiers who 'fought for liberty and justice', he cautioned his listeners, 'we are not here to applaud manly courage, save as it has been displayed in a noble cause' (p. 347). For Douglass writing decades later in *Life and Times*, no more powerful vindication of Civil War military heroism in the service of a 'noble cause' was to be found than in the 'manly courage' displayed, not only by the Union armed forces in general, but by their Black combat regiments, in particular: trailblazing 'fighting units' of Black soldiers who sacrificed their lives and who were the U.S. nation's heroic and 'loyal' but still 'unknown dead'.

As a national conflict predated by many smaller disturbances, the U.S. Civil War officially began on 12 April 1861. Eleven southern states protested the presidential election of Abraham Lincoln that had taken place only months earlier by seceding in order to found their own Confederate States of America. A bloody, terrible, and tragic conflict in which over 10,000 military engagements and battles took place and over 750,000 people lost their lives, the Civil War lasted until 9 April 1865.[19]

[19] For further information, see James M. McPherson, *Battle Cry of Freedom: The Civil War Era* (New York: Penguin, 1990).

While there are many ongoing conflicting positions on the causes of the secession, for the vast majority of historians, including Frederick Douglass, there can be no question that the primary cause of the war was the Southern states' desire to preserve the institution of slavery.[20] Douglass was in no doubt that a fight over the 'institution of slavery' was the sole purpose of the war. Writing for the benefit of the historical record and the education of his readers in *Life and Times*, he recalls, 'From the first, I, for one, saw in this war the end of slavery' (p. 284). Careful to interpret any understanding of the Civil War as a war for the end of slavery from the point of view of enslaved people, he further summarizes that the 'mission of the war was the liberation of the slave, as well as the salvation of the Union' (p. 285).

The government initially sought to deny Black men the right to bear arms in the Civil War. Such discriminatory actions were immediately protested by thousands of social justice campaigners who petitioned the government for the Black man's right to enlist in the Union armed forces as a combat soldier: foremost among these radical activists was Frederick Douglass. As he remembers, 'I reproached the North that they fought the rebels with only one hand, when they might strike effectually with two—that they fought with their soft white hand, while they kept their black iron hand chained and helpless behind them' (p. 285). Here and elsewhere, he and thousands of Black campaigners endorsed the commitment and dedication of Black men over and above that of white men who had always enjoyed their legal freedoms. Two years of ignoring these campaigns for the Black man's right to fight and finally, Douglass writes, by 1863, Abraham Lincoln's government decided that the Union army would now fight by issuing the order to 'raise two colored regiments, the 54th and 55th' (p. 287): all Black combat units that would represent the state of Massachusetts. Douglass immediately shouldered the burden of recruiting thousands of Black men to fill these regiments which were to gain widespread fame for their heroism.

Tirelessly travelling to towns and cities across the northern states, Douglass repeatedly delivered his powerful appeal, 'Men of Color, To Arms!' to audiences in their thousands. 'Better even die free, than to live slaves,' he counsels. Douglass inspired Black men to enlist by issuing the following plea: 'I urge you to fly to arms, and smite with death the power that would bury the government and your liberty in the same

---

[20] John Pierce, 'The Reasons for Secession', *American Battlefield Trust*, available online: https://www.battlefields.org/learn/articles/reasons-secession

hopeless grave' (p. 288). He implored Black men to fight as the sole means by which they would be able to take a leading role, not only in guaranteeing 'the end of slavery', but in protecting their families and their descendants, securing their rights to equal citizenship, and proving their military prowess as trained combat soldiers.

Writing decades later in *Life and Times*, Douglass appointed himself as the accurate memorialist and official historian of the Civil War as a war 'fought for liberty and justice' by deciding to place 'on record' his conviction that the 'raising of these two regiments—the 54th and 55th—and their splendid behavior in South and North Carolina, was the beginning of great things for the colored people of the whole country' (p. 289). At the heart of his exaltation, and in the pride he took in 'contemplating my humble part in raising them', was the 'fact that my two sons, Charles and Lewis, were the first two in the State of New York to enlist in them' (p. 289). While Anna Murray and Frederick Douglass' eldest and youngest sons, Lewis Henry and Charles Remond Douglass, served distinguished military careers as combat soldiers in both of these 'Massachusetts regiments', their middle son, Frederick Douglass Jr, laboured tirelessly in the war effort by 'recruiting colored troops in the Mississippi valley' (p. 295).[21]

In *Life and Times*, Douglass draws attention to the exceptional heroism displayed by Black soldiers of one combat unit in particular: the 54th Massachusetts regiment. As he writes, the 54th 'was not long in the field before it proved itself gallant and strong', and as 'worthy to rank with the most courageous of its white companions in arms' (p. 289). Writing of the regiment's leading participation in the 'assault upon Fort Wagner' (p. 289), a military engagement which took place between northern Union armed forces and the southern Confederate army at Morris Island, South Carolina, on 18 July 1863, Douglass did not have to rely on second-hand testimony. His harrowing description that the regiment 'was so fearfully cut to pieces, and lost nearly half its officers' (p. 289), was heavily indebted to the eye-witness accounts provided by one of the key participants in the conflict: his eldest son, 'Sergeant Major' Lewis Henry Douglass.

Writing a letter from the frontlines on 18 July, the day of the battle, Lewis Henry informed Anna Murray and Frederick Douglass that 'we

[21] For a detailed history of the Douglass sons' military experiences, see Celeste-Marie Bernier and Andrew Taylor, *If I Survive: Frederick Douglass's Family in the Walter O. Evans Collection* (Edinburgh: Edinburgh University Press, 2018).

made the most desperate charge of the war on Fort Wagner'.[22] Sharing his father's awareness regarding the political power of his regiment's heroism, Lewis Henry Douglass celebrates his own and his unit's courage by not only narrating his own death-defying valour, 'I had my sword sheath blown away while on the parapet of the fort', but by relying on graphic language to summarize the 54th's exceptional military prowess: 'Our men fought like tigers, one sergeant killing five men by shooting and bayonetting.' In his refusal to sanitize or censor the atrocities of warfare for either his parents or the wider public—he undoubtedly knew his father would decide to publish his letter in his newspaper, *Douglass' Monthly*—he lends powerful weight to his regiment's exceptionalism by reporting, 'The grape and canister shell and Minnie swept us down like chaff, still our men went on and on.' He is in no doubt that it is his regiment's self-sacrificial courage that secures their military successes. He takes very real pride in the fact that 'The rebels were held in check by our front men long enough to allow the 10th Connecticut to escape being surrounded and captured.' He jubilantly informs his parents that the 54th immediately 'received the highest praise from all parties who knew of it' with the result that their heroism 'earned us our reputation as a fighting regiment'.[23]

As Lewis Henry Douglass, let alone his father and mother, was all too powerfully aware, the 54th's 'reputation' as a 'fighting regiment' came at a terrible cost: 'Our loss in killed wounded and missing was 300.' He shares the very real devastation in the loss of life experienced by his regiment by confiding, 'The splendid Fifty Fourth is cut to pieces, all of our officers with the exception of eight are either killed or wounded.'[24] Douglass' decision to repeat his son's phrase decades later in *Life and Times* by writing that the regiment 'was so fearfully cut to pieces, and lost nearly half its officers', testifies to his painful realization regarding these men's sacrifices in this terrible war for the 'end of slavery'.

This father and son's story of Black military victory as the 'beginning of great things for the colored people of the whole country' was far

[22] Lewis Henry Douglass to Frederick and Anna Murray Douglass, Morris Island, South Carolina, 20 July [1863]. Frederick Douglass Papers, General Correspondence, Manuscript Division, Library of Congress, Washington, D.C. Lewis Henry Douglass' letter was also published in the August 1863 edition of his father's newspaper, *Douglass' Monthly*, edited and printed in Rochester, New York.

[23] Ibid. For further information on the combat heroism of the 54th Massachusetts regiment in this and other battles, see Luis F. Emilio, *A Brave Black Regiment: History of the 54th Massachusetts, 1863–1865* (Boston: Da Capo Press, 1995).

[24] Lewis Henry Douglass to Frederick and Anna Murray Douglass, Morris Island, South Carolina, 20 July [1863].

from the whole story regarding the treatment of Black combat troops by the U.S. armed forces during the Civil War, however. In *Life and Times*, Douglass records that he was soon forced to abandon his recruitment labours not long after the 'assault on Fort Wagner' due to the discriminatory 'attitude of the government at Washington' which 'caused me deep sadness and discouragement' (p. 290). The earliest cause of Douglass' 'deep sadness' undoubtedly came from the testimony provided by his son. In this same letter in which he had informed his parents of the 54th's exceptional reputation as a 'fighting unit', Lewis Henry Douglass was also candid regarding the difficulties and dangers they unnecessarily faced due to the racist actions, not of the enemy, but of white regiments within the Union army. He is careful to explain to his parents that 'if we had been properly supported we would have held the fort. But the white troops could not be ~~driven~~ made to come up, the consequence is we had to fall back dodging shells and other missiles.'[25] The 54th was 'cut to pieces' and forced 'to fall back' as a result not only of enemy fire but of white persecutory practices within their own armed forces. There can be no question that Lewis Henry Douglass' exposure of these white troops' discriminatory actions, which unnecessarily put the lives of an entire Black combat regiment at risk, weighed heavily in Douglass' decision to 'suspend my efforts in that direction' (p. 290).

In *Life and Times*, Douglass reprints the official letter of protest he wrote the U.S. government on 1 August 1863, less than two weeks after he received his son's letter. Lewis Henry Douglass' words are fresh in his mind as he holds the government to account by singling out the injustices experienced by the 54th in the 'assault on Fort Wagner'. In expressing his anger, he condemns an unforgivable injustice: 'No word is said when brave black men, according to the testimony of both friend and foe, fought like heroes to plant the star-spangled banner on the blazing parapets of Fort Wagner and in so doing were captured, mutilated, killed, and sold into slavery' (p. 291). Douglass gives full vent to his despair regarding the nation's failure to protect Black soldiers by rhetorically questioning, 'How many 54ths must be cut to pieces, its mutilated prisoners killed, and its living sold into slavery, to be tortured to death by inches, before Mr. Lincoln shall say, "Hold, enough!"'' (p. 292).

Douglass informs his readers that his letter generated a response from the U.S. government in which officials offered him reassurances that they were 'already taking measures which will secure the captured colored soldiers at Charleston and elsewhere the same protection

[25] Ibid.

against slavery and cruelty that is extended to white soldiers' (p. 292). Too little too late, Douglass interpreted these 'measures' as fundamental human rights acts which 'ought to have been done at the beginning' (p. 292). Laid bare in the government's outright betrayal and wilful disrespect of Black men's lives is incontestable evidence of Douglass' terrible realization that 'The poor colored soldiers have purchased interference dearly' (p. 292).

A 'monumental record' to the unending 'conflict between the spirit of liberty and the spirit of slavery', Douglass' call for 'justice', 'liberty', and 'humanity' in *Life and Times* lives on as a call to arms for all past, present, and future freedom-fighters working within the centuries-long Black revolutionary tradition of radical activism.

## *The Publishing History of* Life and Times

Across both 1881 and 1892 editions, *Life and Times* is burdened by an emotionally challenging and practically difficult relationship between author and publisher. The fact that Douglass was a world-renowned writer had no influence whatsoever on his white U.S. editors who repeatedly disregarded and disrespected his wishes. As his surviving correspondence reveals, he had to fight for his rights at each and every stage of the publication process of both editions of his final autobiography.

On 7 April 1881, Douglass signed a contract with Thomas Belknap and Sylvester M. Betts, the white publishers of the Park Publishing Company located at Hartford, Connecticut. According to the official terms of their legal agreement, Douglass promised 'to write a history of his life' that would be published in a 'book' of '480 to 500 pages', with 'each page to contain on an average about four hundred words'. In return, Belknap and Betts agreed 'to publish said book on good white paper' with 'each book to contain a steel portrait of the author'.[26] Despite the absence of any controversial clauses, only months later and the publishers had already broken the terms of their agreement. They committed a series of actions that violated the terms of the contract and evidenced the very real difficulties that were not only facing Douglass, but were experienced by all Black authors, in his and their ongoing fight to defend their authorial rights and exert their editorial power.

---

[26] See Frederick Douglass, 'Contracts', Financial Papers, Frederick Douglass Papers, Manuscripts Division, Library of Congress, Washington, D.C.

At the heart of Douglass' disapproval of the Park Publishing Company's actions was their decision to commission interior illustrations for inclusion in the book without his knowledge and consent. Just months after signing the contract, on 30 October 1881, Douglass writes Betts a letter in which he feels compelled to restate the terms on which they had both signed in order to lend weight to his critique. 'I beg to remind you', he states, 'that in the contract made with me, for the publication of the book, you say nothing about illustrations.' Having reminded Betts of the original terms of their agreement, he gives full vent to his fury by bitterly protesting, 'This contract does not permit you to load the book with all manner of coarse and shocking wood cuts, such as may be found in the news papers of the day.'

Writing in powerful protest against their violation of their contractual obligations and against their direct and personal attack on his authorial agency, in this same letter Douglass candidly informs Betts, 'If the wood cuts had been submitted to my approval, and I had given it, I should have been stopped from objecting as I now do, but you have gone outside the contract, taken the matter in your own hands, and, I hold, have marred and spoiled my work entirely.' He refuses to concede any ground by not only declaring, 'I am not more reconciled than ever to the publication of my life with the illustrations', but by making a demand: 'I ask and insist, as I have a right to do, that an edition of the book shall be published without illustrations, for Northern circulation.' Anticipating that his demands will be ignored, Douglass threatens Parks Publishing Company with legal action. Issuing an ultimatum, he decides to withhold all further content until this issue is resolved.[27] For Douglass, these 'coarse and shocking wood cuts' in which he, as well as Black women, children, and men living in enslaved communities, are portrayed as dehumanized caricatures are nothing less than a moral abomination. As he understood only too well, the images were the persecutory work of white racism and nothing less than a barbaric act of atrocity purposefully committed against the 'cause of the oppressed'. While the archive is silent regarding whether Douglass received any response from the Park Publishing Company, evidence of their lack of respect or understanding is provided in the emotionally despondent letter Douglass writes Betts over two months later. On 28 January 1882,

[27] Frederick Douglass to Sylvester M. Betts, Washington, D.C., 30 October 1881, General Correspondence, Frederick Douglass Papers, Manuscripts Division, Library of Congress, Washington, D.C.

he had no choice but to admit defeat by confiding, 'I have given up all opposition to the illustrations and am silent about typographical errors and submit to the caracature [*sic*] of my own face.'[28]

While Douglass was denied any agency over the production of *Life and Times*, he exerted full control over the preface he commissioned to accompany both editions. As early as 26 May 1881, he wrote George Lewis Ruffin, a man who had been born free in the southern states in 1834, and who went on to become a renowned lawyer, judge, and social justice campaigner living in the north, with a personal invitation.[29] 'I am going to ask you a favor which will carry our names into History together,' he explains to Ruffin in a letter in which he exalts in his 'talents' which 'eminently fit you for the work I am about to ask you to undertake for me'. Confiding to Ruffin that he was 'writing a volume of the Life and Times of Frederick Douglass—including all my experiences in slavery, my efforts for the freedom and elevation of my people and the vast and wonderful changes through which I have passed embracing my toils and triumphs', he informs him that 'the Publishers tell me that ten pages of the Book should be· occupied with an Introduction'.

Douglass readily admitted that his autobiography needed an introduction but he refused to comply with his publishers' demand that he 'prepare it' himself. Instead, he decided to have it 'done by hands other than mine' in recognition of his conviction that 'I cannot speak of my own career as another can'. For Douglass, this is where Ruffin came in. 'I want you to introduce my story,' he states. He exerts all his powers of persuasion by adding, 'The Life and Times of Frederick Douglass With an Introduction By George L. Ruffin Esq. will look well in print.' Not taking any risks, Douglass expresses his absolute confidence in Ruffin's abilities by stating, 'you will know how to do it if you undertake the work', only to refuse to leave his choice of thematic focus to chance. 'Much of the present work will of course be devoted to my slave life—but I mean to bring my career down through the storms and vicissitudes of the last six and twenty years,' he summarizes immediately prior to offering his suggestion—and one which Ruffin would

---

[28] Frederick Douglass to Sylvester M. Betts, Washington, D.C., 28 January 1882, General Correspondence, Frederick Douglass Papers, Manuscripts Division, Library of Congress, Washington D.C.

[29] For detailed information on Ruffin's life, see J. Clay Smith Jr, 'In Freedom's Birthplace: The Making of George Lewis Ruffin, The First Black Law Graduate of Harvard University', *Howard Law Journal*, 39.1 (1995): 218–29.

have undoubtedly read as a stipulation—that 'An introduction should contrast my former life with the present'.[30]

On 1 June 1881, Ruffin writes Douglass to confirm his acceptance. While he admits, 'I know you might have done better', he confirms, 'I do not feel to decline the service' because 'you in your judgment have made this choice'.[31] Far more than a literary commission, Ruffin understood his role in writing the preface to a work authored by Douglass, an inspirational author who held world-renowned status as 'our most celebrated colored man' (p. 25), as an act of social justice 'service'. Recognizing Douglass as the pre-eminent freedom-fighter Ruffin himself applauded for his 'disposition to carry on the fight for us', he expresses his gratitude in being 'called upon to offer my testimony in a great public matter', and for the 'opportunity' to 'give my full assistance to our cause'.[32] Ruffin's interpretation of the activist importance of his preface as 'testimony' and as a 'service' to 'our cause' vindicates Douglass' faith in his ideal suitability 'for the work'. Ruffin understood all too well that the political power and radical purpose of *Life and Times* derived from its status not solely as a 'monumental' philosophical meditation and epic literary work but as an official record of Douglass' repeated exposure to 'storms and vicissitudes' in his unceasing 'efforts for the freedom and elevation of my people'. Over a month later, on 14 July 1881, Douglass wrote Ruffin, 'You have made me very happy by your willingness to undertake this work of friendship', expressing his belief, 'I have no doubt that the work will be done and well done.'[33]

Self-consciously transforming Douglass from a mortal man into a mythic exemplar and an awe-inspiring hero in his introduction, Ruffin commands his readers' deepest admiration and adulation for his unparalleled life's work as a freedom-fighter, orator, author, intellectual, philosopher, statesman, political leader, and family man. According to Ruffin, these are all accolades which would be exceptional and unprecedented by any measure but which are nothing short of

---

[30] Frederick Douglass to George Lewis Ruffin, 26 May 1881, George Lewis Ruffin, Manuscript Division, Moorland-Spingarn-Research Center, Washington, D.C.

[31] George Lewis Ruffin to Frederick Douglass, 1 June, 1881, General Correspondence, Frederick Douglass Papers, Manuscripts Division, Library of Congress, Washington D.C.

[32] George Lewis Ruffin to Frederick Douglass, 24 May 1881; George Lewis Ruffin to Frederick Douglass, 1 June 1881, General Correspondence, Frederick Douglass Papers, Manuscripts Division, Library of Congress, Washington, D.C.

[33] Frederick Douglass to George Lewis Ruffin, 14 July 1881, George Lewis Ruffin Papers, Manuscript Division, Moorland-Spingarn-Research Center, Washington, D.C.

miraculous when it is remembered that they were achieved by Douglass as an individual whose life was lived under the traumatizing conditions of 'chattel slavery' and the heartbreaking context of 'American prejudice'. In no doubt that 'the life and work of Douglass has been a complete vindication of the colored people' (p. 24), Ruffin's preface exalts in Douglass' power not as a fallible individual but as an immortal icon and an inspirational role model for present and future generations of Black political leaders, activists, authors, and intellectuals. 'I bid my fellow countrymen take new hope and courage' (p. 25), he writes as he concludes with a powerful prediction that 'The near future will bring us other men of worth and genius, and our list of illustrious names will become lengthened' (p. 25). For Ruffin, as for all authors and activists working in the Black liberation movements in the U.S.A. and across the African diaspora, *Life and Times* lives on as the 'monumental record' of a 'man of worth and genius' (p. 25) who fought all his life 'to carry on the fight for us'.[34]

In comparison to his bestselling autobiographies, *Narrative of the Life and Times of Frederick Douglass, An American Slave* and *My Bondage and My Freedom*, *Life and Times* was a financial disappointment. On 19 July 1882, the Park Publishing Company wrote Douglass to inform him of the low sales figures of their second printing of *Life and Times*: 'Your book does not sell quite as well as we expected.'[35] Disheartening sales figures are also the fate of the 1892 and 1895 editions printed by De Wolfe and Fiske Company. On 26 March 1895, over a month following Douglass' death, they write Helen Pitts Douglass, Douglass' second wife, now widow, a white activist-author, 'We must confess that we were very much disappointed after the publication of the book that no more copies were sold.' 'We sent out a number of editorial copies and the book received some very flattering notices,' they confirm only to admit they were to no avail as 'the sale has up to this time been a very great disappointment to us'.[36]

[34] George Lewis Ruffin to Frederick Douglass, 24 May 1881; George Lewis Ruffin to Frederick Douglass, 1 June 1881, General Correspondence, Frederick Douglass Papers, Manuscripts Division, Library of Congress, Washington, D.C.

[35] Park Publishing Company to Frederick Douglass, 19 July 1892, General Correspondence, Frederick Douglass Papers, Manuscripts Division, Library of Congress, Washington, D.C.

[36] De Wolfe and Fiske Company to Helen Pitts Douglass, 26 March 1895, General Correspondence, Frederick Douglass Papers, Manuscripts Division, Library of Congress, Washington, D.C.

The reviews for the book were few and far between with the exception of the vitally important notices of the book published in world-leading African American newspapers and periodicals. Among the rare references to Douglass' volume is the anonymous review which appeared on 1 June 1882, in the pages of *The Christian Recorder*, a newspaper published in Philadelphia by the African Methodist Episcopal Church. As Ruffin eulogized Douglass as 'our most celebrated colored man' with a 'reputation established on both sides of the Atlantic', so this unnamed writer, on reading his 'life and times', was inspired to declare, 'no Scotch Douglass had haughtier steel in him than this Douglass of America'.[37] This author's decision to foreground Douglass' exceptionalism by making a comparison between his unparalleled heroism and the unrivalled military prowess of white Scottish-born war commander Sir James Douglas was deeply indebted to Douglass' own belief systems. As a man who had taken Sir James Douglas' surname as his own and who laboured decades earlier in the 1840s as 'Scotland's Antislavery Agent', Douglass as a young man went so far as to threaten one of his former white U.S. racist persecutors by asserting, 'If I should meet you now, amid the free hills of old Scotland, where the ancient "black Douglas" once met his foes', and 'were you to attempt to make a slave of me, it is possible you might find me almost as disagreeable a subject, as was the Douglas to whom I just referred.'[38]

Over a decade later, on 10 February 1893, and only months after the first publication of Douglass' final edition at the end of 1892, another anonymous review appeared in the Black press: this time in *The Plaindealer*, a pioneering newspaper published in Detroit, Michigan. In an article titled, 'Frederick Douglass: One of the Most Remarkable Of All Living Men—A Nice Tribute', the unnamed author provides a powerful endorsement of *Life and Times* by issuing a recommendation that 'The Autobiography of the Honorable Frederick Douglass should be in the home of every Afro-American in this country'.[39] For

[37] Anon., 'n.t.', *Christian Recorder*, 1 June 1882. Rpt. in 'Reader Responses: 1881–93', in John R. McKivigan (ed.), *The Frederick Douglass Papers: Series Two: Autobiographical Writings:* Volume 3: *Life and Times of Frederick Douglass Book 2. The Text and Editorial Apparatus* (New Haven: Yale University Press, 2012), 1062.

[38] Frederick Douglass, qtd. in Alisdair Pettinger, 'Douglass, Burns and Scott', available online: https://www.bulldozia.com/douglass-in-scotland/douglass-burns-and-scott/

[39] Anon., 'Frederick Douglass. One of the Most Remarkable Of All Living Men—A Nice Tribute', *Plaindealer*, 10 February 1893. Rpt. in 'Reader Responses: 1881–93', in McKivigan (ed.), *The Frederick Douglass Papers: Series Two: Autobiographical Writings:* Volume 3: *Life and Times of Frederick Douglass Book 2*, 1063.

this unnamed writer, as it was for Ruffin and the unidentified reviewer in *The Christian Recorder*, Douglass' 'life and times' was essential reading for all Black families as a source of inspiration, pride, and emulation.

All too aware of the social justice importance of Douglass' final autobiography as *the* 'life and times' of 'one of the most remarkable of all living men', the publishers of *The Plaindealer* had secured a special rate for their readers. ' "The Plaindealer" is enabled to offer this great work in connection with the paper for the price of the book alone,' they proudly declare, instructing their readers that 'To any one sending us $2.50 cash we will forward them *The Plaindealer* one year and a copy of this excellent race book'.[40] As per *The Plaindealer*'s self-proclaimed status as 'a representative weekly newspaper in the interest of the colored race', so Douglass held the unrivalled position as the 'representative' leader labouring 'in the interest of the colored race'.[41] On these grounds, their decision to encourage yearly subscriptions to their newspaper by selling Douglass' book as an added inducement worked to unite his 'life and times' with the 'life and times' of new generations of African American liberators: all fighting for their rights and relying on *The Plaindealer*, as they had relied on Douglass himself, as the 'medium through which to voice the sentiments of the race'.[42]

## Frederick Douglass as Witness, Memorialist, and Advocate

'When the war for the Union was substantially ended, and peace had dawned upon the land' and 'when the gigantic system of American slavery which had defied the march of time and resisted all the appeals and arguments of the abolitionists and the humane testimonies of good men of every generation during two hundred and fifty years, was finally abolished' (p. 314), Frederick Douglass underwent a painful period of personal doubt and uncertainty. Living in the immediate aftermath of the end of the Civil War and following the legal abolition of slavery, he experienced an emotional and existential crisis. He was initially at a loss to decide his future vocation by believing, 'I had reached the end of the noblest and best part of my life' (p. 314). He initially erroneously assumed that 'The anti-slavery platform had performed its work, and my voice was no longer needed' (p. 314). Ever the powerful accuser and

---

[40] Ibid.

[41] See the advertisement for *The Plaindealer* included in anon., *Geo. P. Rowell & Co.'s American Newspaper Directory*, Sixteenth Annual Edition (New York: Geo. P. Rowell & Co., 1884), 793.

[42] Ibid.

incisive diagnostician of the nation's sins, however, he did not hold onto his misplaced hope for long. Almost immediately, he realized the terrible mistake he had made.[43]

A 'monument' to his many lives as a freedom-fighter living in pre- and post-war eras, Douglass' *Life and Times* is the powerful protest vehicle by which he denounces the morally unforgivable 'decision of the United States Supreme Court' in 'declaring the Civil Rights law of 1875, unconstitutional' (p. 449). Here he placed 'on record' the hard-hitting words he delivered at a protest meeting held in Washington, D.C. Among his many searing denunciations of U.S. immorality, injustice, and hypocrisy that he delivered in this address, he proclaimed, 'When a deed is done for slavery, caste and oppression, and a blow is struck at human progress, whether so intended or not, the heart of humanity sickens in sorrow and writhes in pain' (p. 451). He voices his painful emotions: 'It makes us feel as if some one were stamping upon the graves of our mothers' (p. 451). For Douglass, and the millions of 'my people' who had been born to enslaved mothers, there was no greater violence than that committed against the memories and experiences of generations of Black women who had lived lives of sacrifice, struggle, and suffering. All too aware that the 'conflict between the spirit of liberty and the spirit of slavery' was gaining rather than losing momentum in the white supremacist acts of prejudicial legislation, national discrimination, and political disenfranchisement that were being inflicted upon 'my people', Douglass soon realized that the emotional and political power of 'my voice' was 'needed' now more than ever.

As one among untold numbers of present and future generations of Black freedom-fighters, Douglass understood, 'Though slavery was abolished, the wrongs of my people were not ended.' Recognizing that the 'conflict between the spirit of slavery and the spirit of liberty' continued to exert an unforgivable stranglehold over the political and moral life of the U.S. nation, Douglass relied on the emotional power and social justice force of his revolutionary voice to expose the 'wrongs of my people' who had been cruelly emancipated with 'nothing left' with 'which to fight the battle of life, but a slavery-distorted and diseased body and lame and twisted limbs' (p. 318). To the day he died, Douglass relied on the undying power of his voice to condemn the sins of a white U.S. nation that had legally mandated and spiritually defended not only the 'hell-black system of human

[43] Douglass, *My Bondage and My Freedom*, 314.

bondage' but the 'spirit of slavery' that left millions of Black women, children, and men burdened by every form of bodily, psychological, spiritual, and emotional trauma. No more powerful confirmation of Douglass' poignant realization that his life's work was to remain unfinished at his death can be found than in his declaration, 'Forty years of my life have been given to the cause of my people, and if I had forty years more they should all be sacredly given to the same great cause' (p. 400).

In the conclusion to the 1892 edition of *Life and Times* Douglass confides, 'Time and events have summoned me to stand forth both as a witness and an advocate for a people long dumb, not allowed to speak for themselves, yet much misunderstood and deeply wronged' (p. 426). Dedicating his life's work to his self-appointed role as an author-witness-advocate, Douglass ultimately measured the value of his final autobiography, not according to its experimental literary power which it all too self-evidently and incontestably possessed, but as per its social justice value as an educational tract, an anti-racist manifesto, an accurate history, and a work of political consciousness-raising for the benefit of the lives of his Black audiences. Living all his life as a defender and a labourer, no less than as an advocate and a witness, working to right the wrongs of the tragedies and traumas experienced by millions of enslaved people, Douglass readily understood, 'by voice and pen, in season and out of season, it was mine to stand for the free-dom of people of all colors, until in our land the last yoke was broken and the last bondsman was set free' (p. 429). Ultimately, *Life and Times* is Douglass' vehicle for his conviction that a life of authorship is a life of activism.

Working tirelessly to end all inequalities at the close of the nine-teenth century, Douglass concludes *Life and Times* with a powerful appeal. He purposefully calls upon all his readers to draw their atten-tion to the founding history of the United States as a nation 'based upon human brotherhood and the self-evident truths of liberty and equality' (p. 549). He issues clear and direct instructions by command-ing them to 'apply these sublime and glorious truths to the situation now before you' and to 'put away your race prejudice' (p. 549). According to his egalitarian philosophy, it is only when the country is 'based upon the eternal principles of truth, justice and humanity, and with no class having any cause of complaint or grievance', that 'your Republic will stand and flourish forever' (p. 549). No less powerfully, in one of his final speeches he delivers a year later in 1893, Douglass summarizes, 'there is no negro problem. The problem is whether the American people have loyalty enough, honor enough, patriotism enough, to live up to their own constitution.'[44]

For Frederick Douglass, a self-liberated freedom-fighter, philosopher, intellectual, educator, and activist author of thousands of writings and speeches, there was only ever one subject to which he dedicated his entire life: 'the subject of human rights' (p. 139).

[44] Rpt., 'Appendix I: Frederick Douglass's Speech at Colored American Day', in Christopher Robert Reed, *"All The World Is Here!" The Black Presence at White City* (Bloomington: Indiana University Press, 2000), 194.

# NOTE ON THE TEXT

THE most detailed account of the textual history of *Life and Times of Frederick Douglass* is to be found in the 'Textual Afterword: A Critical Edition of *Life and Times of Frederick Douglass*' authored by Joseph R. McElrath Jr and Jesse S. Crisler and published in John R. McKivigan (ed.), *Series Two: Autobiographical Writings*, Volume 3: *Life and Times of Frederick Douglass* (New Haven: Yale University Press, 2012). Readers are advised to consult this resource. We offer a summary of the key stages of the book's publication here and in the Introduction to this edition.

*Life and Times* was first published as a two-part volume in 1881. Douglass signed an agreement with the Park Publishing Company of Hartford, Connecticut, in April of that year to write what would be his third autobiographical narrative. By October Douglass had delivered a manuscript significantly longer than the 480–500 pages stipulated in his contract. His white U.S. editor, Sylvester Betts, wrote in October 1881 asking for more manuscript material, so that the book could grow to 518 pages. Douglass duly obliged, sending Betts a copy of his April 1876 speech commemorating the unveiling of the Freedmen's Monument to Abraham Lincoln, as well as a newspaper article containing his September 1881 eulogy of President James Garfield and a copy of his August 1880 speech commemorating West Indian Emancipation. While Betts wrote to Douglass suggesting ways in which this additional material could be integrated into the volume so as to avoid an awkward abruptness, in the end the additional material appears at the end of the 1881 volume, after chapter 18, with the inclusion of a short 'Conclusion' mid-way through chapter 19 followed by a lengthy appendix. The effect is to disrupt the chronology of the book with material that might have been integrated more successfully into the body of the narrative.

Upon receipt of an advance copy of his book, and as discussed in detail in the Introduction to this edition, Douglass wrote to Betts in January 1882 protesting about the 'coarse and shocking' illustrations, the plates for which Betts had made without Douglass' approval. Douglass asked for them to be removed, to no avail. The first U.S. edition of *Life and Times* had been deposited at the Library of Congress for copyright on 23 November 1881. Douglass' dissatisfaction with the quality of this edition was evidently made clear to the publisher, who financed the resetting of the type and the production of new plates for the second American edition, which appeared in three printings, in 1882, 1883, and 1884. The English edition of *Life and Times* appeared in 1882.

The version of *Life and Times* that we choose to publish here is the expanded second U.S. edition, which was deposited at the Library of Congress for copyright in December 1892 but appears with the date 1893 on its title page. The Boston publishers De Wolfe and Fiske Company bought the plates of the second U.S. edition, complete with the 'coarse and shocking' illustrations and the additional material requested by Betts. In addition, Douglass provided thirteen new chapters, updating his life story, which were added as a 'Third Part' after the appendix of the 1882 edition. Numerous revisions and corrections were made to the First and Second parts, largely focusing on tidying punctuation and enhancing sentence structure, whether by Douglass or another hand it is impossible to say: these amendments were carefully summarized by the editors of the Yale edition. There were three printings of this expanded edition, in 1892, 1895, and a third, undated printing.

Our decision to use the 1892 expanded edition is based, in part, on the fact that it is the last published during Douglass' lifetime, and with the inclusion of the Third Part it brings his story up to date. The substantial revisions made to the text of the 1882 edition are also indicative of his commitment to producing a final testimony of his life. As per the detailed analysis in the Introduction, we have made the decision to omit the illustrations that appeared in both the 1881 and 1892 editions of *Life and Times*, in deepest respect for Douglass' heartfelt protest and moral condemnation of these 'coarse and shocking' white racist grotesque and caricatured illustrations. Every effort has been made to contact the rightsholders and obtain permission to reproduce the archival material. Information regarding any amendments that should be included in future editions of this book would be very gratefully received. Throughout the manuscript, obvious spelling mistakes as well as typesetting and typographical errors in the original volume have been silently corrected.

Douglass first delivered his powerful address 'The Lessons of the Hour' on 9 January 1894 at the African Metropolitan Episcopal Church in Washington, D.C. Later the same year, he arranged for the publication of his speech as a pamphlet in Baltimore by the publisher, Thomas & Evans.

# SELECT BIBLIOGRAPHY

*Selected Writings by Frederick Douglass*

Blassingame, John W., and John R. McKivigan (eds), *The Frederick Douglass Papers: Series one, Speeches, Debates, and Interviews*. 5 vols (New Haven: Yale University Press, 1979–92).

Douglass, Frederick, *Frederick Douglass Collection*, Manuscript Division (Moorland-Spingarn Research Center: Washington, D.C.). Finding Aid Available online: https://dh.howard.edu/finaid:manu/61/

Douglass, Frederick, *Frederick Douglass Papers*, Manuscript Division (Library of Congress: Washington, D.C.). Digital Collections available online: https://www.loc.gov/collections/frederick-douglass-papers/

Douglass, Frederick, *Frederick Douglass' Lif och Samtid*. Trans. *Carl Stenholm* (Stockholm: N. J. Schedins Forlag, 1895).

Douglass, Frederick, *Life and Times of Frederick Douglass, Written By Himself* (Hartford; Park Publishing, 1881, 1882).

Douglass, Frederick, *Life and Times of Frederick Douglass, Written By Himself* (Boston: De Wolfe & Fiske Co., 1892, 1895).

Douglass, Frederick, *Life and Times of Frederick Douglass*, ed. Rayford W. Logan (New York: Collier Books, 1973).

Douglass, Frederick, *Life and Times of Frederick Douglass: Centenary Memorial Subscribers' Edition*. Foreword by Alain Locke (New York: Pathway Press, 1941).

Douglass, Frederick, *Life and Times of Frederick Douglass: The Illustrated Edition*, ed. Henry Louis Gates, Jr (Minneapolis: Zenith Press, 2015).

Douglass, Frederick, *The Life and Times of Frederick Douglass, From 1817 to 1882, Written By Himself. Illustrated. With an Introduction By The Right Hon. John Bright, M.P.*, ed. John Lobb (London: Christian Age Office, 1882).

Douglass, Frederick, *Mes Années D'esclavage Et De Liberté Par Frédérik Douglass Marshal De Colombie (D'Apres L'Anglais)*. Trans. Catherine Valérie Boissier Gasparin (Paris, France: E. Plon et cie, 1883).

Douglass, Frederick, *My Bondage and My Freedom*, ed. Celeste-Marie Bernier (Oxford: Oxford University Press, 2019).

Douglass, Frederick, *Narrative of the Life of Frederick Douglass, An American Slave*, ed. Celeste-Marie Bernier (Peterborough, Ontario: Broadview Press, 2018).

Douglass, Frederick, *Series Two: Autobiographical Writings*, Volume 3: *Life and Times of Frederick Douglass*, ed. John R. McKivigan, 2 vols (New Haven: Yale University Press, 2012).

Douglass, Frederick, *Walter O. Evans Collection of Frederick Douglass and Douglass Family Papers*. Beinecke Rare Book and Manuscript Library, Yale University, New Haven, C.T. Digitized online: https://beinecke.library.

yale.edu/collections/highlights/walter-o-evans-collection-frederick-douglass-and-douglass-family-papers

Foner, Philip S. (ed.), *The Life and Writings of Frederick Douglass*, 5 vols (New York: International Publishers, 1950–75).

McKivigan, John R. (ed.), *The Frederick Douglass Papers: Series Three: Correspondence*, Volume 1: *1842–1852* (New Haven: Yale University Press, 2009).

McKivigan, John R. (ed.), *The Frederick Douglass Papers: Series Three: Correspondence*, Volume 2: *1853–1865* (New Haven: Yale University Press, 2018).

Murray, Hannah-Rose, and John R. McKivigan (eds), *Frederick Douglass in Britain and Ireland, 1845–1895* (Edinburgh: Edinburgh University Press, 2021).

Stauffer, John, and Henry Louis Gates, Jr (eds), *The Portable Frederick Douglass* (New York: Penguin Classics, 2016).

## Biography

Barnes, L. Diane (ed.), *Frederick Douglass: A Life in Documents* (Charlottesville: University of Virginia Press, 2013).

Bernier, Celeste-Marie, *The Anna Murray and Frederick Douglass Family Papers Collection Volume 1 Anna Murray Douglass and Rosetta Douglass Sprague* (Edinburgh: Edinburgh University Press, 2023).

Bernier, Celeste-Marie, *The Anna Murray and Frederick Douglass Family Papers Collection Volume 2 Lewis Henry Douglass* (Edinburgh: Edinburgh University Press, 2023).

Bernier, Celeste-Marie, *The Anna Murray and Frederick Douglass Family Papers Collection Volume 3 Frederick Douglass, Jr.* (Edinburgh: Edinburgh University Press, 2023).

Bernier, Celeste-Marie, *The Anna Murray and Frederick Douglass Family Papers Collection Volume 4 Charles Remond Douglass* (Edinburgh: Edinburgh University Press, 2023).

Bernier, Celeste-Marie, *The Anna Murray and Frederick Douglass Family Papers Collection Volume 5 Annie Douglass and the Douglass Grandchildren* (Edinburgh: Edinburgh University Press, 2023).

Bernier, Celeste-Marie, *The Anna Murray and Frederick Douglass Family Reader* (Edinburgh and Durham: Edinburgh University Press and Duke University Press, 2023).

Bernier, Celeste-Marie, *Douglass Family Lives: The Biography* (Edinburgh and Durham: Edinburgh University Press and Duke University Press, 2023).

Bernier, Celeste-Marie, and Andrew Taylor, *If I Survive: Frederick Douglass's Family in the Walter O. Evans Collection* (Edinburgh: Edinburgh University Press, 2018).

Blight, David, *Frederick Douglass: Prophet of Freedom* (New York: Simon and Schuster, 2018).

Douglas, Joseph L., Jr, *Frederick Douglass: A Family Biography 1733–1936* (Shelbyville: Winterlight Books, 2011).

Fought, Leigh, *Women in the World of Frederick Douglass* (Oxford: Oxford University Press, 2017).

Gregory, James M., *Frederick Douglass, the Orator* (Springfield: Willey Co., 1907).

Holland, Frederic May, *Frederick Douglass: The Colored Orator* (New York: Funk & Wagnalls Company, 1895).

McFeely, William S., *Frederick Douglass* (New York: Norton, 1991).

Martin, Waldo E., Jr, *The Mind of Frederick Douglass* (Chapel Hill: University of North Carolina Press, 1984).

Muller, John, *Frederick Douglass in Washington D.C.: The Lion of Anacostia* (Charleston: The History Press, 2012).

O'Keefe, Rose, *Frederick and Anna Douglass in Rochester, New York* (Charleston: The History Press, 2013).

Preston, Dickson J., *Young Frederick Douglass: The Maryland Years* (Baltimore: Johns Hopkins University Press, 1980).

Quarles, Benjamin, *Frederick Douglass* (Englewood-Cliffs, NJ: Prentice-Hall, 1968).

### Critical Studies, Essays and Art Installations

Andrews, William L. (ed.), *Critical Essays on Frederick Douglass* (Boston: G. K. Hall, 1991).

Bernier, Celeste-Marie, '"The Face of a Fugitive Slave": Representing and Reimagining Frederick Douglass in Popular Illustrations, Fine Art Portraiture and Daguerreotypes', in *Political Memory*, ed. Magnus Brechkten (Göttingen: Vandenhoeck & Ruprecht, 2012), 11–33.

Bernier, Celeste-Marie, 'A "Typical Negro" or a "Work of Art?": The "Inner" via the "Outer Man" in Frederick Douglass' Manuscripts and Daguerreotypes', *Slavery and Abolition*, 33.2 (2012): 287–303.

Bernier, Celeste-Marie, 'A Visual Call to Arms against the "Caracature [sic] of My Own Face": From Fugitive Slave to Fugitive Image in Frederick Douglass's Theory of Portraiture', *Journal of American Studies*, 49.2 (2015): 323–57.

Bernier, Celeste-Marie, *Characters of Blood: Black Heroism in the Transatlantic Imagination* (Charlottesville: University of Virginia Press, 2012).

Bernier, Celeste-Marie, '"His Complete History?": Revisioning, Recreating and Reimagining Multiple Lives in Frederick Douglass's *Life and Times* (1881, 1892)', *Slavery and Abolition*, 33.4 (2012): 595–610.

Bernier, Celeste-Marie, '"Ten Thousand Agonies": Isaac Julien's Frederick and Anna Murray Douglass Paint Pictures of "War and Slavery"', in *Lessons of the Hour*, eds Isaac Julien and Cora Gilroy-Ware with Vladimir Seput (D.A.P. New York: DelMonico Books, 2021).

Bernier, Celeste-Marie, '"To Preserve My Features in Marble": Post-Civil War Paintings, Drawings, Sculpture, and Sketches of Frederick Douglass: An Illustrated Essay', *Callaloo: A Journal of African Diaspora Arts and Letters*, 39.2 (2016): 372–99.

Bernier, Celeste-Marie, and Bill E. Lawson (eds), *Pictures and Power: Imaging and Imagining Frederick Douglass (1818–2018)* (Liverpool: Liverpool University Press, 2018).

Bernier, Celeste-Marie, '"Why not we endure hardship that our race may be free?" *The Anna Murray and Frederick Douglass Family Papers Volume 1*

*(1846–1880) and Volume 2 (1881–1943) and Douglass Family Lives: The Biography'*, New North Star 3 (2021): 59–63.

Condon, Robin L., ' "Finished By The Hand By Which It was Begun": Who Wrote *The Life and Times of Frederick Douglass?*', *Journal of African American History*, 99.1–2 (2014): 12–19.

Ernest, John (ed.), *Douglass in His Own Time* (Iowa City: Iowa University Press, 2014).

Ernest, John (ed.), *The Oxford Handbook of the African American Slave Narrative* (Oxford: Oxford University Press, 2017).

Gates, Henry Louis, Jr, *Figures in Black: Words, Signs and the 'Racial Self'* (New York: Oxford University Press, 1990).

Grandt, Jürgen E., 'A Life and Power Far Beyond the Letter: "Life and Times of Frederick Douglass" and the Authentic Blackness of Autobiography', *CLA Journal*, 45.1 (September 2001): 1–25.

Hooper, M. Clay, ' "Othello's Occupation Was Gone": Tragic Anachronism and the Philosophy of Frederick Douglass's *Life and Times*', *CLA Journal*, 56.1 (September 2012): 82–104.

Jeffrey, Julie Roy, *Abolitionists Remember: Antislavery Autobiographies and the Unfinished Work of Emancipation* (Chapel Hill: University of North Carolina Press, 2012).

Jeffrey, Julie Roy, ' "Mr. Douglass Must Share Our Disappointment": The Commercial, and Aesthetic Failure of Life and Times', *Journal of African American History*, 99.1–2 (2014): 20–33.

Julien, Isaac, *Lessons of the Hour*, 2019. Ten-Screen Installation. Further information available online: https://www.isaacjulien.com/projects/37/

Laski, Gregory, *Untimely Democracy: The Politics of Progress after Slavery* (Oxford: Oxford University Press, 2018).

Lawson, Bill E., and Frank Kirkland (eds), *Frederick Douglass: A Critical Reader* (Malden: Blackwell Publishers, 1999).

Lee, Maurice S. (ed.), *Cambridge Companion to Frederick Douglass* (Cambridge: Cambridge University Press, 2009).

Levine, Robert S., *The Lives of Frederick Douglass* (Cambridge MA: Harvard University Press, 2016).

McKivigan, John R., 'Rediscovering The *Life and Times of Frederick Douglass*', *Journal of African American History*, 99.1–2 (2014): 4–11.

McKivigan, John R., 'Stalwart Douglass: Life and Times as Political Manifesto', *Journal of African American History*, 99.1–2 (2014): 46–55.

Moses, Wilson J., ' "The Ever-Present Now": Frederick Douglass's Pragmatic Constitutionalism', *Journal of African American History*, 99.1–2 (2014): 71–88.

Myers, Peter C., 'Seed-Time and Harvest-Time: Natural Law and Rational Hopefulness in Frederick Douglass's *Life and Times*', *Journal of African American History*, 99.1–2 (2014): 56–70.

Quarles, Ernest J., 'Framing Frederick Douglass: The Female Talented Tenth Who Shaped America', *Kalfou: A Journal of Comparative and Relational Ethnic Studies*, 7.1 (2020).

Redding, J. Saunders, *To Make a Poet Black* (Chapel Hill: University of North Carolina Press, 1939).

Rice, Alan J., and Martin Crawford (eds), *Liberating Sojourn: Frederick Douglass and Transatlantic Reform* (Athens: University of Georgia Press, 1999).

Roy, Michaël (ed.), *Frederick Douglass in Context* (Cambridge: Cambridge University Press, 2021).

Smith, J. Clay, Jr, 'In Freedom's Birthplace: The Making of George Lewis Ruffin, the First Black Law Graduate of Harvard University', *Howard Law Journal*, 39.1 (1995): 218–29.

Sundquist, Eric J. (ed.), *Frederick Douglass: New Literary and Historical Essays* (New York: Cambridge University Press, 1990).

Sweeney, Fionnghuala, *Frederick Douglass and the Atlantic World* (Liverpool: Liverpool University Press, 2007).

Tang, Edward, 'Rebirth of a Nation: Frederick Douglass as Postwar Founder in "Life and Times"', *Journal of American Studies*, 39.1 (2005): 19–39.

Wallace, Maurice O. and Shawn Michelle Smith, eds, *Pictures and Progress: Early Photography and the Making of African American Identity* (Durham: Duke University Press, 2012).

Warren, Kenneth W., 'Frederick Douglass's *Life and Times*: Progressive Rhetoric and the Problem of Constituency', in Adolph Reed Jr and Kenneth W. Warren (eds), *Renewing Black Intellectual History: The Ideological and Material Foundations of African American Thought* (New York: Routledge, 2010), 3–18.

# A CHRONOLOGY OF
# FREDERICK DOUGLASS

*Life*

1818 (Feb.) Frederick Douglass is born Frederick Augustus Washington Bailey to Harriet Bailey (1792–c.1825) and an unidentified white man in Easton, Talbot County, Maryland.

*Historical and Cultural Background*

A Founding Mother of African American literature, Phillis Wheatley (1753–84) is born into slavery in West Africa and transported onto a ship to be inhumanely sold to white enslavers in Boston. In 1773, she publishes her seminal work, *Poems on Various Subjects, Religious and Moral*, shortly after which she secures her legal emancipation.

In 1800, an enslaved man named Gabriel (1776–1800) leads a rebellion in Richmond, Virginia. Tragically, his revolutionary plan is leaked to white racist officials before he and his supporters are able to execute it. White racist reprisals are immediate and terrible: he and many other enslaved people are executed.

In 1807 Britain passes An Act for the Abolition of the Slave Trade which ends the legal slave trade in the British Empire. The illegal traffic continues.

1824 (Aug.) Douglass' grandmother, Betsey Bailey, takes him to live on white enslaver Edward Lloyd's Wye River labour camp in Talbot County, Maryland.

Harriet Tubman (1822–1913) is born into slavery in Dorchester county, very near to Douglass' place of birth on Maryland's Eastern Shore. In 1849, she makes her escape and becomes one of the most important Underground Railroad liberators, activists, freedom-fighters, social justice campaigners, and Civil War commanders in U.S. history.

In 1822, Denmark Vesey (1767–1822) plans a rebellion of enslaved people in Charleston, South Carolina. News of his revolutionary plot is leaked to white enslaving authorities and he and his followers are captured, unjustly tried, and executed.

*Life*

*Historical and Cultural Background*

1825 (14 Feb.) Harriet Bailey visits her son for the last time and dies shortly after.

In 1827, free northern-born editors and journalists Reverend Peter Williams, Jr (1786–1840), John B. Russwurm (1799–1851), and Samuel E. Cornish (1795–1858) publish the first African American newspaper, *Freedom's Journal*, in New York city.

1826 (Mar.) Frederick Douglass learns to read and obtains a copy of the bestselling U.S. educational primer *The Columbian Orator* (1797), by white U.S. author and educator Caleb Bingham (1757–1817).

In 1829, free born radical and revolutionary David Walker (1796–1830) prints the first edition of his seminal political treatise and radical manifesto of Black liberation, *Appeal, in Four Articles; Together with a Preamble, to the Coloured Citizens of the World, but in Particular, and Very Expressly, to Those of the United States of America*. A founding father of Black revolutionary philosophy, Walker is later singled out by Frederick Douglass as *the* pioneering figure in U.S. abolitionist and activist history.

1831

(21 Aug.) Born into slavery, Nathaniel Turner (1800–31) leads an army of enslaved men in a revolution in Southampton County, Virginia. Waging a war for the liberty of all enslaved people, they kill sixty whites, while untold numbers of Black women, children, and men are tortured, persecuted, abused, and murdered in bloody reprisals enacted by white enslaving government officials. Turner is executed on 11 November.

1833 (Mar.) Douglass begins teaching a Sabbath School for enslaved African Americans in St Michaels, Maryland, only to have it shut down by a violent and persecutory white racist mob.

In 1833, Sarah Mapps Douglass (1806–82), a free-born northern woman and pioneering educator and abolitionist, opens a school for African American female children in Philadelphia.

In 1831, white radical William Lloyd Garrison (1805–79) begins publishing his antislavery newspaper, *The Liberator*. In 1833 he and white campaigner Arthur Tappan (1786–1865) found the American Anti-Slavery Society in New York city.

In 1833, white abolitionist, author and newspaper editor Lydia Maria Child (1802–80) publishes *An Appeal in Favor of That Class of Americans Called Africans* in Boston.

*Life*

1834  (1 Jan.) Douglass lives with white 'negro-breaker', Edward Covey (1806–75). He suffers repeated physical abuse, torture, and persecution at the hands of Covey until he defeats him in a fight.

1836  (Apr.) As an enslaved labourer hired to white enslaver William Freeland, Douglass convinces enslaved men Henry Harris, John Harris, Sandy Jenkins, Charles Roberts, and Henry Bailey to join him in a 'runaway plot'. Before they are able to put their plan into action, they are betrayed and incarcerated in Easton jail, Maryland. Douglass' revolutionary collaborators are released from prison while he is threatened with sale to a white enslaver and trader heading south. However, Thomas Auld, his white enslaver, changes his mind and instead hires Douglass out to white business-owner William Gardener as a caulker working in the shipyards on Fell's Point, Baltimore. While he is at work, Douglass is attacked by white carpenters who fear the encroachment on their livelihood by enslaved Black labourers. Douglass plays an active role in the 'East Baltimore Mental Improvement Society' organized by free African American men.

1838  (3 Sept.) Douglass borrows a friend's sailor's identity papers and boards a train to Wilmington where he takes a steamer for Philadelphia and a train to New York. Anna Murray Douglass (1813–82), a free Black woman who was born in Denton, Maryland, and to whom he is engaged to

*Historical and Cultural Background*

(1 Aug.) Britain abolishes slavery in their colonial possessions in the Caribbean, but enslaved people are still not legally free until 1 August 1838.

| *Life* | *Historical and Cultural Background* |
|---|---|

be married, sells a feather bed to raise the funds for his flight. (15 Sept.) Douglass and Anna Murray are married by self-emancipated religious minister, philosopher, intellectual, scholar, and radical activist Reverend James W. C. Pennington (1807–70). On 17 September, they travel to New Bedford, where Douglass becomes a manual labourer, orator in African American churches, and a renowned antislavery lecturer.

1839  (Feb.) Douglass subscribes to William Lloyd Garrison's antislavery newspaper, *The Liberator*.

(24 June) Frederick and Anna Murray Douglass' daughter Rosetta Douglass is born.

(Jan.) Sengbe Pieh (*c*.1814–*c*.1879) (also known as Joseph Cinque) leads a successful rebellion following the illegal capture of himself and fifty-three men and children aboard *La Amistad*. His rebellion results in a series of legal battles in U.S. courts before the eventual return of the survivors to their homeland of Sierra Leone in 1842.

1840  (9 Oct.) Frederick and Anna Murray Douglass' son Lewis Henry Douglass is born.

1841  (11–12 Aug.) Frederick and Anna Murray Douglass attend an antislavery convention in Nantucket. Douglass delivers his first speech before the Massachusetts Antislavery Society and is appointed as their lecturer.

1842  (3 Mar.) Frederick and Anna Murray Douglass' second son, Frederick Douglass Jr, is born.

(Autumn) Frederick, Anna, Rosetta, and Lewis Henry Douglass move to Lynn, Massachusetts.

(7 Nov.) Madison Washington leads a group of enslaved men in rebellion aboard the enslaver *Creole* and they are freed by Black British soldiers on 9 November in Nassau, Bahamas. This revolt sparks a British–U.S. diplomatic conflict.

*Life*

*Historical and Cultural Background*

1843 (16 Sept.) Douglass is viciously attacked by a white racist mob in Indiana.

Self-liberated revolutionary activist, author, philosopher, educator and religious minister Henry Highland Garnet (1815–82) delivers 'An Address to the Slaves of the United States', at the National Negro Convention in Buffalo, New York. He advocates armed resistance by urging his enslaved audiences that they had 'rather die freemen, than live to be slaves'.

1844 (21 Oct.) Frederick and Anna Murray Douglass' final son, Charles Remond Douglass, is born.

1845 (28 May) Douglass publishes *Narrative of the Life of Frederick Douglass, an American Slave*, at the Boston Antislavery office.

(16 Aug.) Fearing for his safety after the publication of his autobiography, in which he names his white enslavers, he undertakes an eighteen-month transatlantic abolitionist tour of Ireland, Scotland, Wales, and England.

(Sept.) The first Dublin edition of Douglass' *Narrative* is published.

(25 Oct.) Thomas Auld sells his ownership in the 'body and bones' of Douglass to his brother Hugh Auld for $100. On 6 October 1846, Hugh Auld releases Douglass' manumission papers for £150 (about $710), following his receipt of funds raised by white British abolitionists, Anna Richardson (1806–92) and Ellen Richardson, of Newcastle-upon-Tyne, England.

1847 (3 Dec.) Douglass moves to Rochester, New York, and begins publishing his antislavery and social justice

newspapers, *The North Star*
(subsequently *Frederick
Douglass' Paper*) (1847–51)
and later *Douglass' Monthly*
(1858–63) funded by British
and Irish monies. Frederick,
Anna Murray, Lewis Henry,
Frederick Jr, and Charles
Remond Douglass work
together on the Underground
Railroad. They run their
family home as a safe house
and offer their support to
enslaved people of all genders
and ages who are making their
escape from 'chattel slavery'
by ensuring that they reach
their new lives in the northern
U.S. states and Canada.

1848  (19–20 June) Douglass attends
the first Women's Rights
Convention at Seneca Falls,
New York.

(3 Sept.) He publishes his letter
'To My old Master, Thomas
Auld' in *The North Star*.

1849  (22 Mar.) Frederick and Anna
Murray Douglass' final daughter,
Annie Douglass, is born.

1850                                  The Fugitive Slave Act is passed which
makes the North a hunting ground for
white enslavers by legalizing the return
of enslaved women, children, and men
who had made it to the free states and
Canada to their enslavers.

1851  (9 May) Douglass breaks with      (29 May) Sojourner Truth (1797–1883),
white U.S. antislavery radical       a self-emancipated orator, philosopher,
William Lloyd Garrison, by           and radical reformer, delivers her speech
newly endorsing the necessity        'Ar'n't I a Woman' at the Women's
for political action to oppose        Convention in Akron, Ohio, in which she
slavery and begins his lifelong      avows, 'I am a woman's rights.'
friendship with white
U.S. abolitionist Gerrit
Smith, a Liberty Party
supporter.

| *Life* | *Historical and Cultural Background* |
|---|---|
| 1852 (5 July) Douglass delivers his speech 'What to the Slave is the Fourth of July?' in Corinthian Hall, Rochester, New York. | Martin Robison Delany (1812–85), a free born novelist, journalist, editor, historian, military officer, and physician, publishes *The Condition, Elevation, Emigration and Destiny of the Colored People of the United States*. Seeing no future for African Americans on U.S. soil, he endorses emigration to the African continent. Throughout his life, he advocates a Black nationalist philosophy. |
| | White U.S. author Harriet Beecher Stowe (1811–96) publishes her antislavery novel *Uncle Tom's Cabin*. While the novel continues to be widely celebrated as a key work in the freedom struggle, it is not without its own political and human rights costs due to the ongoing collateral damage produced by its white racist derogatory and dehumanizing stereotypes of enslaved and self-liberated Black people. |
| 1853 Douglass publishes his novella *The Heroic Slave*, in *Autographs for Freedom*, an antislavery giftbook edited by white British journalist, editor, and author Julia Griffiths (1811–95). | Self-emancipated author, orator, historian, and activist William Wells Brown (1814–84) publishes his antislavery novel *Clotel; or, the President's Daughter*. |
| 1855 (Aug.) Douglass publishes his second autobiography, *My Bondage and My Freedom*. | William Cooper Nell (1816–74), a free-born northern radical reformer and prolific author, publishes *The Colored Patriots of the American Revolution*, a seminal work of African American history. |
| 1856 | (28 June) Born into slavery in Kentucky, Margaret Garner (1834–58) secures her liberation with her husband and children only to be captured by white persecutory authorities in Cincinnati. She murders Mary, her youngest child, and wounds but fails to kill her other children and herself. She and they are returned to slavery. In a speech he delivered in 1857, Frederick Douglass declared, 'Every mother who, like Margaret Garner, plunges a knife into the bosom of her infant to save it from the hell of Christian Slavery, should be held and honored as a benefactress.' |

| *Life* | *Historical and Cultural Background* |
|---|---|
| 1857 | The landmark Dred Scott *v.* John V. A. Sandford legal case takes place, in which the U.S. Supreme Court overrules the legal claim of Dred Scott (1799–1858), an enslaved man fighting for his freedom, by instead writing white supremacist legislation into law by stating that Black people 'had no rights which the white man was bound to respect'. The Douglass family dedicate their lives to opposing and resisting this legislation by every means necessary. |
| 1859 (20 Aug.) Douglass participates in a clandestine meeting with white liberator and warrior John Brown (1800–59) at a stone quarry near Chambersburg, Pennsylvania. Brown asks Douglass to participate in his revolutionary raid on the federal arsenal at Harpers Ferry, West Virginia, and Douglass refuses.<br><br>(17 Oct.) Douglass escapes to Canada in the wake of John Brown's raid in order to evade arrest.<br><br>(12 Nov.) Douglass sails from Quebec to the United Kingdom, and he delivers antislavery and social justice speeches in Scotland and northern England. | (16–18 Oct.) John Brown launches his revolutionary raid on the federal arsenal at Harpers Ferry.<br><br>(2 Dec.) Brown and his men are defeated and Brown is hanged.<br><br>(btw. 1858 and 1859) Austin Read (1823–?) writes his autobiographical manuscript, *The Life and Adventures of a Haunted Convict*, the first prison narrative by an African American author.<br><br>Harriet E. Wilson (1825–1900), a free-born northern author, anonymously publishes her autobiographical novel *Our Nig, or Sketches from the Life of a Free Black* in which she exposes the suffering, torture, and persecution at the hands of white racists endured by African Americans living in northern communities. |
| 1860 (13 Mar.) Annie Douglass dies, and Douglass returns home inconsolably grief-stricken. | White U.S. politician Abraham Lincoln (1809–65) is elected President to the fury of the enslaving southern states. |
| 1861 | Self-liberated author and activist Harriet Ann Jacobs (1813–97) publishes her life story, *Incidents in the Life of A Slave Girl*, under the pseudonym Linda Brent in Boston. |
| 1862 (31 Dec.) Douglass is a speaker at a reception held at Boston's Tremont Temple to celebrate Abraham Lincoln's Emancipation Proclamation which arrives via telegram at midnight on 1 January 1863. | (16 July) Ida B. Wells-Barnett (1862–1931), an anti-lynching crusader and social justice campaigner, is born into slavery in Holly Springs, Mississippi. |

---

*Life*                    *Historical and Cultural Background*

1863 (Feb.–July) Douglass is appointed as an agent to recruit Black combat soldiers into the Union Army during the Civil War.

(2 Mar.) Douglass publishes his appeal, 'Men of Color, To Arms', in *Douglass' Monthly*.

His sons, Lewis Henry and Charles Remond Douglass, enlist in the 54th Massachusetts Regiment. Lewis Henry is promoted to the rank of Sergeant-Major and participates in the Battle of Fort Wagner on 18 July. Charles Remond is transferred to the 5th Cavalry. Frederick Jr is appointed as a recruitment agent in Mississippi.

(July) Douglass meets Abraham Lincoln to protest against the unequal and discriminatory treatment of Black soldiers.

(16 Aug.) Douglass ends the publication of *Douglass' Monthly*.

1865 The Thirteenth Amendment to the U.S. Constitution, which abolishes slavery in the United States, is passed.

(14 Apr.) Abraham Lincoln is assassinated by white stage actor John Wilkes Booth (1838–65).

Reconstruction, the period immediately following Lincoln's death and continuing on through to the late 1870s, is an era in which the U.S. nation ostensibly works to heal the wounds of the Civil War. There is no halcyon period of race relations, however; the U.S. government conciliates and capitulates to the demands of the white U.S. South. As a result, slavery is legally abolished only for its inhumane injustices and persecutory inequalities to live on in white racist reprisals which reach unprecedented levels during these decades and on into the twentieth and

| *Life* | *Historical and Cultural Background* |
|---|---|
| | twenty-first centuries. This era sees the accelerated rise of white supremacist legislation, segregation, persecution, discrimination, torture, murder, and lynch law. |
| | Congress establishes the Bureau of Refugees, Freedmen and Abandoned Lands. This national organization is created with the dedicated goal of supporting Black and white teachers in setting up schools for freed women, children, and men living in the U.S. South. |
| | The white supremacist hate group the Ku Klux Klan is founded. |
| 1866 | The Civil Rights Act is passed by Congress only to be vetoed twice by white U.S. President Andrew Johnson (1808–75). His protest is to no avail, however, as he is outvoted with the result that this act is finally ratified in 1870. |
| 1868 | Elizabeth Keckley (1818–1907), a self-liberated author, activist, social justice campaigner, dress-maker, and seamstress, publishes her autobiography, *Behind the Scenes (or, Thirty Years a Slave and Four Years in the White House)*. |
| | The Fourteenth Amendment to the U.S. Constitution is passed in which it is decreed, 'All persons born or naturalized in the United States, and subject to the jurisdiction thereof, are citizens of the United States and of the State wherein they reside. No State shall make or enforce any law which shall abridge the privileges or immunities of citizens of the United States; nor shall any State deprive any person of life, liberty, or property, without due process of law; nor deny to any person within its jurisdiction the equal protection of the laws.' |
| 1870 (Jan.) Douglass becomes corresponding editor for the *New National Era* (1870–4), a newspaper he edits and publishes with his sons Lewis Henry and Frederick Douglass Jr in Washington, D.C. | The Fifteenth Amendment to the U.S. Constitution, which guarantees the right of all male citizens of the United States to vote regardless of 'race, color or previous condition of servitude', is passed. |

*Life* | *Historical and Cultural Background*

(11 Dec.) Douglass assumes the role of editor and is assisted by Lewis Henry and Frederick Douglass Jr.

Free-born political leader, Hiram Rhodes Revels (1827–1901), becomes the first African American senator elected to the U.S. Congress.

1871 (12 Jan.) Douglass is appointed assistant secretary of the commission of inquiry to Santo Domingo. He endorses the plans of white U.S. President Ulysses S. Grant (1822–85) in favour of annexing Santo Domingo to the United States.

The Enforcement Act is passed by President Ulysses S. Grant in an attempt to protect African American voting rights and in recognition of the fact that Black men are facing widespread acts of torture and murder at the hands of white perscutory mobs.

1872 (1 July) Douglass and his family move to 'A' Street NE in Washington, D.C.

William Still (1821–1902), a Philadelphia-based Black antislavery activist, social justice campaigner, business owner, liberator, and author, publishes *The Underground Railroad*, a definitive history of this resistance movement.

1874 (Mar.) Douglass is appointed as President of the Freedmen's Bank.

(Sept.) Douglass ends publication of the *New National Era* due to ongoing financial difficulties. The Freedmen's Bank is dissolved in financial crisis, and he loses significant amounts of personal funds.

1875

The Civil Rights Act, which has been written by white U.S. Senator Charles Sumner (1811–74), and free-born political leader, author, and educator John Mercer Langston (1829–97), is passed by President Ulysses S. Grant following Sumner's death. This bill is passed in order to 'protect all citizens in their civil and legal rights' and to safeguard African Americans from white racist violence.

1876

(July) The Hamburg Massacre takes place in South Carolina in which a white racist hate group attacks Black men with tragic results: six Black men are killed.

1877 (17 Mar.) Douglass is appointed as U.S. Marshal of the District of Columbia by white U.S. President Rutherford B. Hayes (1822–93).

(17 June) Douglass returns to St Michaels, Maryland, to visit his white enslaver Thomas Auld on his deathbed.

1878 Douglass purchases Cedar Hill in Anacostia, Washington, D.C., with monies saved by Anna Murray Douglass.

1879          The Exodus takes place. Black people leave the South in the thousands to migrate to Kansas to escape white racist persecution, torture, and death.

1881 (Jan.) Douglass publishes his third autobiography, *Life and Times of Frederick Douglass Written By Himself*.

(Mar.) Douglass is appointed as Recorder of Deeds for the District of Columbia by white U.S. President James A. Garfield (1831–81).

(4 July) Booker T. Washington (1856–1915), a world-leading educator and activist who had been born into slavery, founds the Tuskegee Normal and Industrial Institute in Tuskegee, Alabama.

1882 (4 Aug.) Anna Murray Douglass dies. Over three thousand people attend her funeral.

1883          The Civil Rights Act of 1875 is deemed unconstitutional.

1884 (24 Jan.) Douglass marries Helen Pitts (1838–1903), a white political reformer and women's rights campaigner.

Ida B. Wells-Barnett initiates a law suit against the Chesapeake, Ohio and South Western Railroad Company for maintaining racist practices of racial segregation on its carriages.

1886 (Sept.–Aug. 1887) Frederick and Helen Pitts Douglass undertake an extended tour of England, Ireland, France, Switzerland, Italy, Egypt, and Greece.

1889 (1 July) White U.S. President Benjamin Harrison (1833–1901) appoints Douglass as the

| *Life* | *Historical and Cultural Background* |
|---|---|
| | Minister Resident and Consul General to Haiti. |
| | (Sept.) Douglass is appointed as Chargé d'Affaires for Santo Domingo as well as Minister to Haiti. |
| 1891 | (30 July) Douglass resigns as Minister Resident and Consul General to Haiti. |
| 1892 | Douglass completes a final revised, significantly updated edition of his autobiography *Life and Times*. |

1892 · Douglass completes a final revised, significantly updated edition of his autobiography *Life and Times*.

Ida B. Wells-Barnett publishes *Southern Horrors: Lynch Law in All Its Phases*, an unflinching radical tract in which she protests against lynching.

(26 July) Frederick Douglass Jr dies.

(to 1893) Douglass serves as Commissioner of the Haitian exhibit at the World's Fair in Chicago. He contributes an introductory essay to *The Reason Why the Colored American is Not in the World's Columbian Exposition*, edited by anti-lynching campaigner, Ida B. Wells-Barnett.

Born into slavery in Raleigh, North Carolina, renowned educator, scholar, philosopher, and political activist Anna Julia Cooper (1858–1964) publishes her collection of essays, *A Voice from the South*, in which she provides a pioneering theorization of Black feminist ideologies.

1893

Black author, essayist, orator, and performer, Paul Laurence Dunbar (1872–1906), publishes his first collection of poetry, *Oak and Ivy*.

1894 (9 Jan.) Douglass delivers an anti-lynching speech, 'Lessons of the Hour', at the Metropolitan A.M.E. Church in Washington, D.C.

1895 (20 Feb.) Douglass attends the National Council of Women in Washington, D.C. On his return, he collapses in the hallway at Cedar Hill with Helen Pitts Douglass and dies. (25 Feb.) Douglass' memorial service is held at Cedar Hill and his body is on public view at the Metropolitan African Methodist Church in

| *Life* | *Historical and Cultural Background* |
|---|---|
| Washington, D.C. His body is then taken to Rochester, New York, and his funeral is held in Rochester Central Presbyterian Church. Douglass is buried in Mount Hope Cemetery, Rochester. | |
| 1896 | In the Plessy *v.* Ferguson decision, the U.S. Supreme Court establishes the 'separate but equal' rule according to which the white racist and persecutory system of racial segregation is upheld. |
| 1898 | The National Association of Colored Women meets in Washington, D.C. Harriet Tubman attends, and Anna Murray and Frederick Douglass' eldest daughter, Rosetta Douglass Sprague, gives an inspirational speech in which she eulogizes Black female heroism. |
| | TheWilmington Massacre takes place in North Carolina: a white racist mob wreaks a reign of terror by killing and wounding hundreds of Black people. |
| 1901 | Booker T. Washington publishes his autobiography, *Up From Slavery*. |
| 1903 | W. E. B. Du Bois (1868–1963) releases his autobiography, *Souls of Black Folk*. |
| 1906 (25 Nov.) Rosetta Douglass Sprague dies. | |
| 1908 (9 Oct.) Lewis Henry Douglass dies. | |
| 1909 | The National Association for the Advancement of Colored People is established in New York City. |
| 1910 | The National Urban League is founded in New York City. |
| 1918 | Over 200,000 African American soldiers fight in World War I. |
| 1920 (23 Nov.) Charles Remond Douglass dies. Following his combat service in the Civil War, he campaigned for the equal treatment of African American soldiers and an end to white racist discrimination in the U.S. military. | |

Yours truly
Frederick Douglass

# LIFE AND TIMES

OF

# FREDERICK DOUGLASS

## WRITTEN BY HIMSELF.

### HIS EARLY LIFE AS A SLAVE, HIS ESCAPE FROM BONDAGE,

AND

### HIS COMPLETE HISTORY TO THE PRESENT TIME,

INCLUDING

HIS CONNECTION WITH THE ANTI-SLAVERY MOVEMENT; HIS LABORS IN GREAT BRITAIN
AS WELL AS IN HIS OWN COUNTRY; HIS EXPERIENCE IN THE CONDUCT OF AN
INFLUENTIAL NEWSPAPER; HIS CONNECTION WITH THE UNDERGROUND RAILROAD;
HIS RELATIONS WITH JOHN BROWN AND THE HARPER'S FERRY RAID; HIS
RECRUITING THE 54TH AND 55TH MASS. COLORED REGIMENTS; HIS INTER-
VIEWS WITH PRESIDENTS LINCOLN AND JOHNSON; HIS APPOINTMENT
BY GEN. GRANT TO ACCOMPANY THE SANTO DOMINGO COMMISSION—
ALSO TO A SEAT IN THE COUNCIL OF THE DISTRICT OF COLUMBIA;
HIS APPOINTMENT AS UNITED STATES MARSHAL BY PRESIDENT
R. B. HAYES; ALSO HIS APPOINTMENT TO BE RECORDER OF
DEEDS IN WASHINGTON BY PRESIDENT J. A. GARFIELD;
WITH MANY OTHER INTERESTING AND IMPORTANT
EVENTS OF HIS MOST EVENTFUL LIFE;

WITH

## AN INTRODUCTION BY MR. GEORGE L. RUFFIN,

OF BOSTON.

New Revised Edition.

BOSTON:
DE WOLFE & FISKE CO.

# LIFE AND TIMES

OF

# FREDERICK DOUGLASS

WRITTEN BY HIMSELF.

HIS EARLY LIFE AS A SLAVE, HIS ESCAPE FROM BONDAGE,

AND

HIS COMPLETE HISTORY TO THE PRESENT TIME,

INCLUDING

HIS CONNECTION WITH THE ANTI-SLAVERY MOVEMENT; HIS LABORS IN GREAT BRITAIN
AS WELL AS IN HIS OWN COUNTRY; HIS EXPERIENCE IN THE CONDUCT OF AN
INFLUENTIAL NEWSPAPER; HIS CONNECTION WITH THE UNDERGROUND RAILROAD;
HIS RELATIONS WITH JOHN BROWN AND THE HARPER'S FERRY RAID; HIS
RECRUITING THE 54TH AND 55TH MASS. COLORED REGIMENTS; HIS INTER-
VIEWS WITH PRESIDENTS LINCOLN AND JOHNSON; HIS APPOINTMENT
BY GEN. GRANT TO ACCOMPANY THE SANTO DOMINGO COMMISSION —
ALSO TO A SEAT IN THE COUNCIL OF THE DISTRICT OF COLUMBIA;
HIS APPOINTMENT AS UNITED STATES MARSHAL BY PRESIDENT
R. B. HAYES; ALSO HIS APPOINTMENT TO BE RECORDER OF
DEEDS IN WASHINGTON BY PRESIDENT J. A. GARFIELD;
WITH MANY OTHER INTERESTING AND IMPORTANT
EVENTS OF HIS MOST EVENTFUL LIFE;

WITH

AN INTRODUCTION BY MR. GEORGE L. RUFFIN,*

OF BOSTON.

New Revised Edition.

BOSTON:
DE WOLFE & FISKE CO.

# CONTENTS.

of Mrs. Sophia—My hatred of slavery—One Upas tree
overshadows us all.

## CHAPTER XV.
### COVEY, THE NEGRO BREAKER.

Journey to Covey's—Meditations by the way—Covey's house—Family—Awkwardness as a field hand—A cruel beating—Why given—Description of Covey—First attempt at driving oxen—Hair-breadth escape—Ox and man alike property—Hard labor more effective than the whip for breaking down the spirit—Cunning and trickery of Covey—Family worship—Shocking and indecent contempt for chastity—Great mental agitation—Anguish beyond description.

## CHAPTER XVI.
### ANOTHER PRESSURE OF THE TYRANT'S VISE.

Experience at Covey's summed up—First six months severer than the remaining six—Preliminaries to the change—Reasons for narrating the circumstances—Scene in the treading-yard—Author taken ill—Escapes to St. Michaels—The pursuit—Suffering in the woods—Talk with Master Thomas—His beating—Driven back to Covey's—The slaves never sick—Natural to expect them to feign sickness—Laziness of slaveholders.

## CHAPTER XVII.
### THE LAST FLOGGING.

A sleepless night—Return to Covey's—Punished by him—The chase defeated—Vengeance postponed—Musings in the woods—The alternative—Deplorable spectacle—Night in the woods—Expected attack—Accosted by Sandy—A friend, not a master—Sandy's hospitality—The ash-cake supper—Interview with Sandy—His advice—Sandy a conjuror as well as a Christian—The magic root—Strange meeting with Covey—His manner—Covey's Sunday face—Author's defensive resolve—The fight—The victory, and its results.

## CHAPTER XVIII.
### NEW RELATIONS AND DUTIES.

Change of masters—Benefits derived by change—Fame of the fight with Covey—Reckless unconcern—Author's abhorrence of slavery—Ability to read a cause of prejudice—

The holidays—How spent—Sharp hit at slavery—
Effects of holidays—Difference between Covey and
Freeland—An irreligious master preferred to a religious
one—Hard life at Covey's useful to the author—Improved
condition does not bring contentment—Congenial society
at Freeland's—Author's Sabbath-school—Secrecy
necessary—Affectionate relations of tutor and pupils—
Confidence and friendship among slaves—Slavery the
inviter of vengeance.

## CHAPTER XXI.
### ESCAPE FROM SLAVERY.

Closing incidents in my 'Life as a Slave'—Discontent—
Suspicions—Master's generosity—Difficulties in the way
of escape—Plan to obtain money—Allowed to hire my
time—A gleam of hope—Attend camp-meeting—Anger
of Master Hugh—The result—Plans of escape—Day for
departure fixed—Harassing doubts and fears—Painful
thoughts of separation from friends.

## SECOND PART.

## CHAPTER I.
### ESCAPE FROM SLAVERY.

Reasons for not having revealed the manner of
escape—Nothing of romance in the
method—Danger—Free papers—Unjust
tax—Protection papers—'Free trade and sailors'
rights'—American eagle—Railroad train—Unobserving
conductor—Capt. McGowan—Honest German—
Fears—Safe arrival in Philadelphia—Ditto in
New York.

## CHAPTER II.
### LIFE AS A FREEMAN.

Loneliness and insecurity—'Allender's Jake'—Succored
by a sailor—David Ruggles—Marriage—Steamer J. W.
Richmond—Stage to New Bedford—Arrival
there—Driver's detention of baggage—Nathan
Johnson—Change of name—Why called
'Douglass'—Obtaining Work—The *Liberator* and its
Editor.

## CHAPTER III.
### INTRODUCED TO THE ABOLITIONISTS.

Anti-Slavery Convention at Nantucket—First
Speech—Much Sensation—Extraordinary Speech of
Mr. Garrison—Anti-Slavery Agency—Youthful

Enthusiasm—Fugitive Slaveship Doubted—Experience
in slavery written—Danger of Recapture.

## CHAPTER IV.
### RECOLLECTIONS OF OLD FRIENDS.

Work in Rhode Island—Dorr War—Recollections of old
friends—Further labors in Rhode Island and elsewhere
in New England.

## CHAPTER V.
### ONE HUNDRED CONVENTIONS.

Anti-slavery conventions held in parts of New England,
and in some of the Middle and Western
States—Mobs—Incidents, etc.

## CHAPTER VI.
### IMPRESSIONS ABROAD.

Danger to be averted—A refuge sought abroad—Voyage
on the steamship Cambria—Refusal of first-class
passage—Attractions of the forecastle- deck—
Hutchinson family—Invited to make a speech—
Southerners feel insulted—Captain threatens to put them
in irons—Experiences abroad—Attentions
received—Impressions of different members of
Parliament and of other public men—Contrast
with life in America—Kindness of friends—Their
purchase of my person and the gift of the same to
myself—My return.

## CHAPTER VII.
### TRIUMPHS AND TRIALS.

New Experiences—Painful Disagreement of Opinion
with old Friends—Final Decision to publish my Paper in
Rochester—Its Fortunes and its Friends—Change in my
own Views Regarding the Constitution of the United
States—Fidelity to Conviction—Loss of Old
Friends—Support of New Ones—Loss of House, etc.,
by Fire—Triumphs and Trials—Underground
Railroad—Incidents.

rights—President Andy Johnson—Colored delegation—
Their reply to him—National Loyalist Convention, 1866,
and its procession—Not wanted—Meeting with an old
friend—Joy and surprise—The old master's welcome,
and Miss Amanda's friendship—Enfranchisement
debated and accomplished—The negro a citizen.

## CHAPTER XIV.
### LIVING AND LEARNING.

Inducements to a political career—Objections—A
newspaper enterprise—The New National Era—Its
abandonment—The Freedmen's Saving and Trust
Company—Sad experience—Vindication.

## CHAPTER XV.
### WEIGHED IN THE BALANCE.

The Santo Domingo controversy—Decoration Day at
Arlington, 1871—Speech delivered there—National
colored convention at New Orleans, 1872—Elector at large
for the State of New York—Death of Hon. Henry Wilson.

## CHAPTER XVI.
### 'TIME MAKES ALL THINGS EVEN.'

Return to 'old master'—A last interview—Capt. Auld's
admission, 'had I been in your place, I should have done as
you did'—Speech at Easton—The old jail there—Invited
to a sail on the revenue cutter Guthrie—Hon.
John L. Thomas—Visit to the old plantation—Home of
Col. Lloyd—Kind reception and attentions—
Familiar Scenes—Old memories—Burial
ground—Hospitality—Gracious reception from
Mrs. Buchanan—A little girl's floral gift—A promise of
a 'good time coming'—Speech at Harper's Ferry,
Decoration day, 1881—Storer College—Hon.
A. J. Hunter.

## CHAPTER XVII.
### INCIDENTS AND EVENTS.

Hon. Gerrit Smith and Mr. E. C. Delevan—Experiences
at hotels and on steamboats and other modes of

## CHAPTER III.
### DOUBTS AS TO GARFIELD'S COURSE.

Garfield not a stalwart—Encounter of Garfield with
Tucker—Hope in promises of a new departure—
The sorrow-stricken nation.

## CHAPTER IV.
### RECORDER OF DEEDS.

Activity in behalf of his people—Income of the Recorder
of Deeds—False impressions as to his wealth—Appeals
for assistance—Persistent beggars.

## CHAPTER V.
### PRESIDENT CLEVELAND'S ADMINISTRATION.

Circumstances of Cleveland's election—Political standing
of the District of Columbia—Estimate of Cleveland's
character—Respect for Mr. Cleveland—Decline of
strength in the Republican Party—Time of gloom for the
colored people—Reason for the defeat of Blaine.

## CHAPTER VI.
### THE SUPREME COURT DECISION.

Action of the Supreme Court—Its effect on the colored
people—Address at Lincoln Hall.

## CHAPTER VII.
### DEFEAT OF JAMES G. BLAINE.

Causes of the Republican defeat—Tariff and free
trade—No confidence in the Democratic party.

## CHAPTER VIII.
### EUROPEAN TOUR.

Revisits Parliament—Changes in
Parliament—Recollections of Lord Brougham—Listens
to Gladstone—Meeting with old friends.

## CHAPTER IX.
### CONTINUATION OF EUROPEAN TOUR.

Through France—Dijon and Lyons—The palace of the
Popes—The Amphitheater at Arles—Visits Nice—

# INTRODUCTION.

JUST what this country has in store to benefit or to startle the world in the future, no tongue can tell. We know full well the wonderful things which have occurred or have been accomplished here in the past, but the still more wonderful things which we may well say will happen in the centuries of development which lie before us, is vain conjecture; it lies in the domain of speculation.

America will be the field for the demonstration of truths not now accepted and the establishment of a new and higher civilization. Horace Walpole's prophecy will be verified when there shall be a Xenophon at New York and a Thucydides at Boston.* Up to this time the most remarkable contribution this country has given to the world is the Author and subject of this book, now being introduced to the public— Frederick Douglass. The contribution comes naturally and legitimately and to some not unexpectedly, nevertheless it is altogether unique and must be regarded as truly remarkable. Our Pantheon contains many that are illustrious and worthy, but Douglass is unlike all others, he is *sui generis*. For every other great character we can bring forward, Europe can produce another equally as great; when we bring forward Douglass, he cannot be matched.

Douglass was born a slave, he won his liberty; he is of negro extraction, and consequently was despised and outraged; he has by his own energy and force of character commanded the respect of the Nation; he was ignorant, he has, against law and by stealth and entirely unaided, educated himself; he was poor, he has by honest toil and industry become rich and independent, so to speak; he, a chattel slave of a hated and cruelly wronged race, in the teeth of American prejudice and in face of nearly every kind of hindrance and draw-back, has come to be one of the foremost orators of the age, with a reputation established on both sides of the Atlantic; a writer of power and elegance of expression; a thinker whose views are potent in controlling and shaping public opinion; a high officer in the National Government; a cultivated gentleman whose virtues as a husband, father, and citizen are the highest honor a man can have.

Frederick Douglass stands upon a pedestal; he has reached this lofty height through years of toil and strife, but it has been the strife of moral ideas; strife in the battle for human rights. No bitter memories come from this strife; no feelings of remorse can rise to cast their gloomy shadows over his soul; Douglass has now reached and passed the meridian of life, his co-laborers in the strife have now nearly all passed away. Garrison has gone, Gerritt Smith has gone, Giddings and Sumner have gone,*—nearly all the abolitionists are gone to their reward. The culmination of his life work has been reached; the object dear to his heart—the Emancipation of the slaves*—had been accomplished, through the blessings of God; he stands facing the goal, already reached by his co-laborers, with a halo of peace about him, and nothing but serenity and gratitude must fill his breast. To those, who in the past—in *ante-bellum* days—in any degree shared with Douglass his hopes and feelings on the slavery question, this serenity of mind, this gratitude, can be understood and felt. All Americans, no matter what may have been their views on slavery, now that freedom has come and slavery is ended, must have a restful feeling and be glad that the source of bitterness and trouble is removed. The man who is sorry because of the abolition of slavery, has outlived his day and generation; he should have insisted upon being buried with the 'lost cause' at Appomatox.*

We rejoice that Douglass has attained unto this exalted position—this pedestal. It has been honorably reached; it is a just recognition of talent and effort; it is another proof that success attends high and noble aim. With this example, the black boy as well as the white boy can take hope and courage in the race of life.

Douglass' life has been a romance—and a fragrance—to the age. There has been just enough mystery about his origin and escape from slavery to throw a charm about them. The odd proceedings in the purchase of his freedom after his escape from slavery; his movements in connection with the John Brown raid at Harper's Ferry* and his subsequent flight across the ocean are romantic as anything which took place among the crags and the cliffs, the Roderick Dhus and Douglasses of the Lady of the Lake;* while the pure life he has led and his spotless character are sweet by contrast with the lives of mere politicians and time-serving statesmen. It is well to contemplate one like him, who has had 'hair-breadth escapes.'* It is inspiring to know that the day of self-sacrifice and self-development are not passed.

To say that his life has been eventful, is hardly the word. From the time when he first saw the light on the Tuckahoe plantation up to the time he was called to fill a high official position, his life has been crowded with events which in some sense may be called miracles, and now since his autobiography has come to be written, we must understand the hour of retrospect has come—for casting up and balancing accounts as to work done or left undone.

It is more than forty years now that he has been before the world as a writer and speaker—busy, active, wonderful years to him—and we are called upon to pass judgment upon his labors. What can we say? Can he claim the well done good and faithful? The record shows this, and we must state it, generally speaking, his life had been devoted to his race and the cause of his race. The freedom and elevation of his people has been his life work, and it has been done well and faithfully. That is the record, and that is sufficient. No higher eulogium can be pronounced than that Longfellow says of the Village Blacksmith:—

> 'Something attempted, something done,
> Has earned a night's repose.'*

Douglass found his people enslaved and oppressed. He has given the best years of his life to the improvement of their condition, and, now that he looks back upon his labors, may he not say he has 'attempted' and 'done' something? and may he not claim the 'repose' which ought to come in the evening of a well spent life?

The first twenty-three years of Douglass' life were twenty-three years of slavery, obscurity, and degradation, yet doubtless in time to come these years will be regarded by the student of history the most interesting portion of his life; to those who in the future would know the inside history of American slavery, this part of his life will be specially instructive. Plantation life at Tuckahoe as related by him is not fiction, it is fact; it is not the historian's dissertation on slavery, it is slavery itself, the slave's life, acts, and thoughts, and the life, acts, and thoughts of those around him. It is Macauley (I think) who says that a copy of a daily newspaper [if there were such] published at Rome would give more information and be of more value than any history we have. So, too, this photographic view of slave life as given to us in the autobiography of an ex-slave will give to the reader a clearer insight of the system of slavery than can be gained from the examination of general history.

Col. Lloyd's plantation, where Douglass belonged, was very much like other plantations of the south. Here was the great house and the cabins, the old Aunties, and patriarchal Uncles, little picanninies and picanninies not so little, of every shade of complexion, from ebony black to whiteness of the master race; mules, overseers, and broken down fences. Here was the negro Doctor learned in the science of roots and herbs; also the black conjurer with his divination. Here was slave-breeding and slave-selling, whipping, torturing and beating to death. All this came under the observation of Douglass and is a part of the education he received while under the yoke of bondage. He was there in the midst of this confusion, ignorance, and brutality. Little did the overseer on this plantation think that he had in his gang a man of superior order and undaunted spirit, whose mind, far above the minds of the grovelling creatures about him, was at that very time plotting schemes for his liberty; nor did the thought ever enter the mind of Col. Lloyd, the rich slaveholder, that he had upon his estate one who was destined to assail the system of slavery with more power and effect than any other person.

Douglass' fame will rest mainly, no doubt, upon his oratory. His powers in this direction are very great, and, in some respects, unparalleled by our living speakers. His oratory is his own, and apparently formed after the model of no single person. It is not after the Edmund Burke* style, which has been so closely followed by Everett,* Sumner,* and others, and which has resulted in giving us splendid and highly embellished essays rather than natural and not overwrought speeches. If his oratory must be classified, it should be placed somewhere between the Fox* and Henry Clay* schools. Like Clay, Douglass' greatest effect is upon his immediate hearers, those who see him and feel his presence, and, like Clay, a good part of his oratorical fame will be tradition. The most striking feature of Douglass' oratory is his fire, not the quick and flashy kind, but the steady and intense kind. Years ago, on the anti-slavery platform, in some sudden and unbidden outburst of passion and indignation, he has been known to awe-inspire his listeners as though Ætna were there.

If oratory consists of the power to move men by spoken words, Douglass is a complete orator. He can make men laugh or cry, at his will. He has power of statement, logic, withering denunciation, pathos, humor, and inimitable wit. Daniel Webster,* with his immense intellectuality, had no humor, not a particle. It does not appear that he could even see the point of a joke. Douglass is brim full of humor, at times, of the dryest kind. It is of a quiet kind. You can see it coming a long way off in a peculiar twitch of his mouth. It increases and broadens gradually until it becomes irresistible and all-pervading with his audience.

Douglass' rank as a writer is high, and justly so. His writings, if anything, are more meritorious than his speaking. For many years he was the editor of newspapers, doing all of the editorial work. He has contributed largely to magazines. He is a forcible and thoughtful writer. His style is pure and graceful, and he has great felicity of expression. His written productions, in finish, compare favorably with the written productions of our most cultivated writers. His style comes partly, no doubt, from his long and constant practice, but the true source is his clear mind, which is well stored by a close acquaintance with the best authors. His range of reading has been wide and extensive. He has been a hard student. In every sense of the word, he is a self-made man. By dint of hard study he has educated himself, and to-day it may be said he has a well-trained intellect. He has surmounted the disadvantage of not having a university education, by application and well-directed effort. He seems to have realized the fact, that to one who is anxious to become educated and is really in earnest, it is not positively necessary to go to college, and that information may be had outside of college walks; books may be obtained and read elsewhere. They are not chained to desks in college libraries, as they were in early times at Oxford. Professors' lectures may be bought already printed, learned doctors may be listened to in the lyceum, and the printing-press has made it easy and cheap to get information on every subject and topic that is discussed and taught in the university. Douglass never made the mistake (a common one) of considering that his education was finished. He has continued to study, he studies now, and is a growing man, and at this present moment he is a stronger man intellectually than ever before.

Soon after Douglass' escape from Maryland to the Northern States, he commenced his public career. It was at New Bedford, as a local Methodist preacher, and by taking part in small public meetings held by colored people, wherein anti-slavery and other matters were discussed. There he laid the foundation of the splendid career which is now about drawing to a close. In these meetings Douglass gave evidence that he possessed uncommon powers, and it was plainly to be seen that he needed only a field and opportunity to display them. That field and opportunity soon came, as it always does to possessors of genius. He became a member and agent of the American Anti-Slavery society. Then commenced his great crusade against slavery in behalf of his oppressed brethren at the South.

He waged violent and unceasing war against slavery. He went through every town and hamlet in the Free States, raising his voice against the iniquitous system.

Just escaped from the prison-house himself, to tear down the walls of the same and to let the oppressed go free was the mission which engaged the powers of his soul and body. North, East, and West, all through the land went this escaped slave, delivering his warning message against the doomed cities of the South. The ocean did not stop nor hinder him. Across the Atlantic he went, through England, Ireland, and Scotland.

Wherever people could be found to listen to his story, he pleaded the cause of his enslaved and down-trodden brethren with vehemence and great power. From 1840 to 1861, the time of the commencement of the civil war, which extirpated slavery in this country, Douglass was continually speaking on the platform, writing for his newspaper and for magazines, or working in conventions for the abolition of slavery.

The life and work of Douglass has been a complete vindication of the colored people in this respect. It has refuted and overthrown the position taken by some writers, that colored people were deficient in mental qualifications and were incapable of attaining high intellectual position. We may reasonably expect to hear no more of this now, the argument is exploded. Douglass has settled the fact the right way, and it is something to settle a fact.

That Douglass is a brave man there can be little doubt. He has physical as well as moral courage. His encounter with the overseer of the eastern shore plantation attests his pluck. There the odds were against him, everything was against him. There the unwritten rule of law was, that the negro who dared to strike a white man must be killed; but Douglass fought the overseer and whipped him. His plotting with other slaves to escape, writing and giving them passes, and the unequal and desperate fight maintained by him in the Baltimore ship yard, where law and public sentiment were against him, also show that he has courage. But since the day of his slavery, while living here at the North, many instances have happened which show very plainly that he is a man of courage and determination. If he had not been, he would have long since succumbed to the brutality and violence of the low and mean-spirited people found in the Free States.

Up to a very recent date it has been deemed quite safe, even here in the North, to insult and impose on inoffensive colored people, to elbow a colored man from the sidewalk, to jeer at him and apply vile epithets to him. In some localities this has been the rule and not the exception, and to put him out of public conveyances and public places by force was of common occurrence. It made little difference that the colored man was decent, civil, and respectably clad, and had paid his fare. If the proprietor of the place or his patrons took the notion that the presence of the colored man was an affront to their dignity or inconsistent with their notions of self-respect, out he must go. Nor must he stand upon the order of his going, but go at once. It was against this feeling that Douglass had to contend. He met it often. He was a prominent colored man traveling from place to place. A good part of the time he was in strange cities, stopping at strange taverns—that is, when he was allowed to stop. Time and again has he been refused accommodation in hotels. Time and again has he been in a strange place with nowhere to lay his head until some kind anti-slavery person would come forward and give him shelter.

The writer of this remembers well, because he was present and saw the transaction, the John Brown meeting in Tremont Temple,* in 1860, when a violent mob, composed of the rough element from the slums of the city, led and encouraged by bankers and brokers, came into the hall to break up the meeting. Douglass was presiding. The mob was armed; the police were powerless; the mayor could not or would not do anything. On came the mob, surging through the aisles, over benches, and upon the platform. The women in the audience became alarmed and fled. The hirelings were prepared to do anything; they had the power and could with impunity. Douglass sat upon the platform with a few chosen spirits, cool and undaunted. The mob had got about and around him. He did not heed their howling nor was he moved by their threats. It was not until their leader, a rich banker, with his followers, had mounted the platform and wrenched the chair from under him that he was dispossessed. By main force and personal violence (Douglass resisting all the time) they removed him from the platform.

It affords me great pleasure to introduce to the public this book, 'The Life and Times of Frederick Douglass.' I am glad of the opportunity to present a work which tells the story of the rise and progress of our most celebrated colored man. To the names of Toussaint L'Overture* and Alexander Dumas* is to be added that of Frederick Douglass. We point with pride to this trio of illustrious names. I bid my fellow countrymen take new hope and courage. The near future will bring us other men of worth and genius, and our list of illustrious names will become lengthened. Until that time the duty is to work and wait.

Respectfully,
GEORGE L. RUFFIN.

# LIFE AS A SLAVE.

# CHAPTER I.

## AUTHOR'S BIRTH.

*Author's place of birth—Description of country—Its inhabitants—
Genealogical trees—Method of counting time in slave districts—Date
of author's birth—Names of grandparents—Their cabin—Home with
them—Slave practice of separating mothers from their children—
Author's recollections of his mother—Who was his father?*

IN Talbot County, Eastern Shore, State of Maryland, near Easton, the
county town, there is a small district of country, thinly populated, and
remarkable for nothing that I know of more than for the worn-out,
sandy, desert-like appearance of its soil, the general dilapidation of its
farms and fences, the indigent and spiritless character of its inhabitants, and the prevalence of ague and fever. It was in this dull, flat, and
unthrifty district or neighborhood, bordered by the Choptank river,
among the laziest and muddiest of streams, surrounded by a white
population of the lowest order, indolent and drunken to a proverb, and
among slaves who, in point of ignorance and indolence, were fully in
accord with their surroundings, that I, without any fault of my own,
was born, and spent the first years of my childhood.

The reader must not expect me to say much of my family.
Genealogical trees did not flourish among slaves. A person of some
consequence in civilized society, sometimes designated as father, was
literally unknown to slave law and to slave practice. I never met with
a slave in that part of the country who could tell me with any certainty
how old he was. Few at that time knew anything of the months of the
year or of the days of the month. They measured the ages of their children by spring-time, winter-time, harvest-time, planting-time, and the
like. Masters allowed no questions concerning their ages to be put to
them by slaves. Such questions were regarded by the masters as evidence of an impudent curiosity. From certain events, however, the
dates of which I have since learned, I suppose myself to have been born
in February, 1817.*

My first experience of life, as I now remember it, and I remember it
but hazily, began in the family of my grandmother and grandfather,
Betsey and Isaac Bailey.* They were considered old settlers in the
neighborhood, and from certain circumstances I infer that my grandmother, especially, was held in high esteem, far higher than was the lot
of most colored persons in that region. She was a good nurse, and

a capital hand at making nets used for catching shad and herring, and was, withal, somewhat famous as a fisherwoman. I have known her to be in the water waist deep, for hours, seine-hauling. She was a gardener as well as a fisherwoman, and remarkable for her success in keeping her seedling sweet potatoes through the months of winter, and easily got the reputation of being born to 'good luck.' In planting-time Grandmother Betsey was sent for in all directions, simply to place the seedling potatoes in the hills or drills; for superstition had it that her touch was needed to make them grow. This reputation was full of advantage to her and her grandchildren, for a good crop, after her planting for the neighbors, brought her a share of the harvest.

Whether because she was too old for field service, or because she had so faithfully discharged the duties of her station in early life, I know not, but she enjoyed the high privilege of living in a cabin separate from the quarters, having imposed upon her only the charge of the young children and the burden of her own support. She esteemed it great good fortune to live so, and took much comfort in having the children. The practice of separating mothers from their children and hiring them out at distances too great to admit of their meeting, save at long intervals, was a marked feature of the cruelty and barbarity of the slave system; but it was in harmony with the grand aim of that system, which always and everywhere sought to reduce man to a level with the brute. It had no interest in recognizing or preserving any of the ties that bind families together or to their homes.

My grandmother's five daughters were hired out in this way, and my only recollections of my own mother* are of a few hasty visits made in the night on foot, after the daily tasks were over, and when she was under the necessity of returning in time to respond to the driver's call to the field in the early morning. These little glimpses of my mother, obtained under such circumstances and against such odds, meager as they were, are ineffaceably stamped upon my memory. She was tall and finely proportioned, of dark, glossy complexion, with regular features, and amongst the slaves was remarkably sedate and dignified. There is, in 'Prichard's Natural History of Man,' the head of a figure, on page 157,* the features of which so resemble my mother that I often recur to it with something of the feelings which I suppose others experience when looking upon the likenesses of their own dear departed ones.

Of my father I know nothing. Slavery had no recognition of fathers, as none of families. That the mother was a slave was enough for its deadly purpose. By its law the child followed the condition of its mother. The father might be a freeman and the child a slave. The father might be a white man, glorying in the purity of his Anglo-Saxon blood, and the child ranked with the blackest slaves. Father he might be, and not be husband, and could sell his own child without incurring reproach, if in its veins coursed one drop of African blood.

# CHAPTER II.

## REMOVAL FROM GRANDMOTHER'S.

*Author's early home—Its charms—Author's ignorance of 'old master'—His gradual perception of the truth concerning him—His relations to Col. Edward Lloyd—Author's removal to 'old master's' home—His journey thence—His separation from his grandmother—His grief.*

LIVING thus with my grandmother, whose kindness and love stood in place of my mother's, it was some time before I knew myself to be a slave. I knew many other things before I knew that. Her little cabin had to me the attractions of a palace. Its fence-railed floor—which was equally floor and bedstead—up stairs, and its clay floor down stairs, its dirt and straw chimney, and windowless sides, and that most curious piece of workmanship, the ladder stairway, and the hole so strangely dug in front of the fire-place, beneath which grandmamma placed her sweet potatoes, to keep them from frost in winter, were full of interest to my childish observation. The squirrels, as they skipped the fences, climbed the trees, or gathered their nuts, were an unceasing delight to me. There, too, right at the side of the hut, stood the old well, with its stately and skyward-pointing beam, so aptly placed between the limbs of what had once been a tree, and so nicely balanced, that I could move it up and down with only one hand, and could get a drink myself without calling for help. Nor were these all the attractions of the place. At a little distance stood Mr. Lee's mill, where the people came in large numbers to get their corn ground. I can never tell the many things thought and felt, as I sat on the bank and watched that mill, and the turning of its ponderous wheel. The mill-pond, too, had its charms; and with my pin-hook and thread-line, I could get amusing nibbles if I could catch no fish.

It was not long, however, before I began to learn the sad fact that this house of my childhood belonged not to my dear old grandmother, but to some one I had never seen, and who lived a great distance off. I learned, too, the sadder fact, that not only the home and lot, but that grandmother herself and all the little children around her belonged to a mysterious personage, called by grandmother, with every mark of reverence, 'Old Master.'* Thus early did clouds and shadows begin to fall upon my path.

I learned that this old master, whose name seemed ever to be mentioned with fear and shuddering, only allowed the little children to live with grandmother for a limited time, and that as soon as they were big enough they were promptly taken away to live with the said old master. These were distressing revelations, indeed. My grandmother was all the world to me, and the thought of being separated from her was a most unwelcome suggestion to my affections and hopes. This mysterious old master was really a man of some consequence. He owned several farms in Tuckahoe, was the chief clerk and butler on the home plantation of Colonel Lloyd,* had overseers as well as slaves on his own farms, and gave directions to the overseers on the farms owned by Colonel Lloyd. Captain Aaron Anthony, for such is the name and title of my old master, lived on Colonel Lloyd's plantation, which was situated on the Wye river, and which was one of the largest, most fertile, and best appointed in the State.

About this plantation and this old master I was most eager to know everything which could be known; and, unhappily for me, all the information I could get concerning him increased my dread of being separated from my grandmother and grandfather. I wished that it was possible for me to remain small all my life, knowing that the sooner I grew large the shorter would be my time to remain with them. Everything about the cabin became doubly dear and I was sure that there could be no other spot on earth equal to it. But the time came when I must go, and my grandmother, knowing my fears, and in pity for them, kindly kept me ignorant of the dreaded moment up to the morning (a beautiful summer morning) when we were to start; and, indeed, during the whole journey, which, child as I was, I remember as well as if it were yesterday, she kept the unwelcome truth hidden from me. The distance from Tuckahoe to Colonel Lloyd's, where my old master lived, was full twelve miles, and the walk was quite a severe test of the endurance of my young legs. The journey would have proved too severe for me, but that my dear old grandmother (blessings on her memory) afforded occasional relief by 'toteing'* me on her shoulder. Advanced in years as she was, as was evident from the more than one gray hair which peeped from between the ample and graceful folds of her newly and smoothly-ironed bandana turban, grandmother was yet a woman of power and spirit. She was remarkably straight in figure, and elastic and muscular in movement. I seemed hardly to be a burden to her. She would have 'toted' me farther, but I felt myself too much of a man to allow it. Yet while I walked I was not independent of her. She often found me holding her skirts lest something should come out of the woods and eat me up. Several old logs and stumps imposed upon me, and got themselves taken for enormous animals. I could plainly see their legs, eyes, ears, and teeth, till I got close enough to see that the eyes were knots, washed white with rain, and the legs were broken limbs, and the ears and teeth only such because of the point from which they were seen.

As the day advanced the heat increased, and it was not until the afternoon that we reached the much-dreaded end of the journey. Here I found myself in the midst of a group of children of all sizes and of many colors,—black, brown, copper-colored, and nearly white. I had not before seen so many children. As a new-comer I was an object of special interest. After laughing and yelling around me and playing all sorts of wild tricks, they asked me to go out and play with them. This I refused to do. Grandmamma looked sad, and I could not help feeling that our being there boded no good to me. She was soon to lose another object of affection, as she had lost many before. Affectionately patting me on the head, she told me to be a good boy and go out to play with the children. They are 'kin to you,' she said, 'go and play with them.' She pointed out to me my brother Perry,* and my sisters, Sarah and Eliza.* I had never seen them before, and though I had sometimes heard of them and felt a curious interest in them, I really did not understand what they were to me or I to them. Brothers and sisters we were by blood, but slavery had made us strangers. They were already initiated into the mysteries of old master's domicile, and they seemed to look upon me with a certain degree of compassion. I really wanted to play with them, but they were strangers to me, and I was full of fear that my grandmother might leave for home without taking me with her. Entreated to do so, however, and that, too, by my dear grandmother, I went to the back part of the house to play with them and the other children. Play, however, I did not, but stood with my back against the wall witnessing the playing of the others. At last, while standing there, one of the children, who had been in the kitchen, ran up to me in a sort of roguish glee, exclaiming, 'Fed, Fed, grandmamma gone!' I could not believe it. Yet, fearing the worst, I ran into the kitchen to see for myself, and lo! she was indeed gone, and was now far away, and 'clean' out of sight. I need not tell all that happened now. Almost heart-broken at the discovery, I fell upon the ground and wept a boy's bitter tears, refusing to be comforted. My brother gave me peaches and pears to quiet me, but I promptly threw them on the ground. I had never been deceived before and something of resentment mingled with my grief at parting with my grandmother.

It was now late in the afternoon. The day had been an exciting and wearisome one, and I know not where, but I suppose I sobbed myself to sleep; and its balm was never more welcome to any wounded soul than to mine. The reader may be surprised that I relate so minutely an incident apparently so trivial, and which must have occurred when I was less than seven years old; but, as I wish to give a faithful history of my experience in slavery, I cannot withhold a circumstance which at the time affected me so deeply, and which I still remember so vividly. Besides, this was my first introduction to the realities of the slave system.

# CHAPTER III.

## TROUBLES OF CHILDHOOD.

*Col. Lloyd's plantation—Aunt Katy—Her cruelty and ill-nature—*
*Capt. Anthony's partiality to Aunt Katy—Allowance of food—*
*Author's hunger—Unexpected rescue by his mother—The reproof of*
*Aunt Katy—Sleep—A slave-mother's love—Author's inheritance—*
*His mother's acquirements—Her death.*

ONCE established on the home plantation of Col. Lloyd—I was with the children there, left to the tender mercies of Aunt Katy,* a slave woman, who was to my master what he was to Col. Lloyd. Disposing of us in classes or sizes, he left to Aunt Katy all the minor details concerning our management. She was a woman who never allowed herself to act greatly within the limits of delegated power, no matter how broad that authority might be. Ambitious of old master's favor, ill-tempered and cruel by nature, she found in her present position an ample field for the exercise of her ill-omened qualities. She had a strong hold upon old master, for she was a first-rate cook, and very industrious. She was therefore greatly favored by him—and as one mark of his favor she was the only mother who was permitted to retain her children around her, and even to these, her own children, she was often fiendish in her brutality. Cruel, however, as she sometimes was to her own children, she was not destitute of maternal feeling, and in her instinct to satisfy their demands for food she was often guilty of starving me and the other children. Want of food was my chief trouble during my first summer here. Captain Anthony, instead of allowing a given quantity of food to each slave, committed the allowance for all to Aunt Katy, to be divided by her, after cooking, amongst us. The allowance consisted of coarse corn-meal, not very abundant, and which, by passing through Aunt Katy's hands, became more slender still for some of us. I have often been so pinched with hunger as to dispute with old 'Nep,' the dog, for the crumbs which fell from the kitchen table. Many times have I followed, with eager step, the waiting-girl when she shook the table-cloth, to get the crumbs and small bones flung out for the dogs and cats. It was a great thing to have the privilege of dipping a piece of bread into the water in which meat had been boiled, and the skin taken from the rusty bacon was a positive luxury. With this description of the domestic arrangements of my new home, I may here recount a circumstance which is deeply impressed on my memory, as affording a bright gleam of a slave-mother's love, and the earnestness of a mother's care. I had offended Aunt Katy. I do not remember in what way, for my offences were numerous in that quarter, greatly depending upon her moods as to their heinousness, and she had adopted her usual mode of punishing me: namely, making me go all day without food. For the first hour or two after dinner time, I succeeded pretty well in keeping up my spirits; but as the day wore away, I found it quite impossible to do so any longer. Sundown came, but no bread; and in its stead came the threat from Aunt Katy, with a scowl well-suited to its terrible import, that she would starve the life out of me. Brandishing her knife, she chopped off the heavy slices of bread for the other children, and put the loaf away, muttering all the while her savage designs upon myself. Against this disappointment, for I was expecting that her heart would relent at last, I made an extra effort to maintain my dignity, but when I saw the other children around me with satisfied faces, I could stand it no longer. I went out behind the kitchen wall and cried like a fine fellow. When wearied with this, I returned to the kitchen, sat by the fire and brooded over my hard lot. I was too hungry to sleep. While I sat in the corner, I caught sight of an ear of Indian corn upon an upper shelf. I watched my chance and got it; and shelling off a few grains, I put it back again. These grains I quickly put into the hot ashes to roast. I did this at the risk of getting a brutal thumping, for Aunt Katy could beat as well as starve me. My corn was not long in roasting, and I eagerly pulled it from the ashes, and placed it upon a stool in a clever little pile. I began to help myself, when who but my own dear mother should come in. The scene which followed is beyond my power to describe. The friendless and hungry boy, in his extremest need, found himself in the strong, protecting arms of his mother. I have before spoken of my mother's dignified and impressive manner. I shall never forget the indescribable expression of her countenance when I told her that Aunt Katy had said she would starve the life out of me. There was deep and tender pity in her glance at me, and, at the same moment, a fiery indignation at Aunt Katy, and while she took the corn from me, and gave in its stead a large ginger-cake, she read Aunt Katy a lecture which was never forgotten. That night I learned as I had never learned before, that I was not only a child, but somebody's child. I was grander upon my mother's knee than a king upon his throne. But my triumph was short. I dropped off to sleep, and waked in the morning to find my mother gone and myself at the mercy again of the virago in my master's kitchen, whose fiery wrath was my constant dread.

My mother had walked twelve miles to see me, and had the same distance to travel over again before the morning sunrise. I do not remember ever seeing her again. Her death soon ended the little communication that had existed between us, and with it, I believe, a life full of weariness and heartfelt sorrow. To me it has ever been a grief that I knew my mother so little, and have so few of her words treasured in my remembrance. I have since learned that she was the only one of all the colored people of Tuckahoe who could read. How she acquired this knowledge I know not, for Tuckahoe was the last place in the world where she would have been likely to find facilities for learning. I can therefore fondly and proudly ascribe to her an earnest love of knowledge. That in any slave State a field-hand should learn to read is remarkable, but the achievement of my mother, considering the place and circumstances, was very extraordinary. In view of this fact, I am happy to attribute any love of letters I may have, not to my presumed Anglo-Saxon paternity, but to the native genius of my sable, unprotected, and uncultivated mother—a woman who belonged to a race whose mental endowments are still disparaged and despised.

# CHAPTER IV.

## A GENERAL SURVEY OF THE SLAVE PLANTATION.

IT was generally supposed that slavery in the State of Maryland existed
in its mildest form, and that it was totally divested of those harsh
and terrible peculiarities which characterized the slave system in
the Southern and South-Western States of the American Union. The
ground of this opinion was the contiguity of the free States, and the
influence of their moral, religious, and humane sentiments. Public opinion was, indeed, a measurable restraint upon the cruelty and barbarity
of masters, overseers, and slave-drivers, whenever and wherever it could
reach them; but there were certain secluded and out-of-the-way places,
even in the state of Maryland, fifty years ago, seldom visited by a single
ray of healthy public sentiment, where slavery, wrapt in its own congenial darkness, could and did develop all its malign and shocking characteristics, where it could be indecent without shame, cruel without
shuddering, and murderous without apprehension or fear of exposure
or punishment. Just such a secluded, dark, and out-of-the-way place
was the home plantation of Colonel Edward Lloyd, in Talbot county,
eastern shore of Maryland. It was far away from all the great thorough-
fares of travel and commerce, and proximate to no town or village. There
was neither school-house nor town-house in its neighborhood. The
school-house was unnecessary, for there were no children to go to school.
The children and grandchildren of Col. Lloyd were taught in the house
by a private tutor (a Mr. Page* from Greenfield, Massachusetts, a tall,
gaunt sapling of a man, remarkably dignified, thoughtful, and reticent,
and who did not speak a dozen words to a slave in a whole year). The
overseer's children went off somewhere in the State to school, and therefore could bring no foreign or dangerous influence from abroad to
embarrass the natural operation of the slave system of the place. Here,
not even the commonest mechanics, from whom there might have been

an occasional outburst of honest and telling indignation at cruelty and wrong on other plantations, were white men. Its whole public was made up of and divided into three classes, slaveholders, slaves, and overseers. Its blacksmiths, wheelwrights, shoemakers, weavers, and coopers were slaves. Not even commerce, selfish and indifferent to moral considerations as it usually is, was permitted within its secluded precincts. Whether with a view of guarding against the escape of its secrets, I know not, but it is a fact, that every leaf and grain of the products of this plantation and those of the neighboring farms belonging to Col. Lloyd were transported to Baltimore in his own vessels, every man and boy on board of which, except the captain, were owned by him as his property. In return, everything brought to the plantation came through the same channel. To make this isolation more apparent, it may be stated that the estates adjoining Col. Lloyd's were owned and occupied by friends of his, who were as deeply interested as himself in maintaining the slave system in all its rigor. These were the Tilgmans, the Goldboroughs, the Lockermans, the Pacas, the Skinners, Gibsons,* and others of lesser affluence and standing.

Public opinion in such a quarter, the reader must see, was not likely to be very efficient in protecting the slave from cruelty. To be a restraint upon abuses of this nature, opinion must emanate from humane and virtuous communities, and to no such opinion or influence was Col. Lloyd's plantation exposed. It was a little nation by itself, having its own language, its own rules, regulations, and customs. The troubles and controversies arising here were not settled by the civil power of the State. The overseer was the important dignitary. He was generally accuser, judge, jury, advocate, and executioner. The criminal was always dumb, and no slave was allowed to testify other than against his brother slave.

There were, of course, no conflicting rights of property, for all the people were the property of one man, and they could themselves own no property. Religion and politics were largely excluded. One class of the population was too high to be reached by the common preacher, and the other class was too low in condition and ignorance to be much cared for by religious teachers, and yet some religious ideas did enter this dark corner.

This, however, is not the only view which the place presented. Though civilization was, in many respects, shut out, nature could not be. Though separated from the rest of the world, though public opinion, as I have said, could seldom penetrate its dark domain, though the whole place was stamped with its own peculiar iron-like individuality, and though crimes, high-handed and atrocious, could be committed there with strange and shocking impunity, it was, to outward seeming, a most strikingly interesting place, full of life, activity, and spirit, and presented a very favorable contrast to the indolent monotony and languor of Tuckahoe. It resembled, in some respects, descriptions I have since read of the old baronial domains of Europe. Keen as was my regret and great as was my sorrow at leaving my old home, I was not long in adapting myself to this my new one. A man's troubles are always half disposed of when he finds endurance the only alternative. I found myself here, there was no getting away, and naught remained for me but to make the best of it. Here were plenty of children to play with and plenty of pleasant resorts for boys of my age and older. The little tendrils of affection, so rudely broken from the darling objects in and around my grandmother's home, gradually began to extend and twine themselves around the new surroundings. Here, for the first time, I saw a large windmill, with its wide-sweeping white wings, a commanding object to a child's eye. This was situated on what was called Long Point—a tract of land dividing Miles river from the Wye. I spent many hours here watching the wings of this wondrous mill. In the river, or what was called the 'Swash,' at a short distance from the shore, quietly lying at anchor, with her small row boat dancing at her stern, was a large sloop, the Sally Lloyd, called by that name in honor of the favorite daughter of the Colonel. These two objects, the sloop and mill, awakened as I remember, thoughts, ideas, and wondering. Then here were a great many houses, human habitations full of the mysteries of life at every stage of it. There was the little red house up the road, occupied by Mr. Seveir, the overseer. A little nearer to my old master's stood a long, low, rough building literally alive with slaves of all ages, sexes, conditions, sizes, and colors. This was called the long quarter. Perched upon a hill east of our house, was a tall, dilapidated old brick building, the architectural dimensions of which proclaimed its creation for a different purpose, now occupied by slaves, in a similar manner to the long quarters. Besides these, there were numerous other slave houses and huts scattered around in the neighborhood, every nook and corner of which were completely occupied.

Old master's house, a long brick building, plain but substantial, was centrally located, and was an independent establishment. Besides these houses there were barns, stables, store-houses, tobacco-houses, blacksmith shops, wheelwright shops, cooper shops; but above all there stood the grandest building my young eyes had ever beheld, called by every one on the plantation the *great* house.* This was occupied by Col.

Lloyd and his family. It was surrounded by numerous and variously-shaped out-buildings. There were kitchens, wash-houses, dairies, summer-houses, green-houses, hen-houses, turkey-houses, pigeon-houses, and arbors of many sizes and devices, all neatly painted or whitewashed, interspersed with grand old trees, ornamental and primitive, which afforded delightful shade in summer and imparted to the scene a high degree of stately beauty. The *great* house itself was a large white wooden building with wings on three sides of it. In front, extending the entire length of the building and supported by a long range of columns, was a broad portico, which gave to the Colonel's home an air of great dignity and grandeur. It was a treat to my young and gradually opening mind to behold this elaborate exhibition of wealth, power and beauty.

The carriage entrance to the house was by a large gate, more than a quarter of a mile distant. The intermediate space was a beautiful lawn, very neatly kept and tended. It was dotted thickly over with trees and flowers. The road or lane from the gate to the great house was richly paved with white pebbles from the beach and in its course formed a complete circle around the lawn. Outside this select enclosure were parks, as about the residences of the English nobility, where rabbits, deer, and other wild game might be seen peering and playing about, with 'none to molest them or make them afraid.'* The tops of the stately poplars were often covered with red-winged blackbirds, making all nature vocal with the joyous life and beauty of their wild, warbling notes. These all belonged to me as well as to Col. Edward Lloyd, and, whether they did or not, I greatly enjoyed them. Not far from the great house were the stately mansions of the dead Lloyds—a place of somber aspect. Vast tombs, embowered beneath the weeping willow and the fir tree, told of the generations of the family, as well as of their wealth. Superstition was rife among the slaves about this family burying-ground. Strange sights had been seen there by some of the older slaves, and I was often compelled to hear stories of shrouded ghosts, riding on great black horses, and of balls of fire which had been seen to fly there at midnight, and of startling and dreadful sounds that had been repeatedly heard. Slaves knew enough of the Orthodox theology of the time, to consign all bad slaveholders to hell, and they often fancied such persons wishing themselves back again to wield the lash. Tales of sights and sounds strange and terrible, connected with the huge black tombs, were a great security to the grounds about them, for few of the slaves had the courage to approach them during the day time. It was a dark, gloomy, and forbidding place, and it was difficult to feel that the spirits of the sleeping dust there deposited reigned with the blest in the realms of eternal peace.

At Lloyd's, was transacted the business of twenty or thirty different farms, which, with the slaves upon them, numbering, in all, not less than a thousand, all belonged to Col. Lloyd. Each farm was under the management of an overseer, whose word was law.

Mr. Lloyd was, at this time, very rich. His slaves alone, numbering as I have said not less than a thousand, were an immense fortune, and though scarcely a month passed without the sale to the Georgia traders, of one or more lots, there was no apparent diminution in the number of his human stock. The selling of any to the State of Georgia was a sore and mournful event to those left behind, as well as to the victims themselves.

The reader has already been informed of the handicrafts carried on here by the slaves. 'Uncle' Toney was the blacksmith, 'Uncle' Harry the cartwright, and 'Uncle' Abel was the shoemaker, and these had assistants in their several departments. These mechanics were called 'Uncles' by all the younger slaves, not because they really sustained that relationship to any, but according to plantation etiquette, as a mark of respect, due from the younger to the older slaves. Strange and even ridiculous as it may seem, among a people so uncultivated and with so many stern trials to look in the face, there is not to be found among any people a more rigid enforcement of the law of respect to elders than is maintained among them. I set this down as partly constitutional with the colored race and partly conventional. There is no better material in the world for making a gentleman than is furnished in the African.

Among other slave notabilities, I found here one called by everybody, white and colored, 'Uncle' Isaac Copper. It was seldom that a slave, however venerable, was honored with a surname in Maryland, and so completely has the south shaped the manners of the north in this respect that their right to such honor is tardily admitted even now. It goes sadly against the grain to address and treat a negro as one would address and treat a white man. But once in a while, even in a slave state, a negro had a surname fastened to him by common consent. This was the case with 'Uncle' Isaac Copper. When the 'Uncle' was dropped, he was called Doctor Copper. He was both our Doctor of Medicine and our Doctor of Divinity. Where he took his degree I am unable to say, but he was too well established in his profession to permit question as to his native skill or attainments. One qualification he certainly had. He was a confirmed cripple, wholly unable to work, and was worth nothing for sale in the market. Though lame, he was no sluggard. He made his crutches do him good service, and was always on the alert looking up the sick, and such as were supposed to need his aid and counsel. His remedial prescriptions embraced four articles. For diseases of the body, epsom salts and castor oil; for those of the soul, the 'Lord's prayer,' and a few stout hickory switches.

I was, with twenty or thirty other children, early sent to Doctor Isaac Copper, to learn the Lord's prayer. The old man was seated on a huge three-legged oaken stool, armed with several large hickory switches, and from the point where he sat, lame as he was, he could reach every boy in the room. After our standing a while to learn what was expected of us, he commanded us to kneel down. This done, he told us to say everything he said. 'Our Father'—this we repeated after him with promptness and uniformity—'who art in Heaven,' was less promptly and uniformly repeated, and the old gentleman paused in the prayer to give us a short lecture, and to use his switches on our backs.

Everybody in the South seemed to want the privilege of whipping somebody else. Uncle Isaac, though a good old man, shared the common passion of his time and country. I cannot say I was much edified by attendance upon his ministry. There was in my mind, even at that time, something a little inconsistent and laughable in the blending of prayer with punishment.

I was not long in my new home before I found that the dread I had conceived of Captain Anthony was in a measure groundless. Instead of leaping out from some hiding-place and destroying me, he hardly seemed to notice my presence. He probably thought as little of my arrival there as of an additional pig to his stock. He was the chief agent of his employer. The overseers of all the farms composing the Lloyd estate were in some sort under him. The Colonel himself seldom addressed an overseer, or allowed himself to be addressed by one. To Captain Anthony, therefore, was committed the headship of all the farms. He carried the keys of all the store-houses, weighed and measured the allowances of each slave, at the end of each month; superintended the storing of all goods brought to the store-house; dealt out the raw material to the different handicraftsmen; shipped the grain, tobacco, and all other saleable produce of the numerous farms to Baltimore, and had a general oversight of all the workshops of the place. In addition to all this he was frequently called abroad to Easton and elsewhere in the discharge of his numerous duties as chief agent of the estate.

The family of Captain Anthony consisted of two sons—Andrew and Richard,* and his daughter Lucretia and her newly-married husband, Captain Thomas Auld.* In the kitchen were Aunt Katy, Aunt Esther,* and ten or a dozen children, most of them older than myself. Captain Anthony was not considered a rich slave-holder, though he was pretty well off in the world. He owned about thirty slaves and three farms in the Tuckahoe district. The more valuable part of his property was in slaves, of whom he sold one every year, which brought him in seven or eight hundred dollars, besides his yearly salary and other revenue from his lands.

I have been often asked, during the earlier part of my free life at the North, how I happened to have so little of the slave accent in my speech. The mystery is in some measure explained by my association with Daniel Lloyd,* the youngest son of Col. Edward Lloyd. The law of compensation holds here as well as elsewhere. While this lad could not associate with ignorance without sharing its shade, he could not give his black playmates his company without giving them his superior intelligence as well. Without knowing this, or caring about it at the time, I, for some cause or other, was attracted to him, and was much his companion.

I had little to do with the older brothers of Daniel—Edward and Murray.* They were grown up and were fine-looking men. Edward was especially esteemed by the slave children, and by me among the rest—not that he ever said anything to us or for us which could be called particularly kind. It was enough for us that he never looked or acted scornfully toward us. The idea of rank and station was rigidly maintained on this estate. The family of Captain Anthony never visited the great house, and the Lloyds never came to our house. Equal non-intercourse was observed between Captain Anthony's family and the family of Mr. Seveir, the overseer.

Such, kind readers, was the community and such the place in which my earliest and most lasting impressions of the workings of slavery were received, of which impressions you will learn more in the after coming chapters of this book.

# CHAPTER V.

## A SLAVEHOLDER'S CHARACTER.

*Increasing acquaintance with old Master—Evils of unresisted passion—Apparent tenderness—A man of trouble—Custom of muttering to himself—Brutal outrage—A drunken overseer—Slaveholder's impatience—Wisdom of appeal—A base and selfish attempt to break up a courtship.*

ALTHOUGH my old master, Captain Anthony, gave me, at the first of my coming to him from my grandmother's, very little attention, and although that little was of a remarkably mild and gentle description, a few months only were sufficient to convince me that mildness and gentleness were not the prevailing or governing traits of his character. These excellent qualities were displayed only occasionally. He could, when it suited him, appear to be literally insensible to the claims of humanity. He could not only be deaf to the appeals of the helpless against the aggressor, but he could himself commit outrages deep, dark, and nameless. Yet he was not by nature worse than other men. Had he been brought up in a free state, surrounded by the full restraints of civilized society—restraints which are necessary to the freedom of all its members, alike and equally, Capt. Anthony might have been as humane a man as are members of such society generally. A man's character always takes its hue, more or less, from the form and color of things about him. The slaveholder, as well as the slave, was the victim of the slave system. Under the whole heavens there could be no relation more unfavorable to the development of honorable character than that sustained by the slaveholder to the slave. Reason is imprisoned here, and passions run wild. Could the reader have seen Captain Anthony gently leading me by the hand, as he sometimes did, patting me on the head, speaking to me in soft, caressing tones, and calling me his little Indian boy, he would have deemed him a kind-hearted old man, and really almost fatherly to the slave boy. But the pleasant moods of a slaveholder are transient and fitful. They neither come often nor remain long. The temper of the old man was subject to special trials; but since these trials were never borne patiently, they added little to his natural stock of patience. Aside from his troubles with his slaves and those of Mr. Lloyd, he made the impression upon me of being an unhappy man. Even to my child's eye he wore a troubled and at times a haggard aspect. His strange movements excited my curiosity and awakened my compassion. He seldom walked alone without muttering to himself, and he occasionally stormed about as if defying an army of invisible foes. Most of his leisure was spent in walking around, cursing and gesticulating as if possessed by a demon. He was evidently a wretched man, at war with his own soul and all the world around him. To be overheard by the children disturbed him very little. He made no more of our presence than that of the ducks and geese he met on the green. But when his gestures were most violent, ending with a threatening shake of the head and a sharp snap of his middle finger and thumb, I deemed it wise to keep at a safe distance from him.

One of the first circumstances that opened my eyes to the cruelties and wickedness of slavery and its hardening influences upon my old master, was his refusal to interpose his authority to protect and shield a young woman, a cousin of mine,* who had been most cruelly abused and beaten by his overseer in Tuckahoe. This overseer, a Mr. Plummer, was, like most of his class, little less than a human brute; and, in addition to his general profligacy and repulsive coarseness, he was a miserable drunkard, a man not fit to have the management of a drove of mules. In one of his moments of drunken madness he committed the outrage which brought the young woman in question down to my old master's for protection. The poor girl, on her arrival at our house, presented a most pitiable appearance. She had left in haste and without preparation, and probably without the knowledge of Mr. Plummer. She had traveled twelve miles, barefooted, bare-necked, and bare-headed. Her neck and shoulders were covered with scars, newly made; and, not content with marring her neck and shoulders with the cowhide, the cowardly wretch had dealt her a blow on the head with a hickory club, which cut a horrible gash, and left her face literally covered with blood. In this condition the poor young woman came down to implore protection at the hands of my old master. I expected to see him boil over with rage at the revolting deed, and to hear him fill the air with curses upon the brutal Plummer; but I was disappointed. He sternly told her in an angry tone, 'She deserved every bit of it, and if she did not go home instantly he would himself take the remaining skin from her neck and back.' Thus the poor girl was compelled to return without redress, and perhaps to receive an additional flogging for daring to appeal to authority higher than that of the overseer.

I did not at that time understand the philosophy of this treatment of my cousin. I think I now understand it. This treatment was a part of the system, rather than a part of the man. To have encouraged appeals of this kind would have occasioned much loss of time and would have left the overseer powerless to enforce obedience. Nevertheless, when a slave had nerve enough to go straight to his master with a well-founded complaint against an overseer, though he might be repelled and have even that of which he at the time complained repeated, and though he might be beaten by his master, as well as by the overseer, for his temerity, the policy of complaining was, in the end, generally vindicated by the relaxed rigor of the overseer's treatment. The latter became more careful and less disposed to use the lash upon such slaves thereafter.

The overseer very naturally disliked to have the ear of the master disturbed by complaints; and, either for this reason or because of advice privately given him by his employer, he generally modified the rigor of his rule after complaints of this kind had been made against him. For some cause or other, the slaves, no matter how often they were repulsed by their masters, were ever disposed to regard them with less abhorrence than the overseer. And yet these masters would often go beyond their overseers in wanton cruelty. They wielded the lash without any sense of responsibility. They could cripple or kill without fear of consequences. I have seen my old master when in a tempest of wrath, and full of pride, hatred, jealousy and revenge, seem a very fiend.

The circumstances which I am about to narrate and which gave rise to this fearful tempest of passion, were not singular, but very common in our slave-holding community.

The reader will have noticed that, among the names of slaves, that of Esther is mentioned. This was the name of a young woman who possessed that which was ever a curse to the slave girl—namely, personal beauty. She was tall, light-colored, well formed, and made a fine appearance. Esther was courted by 'Ned Roberts,' the son of a favorite slave of Col. Lloyd, and who was as fine-looking a young man as Esther was a woman. Some slave holders would have been glad to have promoted the marriage of two such persons, but for some reason Captain Anthony disapproved of their courtship. He strictly ordered her to quit the society of young Roberts, telling her that he would punish her severely if he ever found her again in his company. But it was impossible to keep this couple apart. Meet they would and meet they did. Had Mr. Anthony himself been a man of honor, his motives in this matter might have appeared more favorably. As it was, they appeared as abhorrent as they were contemptible. It was one of the damning characteristics of slavery that it robbed its victims of every earthly incentive to a holy life. The fear of God and the hope of heaven were sufficient to sustain many slave women amidst the snares and dangers of their strange lot; but they were ever at the mercy of the power, passion and caprice of their owners. Slavery provided no means for the honorable perpetuation of the race. Yet, despite of this destitution, there were many men and women among the slaves who were true and faithful to each other through life.

But to the case in hand. Abhorred and circumvented as he was, Captain Anthony, having the power, was determined on revenge. I happened to see its shocking execution, and shall never forget the scene. It was early in the morning, when all was still, and before any of the family in the house or kitchen had risen. I was, in fact, awakened by the heart-rending shrieks and piteous cries of poor Esther. My sleeping-place was on the dirt floor of a little rough closet which opened into the kitchen, and through the cracks in its unplaned boards I could distinctly see and hear what was going on, without being seen. Esther's wrists were firmly tied, and the twisted rope was fastened to a strong iron staple in a heavy wooden beam above, near the fire-place. Here she stood on a bench, her arms tightly drawn above her head. Her back and shoulders were perfectly bare. Behind her stood old master, cowhide in hand, pursuing his barbarous work with all manner of harsh, coarse, and tantalizing epithets. He was cruelly deliberate, and protracted the torture as one who was delighted with the agony of his victim. Again and again he drew the hateful scourge through his hand, adjusting it with a view of dealing the most pain-giving blow his strength and skill could inflict. Poor Esther had never before been severely whipped. Her shoulders were plump and tender. Each blow, vigorously laid on, brought screams from her as well as blood. 'Have mercy! Oh, mercy!' she cried. 'I won't do so no more.' But her piercing cries seemed only to increase his fury. The whole scene, with all its attendant circumstances, was revolting and shocking to the last degree, and when the motives for the brutal castigation are known, language has no power to convey a just sense of its dreadful criminality. After laying on I dare not say how many stripes, old master untied his suffering victim. When let down she could scarcely stand. From my heart I pitied her, and child as I was, and new to such scenes, the shock was tremendous. I was terrified, hushed, stunned and bewildered. The scene here described was often repeated, for Edward and Esther continued to meet, notwithstanding all efforts to prevent their meeting.

# CHAPTER VI.

## A CHILD'S REASONING.

*The author's early reflections on Slavery—Aunt Jennie and Uncle Noah—Presentiment of one day becoming a freeman—Conflict between an overseer and a slave woman—Advantage of resistance—Death of an overseer—Col. Lloyd's plantation home—Monthly distribution of food—Singing of Slaves—An explanation—The slaves' food and clothing—Naked children—Life in the quarter—Sleeping-places—not beds—Deprivation of sleep—Care of nursing babies—Ash cake—Contrast.*

THE incidents related in the foregoing chapter led me thus early to inquire into the origin and nature of slavery. Why am I a slave? Why are some people slaves and others masters? These were perplexing questions and very troublesome to my childhood. I was very early told by some one that '*God up in the sky*' had made all things, and had made black people to be slaves and white people to be masters. I was told too that God was good, and that He knew what was best for everybody. This was, however, less satisfactory than the first statement. It came point blank against all my notions of goodness. The case of Aunt Esther was in my mind. Besides, I could not tell how anybody could know that God made black people to be slaves. Then I found, too, that there were puzzling exceptions to this theory of slavery, in the fact that all black people were not slaves, and all white people were not masters.

An incident occurred about this time that made a deep impression on my mind. My Aunt Jennie and one of the men slaves of Captain Anthony ran away. A great noise was made about it. Old master was furious. He said he would follow them and catch them and bring them back, but he never did, and somebody told me that Uncle Noah and Aunt Jennie had gone to the free states and were free. Besides this occurrence, which brought much light to my mind on the subject, there were several slaves on Mr. Lloyd's place who remembered being brought from Africa. There were others who told me that their fathers and mothers were stolen from Africa.

This to me was important knowledge, but not such as to make me feel very easy in my slave condition. The success of Aunt Jennie and Uncle Noah in getting away from slavery was, I think, the first fact that made me seriously think of escape for myself. I could not have been more than seven or eight years old at the time of this occurrence, but young as I was I was already, in spirit and purpose, a fugitive from slavery.

Up to the time of the brutal treatment of my Aunt Esther, already narrated, and the shocking plight in which I had seen my cousin from Tuckahoe, my attention had not been especially directed to the grosser and more revolting features of slavery. I had, of course, heard of whippings and savage mutilations of slaves by brutal overseers, but happily for me I had always been out of the way of such occurrences. My play time was spent outside of the corn and tobacco fields, where the overseers and slaves were brought together and in conflict. But after the case of my Aunt Esther I saw others of the same disgusting and shocking nature. The one of these which agitated and distressed me most was the whipping of a woman, not belonging to my old master, but to Col. Lloyd. The charge against her was very common and very indefinite, namely, 'impudence.' This crime could be committed by a slave in a hundred different ways, and depended much upon the temper and caprice of the overseer as to whether it was committed at all. He could create the offense whenever it pleased him. A look, a word, a gesture, accidental or intentional, never failed to be taken as impudence when he was in the right mood for such an offense. In this case there were all the necessary conditions for the commission of the crime charged. The offender was nearly white, to begin with; she was the wife of a favorite hand on board of Mr. Lloyd's sloop, and was besides, the mother of five sprightly children. Vigorous and spirited woman that she was, a wife and a mother, with a predominating share of the blood of the master running in her veins, Nellie (for that was her name) had all the qualities essential to impudence to a slave overseer. My attention was called to the scene of the castigation by the loud screams and curses that proceeded from the direction of it. When I came near the parties engaged in the struggle the overseer had hold of Nellie, endeavoring with his whole strength to drag her to a tree against her resistance. Both his and her faces were bleeding, for the woman was doing her best. Three of her children were present, and though quite small, (from seven to ten years old, I should think), they gallantly took the side of their mother against the overseer, and pelted him well with stones and epithets. Amid the screams of the children, '*Let my mammy go! Let my mammy go!*' the hoarse voice of the maddened overseer was heard in terrible oaths that he would teach her how to give a white man '*impudence*.' The blood on his face and on hers attested her skill in the use of her nails, and his dogged determination to conquer. His purpose was to tie her up to a tree and give her, in slave-holding parlance, a 'genteel flogging,' and he evidently had not expected the stern and protracted resistance he was meeting, or the strength and skill needed to its execution. There were times when she seemed likely to get the better of the brute, but he finally overpowered her and succeeded in getting her arms firmly tied to the tree towards which he had been dragging her. The victim was now at the mercy of his merciless lash. What followed I need not here describe. The cries of the now helpless woman, while undergoing the terrible infliction, were mingled with the hoarse curses of the overseer and the wild cries of her distracted children. When the poor woman was untied her back was covered with blood. She was whipped, terribly whipped, but she was not subdued, and continued to denounce the overseer and to pour upon him every vile epithet of which she could think. Such floggings are seldom repeated on the same persons by overseers. They prefer to whip those who are the most easily whipped. The doctrine that submission to violence is the best cure for violence did not hold good as between slaves and overseers. He was whipped oftener who was whipped easiest. That slave who had the courage to stand up for himself against the overseer, although he might have many hard stripes at first, became while legally a slave virtually a freeman. 'You can shoot me,' said a slave to Rigby Hopkins,* 'but you can't whip me,' and the result was he was neither whipped nor shot. I do not know that Mr. Sevier ever attempted to whip Nellie again. He probably never did, for he was taken sick not long after and died. It was commonly said that his death-bed was a wretched one, and that, the ruling passion being strong in death, he died flourishing the slave whip and with horrid oaths upon his lips. This death-bed scene may only be the imagining of the slaves. One thing is certain, that when he was in health his profanity was enough to chill the blood of an ordinary man. Nature, or habit, had given to his face an expression of uncommon savageness. Tobacco and rage had ground his teeth short, and nearly every sentence that he uttered was commenced or completed with an oath. Hated for his cruelty, despised for his cowardice, he went to his grave lamented by nobody on the place outside of his own house, if, indeed, he was even lamented there.

In Mr. James Hopkins, the succeeding overseer, we had a different and a better man; as good perhaps as any man could be in the position of a slave overseer. Though he sometimes wielded the lash, it was evident that he took no pleasure in it and did it with much reluctance. He stayed but a short time here, and his removal from the position was much regretted by the slaves generally. Of the successor of Mr. Hopkins I shall have something to say at another time and in another place.

For the present we will attend to a further description of the business-like aspect of Col. Lloyd's '*Great House*' farm. There was always much bustle and noise here on the two days at the end of each month, for then the slaves belonging to the different branches of this great estate assembled here by their representatives, to obtain their monthly allowances of corn-meal and pork. These were gala days for the slaves of the outlying farms, and there was much rivalry among them as to who should be elected to go up to the Great House farm for the '*Allowances*,' and indeed to attend to any other business at this great place, to them the capital of a little nation. Its beauty and grandeur, its immense wealth, its numerous population, and the fact that uncles Harry, Peter, and Jake, the sailors on board the sloop, usually kept on sale trinkets which they bought in Baltimore to sell to their less fortunate fellow-servants, made a visit to the Great House farm a high privilege, and eagerly sought. It was valued, too, as a mark of distinction and confidence; but probably the chief motive among the competitors for the office was the opportunity it afforded to shake off the monotony of the field and to get beyond the overseer's eye and lash. Once on the road with an ox-team, and seated on the tongue of the cart, with no overseer to look after him, one felt comparatively free.

Slaves were expected to sing as well as to work. A silent slave was not liked, either by masters or overseers. '*Make a noise there! Make a noise there!*' and 'bear a hand,' were words usually addressed to slaves when they were silent. This, and the natural disposition of the negro to make a noise in the world, may account for the almost constant singing among them when at their work. There was generally more or less singing among the teamsters, at all times. It was a means of telling the overseer, in the distance, where they were and what they were about. But on the allowance days those commissioned to the Great House farm were peculiarly vocal. While on the way they would make the grand old woods for miles around reverberate with their wild and plaintive notes. They were indeed both merry and sad. Child as I was, these wild songs greatly depressed my spirits. Nowhere outside of dear old Ireland,* in the days of want and famine, have I heard sounds so mournful.

In all these slave songs there was ever some expression of praise of the Great House farm—something that would please the pride of the Lloyds.

> I am going away to the Great House farm,
> O, yea! O, yea! O, yea!
> My old master is a good old master,
> O, yea! O, yea! O, yea!

These words would be sung over and over again, with others, improvised as they went along—jargon, perhaps, to the reader, but full of meaning to the singers. I have sometimes thought that the mere hearing of these songs would have done more to impress the good people of the north with the soul-crushing character of slavery than whole volumes exposing the physical cruelties of the slave system; for the heart has no language like song. Many years ago, when recollecting my experience in this respect, I wrote of these slave songs in the following strain:

'I did not, when a slave, fully understand the deep meaning of those rude and apparently incoherent songs. I was, myself, within the circle, so that I could then neither hear nor see as those without might see and hear. They breathed the prayer and complaint of souls over-flowing with the bitterest anguish. They depressed my spirits and filled my heart with ineffable sadness.'*

The remark in the olden time was not unfrequently made, that slaves were the most contented and happy laborers in the world, and their dancing and singing were referred to in proof of this alleged fact; but it was a great mistake to suppose them happy because they sometimes made those joyful noises. The songs of the slaves represented their sorrows, rather than their joys. Like tears, they were a relief to aching hearts. It is not inconsistent with the constitution of the human mind that it avails itself of one and the same method for expressing opposite emotions. Sorrow and desolation have their songs, as well as joy and peace.

It was the boast of slaveholders that their slaves enjoyed more of the physical comforts of life than the peasantry of any country in the world. My experience contradicts this. The men and the women slaves on Col. Lloyd's farm received as their monthly allowance of food, eight pounds of pickled pork, or its equivalent in fish. The pork was often tainted, and the fish were of the poorest quality. With their pork or fish, they had given them one bushel of Indian meal, unbolted, of which quite fifteen per cent. was more fit for pigs than for men. With this one pint of salt was given, and this was the entire monthly allowance of a full-grown slave, working constantly in the open field from morning till night every day in the month except Sunday. There is no kind of work which really requires a better supply of food to prevent physical exhaustion than the field work of a slave. The yearly allowance of clothing was not more ample than the supply of food. It consisted of two tow-linen shirts, one pair of trowsers of the same coarse material, for summer, and a woolen pair of trowsers and a woolen jacket for winter, with one pair of yarn stockings and a pair of shoes of the coarsest description. Children under ten years old had neither shoes, stockings, jackets, nor trowsers. They had two coarse tow-linen shirts per year, and when these were worn out they went naked till the next allowance day—and this was the condition of the little girls as well as of the boys. As to beds, they had none. One coarse blanket was given them, and this only to the men and women. The children stuck themselves in holes and corners about the quarters, often in the corners of huge chimneys, with their feet in the ashes to keep them warm. The want of beds, however, was not considered a great privation by the field hands. Time to sleep was of far greater importance. For when the day's work was done most of these had their washing, mending, and cooking to do, and having few or no facilities for doing such things, very many of their needed sleeping hours were consumed in necessary preparations for the labors of the coming day. The sleeping apartments, if they could have been properly called such, had little regard to comfort or decency. Old and young, male and female, married and single, dropped down upon the common clay floor, each covering up with his or her blanket, their only protection from cold or exposure. The night, however, was shortened at both ends. The slaves worked often as long as they could see, and were late in cooking and mending for the coming day, and at the first gray streak of the morning they were summoned to the field by the overseer's horn. They were whipped for over-sleeping more than for any other fault. Neither age nor sex found any favor. The overseer stood at the quarter door, armed with stick and whip, ready to deal heavy blows upon any who might be a little behind time. When the horn was blown there was a rush for the door, for the hindermost one was sure to get a blow from the overseer. Young mothers who worked in the field were allowed an hour about ten o'clock in the morning to go home to nurse their children. This was when they were not required to take them to the field with them, and leave them upon 'turning row,' or in the corner of the fences.

As a general rule the slaves did not come to their quarters to take their meals, but took their ash-cake (called thus because baked in the ashes) and piece of pork, or their salt herrings, where they were at work.

But let us now leave the rough usage of the field, where vulgar coarseness and brutal cruelty flourished as rank as weeds in the tropics and where a vile wretch, in the shape of a man, rides, walks and struts about, with whip in hand, dealing heavy blows and leaving deep gashes on the flesh of men and women, and turn our attention to the less repulsive slave life as it existed in the home of my childhood. Some idea of the splendor of that place sixty years ago has already been given. The contrast between the condition of the slaves and that of their masters was marvelously sharp and striking. There were pride, pomp, and luxury on the one hand, servility, dejection, and misery on the other.

# CHAPTER VII.

## LUXURIES AT THE GREAT HOUSE.

*Contrasts—Great House luxuries—Its hospitality—Entertainments—
Fault-finding—Shameful humiliation of an old and faithful coachman—
William Wilks—Curious incident—Expressed satisfaction not always
genuine—Reasons for suppressing the truth.*

THE close-fisted stinginess that fed the poor slave on coarse corn-
meal and tainted meat, that clothed him in crashy tow-linen and hurried him on to toil through the field in all weathers, with wind and
rain beating through his tattered garments, and that scarcely gave
even the young slave-mother time to nurse her infant in the fence-
corner, wholly vanished on approaching the sacred precincts of the
'Great House' itself. There the scriptural phrase descriptive of the
wealthy found exact illustration. The highly-favored inmates of this
mansion were literally arrayed in 'purple and fine linen, and fared
sumptuously every day.'* The table of this house groaned under the
blood-bought luxuries gathered with pains-taking care at home and
abroad. Fields, forests, rivers, and seas were made tributary. Immense
wealth and its lavish expenditures filled the Great House with all that
could please the eye or tempt the taste. Fish, flesh, and fowl were here
in profusion. Chickens of all breeds; ducks of all kinds, wild and
tame, the common and the huge Muscovite; Guinea fowls, turkeys,
geese and pea-fowls; all were fat and fattening for the destined vortex.
Here the graceful swan, the mongrel, the black-necked wild goose,
partridges, quails, pheasants, pigeons and choice waterfowl, with all
their strange varieties, were caught in this huge net. Beef, veal, mut-
ton, and venison, of the most select kinds and quality, rolled in bounteous profusion to this grand consumer. The teeming riches of the
Chesapeake Bay, its rock perch, drums, crocus, trout, oysters, crabs,
and terrapin were drawn hither to adorn the glittering table. The
dairy, too, the finest then on the eastern shore of Maryland, supplied
by cattle of the best English stock, imported for the express purpose,
poured its rich donations of fragrant cheese, golden butter, and deli-
cious cream to heighten the attractions of the gorgeous, unending
round of feasting. Nor were the fruits of the earth overlooked. The
fertile garden, many acres in size, constituting a separate establishment distinct from the common farm, with its scientific gardener
direct from Scotland, a Mr. McDermott, and four men under his

direction, was not behind, either in the abundance or in the delicacy of its contributions. The tender asparagus, the crispy celery, and the delicate cauliflower, egg plants, beets, lettuce, parsnips, peas, and French beans, early and late; radishes, cantelopes, melons of all kinds; and the fruits of all climes and of every description, from the hardy apples of the north to the lemon and orange of the south, culminated at this point. Here were gathered figs, raisins, almonds, and grapes from Spain, wines and brandies from France, teas of various flavor from China, and rich, aromatic coffee from Java, all conspiring to swell the tide of high life, where pride and indolence lounged in magnificence and satiety.

Behind the tall-backed and elaborately wrought chairs stood the servants, fifteen in number, carefully selected, not only with a view to their capacity and adeptness, but with especial regard to their personal appearance, their graceful agility, and pleasing address. Some of these servants, armed with fans, wafted reviving breezes to the over-heated brows of the alabaster ladies, whilst others watched with eager eye and fawn-like step, anticipating and supplying wants before they were sufficiently formed to be announced by word or sign.

These servants constituted a sort of black aristocracy. They resembled the field hands in nothing except their color, and in this they held the advantage of a velvet-like glossiness, rich and beautiful. The hair, too, showed the same advantage. The delicately-formed colored maid rustled in the scarcely-worn silk of her young mistress, while the servant men were equally well attired from the overflowing wardrobe of their young masters, so that in dress, as well as in form and feature, in manner and speech, in tastes and habits, the distance between these favored few and the sorrow and hunger-smitten multitudes of the quarter and the field was immense.

In the stables and carriage-houses were to be found the same evidences of pride and luxurious extravagance. Here were three splendid coaches, soft within and lustrous without. Here, too, were gigs, phaetons, barouches, sulkeys, and sleighs. Here were saddles and harnesses, beautifully wrought and richly mounted. Not less than thirty-five horses of the best approved blood, both for speed and beauty, were kept only for pleasure. The care of these horses constituted the entire occupation of two men, one or the other of them being always in the stable to answer any call which might be made from the Great House. Over the way from the stable was a house built expressly for the hounds, a pack of twenty-five or thirty, the fare for which would have made glad the hearts of a dozen slaves. Horses and hounds, however, were not the only consumers of the slave's toil. The hospitality practiced at the Lloyd's would have astonished and charmed many a health-seeking divine or merchant from the north. Viewed from his table, and *not* from the field, Colonel Lloyd was, indeed, a model of generous hospitality. His house was literally a hotel for weeks, during the summer months. At these times, especially, the air was freighted with the rich fumes of baking, boiling, roasting, and broiling. It was something to me that I could share these odors with the winds, even if the meats themselves were under a more stringent monopoly. In master Daniel I had a friend at court, who would sometimes give me a cake, and who kept me well informed as to their guests and their entertainments. Viewed from Col. Lloyd's table, who could have said that his slaves were not well clad and well cared for? Who would have said they did not glory in being the slaves of such a master? Who but a fanatic could have seen any cause for sympathy for either master or slave? Alas, this immense wealth, this gilded splendor, this profusion of luxury, this exemption from toil, this life of ease, this sea of plenty were not the pearly gates they seemed to a world of happiness and sweet content to be. The poor slave, on his hard pine plank, scantily covered with his thin blanket, slept more soundly than the feverish voluptuary who reclined upon his downy pillow. Food to the indolent is poison, not sustenance. Lurking beneath the rich and tempting viands were invisible spirits of evil, which filled the self-deluded gormandizer with aches and pains, passions uncontrollable, fierce tempers, dyspepsia, rheumatism, lumbago, and gout, and of these the Lloyds had a full share.

I had many opportunities of witnessing the restless discontent and capricious irritation of the Lloyds. My fondness for horses attracted me to the stable much of the time. The two men in charge of this establishment were old and young Barney—father and son. Old Barney was a fine-looking, portly old man of a brownish complexion, and a respectful and dignified bearing. He was much devoted to his profession, and held his office as an honorable one. He was a farrier as well as an ostler, and could bleed horses, remove lampers from their mouths and administer medicine to them. No one on the farm knew so well as old Barney what to do with a sick horse; but his office was not an enviable one, and his gifts and acquirements were of little advantage to him. In nothing was Col. Lloyd more unreasonable and exacting than in respect to the management of his horses. Any supposed inattention to these animals was sure to be visited with degrading punishment. His horses and dogs fared better than his men. Their beds were far softer and cleaner than those of his human cattle. No excuse could shield old

Barney if the Colonel only suspected something wrong about his horses, and consequently he was often punished when faultless. It was painful to hear the unreasonable and fretful scoldings administered by Col. Lloyd, his son Murray, and his sons-in-law, to this poor man. Three of the daughters of Col. Lloyd were married, and they with their husbands remained at the great house a portion of the year, and enjoyed the luxury of whipping the servants when they pleased. A horse was seldom brought out of the stable to which no objection could be raised. 'There was dust in his hair;' 'there was a twist in his reins;' 'his foretop was not combed;' 'his mane did not lie straight;' 'his head did not look well;' 'his fetlocks had not been properly trimmed.' Something was always wrong. However groundless the complaint, Barney must stand, hat in hand, lips sealed, never answering a word in explanation or excuse. In a free State, a master thus complaining without cause, might be told by his ostler: 'Sir, I am sorry I cannot please you, but since I have done the best I can and fail to do so, your remedy is to dismiss me.' But here the ostler must listen and tremblingly abide his master's behest. One of the most heart-suddening and humiliating scenes I ever witnessed was the whipping of old Barney by Col. Lloyd. These two men were both advanced in years; there were the silver locks of the master, and the bald and toil-worn brow of the slave—superior and inferior here, powerful and weak here, but *equals* before God. 'Uncover your head,' said the imperious master; he was obeyed. 'Take off your jacket, you old rascal!' and off came Barney's jacket. 'Down on your knees!' Down knelt the old man, his shoulders bare, his bald head glistening in the sunshine, and his aged knees on the cold, damp ground. In this humble and debasing attitude, that master, to whom he had devoted the best years and the best strength of his life, came forward and laid on thirty lashes with his horsewhip. The old man made no resistance, but bore it patiently, answering each blow with only a shrug of the shoulders and a groan. I do not think that the physical suffering from this infliction was severe, for the whip was a light riding-whip; but the spectacle of an aged man—a husband and a father—humbly kneeling before his fellowman, shocked me at the time; and since I have grown older, few of the features of slavery have impressed me with a deeper sense of its injustice and barbarity than did this existing scene. I owe it to the truth, however, to say that this was the first and last time I ever saw a slave compelled to kneel to receive a whipping.

Another incident, illustrating a phase of slavery to which I have referred in another connection, I may here mention. Besides two other coachmen, Col. Lloyd owned one named William Wilks, and his was one of the exceptionable cases where a slave possessed a surname, and was recognized by it, by both colored and white people. Wilks was a very fine-looking man. He was about as white as any one on the plantation, and in form and feature bore a very striking resemblance to Murray Lloyd. It was whispered and generally believed that William Wilks was a son of Col. Lloyd, by a highly favored slavewoman, who was still on the plantation. There were many reasons for believing this whisper, not only from his personal appearance, but from the undeniable freedom which he enjoyed over all others, and his apparent consciousness of being something more than a slave to his master. It was notorious too that William had a deadly enemy in Murray Lloyd, whom he so much resembled, and that the latter greatly worried his father with importunities to sell William. Indeed, he gave his father no rest, until he did sell him to Austin Woldfolk,* the great slave-trader at that time. Before selling him, however, he tried to make things smooth by giving William a whipping, but it proved a failure. It was a compromise, and like most such, defeated itself,—for Col. Lloyd soon after atoned to William for the abuse by giving him a gold watch and chain. Another fact somewhat curious was, that though sold to the remorseless Woldfolk, taken in irons to Baltimore, and cast into prison, with a view to being sent to the South, William outbid all his purchasers, paid for himself, and afterwards resided in Baltimore. How this was accomplished was a great mystery at the time, explained only on the supposition that the hand which had bestowed the gold watch and chain had also supplied the purchase-money, but I have since learned that this was not the true explanation. Wilks had many friends in Baltimore and Annapolis, and they united to save him from a fate which was one of all others most dreaded by the slaves. Practical amalgamation was however so common at the South, and so many circumstances pointed in that direction, that there was little reason to doubt that William Wilks was the son of Edward Lloyd.

The real feelings and opinions of the slaves were not much known or respected by their masters. The distance between the two was too great to admit of such knowledge, and in this respect Col. Lloyd was no exception to the rule. His slaves were so numerous that he did not know them when he saw them. Nor, indeed, did all his slaves know him. It is reported of him, that, riding along the road one day, he met a colored man, and addressed him in what was the usual way of speaking to colored people on the public highways of the South: 'Well, boy, who do you belong to?' 'To Col. Lloyd,' replied the slave. 'Well, does the

Colonel treat you well?' 'No, sir,' was the ready reply. 'What, does he work you hard?' 'Yes, sir.' 'Well, don't he give you enough to eat?' 'Yes, sir, he gives me enough to eat, such as it is.' The Colonel rode on; the slave also went on about his business, not dreaming that he had been conversing with his master. He thought and said nothing of the matter, until, two or three weeks afterwards, he was informed by his overseer that, for having found fault with his master, he was now to be sold to a Georgia trader. He was immediately chained and handcuffed; and thus, without a moment's warning, he was snatched away, and forever sundered from his family and friends by a hand as unrelenting as that of death. This was the penalty of telling the simple truth, in answer to a series of plain questions. It was partly in consequence of such facts, that slaves, when inquired of as to their condition and the character of their masters, would almost invariably say that they were contented and their masters kind. Slaveholders are known to have sent spies among their slaves to ascertain, if possible, their views and feelings in regard to their condition; hence the maxim established among them, that 'a still tongue makes a wise head.' They would suppress the truth rather than take the consequences of telling it, and in so doing they prove themselves a part of the human family. I was frequently asked if I had a kind master, and I do not remember ever to have given a negative reply. I did not consider myself as uttering that which was strictly untrue, for I always measured the kindness of my master by the standard of kindness set up by the slaveholders around us.

# CHAPTER VIII.

## CHARACTERISTICS OF OVERSEERS.

*Austin Gore—Sketch of his character—Overseers as a class—Their peculiar characteristics—The marked individuality of Austin Gore—His sense of duty—Murder of poor Denby—Sensation—How Gore made his peace with Col. Lloyd—Other horrible murders—No laws for the protection of slaves possible of being enforced.*

THE comparatively moderate rule of Mr. Hopkins as overseer on Col. Lloyd's plantation was succeeded by that of another, whose name was Austin Gore.\* I hardly know how to bring this man fitly before the reader; for under him there was more suffering from violence and bloodshed than had, according to the older slaves, ever been experienced before at this place. He was an overseer, and possessed the peculiar characteristics of his class; yet to call him merely an overseer would not give one a fair conception of the man. I speak of overseers as a class, for they were such. They were as distinct from the slaveholding gentry of the South as are the fish-women of Paris and the coal-heavers of London distinct from other grades of society. They constituted, at the South, a separate fraternity. They were arranged and classified by that great law of attraction which determines the sphere and affinities of men and which ordains that men whose malign and brutal propensities preponderate over their moral and intellectual endowments shall naturally fall into the employments which promise the largest gratification to their predominating instincts or propensities. The office of overseer took this raw material of vulgarity and brutality and stamped it as a distinct class in southern life. But in this class, as in all other classes, there were sometimes persons of marked individuality, yet with a general resemblance to the mass. Mr. Gore was one of those to whom a general characterization would do no manner of justice. He was an overseer, but he was something more. With the malign and tyrannical qualities of an overseer he combined something of the lawful master. He had the artfulness and mean ambition of his class, without its disgusting swagger and noisy bravado. There was an easy air of independence about him, a calm self-possession, and at the same time a sternness of glance which well might daunt less timid hearts than those of poor slaves accustomed from childhood to cower before a driver's lash. He was one of those overseers who could torture the slightest word or look into impudence, and he had the nerve not only to resent, but to punish promptly and severely. There could be no answering back. Guilty or not guilty, to be accused was to be sure of a flogging. His very presence was fearful, and I shunned him as I would have shunned a rattlesnake. His piercing black eyes and sharp, shrill voice ever awakened sensations of dread. Other overseers, how brutal soever they might be, would sometimes seek to gain favor with the slaves by indulging in a little pleasantry; but Gore never said a funny thing or perpetrated a joke. He was always cold, distant, and unapproachable—the *overseer* on Col. Edward Lloyd's plantation—and needed no higher pleasure than the performance of the duties of his office. When he used the lash, it was from a sense of duty, without fear of consequences. There was a stern will, an iron-like reality about him, which would easily have made him chief of a band of pirates, had his environments been favorable to such a sphere. Among many other deeds of shocking cruelty committed by him was the murder of a young colored man named Bill Denby.* He was a powerful fellow, full of animal spirits, and one of the most valuable of Col. Lloyd's slaves. In some way, I know not what, he offended this Mr. Austin Gore, and, in accordance with the usual custom, the latter undertook to flog him. He had given him but a few stripes when Denby broke away from him, plunged into the creek, and, standing there with the water up to his neck, refused to come out; whereupon, for this refusal, Gore *shot him dead!* It was said that Gore gave Denby three calls to come out, telling him that if he did not obey the last call he should shoot him. When the last call was given Denby still stood his ground, and Gore, without further parley or making any further effort to induce obedience, raised his gun deliberately to his face, took deadly aim at his standing victim, and with one click of the gun the mangled body sank out of sight, and only his warm red blood marked the place where he had stood.

This fiendish murder produced, as it could not help doing, a tremendous sensation. The slaves were panic-stricken, and howled with alarm. The atrocity roused my old master, and he spoke out in reprobation of it. Both he and Col. Lloyd arraigned Gore for his cruelty; but the latter, calm and collected as though nothing unusual had happened, declared that Denby had become unmanageable; that he set a dangerous example to the other slaves, and that unless some such prompt measure was resorted to there would be an end of all rule and order on the plantation. That convenient covert for all manner of villainy and outrage; that cowardly alarm-cry that the slaves would 'take the place,' was pleaded, just as it had before been in thousands of similar cases. Gore's defense was evidently considered satisfactory, for he was continued in his office without being subjected to a judicial investigation. The murder was committed in the presence of slaves only, and they, being slaves, could neither institute a suit nor testify against the murderer. Mr. Gore lived in St. Michaels, Talbot Co., Maryland, and I have no reason to doubt, from what I know to have been the moral sentiment of the place, that he was as highly esteemed and as much respected as though his guilty soul had not been stained with innocent blood.

I speak advisedly when I say that in Talbot Co., Maryland, killing a slave, or any colored person, was not treated as a crime, either by the courts or the community. Mr. Thomas Lanman, ship carpenter of St. Michaels, killed two slaves, one of whom he butchered with a hatchet by knocking out his brains. He used to boast of having committed the awful and bloody deed. I have heard him do so laughingly, declaring himself a benefactor of his country and that 'when others would do as much as he had done, they would be rid of the d—d niggers.'

Another notorious fact which I may here state was the murder of a young girl between fifteen and sixteen years of age, by her mistress, Mrs. Giles Hicks, who lived but a short distance from Col. Lloyd's. This wicked woman, in the paroxysm of her wrath, not content with killing her victim, literally mangled her face and broke her breastbone. Wild and infuriated as she was, she took the precaution to cause the burial of the girl; but, the facts of the case getting abroad, the remains were disinterred and a coroner's jury assembled, who, after due deliberation, decided that 'the girl had come to her death from severe beating.' The offense for which this girl was thus hurried out of the world was this: she had been set that night, and several preceding nights, to mind Mrs. Hicks' baby, and, having fallen into a sound sleep, the crying of the baby did not wake her, as it did its mother. The tardiness of the girl excited Mrs. Hicks, who, after calling her several times, seized a piece of fire-wood from the fire-place and pounded in her skull and breast-bone till death ensued. I will not say that this murder most foul produced no sensation. It *did* produce a sensation. A warrant was issued for the arrest of Mrs. Hicks, but incredible to tell, for some reason or other, that warrant was never served, and she not only escaped condign punishment, but the pain and mortification as well, of being arraigned before a court of justice.

While I am detailing the bloody deeds that took place during my stay on Col. Lloyd's plantation, I will briefly narrate another dark transaction, which occurred about the time of the murder of Denby.

On the side of the river Wye opposite from Col. Lloyd's, there lived a Mr. Beal Bondley,* a wealthy slaveholder. In the direction of his land,

and near the shore, there was an excellent oyster fishing-ground, and to this some of Lloyd's slaves occasionally resorted in their little canoes, at night, with a view to make up the deficiency of their scanty allowance of food by the oysters that they could easily get there. Mr. Bondley took it into his head to regard this as a trespass, and while an old man slave was engaged in catching a few of the many millions of oysters that lined the bottom of the creek, to satisfy his hunger, the rascally Bondley, lying in ambush, without the slightest warning, discharged the contents of his musket into the back of the poor old man. As good fortune would have it, the shot did not prove fatal, and Mr. Bondley came over the next day to see Col. Lloyd about it. What happened between them I know not, but there was little said about it and nothing publicly done. One of the commonest sayings to which my ears early became accustomed, was, that it was 'worth but a half a cent to kill a nigger, and half a cent to bury one.' While I heard of numerous murders committed by slaveholders on the eastern shore of Maryland, I never knew a solitary instance where a slaveholder was either hung or imprisoned for having murdered a slave. The usual pretext for such crimes was that the slave had offered resistance. Should a slave, when assaulted, but raise his hand in self-defense, the white assaulting party was fully justified by southern law and southern public opinion in shooting the slave down, and for this there was no redress.

# CHAPTER IX.

## CHANGE OF LOCATION.

I HAVE nothing cruel or shocking to relate of my own personal experience while I remained on Col. Lloyd's plantation, at the home of my old master. An occasional cuff from Aunt Katy, and a regular whipping from old master, such as any heedless and mischievous boy might get from his father, is all that I have to say of this sort. I was not old enough to work in the field, and there being little else than field-work to perform, I had much leisure. The most I had to do was to drive up the cows in the evening, to keep the front yard clean, and to perform small errands for my young mistress, Lucretia Auld. I had reasons for thinking this lady was very kindly disposed towards me, and although I was not often the object of her attention, I constantly regarded her as my friend, and was always glad when it was my privilege to do her a service. In a family where there was so much that was harsh and indifferent, the slightest word or look of kindness was of great value. Miss Lucretia—as we all continued to call her long after her marriage—had bestowed on me such looks and words as taught me that she pitied me, if she did not love me. She sometimes gave me a piece of bread and butter, an article not set down in our bill of fare, but an extra ration aside from both Aunt Katy and old master, and given as I believed solely out of the tender regard she had for me. Then, too, I one day got into the wars with Uncle Abel's son 'Ike,' and got sadly worsted; the little rascal struck me directly in the forehead with a sharp piece of cinder, fused with iron, from the old blacksmith's forge, which made a cross in my forehead very plainly to be seen even now. The gash bled very freely, and I roared and betook myself home. The cold-hearted Aunt Katy paid no attention either to my wound or my roaring except to tell me it 'served me right; I had no business with Ike; it would do me good; I would now keep away from "dem Lloyd niggers."' Miss Lucretia in this state of the case came forward, and called me into the parlor (an extra privilege of itself), and without using toward me any of the hard and reproachful epithets of Aunt Katy, quietly acted the good Samaritan. With her own soft hand she washed the blood from my head and face, brought her own bottle of balsam, and with the balsam wetted a nice piece of white linen and bound up my head. The balsam was not more healing to the wound in my head, than her kindness was healing to the wounds in my spirit, induced by the unfeeling words of Aunt Katy.

Miss Lucretia was after this yet more my friend. I felt her to be such and I have no doubt that the simple act of binding up my head did much to awaken in her heart an interest in my welfare. It is quite true that this interest seldom showed itself in anything more than in giving me a piece of bread and butter, but this was a great favor on a slave plantation, and I was the only one of the children to whom such attention was paid. When very severely pinched with hunger, I had the habit of singing, which the good lady very soon came to understand, and when she heard me singing under her window I was very apt to be paid for my music.

Thus I had two friends, both at important points—Mas'r Daniel at the great house, and Miss Lucretia at home. From Mas'r Daniel I got protection from the bigger boys, and from Miss Lucretia I got bread by singing when I was hungry, and sympathy when I was abused by the termagant in the kitchen. For such friendship I was deeply grateful, and bitter as are my recollections of slavery, it is a true pleasure to recall any instances of kindness, any sunbeams of humane treatment, which found way to my soul, through the iron grating of my house of bondage. Such beams seem all the brighter from the general darkness into which they penetrate, and the impression they make there is vividly distinct.

As before intimated, I received no severe treatment from the hands of my master, but the insufficiency of both food and clothing was a serious trial to me, especially the lack of clothing. In hottest summer and coldest winter I was kept almost in a state of nudity. My only clothing—a little coarse sack-cloth or tow-linen sort of shirt, scarcely reaching to my knees, was worn night and day and changed once a week. In the day time I could protect myself by keeping on the sunny side of the house, or, in stormy weather, in the corner of the kitchen chimney. But the great difficulty was to keep warm during the night. The pigs in the pen had leaves, and the horses in the stable had straw, but the children had no beds. They lodged anywhere in the ample kitchen. I slept generally in a little closet, without even a blanket to cover me. In very cold weather

I sometimes got down the bag in which corn was carried to the mill, and crawled into that. Sleeping there with my head in and my feet out, I was partly protected, though never comfortable. My feet have been so cracked with the frost that the pen with which I am writing might be laid in the gashes. Our corn meal mush, which was our only regular if not all-sufficing diet, was, when sufficiently cooled from the cooking, placed in a large tray or trough. This was set down either on the floor of the kitchen, or out of doors on the ground, and the children were called like so many pigs, and like so many pigs would come, some with oyster-shells, some with pieces of shingles, but none with spoons, and literally devour the mush. He who could eat fastest got most, and he who was strongest got the best place, but few left the trough really satisfied. I was the most unlucky of all, for Aunt Katy had no good feeling for me, and if I pushed the children, or if they told her anything unfavorable of me, she always believed the worst and was sure to whip me.

As I grew older and more thoughtful, I became more and more filled with a sense of my wretchedness. The unkindness of Aunt Katy, the hunger and cold I suffered, and the terrible reports of wrongs and out-rages which came to my ear, together with what I almost daily wit-nessed, led me to wish I had never been born. I used to contrast my condition with that of the black-birds, in whose wild and sweet songs I fancied them so happy. Their apparent joy only deepened the shades of my sorrow. There are thoughtful days in the lives of children—at least there were in mine—when they grapple with the great primary subjects of knowledge, and reach in a moment conclusions which no subsequent experience can shake. I was just as well aware of the unjust, unnatural, and murderous character of slavery, when nine years old, as I am now. Without any appeals to books, to laws, or to authorities of any kind, to regard God as 'Our Father,' condemned slavery as a crime.

I was in this unhappy state when I received from Miss Lucretia the joyful intelligence that my old master had determined to let me go to Baltimore to live with Mr. Hugh Auld,* a brother to Mr. Thomas Auld, Miss Lucretia's husband. I shall never forget the ecstacy with which I received this information, three days before the time set for my departure. They were the three happiest days I had ever known. I spent the largest part of them in the creek, washing off the plantation scurf, and thus preparing for my new home. Miss Lucretia took a lively inter-est in getting me ready. She told me I must get all the dead skin off my feet and knees, for the people in Baltimore were very cleanly, and would laugh at me if I looked dirty; and besides she was intending to give me a pair of trowsers, but which I could not put on unless I got off all the dirt. This was a warning which I was bound to heed, for the thought of owning and wearing a pair of trowsers was great indeed. So I went at it in good earnest, working for the first time in my life in the hope of reward. I was greatly excited, and could hardly consent to sleep lest I should be left.

The ties that ordinarily bind children to their homes had no existence in my case, and in thinking of a home elsewhere, I was confident of finding none that I should relish less than the one I was leaving. If I should meet with hardship, hunger, and nakedness, I had known them all before, and I could endure them elsewhere, especially in Baltimore, for I had something of the feeling about that city that is expressed in the saying that 'being hanged in England is better than dying a natural death in Ireland.' I had the strongest desire to see Baltimore. My cousin Tom,* a boy two or three years older than I, had been there, and, though not fluent in speech (he stuttered immoderately), he had inspired me with that desire by his eloquent descriptions of the place. Tom was sometimes cabin-boy on board the sloop 'Sally Lloyd' (which Capt. Thomas Auld commanded), and when he came home from Baltimore he was always a sort of hero amongst us, at least till his trip to Baltimore was forgotten. I could never tell him anything, or point out anything that struck me as beautiful or powerful, but that he had seen something in Baltimore far surpassing it. Even the 'great house,' with all its pictures within and pillars without, he had the hardihood to say, 'was nothing to Baltimore.' He bought a trumpet (worth sixpence) and brought it home; told what he had seen in the windows of the stores; that he had heard shooting-crackers, and seen soldiers; that he had seen a steamboat, and that there were ships in Baltimore that could carry four such sloops as the 'Sally Lloyd.' He said a great deal about the Market house; of the ringing of the bells, and of many other things which roused my curiosity very much, and indeed brightened my hopes of happiness in my new home.

We sailed out of Miles River for Baltimore early on a Saturday morning. I remember only the day of the week, for at that time I had no knowledge of the days of the month, nor indeed of the months of the year. On setting sail I walked aft and gave to Col. Lloyd's plantation what I hoped would be the last look I should give to it, or to any place like it. After taking this last view, I quitted the quarter-deck, made my way to the bow of the boat, and spent the remainder of the day in looking ahead; interesting myself in what was in the distance, rather than in what was near by, or behind. The vessels sweeping along the bay were objects full of interest to me. The broad bay opened like a shoreless ocean on my boyish vision, filling me with wonder and admiration.

Late in the afternoon we reached Annapolis,* but not stopping there long enough to admit of going ashore. It was the first large town I had ever seen, and though it was inferior to many a factory village in New England, my feelings on seeing it were excited to a pitch very little below that reached by travelers at the first view of Rome. The dome of the State house* was especially imposing, and surpassed in grandeur the appearance of the 'great house' I had left behind. So the great world was opening upon me, and I was eagerly acquainting myself with its multifarious lessons.

We arrived in Baltimore on Sunday morning, and landed at Smith's wharf, not far from Bowly's wharf. We had on board a large flock of sheep for the Baltimore market; and after assisting in driving them to the slaughter house of Mr. Curtiss, on Loudon Slater's hill, I was conducted by Rich—one of the hands belonging to the sloop—to my new home on Alliciana street, near Gardiner's ship yard, on Fell's point.* Mr. and Mrs. Hugh Auld, my new master and mistress, were both at home, and met me at the door, together with their rosy-cheeked little son Thomas,* to take care of whom was to constitute my future occupation. In fact it was to 'little Tommy,' rather than to his parents, that old master made a present of me, and, though there was no *legal* form or arrangement entered into, I have no doubt that Mr. and Mrs. Auld felt that in due time I should be the legal property of their bright-eyed and beloved boy Tommy. I was especially struck with the appearance of my new mistress. Her face was lighted with the kindliest emotions; and the reflex influence of her countenance, as well as the tenderness with which she seemed to regard me, while asking me sundry little questions, greatly delighted me, and lit up, to my fancy, the pathway of my future. Little Thomas was affectionately told by his mother, that 'there was his Freddy,' and that 'Freddy would take care of him;' and I was told to 'be kind to little Tommy,' an injunction I scarcely needed, for I had already fallen in love with the dear boy. With these little ceremonies I was initiated into my new home, and entered upon my peculiar duties, then unconscious of a cloud to dim its broad horizon.

I may say here that I regard my removal from Col. Lloyd's plantation as one of the most interesting and fortunate events of my life. Viewing it in the light of human likelihoods, it is quite probable that but for the mere circumstance of being thus removed, before the rigors of slavery had fully fastened upon me; before my young spirit had been crushed under the iron control of the slave-driver; I might have continued in slavery until emancipated by the war.

# CHAPTER X.

## LEARNING TO READ.

*City annoyances—Plantation regrets—My mistress—Her history—Her kindness—My master—His sourness—My comforts—Increased sensitiveness—My occupation—Learning to read—Baneful effects of slaveholding on my dear, good mistress—Mr. Hugh forbids Mrs. Sophia to teach me further—Clouds gather on my bright prospects—Master Auld's exposition of the Philosophy of Slavery—City slaves—Country slaves—Contrasts—Exceptions—Mr. Hamilton's two slaves—Mrs. Hamilton's cruel treatment of them—Piteous aspect presented by them—No power to come between the slave and slaveholder.*

ESTABLISHED in my new home in Baltimore, I was not very long in perceiving that in picturing to myself what was to be my life there, my imagination had painted only the bright side; and that the reality had its dark shades as well as its light ones. The open country which had been so much to me was all shut out. Walled in on every side by towering brick buildings, the heat of the summer was intolerable to me, and the hard brick pavements almost blistered my feet. If I ventured out on to the streets, new and strange objects glared upon me at every step, and startling sounds greeted my ears from all directions. My country eyes and ears were confused and bewildered. Troops of hostile boys pounced upon me at every corner. They chased me, and called me 'Eastern-Shore man,' till really I almost wished myself back on the Eastern Shore. My new mistress happily proved to be all she had seemed, and in her presence I easily forgot all outside annoyances. Mrs. Sophia was naturally of an excellent disposition—kind, gentle, and cheerful. The supercilious contempt for the rights and feelings of others, and the petulance and bad humor which generally characterized slaveholding ladies, were all quite absent from her manner and bearing toward me.

She had never been a slaveholder—a thing then quite unusual at the South—but had depended almost entirely upon her own industry for a living. To this fact the dear lady no doubt owed the excellent preservation of her natural goodness of heart, for slavery could change a saint into a sinner, and an angel into a demon. I hardly knew how to behave towards 'Miss Sopha,' as I used to call Mrs. Hugh Auld. I could not approach her even as I had formerly approached Mrs. Thomas Auld.

Why should I hang down my head, and speak with bated breath, when there was no pride to scorn me, no coldness to repel me, and no hatred to inspire me with fear? I therefore soon came to regard her as something more akin to a mother than a slaveholding mistress. So far from deeming it impudent in a slave to look her straight in the face, she seemed ever to say, 'look up, child; don't be afraid.' The sailors belonging to the sloop esteemed it a great privilege to be the bearers of parcels or messages for her, for whenever they came, they were sure of a most kind and pleasant reception. If little Thomas was her son, and her most dearly loved child, she made me something like his half-brother in her affections. If dear Tommy was exalted to a place on his mother's knee, 'Freddy' was honored by a place at the mother's side. Nor did the slave-boy lack the caressing strokes of her gentle hand, soothing him into the consciousness that, though motherless, he was not friendless. Mrs. Auld was not only kind-hearted, but remarkably pious; frequent in her attendance at public worship and much given to reading the Bible and to chanting hymns of praise when alone. Mr. Hugh was altogether a different character. He cared very little about religion; knew more of the world and was more a part of the world, than his wife. He doubtless set out to be, as the world goes, a respectable man and to get on by becoming a successful ship-builder, in that city of ship-building. This was his ambition, and it fully occupied him. I was of course of very little consequence to him, and when he smiled upon me, as he sometimes did, the smile was borrowed from his lovely wife, and like borrowed light, was transient, and vanished with the source whence it was derived. Though I must in truth characterize Master Hugh as a sour man of forbidding appearance, it is due to him to acknowledge that he was never cruel to me, according to the notion of cruelty in Maryland. During the first year or two, he left me almost exclusively to the management of his wife. She was my law-giver. In hands so tender as hers, and in the absence of the cruelties of the plantation, I became both physically and mentally much more sensitive, and a frown from my mistress caused me far more suffering than had Aunt Katy's hardest cuffs. Instead of the cold, damp floor of my old master's kitchen, I was on carpets; for the corn bag in winter, I had a good straw bed, well furnished with covers; for the coarse corn meal in the morning, I had good bread and mush occasionally; for my old tow-linen shirt, I had good clean clothes. I was really well off. My employment was to run of errands, and to take care of Tommy; to prevent his getting in the way of carriages, and to keep him out of harm's way generally.

So for a time everything went well. I say for a time, because the fatal poison of irresponsible power, and the natural influence of slave customs, were not very long in making their impression on the gentle and loving disposition of my excellent mistress. She at first regarded me as a child, like any other. This was the natural and spontaneous thought; afterwards, when she came to consider me as property, our relations to each other were changed, but a nature so noble as hers could not instantly become perverted, and it took several years before the sweetness of her temper was wholly lost.

The frequent hearing of my mistress reading the Bible aloud, for she often read aloud when her husband was absent, awakened my curiosity in respect to this *mystery* of reading, and roused in me the desire to learn. Up to this time I had known nothing whatever of this wonderful art, and my ignorance and inexperience of what it could do for me, as well as my confidence in my mistress, emboldened me to ask her to teach me to read. With an unconsciousness and inexperience equal to my own, she readily consented, and in an incredibly short time, by her kind assistance, I had mastered the alphabet and could spell words of three or four letters. My mistress seemed almost as proud of my progress as if I had been her own child, and supposing that her husband would be as well pleased, she made no secret of what she was doing for me. Indeed, she exultingly told him of the aptness of her pupil and of her intention to persevere, as she felt it her duty to do, in teaching me, at least, to read the Bible. And here arose the first dark cloud over my Baltimore prospects, the precursor of chilling blasts and drenching storms. Master Hugh was astounded beyond measure and, probably for the first time, proceeded to unfold to his wife the true philosophy of the slave system, and the peculiar rules necessary in the nature of the case to be observed in the management of human chattels. Of course he forbade her to give me any further instruction, telling her in the first place that to do so was unlawful, as it was also unsafe; 'for,' said he, 'if you give a nigger an inch he will take an ell.* Learning will spoil the best nigger in the world. If he learns to read the Bible it will forever unfit him to be a slave. He should know nothing but the will of his master, and learn to obey it. As to himself, learning will do him no good, but a great deal of harm, making him disconsolate and unhappy. If you teach him how to read, he'll want to know how to write, and this accomplished, he'll be running away with himself.' Such was the tenor of Master Hugh's oracular exposition; and it must be confessed that he very clearly comprehended the nature and the requirements of the relation of master and slave. His discourse was the first decidedly anti-slavery lecture to which it had been my lot to listen. Mrs. Auld evidently felt the force of what he said, and, like an obedient wife, began to shape her course in the direction indicated by him. The effect of his words on me was neither slight nor transitory. His iron sentences, cold and harsh, sunk like heavy weights deep into my heart, and stirred up within me a rebellion not soon to be allayed.

This was a new and special revelation, dispelling a painful mystery against which my youthful understanding had struggled, and struggled in vain, to wit, the white man's power to perpetuate the enslavement of the black man. 'Very well,' thought I. 'Knowledge unfits a child to be a slave.' I instinctively assented to the proposition, and from that moment I understood the direct pathway from slavery to freedom. It was just what I needed, and it came to me at a time and from a source whence I least expected it. Of course I was greatly saddened at the thought of losing the assistance of my kind mistress, but the information so instantly derived, to some extent compensated me for the loss I had sustained in this direction. Wise as Mr. Auld was, he underrated my comprehension, and had little idea of the use to which I was capable of putting the impressive lesson he was giving to his wife. He wanted me to be a slave; I had already voted against that on the home plantation of Col. Lloyd. That which he most loved I most hated; and the very determination which he expressed to keep me in ignorance only rendered me the more resolute to seek intelligence. In learning to read, therefore, I am not sure that I do not owe quite as much to the opposition of my master as to the kindly assistance of my amiable mistress. I acknowledge the benefit rendered me by the one, and by the other, believing that but for my mistress I might have grown up in ignorance.

# CHAPTER XI.

## GROWING IN KNOWLEDGE.

*My mistress—Her slaveholding duties—Their effects on her originally
noble nature—The conflict in her mind—She opposes my learning to
read—Too late—She had given me the 'inch,' I was resolved to take
the 'ell'—How I pursued my study to read—My tutors—What progress I made—Slavery—What I heard said about it—Thirteen
years old—Columbian Orator—Dialogue—Speeches—Sheridan—
Pitt—Lords Chatham and Fox—Knowledge increasing—Liberty—
Singing—Sadness—Unhappiness of Mrs. Sophia—My hatred of
slavery—One Upas tree overshadows us all.*

I LIVED in the family of Mr. Auld, at Baltimore, seven years, during
which time, as the almanac makers say of the weather, my condition was
variable. The most interesting feature of my history here was my learning, under somewhat marked disadvantages, to read and write. In
attaining this knowledge I was compelled to resort to indirections by no
means congenial to my nature, and which were really humiliating to my
sense of candor and uprightness. My mistress, checked in her benevolent designs toward me, not only ceased instructing me herself, but set
her face as a flint against my learning to read by any means. It is due to
her to say, however, that she did not adopt this course in all its strin-
gency at first. She either thought it unnecessary, or she lacked the
depravity needed to make herself forget at once my human nature. She
was, as I have said, naturally a kind and tender-hearted woman, and in
the humanity of her heart and the simplicity of her mind, she set out,
when I first went to live with her, to treat me as she supposed one
human being ought to treat another.

Nature never intended that men and women should be either slaves
or slaveholders, and nothing but rigid training long persisted in, can
perfect the character of the one or the other.

Mrs. Auld was singularly deficient in the qualities of a slaveholder. It
was no easy matter for her to think or to feel that the curly-headed boy,
who stood by her side, and even leaned on her lap, who was loved by
little Tommy, and who loved little Tommy in turn, sustained to her only
the relation of a chattel. I was more than that; she felt me to be more
than that. I could talk and sing; I could laugh and weep; I could reason
and remember; I could love and hate. I was human, and she, dear lady,
knew and felt me to be so. How could she then treat me as a brute,

without a mighty struggle with all the noblest powers of her soul? That struggle came, and the will and power of the husband were victorious. Her noble soul was overcome, and he who wrought the wrong was injured in the fall no less than the rest of the household. When I went into that household, it was the abode of happiness and contentment. The wife and mistress there was a model of affection and tenderness. Her fervent piety and watchful uprightness made it impossible to see her without thinking and feeling that 'that woman is a Christian.' There was no sorrow nor suffering for which she had not a tear, and there was no innocent joy for which she had not a smile. She had bread for the hungry, clothes for the naked, and comfort for every mourner who came within her reach.

But slavery soon proved its ability to divest her of these excellent qualities, and her home of its early happiness. Conscience cannot stand much violence. Once thoroughly injured, who is he who can repair the damage? If it be broken toward the slave on Sunday, it will be toward the master on Monday. It cannot long endure such shocks. It must stand unharmed, or it does not stand at all. As my condition in the family waxed bad, that of the family waxed no better. The first step in the wrong direction was the violence done to nature and to conscience in arresting the benevolence that would have enlightened my young mind. In ceasing to instruct me, my mistress had to seek to justify herself to herself, and once consenting to take sides in such a debate, she was compelled to hold her position. One needs little knowledge of moral philosophy to see where she inevitably landed. She finally became even more violent in her opposition to my learning to read than was Mr. Auld himself. Nothing now appeared to make her more angry than seeing me, seated in some nook or corner, quietly reading a book or newspaper. She would rush at me with the utmost fury, and snatch the book or paper from my hand, with something of the wrath and consternation which a traitor might be supposed to feel on being discovered in a plot by some dangerous spy. The conviction once thoroughly established in her mind, that education and slavery were incompatible with each other, I was most narrowly watched in all my movements. If I remained in a separate room from the family for any considerable length of time, I was sure to be suspected of having a book, and was at once called to give an account of myself. But this was too late: the first and never-to-be-retraced step had been taken. Teaching me the alphabet had been the 'inch' given, I was now waiting only for the opportunity to 'take the ell.'

Filled with the determination to learn to read at any cost, I hit upon many expedients to accomplish that much desired end. The plan which

I mainly adopted, and the one which was the most successful, was that of using as teachers my young white playmates, with whom I met on the streets. I used almost constantly to carry a copy of Webster's spelling-book* in my pocket, and when sent of errands, or when play-time was allowed me, I would step aside with my young friends and take a lesson in spelling. I am greatly indebted to these boys—Gustavus Dorgan, Joseph Bailey, Charles Farity, and William Cosdry.

Although slavery was a delicate subject and, in Maryland, very cautiously talked about among grown up people, I frequently talked with the white boys about it, and that very freely. I would sometimes say to them, while seated on a curbstone or a cellar door, 'I wish I could be free, as you will be when you get to be men.' 'You will be free, you know, as soon as you are twenty-one, and can go where you like, but I am a slave for life. Have I not as good a right to be free as you have?' Words like these, I observed, always troubled them; and I had no small satisfaction in drawing out from them, as I occasionally did, that fresh and bitter condemnation of slavery which ever springs from natures unseared and unperverted. Of all consciences, let me have those to deal with, which have not been seared and bewildered with the cares and perplexities of life. I do not remember ever while I was in slavery, to have met with a *boy* who defended the system, but I do remember many times, when I was consoled by them, and by them encouraged to hope that something would yet occur by which I would be made free. Over and over again, they have told me that 'they believed I had as good a right to be free as *they* had,' and that 'they did not believe God ever made any one to be a slave.' It is easily seen that such little conversations with my playfellows had no tendency to weaken my love of liberty, nor to render me contented as a slave.

When I was about thirteen years old, and had succeeded in learning to read, every increase of knowledge, especially anything respecting the free states, was an additional weight to the almost intolerable burden of my thought—'*I am a slave for life.*' To my bondage I could see no end. It was a terrible reality, and I shall never be able to tell how sadly that thought chafed my young spirit. Fortunately or unfortunately, I had, by blacking boots for some gentlemen, earned a little money with which I purchased of Mr. Knight, on Thames street, what was then a very popular school book, viz., 'The Columbian Orator,'* for which I paid fifty cents. I was led to buy this book by hearing some little boys say that they were going to learn some pieces out of it for the exhibition. This volume was indeed a rich treasure, and, for a time, every opportunity afforded me was spent in diligently perusing it. Among much other interesting matter, that which I read again and again with unflagging satisfaction was a short dialogue between a master and his slave.* The slave is represented as having been recaptured in a second attempt to run away; and the master opens the dialogue with an upbraiding speech, charging the slave with ingratitude, and demanding to know what he has to say in his own defense. Thus upbraided and thus called upon to reply, the slave rejoins that he knows how little anything that he can say will avail, seeing that he is completely in the hands of his owner; and with noble resolution, calmly says, 'I submit to my fate.' Touched by the slave's answer, the master insists upon his further speaking, and recapitulates the many acts of kindness which he has performed toward the slave, and tells him he is permitted to speak for himself. Thus invited, the quondam slave made a spirited defense of himself, and thereafter the whole argument for and against slavery is brought out. The master was vanquished at every turn in the argument, and, appreciating the fact, he generously and meekly emancipates the slave, with his best wishes for his prosperity.

It is unnecessary to say that a dialogue with such an origin and such an end, read by me when every nerve of my being was in revolt at my own condition as a slave, affected me most powerfully. I could not help feeling that the day might yet come when the well-directed answers made by the slave to the master, in this instance, would find a counterpart in my own experience. This, however, was not all the fanaticism which I found in the Columbian Orator. I met there one of Sheridan's mighty speeches on the subject of Catholic Emancipation,* Lord Chatham's speech on the American War,* and speeches by the great William Pitt,* and by Fox.* These were all choice documents to me, and I read them over and over again, with an interest ever increasing, because it was ever gaining in intelligence; for the more I read them the better I understood them. The reading of these speeches added much to my limited stock of language, and enabled me to give tongue to many interesting thoughts which had often flashed through my mind and died away for want of words in which to give them utterance. The mighty power and heart-searching directness of truth penetrating the heart of a slave-holder and compelling him to yield up his earthly interests to the claims of eternal justice, were finely illustrated in the dialogue, and from the speeches of Sheridan I got a bold and powerful denunciation of oppression and a most brilliant vindication of the rights of man.

Here was indeed a noble acquisition. If I had ever wavered under the consideration that the Almighty, in some way, had ordained slavery and willed my enslavement for His own glory, I wavered no longer. I had now penetrated to the secret of all slavery and of all oppression, and had ascertained their true foundation to be in the pride, the power and the avarice of man. With a book in my hand so redolent of the principles of liberty, and with a perception of my own human nature and of the facts of my past and present experience, I was equal to a contest with the religious advocates of slavery, whether white or black; for blindness in this matter was not confined to the white people. I have met, at the south, many good, religious colored people who were under the delusion that God required them to submit to slavery and to wear their chains with meekness and humility. I could entertain no such nonsense as this, and I quite lost my patience when I found a colored man weak enough to believe such stuff. Nevertheless, eager as I was to partake of the tree of knowledge, its fruits were bitter as well as sweet. 'Slaveholders,' thought I, 'are only a band of successful robbers, who, leaving their own homes, went into Africa for the purpose of stealing and reducing my people to slavery.' I loathed them as the meanest and the most wicked of men. And as I read, behold! the very discontent so graphically predicted by Master Hugh had already come upon me. I was no longer the light-hearted, gleesome boy full of mirth and play, that I was when I landed in Baltimore. Light had penetrated the moral dungeon where I had lain, and I saw the bloody whip for my back and the iron chain for my feet, and my *good*, *kind* master was the author of my situation. The revelation haunted me, stung me, and made me gloomy and miserable. As I writhed under the sting and torment of this knowledge I almost envied my fellow slaves their stupid indifference. It opened my eyes to the horrible pit, and revealed the teeth of the frightful dragon that was ready to pounce upon me; but alas, it opened no way for my escape. I wished myself a beast, a bird, anything rather than a slave. I was wretched and gloomy beyond my ability to describe. This everlasting thinking distressed and tormented me; and yet there was no getting rid of this subject of my thoughts. Liberty, as the inestimable birthright of every man, converted every object into an asserter of this right. I heard it in every sound, and saw it in every object. It was ever present to torment me with a sense of my wretchedness. The more beautiful and charming were the smiles of nature, the more horrible and desolate was my condition. I saw nothing without seeing it, and I heard nothing without hearing it. I do not exaggerate when I say that it looked at me in every star, smiled in every calm, breathed in every wind and moved in every storm. I have no doubt that my state of mind had something to do with the change in treatment which my mistress adopted towards me. I can easily believe that my leaden, downcast, and disconsolate look was very offensive to her. Poor lady! She did not understand my trouble, and I could not tell her. Could I have made her acquainted with the real state of my mind and given her the reasons therefor, it might have been well for both of us. As it was, her abuse fell upon me like the blows of the false prophet upon his ass;* she did not know that an angel stood in the way. Nature made us friends, but slavery had made us enemies. My interests were in a direction opposite to hers, and we both had our private thoughts and plans. She aimed to keep me ignorant, and I resolved to *know*, although knowledge only increased my misery. My feelings were not the result of any marked cruelty in the treatment I received; they sprung from the consideration of my being a slave at all. It was *slavery*, not its mere *incidents* that I hated. I had been cheated. I saw through the attempt to keep me in ignorance. I saw that slaveholders would have gladly made me believe that, in making a slave of me and in making slaves of others, they were merely acting under the authority of God, and I felt to them as to robbers and deceivers. The feeding and clothing me well could not atone for taking my liberty from me. The smiles of my mistress could not remove the deep sorrow that dwelt in my young bosom. Indeed, these came, in time, but to deepen my sorrow. She had changed, and the reader will see that I too, had changed. We were both victims to the same overshadowing evil, *she* as mistress, I as slave. I will not censure her harshly.

# CHAPTER XII.

### RELIGIOUS NATURE AWAKENED.

*Abolitionists spoken of—Eagerness to know the meaning of word—Consults the dictionary—Incendiary information—The enigma solved—'Nat Turner' insurrection—Cholera—Religion—Methodist minister—Religious impressions—Father Lawson—His character and occupation—His influence over me—Our mutual attachment—New hopes and aspirations—Heavenly light—Two Irishmen on wharf—Conversation with them—Learning to write—My aims.*

IN the unhappy state of mind described in the foregoing chapter, regretting my very existence because doomed to a life of bondage, and so goaded and wretched as to be even tempted at times to take my own life, I was most keenly sensitive to know any and everything possible that had any relation to the subject of slavery. I was all ears, all eyes, whenever the words slave or slavery dropped from the lips of any white person, and more and more frequently occasions occurred when these words became leading ones in high, social debate at our house. Very often I would overhear Master Hugh, or some of his company, speak with much warmth of the '*abolitionists.*' *Who* or what the *abolitionists* were, I was totally ignorant. I found, however, that whoever or whatever they might be, they were most cordially hated and abused by slaveholders of every grade. I very soon discovered too, that slavery was, in some sort, under consideration whenever the abolitionists were alluded to. This made the term a very interesting one to me. If a slave had made good his escape from slavery, it was generally alleged that he had been persuaded and assisted to do so by the abolitionists. If a slave killed his master, or struck down his overseer, or set fire to his master's dwelling, or committed any violence or crime, out of the common way, it was certain to be said that such a crime was the legitimate fruits of the abolition movement. Hearing such charges often repeated, I, naturally enough, received the impression that abolition—whatever else it might be—was not unfriendly to the slave, nor very friendly to the slaveholder. I therefore set about finding out, if possible, *who* and *what* the abolitionists were, and *why* they were so obnoxious to the slaveholders. The dictionary offered me very little help. It taught me that abolition was 'the act of abolishing;' but it left me in ignorance at the very point where I most wanted information, and that was, as to the thing to be abolished. A city newspaper—the 'Baltimore *American*'*—gave me the incendiary information denied me by the dictionary. In its columns I found that on a certain day a vast number of petitions and memorials had been presented to Congress, praying for the abolition of slavery in the District of Columbia, and for the abolition of the slave trade between the States of the Union. This was enough. The vindictive bitterness, the marked caution, the studied reserve, and the ambiguity practiced by our white folks when alluding to this subject, was now fully explained. Ever after that, when I heard the word abolition, I felt the matter one of a personal concern, and I drew near to listen whenever I could do so, without seeming too solicitous and prying. There was HOPE in those words. Ever and anon too, I could see some terrible denunciation of slavery in our papers,—copied from abolition papers at the North,—and the injustice of such denunciation commented on. These I read with avidity. I had a deep satisfaction in the thought that the rascality of slaveholders was not concealed from the eyes of the world, and that I was not alone in abhorring the cruelty and brutality of slavery. A still deeper train of thought was stirred. I saw that there was fear as well as rage in the manner of speaking of the abolitionists, and from this I inferred that they must have some power in the country, and I felt that they might perhaps succeed in their designs. When I met with a slave to whom I deemed it safe to talk on the subject, I would impart to him so much of the mystery as I had been able to penetrate. Thus the light of this grand movement broke in upon my mind by degrees; and I must say that ignorant as I was of the philosophy of that movement, I believed in it from the first, and I believed in it, partly, because I saw that it alarmed the consciences of the slaveholders. The insurrection of Nat. Turner* had been quelled, but the alarm and terror which it occasioned had not subsided. The cholera was then on its way to this country, and I remember thinking that God was angry with the white people because of their slaveholding wickedness, and therefore his judgments were abroad in the land. Of course it was impossible for me not to hope much for the abolition movement when I saw it supported by the Almighty, and armed with DEATH.

Previously to my contemplation of the anti-slavery movement and its probable results, my mind had been seriously awakened to the subject of religion. I was not more than thirteen years old, when, in my loneliness and destitution, I longed for some one to whom I could go, as to a father and protector. The preaching of a white Methodist minister, named Hanson,* was the means of causing me to feel that in God I had such a friend. He thought that all men, great and small, bond and free, were sinners in the sight of God: that they were by nature rebels against his government: and that they must repent of their sins, and be reconciled to God through Christ. I cannot say that I had a very distinct notion of what was required of me, but one thing I did know well: that I was wretched and had no means of making myself otherwise. I consulted a good colored man named Charles Lawson,* and in tones of holy affection he told me to pray, and to 'cast all my care upon God.'* This I sought to do; and though for weeks I was a poor, broken-hearted mourner, traveling through doubts and fears, I finally found my burden lightened, and my heart relieved. I loved all mankind, slaveholders not excepted, though I abhorred slavery more than ever. I saw the world in a new light, and my great concern was to have everybody converted. My desire to learn increased, and especially did I want a thorough acquaintance with the contents of the Bible. I have gathered scattered pages of the Bible from the filthy street-gutters, and washed and dried them, that in moments of leisure I might get a word or two of wisdom from them. While thus religiously seeking knowledge, I became acquainted with a good old colored man named Lawson. This man not only prayed three times a day, but he prayed as he walked through the streets, at his work, on his dray—everywhere. His life was a life of prayer, and his words when he spoke to any one, were about a better world. Uncle Lawson lived near Master Hugh's house, and becoming deeply attached to him, I went often with him to prayer-meeting and spent much of my leisure time on Sunday with him. The old man could read a little, and I was a great help to him in making out the hard words, for I was a better reader than he. I could teach him 'the letter,' but he could teach me 'the spirit,' and refreshing times we had together, in singing and praying. These meetings went on for a long time without the knowledge either of Master Hugh or my mistress. Both knew, however, that I had become religious, and seemed to respect my conscientious piety. My mistress was still a professor of religion, and belonged to class. Her leader was no less a person than Rev. Beverly Waugh,* the presiding elder, and afterwards one of the bishops of the Methodist Episcopal church.

In view of the cares and anxieties incident to the life she was leading, and especially in view of the separation from religious associations to which she was subjected, my mistress had, as I have before stated, become lukewarm, and needed to be looked up by her leader. This often brought Mr. Waugh to our house, and gave me an opportunity to hear him exhort and pray. But my chief instructor in religious matters was Uncle Lawson. He was my spiritual father and I loved him intensely, and was at his house every chance I could get. This pleasure, however, was not long unquestioned. Master Hugh became averse to our intimacy, and threatened to whip me if I ever went there again. I now felt myself persecuted by a wicked man, and I *would* go. The good old man had told me that the 'Lord had great work for me to do,' and I must prepare to do it; that he had been shown that I must preach the gospel. His words made a very deep impression upon me, and I verily felt that some such work was before me, though I could not see how I could ever engage in its performance. 'The good Lord would bring it to pass in his own good time,' he said, and that I must go on reading and studying the Scriptures. This advice and these suggestions were not without their influence on my character and destiny. He fanned my already intense love of knowledge into a flame by assuring me that I was to be a useful man in the world. When I would say to him, 'How can these things be? and what can I do?' his simple reply was, '*Trust in the Lord.*' When I would tell him, 'I am a slave, and a slave for life, how can I do anything?' he would quietly answer, 'The *Lord* can make you free, my dear; all things are possible with Him; only have *faith* in God. "Ask, and it shall be given you."* If you want liberty, ask the Lord for it *in* FAITH, *and He will give it to you.*'

Thus assured and thus cheered on under the inspiration of hope, I worked and prayed with a light heart, believing that my life was under the guidance of a wisdom higher than my own. With all other blessings sought at the mercy seat, I always prayed that God would, of His great mercy, and in His own good time, deliver me from my bondage.

I went, one day, on the wharf of Mr. Waters, and seeing two Irishmen unloading a scow of stone or ballast, I went on board unasked, and helped them. When we had finished the work one of the men came to me, aside, and asked me a number of questions, and among them if I were a slave? I told him 'I was a slave for life.' The good Irishman gave a shrug, and seemed deeply affected. He said it was a pity so fine a little fellow as I should be a slave for life. They both had much to say about the matter, and expressed the deepest sympathy with me, and the most decided hatred of slavery. They went so far as to tell me that I ought to run away and go to the north; that I should find friends there, and that I should then be as free as anybody. I pretended not to be interested in what they said, for I feared they might be treacherous. White men were not unfrequently known to encourage slaves to escape, and then, to get the reward, they would kidnap them and return them to their masters. While I mainly inclined to the notion that these men were honest and meant me no ill, I feared it might be otherwise. I nevertheless remembered their words and their advice, and looked forward to an escape to the north as a possible means of gaining the liberty for which my heart panted. It was not my enslavement at the then present time which most affected me; the being a slave *for life* was the saddest thought. I was too young to think of running away immediately; besides, I wished to learn to write before going, as I might have occasion to write my own pass. I now not only had the hope of freedom, but a foreshadowing of the means by which I might some day gain that inestimable boon. Meanwhile I resolved to add to my educational attainments the art of writing.

After this manner I began to learn to write. I was much in the ship-yard—Master Hugh's, and that of Durgan & Bailey, and I observed that the carpenters, after hewing and getting ready a piece of timber to use, wrote on it the initials of the name of that part of the ship for which it was intended. When, for instance, a piece of timber was ready for the starboard side, it was marked with a capital 'S.' A piece for the larboard side was marked 'L.'; larboard forward was marked 'L. F.'; larboard aft was marked 'L. A.'; starboard aft, 'S. A.'; and starboard forward, 'S. F.' I soon learned these letters, and for what they were placed on the timbers.

My work now was to keep fire under the steam-box, and to watch the ship-yard while the carpenters had gone to dinner. This interval gave me a fine opportunity for copying the letters named. I soon astonished myself with the ease with which I made the letters, and the thought was soon present, 'If I can make four letters I can make more.' Having made these readily and easily, when I met boys about the Bethel church or on any of our play-grounds, I entered the lists with them in the art of writing, and would make the letters which I had been so fortunate as to learn, and ask them to 'beat that if they could.' With play-mates for my teachers, fences and pavements for my copy-books, and chalk for my pen and ink, I learned to write. I however adopted, afterward, various methods for improving my hand. The most successful was copying the *italics* in Webster's spelling-book until I could make them all without looking on the book. By this time my little 'Master Tommy' had grown to be a big boy, and had written over a number of copy-books and brought them home. They had been shown to the neighbors, had elicited due praise, and had been laid carefully away. Spending parts of my time both at the shipyard and the house, I was often the lone keeper of the latter as of the former. When my mistress left me in charge of the house I had a grand time. I got Master Tommy's copy-books and a pen and ink, and in the ample spaces between the lines I wrote other lines as nearly like his as possible. The process was a tedious one, and I ran the risk of getting a flogging for marking the highly-prized copy-books of the oldest son. In addition to these opportunities, sleeping as I did in the kitchen loft, a room seldom visited by any of the family, I contrived to get a flour-barrel up there and a chair, and upon the head of that barrel I have written, or endeavored to write, copying from the Bible and the Methodist hymn-book, and other books which I had accumulated, till late at night, and when all the family were in bed and asleep. I was supported in my endeavors by renewed advice and by holy promises from the good father Lawson, with whom I continued to meet and pray and read the Scriptures. Although Master Hugh was aware of these meetings, I must say for his credit that he never executed his threats to whip me for having thus innocently employed my leisure time.

# CHAPTER XIII.

## THE VICISSITUDES OF SLAVE LIFE.

*Death of old Master's son Richard, speedily followed by that of old Master—Valuation and division of all the property, including the slaves—Sent for to come to Hillsborough to be valued and divided—Sad prospects and grief—Parting—Slaves have no voice in deciding their own destinies—General dread of falling into Master Andrew's hands—His drunkenness—Good fortune in falling to Miss Lucretia—She allows my return to Baltimore—Joy at Master Hugh's—Death of Miss Lucretia—Master Thomas Auld's second marriage—The new wife unlike the old—Again removed from Master Hugh's—Reasons for regret—Plan of escape.*

I MUST now ask the reader to go back with me a little in point of time, in my humble story, and notice another circumstance that entered into my slavery experience, and which, doubtless, has had a share in deepening my horror of slavery and of my hostility toward those men and measures that practically uphold the slave system.

It has already been observed that though I was, after my removal from Col. Lloyd's plantation, in *form* the slave of Master Hugh Auld, I was in *fact* and in *law* the slave of my old master, Capt. Anthony. Very well. In a very short time after I went to Baltimore my old master's youngest son, Richard, died; and in three years and six months after, my old master himself died,* leaving, to share the estate, only his daughter Lucretia and his son Andrew. The old man died while on a visit to his daughter in Hillsborough, where Capt. Auld and Mrs. Lucretia now lived. Master Thomas, having given up the command of Col. Lloyd's sloop, was now keeping store in that town.

Cut off thus unexpectedly, Capt. Anthony died intestate, and his property must be equally divided between his two children, Andrew and Lucretia.

The valuation and division of slaves among contending heirs was a most important incident in slave life. The characters and tendencies of the heirs were generally well understood by the slaves who were to be divided, of whom all had their aversions and their preferences. But neither their aversions nor their preferences availed anything.

On the death of old master I was immediately sent for to be valued and divided with the other property. Personally, my concern was mainly about my possible removal from the home of Master Hugh, for up to this time there had no dark clouds arisen to darken the sky of that happy abode. It was a sad day to me when I left for the Eastern Shore, to be valued and divided, as it was for my dear mistress and teacher, and for little Tommy. We all three wept bitterly, for we were parting, and it might be we were parting forever. No one could tell amongst which pile of chattels I might be flung. Thus early, I got a foretaste of that painful uncertainty which in one form or another was ever obtruding itself in the pathway of the slave. It furnished me a new insight into the unnatural power to which I was subjected. Sickness, adversity, and death may interfere with the plans and purposes of all, but the slave had the added danger of changing homes, in the separations unknown to other men. Then, too, there was the intensified degradation of the spectacle. What an assemblage! Men and women, young and old, married and single; moral and thinking human beings, in open contempt of their humanity, leveled at a low with horses, sheep, horned cattle, and swine. Horses and men, cattle and women, pigs and children—all holding the same rank in the scale of social existence, and all subjected to the same narrow inspection, to ascertain their value in gold and silver—the only standard of worth applied by slaveholders to their slaves. Personality swallowed up in the sordid idea of property! Manhood lost in chattelhood!

The valuation over, then came the division and apportionment. Our destiny was to be *fixed for life*, and we had no more voice in the decision of the question than the oxen and cows that stood chewing at the haymow. One word of the appraisers, against all preferences and prayers, could sunder all the ties of friendship and affection, even to separating husbands and wives, parents and children. We were all appalled before that power which, to human seeming, could, in a moment, bless or blast us. Added to this dread of separation, most painful to the majority of the slaves, we all had a decided horror of falling into the hands of Master Andrew, who was distinguished for his cruelty and intemperance.

Slaves had a great dread, very naturally, of falling into the hands of drunken owners. Master Andrew was a confirmed sot, and had already by his profligate dissipation wasted a large portion of his father's property. To fall into his hands, therefore, was considered as the first step toward being sold away to the far South. He would no doubt spend his fortune in a few years, it was thought, and his farms and slaves would be sold at public auction, and the slaves hurried away to the cotton-fields and rice-swamps of the burning South. This was cause of deep consternation.

The people of the North, and free people generally, I think, have less attachment to the places where they are born and brought up than had the slaves. Their freedom to come and go, to be here or there, as they list, prevents any extravagant attachment to any one particular place. On the other hand, the slave was a fixture; he had no choice, no goal, but was pegged down to one single spot, and must take root there or nowhere. The idea of removal elsewhere came generally in shape of a threat, and in punishment for crime. It was therefore attended with fear and dread. The enthusiasm which animates the bosoms of young freemen, when they contemplate a life in the far West, or in some distant country, where they expect to rise to wealth and distinction, could have no place in the thought of the slave; nor could those from whom they separated know anything of that cheerfulness with which friends and relations yield each other up, when they feel that it is for the good of the departing one that he is removed from his native place. Then, too, there is correspondence and the hope of reunion, but with the slaves, all these mitigating circumstances were wanting. There was no improvement in condition *probable*—no correspondence *possible*—no reunion attainable. His going out into the world was like a living man going into the tomb, who, with open eyes, sees himself buried out of sight and hearing of wife, children, and friends of kindred tie.

In contemplating the likelihoods and possibilities of our circumstances, I probably suffered more than most of my fellow-servants. I had known what it was to experience kind and even tender treatment; they had known nothing of the sort. Life to them had been rough and thorny, as well as dark. They had—most of them—lived on my old master's farm in Tuckahoe, and had felt the rigors of Mr. Plummer's rule. He had written his character on the living parchment of most of their backs, and left them seamed and callous; my back (thanks to my early removal to Baltimore) was yet tender. I had left a kind mistress in tears when we parted, and the probability of ever seeing her again, trembling in the balance, as it were, could not fail to excite in me alarm and agony. The thought of becoming the slave of Andrew Anthony—who but a few days before the division, had, in my presence, seized my brother Perry by the throat, dashed him on the ground, and with the heel of his boot stamped him on the head, until the blood gushed from his nose and ears—was terrible! This fiendish proceeding had no better apology than the fact that Perry had gone to play when Master Andrew wanted him for some trifling service. After inflicting this cruel treatment on my brother, observing me, as I looked at him in astonishment, he said, '*That's* the way I'll serve you, one of these days'; meaning, probably, when I should come into his possession. This threat, the reader may well suppose, was not very tranquilizing to my feelings.

At last the anxiety and suspense were ended; and ended, thanks to a kind Providence, in accordance with my wishes. I fell to the portion of Mrs. Lucretia, the dear lady who bound up my head in her father's kitchen, and shielded me from the maledictions of Aunt Katy.

Capt. Thomas Auld and Mrs. Lucretia at once decided on my return to Baltimore. They knew how warmly Mrs. Hugh Auld was attached to me, and how delighted Tommy would be to see me, and withal, having no immediate use for me, they willingly concluded this arrangement.

I need not stop to narrate my joy on finding myself back in Baltimore. I was just one month absent, but the time seemed fully six months.

I had returned to Baltimore but a short time when the tidings reached me that my kind friend, Mrs. Lucretia, was dead. She left one child, a daughter, named Amanda,* of whom I shall speak again. Shortly after the death of Mrs. Lucretia, Master Andrew died, leaving a wife and one child. Thus the whole family of Anthonys, as it existed when I went to Col. Lloyd's place, was swept away during the first five years' time of my residence at Master Hugh Auld's in Baltimore.

No especial alternation took place in the condition of the slaves, in consequence of these deaths, yet I could not help the feeling that I was less secure now that Mrs. Lucretia was gone. While she lived, I felt that I had a strong friend to plead for me in any emergency.

In a little book which I published six years after my escape from slavery, entitled, 'Narrative of Frederick Douglass,'—when the distance between the past then described and the present was not so great as it is now—speaking of these changes in my master's family, and their results, I used this language: 'Now all the property of my old master, slaves included, was in the hands of strangers—strangers who had had nothing to do in its accumulation. Not a slave was left free. All remained slaves, from the youngest to the oldest. If any one thing more than another in my experience has served to deepen my conviction of the infernal character of slavery and fill me with unutterable loathing of slaveholders, it is their base ingratitude to my poor old grandmother. She had served my old master faithfully from youth to old age. She had been the source of all his wealth; she had peopled his plantation with slaves; she had become a great-grandmother in his service. She had rocked him in his infancy, attended him in his childhood, served him through life, and at his death wiped from his icy brow the cold death-sweat, and closed his eyes forever. She was nevertheless a slave—a slave for life—a slave in the hands of strangers; and in their hands she saw her children, her grandchildren, and her great-grandchildren, divided like so many sheep; and this without being gratified with the small privilege of a single word as to their or her own destiny. And to cap the climax of their base ingratitude, my grandmother, who was now very old, having outlived my old master and all his children, having seen the beginning and end of them, her present owner—his grandson—finding that she was of but little value; that her frame was already racked with the pains of old age and that complete helplessness was fast stealing over her once active limbs—took her to the woods, built her a little hut with a mud chimney and then gave her the *bounteous* privilege of there supporting herself in utter loneliness; thus virtually turning her out to die. If my poor, dear old grandmother now lives, she lives to remember and mourn over the loss of children, the loss of grandchildren and the loss of great-grandchildren. They are, in the language of Whittier, the slave's poet:

'Gone, gone, sold and gone,
To the rice-swamp dank and lone;
Where the slave-whip ceaseless swings,
Where the noisome insect stings,
Where the fever-demon strews
Poison with the falling dews,
Where the sickly sunbeams glare
Through the hot and misty air:—

Gone, gone, sold and gone,
To the rice-swamp, dank and lone,
From Virginia's hills and waters—
Woe is me, my stolen daughters!'*

'The hearth is desolate. The unconscious children who once sang and danced in her presence are gone. She gropes her way, in the darkness of age, for a drink of water. Instead of the voices of her children, she hears by day the moans of the dove, and by night the screams of the hideous owl. All is gloom. The grave is at the door; and now, weighed down by the pains and aches of old age, when the head inclines to the feet, when the beginning and ending of human existence meet, and helpless infancy, and painful old age combine together, at this time,—this most needed time for the exercise of that tenderness and affection which children only can bestow on a declining parent,—my poor old grandmother, the devoted mother of twelve children, is left all alone, in yonder little hut, before a few dim cinders.'

Two years after the death of Mrs. Lucretia, Master Thomas married his second wife. Her name was Rowena Hamilton,* the eldest daughter of Mr. William Hamilton,* a rich slaveholder on the Eastern Shore of Maryland, who lived about five miles from St. Michaels, the then place of Master Thomas Auld's residence.

Not long after his marriage, Master Thomas had a misunderstanding with Master Hugh, and, as a means of punishing him, ordered him to send me home. As the ground of the misunderstanding will serve to illustrate the character of Southern chivalry and Southern humanity, fifty years ago, I will relate it.

Among the children of my Aunt Milly was a daughter named Henny. When quite a child, Henny had fallen into the fire and had burnt her hands so badly that they were of very little use to her. Her fingers were drawn almost into the palms of her hands. She could make out to do something, but she was considered hardly worth the having—of little more value than a horse with a broken leg. This unprofitable piece of property, ill-shapen, and disfigured, Capt. Auld sent off to Baltimore.

After giving poor Henny a fair trial, Master Hugh and his wife came to the conclusion that they had no use for the poor cripple, and they sent her back to Master Thomas. This the latter took as an act of ingratitude on the part of his brother and, as a mark of his displeasure, required him to send me immediately to St. Michaels, saying, 'if he cannot keep Hen., he shan't have Fred.'

Here was another shock to my nerves, another breaking up of my plans, and another severance of my religious and social alliances. I was now a big boy. I had become quite useful to several young colored men, who had made me their teacher. I had taught some of them to read, and was accustomed to spend many of my leisure hours with them. Our attachment was strong, and I greatly dreaded the separation. But, with slaves, regrets are unavailing; my wishes were nothing; my happiness was the sport of my master.

My regrets at leaving Baltimore now were not for the same reasons as when I before left the city to be valued and handed over to a new owner.

A change had taken place, both in Master Hugh and in his once pious and affectionate wife. The influence of brandy and bad company on him, and of slavery and social isolation on her, had wrought disastrously upon the characters of both. Thomas was no longer 'little Tommy,' but was a big boy and had learned to assume towards me the airs of his class. My condition, therefore, in the house of Master Hugh was not by any means so comfortable as in former years. My attachments were now outside of our family. They were to those to whom I imparted instruction, and to those little white boys from whom I received instruction. There, too, was my dear old father, the pious Lawson, who was in all the Christian graces the very counterpart of 'Uncle Tom'—the resemblance so perfect that he might have been the original of Mrs. Stowe's Christian hero.\* The thought of leaving these dear friends greatly troubled me, for I was going without the hope of ever returning again; the feud being most bitter, and apparently wholly irreconcilable.

In addition to the pain of parting from friends, as I supposed, for-ever, I had the added grief of neglected chances of escape to brood over. I had put off running away until I was now to be placed where oppor-tunities for escape would be much more difficult, and less frequent.

As we sailed down the Chesapeake bay, on board the sloop Amanda, to St. Michaels, and were passed by the steamers plying between Baltimore and Philadelphia, I formed many a plan for my future, begin-ning and ending in the same determination—to find some way yet of escape from slavery.

# CHAPTER XIV.

## EXPERIENCE IN ST. MICHAELS.

*St. Michaels and its inhabitants—Capt. Auld—His new wife—
Sufferings from hunger—Forced to steal—Argument in vindication
thereof—Southern camp-meeting—What Capt. Auld did there—
Hopes—Suspicions—The result—Faith and works at variance—
Position in the church—Poor Cousin Henny—Methodist Preachers—
Their disregard of the slaves—One exception—Sabbath-school—How
and by whom broken up—Sad change in my prospects—Covey, the
negro-breaker.*

ST. MICHAELS, the village in which was now my new home, compared
favorably with villages in slave States generally, at this time—1833.
There were a few comfortable dwellings in it, but the place as a whole
wore a dull, slovenly, enterprise-forsaken aspect. The mass of the
buildings were of wood; they had never enjoyed the artificial adornment
of paint, and time and storms had worn off the bright color of the wood,
leaving them almost as black as buildings charred by a conflagration.

St. Michaels had, in former years, enjoyed some reputation as a ship-
building community, but that business had almost entirely given place
to oyster-fishing for the Baltimore and Philadelphia markets, a course
of life highly unfavorable to morals, industry, and manners. Miles river
was broad, and its oyster-fishing grounds were extensive, and the fishermen were, during autumn, winter and spring, often out all day and
a part of the night. This exposure was an excuse for carrying with them,
in considerable quantities, spirituous liquors, the then supposed best
antidote for cold. Each canoe was supplied with its jug of rum, and
tippling among this class of the citizens became general. This drinking
habit, in an ignorant population, fostered coarseness, vulgarity, and an
indolent disregard for the social improvement of the place, so that it
was admitted by the few sober thinking people who remained there,
that St. Michaels was an unsaintly, as well as unsightly place.

I went to St. Michaels to live in March, 1833. I know the year,
because it was the one succeeding the first cholera in Baltimore, and
was also the year of that strange phenomenon when the heavens seemed
about to part with their starry train. I witnessed this gorgeous spectacle, and was awe-struck. The air seemed filled with bright descending
messengers from the sky. It was about daybreak when I saw this sublime
scene. I was not without the suggestion, at the moment, that it might be

the harbinger of the coming of the Son of Man; and in my then state of mind I was prepared to hail Him as my friend and deliverer. I had read that the 'stars shall fall from heaven,'* and they were now falling. I was suffering very much in my mind. It did seem that every time the young tendrils of my affection became attached they were rudely broken by some unnatural outside power; and I was looking away to heaven for the rest denied me on earth.

But to my story. It was now more than seven years since I had lived with Master Thomas Auld, in the family of my old master, Capt. Anthony, on the home plantation of Col. Lloyd. I knew him then as the husband of old master's daughter; I had now to know him as my master. All my lessons concerning his temper and disposition, and the best methods of pleasing him, were yet to be learned. Slaveholders, however, were not very ceremonious in approaching a slave, and my ignorance of the new material in the shape of a master was but transient. Nor was my new mistress long in making known her animus. Unlike Miss Lucretia, whom I remembered with the tenderness which departed blessings leave, Mrs. Rowena Auld was as cold and cruel as her husband was stingy, and possessed the power to make him as cruel as herself, while she could easily descend to the level of his meanness.

As long as I lived in Mr. Hugh Auld's family, in whatever changes came over them there had always been a bountiful supply of food. Now, for the first time in seven years, I realized the pitiless pinchings of hunger. So wretchedly starved were we that we were compelled to live at the expense of our neighbors, or to steal from the home larder. This was a hard thing to do; but after much reflection I reasoned myself into the conviction that there was no other way to do, and that after all there was no wrong in it. Considering that my labor and person were the property of Master Thomas, and that I was deprived of the necessaries of life—necessaries obtained by my own labor—it was easy to deduce the right to supply myself with what was my own. It was simply appropriating what was my own to the use of my master, since the health and strength derived from such food were exerted in his service. To be sure, this was stealing, according to the law and gospel I heard from the pulpit; but I had begun to attach less importance to what dropped from that quarter on such points. It was not always convenient to steal from Master, and the same reason why I might innocently steal from him did not seem to justify me in stealing from others. In the case of my Master it was a question of removal—the taking his meat out of one tub and putting it in another; the ownership of the meat was not affected by the transaction. At first he owned it in the tub, and last he owned it in me.

His meat-house was not always open. There was a strict watch kept in that point, and the key was carried in Mrs. Auld's pocket. We were often-times severely pinched with hunger, when meat and bread were mouldering under lock and key. This was so, when she knew we were nearly half starved; and yet with saintly air she would each morning kneel with her husband and pray that a merciful God would 'bless them in basket and store, and save them at last in His kingdom.'* But I proceed with my argument.

It was necessary that the right to steal from others should be established; and this could only rest upon a wider range of generalization than that which supposed the right to steal from my master. It was some time before I arrived at this clear right. To give some idea of my train of reasoning, I will state the case as I laid it out in my mind. 'I am,' I thought, 'not only the slave of Master Thomas, but I am the slave of society at large. Society at large has bound itself, in form and in fact, to assist Master Thomas in robbing me of my rightful liberty, and of the just reward of my labor; therefore, whatever rights I have against Master Thomas I have equally against those confederated with him in robbing me of liberty. As society has marked me out as privileged plunder, on the principle of self-preservation, I am justified in plundering in turn. Since each slave belongs to all, all must therefore belong to each.' I reasoned further, that within the bounds of his just earnings the slave was fully justified in helping himself to the gold and silver, and the best apparel of his master, or that of any other slave-holder; and that such taking was not stealing, in any just sense of the word.

The morality of free society could have no application to slave society. Slaveholders made it almost impossible for the slave to commit any crime, known either to the laws of God or to the laws of man. If he stole, he but took his own; if he killed his master, he only imitated the heroes of the revolution. Slaveholders I held to be individually and collectively responsible for all the evils which grew out of the horrid relation, and I believed they would be so held in the sight of God. To make a man a slave was to rob him of moral responsibility. Freedom of choice is the essence of all accountability. But my kind readers are probably less concerned about what were my opinions than about that which more nearly touched my personal experience, albeit my opinions have, in some sort, been the outgrowth of my experience.

When I lived with Capt. Auld I thought him incapable of a noble action. His leading characteristic was intense selfishness. I think he was himself fully aware of this fact, and often tried to conceal it. Capt. Auld was not born a slaveholder. He was not a birthright member of the slaveholding oligarchy. He was only a slaveholder by marriage-right; and of all slaveholders these were by far the most exacting. There was in him all the love of domination, the pride of mastery, and the swagger of authority; but his rule lacked the vital element of consistency. He could be cruel; but his methods of showing it were cowardly, and evinced his meanness, rather than his spirit. His commands were strong, his enforcements weak.

Slaves were not insensible to the whole-souled qualities of a generous, dashing slaveholder, who was fearless of consequences, and they preferred a master of this bold and daring kind, even with the risk of being shot down for impudence, to the fretful little soul who never used the lash but at the suggestion of a love of gain.

Slaves too, readily distinguish between the birthright bearing of the original slaveholder, and the assumed attitudes of the accidental slaveholder; and while they could have no respect for either, they despised the latter more than the former.

The luxury of having slaves to wait upon him was new to Master Thomas, and for it he was wholly unprepared. He was a slaveholder, without the ability to hold or manage his slaves. Failing to command their respect, both himself and wife were ever on the alert lest some indignity should be offered them by the slaves.

It was in the month of August, 1833, when I had become almost desperate under the treatment of Master Thomas, and entertained more strongly than ever the oft-repeated determination to run away, that a circumstance occurred which seemed to promise brighter and better days for us all. At a Methodist camp-meeting, held in the Bay side (a famous place for camp-meetings), about eight miles from St. Michaels, Master Thomas came out with a profession of religion. He had long been an object of interest to the church, and to the ministers, as I had seen by the repeated visits and lengthy exhortations of the latter. He was a fish quite worth catching, for he had money and standing. In the community of St. Michaels he was equal to the best citizen. He was strictly temperate, and there was little to do for him in order to give him the appearance of piety and to make him a pillar of the church. Well, the camp-meeting continued a week; people gathered from all parts of the country, and two steamboats came loaded from Baltimore. The ground was happily chosen; seats were arranged, a stand erected and a rude altar fronting the preacher's stand, fenced in, with straw in it, making a soft kneeling place for the accommodation of mourners. This place would have held at least one hundred persons. In front and on the sides of the preacher's stand, and outside the long rows of seats, rose the first class of stately tents, each vieing with the other in strength, neatness, and capacity for accommodation. Behind this first circle of tents was another, less imposing, which reached around the camp-ground to the speaker's stand. Outside this second class of tents were covered wagons, ox-carts, and vehicles of every shape and size. These served as tents for their owners. Outside of these, huge fires were burning in all directions, where roasting and boiling and frying were going on, for the benefit of those who were attending to their spiritual welfare within the circle. *Behind* the preacher's stand, a narrow space was marked out for the use of the colored people. There were no seats provided for this class of persons, and if the preachers addressed them at all, it was in an *aside*. After the preaching was over, at every service, an invitation was given to mourners to come forward into the pen; and in some cases, ministers went out to persuade men and women to come in. By one of these ministers Master Thomas was persuaded to go inside the pen. I was deeply interested in that matter, and followed; and though colored people were not allowed either in the pen, or in front of the preacher's stand, I ventured to take my stand at a sort of half-way place between the blacks and whites, where I could distinctly see the movements of the mourners, and especially the progress of Master Thomas. 'If he has got religion,' thought I, 'he will emancipate his slaves; or, if he should not do so much as this, he will at any rate behave towards us more kindly, and feed us more generously than he has heretofore done.' Appealing to my own religious experience, and judging my master by what was true in my own case, I could not regard him as soundly converted, unless some such good results followed his profession of religion. But in my expectations I was doubly disappointed: Master Thomas was *Master Thomas* still. The fruits of his righteousness were to show themselves in no such way as I had anticipated. His conversion was not to change his relation toward men—at any rate not toward BLACK men—but toward God. My faith, I confess, was not great. There was something in his appearance that in my mind cast a doubt over his conversion. Standing where I did, I could see his every movement. I watched very narrowly while he remained in the pen; and although I saw that his face was extremely red, and his hair disheveled, and though I heard him groan, and saw a stray tear halting on his cheek, as if inquiring, 'which way shall I go?'—I could not wholly confide in the genuineness of the conversion. The hesitating behavior of that teardrop, and its loneliness, distressed me, and cast a doubt upon the whole transaction, of which it was a part. But people said, 'Capt. Auld has come through,' and it was for me to hope for the best. I was bound in charity to do this, for I, too, was religious, and had been in the church full three years, although now I was not more than sixteen years old. Slaveholders may sometimes have confidence in the piety of some of their slaves, but slaves seldom have confidence in the piety of their masters. 'He can't go to heaven without blood on his skirts,' was a settled point in the creed of every slave; one which rose superior to all teachings to the contrary and stood forever as a fixed fact. The highest evidence of his acceptance with God which the slaveholder could give the slave, was the emancipation of his slaves. This was proof to us that he was willing to give up all to God, and for the sake of God, and not to do this was, in our estimation, an evidence of hard-heartedness, and was wholly inconsistent with the idea of genuine conversion. I had read somewhere, in the Methodist Discipline,* the following question and answer: 'Question. What shall be done for the extirpation of slavery?' 'Answer. We declare that we are as much as ever convinced of the great evil of slavery; therefore, no slaveholder shall be eligible to any official station in our church.' These words sounded in my ears for a long time, and encouraged me to hope. But, as I have before said, I was doomed to disappointment. Master Thomas seemed to be aware of my hopes and expectations concerning him. I have thought before now that he looked at me in answer to my glances, as much as to say, 'I will teach you, young man, that though I have parted with my sins, I have not parted with my sense. I shall hold my slaves, and go to heaven too.'

There was always a scarcity of good-nature about the man; but now his whole countenance was soured all over with the seemings of piety, and he became more rigid and stringent in his exactions. If religion had any effect at all on him, it made him more cruel and hateful in all his ways. Do I judge him harshly? God forbid. Capt. Auld made the greatest professions of piety. His house was literally a house of prayer. In the morning and in the evening loud prayers and hymns were heard there, in which both himself and wife joined; yet no more nor better meal was distributed at the quarters, no more attention was paid to the moral welfare of the kitchen, and nothing was done to make us feel that the heart of Master Thomas was one whit better than it was before he went into the little pen, opposite the preacher's stand on the camp-ground. Our hopes, too, founded on the discipline, soon vanished; for he was taken into the church at once, and before he was out of his term of probation he led in class. He quite distinguished himself among the brethren as a fervent exhorter. His progress was almost as rapid as the growth of the fabled vine of Jack and the Bean-Stalk. No man was more active in revivals, or would go more miles to assist in carrying them on, and in getting outsiders interested in religion. His house, being one of the holiest in St. Michaels, became the 'preachers' home.' They evidently liked to share his hospitality; for while he starved us, he stuffed them—three or four of these 'ambassadors' not unfrequently being there at a time and all living on the fat of the land while we in the kitchen were worse than hungry. Not often did we get a smile of recognition from these holy men. They seemed about as unconcerned about our getting to heaven as about our getting out of slavery. To this general charge I must make one exception—the Reverend George Cookman.* Unlike Rev. Messrs. Storks, Ewry, Nicky, Humphrey, and Cooper (all of whom were on the St. Michaels circuit), he kindly took an interest in our temporal and spiritual welfare. Our souls and our bodies were alike sacred in his sight, and he really had a good deal of genuine anti-slavery feeling mingled with his colonization ideas.* There was not a slave in our neighborhood who did not love and venerate Mr. Cookman. It was pretty generally believed that he had been instrumental in bringing one of the largest slaveholders in that neighborhood—Mr. Samuel Harrison*—to emancipate all his slaves, and the general impression about Mr. Cookman was, that whenever he met slaveholders he labored faithfully with them, as a religious duty, to induce them to liberate their bondmen. When this good man was at our house, we were all sure to be called in to prayers in the morning; and he was not slow in making inquiries as to the state of our minds, nor in giving us a word of exhortation and of encouragement. Great was the sorrow of all the slaves when this faithful preacher of the gospel was removed from the circuit. He was an eloquent preacher, and possessed what few ministers, south of Mason and Dixon's line,* possessed or dared to show; viz., a warm and philanthropic heart. This Mr. Cookman was an Englishman by birth, and perished on board the ill-fated steamship 'President,' while on his way to England.

But to my experience with Master Thomas after his conversion. In Baltimore I could occasionally get into a Sabbath-school amongst the free children and receive lessons with the rest; but having already learned to read and write I was more a teacher than a scholar, even there. When, however, I went back to the eastern shore and was at the house of Master Thomas, I was not allowed either to teach or to be taught. The whole community among the whites, with but one single exception, frowned upon everything like imparting instruction, either to slaves or to free colored persons. That single exception, a pious young man named Wilson, asked me one day if I would like to assist him in teaching a little Sabbath-school at the house of a free colored man named James Mitchell. The idea to me was a delightful one and I told him that I would gladly devote to that most laudable work as many of my Sabbaths as I could command. Mr. Wilson soon mustered up a dozen old spelling-books and a few Testaments, and we commenced operations with some twenty pupils in our school. Here, thought I, is something worth living for. Here is a chance for usefulness. The first Sunday passed delightfully, and I spent the week after very joyously. I could not go to Baltimore, where was the little company of young friends who had been so much to me there, and from whom I felt parted forever, but I could make a little Baltimore here. At our second meeting I learned there were some objections to the existence of our school; and, surely enough, we had scarcely got to work—good work, simply teaching a few colored children how to read the gospel of the Son of God—when in rushed a mob, headed by two class-leaders, Mr. Wright Fairbanks and Mr. Garrison West, and with them Master Thomas. They were armed with sticks and other missiles and drove us off, commanding us never again to meet for such a purpose. One of this pious crew told me that as for me, I wanted to be another Nat. Turner, and that, if I did not look out, I should get as many balls in me as Nat. did into him. Thus ended the Sabbath-school; and the reader will not be surprised that this conduct, on the part of class-leaders and professedly holy men, did not serve to strengthen my religious convictions. The cloud over my St. Michaels home grew heavier and blacker than ever.

It was not merely the agency of Master Thomas in breaking up our Sabbath-school, that shook my confidence in the power of that kind of southern religion to make men wiser or better, but I saw in him all the cruelty and meanness after his conversion which he had exhibited before that time. His cruelty and meanness were especially displayed in his treatment of my unfortunate cousin Henny, whose lameness made her a burden to him. I have seen him tie up this lame and maimed woman and whip her in a manner most brutal and shocking; and then with blood-chilling blasphemy he would quote the passage of scripture, 'That servant which knew his lord's will and prepared not himself, neither did according to his will, shall be beaten with many stripes.'* He would keep this lacerated woman tied up by her wrists to a bolt in the joist, three, four, and five hours at a time. He would tie her up early in the morning, whip her with a cowskin before breakfast, leave her tied up, go to his store, and, returning to dinner, repeat the castigation, laying the rugged lash on flesh already raw by repeated blows. He seemed desirous to get the poor girl out of existence, or at any rate off his hands.

In proof of this, he afterwards gave her away to his sister Sarah (Mrs. Cline),* but as in the case of Mr. Hugh, Henny was soon returned on his hands. Finally, upon a pretense that he could do nothing for her (I use his own words), he 'set her adrift to take care of herself.' Here was a recently converted man, holding with tight grasp the well-framed and able-bodied slaves left him by old master—the persons who in freedom could have taken care of themselves; yet turning loose the only cripple among them, virtually to starve and die.

No doubt, had Master Thomas been asked by some pious northern brother, why he held slaves? his reply would have been precisely that which many another slaveholder has returned to the same inquiry, viz.: 'I hold my slaves for their own good.'

The many differences springing up between Master Thomas and myself, owing to the clear perception I had of his character, and the boldness with which I defended myself against his capricious complaints, led him to declare that I was unsuited to his wants; that my city life had affected me perniciously; that in fact it had almost ruined me for every good purpose, and had fitted me for everything bad. One of my greatest faults, or offences, was that of letting his horse get away and go down to the farm which belonged to his father-in-law. The animal had a liking for that farm with which I fully sympathized. Whenever I let it out it would go dashing down the road to Mr. Hamilton's, as if going on a grand frolic. My horse gone, of course I must go after it. The explanation of our mutual attachment to the place is the same—the horse found good pasturage, and I found there plenty of bread. Mr. Hamilton had his faults, but starving his slaves was not one of them. He gave food in abundance, and of excellent quality. In Mr. Hamilton's cook—Aunt Mary—I found a generous and considerate friend. She never allowed me to go there without giving me bread enough to make good the deficiencies of a day or two. Master Thomas at last resolved to endure my behavior no longer; he could keep neither me nor his horse, we liked so well to be at his father-in-law's farm. I had lived with him nearly nine months and he had given me a number of severe whippings, without any visible improvement in my character or conduct, and now he was resolved to put me out, as he said, 'to be broken.'

There was, in the Bay-side, very near the camp-ground where my master received his religious impressions, a man named Edward Covey,* who enjoyed the reputation of being a first rate hand at breaking young negroes. This Covey was a poor man, a farm renter; and his reputation of being a good hand to break in slaves was of immense pecuniary advantage to him, since it enabled him to get his farm tilled with very little expense, compared with what it would have cost him otherwise. Some slaveholders thought it an advantage to let Mr. Covey have the government of their slaves a year or two, almost free of charge, for the sake of the excellent training they had under his management. Like some horse-breakers noted for their skill, who ride the best horses in the country without expense, Mr. Covey could have under him the most fiery bloods of the neighborhood, for the simple reward of returning them to their owners well broken. Added to the natural fitness of Mr. Covey for the duties of his profession, he was said 'to enjoy religion,' and he was as strict in the cultivation of piety as he was in the cultivation of his farm. I was made aware of these traits in his character by some one who had been under his hand, and while I could not look forward to going to him with any degree of pleasure, I was glad to get away from St. Michaels. I believed I should get enough to eat at Covey's, even if I suffered in other respects, and this to a hungry man is not a prospect to be regarded with indifference.

# CHAPTER XV.

## COVEY, THE NEGRO BREAKER.

*Journey to Covey's—Meditations by the way—Covey's house—
Family—Awkwardness as a field hand—A cruel beating—Why
given—Description of Covey—First attempt at driving oxen—Hair-
breadth escape—Ox and man alike property—Hard labor more
effective than the whip for breaking down the spirit—Cunning and
trickery of Covey—Family worship—Shocking and indecent contempt for chastity—Great mental agitation—Anguish beyond
description.*

THE morning of January 1, 1834, with its chilling wind and pinching
frost, quite in harmony with the winter in my own mind, found me,
with my little bundle of clothing on the end of a stick swung across my
shoulder, on the main road bending my way towards Covey's, whither
I had been imperiously ordered by Master Thomas. He had been as
good as his word, and had committed me without reserve to the mastery of that hard man. Eight or ten years had now passed since I had
been taken from my grandmother's cabin in Tuckahoe; and these years,
for the most part, I had spent in Baltimore, where, as the reader has
already seen, I was treated with comparative tenderness. I was now
about to sound profounder depths in slave life. My new master was
notorious for his fierce and savage disposition, and my only consolation
in going to live with him, was the certainty of finding him precisely as
represented by common fame. There was neither joy in my heart nor
elasticity in my frame as I started for the tyrant's home. Starvation
made me glad to leave Thomas Auld's, and the cruel lash made me
dread to go to Covey's. Escape, however, was impossible; so, heavy
and sad, I paced the seven miles which lay between his house and
St. Michaels, thinking much by the solitary way, of my adverse condition.
But thinking was all I could do. Like a fish in a net, allowed to play for
a time, I was now drawn rapidly to the shore and secured at all points.
'I am,' thought I, 'but the sport of a power which makes no account,
either of my welfare or of my happiness. By a law which I can comprehend, but cannot evade or resist, I am ruthlessly snatched from the
hearth of a fond grandmother and hurried away to the home of a mysterious old master; again I am removed from there to a master in
Baltimore; thence am I snatched away to the eastern shore to be valued
with the beasts of the field, and with them divided and set apart for

a possessor; then I am sent back to Baltimore, and by the time I have formed new attachments and have begun to hope that no more rude shocks shall touch me, a difference arises between brothers, and I am again broken up and sent to St. Michaels; and now from the latter place I am footing my way to the home of another master, where, I am given to understand, like a wild young working animal I am to be broken to the yoke of a bitter and life-long bondage.' With thoughts and reflections like these I came in sight of a small wood-colored building, about a mile from the main road, and which, from the description I had received at starting, I easily recognized as my new home. The Chesapeake bay, upon the jutting banks of which the little wood colored house was standing, white with foam raised by the heavy northwest wind; Poplar Island, covered with a thick black pine forest, standing out amid this half ocean; and Keat Point, stretching its sandy, desert-like shores out into the foam-crested bay, were all in sight, and served to deepen the wild and desolate scene.

The good clothes I had brought with me from Baltimore were now worn thin, and had not been replaced; for Master Thomas was as little careful to provide against cold as against hunger. Met here by a north wind sweeping through an open space of forty miles, I was glad to make any port, and, therefore, I speedily pressed on to the wood-colored house. The family consisted of Mr. and Mrs. Covey; Mrs. Kemp (a broken-backed woman), sister to Mrs. Covey; William Hughes, cousin to Mr. Covey; Caroline, the cook; Bill Smith, a hired man, and myself. Bill Smith, Bill Hughes, and myself were the working force of the farm, which comprised three or four hundred acres. I was now for the first time in my life to be a field-hand; and in my new employment I found myself even more awkward than a green country boy may be supposed to be upon his first entrance into the bewildering scenes of city life. My awkwardness gave me much trouble. Strange and unnatural as it may seem, I had been in my new home but three days before Mr. Covey (my brother in the Methodist church,) gave me a bitter foretaste of what was in reserve for me. I presume he thought that, since he had but a single year in which to complete his work, the sooner he began the better. Perhaps he thought that by coming to blows at once we should mutually better understand our relations to each other. But to whatever motive, direct or indirect, the cause may be referred, I had not been in his possession three whole days before he subjected me to a most brutal chastisement. Under his heavy blows blood flowed freely, and wales were left on my back as large as my little finger. The sores from this flogging continued for weeks, for they were kept open by the rough and coarse cloth which I wore for shirting. The occasion and details of this first chapter of my experience as a field-hand must be told, that the reader may see how unreasonable, as well as how cruel, my new Master Covey was. The whole thing I found to be characteristic of the man, and I was probably treated no worse by him than had been scores of lads previously committed to him for reasons similar to those which induced my master to place me with him. But here are the facts connected with the affair, precisely as they occurred.

On one of the coldest mornings of the whole month of January, 1834, I was ordered at daybreak to get a load of wood, from a forest about two miles from the house. In order to perform this work, Mr. Covey gave me a pair of unbroken oxen, for it seemed that his breaking abilities had not been turned in that direction. In due form, and with all proper ceremony, I was introduced to this huge yoke of unbroken oxen, and was carefully made to understand which was 'Buck,' and which was 'Darby,'—which was the 'in hand' ox, and which was the 'off hand.' The master of this important ceremony was no less a person than Mr. Covey himself, and the introduction was the first of the kind I had ever had.

My life, hitherto, had been quite away from horned cattle, and I had no knowledge of the art of managing them. What was meant by the 'in ox,' as against the 'off ox,' when both were equally fastened to one cart, and under one yoke, I could not very easily divine; and the difference implied by the names, and the peculiar duties of each, were alike Greek to me. Why was not the 'off ox' called the 'in ox?' Where and what is the reason for this distinction in names, when there is none in the things themselves? After initiating me into the use of the 'whoa,' 'back,' 'gee,' 'hither,'—the entire language spoken between oxen and driver,— Mr. Covey took a rope about ten feet long and one inch thick, and placed one end of it around the horns of the 'in hand ox,' and gave the other end to me, telling me that if the oxen started to run away (as the scamp knew they would), I must hold on to the rope and stop them. I need not tell any one who is acquainted with either the strength or the dispos-ition of an untamed ox, that this order was about as unreasonable as a command to shoulder a mad bull. I had never before driven oxen and I was as awkward a driver as it is possible to conceive. I could not plead my ignorance to Mr. Covey. There was that in his manner which for-bade any reply. Cold, distant, morose, with a face wearing all the marks of captious pride and malicious sternness, he repelled all advances. He was not a large man—not more than five feet ten inches in height, I should think; short-necked, round-shouldered, of quick and wiry motion, of thin and wolfish visage, with a pair of small, greenish-gray eyes, set well back under a forehead without dignity, and which were constantly in motion, expressing his passions rather than his thoughts, in sight, but denying them utterance in words. The creature presented an appearance altogether ferocious and sinister, disagreeable and forbidding, in the extreme. When he spoke, it was from the corner of his mouth, and in a sort of light growl like that of a dog when an attempt is made to take a bone from him. I already believed him a worse fellow than he had been represented to be. With his directions, and without stopping to question, I started for the woods, quite anxious to perform in a creditable manner, my first exploit in driving. The distance from the house to the wood's gate—a full mile, I should think—was passed over with little difficulty: for, although the animals ran, I was fleet enough in the open field to keep pace with them, especially as they pulled me along at the end of the rope; but on reaching the woods, I was speedily thrown into a distressing plight. The animals took fright, and started off ferociously into the woods, carrying the cart full tilt against trees, over stumps, and dashing from side to side in a manner altogether frightful. As I held the rope I expected every moment to be crushed between the cart and the huge trees, among which they were so furiously dashing. After running thus for several minutes, my oxen were finally brought to a stand, by a tree, against which they dashed themselves with great violence, upsetting the cart, and entangling themselves among sundry young saplings. By the shock the body of the cart was flung in one direction and the wheels and tongue in another, and all in the greatest confusion. There I was, all alone in a thick wood to which I was a stranger; my cart upset and shattered, my oxen, wild and enraged, were entangled, and I, poor soul, was but a green hand to set all this disorder right. I knew no more of oxen than the ox-driver is supposed to know of wisdom.

After standing a few minutes, surveying the damage, and not without a presentiment that this trouble would draw after it others, even more distressing, I took one end of the cart-body and, by an extra outlay of strength, I lifted it toward the axle-tree, from which it had been violently flung. After much pulling and straining, I succeeded in getting the body of the cart in its place. This was an important step out of the difficulty, and its performance increased my courage for the work which remained to be done. The cart was provided with an ax, a tool with which I had become pretty well acquainted in the ship-yard at Baltimore. With this I cut down the saplings by which my oxen were entangled, and again pursued my journey, with my heart in my mouth, lest the oxen should again take it into their senseless heads to cut up a caper. But their spree was over for the present, and the rascals now moved off as soberly as though their behavior had been natural and exemplary. On reaching the part of the forest where I had, the day before, been chopping wood, I filled the cart with a heavy load, as a security against another runaway. But the neck of an ox is equal in strength to iron. It defies ordinary burdens. Tame and docile to a proverb, when well trained, when but half broken to the yoke, the ox is the most sullen and intractable of animals. I saw in my own situation several points of similarity with that of the oxen. They were property; so was I. Covey was to break me—I was to break them. Break and be broken was the order.

Half of the day was already gone and I had not yet turned my face homeward. It required only two days' experience and observation to teach me that no such apparent waste of time would be lightly overlooked by Covey. I therefore hurried toward home; but in reaching the lane gate I met the crowning disaster of the day. This gate was a fair specimen of southern handicraft. There were two huge posts eighteen inches in diameter, rough hewed and square, and the heavy gate was so hung on one of these that it opened only about half the proper distance. On arriving here it was necessary for me to let go the end of the rope on the horns of the 'in-hand ox'; and as soon as the gate was open and I let go of it to get the rope again, off went my oxen, full tilt; making nothing of their load, as, catching the huge gate between the wheel and the cart-body, they literally crushed it to splinters and came within only a few inches of subjecting me to a similar catastrophe, for I was just in advance of the wheel when it struck the left gate-post. With these two hair-breadth escapes I thought I could successfully explain to Mr. Covey the delay and avert punishment—I was not without a faint hope of being commended for the stern resolution which I had displayed in accomplishing the difficult task—a task which I afterwards learned even Covey himself would not have undertaken without first driving the oxen for some time in the open field, preparatory to their going to the woods. But in this hope I was disappointed. On coming to him his countenance assumed an aspect of rigid displeasure, and as I gave him a history of the casualties of my trip, his wolfish face, with his greenish eyes, became intensely ferocious. 'Go back to the woods again,' he said, muttering something else about wasting time. I hastily obeyed, but I had not gone far on my way when I saw him coming after me. My oxen now behaved themselves with singular propriety, contrasting their present conduct to my representation of their former antics. I almost wished, now that Covey was coming, they would do something in keeping with the character I had given them; but no, they had already had their spree, and they could afford now to be extra good, readily obeying orders, and seeming to understand them quite as well as I did myself. On reaching the woods, my tormenter, who seemed all the time to be remarking to himself upon the good behavior of the oxen, came up to me and ordered me to stop the cart, accompanying the same with the threat that he would now teach me how to break gates and idle away my time when he sent me to the woods. Suiting the action to the words, Covey paced off, in his own wiry fashion, to a large black gum tree, the young shoots of which are generally used for ox-goads, they being exceedingly tough. Three of these goads, from four to six feet long, he cut off and trimmed up with his large jack-knife. This done, he ordered me to take off my clothes. To this unreasonable order I made no reply, but in my apparent unconsciousness and inattention to this command I indicated very plainly a stern determination to do no such thing. 'If you will beat me,' thought I, 'you shall do so over my clothes.' After many threats, which made no impression upon me, he rushed at me with something of the savage fierceness of a wolf, tore off the few and thinly worn clothes I had on, and proceeded to wear out on my back the heavy goads which he had cut from the gum tree. This flogging was the first of a series of floggings, and though very severe, it was less so than many which came after it, and these for offences far lighter than the gate-breaking.

I remained with Mr. Covey one year (I cannot say I lived with him), and during the first six months that I was there I was whipped, either with sticks or cow-skins, every week. Aching bones and a sore back were my constant companions. Frequent as the lash was used, Mr. Covey thought less of it as a means of breaking down my spirit than that of hard and continued labor. He worked me steadily up to the point of my powers of endurance. From the dawn of day in the morning till the darkness was complete in the evening, I was kept hard at work in the field or the woods. At certain seasons of the year we were all kept in the field till eleven and twelve o'clock at night. At these times Covey would attend us in the field and urge us on with words or blows, as it seemed best to him. He had in his life been an overseer, and he well understood the business of slave-driving. There was no deceiving him. He knew just what a man or boy could do, and he held both to strict account. When he pleased he would work himself like a very Turk, making everything fly before him. It was, however, scarcely necessary for Mr. Covey to be really present in the field to have his work go on industriously. He had the faculty of making us feel that he was always present. By a series of adroitly managed surprises which he practiced, I was prepared to expect him at any moment. His plan was never to approach in an open, manly and direct manner the spot where his hands were at work. No thief was ever more artful in his devices than this man Covey. He would creep and crawl in ditches and gullies, hide behind stumps and bushes, and practice so much of the cunning of the serpent, that Bill Smith and I, between ourselves, never called him by any other name than 'the snake.' We fancied that in his eyes and his gait we could see a snakish resemblance. One-half of his proficiency in the art of negro-breaking consisted, I should think, in this species of cunning. We were never secure. He could see or hear us nearly all the time. He was, to us, behind every stump, tree, bush, and fence on the plantation. He carried this kind of trickery so far that he would sometimes mount his horse and make believe he was going to St. Michaels, and in thirty minutes after-wards you might find his horse tied in the woods, and the snake-like Covey lying flat in the ditch with his head lifted above its edge, or in a fence-corner, watching every movement of the slaves. I have known him walk up to us and give us special orders as to our work in advance, as if he were leaving home with a view to being absent several days, and before he got half way to the house he would avail himself of our inattention to his movements to turn short on his heel, conceal himself behind a fence-corner or a tree, and watch us until the going down of the sun. Mean and contemptible as is all this, it is in keeping with the character which the life of a slaveholder was calculated to produce. There was no earthly inducement in the slave's condition to incite him to labor faithfully. The fear of punishment was the sole motive of any sort of industry with him. Knowing this fact as the slaveholder did, and judging the slave by himself, he naturally concluded that the slave would be idle whenever the cause for this fear was absent. Hence all sorts of petty deceptions were practiced to inspire fear.

But with Mr. Covey trickery was natural. Everything in the shape of learning or religion which he possessed was made to conform to this semi-lying propensity. He did not seem conscious that the practice had anything unmanly, base or contemptible about it. It was with him a part of an import-ant system essential to the relation of master and slave. I thought I saw, in his very religious devotions, this controlling element of his character. A long prayer at night made up for a short prayer in the morning, and few men could seem more devotional than he when he had nothing else to do.

Mr. Covey was not content with the cold style of family worship adopted in the cold latitudes, which begin and end with a simple prayer.

No! the voice of praise as well as of prayer must be heard in his house night and morning. At first I was called upon to bear some part in these exercises; but the repeated floggings given me turned the whole thing into mockery. He was a poor singer and relied mainly upon me for raising the hymn for the family, and when I failed to do so he was thrown into much confusion. I do not think he ever abused me on account of these vexations. His religion was a thing altogether apart from his worldly concerns. He knew nothing of it as a holy principle directing and controlling his daily life and making the latter conform to the requirements of the gospel. One or two facts will illustrate his character better than a volume of generalities.

I have already implied that Mr. Edward Covey was a poor man. He was, in fact, just commencing to lay the foundation of his fortune, as fortune was regarded in a slave state. The first condition of wealth and respectability there being the ownership of human property, every nerve was strained by the poor man to obtain it, with little regard sometimes as to the means. In pursuit of this object, pious as Mr. Covey was, he proved himself as unscrupulous and base as the worst of his neighbors. In the beginning he was only able—as he said—'to buy one slave;' and scandalous and shocking as is the fact, he boasted that he bought her simply 'as a breeder.' But the worst of this is not told in this naked statement. This young woman (Caroline was her name) was virtually compelled by Covey to abandon herself to the object for which he had purchased her; and the result was the birth of twins at the end of the year. At this addition to his human stock Covey and his wife were ecstatic with joy. No one dreamed of reproaching the woman or of finding fault with the hired man, Bill Smith, the father of the children, for Mr. Covey himself had locked the two up together every night, thus inviting the result.

But I will pursue this revolting subject no farther. No better illustration of the unchaste, demoralizing, and debasing character of slavery can be found, than is furnished in the fact that this professedly Christian slave-holder, amidst all his prayers and hymns, was shamelessly and boastfully encouraging and actually compelling, in his own house, undisguised and unmitigated fornication, as a means of increasing his stock. It was the system of slavery which made this allowable, and which no more condemned the slaveholder for buying a slave woman and devoting her to this life, than for buying a cow and raising stock from her, and the same rules were observed, with a view to increasing the number and quality of the one, as of the other.

If at any one time of my life, more than another, I was made to drink the bitterest dregs of slavery, that time was during the first six months of my stay with this man Covey. We worked all weathers. It was never too hot, or too cold; it could never rain, blow, snow, or hail too hard for us to work in the field. Work, work, work, was scarcely more the order of the day than of the night. The longest days were too short for him, and the shortest nights were too long for him. I was somewhat unmanageable at the first, but a few months of this discipline tamed me. Mr. Covey succeeded in breaking me—in body, soul, and spirit. My natural elasticity was crushed; my intellect languished; the disposition to read departed, the cheerful spark that lingered about my eye died out; the dark night of slavery closed in upon me, and behold a man transformed to a brute!

Sunday was my only leisure time. I spent this under some large tree, in a sort of beast-like stupor between sleeping and waking. At times I would rise up and a flash of energetic freedom would dart through my soul, accompanied with a faint beam of hope that flickered for a moment, and then vanished. I sank down again, mourning over my wretched condition. I was sometimes tempted to take my life and that of Covey, but was prevented by a combination of hope and fear. My sufferings, as I remember them now, seem like a dream rather than like a stern reality.

Our house stood within a few rods of the Chesapeake bay, whose broad bosom was ever white with sails from every quarter of the habitable globe. Those beautiful vessels, robed in white, and so delightful to the eyes of freemen, were to me so many shrouded ghosts, to terrify and torment me with thoughts of my wretched condition. I have often, in the deep stillness of a summer's Sabbath, stood all alone upon the banks of that noble bay, and traced, with saddened heart and tearful eye, the countless number of sails moving off to the mighty ocean. The sight of these always affected me powerfully. My thoughts would compel utterance; and there, with no audience but the Almighty, I would pour out my soul's complaint in my rude way with an apostrophe to the moving multitude of ships.

'You are loosed from your moorings, and free. I am fast in my chains, and am a slave! You move merrily before the gentle gale, and I sadly before the bloody whip. You are freedom's swift-winged angels, that fly around the world; I am confined in bonds of iron. O, that I were free! O, that I were on one of your gallant decks, and under your protecting wing! Alas! betwixt me and you the turbid waters roll. Go on, go on; O, that I could also go! Could I but swim! If I could fly! O, why was I born a man, of whom to make a brute! The glad ship is gone: she hides in the dim distance. I am left in the hell of unending slavery. O, God, save me!

God, deliver me! Let me be free!—Is there any God? Why am I a slave? I will run away. I will not stand it. Get caught or get clear, I'll try it. I had as well die with ague as with fever. I have only one life to lose. I had as well be killed running as die standing. Only think of it: one hundred miles north, and I am free! Try it? Yes! God helping me, I will. It cannot be that I shall live and die a slave. I will take to the water. This very bay shall yet bear me into freedom. The steamboats steer in a northeast course from North Point; I will do the same; and when I get to the head of the bay, I will turn my canoe adrift, and walk straight through Delaware into Pennsylvania. When I get there I shall not be required to have a pass: I will travel there without being disturbed. Let but the first opportunity offer, and come what will, I am off. Meanwhile I will try to bear the yoke. I am not the only slave in the world. Why should I fret? I can bear as much as any of them. Besides I am but a boy yet, and all boys are bound out to some one. It may be that my misery in slavery will only increase my happiness when I get free. There is a better day coming.'

I shall never be able to narrate half the mental experience through which it was my lot to pass, during my stay at Covey's. I was completely wrecked, changed, and bewildered; goaded almost to madness at one time, and at another reconciling myself to my wretched condition. All the kindness I had received at Baltimore, all my former hopes and aspirations for usefulness in the world, and even the happy moments spent in the exercises of religion, contrasted with my then present lot, served but to increase my anguish.

I suffered bodily as well as mentally. I had neither sufficient time in which to eat, or to sleep, except on Sundays. The over-work, and the brutal chastisements of which I was the victim, combined with that ever-gnawing and soul-devouring thought—'I am a slave—a slave for life—a slave with no rational ground to hope for freedom'—rendered me a living embodiment of mental and physical wretchedness.

# CHAPTER XVI.

## ANOTHER PRESSURE OF THE TYRANT'S VISE.

*Experience at Covey's summed up—First six months severer than the remaining six—Preliminaries to the change—Reasons for narrating the circumstances—Scene in the treading-yard—Author taken ill—Escapes to St. Michaels—The pursuit—Suffering in the woods—Talk with Master Thomas—His beating—Driven back to Covey's—The slaves never sick—Natural to expect them to feign sickness—Laziness of slaveholders.*

THE reader has but to repeat, in his mind, once a week the scene in the woods, where Covey subjected me to his merciless lash, to have a true idea of my bitter experience, during the first six months of the breaking process through which he carried me. I have no heart to repeat each separate transaction. Such a narration would fill a volume much larger than the present one. I aim only to give the reader a truthful impression of my slave-life, without unnecessarily affecting him with harrowing details.

As I have intimated that my hardships were much greater during the first six months of my stay at Covey's than during the remainder of the year, and as the change in my condition was owing to causes which may help the reader to a better understanding of human nature, when subjected to the terrible extremities of slavery, I will narrate the circumstances of this change, although I may seem thereby to applaud my own courage.

You have, dear reader, seen me humbled, degraded, broken down, enslaved, and brutalized; and you understand how it was done; now let us see the converse of all this, and how it was brought about; and this will take us through the year 1834.

On one of the hottest days of the month of August of the year just mentioned, had the reader been passing through Covey's farm, he might have seen me at work in what was called the 'treading-yard'—a yard upon which wheat was trodden out from the straw by the horses' feet. I was there at work feeding the 'fan,' or rather bringing wheat to the fan, while Bill Smith was feeding. Our force consisted of Bill Hughes, Bill Smith, and a slave by the name of Eli, the latter having been hired for the occasion. The work was simple, and required strength and activity, rather than any skill or intelligence; and yet to one entirely unused to such work, it came very hard. The heat was intense and overpowering, and there was much hurry to get the wheat trodden out that day, through the fan; since if that work was done an hour before sundown, the hands would have, according to a promise of Covey, that hour added to their night's rest. I was not behind any of them in the wish to complete the day's work before sundown, and hence I struggled with all my might to get it forward. The promise of one hour's repose on a week day was sufficient to quicken my pace, and to spur me on to extra endeavor. Besides, we had all planned to go fishing, and I certainly wished to have a hand in that. But I was disappointed, and the day turned out to be one of the bitterest I ever experienced. About three o'clock, while the sun was pouring down his burning rays, and not a breeze was stirring, I broke down; my strength failed me; I was seized with a violent aching of the head, attended with extreme dizziness, and trembling in every limb. Finding what was coming, and feeling that it would never do to stop work, I nerved myself up and staggered on, until I fell by the side of the wheat fan, with a feeling that the earth had fallen in upon me. This brought the entire work to a dead stand. There was work for four: each one had his part to perform, and each part depended on the other, so that when one stopped, all were compelled to stop. Covey, who had become my dread, was at the house, about a hundred yards from where I was fanning, and instantly, upon hearing the fan stop, he came down to the treading-yard to inquire into the cause of the interruption. Bill Smith told him that I was sick and unable longer to bring wheat to the fan.

I had by this time crawled away in the shade, under the side of a post-and-rail fence, and was exceedingly ill. The intense heat of the sun, the heavy dust rising from the fan, and the stooping to take up the wheat from the yard, together with the hurrying to get through, had caused a rush of blood to my head. In this condition Covey, finding out where I was, came to me, and after standing over me a while asked what the matter was. I told him as well as I could, for it was with difficulty that I could speak. He gave me a savage kick in the side which jarred my whole frame, and commanded me to get up. The monster had obtained complete control over me, and if he had commanded me to do any possible thing I should, in my then state of mind, have endeavored to comply. I made an effort to rise, but fell back in the attempt before gaining my feet. He gave me another heavy kick, and again told me to rise. I again tried, and succeeded in standing up; but upon stooping to get the tub with which I was feeding the fan I again staggered and fell to the ground. I must have so fallen had I been sure that a hundred bullets would have pierced me through as the consequence. While down in this sad condition, and perfectly helpless, the merciless negro-breaker took up the hickory slab with which Hughes had been striking off the wheat to a level with the sides of the half-bushel measure, (a very hard weapon), and, with the edge of it, he dealt me a heavy blow on my head which made a large gash, and caused the blood to run freely, saying at the same time, 'If you have got the headache I'll cure you.' This done, he ordered me again to rise, but I made no effort to do so, for I had now made up my mind that it was useless and that the heartless villain might do his worst. He could but kill me and that might put me out of my misery. Finding me unable to rise, or rather despairing of my doing so, Covey left me, with a view to getting on with the work without me. I was bleeding very freely, and my face was soon covered with my warm blood. Cruel and merciless as was the motive that dealt that blow, the wound was a fortunate one for me. Bleeding was never more efficacious. The pain in my head speedily abated, and I was soon able to rise. Covey had, as I have said, left me to my fate, and the question was, shall I return to my work, or shall I find my way to St. Michaels and make Capt. Auld acquainted with the atrocious cruelty of his brother Covey, and beseech him to get me another master? Remembering the object he had in view in placing me under the management of Covey, and further, his cruel treatment of my poor crippled cousin Henny, and his meanness in the matter of feeding and clothing his slaves, there was little ground to hope for a favorable reception at the hands of Capt. Thomas Auld. Nevertheless, I resolved to go straight to him, thinking that, if not animated by motives of humanity, he might be induced to interfere on my behalf from selfish considerations. 'He cannot,' I thought, 'allow his property to be thus bruised and battered, marred and defaced, and I will go to him about the matter.' In order to get to St. Michaels by the most favorable and direct road I must walk seven miles, and this, in my sad condition, was no easy performance. I had already lost much blood, I was exhausted by over-exertion, my sides were sore from the heavy blows planted there by the stout boots of Mr. Covey, and I was in every way in an unfavorable plight for the journey. I however watched my chance while the cruel and cunning Covey was looking in an opposite direction, and started off across the field for St. Michaels. This was a daring step. If it failed it would only exasperate Covey and increase during the remainder of my term of service under him, the rigors of my bondage. But the step was taken and I must go forward. I succeeded in getting nearly half way across the broad field toward the woods, when Covey observed me. I was still bleeding and the exertion of running had started the blood afresh. '*Come back! Come back!*' he vociferated, with

threats of what he would do if I did not instantly return. But, disre-
garding his calls and threats, I pressed on toward the woods as fast as
my feeble state would allow. Seeing no signs of my stopping, he caused
his horse to be brought out and saddled, as if he intended to pursue me.
The race was now to be an unequal one, and thinking I might be over-
hauled by him if I kept the main road, I walked nearly the whole distance in the woods, keeping far enough from the road to avoid detection
and pursuit. But I had not gone far before my little strength again
failed me, and I was obliged to lie down. The blood was still oozing
from the wound in my head, and for a time I suffered more than I can
describe. There I was in the deep woods, sick and emaciated, bleeding
and almost bloodless, and pursued by a wretch whose character for
revolting cruelty beggars all opprobrious speech. I was not without the
fear of bleeding to death. The thought of dying all alone in the woods,
and of being torn in pieces by the buzzards, had not yet been rendered
tolerable by my many troubles and hardships, and I was glad when the
shade of the trees and the cool evening breeze combined with my mat-
ted hair to stop the flow of blood. After lying there about three-quarters
of an hour, brooding over the singular and mournful lot to which I was
doomed, my mind passing over the whole scale or circle of belief and
unbelief, from faith in the overruling Providence of God, to the blackest atheism, I again took up my journey toward St. Michaels, more
weary and sad than on the morning when I left Thomas Auld's for the
home of Covey. I was bare-footed, bare-headed, and in my shirt-sleeves.
The way was through briers and bogs, and I tore my feet often during
the journey. I was full five hours in going the seven or eight miles;
partly because of the difficulties of the way, and partly because of the
feebleness induced by my illness, bruises, and loss of blood.

On gaining my master's store, I presented an appearance of wretchedness and woe calculated to move any but a heart of stone. From the
crown of my head to the sole of my feet, there were marks of blood. My
hair was all clotted with dust and blood, and the back of my shirt was
literally stiff with the same. Briers and thorns had scarred and torn my
feet and legs. Had I escaped from a den of tigers, I could not have
looked worse. In this plight I appeared before my professedly *Christian*
master, humbly to invoke the interposition of his power and authority,
to protect me from further abuse and violence. During the latter part of
my tedious journey I had begun to hope that my master would now
show himself in a nobler light than I had before seen him. But I was
disappointed. I had jumped from a sinking ship into the sea. I had fled
from a tiger to something worse. I told him as well as I could, all the

circumstances; how I was endeavoring to please Covey; how hard I was at work in the present instance; how unwillingly I sank down under the heat, toil, and pain; the brutal manner in which Covey had kicked me in the side, the gash cut in my head; my hesitation about troubling him (Capt. Auld) with complaints; but that now I felt it would not be best longer to conceal from him the outrages committed from time to time upon me. At first Master Thomas seemed somewhat affected by the story of my wrongs, but he soon repressed whatever feeling he may have had, and became as cold and hard as iron. It was impossible, *at first*, as I stood before him, to seem indifferent. I distinctly saw his human nature asserting its conviction against the slave system, which made cases like mine *possible*; but, as I have said, humanity fell before the systematic tyranny of slavery. He first walked the floor, apparently much agitated by my story, and the spectacle I presented; but soon it was his turn to talk. He began moderately by finding excuses for Covey, and ended with a full justification of him, and a passionate condemnation of me. He had no doubt I deserved the flogging. He did not believe I was sick; I was only endeavoring to get rid of work. My dizziness was laziness, and Covey did right to flog me as he had done. After thus fairly annihilating me, and arousing himself by his eloquence, he fiercely demanded what I wished *him* to do in the case! With such a knock-down to all my hopes, and feeling as I did my entire subjection to his power, I had very little heart to reply. I must not assert my innocence of the allegations he had piled up against me, for that would be impudence. The guilt of a slave was always and everywhere presumed, and the innocence of the slaveholder, or employer, was always asserted. The word of the slave against this presumption was generally treated as impudence, worthy of punishment. 'Do you dare to contradict me, you rascal?' was a final silencer of counter-statements from the lips of a slave. Calming down a little, in view of my silence and hesitation, and perhaps a little touched at my forlorn and miserable appearance, he inquired again, what I wanted him to do? Thus invited a second time, I told him I wished him to allow me to get a new home, and to find a new master; that as sure as I went back to live again with Mr. Covey, I should be killed by him; that he would never forgive my coming home with complaints; that since I had lived with him he had almost crushed my spirit, and I believed he would ruin me for future service and that my life was not safe in his hands. This Master Thomas (*my brother in the church*) regarded as 'non-sense.' There was no danger that Mr. Covey would kill me; he was a good man, industrious and religious, and he would not think of removing me from that home; 'besides,' said he—and this I found was the most distressing thought of all to him—'if you should leave Covey now that your year is but half expired, I should lose your wages for the entire year. You belong to Mr. Covey for one year, and you *must go back* to him, come what will; and you must not trouble me with any more stories; and if you don't go immediately home, I'll get hold of you myself.' This was just what I expected when I found he had *prejudged* the case against me. 'But, sir,' I said, 'I am sick and tired, and I *cannot* get home to-night.' At this he somewhat relented, and finally allowed me to stay the night, but said I must be off early in the morning, and concluded his directions by making me swallow a huge dose of Epsom salts, which was about the only medicine ever administered to slaves.

It was quite natural for Master Thomas to presume I was feigning sickness to escape work, for he probably thought that were he in the place of a slave, with no wages for his work, no praise for well-doing, no motive for toil but the lash, he would try every possible scheme by which to escape labor. I say I have no doubt of this; the reason is, that there were not, under the whole heavens, a set of men who cultivated such a dread of labor as did the slaveholders. The charge of laziness against the slaves was ever on their lips and was the standing apology for every species of cruelty and brutality. These men did indeed literally 'bind heavy burdens, grievous to be borne, and laid them upon men's shoulders, but they themselves would not move them with one of their fingers.'*

# CHAPTER XVII.

## THE LAST FLOGGING.

*A sleepless night—Return to Covey's—Punished by him—The chase defeated—Vengeance postponed—Musings in the woods—The alternative—Deplorable spectacle—Night in the woods—Expected attack—Accosted by Sandy—A friend, not a master—Sandy's hospitality—The ash-cake supper—Interview with Sandy—His advice—Sandy a conjuror as well as a Christian—The magic root—Strange meeting with Covey—His manner—Covey's Sunday face—Author's defensive resolve—The fight—The victory, and its results.*

SLEEP does not always come to the relief of the weary in body, and broken in spirit; especially is it so when past troubles only foreshadow coming disasters. My last hope had been extinguished. My master, who I did not venture to hope would protect me *as a* MAN, had now refused to protect me as *his property*, and had cast me back, covered with reproaches and bruises, into the hands of one who was a stranger to that mercy which is the soul of the religion he professed. May the reader never know what it is to spend such a night as to me was that which heralded my return to the den of horrors from which I had made a temporary escape.

I remained—sleep I did not—all night at St. Michaels, and in the morning (Saturday) I started off, obedient to the order of Master Thomas, feeling that I had no friend on earth, and doubting if I had one in heaven. I reached Covey's about nine o'clock; and just as I stepped into the field, before I had reached the house, true to his snakish habits, Covey darted out at me from a fence corner, in which he had secreted himself for the purpose of securing me. He was provided with a cowskin and a rope, and he evidently intended to tie me up, and wreak his vengeance on me to the fullest extent. I should have been an easy prey had he succeeded in getting his hands upon me, for I had taken no refreshment since noon on Friday; and this, with the other trying circumstances, had greatly reduced my strength. I, however, darted back into the woods before the ferocious hound could reach me, and buried myself in a thicket, where he lost sight of me. The cornfield afforded me shelter in getting to the woods. But for the tall corn, Covey would have overtaken me, and made me his captive. He was much chagrined that I did not, and gave up the chase very reluctantly, as I could see by his angry movements, as he returned to the house.

For a little time I was clear of Covey and his lash. I was in the wood, buried in its somber gloom and hushed in its solemn silence; hidden from all human eyes; shut in with nature and with nature's God, and absent from all human contrivances. Here was a good place to pray; to pray for help, for deliverance—a prayer I had often before made. But how could I pray? Covey could pray—Capt. Auld could pray. I would fain pray; but doubts arising, partly from my neglect of the means of grace and partly from the sham religion which everywhere prevailed, there was awakened in my mind a distrust of all religion and the conviction that prayers were unavailing and delusive.

Life in itself had almost become burdensome to me. All my outward relations were against me. I must stay here and starve, or go home to Covey's and have my flesh torn to pieces and my spirit humbled under his cruel lash. These were the alternatives before me. The day was long and irksome. I was weak from the toils of the previous day and from want of food and sleep, and I had been so little concerned about my appearance that I had not yet washed the blood from my garments. I was an object of horror, even to myself. Life in Baltimore, when most oppressive, was a paradise to this. What had I done, what had my parents done, that such a life as this should be mine? That day, in the woods, I would have exchanged my manhood for the brutehood of an ox.

Night came. I was still in the woods, and still unresolved what to do. Hunger had not yet pinched me to the point of going home, and I laid myself down in the leaves to rest; for I had been watching for hunters all day, but not being molested by them during the day, I expected no disturbance from them during the night. I had come to the conclusion that Covey relied upon hunger to drive me home, and in this I was quite correct, for he made no effort to catch me after the morning.

During the night I heard the step of a man in the woods. He was coming toward the place where I lay. A person lying still in the woods in the day-time has the advantage over one walking, and this advantage is much greater at night. I was not able to engage in a physical struggle, and I had recourse to the common resort of the weak. I hid myself in the leaves to prevent discovery. But as the night rambler in the woods drew nearer I found him to be a *friend*, not an enemy; a slave of Mr. William Groomes of Easton, a kind-hearted fellow named 'Sandy.' Sandy lived that year with Mr. Kemp, about four miles from St. Michaels. He, like myself, had been hired out, but unlike myself had not been hired out to be broken. He was the husband of a free woman who lived in the lower part of 'Poppie Neck,' and he was now on his way through the woods to see her and to spend the Sabbath with her.

As soon as I had ascertained that the disturber of my solitude was not an enemy, but the good-hearted Sandy,—a man as famous among the slaves of the neighborhood for his good nature as for his good sense— I came out from my hiding-place and made myself known to him. I explained the circumstances of the past two days which had driven me to the woods, and he deeply compassionated my distress. It was a bold thing for him to shelter me, and I could not ask him to do so, for had I been found in his hut he would have suffered the penalty of thirty-nine lashes on his bare back, if not something worse. But Sandy was too generous to permit the fear of punishment to prevent his relieving a brother bondman from hunger and exposure, and therefore, on his own motion, I accompanied him home to his wife—for the house and lot were hers, as she was a free woman. It was about midnight, but his wife was called up, a fire was made, some Indian meal was soon mixed with salt and water, and an ash-cake was baked in a hurry, to relieve my hunger. Sandy's wife was not behind him in kindness; both seemed to esteem it a privilege to succor me, for although I was hated by Covey and by my master I was loved by the colored people, because they thought I was hated for my knowledge, and persecuted because I was feared. I was the only slave in that region who could read or write. There had been one other man, belonging to Mr. Hugh Hamilton, who could read, but he, poor fellow, had, shortly after coming into the neighborhood, been sold off to the far south. I saw him in the cart, to be carried to Easton for sale, ironed and pinioned like a yearling for the slaughter. My knowledge was now the pride of my brother slaves, and no doubt Sandy felt on that account something of the general interest in me. The supper was soon ready, and though over the sea I have since feasted with honorables, lord mayors and aldermen, my supper on ash-cake and cold water, with Sandy, was the meal of all my life most sweet to my taste and now most vivid to my memory.

Supper over, Sandy and I went into a discussion of what was *possible* for me, under the perils and hardships which overshadowed my path. The question was, must I go back to Covey, or must I attempt to run away? Upon a careful survey the latter was found to be impossible; for I was on a narrow neck of land, every avenue from which would bring me in sight of pursuers. There was Chesapeake Bay to the right, and 'Pot-pie' river to the left, and St. Michaels and its neighborhood occupied the only space through which there was any retreat.

I found Sandy an old adviser. He was not only a religious man, but he professed to believe in a system for which I have no name. He was a genuine African, and had inherited some of the so-called magical powers said to be possessed by the eastern nations. He told me that he could help me; that in those very woods there was an herb which in the morning might be found, possessing all the powers required for my protection (I put his words in my own language), and that if I would take his advice he would procure me the root of the herb of which he spoke. He told me, further, that if I would take that root and wear it on my right side it would be impossible for Covey to strike me a blow, and that, with this root about my person, no white man could whip me. He said he had carried it for years, and that he had fully tested its virtues. He had never received a blow from a slave-holder since he carried it, and he never expected to receive one, for he meant always to carry that root for protection. He knew Covey well, for Mrs. Covey was the daughter of Mrs. Kemp; and he (Sandy) had heard of the barbarous treatment to which I had been subjected, and he wanted to do something for me.

Now all this talk about the root was to me very absurd and ridiculous, if not positively sinful. I at first rejected the idea that the simple carrying a root on my right side (a root, by the way, over which I walked every time I went into the woods) could possess any such magic power as he ascribed to it, and I was, therefore, not disposed to cumber my pocket with it. I had a positive aversion to all pretenders to '*divination*.' It was beneath one of my intelligence to countenance such dealings with the devil as this power implied. But with all my learning—it was really precious little—Sandy was more than a match for me. 'My book-learning,' he said, 'had not kept Covey off me' (a powerful argument just then), and he entreated me, with flashing eyes, to try this. If it did me no good it could do me no harm, and it would cost me nothing any way. Sandy was so earnest and so confident of the good qualities of this weed that, to please him, I was induced to take it. He had been to me the good Samaritan, and had, almost providentially, found me and helped me when I could not help myself; how did I know but that the hand of the Lord was in it? With thoughts of this sort I took the roots from Sandy and put them in my right-hand pocket.

This was of course Sunday morning. Sandy now urged me to go home with all speed, and to walk up bravely to the house, as though nothing had happened. I saw in Sandy, with all his superstition, too deep an insight into human nature not to have some respect for his advice; and perhaps, too, a slight gleam or shadow of his superstition had fallen on me. At any rate, I started off toward Covey's, as directed. Having, the previous night, poured my griefs into Sandy's ears and enlisted him in my behalf, having made his wife a sharer in my sorrows, and having also become well refreshed by sleep and food, I moved off quite courageously toward the dreaded Covey's. Singularly enough, just as I entered the yard-gate I met him and his wife on their way to church, dressed in their Sunday best, and looking as smiling as angels. His manner perfectly astonished me. There was something really benignant in his countenance. He spoke to me as never before, told me that the pigs had got into the lot and he wished me to go to drive them out; inquired how I was, and seemed an altered man. This extraordinary conduct really made me begin to think that Sandy's herb had more virtue in it than I, in my pride, had been willing to allow, and, had the day been other than Sunday, I should have attributed Covey's altered manner solely to the power of the root. I suspected, however, that the *Sabbath*, not the root, was the real explanation of the change. His religion hindered him from breaking the Sabbath, but not from breaking my skin on any other day than Sunday. He had more respect for the day than for the man for whom the day was mercifully given;* for while he would cut and slash my body during the week, he would on Sunday teach me the value of my soul, and the way of life and salvation by Jesus Christ.

All went well with me till Monday morning; and then, whether the root had lost its virtue, or whether my tormentor had gone deeper into the black art than I had, (as was sometimes said of him), or whether he had obtained a special indulgence for his faithful Sunday's worship, it is not necessary for me to know or to inform the reader; but this much I may say, the pious and benignant smile which graced the face of Covey on *Sunday* wholly disappeared on *Monday*.

Long before daylight I was called up to go feed, rub, and curry the horses. I obeyed the call, as I should have done had it been made at an earlier hour, for I had brought my mind to a firm resolve during that Sunday's reflection to obey every order, however unreasonable, if it were possible, and if Mr. Covey should then undertake to beat me to defend and protect myself to the best of my ability. My religious views on the subject of resisting my master had suffered a serious shock by the savage persecution to which I had been subjected, and my hands were no longer tied by my religion. Master Thomas's indifference had severed the last link. I had backslidden from this point in the slaves' religious creed, and I soon had occasion to make my fallen state known to my Sunday-pious brother, Covey.

While I was obeying his order to feed and get the horses ready for the field, and when I was in the act of going up the stable-loft, for the purpose of throwing down some blades, Covey sneaked into the stable, in his peculiar way, and seizing me suddenly by the leg, he brought me to the stable-floor, giving my newly-mended body a terrible jar. I now forgot all about my *roots*, and remembered my pledge to stand up in my own defense. The brute was skillfully endeavoring to get a slip-knot on my legs, before I could draw up my feet. As soon as I found what he was up to, I gave a sudden spring (my two days' rest had been of much service to me) and by that means, no doubt, he was able to bring me to the floor so heavily. He was defeated in his plan of tying me. While down, he seemed to think that he had me very securely in his power. He little thought he was—as the rowdies say—'in' for a 'rough and tumble' fight; but such was the fact. Whence came the daring spirit necessary to grapple with a man who, eight-and-forty hours before, could, with his slightest word, have made me tremble like a leaf in a storm, I do not know; at any rate, I *was resolved to fight*, and what was better still, I actually was hard at it. The fighting madness had come upon me, and I found my strong fingers firmly attached to the throat of the tyrant, as heedless of consequences, at the moment, as if we stood as equals before the law. The very color of the man was forgotten. I felt supple as a cat, and was ready for him at every turn. Every blow of his was parried, though I dealt no blows in return. I was strictly on the defensive, preventing him from injuring me, rather than trying to injure him. I flung him on the ground several times when he meant to have hurled me there. I held him so firmly by the throat that his blood followed my nails. He held me, and I held him.

All was fair thus far, and the contest was about equal. My resistance was entirely unexpected and Covey was taken all aback by it. He trembled in every limb. '*Are you going to resist*, you scoundrel?' said he. To which I returned a polite '*Yes, sir*,' steadily gazing my interrogator in the eye, to meet the first approach or dawning of the blow which I expected my answer would call forth. But the conflict did not long remain equal. Covey soon cried lustily for help; not that I was obtaining any marked advantage over him, or was injuring him but because he was gaining none over me, and was not able, single-handed, to conquer me. He called for his cousin Hughes to come to his assistance, and now the scene was changed. I was compelled to give blows, as well as to parry them, and since I was in any case to suffer for resistance, I felt (as the musty proverb goes) that I 'might as well be hanged for an old sheep as a lamb.' I was still defensive toward Covey, but aggressive toward Hughes, on whom, at his first approach, I dealt a blow which fairly sickened him. He went off, bending over with pain, and manifesting no disposition to come again within my reach. The poor fellow was in the act of trying to catch and tie my right hand, and while flattering himself with success, I gave him the kick which sent him staggering away in pain, at the same time that I held Covey with a firm hand.

Taken completely by surprise, Covey seemed to have lost his usual strength and coolness. He was frightened, and stood puffing and blowing, seemingly unable to command words or blows. When he saw that Hughes was standing half bent with pain, his courage quite gone, the cowardly tyrant asked if I 'meant to persist in my resistance.' I told him I '*did mean to resist*, come what might; that I had been treated like a brute during the last six months, and that I should stand it no longer.' With that he gave me a shake, and attempted to drag me toward a stick of wood that was lying just outside the stable-door. He meant to knock me down with it; but, just as he leaned over to get the stick, I seized him with both hands, by the collar, and with a vigorous and sudden snatch brought my assailant harmlessly, his full length, on the not over-clean ground, for we were now in the cow-yard. He had selected the place for the fight, and it was but right that he should have all the advantages of his own selection.

By this time Bill, the hired man, came home. He had been to Mr. Helmsley's to spend Sunday with his nominal wife. Covey and I had been skirmishing from before daybreak till now. The sun was shooting his beams almost over the eastern woods, and we were still at it. I could not see where the matter was to terminate. He evidently was afraid to let me go, lest I should again make off to the woods, otherwise he would probably have obtained arms from the house to frighten me. Holding me, he called upon Bill to assist him. The scene here had something comic about it. Bill, who knew precisely what Covey wished him to do, affected ignorance, and pretended he did not know what to do. 'What shall I do, Master Covey?' said Bill. 'Take hold of him!—take hold of him!' cried Covey. With a toss of his head, peculiar to Bill, he said: 'Indeed, Master Covey, I want to go to work.' '*This is your work*,' said Covey; 'take hold of him.' Bill replied, with spirit: 'My master hired me here to work, and not to help you whip Frederick.' It was my turn to speak. 'Bill,' said I, 'don't put your hands on me.' To which he replied: 'My God, Frederick, I ain't goin' to tech ye'; and Bill walked off, leaving Covey and myself to settle our differences as best we might.

But my present advantage was threatened when I saw Caroline (the slave woman of Covey) coming to the cow-yard to milk, for she was a powerful woman, and could have mastered me easily, exhausted as I was.

As soon as she came near, Covey attempted to rally her to his aid. Strangely and fortunately, Caroline was in no humor to take a hand in any such sport. We were all in open rebellion that morning. Caroline answered the command of her master to 'take hold of me,' precisely as Bill had done, but in her it was at far greater peril, for she was the slave of Covey, and he could do what he pleased with her. It was not so with Bill, and Bill knew it. Samuel Harris, to whom Bill belonged, did not allow his slaves to be beaten unless they were guilty of some crime which the law would punish. But poor Caroline, like myself, was at the mercy of the merciless Covey, nor did she escape the dire effects of her refusal: he gave her several sharp blows.

At length (two hours had elapsed) the contest was given over. Letting go of me, puffing and blowing at a great rate, Covey said: 'Now, you scoundrel, go to your work; I would not have whipped you half so hard if you had not resisted.' The fact was, he had not whipped me at all. He had not, in all the scuffle, drawn a single drop of blood from me. I had drawn blood from him, and should even without this satisfaction have been victorious, because my aim had not been to injure him, but to prevent his injuring me.

During the whole six months that I lived with Covey after this transaction, he never again laid the weight of his finger on me in anger. He would occasionally say he did not want to have to get hold of me again—a declaration which I had no difficulty in believing; and I had a secret feeling which answered, 'You had better not wish to get hold of me again, for you will be likely to come off worse in a second fight than you did in the first.'

This battle with Mr. Covey, undignified as it was and as I fear my narration of it is, was the turning-point in my 'life as a slave.' It rekindled in my breast the smouldering embers of liberty. It brought up my Baltimore dreams and revived a sense of my own manhood. I was a changed being after that fight. I was *nothing* before; *I was a man* now. It recalled to life my crushed self-respect, and my self-confidence, and inspired me with a renewed determination to be a *free man*. A man without force is without the essential dignity of humanity. Human nature is so constituted, that it cannot *honor* a helpless man, though it can *pity* him, and even this it cannot do long if signs of power do not arise.

He only can understand the effect of this combat on my spirit, who has himself incurred something, or hazarded something, in repelling the unjust and cruel aggressions of a tyrant. Covey was a tyrant and a cowardly one withal. After resisting him, I felt as I had never felt before. It was a resurrection from the dark and pestiferous tomb of slavery, to the heaven of comparative freedom. I was no longer a servile coward, trembling under the frown of a brother worm of the dust, but my long-cowed spirit was roused to an attitude of independence. I had reached the point at which I was *not afraid to die*. This spirit made me a freeman in *fact*, though I still remained a slave in *form*. When a slave cannot be flogged, he is more than half free. He has a domain as broad as his own manly heart to defend, and he is really 'a power on earth.' From this time until my escape from slavery, I was never fairly whipped. Several attempts were made, but they were always unsuccessful. Bruised I did get, but the instance I have described was the end of the brutification to which slavery had subjected me.

The reader may like to know why, after I had so grievously offended Mr. Covey, he did not have me taken in hand by the authorities; indeed, why the law of Maryland, which assigned hanging to the slave who resisted his master, was not put in force against me, at any rate why I was not taken up, as was usual in such cases, and publicly whipped as an example to other slaves, and as a means of deterring me from again committing the same offence. I confess that the easy manner in which I got off was always a surprise to me, and even now I cannot fully explain the cause, though the probability is that Covey was ashamed to have it known that he had been mastered by a boy of sixteen. He enjoyed the unbounded and very valuable reputation of being a first-rate overseer and negro-breaker, and by means of this reputation he was able to procure his hands at very trifling compensation and with very great ease. His interest and his pride would mutually suggest the wisdom of passing the matter by in silence. The story that he had undertaken to whip a lad and had been resisted, would of itself be damaging to him in the estimation of slaveholders.

It is perhaps not altogether creditable to my natural temper that after this conflict with Mr. Covey I did, at times, purposely aim to provoke him to an attack, by refusing to keep with the other hands in the field; but I could never bully him to another battle. I was determined on doing him serious damage if he ever again attempted to lay violent hands on me.

> 'Hereditary bondmen, know ye not
> Who would be free, themselves must strike the blow?'*

# CHAPTER XVIII.

## NEW RELATIONS AND DUTIES.

*Change of masters—Benefits derived by change—Fame of the fight with Covey—Reckless unconcern—Author's abhorrence of slavery—Ability to read a cause of prejudice—The holidays—How spent—Sharp hit at slavery—Effects of holidays—Difference between Covey and Freeland—An irreligious master preferred to a religious one—Hard life at Covey's useful to the author—Improved condition does not bring contentment—Congenial society at Freeland's—Author's Sabbath-school—Secrecy necessary—Affectionate relations of tutor and pupils—Confidence and friendship among slaves—Slavery the inviter of vengeance.*

MY term of service with Edward Covey expired on Christmas day, 1834. I gladly-enough left him, although he was by this time as gentle as a lamb. My home for the year 1835 was already secured, my next master selected. There was always more or less excitement about the changing of hands, but determined to fight my way, I had become somewhat reckless and cared little into whose hands I fell. The report got abroad that I was hard to whip; that I was guilty of kicking back, and that, though generally a good-natured negro, I sometimes 'got the devil in me.' These sayings were rife in Talbot County and distinguished me among my servile brethren. Slaves would sometimes fight with each other, and even die at each other's hands, but there were very few who were not held in awe by a white man. Trained from the cradle up to think and feel that their masters were superiors, and invested with a sort of sacredness, there were few who could rise above the control which that sentiment exercised. I had freed myself from it, and the thing was known. One bad sheep will spoil a whole flock. I was a bad sheep. I hated slavery, slaveholders, and all pertaining to them; and I did not fail to inspire others with the same feeling wherever and whenever opportunity was presented. This made me a marked lad among the slaves, and a suspected one among slaveholders. A knowledge also of my ability to read and write got pretty widely spread, which was very much against me.

The days between Christmas day and New Year's were allowed the slaves as holidays. During these days all regular work was suspended, and there was nothing to do but to keep fires and look after the stock. We regarded this time as our own by the grace of our masters, and we therefore used it or abused it as we pleased. Those who had families at a distance were expected to visit them and spend with them the entire week. The younger slaves or the unmarried ones were expected to see to the animals and attend to incidental duties at home. The holidays were variously spent. The sober, thinking, industrious ones would employ themselves in manufacturing corn-brooms, mats, horse-collars, and baskets, and some of these were very well made. Another class spent their time in hunting opossums, coons, rabbits, and other game. But the majority spent the holidays in sports, ball-playing, wrestling, boxing, running, foot-races, dancing, and drinking whisky; and this latter mode was generally most agreeable to their masters. A slave who would work during the holidays was thought by his master undeserving of holidays. There was in this simple act of continued work an accusation against slaves, and a slave could not help thinking that if he made three dollars during the holidays he might make three hundred during the year. Not to be drunk during the holidays was disgraceful.

The fiddling, dancing, and 'jubilee beating'* was carried on in all directions. This latter performance was strictly southern. It supplied the place of violin or other musical instruments and was played so easily that almost every farm had its 'Juba' beater. The performer improvised as he beat the instrument, marking the words as he sang so as to have them fall pat with the movement of his hands. Once in a while among a mass of nonsense and wild frolic, a sharp hit was given to the meanness of slaveholders. Take the following for example:

| | |
|---|---|
| We raise de wheat, | We peel de meat, |
| Dey gib us de corn: | Dey gib us de skin; |
| We bake de bread, | And dat's de way |
| Dey gib us de crust; | Dey take us in; |
| We sif de meal, | We skim de pot, |
| Dey gib us de huss; | Dey gib us de liquor, |

And say dat's good enough for nigger.
Walk over! walk over!
Your butter and de fat;
Poor nigger, you can't get over dat!
Walk over—

This is not a bad summary of the palpable injustice and fraud of slavery, giving, as it does, to the lazy and idle the comforts which God designed should be given solely to the honest laborer. But to the holidays. Judging from my own observation and experience, I believe those holidays were among the most effective means in the hands of slaveholders of keeping down the spirit of insurrection among the slaves.

To enslave men successfully and safely it is necessary to keep their minds occupied with thoughts and aspirations short of the liberty of which they are deprived. A certain degree of attainable good must be kept before them. These holidays served the purpose of keeping the minds of the slaves occupied with prospective pleasure within the limits of slavery. The young man could go wooing, the married man to see his wife, the father and mother to see their children, the industrious and money-loving could make a few dollars, the great wrestler could win laurels, the young people meet and enjoy each other's society, the drinking man could get plenty of whisky, and the religious man could hold prayer-meetings, preach, pray, and exhort. Before the holidays there were pleasures in prospect; after the holidays they were pleasures of memory, and they served to keep out thoughts and wishes of a more dangerous character. These holidays were also used as conductors or safety-valves, to carry off the explosive elements inseparable from the human mind when reduced to the condition of slavery. But for these the rigors of bondage would have become too severe for endurance, and the slave would have been forced to a dangerous desperation.

Thus they became a part and parcel of the gross wrongs and inhumanity of slavery. Ostensibly they were institutions of benevolence designed to mitigate the rigors of slave-life, but practically they were a fraud instituted by human selfishness, the better to secure the ends of injustice and oppression. Not the slave's happiness but the master's safety, was the end sought. It was not from a generous unconcern for the slave's labor, but from a prudent regard for the slave system. I am strengthened in this opinion from the fact that most slaveholders liked to have their slaves spend the holidays in such manner as to be of no real benefit to them. Everything like rational enjoyment was frowned upon, and only those wild and low sports peculiar to semi-civilized people were encouraged. The license allowed appeared to have no other object than to disgust the slaves with their temporary freedom, and to make them as glad to return to their work as they had been to leave it. I have known slaveholders resort to cunning tricks, with a view of getting their slaves deplorably drunk. The usual plan was to make bets on a slave that he could drink more whisky than any other, and so induce a rivalry among them for the mastery in this degradation. The scenes brought about in this way were often scandalous and loathsome in the extreme. Whole multitudes might be found stretched out in brutal drunkenness, at once helpless and disgusting. Thus, when the slave asked for hours of 'virtuous liberty,' his cunning master took advantage of his ignorance and cheered him with a dose of vicious and revolting dissipation artfully labeled with the name of '*liberty.*'

We were induced to drink, I among the rest, and when the holidays were over we all staggered up from our filth and wallowing, took a long breath, and went away to our various fields of work, feeling, upon the whole, rather glad to go from that which our masters had artfully deceived us into the belief was freedom, back again to the arms of slavery. It was not what we had taken it to be, nor what it would have been, had it not been abused by us. It was about as well to be a slave to master, as to be a slave to whisky and rum. When the slave was drunk the slaveholder had no fear that he would plan an insurrection, or that he would escape to the North. It was the sober, thoughtful slave who was dangerous and needed the vigilance of his master to keep him a slave.

On the first of January, 1835, I proceeded from St. Michaels to Mr. William Freeland's—my new home. Mr. Freeland lived only three miles from St. Michaels, on an old, worn-out farm, which required much labor to render it anything like a self-supporting establishment.

I found Mr. Freeland a different man from Covey. Though not rich, he was what might have been called a well-bred Southern gentleman. Though a slaveholder and sharing in common with them many of the vices of his class, he seemed alive to the sentiment of honor, and had also some sense of justice, and some feelings of humanity. He was fretful, impulsive, and passionate, but free from the mean and selfish characteristics which distinguished the creature from which I had happily escaped. Mr. Freeland was open, frank, and imperative. He practiced no concealments and disdained to play the spy. He was, in all these qualities, the opposite of Covey.

My poor weather-beaten bark now reached smoother water and gentler breezes. My stormy life at Covey's had been of service to me. The things that would have seemed very hard had I gone directly to Mr. Freeland's from the home of Master Thomas, were now 'trifles light as air.'* I was still a field-hand, and had come to prefer the severe labor of the field to the enervating duties of a house-servant. I had become large and strong, and had begun to take pride in the fact that I could do as much hard work as some of the older men. There was much rivalry among slaves at times as to which could do the most work, and masters generally sought to promote such rivalry. But some of us were too wise to race with each other very long. Such racing, we had the sagacity to see, was not likely to pay. We had our times for measuring each other's strength, but we knew too much to keep up the competition so long as to produce an extraordinary day's work. We knew that if by extraordinary exertion a large quantity of work was done in one day, and it became known to the master, it might lead him to require the same amount every day. This thought was enough to bring us to a dead halt when ever so much excited for the race.

At Mr. Freeland's my condition was every way improved. I was no longer the scapegoat that I was when at Covey's, where every wrong thing done was saddled upon me, and where other slaves were whipped over my shoulders. Bill Smith was protected by a positive prohibition, made by his rich master (and the command of the *rich* slaveholder was *law* to the poor one). Hughes was favored by his relationship to Covey, and the hands hired temporarily escaped flogging. I was the general pack-horse; but Mr. Freeland held every man individually responsible for his own conduct. Mr. Freeland, like Mr. Covey, gave his hands enough to eat, but, unlike Mr. Covey, he gave them time to take their meals. He worked us hard during the day, but gave us the night for rest. We were seldom in the field after dark in the evening, or before sunrise in the morning. Our implements of husbandry were of the most improved pattern, and much superior to those used at Covey's.

Notwithstanding all the improvement in my relations, notwithstanding the many advantages I had gained by my new home and my new master, I was still restless and discontented. I was about as *difficult* to be pleased by a master as a master is by a slave. The freedom from bodily torture and unceasing labor had given my mind an increased sensibility and imparted to it greater activity. I was not yet exactly in right relations. 'Howbeit, that was not first which is spiritual, but that which is natural, and afterward that which is spiritual.'* When entombed at Covey's and shrouded in darkness and physical wretchedness, temporal well-being was the grand desideratum; but, temporal wants supplied, the spirit put in its claims. Beat and cuff the slave, keep him hungry and spiritless, and he will follow the chain of his master like a dog; but feed and clothe him well, work him moderately and surround him with physical comfort, and dreams of freedom will intrude. Give him a *bad* master and he aspires to a good master; give him a good master, and he wishes to become his own master. Such is human nature. You may hurl a man so low beneath the level of his kind, that he loses all just ideas of his natural position, but elevate him a little, and the clear conception of rights rises to life and power, and leads him onward. Thus elevated a little at Freeland's, the dreams called into being by that good man, Father Lawson, when in Baltimore, began to visit me again. Shoots from the tree of liberty began to put forth buds, and dim hopes of the future began to dawn.

I found myself in congenial society. There were Henry Harris, John Harris, Handy Caldwell, and Sandy Jenkins (this last, of the root-preventive memory).

Henry and John Harris were brothers, and belonged to Mr. Freeland. They were both remarkably bright and intelligent, though neither of them could read. Now for mischief! I began to address my companions on the subject of education and the advantages of intelligence over ignorance, and, as far as I dared, I tried to show the agency of ignorance in keeping men in slavery. Webster's spelling-book and the Columbian Orator were looked into again. As summer came on and the long Sabbath days stretched themselves over our idleness, I became uneasy and wanted a Sabbath-school in which to exercise my gifts and to impart to my brother-slaves the little knowledge I possessed. A house was hardly necessary in the summer time; I could hold my school under the shade of an old oak tree as well as any where else. The thing was to get the scholars, and to have them thoroughly imbued with the idea to learn. Two such boys were quickly found in Henry and John, and from them the contagion spread. I was not long in bringing around me twenty or thirty young men, who enrolled themselves gladly in my Sabbath-school, and were willing to meet me regularly under the trees or elsewhere, for the purpose of learning to read. It was surprising with what ease they provided themselves with spelling-books. These were mostly the cast-off books of their young masters or mistresses. I taught at first on our own farm. All were impressed with the necessity of keeping the matter as private as possible, for the fate of the St. Michaels attempt was still fresh in the minds of all. Our pious masters at St. Michaels must not know that a few of their dusky brothers were learning to read the Word of God, lest they should come down upon us with the lash and chain. We might have met to drink whisky, to wrestle, fight, and to do other unseemly things, with no fear of interruption from the saints or the sinners of St. Michaels. But to meet for the purpose of improving the mind and heart, by learning to read the sacred scriptures, was a nuisance to be instantly stopped. The slave holders there, like slaveholders elsewhere, preferred to see the slaves engaged in degrading sports, rather than acting like moral and accountable beings. Had any one, at that time, asked a religious white man in St. Michaels, the names of three men in that town whose lives were most after the pattern of our Lord and Master Jesus Christ, the reply would have been: Garrison West, class-leader, Wright Fairbanks and Thomas Auld, both also class-leaders; and yet these men, armed with mob-like missiles, ferociously rushed in upon my Sabbath-school and forbade our meeting again on pain of having our backs subjected to the bloody lash. This same Garrison West was my class-leader, and I had thought him a Christian until he took part in breaking up my school. He led me no more after that.

The plea for this outrage was then, as it is always, the tyrant's plea of necessity. If the slaves learned to read they would learn something more and something worse. The peace of slavery would be disturbed. Slave rule would be endangered. I do not dispute the soundness of the reasoning. If slavery were right, Sabbath-schools for teaching slaves to read were wrong, and ought to have been put down. These Christian class-leaders were, to this extent, consistent. They had settled the question that slavery was right, and by that standard they determined that Sabbath-schools were wrong. To be sure they were Protestants and held to the great Protestant right of every man to 'search the Scriptures'* for himself; but then, to all general rules there are exceptions. How convenient! What crimes may not be committed under such ruling! But my dear class-leading Methodist brethren did not condescend to give me a reason for breaking up the school at St. Michaels. They had determined its destruction, and that was enough.

After getting the school nicely started a second time, holding it in the woods behind the barn, and in the shade of trees, I succeeded in inducing a free colored man who lived several miles from our house to permit me to hold my school in a room at his house. He incurred much peril in doing so, for the assemblage was an unlawful one. I had at one time more than forty pupils, all of the right sort, and many of them succeeded in learning to read. I have had various employments during my life, but to none do I look back with more satisfaction than to this one. An attachment, deep and permanent, sprang up between me and my persecuted pupils, which made my parting from them intensely painful.

Besides my Sunday-school, I devoted three evenings a week to my other fellow slaves during the winter. Those dear souls who came to my Sabbath-school came not because it was popular or reputable to do so, for they came with a liability of having forty stripes laid on their naked backs. In this Christian country men and women were obliged to hide in barns and woods and trees from professing Christians, in order to learn to read the *Holy Bible*. Their minds had been cramped and starved by their cruel masters. The light of education had been completely excluded and their hard earnings had been taken to educate their master's children. I felt a delight in circumventing the tyrants and in blessing the victims of their curses.

To outward seeming the year at Mr. Freeland's passed off very smoothly. Not a blow was given me during the whole year. To the credit of Mr. Freeland, irreligious though he was, it must be stated that he was the best master I ever had until I became my own master and assumed for myself, as I had a right to do, the responsibility of my own existence and the exercise of my own powers.

For much of the happiness, or absence of misery, with which I passed this year, I am indebted to the genial temper and ardent friendship of my brother slaves. They were every one of them manly, generous and brave. Yes, I say they were brave, and I will add, fine-looking. It is seldom the lot of any one to have truer and better friends than were the slaves on this farm. It was not uncommon to charge slaves with great treachery toward each other, but I must say I never loved, esteemed, or confided in men more than I did in these. They were as true as steel, and no band of brothers could be more loving. There were no mean advantages taken of each other, no tattling, no giving each other bad names to Mr. Freeland, and no elevating one at the expense of the other. We never undertook anything of any importance which was likely to affect each other, without mutual consultation. We were generally a unit, and moved together. Thoughts and sentiments were exchanged between us which might well have been considered incendiary had they been known by our masters. The slaveholder, were he kind or cruel, was a slaveholder still, the every-hour violator of the just and inalienable rights of man, and he was therefore every hour silently but surely whetting the knife of vengeance for his own throat. He never lisped a syllable in commendation of the fathers of this republic without inviting the sword, and asserting the right of rebellion for his own slaves.

# CHAPTER XIX.

## THE RUNAWAY PLOT.

*New Year's thoughts and meditations—Again hired by Freeland—Kindness no compensation for slavery—Incipient steps toward escape—Considerations leading thereto—Hostility to slavery—Solemn vow taken—Plan divulged to slaves—Columbian Orator again—Scheme gains favor—Danger of discovery—Skill of slaveholders—Suspicion and coercion—Hymns with double meaning—Consultation—Pass-word—Hope and fear—Ignorance of geography—Imaginary difficulties—Patrick Henry—Sandy a dreamer—Route to the north mapped out—Objections—Frauds—Passes—Anxieties—Fear of failure—Strange presentiment—Coincidence—Betrayal—Arrests—Resistance—Mrs. Freeland—Prison—Brutal jests—Passes eaten—Denial—Sandy—Dragged behind horses—Slave-traders—Alone in prison—Sent to Baltimore.*

I AM now at the beginning of the year 1836. At the opening year the mind naturally occupies itself with the mysteries of life in all its phases—the ideal, the real, and the actual. Sober people then look both ways, surveying the errors of the past and providing against the possible errors of the future. I, too, was thus exercised. I had little pleasure in retrospect, and the future prospect was not brilliant. 'Notwithstanding,' thought I, 'the many resolutions and prayers I have made in behalf of freedom, I am, this first day of the year 1836, still a slave, still wandering in the depths of a miserable bondage. My faculties and powers of body and soul are not my own, but are the property of a fellow-mortal in no sense superior to me, except that he has the physical power to compel me to be owned and controlled by him. By the combined physical force of the community I am his slave—a slave for life.' With thoughts like these I was chafed and perplexed, and they rendered me gloomy and disconsolate. The anguish of my mind cannot be written.

At the close of the year, Mr. Freeland renewed the purchase of my services of Mr. Auld for the coming year. His promptness in doing so would have been flattering to my vanity had I been ambitious to win the reputation of being a valuable slave. Even as it was, I felt a slight degree of complacency at the circumstance. It showed him to be as well pleased with me as a slave as I was with him as a master. But the kindness of the slave-master only gilded the chain. It detracted nothing from its weight or strength. The thought that men are made for other and better uses than slavery, throve best under the gentle treatment of a kind master. Its grim visage could assume no smiles able to fascinate the partially enlightened slave into a forgetfulness of his bondage, or of the desirableness of liberty.

I was not through the first month of my second year with the kind and gentlemanly Mr. Freeland before I was earnestly considering and devising plans for gaining that freedom which, when I was but a mere child, I had ascertained to be the natural and inborn right of every member of the human family. The desire for this freedom had been benumbed while I was under the brutalizing dominion of Covey, and it had been postponed and rendered inoperative by my truly pleasant Sunday-school engagements with my friends during the year at Mr. Freeland's. It had, however, never entirely subsided. I hated slavery *always*, and my desire for freedom needed only a favorable breeze to fan it to a blaze at any moment. The thought of being only a creature of the *present* and the *past* troubled me, and I longed to have a *future*— a future with hope in it. To be shut up entirely to the past and present is to the soul whose life and happiness in unceasing progress—what the prison is to the body—a blight and a mildew, a hell of horrors. The dawning of this, another year, awakened me from my temporary slumber, and roused into life my latent but long-cherished aspirations for freedom. I became not only ashamed to be contented in slavery, but ashamed to seem to be contented, and in my present favorable condition under the mild rule of Mr. Freeland, I am not sure that some kind reader will not condemn me for being over-ambitious, and greatly wanting in humility, when I say the truth, that I now drove from me all thoughts of making the best of my lot, and welcomed only such thoughts as led me away from the house of bondage. The intensity of my desire to be free, quickened by my present favorable circumstances, brought me to the determination to *act* as well as to think and speak.

Accordingly, at the beginning of this year 1836, I took upon me a solemn vow, that the year which had just now dawned upon me should not close without witnessing an earnest attempt, on my part, to gain my liberty. This vow only bound me to make good my own individual escape, but my friendship for my brother-slaves was so affectionate and confiding that I felt it my duty, as well as my pleasure, to give them an opportunity to share in my determination. Toward Henry and John Harris I felt a friendship as strong as one man can feel for another, for I could have died with and for them. To them, therefore, with suitable caution, I began to disclose my sentiments and plans, sounding them the while on the subject of running away, provided a good chance should offer. I need not say that I did my *very best* to imbue the minds of my dear friends with my own views and feelings. Thoroughly awakened now, and with a definite vow upon me, all my little reading which had any bearing on the subject of human rights was rendered available in my communications with my friends. That gem of a book, the Columbian Orator, with its eloquent orations and spicy dialogues denouncing oppression and slavery—telling what had been dared, done, and suffered by men, to obtain the inestimable boon of liberty,—was still fresh in my memory, and its nobly expressed sentiments whirled into the ranks of my speech with the aptitude of well-trained soldiers going through the drill. I here began my public speaking. I canvassed with Henry and John the subject of slavery and dashed against it the condemning brand of God's eternal justice. My fellow-servants were neither indifferent, dull nor inapt. Our feelings were more alike than our opinions. All, however, were ready to act when a feasible plan should be proposed. 'Show us how the thing is to be done,' said they, 'and all else is clear.'

We were all, except Sandy, quite clear from slaveholding priestcraft. It was in vain that we had been taught from the pulpit at St. Michaels the duty of obedience to our masters; to recognize God as the author of our enslavement; to regard running away as an offense, alike against God and man; to deem our enslavement a merciful and beneficial arrangement; to esteem our condition in this country a paradise to that from which we had been snatched in Africa; to consider our hard hands and dark color as God's displeasure, and as pointing us out as the proper subjects of slavery; that the relation of master and slave was one of reciprocal benefits and that our work was not more serviceable to our masters than our master's thinking was to us. I say it was in vain that the pulpit of St. Michaels had constantly inculcated these plausible doctrines. Nature laughed them to scorn. For my part, I had become altogether too big for my chains. Father Lawson's solemn words of what I ought to be, and what I might be in the providence of God, had not fallen dead on my soul. I was fast verging toward manhood, and the prophesies of my childhood were still unfulfilled. The thought that year after year had passed away, and that my best resolutions to run away had failed and faded and that I was still a slave, with chances for gaining my freedom diminished and still diminishing—was not a matter to be slept over easily. But here came a trouble. Such thoughts and purposes as I now cherished could not agitate the mind long without making themselves manifest to scrutinizing and unfriendly observers. I had reason to fear that my sable face might prove altogether too transparent for the safe concealment of my hazardous enterprise. Plans of great moment have leaked through stone walls, and revealed their projectors. But here was no stone wall to hide my purpose. I would have given my poor tell-tale face for the immovable countenance of an Indian, for it was far from proof against the daily searching glances of those whom I met.

It was the interest and business of slaveholders to study human nature, and the slave nature in particular, with a view to practical results; and many of them attained astonishing proficiency in this direction. They had to deal not with earth, wood, and stone, but with *men*; and by every regard they had for their own safety and prosperity they had need to know the material on which they were to work. So much intellect as that surrounding them, required watching. Their safety depended on their vigilance. Conscious of the injustice and wrong they were every hour perpetrating and knowing what they themselves would do were they the victims of such wrongs, they were constantly looking out for the first signs of the dread retribution. They watched, therefore, with skilled and practiced eyes, and learned to read, with great accuracy, the state of mind and heart of the slave, through his sable face. Unusual sobriety, apparent abstraction, sullenness, and indifference,—indeed, any mood out of the common way,—afforded ground for suspicion and inquiry. Relying upon their superior position and wisdom, they would often hector slaves into a confession by affecting to know the truth of their accusations. 'You have got the devil in you, and we'll whip him out of you,' they would say. I have often been put thus to the torture on bare suspicion. This system had its disadvantages as well as its opposite—the slave being sometimes whipped into the confession of offenses which he never committed. It will be seen that the good old rule, 'A man is to be held innocent until proved to be guilty,' did not hold good on the slave plantation. Suspicion and torture were there the approved methods of getting at the truth. It was necessary, therefore, for me to keep a watch over my deportment, lest the enemy should get the better of me. But with all our caution and studied reserve, I am not sure that Mr. Freeland did not suspect that all was not right with us. It *did* seem that he watched us more narrowly after the plan of escape had been conceived and discussed amongst us. Men seldom see themselves as others see them; and while to ourselves everything connected with our contemplated escape appeared concealed, Mr. Freeland may, with the peculiar prescience of a slaveholder, have mastered the huge thought which was disturbing our peace.

As I now look back, I am the more inclined to think that he suspected us, because, prudent as we were, I can see that we did many silly things well calculated to awaken suspicion. We were at times remarkably buoyant, singing hymns, and making joyous exclamations, almost as triumphant in their tone as if we had reached a land of freedom and safety. A keen observer might have detected in our repeated singing of

> 'O Canaan, sweet Canaan,
> I am bound for the land of Canaan,'*

something more than a hope of reaching heaven. We meant to reach the *North*, and the North was our Canaan.

> 'I thought I heard them say
> There were lions in the way;
> I don't expect to stay
>         Much longer here.
> Run to Jesus, shun the danger.
>         I don't expect to stay
>         Much longer here,'*

was a favorite air, and had a double meaning. On the lips of some it meant the expectation of speedy summons to a world of spirits; but on the lips of our company it simply meant a speedy pilgrimage to a free State, and deliverance from all the evils and dangers of slavery.

I had succeeded in winning to my scheme a company of five young men, the very flower of the neighborhood, each one of whom would have commanded one thousand dollars in the home market. At New Orleans they would have brought fifteen hundred dollars apiece, and perhaps more. Their names were as follows: Henry Harris, John Harris, Sandy Jenkins, Charles Roberts, and Henry Bailey. I was the youngest but one of the party. I had, however, the advantage of them all in experience, and in a knowledge of letters. This gave me a great influence over them. Perhaps not one of them, left to himself, would have dreamed of escape as a possible thing. They all wanted to be free, but the serious thought of running away had not entered into their minds until I won them to the undertaking. They were all tolerably well off—for slaves—and had dim hopes of being set free some day by their masters. If any one is to blame for disturbing the quiet of the slaves and slave-masters of the neighborhood of St. Michaels, I AM THE MAN. I claim to be the instigator of the high crime (as the slaveholders regarded it), and I kept life in it till life could be kept in it no longer.

Pending the time of our contemplated departure out of our Egypt, we met often by night, and on every Sunday. At these meetings we talked the matter over, told our hopes and fears, and the difficulties discovered or imagined; and, like men of sense, counted the cost of the enterprise to which we were committing ourselves. These meetings must have resembled, on a small scale, the meetings of the revolutionary conspirators in their primary condition. We were plotting against our (so-called) lawful rulers, with this difference—we sought our own good, and not the harm of our enemies. We did not seek to overthrow them, but to escape from them. As for Mr. Freeland, we all liked him, and would gladly have remained with him *as free men*. *Liberty* was our aim, and we had now come to think that we had a right to it against every obstacle, even against the lives of our enslavers.

We had several words, expressive of things important to us, which we understood, but which, even if distinctly heard by an outsider, would have conveyed no certain meaning. I hated this secrecy, but where slavery was powerful, and liberty weak, the latter was driven to concealment or destruction.

The prospect was not always bright. At times we were almost tempted to abandon the enterprise, and to try to get back to that comparative peace of mind which even a man under the gallows might feel when all hope of escape had vanished. We were, at times, confident, bold and determined, and again, doubting, timid and wavering; whistling, as did the boy in the grave-yard to keep away the spirits.

To look at the map and observe the proximity of Eastern shore, Maryland, to Delaware and Pennsylvania, it may seem to the reader quite absurd to regard the proposed escape as a formidable undertaking. But to *understand*, some one has said, a man must *stand under*. The real distance was great enough, but the imagined distance was, to our ignorance, much greater. Slaveholders sought to impress their slaves with a belief in the boundlessness of slave territory, and of their own limitless power. Our notions of the geography of the country were very vague and indistinct. The distance, however, was not the chief trouble, for the nearer were the lines of a slave state to the borders of a free state the greater was the trouble. Hired kidnappers infested the borders. Then, too, we knew that merely reaching a free state did not free us, that wherever caught we could be returned to slavery. We knew of no spot this side the ocean where we could be safe. We had heard of Canada, then the only real Canaan of the American bondman, simply as a country to which the wild goose and the swan repaired at the end of winter to escape the heat of summer, but not as the home of man. I knew something of theology, but nothing of geography. I really did not know that there was a State of New York, or a State of Massachusetts. I had heard of Pennsylvania, Delaware, and New Jersey, and all the Southern States, but was utterly ignorant of the free States. New York City was our northern limit, and to go there and to be forever harassed with the liability of being hunted down and returned to slavery, with the certainty of being treated ten times worse than ever before, was a prospect which might well cause some hesitation. The case sometimes, to our excited visions, stood thus: At every gate through which we had to pass we saw a watchman; at every ferry a guard; on every bridge a sentinel, and in every wood a patrol or slave-hunter. We were hemmed in on every side. The good to be sought and the evil to be shunned were flung in the balance and weighed against each other. On the one hand stood slavery, a stern reality glaring frightfully upon us, with the blood of millions in its polluted skirts, terrible to behold, greedily devouring our hard earnings and feeding upon our flesh. This was the evil from which to escape. On the other hand, far away, back in the hazy distance where all forms seemed but shadows under the flickering light of the north star, behind some craggy hill or snow-capped mountain, stood a doubtful freedom, half frozen, and beckoning us to her icy domain. This was the good to be sought. The inequality was as great as that between certainty and uncertainty. This in itself was enough to stagger us; but when we came to survey the untrodden road and conjecture the many possible difficulties, we were appalled, and at times, as I have said, were upon the point of giving over the struggle altogether. The reader can have little idea of the phantoms which would flit, in such circumstances, before the uneducated mind of the slave. Upon either side we saw grim death, assuming a variety of horrid shapes. Now it was starvation, causing us, in a strange and friendless land, to eat our own flesh. Now we were contending with the waves and were drowned. Now we were hunted by dogs and overtaken, and torn to pieces by their merciless fangs. We were stung by scorpions, chased by wild beasts, bitten by snakes, and, worst of all, after having succeeded in swimming rivers, encountering wild beasts, sleeping in the woods, and suffering hunger, cold, heat and nakedness, were overtaken by hired kidnappers, who, in the name of law and for the thrice-cursed reward, would, perchance, fire upon us, kill some, wound others and capture all. This dark picture, drawn by ignorance and fear, at times greatly shook our determination, and not unfrequently caused us to

'Rather bear the ills we had,
Than flee to others which we knew not of.'*

I am not disposed to magnify this circumstance in my experience, and yet I think that, to the reader, I shall seem to be so disposed. But no man can tell the intense agony which was felt by the slave when wavering on the point of making his escape. All that he has is at stake, and even that which he has not is at stake also. The life which he has may be lost and the liberty which he seeks may not be gained.

Patrick Henry,* to a listening senate which was thrilled by his magic eloquence and ready to stand by him in his boldest flights, could say, 'Give me liberty or give me death;'* and this saying was a sublime one, even for a freeman; but incomparably more sublime is the same sentiment when *practically* asserted by men accustomed to the lash and chain, men whose sensibilities must have become more or less deadened by their bondage. With us it was a doubtful liberty, at best, that we sought, and a certain lingering death in the rice-swamps and sugar-fields if we failed. Life is not lightly regarded by men of sane minds. It is precious both to the pauper and to the prince, to the slave and to his master; and yet I believe there was not one among us who would not rather have been shot down than pass away life in hopeless bondage.

In the progress of our preparations Sandy (the root man) became troubled. He began to have distressing dreams. One of these, which happened on a Friday night, was to him of great significance, and I am quite ready to confess that I myself felt somewhat damped by it. He said: 'I dreamed last night that I was roused from sleep by strange noises, like the noises of a swarm of angry birds that caused as they passed, a roar which fell upon my ear like a coming gale over the tops of the trees. Looking up to see what it could mean, I saw you, Frederick, in the claws of a huge bird, surrounded by a large number of birds of all colors and sizes. These were all pecking at you, while you, with your arms, seemed to be trying to protect your eyes. Passing over me, the birds flew in a southwesterly direction, and I watched them until they were clean out of sight. Now I saw this as plainly as I now see you; and furder, honey, watch de Friday night dream; dere is sumpon in it shose you born; dere is indeed, honey.' I did not like the dream, but I showed no concern, attributing it to the general excitement and perturbation consequent upon our contemplated plan to escape. I could not, however, at once shake off its effect. I felt that it boded no good. Sandy was unusually emphatic and oracular and his manner had much to do with the impression made upon me.

The plan for our escape, which I recommended and to which my comrades consented, was to take a large canoe owned by Mr. Hamilton, and on the Saturday night previous to the Easter holidays launch out into the Chesapeake bay and paddle with all our might for its head, a distance of seventy miles. On reaching this point we were to turn the canoe adrift and bend our steps toward the north-star till we reached a free state.

There were several objections to this plan. In rough weather the waters of the Chesapeake are much agitated, and there would be danger, in a canoe, of being swamped by the waves. Another objection was that the canoe would soon be missed, the absent slaves would at once be suspected of having taken it, and we should be pursued by some of the fast-sailing craft out of St. Michaels. Then again, if we reached the head of the bay and turned the canoe adrift, she might prove a guide to our track and bring the hunters after us.

These and other objections were set aside by the stronger ones, which could be urged against every other plan that could then be suggested. On the water we had a chance of being regarded as fishermen, in the service of a master. On the other hand, by taking the land route, through the counties adjoining Delaware, we should be subjected to all manner of interruptions, and many disagreeable questions, which might give us serious trouble. Any white man, if he pleased, was authorized to stop a man of color on any road, and examine and arrest him. By this arrangement many abuses (considered such even by slaveholders) occurred. Cases have been known where freemen, being called upon by a pack of ruffians to show their free papers, have presented them, when the ruffians have torn them up, seized the victim and sold him to a life of endless bondage.

The week before our intended start, I wrote a pass for each of our party, giving him permission to visit Baltimore during the Easter holidays. The pass ran after this manner:

'This is to certify that I, the undersigned, have given the bearer, my servant John, full liberty to go to Baltimore to spend the Easter holidays.                                                                    W. H.

NEAR ST. MICHAELS, Talbot Co., Md.'

Although we were not going to Baltimore, and were intending to land east of North Point, in the direction I had seen the Philadelphia steamers go, these passes might be useful to us in the lower part of the bay, while steering towards Baltimore. These were not, however, to be shown by us until all our answers had failed to satisfy the inquirer. We were all fully alive to the importance of being calm and self-possessed when accosted, if accosted we should be; and we more than once rehearsed to each other how we should behave in the hour of trial.

Those were long, tedious days and nights. The suspense was painful in the extreme. To balance probabilities, where life and liberty hang on the result, requires steady nerves. I panted for action, and was glad when the day, at the close of which we were to start, dawned upon us. Sleeping, the night before, was out of the question. I probably felt more deeply than any of my companions, because I was the instigator of the movement. The responsibility of the whole enterprise rested upon my shoulders. The glory of success and the shame and confusion of failure, could not be matters of indifference to me. Our food was prepared, our clothes were packed; we were already to go, and impatient for Saturday morning—considering *that* the last of our bondage.

I cannot describe the tempest and tumult of my brain that morning. The reader will please bear in mind that in a slave State an unsuccessful runaway was not only subjected to cruel torture, and sold away to the far South, but he was frequently execrated by the other slaves. He was charged with making the condition of the other slaves intolerable by laying them all under the suspicion of their masters—subjecting them to greater vigilance, and imposing greater limitations on their privileges. I dreaded murmurs from this quarter. It was difficult, too, for a slave-master to believe that slaves escaping had not been aided in their flight by some one of their fellow-slaves. When, therefore, a slave was missing, every slave on the place was closely examined as to his knowledge of the undertaking.

Our anxiety grew more and more intense, as the time of our intended departure drew nigh. It was truly felt to be a matter of life and death with us, and we fully intended to *fight*, as well as *run*, if necessity should occur for that extremity. But the trial-hour had not yet come. It was easy to resolve, but not so easy to act. I expected there might be some drawing back at the last; it was natural there should be; therefore, during the intervening time, I lost no opportunity to explain away difficulties, remove doubts, dispel fears, and inspire all with firmness. It was too late to look back, and now was the time to go forward. I appealed to the pride of my comrades by telling them that if, after having solemnly promised to go, as they had done, they now failed to make the attempt, they would in effect brand themselves with cowardice, and might well sit down, fold their arms, and acknowledge themselves fit only to be slaves. This detestable character all were unwilling to assume. Every man except Sandy (he, much to our regret, withdrew) stood firm, and at our last meeting we pledged ourselves afresh, and in the most solemn manner, that at the time appointed we *would* certainly start on our long journey for a free country. This meeting was in the middle of the week, at the end of which we were to start.

Early on the appointed morning we went as usual to the field, but with hearts that beat quickly and anxiously. Any one intimately acquainted with us might have seen that all was not well with us, and that some monster lingered in our thoughts. Our work that morning was the same that it had been for several days past—drawing out and spreading manure. While thus engaged, I had a sudden presentiment, which flashed upon me like lightning in a dark night, revealing to the lonely traveler the gulf before and the enemy behind. I instantly turned to Sandy Jenkins, who was near me, and said: '*Sandy, we are betrayed!*—something has just told me so.' I felt as sure of it as if the officers were in sight. Sandy said: 'Man, dat is strange; but I feel just as you do.' If my mother—then long in her grave—had appeared before me and told me that we were betrayed, I could not at that moment have felt more certain of the fact.

In a few minutes after this, the long, low, and distant notes of the horn summoned us from the field to breakfast. I felt as one may be supposed to feel before being led forth to be executed for some great offense. I wanted no breakfast, but for form's sake I went with the other slaves toward the house. My feelings were not disturbed as to the right of running away; on that point I had no misgiving whatever, but from a sense of the consequences of failure.

In thirty minutes after that vivid impression came the apprehended crash. On reaching the house, and glancing my eye toward the lane gate, the worst was at once made known. The lane gate to Mr. Freeland's house was nearly half a mile from the door, and much shaded by the heavy wood which bordered the main road. I was, however, able to descry four white men and two colored men approaching. The white men were on horseback, and the colored men were walking behind, and seemed to be tied. '*It is indeed all over with us; we are surely betrayed,*' I thought to myself. I became composed, or at least comparatively so, and calmly awaited the result. I watched the ill-omened company entering the gate. Successful flight was impossible, and I made up my mind to stand and meet the evil, whatever it might be, for I was not altogether without a slight hope that things might turn differently from what I had at first feared. In a few moments in came Mr. William Hamilton, riding very rapidly and evidently much excited. He was in the habit of riding very slowly, and was seldom known to gallop his horse. This time his horse was nearly at full speed, causing the dust to roll thick behind him. Mr. Hamilton, though one of the most resolute men in the whole neighborhood, was, nevertheless, a remarkably mild-spoken man, and even when greatly excited his language was cool and circumspect. He came to the door, and inquired if Mr. Freeland was in. I told him that Mr. Freeland was at the barn. Off the old gentleman rode toward the barn, with unwonted speed. In a few moments Mr. Hamilton and Mr. Freeland came down from the barn to the house, and just as they made their appearance in the front-yard, three men, who proved to be constables, came dashing into the lane on horse-back, as if summoned by a sign requiring quick work. A few seconds brought them into the front-yard, where they hastily dismounted and tied their horses. This done, they joined Mr. Freeland and Mr. Hamilton, who were standing a short distance from the kitchen. A few moments were spent as if in consulting how to proceed, and then the whole party walked up to the kitchen-door. There was now no one in the kitchen but myself and John Harris; Henry and Sandy were yet in the barn. Mr. Freeland came inside the kitchen-door, and, with an agitated voice, called me by name, and told me to come forward; that there were some gentlemen who wished to see me. I stepped toward them at the door, and asked what they wanted; when the constables grabbed me, and told me that I had better not resist; that I had been in a scrape, or was said to have been in one; that they were merely going to take me where I could be examined; that they would have me brought before my master at St. Michaels, and if the evidence against me was not proved true I should be acquitted. I was now firmly tied, and completely at the mercy of my captors. Resistance was idle. They were five in number and armed to the teeth. When they had secured me, they turned to John Harris and in a few moments succeeded in tying him as firmly as they had tied me. They next turned toward Henry Harris, who had now returned from the barn. 'Cross your hands,' said the constable to Henry. 'I won't,' said Henry, in a voice so firm and clear, and in a manner so determined, as for a moment to arrest all proceedings. 'Won't you cross your hands?' said Tom Graham, the constable. '*No, I won't,*' said Henry, with increasing emphasis. Mr. Hamilton, Mr. Freeland, and the officers now came near to Henry. Two of the constables drew out their shining pistols, and swore, by the name of God, that he should cross his hands or they would shoot him down. Each of these hired ruffians now cocked his pistol, and, with fingers apparently on the triggers, presented his deadly weapon to the breast of the unarmed slave, saying, that if he did not cross his hands, he would 'blow his d———d heart out of him.' '*Shoot me, shoot me,*' said Henry; 'you can't kill me but once. *Shoot, shoot*, and be damned! I won't be tied!' This the brave fellow said in a voice as defiant and heroic in its tone as was the language itself; and at the moment of saying it, with the pistols at his very breast, he quickly raised his arms and dashed them from the puny hands of his assassins, the weapons flying in all directions. Now came the struggle. All hands rushed upon the brave fellow and after beating him for some time succeeded in overpowering and tying him. Henry put me to shame; he fought, and fought bravely. John and I had made no resistance. The fact is, I never saw much use of fighting where there was no reasonable probability of whipping anybody. Yet there was something almost providential in the resistance made by Henry. But for that resistance every soul of us would have been hurried off to the far South. Just a moment previous to the trouble with Henry, Mr. Hamilton *mildly* said,—and this gave me the unmistakable clue to the cause of our arrest,—'Perhaps we had now better make a search for those protections, which we understand Frederick has written for himself and the rest.' Had these passes been found, they would have been point-blank evidence against us, and would have confirmed all the statements of our betrayer. Thanks to the resistance of Henry, the excitement produced by the scuffle drew all attention in that direction, and I succeeded in flinging my pass, unobserved, into the fire. The confusion attendant on the scuffle, and the apprehension of still further trouble, perhaps, led our captors to forego, for the time, any search for '*those protections* which Frederick was said to have written for his companions'; so we were not yet convicted of the purpose to run away, and it was evident that there was some doubt on the part of all whether we had been guilty of such purpose.

Just as we were all completely tied, and about ready to start toward St. Michaels, and thence to jail, Mrs. Betsey Freeland (mother to William, who was much attached, after the Southern fashion, to Henry and John, they having been reared from childhood in her house) came to the kitchen-door with her hands full of biscuits, for we had not had our breakfast that morning, and divided them between Henry and John. This done, the lady made the following parting address to me, pointing her bony finger at me: 'You devil! you yellow devil! It was you who put it into the heads of Henry and John to run away. But for *you, you long-legged, yellow devil*, Henry and John would never have thought of running away.' I gave the lady a look which called forth from her a scream of mingled wrath and terror, as she slammed the kitchen-door and went in, leaving, me, with the rest, in hands as harsh as her own broken voice.

Could the kind reader have been riding along the main road to or from Easton that morning, his eye would have met a painful sight. He would have seen five young men, guilty of no crime save that of preferring *liberty* to *slavery*, drawn along the public highway—firmly bound together, tramping through dust and heat, bare-footed and bare-headed—fastened to three strong horses, whose riders were armed with pistols and daggers, and on their way to prison like felons, and suffering every possible insult from the crowds of idle, vulgar people who clustered round, and heartlessly made their failure to escape the occasion for all manner of ribaldry and sport. As I looked upon this crowd of vile persons, and saw myself and friends thus assailed and persecuted, I could not help seeing the fulfillment of Sandy's dream. I was in the hands of moral vultures, and held in their sharp talons, and was being hurried away toward Easton, in a south-easterly direction, amid the jeers of new birds of the same feather, through every neighborhood we passed. It seemed to me that everybody was out, and knew the cause of our arrest, and awaited our passing in order to feast their vindictive eyes on our misery.

Some said '*I ought to be hanged*,' and others, '*I ought to be burned*'; others, I ought to have the 'hide' taken off my back; while no one gave us a kind word or sympathizing look, except the poor slaves who were lifting their heavy hoes, and who cautiously glanced at us through the post-and-rail fences, behind which they were at work. Our sufferings that morning can be more easily imagined than described. Our hopes were all blasted at one blow. The cruel injustice, the victorious crime, and the helplessness of innocence, led me to ask in my ignorance and weakness: Where is now the God of justice and mercy? and why have these wicked men the power thus to trample upon our rights, and to insult our feelings? and yet in the next moment came the consoling thought, 'the day of the oppressor will come at last.' Of one thing I could be glad: not one of my dear friends upon whom I had brought this great calamity, reproached me, either by word or look, for having led them into it. We were a band of brothers, and never dearer to each other than now. The thought which gave us the most pain was the probable separation which would now take place in case we were sold off to the far South, as we were likely to be. While the constables were looking forward, Henry and I being fastened together, could occasionally exchange a word without being observed by the kidnappers who had us in charge. 'What shall I do with my pass?' said Henry. 'Eat it with your biscuit,' said I; 'it won't do to tear it up.' We were now near St. Michaels. The direction concerning the passes was passed around, and executed.

'Own nothing,' said I. 'Own nothing' was passed round, enjoined, and assented to. Our confidence in each other was unshaken, and we were quite resolved to succeed or fail together; as much after the calamity which had befallen us as before.

On reaching St. Michaels we underwent a sort of examination at my master's store, and it was evident to my mind that Master Thomas suspected the truthfulness of the evidence upon which they had acted in arresting us, and that he only affected, to some extent, the positiveness with which he asserted our guilt. There was nothing said by any of our company which could, in any manner, prejudice our cause, and there was hope yet that we should be able to return to our homes, if for nothing else, at least to find out the guilty man or woman who betrayed us.

To this end we all denied that we had been guilty of intended flight. Master Thomas said that the evidence he had of our intention to run away was strong enough to hang us in a case of murder. 'But,' said I, 'the cases are not equal; if murder were committed,—the thing is done! but we have not run away. Where is the evidence against us? We were quietly at our work.' I talked thus with unusual freedom, in order to bring out the evidence against us, for we all wanted, above all things, to know who had betrayed us, that we might have something tangible on which to pour our execrations. From something which dropped, in the course of the talk, it appeared that there was but one witness against us, and that that witness could not be produced. Master Thomas would not tell us who his informant was, but we suspected, and suspected one person only. Several circumstances seemed to point Sandy out as our betrayer. His entire knowledge of our plans, his participation in them, his withdrawal from us, his dream and his simultaneous presentiment that we were betrayed, the taking us and the leaving him, were calculated to turn suspicion toward him, and yet we could not suspect him. We all loved him too well to think it possible that he could have betrayed us. So we rolled the guilt on other shoulders.

We were literally dragged, that morning, behind horses, a distance of fifteen miles, and placed in the Easton jail. We were glad to reach the end of our journey, for our pathway had been full of insult and mortification. Such is the power of public opinion, that it is hard, even for the innocent, to feel the happy consolation of innocence when they fall under the maledictions of this power. How could we regard ourselves as in the right, when all about us denounced us as criminals, and had the power and the disposition to treat us as such.

In jail we were placed under the care of Mr. Joseph Graham, the sheriff of the county. Henry and John and myself were placed in one room, and Henry Bailey and Charles Roberts in another by themselves. This separation was intended to deprive us of the advantage of concert, and to prevent trouble in jail.

Once shut up, a new set of tormentors came upon us. A swarm of imps in human shape—the slave-traders and agents of slave-traders—who gathered in every country town of the State watching for chances to buy human flesh (as buzzards watch for carrion), flocked in upon us to ascertain if our masters had placed us in jail to be sold. Such a set of debased and villainous creatures I never saw before and hope never to see again. I felt as if surrounded by a pack of *fiends* fresh from *perdition*. They laughed, leered, and grinned at us, saying, 'Ah, boys, we have got you, haven't we? So you were going to make your escape? Where were you going to?' After taunting us in this way as long as they liked, they one by one subjected us to an examination, with a view to ascertain our value, feeling our arms and legs and shaking us by the shoulders, to see if we were sound and healthy, impudently asking us, 'how we would like to have them for masters?' To such questions we were quite dumb (much to their annoyance). One fellow told me, 'if he had me he would cut the devil out of me pretty quick.'

These negro-buyers were very offensive to the genteel southern Christian public. They were looked upon in respectable Maryland society as necessary but detestable characters. As a class, they were hardened ruffians, made such by nature and by occupation. Yes, they were the legitimate fruit of slavery, and were second in villainy only to the slaveholders themselves who made such a class *possible*. They were mere hucksters of the slave produce of Maryland and Virginia—coarse, cruel, and swaggering bullies, whose very breathing was of blasphemy and blood.

Aside from these slave-buyers who infested the prison from time to time, our quarters were much more comfortable than we had any right to expect them to be. Our allowance of food was small and coarse, but our room was the best in the jail—neat and spacious, and with nothing about it necessarily reminding us of being in prison but its heavy locks and bolts and the black iron lattice-work at the windows. We were prisoners of state compared with most slaves who were put into that Easton jail. But the place was not one of contentment. Bolts, bars, and grated windows are not acceptable to freedom-loving people of any color. The suspense, too, was painful. Every step on the stairway was listened to, in the hope that the comer would cast a ray of light on our fate. We would have given the hair of our heads for half a dozen words with one of the waiters in Sol. Lowe's hotel. Such waiters were in the way of hearing, at the table, the probable course of things. We could see them flitting about in their white jackets in front of this hotel, but could speak to none of them.

Soon after the holidays were over, contrary to all our expectations, Messrs. Hamilton and Freeland came up to Easton; not to make a bargain with 'Georgia traders,' nor to send us up to Austin Woldfolk, as was usual in the case of runaway-slaves, but to release, from prison, Charles, Henry Harris, Henry Bailey and John Harris, and this, too, without the infliction of a single blow. I was left alone in prison. The innocent had been taken and the guilty left. My friends were separated from me, and apparently forever. This circumstance caused me more pain than any other incident connected with our capture and imprisonment. Thirty-nine lashes on my naked and bleeding back would have been joyfully borne, in preference to this separation from these, the friends of my youth. And yet I could not but feel that I was the victim of something like justice. Why should these young men, who were led into this scheme by me, suffer as much as the instigator? I felt glad that they were released from prison, and from the dread prospect of a life (or death I should rather say) in the rice-swamps. It is due to the noble Henry to say that he was almost as reluctant to leave the prison with me in it as he had been to be tied and dragged to prison. But he and we all knew that we should, in all the likelihoods of the case, be separated, in the event of being sold; and since we were completely in the hands of our owners they concluded it would be best to go peaceably home.

Not until this last separation, dear reader, had I touched those profounder depths of desolation which it is the lot of slaves often to reach. I was solitary and alone within the walls of a stone prison, left to a fate of life-long misery. I had hoped and expected much, for months before, but my hopes and expectations were now withered and blasted. The ever-dreaded slave life in Georgia, Louisiana, and Alabama—from which escape was next to impossible—now in my loneliness stared me in the face. The possibility of ever becoming anything but an abject slave, a mere machine in the hands of an owner, had now fled, and it seemed to me it had fled forever. A life of living death, beset with the innumerable horrors of the cotton-field and the sugar-plantation, seemed to be my doom. The fiends who rushed into the prison when we were first put there continued to visit me and ply me with questions and tantalizing remarks. I was insulted, but helpless; keenly alive to the demands of justice and liberty, but with no means of asserting them. To talk to those imps about justice or mercy would have been as absurd as to reason with bears and tigers. Lead and steel were the only arguments that they were capable of appreciating, as the events of the subsequent years have proved.

After remaining in this life of misery and despair about a week, which seemed a month, Master Thomas, very much to my surprise and greatly to my relief, came to the prison and took me out, for the purpose, as he said, of sending me to Alabama with a friend of his, who would emancipate me at the end of eight years. I was glad enough to get out of prison, but I had no faith in the story that his friend would emancipate me. Besides, I had never heard of his having a friend in Alabama, and I took the announcement simply as an easy and comfortable method of shipping me off to the far south. There was a little scandal, too, connected with the idea of one Christian selling another to Georgia traders, while it was deemed every way proper for them to sell to others. I thought this friend in Alabama was an invention to meet this difficulty, for Master Thomas was quite jealous of his religious reputation, however unconcerned he might have been about his real Christian character. In these remarks it is possible I do him injustice. He certainly did not exert his power over me as in the case he might have done, but acted, upon the whole, very generously, considering the nature of my offense. He had the power and the provocation to send me, without reserve, into the very Everglades of Florida, beyond the remotest hope of emancipation; and his refusal to exercise that power must be set down to his credit.

After lingering about St. Michaels a few days, and no friend from Alabama appearing, Master Thomas decided to send me back again to Baltimore, to live with his brother Hugh, with whom he was now at peace. Possibly he became so by his profession of religion at the camp-meeting in the Bay-side. Master Thomas told me that he wished me to go to Baltimore and learn a trade; and that if I behaved myself properly he would *emancipate me at twenty-five*. Thanks for this one beam of hope in the future! The promise had but one fault—it seemed too good to be true.

# CHAPTER XX.

## APPRENTICESHIP LIFE.

*Nothing lost in my attempt to run away—Comrades at home—Reasons for sending me away—Return to Baltimore—Tommy changed—Caulking in Gardiner's ship-yard—Desperate fight—Its causes—Conflict between white and black labor—Outrage—Testimony—Master Hugh—Slavery in Baltimore—My condition improves—New associations—Slaveholder's right to the slave's wages—How to make a discontented slave.*

WELL, dear reader, I am not, as you have probably inferred, a loser by the general upstir described in the foregoing chapter. The little domestic revolution, notwithstanding the sudden snub it got by the treachery of somebody, did not, after all, end so disastrously as when in the iron cage at Easton I conceived it would. The prospect from that point did look about as dark as any that ever cast its gloom over the vision of the anxious, out-looking human spirit. 'All's well that ends well!' My affectionate friends, Henry and John Harris, are still with Mr. Freeland. Charles Roberts and Henry Bailey are safe at their homes. I have not, therefore, anything to regret on their account. Their masters have mercifully forgiven them, probably on the ground suggested in the spirited little speech of Mrs. Freeland, made to me just before leaving for the jail. My friends had nothing to regret, either: for while they were watched more closely, they were doubtless treated more kindly than before, and got new assurances that they should some day be legally emancipated, provided their behavior from that time forward should make them deserving. Not a blow was struck any one of them. As for Master Freeland, good soul, he did not believe we were intending to run away at all. Having given—as he thought—no occasion to his boys to leave him, he could not think it probable that they had entertained a design so grievous. This, however, was not the view taken of the matter by 'Mas' Billy,' as we used to call the soft-spoken but crafty and resolute Mr. William Hamilton. He had no doubt that the crime had been meditated, and regarding me as the instigator of it, he frankly told Master Thomas that he must remove me from that neighborhood or he would shoot me. He would not have one so dangerous as 'Frederick' tampering with his slaves. William Hamilton was not a man whose threat might be safely disregarded. I have no doubt that, had his warning been disregarded, he would have proved as good as his word. He was furious at the thought of such a piece of high-handed *theft* as we were about to perpetrate—the stealing of our own bodies and souls. The feasibility of the plan, too, could the first steps have been taken, was marvelously plain. Besides, this was a *new* idea, this use of the Bay. Slaves escaping, until now, had taken to the woods; they had never dreamed of profaning and abusing the waters of the noble Chesapeake by making them the highway from slavery to freedom. Here was a broad road leading to the destruction of slavery, which had hitherto been looked upon as a wall of security by the slaveholders. But Master Billy could not get Mr. Freeland to see matters precisely as he did, nor could he get Master Thomas, excited as he was, to so see them. The latter, I must say it to his credit, showed much humane feeling, and atoned for much that had been harsh, cruel, and unreasonable in his former treatment of me and of others. My 'Cousin Tom' told me that while I was in jail Master Thomas was very unhappy, and that the night before his going up to release me he had walked the floor nearly all night, evincing great distress; that very tempting offers had been made to him by the negro-traders, but he had rejected them all, saying that *money could not tempt him to sell me to the far south.* I can easily believe all this, for he seemed quite reluctant to send me away at all. He told me that he only consented to do so because of the very strong prejudice against me in the neighborhood, and that he feared for my safety if I remained there.

Thus, after three years spent in the country, roughing it in the field, and experiencing all sorts of hardships, I was again permitted to return to Baltimore, the very place of all others, short of a free State, where I most desired to live. The three years spent in the country had made some difference in me, and in the household of Master Hugh. 'Little Tommy' was no longer little Tommy, and I was not the slender lad who had left the Eastern Shore just three years before. The loving relations between Master Tommy and myself were broken up. He was no longer dependent on me for protection, but felt himself a *man*, and had other and more suitable associates. In childhood he had considered me scarcely inferior to himself,—certainly quite as good as any other boy with whom he played; but the time had come when his *friend* must be his slave. So we were cold to each other, and parted. It was a sad thing to me, that, loving each other as we had done, we must now take different roads. To him a thousand avenues were open. Education had made him acquainted with all the treasures of the world and liberty had flung open the gates thereunto; but I who had attended him seven years; who had watched over him with the care of a big brother, fighting his battles in the street and shielding him from harm to an extent which induced his mother to say, 'Oh, Tommy is always safe when he is with Freddy'— I must be confined to a single condition. He had grown and become a *man*: I, though grown to the stature of manhood, must all my life remain a minor—a mere boy. Thomas Auld, junior, obtained a situation on board the brig Tweed, and went to sea. I have since heard of his death.

There were few persons to whom I was more sincerely attached than to him.

Very soon after I went to Baltimore to live, Master Hugh succeeded in getting me hired to Mr. William Gardiner, an extensive ship-builder on Fell's Point. I was placed there to learn to calk, a trade of which I already had some knowledge, gained while in Mr. Hugh Auld's ship-yard. Gardiner's, however, proved a very unfavorable place for the accomplishment of the desired object. Mr. Gardiner was that season engaged in building two large man-of-war vessels, professedly for the Mexican government. These vessels were to be launched in the month of July of that year, and in failure thereof Mr. Gardiner would forfeit a very considerable sum of money. So, when I entered the ship-yard, all was hurry and driving. There were in the yard about one hundred men; of these, seventy or eighty were regular carpenters—privileged men. There was no time for a raw hand to learn anything. Every man had to do that which he knew how to do, and in entering the yard Mr. Gardiner had directed me to do whatever the carpenters told me to do. This was placing me at the beck and call of about seventy-five men. I was to regard all these as my masters. Their word was to be my law. My situation was a trying one. I was called a dozen ways in the space of a single minute. I needed a dozen pairs of hands. Three or four voices would strike my car ear at the same moment. It was 'Fred, come help me to cant this timber here,'—'Fred, come carry this timber yonder,'—'Fred, bring that roller here,'—'Fred, go get a fresh can of water,'—'Fred, come help saw off the end of this timber,'—'Fred, go quick and get the crow-bar,'—'Fred, hold on the end of this fall,'—'Fred, go to the blacksmith's shop and get a new punch,'—'Halloo, Fred! run and bring me a cold-chisel,'—'I say, Fred, bear a hand, and get up a fire under the steam-box as quick as lightning,'—'Hullo, nigger! come turn this grindstone,'—'Come, come; move, move! and *bowse*\* this timber forward,'—'I say, darkey, blast your eyes! why don't you heat up some pitch?'—'Halloo! halloo! halloo! (three voices at the same time)'—'Come here; go there; hold on where you are. D—n you, if you move I'll knock your brains out!' Such, my dear reader, is a glance at the school which was mine during the first eight months of my stay at Gardiner's ship-yard. At the end of eight months Master Hugh refused longer to allow me to remain with Gardiner. The circumstance which led to this refusal was the committing of an outrage upon me, by the white apprentices of the ship-yard. The fight was a desperate one, and I came out of it shockingly mangled. I was cut and bruised in sundry places, and my left eye was nearly knocked out of its socket. The facts which led to this brutal outrage upon me illustrate a phase of slavery which was destined to become an important element in the overthrow of the slave system, and I may therefore state them with some minuteness. That phase was this—the conflict of slavery with the interests of white mechanics and laborers. In the country this conflict was not so apparent; but in cities, such as Baltimore, Richmond, New Orleans, Mobile, etc., it was seen pretty clearly. The slaveholders, with a craftiness peculiar to themselves, by encouraging the enmity of the poor laboring white man against the blacks, succeeded in making the said white man almost as much a slave as the black slave himself. The difference between the white slave and the black slave was this: the latter belonged to one slave-holder, while the former belonged to the slaveholders collectively. The white slave had taken from him by indirection what the black slave had taken from him directly and without ceremony. Both were plundered, and by the same plunderers. The slave was robbed by his master of all his earnings, above what was required for his bare physical necessities, and the white laboring man was robbed by the slave system of the just results of his labor, because he was flung into competition with a class of laborers who worked without wages. The slaveholders blinded them to this competition by keeping alive their prejudice against the slaves as *men*—not against them as *slaves*. They appealed to their pride, often denouncing emancipation as tending to place the white working man on an equality with negroes, and by this means they succeeded in drawing off the minds of the poor whites from the real fact, that by the rich slave master they were already regarded as but a single remove from equality with the slave. The impression was cunningly made that slavery was the only power that could prevent the laboring white man from falling to the level of the slave's poverty and degradation. To make this enmity deep and broad between the slave and the poor white man, the latter was allowed to abuse and whip the former without hindrance. But, as I have said, this state of affairs prevailed *mostly* in the country. In the city of Baltimore there were not unfrequent murmurs that educating slaves to be mechanics might, in the end, give slave-masters power to dispense altogether with the services of the poor white man. But with characteristic dread of offending the slaveholders, these poor white mechanics in Mr. Gardiner's ship-yard, instead of applying the natural, honest remedy for the apprehended evil, and objecting at once to work there by the side of slaves, made a cowardly attack upon the free colored mechanics, saying they were eating the bread which should be eaten by American freemen, and swearing that they, the mechanics, would not work with them. The feeling was *really* against having their labor brought into competition with that of the colored freeman, and aimed to prevent him from serving himself, in the evening of life, with the trade with which he had served his master, during the more vigorous portion of his days. Had they succeeded in driving the black freemen out of the ship-yard, they would have determined also upon the removal of the black slaves. The feeling was, about this time, very bitter toward all colored people in Baltimore (1836), and they—free and slave—suffered all manner of insult and wrong.

Until a very little while before I went there, white and black carpenters worked side by side in the shipyards of Mr. Gardiner, Mr. Duncan, Mr. Walter Price and Mr. Robb. Nobody seemed to see any impropriety in it. Some of the blacks were first-rate workmen and were given jobs requiring the highest skill. All at once, however, the white carpenters swore that they would no longer work on the same stage with negroes. Taking advantage of the heavy contract resting upon Mr. Gardiner to have the vessels for Mexico ready to launch in July, and of the difficulty of getting other hands at that season of the year, they swore that they would not strike another blow for him unless he would discharge his free colored workmen. Now, although this movement did not extend to me *in form*, it did reach me in *fact*. The spirit which it awakened was one of malice and bitterness toward colored people *generally*, and I suffered with the rest, and suffered severely. My fellow-apprentices very soon began to feel it to be degrading to work with me. They began to put on high looks and to talk contemptuously and maliciously of 'the niggers,' saying that they would take the 'country,' and that they 'ought to be killed.' Encouraged by workmen who, knowing me to be a slave, made no issue with Mr. Gardiner about my being there, these young men did their utmost to make it impossible for me to stay. They seldom called me to do anything without coupling the call with a curse, and Edward North, the biggest in everything, rascality included, ventured to strike me, whereupon I picked him up and threw him into the dock. Whenever any of them struck me I struck back again, regardless of consequences. I could manage any of them *singly*, and so long as I could keep them from combining I got on very well. In the conflict which ended my stay at Mr. Gardiner's I was beset by four of them at once—Ned North, Ned Hayes, Bill Stewart, and Tom Humphreys. Two of them were as large as myself, and they came near killing me, in broad daylight. One came in front, armed with a brick; there was one at each side and one behind, and they closed up all around me. I was struck on all sides; and while I was attending to those in front I received a blow on my head from behind, dealt with a heavy hand-spike. I was completely stunned by the blow, and fell heavily on the ground among the timbers. Taking advantage of my fall they rushed upon me and began to pound me with their fists. With a view of gaining strength, I let them lay on for a while after I came to myself. They had done me little damage, so far; but finally getting tired of that sport I gave a sudden surge, and despite their weight I rose to my hands and knees. Just as I did this one of their number planted a blow with his boot in my left eye, which for a time seemed to have burst my eye-ball. When they saw my eye completely closed, my face covered with blood, and I staggering under the stunning blows they had given me, they left me. As soon as I gathered strength I picked up the hand-spike and madly enough attempted to pursue them; but there the carpenters interfered and compelled me to give up my pursuit. It was impossible to stand against so many.

Dear reader, you can hardly believe the statement, but it is true and therefore I write it down; that no fewer than fifty white men stood by and saw this brutal and shameful outrage committed, and not a man of them all interposed a single word of mercy. There were four against one, and that one's face was beaten and battered most horribly, and no one said, 'that is enough;' but some cried out, 'Kill him! kill him! kill the d——n nigger! knock his brains out! he struck a white person!' I mention this inhuman outcry to show the character of the men and the spirit of the times at Gardiner's ship-yard; and, indeed, in Baltimore generally, in 1836. As I look back to this period, I am almost amazed that I was not murdered outright, so murderous was the spirit which prevailed there. On two other occasions while there I came near losing my life. On one of these, I was driving bolts in the hold through the keelson, with Hayes. In its course the bolt bent. Hayes cursed me and said that it was my blow which bent the bolt. I denied this and charged it upon him. In a fit of rage he seized an adze and darted toward me. I met him with a maul and parried his blow, or I should have lost my life.

After the united attack of North, Stewart, Hayes, and Humphreys, finding that the carpenters were as bitter toward me as the apprentices, and that the latter were probably set on by the former, I found my only chance for life was in flight. I succeeded in getting away without an additional blow. To strike a white man was death by lynch law, in

Gardiner's ship-yard; nor was there much of any other law toward the colored people at that time in any other part of Maryland.

After making my escape from the ship-yard I went straight home and related my story to Master Hugh; and to his credit I say it, that his conduct, though he was not a religious man, was every way more humane than that of his brother Thomas, when I went to him in a somewhat similar plight, from the hands of his 'Brother Edward Covey.' Master Hugh listened attentively to my narration of the circumstances leading to the ruffianly assault, and gave many evidences of his strong indignation at what was done. He was a rough but manly-hearted fellow, and at this time his best nature showed itself.

The heart of my once kind mistress Sophia was again melted in pity towards me. My puffed-out eye and my scarred and blood-covered face moved the dear lady to tears. She kindly drew a chair by me, and with friendly and consoling words, she took water and washed the blood from my face. No mother's hand could have been more tender than hers. She bound up my head and covered my wounded eye with a lean piece of fresh beef. It was almost compensation for all I suffered, that it occasioned the manifestation once more of the originally characteristic kindness of my mistress. Her affectionate heart was not yet dead, though much hardened by time and circumstances.

As for Master Hugh, he was furious, and gave expression to his feelings in the forms of speech usual in that locality. He poured curses on the whole of the ship-yard company, and swore that he would have satisfaction. His indignation was really strong and healthy; but unfortunately it resulted from the thought that his rights of property, in my person, had not been respected, more than from any sense of the outrage perpetrated upon me *as a man*. I had reason to think this from the fact that he could, himself, beat and mangle when it suited him to do so.

Bent on having satisfaction, as he said, just as soon as I got a little the better of my bruises Master Hugh took me to Esquire Watson's office on Bond street, Fell's Point, with a view to procuring the arrest of those who had assaulted me. He gave to the magistrate an account of the outrage as I had related it to him, and seemed to expect that a warrant would at once be issued for the arrest of the lawless ruffians. Mr. Watson heard all that he had to say, then coolly inquired, 'Mr. Auld, who saw this assault of which you speak?' 'It was done, sir, in the presence of a ship-yard full of hands.' 'Sir,' said Mr. Watson, 'I am sorry, but I cannot move in this matter, except upon the oath of white witnesses.' 'But here's the boy; look at his head and face,' said the excited Master Hugh; '*they* show *what* has been done.' But Watson insisted that he was not authorized to do anything, unless white witnesses of the transaction would come forward and testify to what had taken place. He could issue no warrant, on my word, against white persons, and if I had been killed in the presence of a *thousand blacks*, their testimony combined would have been insufficient to condemn a single murderer. Master Hugh was compelled to say, for once, that this state of things was *too* bad, and he left the office of the magistrate disgusted.

Of course it was impossible to get any white man to testify against my assailants. The carpenters saw what was done; but the actors were but the agents of their malice, and did only what the carpenters sanctioned. They had cried with one accord, 'Kill the nigger! kill the nigger!' Even those who may have pitied me, if any such were among them, lacked the moral courage to volunteer their evidence. The slightest show of sympathy or justice toward a person of color was denounced as abolitionism; and the name of abolitionist subjected its hearer to frightful liabilities. 'D——n abolitionists,' and 'kill the niggers,' were the watch-words of the foul-mouthed ruffians of those days. Nothing was done, and probably would not have been, had I been killed in the affray. The laws and the morals of the Christian city of Baltimore afforded no protection to the sable denizens of that city.

Master Hugh, on finding that he could get no redress for the cruel wrong, withdrew me from the employment of Mr. Gardiner and took me into his own family, Mrs. Auld kindly taking care of me and dressing my wounds until they were healed and I was ready to go to work again.

While I was on the Eastern Shore, Master Hugh had met with reverses which overthrew his business and had given up ship-building in his own yard, on the City Block, and was now acting as foreman of Mr. Walter Price. The best that he could do for me was to take me into Mr. Price's yard, and afford me the facilities there for completing the trade which I began to learn at Gardiner's. Here I rapidly became expert in the use of calkers' tools, and in the course of a single year, I was able to command the highest wages paid to journeymen calkers in Baltimore.

The reader will observe that I was now of some pecuniary value to my master. During the busy season I was bringing six and seven dollars per week. I have sometimes brought him as much as nine dollars a week, for wages were a dollar and a half per day.

After learning to calk, I sought my own employment, made my own contracts, and collected my own earnings—giving Master Hugh no trouble in any part of the transactions to which I was a party.

Here, then, were better days for the Eastern Shore *slave*. I was free from the vexatious assaults of the apprentices at Gardiner's; free from the perils of plantation life and once more in favorable condition to increase my little stock of education, which had been at a dead stand since my removal from Baltimore. I had on the Eastern Shore been only a teacher, when in company with other slaves, but now there were colored persons here who could instruct me. Many of the young calkers could read, write, and cipher. Some of them had high notions about mental improvement, and the free ones on Fell's Point organized what they called the 'East Baltimore Mental Improvement Society.'* To this society, notwithstanding it was intended that only free persons should attach themselves, I was admitted, and was several times assigned a prominent part in its debates. I owe much to the society of these young men.

The reader already knows enough of the *ill* effects of good treatment on a slave to anticipate what was now the case in my improved condition. It was not long before I began to show signs of disquiet with slavery, and to look around for means to get out of it by the shortest route. I was living among *freemen*, and was in all respects equal to them by nature and attainments. *Why should I be a slave?* There was no reason why I should be the thrall of any man. Besides, I was now getting, as I have said, a dollar and fifty cents per day. I contracted for it, worked for it, collected it; it was paid to me, and it was *rightfully* my own; and yet upon every returning Saturday night, this money—my own hard earnings, every cent of it,—was demanded of me and taken from me by Master Hugh. He did not earn it; he had no hand in earning it; why, then should he have it? I owed him nothing. He had given me no schooling, and I had received from him only my food and raiment; and for these, my services were supposed to pay from the first. The right to take my earnings was the right of the robber. He had the power to compel me to give him the fruits of my labor, and this *power* was his only right in the case. I became more and more dissatisfied with this state of things, and in so becoming I only gave proof of the same human nature which every reader of this chapter in my life—slaveholder, or non-slaveholder—is conscious of possessing.

To make a contented slave, you must make a thought-less one. It is necessary to darken his moral and mental vision, and, as far as possible, to annihilate his power of reason. He must be able to detect no inconsistencies in slavery. The man who takes his earnings must be able to convince him that he has a perfect right to do so. It must not depend upon mere force: the slave must know no higher law than his master's will. The whole relationship must not only demonstrate to his mind its necessity, but its absolute rightfulness. If there be one crevice through which a single drop can fall, it will certainly rust off the slave's chain.

# CHAPTER XXI.

## ESCAPE FROM SLAVERY.

*Closing incidents in my 'Life as a Slave'—Discontent—Suspicions—
Master's generosity—Difficulties in the way of escape—Plan to
obtain money—Allowed to hire my time—A gleam of hope—Attend
camp-meeting—Anger of Master Hugh—The result—Plans of Escape—
Day for departure fixed—Harassing doubts and fears—Painful
thoughts of separation from friends.*

MY condition during the year of my escape (1838) was comparatively
a free and easy one, so far, at least, as the wants of the physical man were
concerned; but the reader will bear in mind that my troubles from the
beginning had been less physical than mental, and he will thus be prepared to find that slave life was adding nothing to its charms for me as
I grew older, and became more and more acquainted with it. The practice
of openly robbing me, from week to week, of all my earnings, kept the
nature and character of slavery constantly before me. I could be robbed
by indirection, but this was too open and barefaced to be endured. I could
see no reason why I should, at the end of each week, pour the reward of
my honest toil into the purse of my master. My obligation to do this
vexed me, and the manner in which Master Hugh received my wages
vexed me yet more. Carefully counting the money, and rolling it out dollar by dollar, he would look me in the face, as if he would search my heart
as well as my pocket, and reproachfully ask me, 'Is that all?'—implying
that I had perhaps kept back part of my wages; or, if not so, the demand
was made possibly to make me feel that after all, I was an 'unprofitable
servant.' Draining me of the last cent of my hard earnings, he would,
however, occasionally, when I brought home an extra large sum, dole out
to me a sixpence or shilling, with a view, perhaps, of kindling my gratitude. But it had the opposite effect. It was an admission of my right to the
whole sum. The fact that he gave me any part of my wages, was proof that
he suspected I had a right to the whole of them; and I always felt uncomfortable after having received anything in this way, lest his giving me
a few cents might possibly ease his conscience, and make him feel himself
to be a pretty honorable robber after all.

Held to a strict account, and kept under a close watch,—the old suspicion of my running away not having been entirely removed,—to
accomplish my escape seemed a very difficult thing. The railroad from
Baltimore to Philadelphia was under regulations so stringent that even

*free* colored travelers were almost excluded. They must have free papers; they must be measured and carefully examined before they could enter the cars, and could go only in the day time, even when so examined. The steamboats were under regulations equally stringent. And still more, and worse than all, all the great turnpikes leading northward were beset with kidnappers; a class of men who watched the newspapers for advertisements for runaway slaves, thus making their living by the accursed reward of slave-hunting.

My discontent grew upon me, and I was on a constant look-out for means to get away. With money I could easily have managed the matter, and from this consideration I hit upon the plan of soliciting the privilege of hiring my time. It was quite common in Baltimore to allow slaves this privilege, and was the practice also in New Orleans. A slave who was considered trustworthy could, by regularly paying his master a definite sum at the end of each week, dispose of his time as he liked. It so happened that I was not in very good odor, and was far from being a trustworthy slave. Nevertheless, I watched my opportunity when Master Thomas came to Baltimore (for I was still his property, Hugh only acting as his agent,) in the spring of 1838, to purchase his spring supply of goods, and applied to him directly for the much-coveted privilege of hiring my time. This request Master Thomas unhesitatingly refused to grant and charged me, with some sternness, with inventing this stratagem to make my escape. He told me I could go *nowhere* but he would catch me; and, in the event of my running away, I might be assured that he should spare no pains in his efforts to recapture me. He recounted, with a good deal of eloquence, the many kind offices he had done me, and exhorted me to be contented and obedient. 'Lay out no plans for the future,' said he. 'If you behave yourself properly, I will take care of you.' Kind and considerate as this offer was, it failed to soothe me into repose. In spite of all Master Thomas had said and in spite of my own efforts to the contrary, the injustice and wickedness of slavery were always uppermost in my thoughts and strengthening my purpose to make my escape at the earliest moment possible.

About two months after applying to Master Thomas for the privilege of hiring my time, I applied to Master Hugh for the same liberty, supposing him to be unacquainted with the fact that I had made a similar application to Master Thomas and had been refused. My boldness in making this request fairly astounded him at first. He gazed at me in amazement. But I had many good reasons for pressing the matter, and, after listening to them awhile, he did not absolutely refuse but told me that he would think of it. There was hope for me in this. Once master of my own time, I felt sure that I could make, over and above my obligation to him, a dollar or two every week. Some slaves had, in this way, made enough to purchase their freedom. It was a sharp spur to their industry; and some of the most enterprising colored men in Baltimore hired themselves in that way.

After mature reflection, as I suppose it was, Master Hugh granted me the privilege in question, on the following terms: I was to be allowed all my time; to make all bargains for work, and to collect my own wages; and in return for this liberty, I was required or obliged to pay him three dollars at the end of each week, and to board and clothe myself, and buy my own calking tools. A failure in any of these particulars would put an end to the privilege. This was a hard bargain. The wear and tear of clothing, the losing and breaking of tools, and the expense of board, made it necessary for me to earn at least six dollars per week to keep even with the world. All who are acquainted with calking know how uncertain and irregular that employment is. It can be done to advantage only in dry weather, for it is useless to put wet oakum into a ship's seam. Rain or shine, however, work or no work, at the end of each week the money must be forthcoming.

Master Hugh seemed, for a time, much pleased with this arrangement; and well he might be, for it was decidedly in his favor. It relieved him of all anxiety concerning me. His money was sure. He had armed my love of liberty with a lash and a driver far more efficient than any I had before known; for, while by this arrangement, he derived all the benefits of slaveholding without its evils, I endured all the evils of being a slave, and yet suffered all the care and anxiety of a responsible freeman. 'Nevertheless,' thought I, 'it is a valuable privilege—another step in my career toward freedom.' It was something even to be permitted to stagger under the disadvantages of liberty, and I was determined to hold on to the newly gained footing by all proper industry. I was ready to work by night as by day, and being in the possession of excellent health, I was not only able to meet my current expenses, but also to lay by a small sum at the end of each week. All went on thus from the month of May till August; then, for reasons which will become apparent as I proceed, my much-valued liberty was wrested from me.

During the week previous to this calamitous event, I had made arrangements with a few young friends to accompany them on Saturday night to a camp-meeting, to be held about twelve miles from Baltimore. On the evening of our intended start for the camp-ground, something occurred in the ship-yard where I was at work which detained me unusually late, and compelled me either to disappoint my friends, or to

neglect carrying my weekly dues to Master Hugh. Knowing that I had
the money and could hand it to him on another day, I decided to go to
camp-meeting and, on my return, to pay him the three dollars for the
past week. Once on the camp-ground, I was induced to remain one day
longer than I had intended when I left home. But as soon as I returned
I went directly to his home on Fell street to hand him his (my) money.
Unhappily the fatal mistake had been made. I found him exceedingly
angry. He exhibited all the signs of apprehension and wrath which
a slave-holder might be surmised to exhibit on the supposed escape of
a favorite slave. 'You rascal! I have a great mind to give you a sound
whipping. How dare you go out of the city without first asking and
obtaining my permission?' 'Sir,' I said, 'I hired my time and paid you
the price you asked for it. I did not know that it was any part of the
bargain that I should ask you when or where I should go.' 'You did not
know, you rascal! You are bound to show yourself here every Saturday
night.' After reflecting a few moments, he became somewhat cooled
down, but, evidently greatly troubled, said: 'Now, you scoundrel, you
have done for yourself; you shall hire your time no longer. The next
thing I shall hear of will be your running away. Bring home your tools
at once. I'll teach you how to go off in this way.'

Thus ended my partial freedom. I could hire my time no longer.
I obeyed my master's orders at once. The little taste of liberty which
I had had—although as it will be seen, that taste was far from being
unalloyed,—by no means enhanced my contentment with slavery.
Punished by Master Hugh, it was now my turn to punish him. 'Since,'
thought I, 'you *will* make a slave of me, I will await your order in all
things.' So, instead of going to look for work on Monday morning, as
I had formerly done, I remained at home during the entire week, without the performance of a single stroke of work. Saturday night came,
and he called upon me as usual for my wages. I, of course, told him
I had done no work, and had no wages. Here we were at the point of
coming to blows. His wrath had been accumulating during the whole
week; for he evidently saw that I was making no effort to get work, but
was most aggravatingly awaiting his orders in all things. As I look back
to this behavior of mine, I scarcely know what possessed me, thus to
trifle with one who had such unlimited power to bless or blast me.
Master Hugh raved, and swore he would 'get hold of me,' but wisely
for *him*, and happily for *me*, his wrath employed only those harmless,
impalpable missiles which roll from a limber tongue. In my desperation
I had fully made up my mind to measure strength with him in case he
should attempt to execute his threat. I am glad there was no occasion

for this, for resistance to him could not have ended so happily for me as it did in the case of Covey. Master Hugh was not a man to be safely resisted by a slave; and I freely own that in my conduct toward him, in this instance, there was more folly than wisdom. He closed his reproofs by telling me that hereafter I need give myself no uneasiness about getting work; he 'would himself see to getting work for me, and enough of it at that.' This threat, I confess, had some terror in it, and on thinking the matter over during the Sunday, I resolved not only to save him the trouble of getting me work, but that on the third day of September I would attempt to make my escape. His refusal to allow me to hire my time therefore hastened the period of my flight. I had three weeks in which to prepare for my journey.

Once resolved, I felt a certain degree of repose, and on Monday morning, instead of waiting for Master Hugh to seek employment for me, I was up by break of day, and off to the ship-yard of Mr. Butler, on the City Block, near the draw-bridge. I was a favorite with Mr. Butler, and, young as I was, I had served as his foreman, on the float-stage, at calking. Of course I easily obtained work, and at the end of the week, which, by the way, was exceedingly fine, I brought Master Hugh nine dollars. The effect of this mark of returning good sense on my part was excellent. He was very much pleased; he took the money, commended me and told me that I might have done the same thing the week before. It is a blessed thing that the tyrant may not always know the thoughts and purposes of his victim. Master Hugh little knew my plans. The going to camp-meeting without asking his permission; the insolent answers to his reproaches and the sulky deportment of the week after being deprived of the privilege of hiring my time, had awakened the suspicion that I might be cherishing disloyal purposes. My object, therefore, in working steadily was to remove suspicion; and in this I succeeded admirably. He probably thought that I was never better satisfied with my condition than at the very time I was planning my escape. The second week passed, and I again carried him my full week's wages—*nine dollars*; and so well pleased was he that he gave me *twenty-five cents!* and bade me 'make good use of it.' I told him I would do so, for one of the uses to which I intended to put it was to pay my fare on the 'underground railroad.'*

Things without went on as usual; but I was passing through the same internal excitement and anxiety which I had experienced two years and a half before. The failure in that instance was not calculated to increase my confidence in the success of this, my second attempt; and I knew that a second failure could not leave me where my first did. I must either get to the *far North* or *be sent* to the far *South*. Besides the exercise of mind from this state of facts, I had the painful sensation of being about to separate from a circle of honest and warmhearted friends. The thought of such a separation, where the hope of ever meeting again was excluded, and where there could be no correspondence, was very painful. It is my opinion that thousands more would have escaped from slavery but for the strong affection which bound them to their families, relatives, and friends. The daughter was hindered by the love she bore her mother and the father by the love he bore his wife and children, and so on to the end of the chapter. I had no relations in Baltimore, and I saw no probability of ever living in the neighborhood of sisters and brothers; but the thought of leaving my friends was the strongest obstacle to my running away. The last two days of the week, Friday and Saturday, were spent mostly in collecting my things together for my journey. Having worked four days that week for my master. I handed him six dollars on Saturday night. I seldom spent my Sundays at home, and for fear that something might be discovered in my conduct, I kept up my custom and absented myself all day. On Monday, the third day of September, 1838, in accordance with my resolution, I bade farewell to the city of Baltimore, and to that slavery which had been my abhorrence from childhood.

# SECOND PART.

# CHAPTER I.

## ESCAPE FROM SLAVERY.

*Reasons for not having revealed the manner of escape—Nothing of romance in the method—Danger—Free papers—Unjust tax—Protection papers—'Free trade and Sailors' rights'—American eagle—Railroad train—Unobserving conductor—Capt. McGowan—Honest German—Fears—Safe arrival in Philadelphia—Ditto in New York.*

IN the first narrative of my experience in slavery, written nearly forty years ago, and in various writings since, I have given the public what I considered very good reasons for withholding the manner of my escape. In substance these reasons were, first, that such publication at any time during the existence of slavery might be used by the master against the slave, and prevent the future escape of any who might adopt the same means that I did. The second reason was, if possible, still more binding to silence—for publication of details would certainly have put in peril the persons and property of those who assisted. Murder itself was not more sternly and certainly punished in the State of Maryland than was the aiding and abetting the escape of a slave. Many colored men, for no other crime than that of giving aid to a fugitive slave, have, like Charles T. Torrey,* perished in prison. The abolition of slavery in my native State and throughout the country, and the lapse of time, render the caution hitherto observed no longer necessary. But, even since the abolition of slavery, I have sometimes thought it well enough to baffle curiosity by saying that while slavery existed there were good reasons for not telling the manner of my escape, and since slavery had ceased to exist there was no reason for telling it. I shall now, however, cease to avail myself of this formula, and, as far as I can, endeavor to satisfy this very natural curiosity. I should perhaps have yielded to that feeling sooner, had there been anything very heroic or thrilling in the incidents connected with my escape, for I am sorry to say I have nothing of that sort to tell; and yet the courage that could risk betrayal and the bravery which was ready to encounter death if need be, in pursuit of freedom, were essential features in the undertaking. My success was due to address rather than to courage; to good luck rather than to bravery. My means of escape were provided for me by the very men who were making laws to hold and bind me more securely in slavery. It was the custom in the State of Maryland to require of the free colored people to have what were called free papers. This instrument they were required to renew very often, and by charging a fee for this writing, considerable sums from time to time were collected by the State. In these papers the name, age, color, height and form of the free man were described, together with any scars or other marks upon his person which could assist in his identification. This device of slaveholding ingenuity, like other devices of wickedness, in some measure defeated itself—since more than one man could be found to answer the same general description. Hence many slaves could escape by personating the owner of one set of papers; and this was often done as follows: A slave nearly or sufficiently answering the description set forth in the papers, would borrow or hire them till he could by their means escape to a free state, and then, by mail or otherwise, return them to the owner. The operation was a hazardous one for the lender as well as for the borrower. A failure on the part of the fugitive to send back the papers would imperil his benefactor, and the discovery of the papers in possession of the wrong man would imperil both the fugitive and his friend. It was therefore an act of supreme trust on the part of a freeman of color thus to put in jeopardy his own liberty that another might be free. It was, however, not unfrequently bravely done, and was seldom discovered. I was not so fortunate as to sufficiently resemble any of my free acquaintances as to answer the description of their papers. But I had one friend—a sailor—who owned a sailor's protection,* which answered somewhat the purpose of free papers—describing his person and certifying to the fact that he was a free American sailor. The instrument had at its head the American eagle, which at once gave it the appearance of an authorized document. This protection did not, when in my hands, describe its bearer very accurately. Indeed, it called for a man much darker than myself, and close examination of it would have caused my arrest at the start. In order to avoid this fatal scrutiny on the part of the railroad official, I had arranged with Isaac Rolls, a hackman, to bring my baggage to the train just on the moment of starting, and jumped upon the car myself when the train was already in motion. Had I gone into the station and offered to purchase a ticket, I should have been instantly and carefully examined, and undoubtedly arrested. In choosing this plan upon which to act, I considered the jostle of the train, and the natural haste of the conductor in a train crowded with passengers, and relied upon my skill and address in playing the sailor as described in my protection, to do the rest. One element in my favor was the kind feeling which prevailed in Baltimore and other seaports at the time, towards 'those who go down to the sea in ships.'* 'Free trade and sailors' rights'* expressed the sentiment of the country just then. In my clothing I was rigged out in sailor style. I had on a red shirt and a tarpaulin hat and black cravat, tied in sailor fashion, carelessly and loosely about my neck. My knowledge of ships and sailor's talk came much to my assistance, for I knew a ship from stem to stern, and from keelson to cross-trees, and could talk sailor like an 'old salt.' On sped the train, and I was well on the way to Havre de Grace before the conductor came into the negro car to collect tickets and examine the papers of his black passengers. This was a critical moment in the drama. My whole future depended upon the decision of this conductor. Agitated I was while this ceremony was proceeding, but still, externally at least, I was apparently calm and self-possessed. He went on with his duty—examining several colored passengers before reaching me. He was somewhat harsh in tone and peremptory in manner until he reached me, when, strangely enough, and to my surprise and relief, his whole manner changed. Seeing that I did not readily produce my free papers, as the other colored persons in the car had done, he said to me in a friendly contrast with that observed towards the others: 'I suppose you have your free papers?' To which I answered: 'No, sir; I never carry my free papers to sea with me.' 'But you have something to show that you are a free man, have you not?' 'Yes, sir,' I answered; 'I have a paper with the American eagle on it, that will carry me round the world.' With this I drew from my deep sailor's pocket my seaman's protection, as before described. The merest glance at the paper satisfied him, and he took my fare and went on about his business. This moment of time was one of the most anxious I ever experienced. Had the conductor looked closely at the paper, he could not have failed to discover that it called for a very different looking person from myself, and in that case it would have been his duty to arrest me on the instant and send me back to Baltimore from the first station. When he left me with the assurance that I was all right, though much relieved, I realized that I was still in great danger: I was still in Maryland, and subject to arrest at any moment. I saw on the train several persons who would have known me in any other clothes, and I feared they might recognize me, even in my sailor 'rig,' and report me to the conductor, who would then subject me to a closer examination, which I knew well would be fatal to me.

Though I was not a murderer fleeing from justice, I felt, perhaps, quite as miserable as such a criminal. The train was moving at a very high rate of speed for that time of railroad travel, but to my anxious mind, it was moving far too slowly. Minutes were hours, and hours were days during this part of my flight. After Maryland I was to pass through

Delaware—another slave State, where slave-catchers generally awaited their prey, for it was not in the interior of the State, but on its borders, that these human hounds were most vigilant and active. The border lines between slavery and freedom were the dangerous ones, for the fugitives. The heart of no fox or deer, with hungry hounds on his trail, in full chase, could have beaten more anxiously or noisily than did mine from the time I left Baltimore till I reached Philadelphia. The passage of the Susquehanna river at Havre de Grace was at that time made by ferry-boat, on board of which I met a young colored man by the name of Nichols, who came very near betraying me. He was a 'hand' on the boat, but instead of minding his business, he insisted upon knowing me, and asking me dangerous questions as to where I was going, and when I was coming back, etc. I got away from my old and inconvenient acquaintance as soon as I could decently do so, and went to another part of the boat. Once across the river I encountered a new danger. Only a few days before I had been at work on a revenue cutter, in Mr. Price's ship-yard, under the care of Captain McGowan. On the meeting at this point of the two trains, the one going south stopped on the track just opposite to the one going north, and it so happened that this Captain McGowan sat at a window where he could see me very distinctly, and would certainly have recognized me had he looked at me but for a second. Fortunately, in the hurry of the moment, he did not see me, and the trains soon passed each other on their respective ways. But this was not the only hair-breadth escape. A German blacksmith, whom I knew well, was on the train with me, and looked at me very intently, as if he thought he had seen me somewhere before in his travels. I really believe he knew me, but had no heart to betray me. At any rate he saw me escaping and held his peace.

The last point of imminent danger, and the one I dreaded most, was Wilmington. Here we left the train and took the steamboat for Philadelphia. In making the change I again apprehended arrest, but no one disturbed me, and I was soon on the broad and beautiful Delaware, speeding away to the Quaker City. On reaching Philadelphia in the afternoon I inquired of a colored man how I could get on to New York? He directed me to the Willow street depot, and thither I went, taking the train that night. I reached New York Tuesday morning, having completed the journey in less than twenty-four hours. Such is briefly the manner of my escape from slavery—and the end of my experience as a slave. Other chapters will tell the story of my life as a freeman.

# CHAPTER II.

## LIFE AS A FREEMAN.

*Loneliness and Insecurity—'Allender's Jake'—Succored by a sailor—David Ruggles—Marriage—Steamer J. W. Richmond—Stage to New Bedford—Arrival there—Driver's detention of baggage—Nathan Johnson—Change of name—Why called 'Douglass'—Obtaining work—The* Liberator *and its editor.*

MY free life began on the third of September, 1838. On the morning of the 4th of that month, after an anxious and most perilous but safe journey, I found myself in the big city of New York, a *free man*; one more added to the mighty throng which, like the confused waves of the troubled sea, surged to and fro between the lofty walls of Broadway. Though dazzled with the wonders which met me on every hand, my thoughts could not be much withdrawn from my strange situation. For the moment the dreams of my youth and the hopes of my manhood were completely fulfilled. The bonds that had held me to 'old master' were broken. No man now had a right to call me his slave or assert mastery over me. I was in the rough and tumble of an outdoor world, to take my chance with the rest of its busy number. I have often been asked, how I felt when first I found myself on free soil. My readers may share the same curiosity. There is scarcely anything in my experience about which I could not give a more satisfactory answer. A new world had opened upon me. If life is more than breath, and the 'quick round of blood,'* I lived more in one day than in a year of my slave life. It was a time of joyous excitement which words can but tamely describe. In a letter written to a friend soon after reaching New York, I said: 'I felt as one might feel upon escape from a den of hungry lions.'* Anguish and grief, like darkness and rain, may be depicted; but gladness and joy, like the rainbow, defy the skill of pen or pencil. During ten or fifteen years I had, as it were, been dragging a heavy chain which no strength of mine could break I was not only a slave, but a slave for life. I might become a husband, a father, an aged man, but through all, from the cradle to the grave, I had felt myself doomed. All efforts I had previously made to secure my freedom, had not only failed, but had seemed only to rivet my fetters the more firmly and to render my escape more difficult. Baffled, entangled and discouraged, I had at times asked myself the question, May not my condition after all be God's work and ordered for a wise purpose, and if so, was not submission my duty?

A contest had in fact been going on in my mind for a long time, between the clear consciousness of right and the plausible make-shifts of theology and superstition. The one held me an abject slave—a prisoner for life, punished for some transgression in which I had no lot or part; the other counseled me to manly endeavor to secure my freedom. This contest was now ended; my chains were broken, and the victory brought me unspeakable joy. But my gladness was short lived, for I was not yet out of the reach and power of the slaveholders. I soon found that New York was not quite so free or so safe a refuge as I had supposed, and a sense of loneliness and insecurity again oppressed me most sadly. I chanced to meet on the street, a few hours after my landing, a fugitive slave whom I had once known well in slavery. The information received from him alarmed me. The fugitive in question was known in Baltimore as 'Allender's Jake,' but in New York he wore the more respectable name of 'William Dixon.' Jake, in law, was the property of Doctor Allender, and Tolly Allender, the son of the doctor, had once made an effort to recapture *Mr. Dixon*, but had failed for want of evidence to support his claim. Jake told me the circumstances of this attempt and how narrowly he escaped being sent back to slavery and torture. He told me that New York was then full of southerners returning from the watering-places north; that the colored people of New York were not to be trusted; that there were hired men of my own color who would betray me for a few dollars; that there were hired men ever on the look-out for fugitives; that I must trust no man with my secret; that I must not think of going either upon the wharves, or into any colored boarding-house, for all such places were closely watched; that he was himself unable to help me; and, in fact, he seemed while speaking to me, to fear lest I myself might be a spy and a betrayer. Under this apprehension, as I suppose, he showed signs of wishing to be rid of me, and with whitewash brush in hand, in search of work, he soon disappeared. This picture, given by poor 'Jake,' of New York, was a damper to my enthusiasm. My little store of money would soon be exhausted, and since it would be unsafe for me to go on the wharves for work and I had no introductions elsewhere, the prospect for me was far from cheerful. I saw the wisdom of keeping away from the ship-yards, for, if pursued, as I felt certain I would be, Mr. Auld would naturally seek me there among the calkers. Every door seemed closed against me. I was in the midst of an ocean of my fellow-men, and yet a perfect stranger to every one. I was without home, without acquaintance, without money, without credit, without work, and without any definite knowledge as to what course to take or where to look for succor. In such an extremity, a man has something beside his new-born freedom of which to think. While wandering about the streets of New York, and lodging at least one night among the barrels on one of the wharves, I was indeed free—from slavery, but free from food and shelter as well. I kept my secret to myself as long as I could, but was compelled at last to seek some one who should befriend me without taking advantage of my destitution to betray me. Such an one I found in a sailor named Stuart, a warm-hearted and generous fellow, who, from his humble home on Center street, saw me standing on the opposite sidewalk, near 'The Tombs.'* As he approached me I ventured a remark to him which at once enlisted his interest in me. He took me to his home to spend the night, and in the morning went with me to Mr. David Ruggles,* the secretary of the New York vigilance committee, a co-worker with Isaac T. Hopper,* Lewis and Arthur Tappan,* Theodore S. Wright,* Samuel Cornish,* Thomas Downing,* Philip A. Bell,* and other true men of their time. All these (save Mr. Bell, who still lives, and is editor and publisher of a paper called the *Elevator*,* in San Francisco) have finished their work on earth. Once in the hands of these brave and wise men, I felt comparatively safe. With Mr. Ruggles, on the corner of Lispenard and Church streets, I was hidden several days, during which time my intended wife* came on from Baltimore at my call, to share the burdens of life with me. She was a free woman, and came at once on getting the good news of my safety. We were married by Rev. J. W. C. Pennington,* then a well-known and respected Presbyterian minister. I had no money with which to pay the marriage fee, but he seemed well pleased with our thanks.

Mr. Ruggles was the first officer on the underground railroad with whom I met after coming North, and was indeed the only one with whom I had anything to do, till I became *such* an officer myself. Learning that my trade was that of a calker, he promptly decided that the best place for me was in New Bedford, Mass. He told me that many ships for whaling voyages were fitted out there, and that I might there find work at my trade and make a good living. So, on the day of the marriage ceremony, we took our little luggage to the steamer John W. Richmond, which at that time was one of the line running between New York and Newport, R. I. Forty-three years ago colored travelers were not permitted in the cabin, nor allowed abaft the paddle-wheels of a steam vessel. They were compelled, whatever the weather might be, whether cold or hot, wet or dry, to spend the night on deck. Unjust as this regulation was, it did not trouble us much. We had fared much harder before. We arrived at Newport the next morning, and soon after an old-fashioned stage-coach with 'New Bedford' in large, yellow letters on its sides, came down to the wharf. I had not money enough to pay our fare and stood hesitating to know what to do. Fortunately for us, there were two Quaker gentlemen who were about to take passage on the stage,—Friends William C. Taber and Joseph Ricketson,—who at once discerned our true situation, and in a peculiarly quiet way, addressing me, Mr. Taber said: 'Thee get in.' I never obeyed an order with more alacrity, and we were soon on our way to our new home. When we reached 'Stone Bridge' the passengers alighted for breakfast and paid their fares to the driver. We took no breakfast, and when asked for our fares I told the driver I would make it right with him when we reached New Bedford. I expected some objection to this on his part, but he made none. When, however, we reached New Bedford he took our baggage, including three music books,—two of them collections by Dyer,* and one by Shaw,*—and held them until I was able to redeem them by paying to him the sums due for our rides. This was soon done, for Mr. Nathan Johnson* not only received me kindly and hospitably, but, on being informed about our baggage, at once loaned me the two dollars with which to square accounts with the stage-driver. Mr. and Mrs. Nathan Johnson reached a good old age and now rest from their labors. I am under many grateful obligations to them. They not only 'took me in when a stranger,' and 'fed me when hungry,'* but taught me how to make an honest living.

Thus, in a fortnight after my flight from Maryland, I was safe in New Bedford,—a citizen of the grand old commonwealth of Massachusetts.

Once initiated into my new life of freedom and assured by Mr. Johnson that I need not fear recapture in that city, a comparatively unimportant question arose, as to the name by which I should be known thereafter, in my new relation as a free man. The name given me by my dear mother was no less pretentious and long than Frederick Augustus Washington Bailey. I had, however, while living in Maryland, disposed of the Augustus Washington, and retained only Frederick Bailey. Between Baltimore and New Bedford, the better to conceal myself from the slave-hunters, I had parted with Bailey and called myself Johnson; but finding that in New Bedford the Johnson family was already so numerous as to cause some confusion in distinguishing one from another, a change in this name seemed desirable. Nathan Johnson, mine host, was emphatic as to this necessity, and wished me to allow him to select a name for me. I consented, and he called me by my present name,—the one by which I have been known for three and forty years,—Frederick Douglass. Mr. Johnson had just been reading the 'Lady of the Lake,'* and so pleased was he with its great character that he wished me to bear his name. Since reading that charming poem myself, I have often thought that considering the noble hospitality and manly character of Nathan Johnson, black man though he was, he, far more than I, illustrated the virtues of the Douglas of Scotland. Sure am I that if any slave-catcher had entered his domicile with a view to my recapture, Johnson would have been like him of the 'stalwart hand.'*

Living in Baltimore as I had done for many years, the reader may be surprised, when I tell the honest truth of the impressions I had in some way conceived of the social and material condition of the people at the north. I had no proper idea of the wealth, refinement, enterprise, and high civilization of this section of the country. My Columbian Orator, almost my only book, had done nothing to enlighten me concerning northern society. I had been taught that slavery was the bottom-fact of all wealth. With this foundation idea, I came naturally to the conclusion that poverty must be the general condition of the people of the free States. A white man holding no slaves in the country from which I came, was usually an ignorant and poverty-stricken man. Men of this class were contemptuously called 'poor white trash.' Hence I supposed that since the non-slaveholders at the south were, as a class, ignorant, poor and degraded, the non-slaveholders at the north must be in a similar condition. New Bedford, therefore, which at that time was in proportion to its population, really the richest city in the Union, took me greatly by surprise, in the evidences it gave of its solid wealth and grandeur. I found that even the laboring classes lived in better houses, that their houses were more elegantly furnished and were more abundantly supplied with conveniences and comforts, than the houses of many who owned slaves on the Eastern Shore of Maryland. This was true not only of the white people of that city, but it was so of my friend, Mr. Johnson. He lived in a nicer house, dined at a more ample board, was the owner of more books, the reader of more newspapers, was more conversant with the moral, social and political condition of the country and the world, than nine-tenths of the slaveholders in all Talbot county. I was not long in finding the cause of the difference, in these respects, between the people of the north and south. It was the superiority of educated mind over mere brute force. I will not detain the reader by extended illustrations as to how my understanding was enlightened on this subject. On the wharves of New Bedford I received my first light. I saw there industry without bustle, labor without noise, toil—honest, earnest and exhaustive—without the whip. There was no loud singing or hallooing, as at the wharves of southern ports when ships were loading or unloading; no loud cursing or quarreling; everything went on as smoothly as well-oiled machinery. One of the first incidents which impressed me with the superior mental character of labor in the north over that of the south, was the manner of loading and unloading vessels. In a southern port twenty or thirty hands would be employed to do what five or six men, with the help of one ox, would do at the wharf in New Bedford. Main strength—human muscle—unassisted by intelligent skill, was slavery's method of labor. With a capital of about sixty dollars in the shape of a good-natured old ox attached to the end of a stout rope, New Bedford did the work of ten or twelve thousand dollars, represented in the bones and muscles of slaves, and did it far better. In a word, I found everything managed with a much more scrupulous regard to economy, both of men and things, time and strength, than in the country from which I had come. Instead of going a hundred yards to the spring, the maid-servant had a well or pump at her elbow. The wood used for fuel was kept dry and snugly piled away for winter. Here were sinks, drains, self-shutting gates, pounding-barrels, washing-machines, wringing machines, and a hundred other contrivances for saving time and money. The ship-repairing docks showed the same thoughtful wisdom as seen elsewhere. Everybody seemed in earnest. The carpenter struck the nail on its *head*, and the calkers wasted no strength in idle flourishes of their mallets. Ships brought here for repairs were made stronger and better than when new. I could have landed in no part of the United States where I should have found a more striking and gratifying contrast, not only to life generally in the South, but in the condition of the colored people there, than in New Bedford. No colored man was really free while residing in a slave State. He was ever more or less subject to the condition of his slave brother. In his color was his badge of bondage. I saw in New Bedford the nearest approach to freedom and equality that I had ever seen. I was amazed when Mr. Johnson told me that there was nothing in the laws or constitution of Massachusetts that would prevent a colored man from being governor of the State, if the people should see fit to elect him. There, too, the black man's children attended the same public schools with the white man's children, and apparently without objection from any quarter. To impress me with my security from recapture and return to slavery, Mr. Johnson assured me that no slaveholder could take a slave out of New Bedford; that there were men there who would lay down their lives to save me from such a fate. A threat was once made by a colored man to inform a southern master where his runaway slave could be found. As soon as this threat became known to the colored people they were furious. A notice was read from the pulpit of the Third Christian Church (colored) for a public meeting, when important business would be transacted (not stating what the important business was). In the meantime special measures had been taken to secure the attendance of the would-be Judas, and these had proved successful, for when the hour of meeting arrived, ignorant of the object for which it was called, the offender was promptly in attendance. All the usual formalities were gone through with, the prayer, appointments of president, secretaries, etc. Then the president, with an air of great solemnity, rose and said: 'Well, friends and brethren, we have got him here, and I would recommend that you, young men, should take him outside the door and kill him.' This was enough; there was a rush for the villain, who would probably have been killed but for his escape by an open window. He was never seen again in New Bedford.

The fifth day after my arrival I put on the clothes of a common laborer, and went upon the wharves in search of work. On my way down Union street I saw a large pile of coal in front of the house of Rev. Ephraim Peabody, the Unitarian minister. I went to the kitchen-door and asked the privilege of bringing in and putting away this coal. 'What will you charge?' said the lady. 'I will leave that to you, madam.' 'You may put it away,' she said. I was not long in accomplishing the job, when the dear lady put into my hand *two silver half-dollars*. To understand the emotion which swelled my heart as I clasped this money, realizing that I had no master who could take it from me—*that it was mine—that my hands were my own*, and could earn more of the precious coin—one must have been in some sense himself a slave. My next job was stowing a sloop at Uncle Gid. Howland's wharf with a cargo of oil for New York. I was not only a freeman but a free-working man, and no master Hugh stood ready at the end of the week to seize my hard earnings.

The season was growing late and work was plenty. Ships were being fitted out for whaling, and much wood was used in storing them. The sawing this wood was considered a good job. With the help of old Friend Johnson (blessings on his memory!) I got a 'saw' and 'buck' and went at it. When I went into a store to buy a cord with which to brace up my saw in the frame, I asked for a 'fip's' worth of cord. The man behind the counter looked rather sharply at me and said with equal sharpness, 'You don't belong about here.' I was alarmed, and thought I had betrayed myself. A fip in Maryland was six and a quarter cents, called fourpence in Massachusetts. But no harm came, except my fear, from the 'fipenny-bit' blunder, and I confidently and cheerfully went to work with my saw and buck. It was new business to me, but I never, in the same space of time, did for Covey, the negro-breaker, better work, or more of it, than I did for myself in these earliest years of my freedom.

Notwithstanding the just and humane sentiment of New Bedford three-and-forty years ago, the place was not entirely free from race and color prejudice. The good influence of the Roaches, Rodmans, Arnolds, Grinnells and Robesons did not pervade all classes of its people. The test of the real civilization of the community came when I applied for work at my trade, and then my repulse was emphatic and decisive. It so happened that Mr. Rodney French,* a wealthy and enterprising citizen, distinguished as an anti-slavery man, was fitting out a vessel for a whaling voyage, upon which there was a heavy job of calking and coppering to be done. I had some skill in both branches, and applied to Mr. French for work. He, generous man that he was, told me he would employ me, and I might go at once to the vessel. I obeyed him, but upon reaching the float-stage, where other calkers were at work, I was told that every white man would leave the ship in her unfinished condition if I struck a blow at my trade upon her. This uncivil, inhuman and selfish treatment was not so shocking and scandalous in my eyes at the time as it now appears to me. Slavery had inured me to hardships that made ordinary trouble sit lightly upon me. Could I have worked at my trade I could have earned two dollars a day, but as a common laborer I received but one dollar. The difference was of great importance to me, but if I could not get two dollars I was glad to get one; and so I went to work for Mr. French as a common laborer. The consciousness that I was free—no longer a slave—kept me cheerful under this and many similar proscriptions which I was destined to meet in New Bedford and elsewhere on the free soil of Massachusetts. For instance, though white and colored children attended the same schools and were treated kindly by their teachers, the New Bedford Lyceum* refused till several years after my residence in that city to allow any colored person to attend the lectures delivered in its hall. Not until such men as Hon. Chas. Sumner,* Theodore Parker,* Ralph W. Emerson,* and Horace Mann* refused to lecture in their course while there was such a restriction was it abandoned.

Becoming satisfied that I could not rely on my trade in New Bedford to give me a living, I prepared myself to do any kind of work that came to hand. I sawed wood, shoveled coal, dug cellars, moved rubbish from back-yards, worked on the wharves, loaded and unloaded vessels, and scoured their cabins.

This was an uncertain and unsatisfactory mode of life, for it kept me too much of the time in search of work. Fortunately it was not to last long. One of the gentlemen of whom I have spoken as being in company with Mr. Taber on the Newport wharf when he said to me, 'Thee get in,' was Mr. Joseph Ricketson, and he was the proprietor of a large candle-works in the south part of the city. By the kindness of Mr. Ricketson I found in this 'candle-works,' as it was called, though no *candles* were manufactured there, what is of the utmost importance to a young man just starting in life—constant employment and regular wages. My work in this oil-refinery required good wind and muscle. Large casks of oil were to be moved from place to place and much heavy lifting to be done. Happily I was not deficient in the requisite qualities. Young (21 years), strong and active, and ambitious to do my full share, I soon made myself useful, and I think liked by the men who worked with me, though they were all white. I was retained here as long as there was anything for me to do, when I went again to the wharves and, as a laborer, obtained work on two vessels which belonged to Mr. George Howland, and which were being repaired and fitted up for whaling. My employer was a man of great industry; a hard driver, but a good pay master, and I got on well with him. I was not only fortunate in finding work with Mr. Howland, but fortunate in my work-fellows. I have seldom met three working men more intelligent than were John Briggs, Abraham Rodman, and Solomon Pennington, who labored with me on the 'Java' and 'Golconda.' They were sober, thoughtful and upright, thoroughly imbued with the spirit of liberty, and I am much indebted to them for many valuable ideas and impressions. They taught me that all colored men were not light-hearted triflers, incapable of serious thought or effort. My next place of work was at the brass-foundry owned by Mr. Richmond. My duty here was to blow the bellows, swing the crane and empty the flasks in which castings were made; and at times this was hot and heavy work. The articles produced here were mostly for ship-work, and in the busy season the foundry was in operation night and day. I have often worked two nights and each working day of the week. My foreman, Mr. Cobb, was a good man, and more than once protected me from abuse that one or more of the hands were disposed to throw upon me. While in this situation I had little time for mental improvement. Hard work, night and day, over a furnace hot enough to keep the metal running like water, was more favorable to action than thought, yet here I often nailed a newspaper to the post near my bellows, and read while I was performing the up and down motion of the heavy beam by which the bellows was inflated and discharged.

It was the pursuit of knowledge under difficulties, and I look back to it now after so many years with some complacency and a little wonder that I could have been so earnest and persevering in any pursuit other than for my daily bread. I certainly saw nothing in the conduct of those around to inspire me with such interest; they were all devoted exclusively to what their hands found to do. I am glad to be able to say that during my engagement in this foundry no complaint was ever made against me that I did not do my work, and do it well. The bellows which I worked by main strength was, after I left, moved by a steam-engine.

I had been living four or five months in New Bedford when there came a young man to me with a copy of the *Liberator*,* the paper edited by William Lloyd Garrison and published by Isaac Knapp,* and asked me to subscribe for it. I told him I had but just escaped from slavery and was of course very poor, and had no money then to pay for it. He was very willing to take me as a subscriber, notwithstanding, and from this time I was brought into contact with the mind of Mr. Garrison, and his paper took a place in my heart second only to the Bible. It detested slavery and made no truce with the traffickers in the bodies and souls of men. It preached human brotherhood; it exposed hypocrisy and wickedness in high places; it denounced oppression and with all the solemnity of 'Thus saith the Lord,' demanded the complete emancipation of my race. I loved this paper and its editor. He seemed to me an all-sufficient match to every opponent, whether they spoke in the name of the law or the gospel. His words were full of holy fire, and straight to the point. Something of a hero-worshiper by nature, here was one to excite my admiration and reverence.

Soon after becoming a reader of the *Liberator*, it was my privilege to listen to a lecture in Liberty Hall* by Mr. Garrison, its editor. He was then a young man, of a singularly pleasing countenance, and earnest and impressive manner. On this occasion he announced nearly all his heresies. His Bible was his text-book—held sacred as the very word of the Eternal Father. He believed in sinless perfection, complete submission to insults and injuries, and literal obedience to the injunction if smitten 'on one cheek to turn the other also.'* Not only was Sunday a Sabbath, but all days were Sabbaths, and to be kept holy. All sectarianism was false and mischievous—the regenerated throughout the world being members of one body, and the head Christ Jesus. *Prejudice against color was rebellion against God*. Of all men beneath the sky, the slaves, because most neglected and despised, were nearest and dearest to his great heart. Those ministers who defended slavery from the Bible were of their 'father the devil';* and those churches which fellowshiped slaveholders as Christians, were synagogues of Satan, and our nation was a nation of liars. He was never loud and noisy, but calm and serene as a summer sky, and as pure. 'You are the man—the Moses, raised up by God, to deliver his modern Israel from bondage,' was the spontaneous feeling of my heart, as I sat away back in the hall and listened to his mighty words,—mighty in truth,—mighty in their simple earnestness. I had not long been a reader of the *Liberator*, and a listener to its editor, before I got a clear comprehension of the principles of the anti-slavery movement. I had already its spirit, and only needed to understand its principles and measures, and as I became acquainted with these my hope for the ultimate freedom of my race increased. Every week the *Liberator* came, and every week I made myself master of its contents. All the anti-slavery meetings held in New Bedford I promptly attended, my heart bounding at every true utterance against the slave system and every rebuke of its friends and supporters. Thus passed the first three years of my free life. I had not then dreamed of the possibility of my becoming a public advocate of the cause so deeply imbedded in my heart. It was enough for me to listen, to receive, and applaud the great words of others, and only whisper in private, among the white laborers on the wharves and elsewhere, the truths which burned in my heart.

# CHAPTER III.

## INTRODUCED TO THE ABOLITIONISTS.

*Anti-Slavery Convention at Nantucket—First Speech—Much Sensation—Extraordinary Speech of Mr. Garrison—Anti-Slavery Agency—Youthful Enthusiasm—Fugitive Slaveship doubted—Experience in Slavery written—Danger of Recapture.*

IN the summer of 1841 a grand anti-slavery convention* was held in Nantucket, under the auspices of Mr. Garrison and his friends. I had taken no holiday since establishing myself in New Bedford, and feeling the need of a little rest, I determined on attending the meeting, though I had no thought of taking part in any of its proceedings. Indeed, I was not aware that any one connected with the convention so much as knew my name. Mr. William C. Coffin,* a prominent abolitionist in those days of trial, had heard me speaking to my colored friends in the little school-house on Second street, where we worshiped. He sought me out in the crowd and invited me to say a few words to the convention. Thus sought out, and thus invited, I was induced to express the feelings inspired by the occasion, and the fresh recollection of the scenes through which I had passed as a slave. It was with the utmost difficulty that I could stand erect, or that I could command and articulate two words without hesitation and stammering. I trembled in every limb. I am not sure that my embarrassment was not the most effective part of my speech, if speech it could be called. At any rate, this is about the only part of my performance that I now distinctly remember. The audience sympa-thized with me at once, and from having been remarkably quiet, became much excited. Mr. Garrison followed me, taking me as his text, and now, whether *I* had made an eloquent plea in behalf of freedom, or not, his was one, never to be forgotten. Those who had heard him oftenest and had known him longest, were astonished at his masterly effort. For the time he possessed that almost fabulous inspiration often referred to, but seldom attained, in which a public meeting is transformed, as it were, into a single individuality, the orator swaying a thousand heads and hearts at once and, by the simple majesty of his all-controlling thought, converting his hearers into the express image of his own soul. That night there were at least a thousand Garrisonians in Nantucket!

At the close of this great meeting I was duly waited on by Mr. John A. Collins,* then the general agent of the Massachusetts Anti-Slavery Society, and urgently solicited by him to become an agent of that society and publicly advocate its principles. I was reluctant to take the proffered position. I had not been quite three years from slavery and was honestly distrustful of my ability, and I wished to be excused. Besides, publicity might discover me to my master, and many other objections presented themselves. But Mr. Collins was not to be refused, and I finally consented to go out for three months, supposing I should in that length of time come to the end of my story and my consequent usefulness.

Here opened for me a new life—a life for which I had had no preparation. Mr. Collins used to say when introducing me to an audience, I was a 'graduate from the peculiar institution, with my diploma *written on my back*.' The three years of my freedom had been spent in the hard school of adversity. My hands seemed to be furnished with something like a leather coating, and I had marked out for myself a life of rough labor, suited to the hardness of my hands, as a means of supporting my family and rearing my children.

Young, ardent and hopeful, I entered upon this new life in the full gush of unsuspecting enthusiasm. The cause was good, the men engaged in it were good, the means to attain its triumph, good. Heaven's blessing must attend all, and freedom must soon be given to the millions pining under a ruthless bondage. My whole heart went with the holy cause, and my most fervent prayer to the Almighty Disposer of the hearts of men was continually offered for its early triumph. In this enthusiastic spirit I dropped into the ranks of freedom's friends and went forth to the battle. For a time I was made to forget that my skin was dark and my hair crisped. For a time I regretted that I could not have shared the hardships and dangers endured by the earlier workers for the slave's release. I found, however, full soon that my enthusiasm had been extravagant, that hardships and dangers were not all over, and that the life now before me had its shadows also, as well as its sunbeams.

Among the first duties assigned me on entering the ranks was to travel in company with Mr. George Foster* to secure subscribers to the *Anti-Slavery Standard*\* and the *Liberator*. With him I traveled and lectured through the eastern counties of Massachusetts. Much interest was awakened—large meetings assembled. Many came, no doubt from curiosity to hear what a negro could say in his own cause. I was generally introduced as a 'chattel'—a 'thing'—a piece of southern property—the chairman assuring the audience that *it* could speak. *Fugitive slaves* were rare then, and as a fugitive slave lecturer, I had the advantage of being a 'bran new fact'—the first one out. Up to that time, a colored man was deemed a fool who confessed himself a runaway slave, not only because of the danger to which he exposed himself of being retaken, but because it was a confession of a very low origin. Some of my colored friends in New Bedford thought very badly of my wisdom in thus exposing and degrading myself. The only precaution I took at the beginning, to prevent Master Thomas from knowing where I was and what I was about, was the withholding my former name, my master's name, and the name of the State and county from which I came. During the first three or four months my speeches were almost exclusively made up of narrations of my own personal experience as a slave. 'Let us have the facts,' said the people. So also said Friend George Foster, who always wished to pin me down to a simple narrative. 'Give us the facts,' said Collins, 'we will take care of the philosophy.' Just here arose some embarrassment. It was impossible for me to repeat the same old story month after month and keep up my interest in it. It was new to the people, it is true, but it was an old story to me; and to go through with it night after night was a task altogether too mechanical for my nature. 'Tell your story, Frederick,' would whisper my revered friend, Mr. Garrison, as I stepped upon the platform. I could not always follow the injunction, for I was now reading and thinking. New views of the subject were being presented to my mind. It did not entirely satisfy me to *narrate* wrongs; I felt like *denouncing* them. I could not always curb my moral indignation for the perpetrators of slaveholding villainy long enough for a circumstantial statement of the facts which I felt almost sure everybody must know. Besides, I was growing and needed room. 'People won't believe you ever were a slave, Frederick, if you keep on this way,' said friend Foster. 'Be yourself,' said Collins, 'and tell your story.' 'Better have a little of the plantation speech than not,' was said to me; 'it is not best that you seem too learned.' These excellent friends were actuated by the best of motives and were not altogether wrong in their advice; and still I must speak just the word that seemed to *me* the word to be spoken *by* me.

At last the apprehended trouble came. People doubted if I had ever been a slave. They said I did not talk like a slave, look like a slave, or act like a slave, and that they believed I had never been south of Mason and Dixon's line. 'He don't tell us where he came from, what his master's name was, or how he got away; besides, he is educated, and is in this a contradiction of all the facts we have concerning the ignorance of the slaves.' Thus I was in a pretty fair way to be denounced as an impostor. The committee of the Massachusetts Anti-Slavery Society knew all the facts in my case and agreed with me thus far in the prudence of keeping them private; but going down the aisles of the churches in which my meetings were held, and hearing the outspoken Yankees repeatedly saying, 'He's never been a slave, I'll warrant you,' I resolved that at no distant day, and by such a revelation of facts as could not be made by any other than a genuine fugitive, I would dispel all doubt. In a little less than four years, therefore, after becoming a public lecturer, I was induced to write out the leading facts connected with my experience in slavery, giving names of persons, places, and dates, thus putting it in the power of any who doubted, to ascertain the truth or falsehood of my story. This statement soon became known in Maryland, and I had reason to believe that an effort would be made to recapture me.

It is not probable that any open attempt to secure me as a slave could have succeeded further than the obtainment by my master of the money value of my bones and sinews. Fortunately for me, in the four years of my labors in the abolition cause I had gained many friends who would have suffered themselves to be taxed to almost any extent to save me from slavery. It was felt that I had committed the double offense of running away and exposing the secrets and crimes of slavery and slaveholders. There was a double motive for seeking my re-enslavement—avarice and vengeance; and while, as I have said, there was little probability of successful recapture, if attempted openly, I was constantly in danger of being spirited away at a moment when my friends could render me no assistance. In traveling about from place to place, often alone, I was much exposed to this sort of attack. Any one cherishing the desire to betray me could easily do so by simply tracing my whereabouts through the anti-slavery journals, for my movements and meetings were made through these in advance. My friends Mr. Garrison and Mr. Phillips* had no faith in the power of Massachusetts to protect me in my right to liberty. Public sentiment and the law, in their opinion, would hand me over to the tormentors. Mr. Phillips especially considered me in danger, and said, when I showed him the manuscript of my story, if in my place he would 'throw it into the fire.' Thus the reader will observe that the overcoming of one difficulty only opened the way for another, and that though I had reached a free State, and had attained a position for public usefulness, I was still under the liability of losing all I had gained.

# CHAPTER IV.

## RECOLLECTIONS OF OLD FRIENDS.

*Work in Rhode Island—Dorr War—Recollections of old friends—Further labors in Rhode Island and elsewhere in New England.*

In the State of Rhode Island, under the leadership of Thomas W. Dorr,* an effort was made in 1841 to set aside the old colonial charter, under which that State had lived and flourished since the Revolution, and to replace it with a new constitution having such improvements as it was thought that time and experience had shown to be wise and necessary. This new constitution was especially framed to enlarge the basis of representation so far as the white people of the State were concerned—to abolish an odious property qualification and to confine the right of suffrage to white male citizens only. Mr. Dorr was himself a well-meaning man, and, after his fashion, a man of broad and progressive views quite in advance of the party with which he acted. To gain their support he consented to this restriction to a class a right which ought to be enjoyed by all citizens. In this he consulted policy rather than right, and at last shared the fate of all compromisers and trimmers, for he was disastrously defeated. The proscriptive features of his constitution shocked the sense of right and roused the moral indignation of the abolitionists of the State, a class which would otherwise have gladly co-operated with him, at the same time that it did nothing to win support from the conservative class which clung to the old charter. Anti-slavery men wanted a new constitution, but they did not want a defective instrument which required reform at the start. The result was that such men as William M. Chase, Thomas Davis, George L. Clark, Asa Fairbanks, Alphonso Janes, and others of Providence, the Perry brothers of Westerly, John Brown and C. C. Eldridge of East Greenwich, Daniel Mitchell, William Adams, and Robert Shove of Pawtucket, Peleg Clark, Caleb Kelton, G. J. Adams, and the Anthonys and Goulds of Coventry and vicinity, Edward Harris of Woonsocket, and other abolitionists of the State, decided that the time had come when the people of Rhode Island might be taught a more comprehensive gospel of human rights than had gotten itself into this Dorr constitution. The public mind was awake, and one class of its people at least was ready to work with us to the extent of seeking to defeat the proposed constitution, though their

reasons for such work were far different from ours. Stephen S. Foster,*
Parker Pillsbury,* Abby Kelley,* James Monroe,* and myself were called
into the State to advocate equal rights as against this narrow and proscriptive constitution. The work to which we were invited was not free
from difficulty. The majority of the people were evidently with the new
constitution; even the word *white* in it chimed well with the popular
prejudice against the colored race, and at the first helped to make the
movement popular. On the other hand, all the arguments which the
Dorr men could urge against a property qualification for suffrage were
equally cogent against a color qualification, and this was our advantage.
But the contest was intensely bitter and exciting. We were as usual
denounced as intermeddlers (carpet-bagger had not come into use at
that time), and were told to mind our own business, and the like, a mode
of defense common to men when called to account for mean and dis-
creditable conduct. Stephen S. Foster, Parker Pillsbury, and the rest of
us were not the kind of men to be ordered off by that sort of opposition.
We cared nothing for the Dorr party on the one hand, nor the 'law and
order party' on the other. What we wanted, and what we labored to
obtain, was a constitution free from the narrow, selfish, and senseless
limitation of the word *white*. Naturally enough, when we said a strong
and striking word against the Dorr Constitution the conservatives were
pleased and applauded, while the Dorr men were disgusted and indignant. Foster and Pillsbury were like the rest of us, young, strong, and at
their best in this contest. The splendid vehemence of the one, and the
weird and terrible denunciations of the other, never failed to stir up
mobocratic wrath wherever they spoke. Foster, especially, was effective
in this line. His theory was that he must make converts or mobs. If neither came he charged it either to his want of skill or his unfaithfulness.
I was much with Mr. Foster during the tour in Rhode Island, and though
at times he seemed to me extravagant and needlessly offensive in his
manner of presenting his ideas, yet take him for all in all, he was one of
the most impressive advocates the cause of the American slave ever had.
No white man ever made the black man's cause more completely his
own. Abby Kelley, since Abby Kelley Foster, was perhaps the most successful of any of us. Her youth and simple Quaker beauty, combined
with her wonderful earnestness, her large knowledge and great logical
power, bore down all opposition to the end, wherever she spoke, though
she was before pelted with foul eggs, and no less foul words, from the
noisy mobs which attended us.

Monroe and I were less aggressive than either of our co-workers, and
of course did not provoke the same resistance. He, at least, had the

eloquence that charms, and the skill that disarms. I think that our labors in Rhode Island during this Dorr excitement did more to abolitionize the State than any previous or subsequent work. It was the 'tide,' 'taken at the flood.' One effect of those labors was to induce the old 'Law and Order' party, when it set about making its new constitution, to avoid the narrow folly of the Dorrites, and make a constitution which should not abridge any man's rights on account of race or color. Such a constitution was finally adopted.

Owing perhaps to my efficiency in this campaign I was for awhile employed in further labors in Rhode Island by the State Anti-Slavery Society, and made there many friends to my cause as well as to myself. As a class the abolitionists of this State partook of the spirit of its founder.* They had their own opinions, were independent, and called no man master. I have reason to remember them most gratefully. They received me as a man and a brother, when I was new from the house of bondage and had few of the graces derived from free and refined society. They took me with earnest hand to their homes and hearths, and made me feel that though I wore the burnished livery of the sun I was still a countryman and kinsman of whom they were never ashamed. I can never forget the Clarks, Keltons, Chases, Browns, Adams, Greenes, Sissons, Eldredges, Mitchells, Shoves, Anthonys, Applins, Janes, Goulds, Fairbanks, and many others.

While thus remembering the noble anti-slavery men and women of Rhode Island, I do not forget that I suffered much rough usage within her borders. It was like all the northern States at that time, under the influence of slave power, and often showed a proscriptive and persecuting spirit, especially upon its railways, steamboats, and in its public houses. The Stonington route was a 'hard road' for a colored man 'to travel' in that day. I was several times dragged from the cars for the *crime* of being colored. On the Sound between New York and Stonington, there were the same proscriptions which I have before named as enforced on the steamboats running between New York and Newport. No colored man was allowed abaft the wheel, and in all seasons of the year, in heat or cold, wet or dry, the deck was his only place. If I would lie down at night I must do so upon the freight on deck, and this in cold weather was not a very comfortable bed. When traveling in company with my white friends I always urged them to leave me and go into the cabin and take their comfortable births. I saw no reason why they should be miserable because I was. Some of them took my advice very readily. I confess, however, that while I was entirely honest in urging them to go, and saw no principle that should bind them to stay and suffer with me, I always felt a little nearer to those who did not take my advice and persisted in sharing my hardships with me.

There is something in the world above fixed rules and the logic of right and wrong, and there is some foundation for recognizing works, which may be called works of supererogation. Wendell Phillips, James Monroe, and William White,* were always dear to me for their nice feeling at this point. I have known James Monroe to pull his coat about him and crawl upon the cotton bales between decks and pass the night with me, without a murmur. Wendell Phillips would never go into a first-class car while I was forced into what was called the Jim Crow car.* True men they were, who could accept welcome at no man's table where I was refused. I speak of these gentlemen, not as singular or exceptional cases, but as representatives of a large class of the early workers for the abolition of slavery. As a general rule there was in New England after 1840, little difficulty in obtaining suitable places where I could plead the cause of my people. The abolitionists had passed the Red Sea of mobs and had conquered the right to a respectful hearing. I, however, found several towns in which the people closed their doors and refused to entertain the subject. Notably among these was Hartford, Conn., and Grafton, Mass. In the former place Messrs. Garrison, Hudson, Foster, Abby Kelley and myself determined to hold our meetings under the open sky, which we did in a little court under the eaves of the 'sanctuary' ministered unto by the Rev. Dr. Hawes, with much satisfaction to ourselves, and I think with advantage to our cause. In Grafton I was alone, and there was neither house, hall, church, nor market-place in which I could speak to the people; but, *determined to speak*, I went to the hotel and borrowed a dinner-bell, with which in hand I passed through the principal streets, ringing the bell and crying out, '*Notice!* Frederick Douglass, recently a slave, will lecture on American Slavery, on Grafton Common, this evening, at 7 o'clock. Those who would like to hear of the workings of slavery by one of the slaves are respectfully invited to attend.' This notice brought out a large audience, after which the largest church in town was open to me. Only in one instance was I compelled to pursue this course thereafter, and that was in Manchester, N. H., and my labors there were followed by similar results. When people found that I would be heard, they saw it was the part of wisdom to open the way for me.

My treatment in the use of public conveyances about these times was extremely rough, especially on the 'Eastern Railroad, from Boston to Portland.' On that road, as on many others, there was a mean, dirty and uncomfortable car set apart for colored travelers called the 'Jim Crow' car. Regarding this as the fruit of slaveholding prejudice and being determined to fight the spirit of slavery wherever I might find it, I resolved to avoid this car, though it sometimes required some courage to do so. The colored people generally accepted the situation and complained of me as making matters worse rather than better by refusing to submit to this proscription. I, however, persisted, and sometimes was soundly beaten by conductor and brakeman. On one occasion six of these 'fellows of the baser sort,' under the direction of the conductor, set out to eject me from my seat. As usual, I had purchased a first-class ticket and paid the required sum for it, and on the requirement of the conductor to leave, refused to do so, when he called on these men to 'snake me out.' They attempted to obey with an air which plainly told me they relished the job. They however found me *much attached* to my seat, and in removing me I tore away two or three of the surrounding ones, on which I held with a firm grasp, and did the car no service in some other respects. I was strong and muscular, and the seats were not then so firmly attached or of as solid make as now. The result was that Stephen A. Chase, superintendent of the road, ordered all passenger trains to pass through Lynn, where I then lived, without stopping. This was a great inconvenience to the people, large numbers of whom did business in Boston and at other points on the road. Led on, however, by James N. Buffum,* Jonathan Buffum, Christopher Robinson, William Bassett, and others, the people of Lynn stood bravely by me and denounced the railroad management in emphatic terms. Mr. Chase made reply that a railroad corporation was neither a religious nor reformatory body; that the road was run for the accommodation of the public, and that *it* required the exclusion of colored people from its cars. With an air of triumph he told us that we ought not to expect a railroad company to be better than the evangelical church, and that until the churches abolished the 'negro pew' we ought not to expect the railroad company to abolish the negro car. This argument was certainly good enough as against the church, but good for nothing as against the demands of justice and equality. My old and dear friend J. N. Buffum made a point against the company that they 'often allowed dogs and monkeys to ride in first-class cars, and yet excluded a man like Frederick Douglass!' In a very few years this barbarous practice was put away, and I think there have been no instances of such exclusion during the past thirty years; and colored people now, everywhere in New England, ride upon equal terms with other passengers.

# CHAPTER V.

## ONE HUNDRED CONVENTIONS.

*Anti-slavery conventions held in parts of New England, and in some of the Middle and Western States—Mobs—Incidents, etc.*

THE year 1843 was one of remarkable anti-slavery activity. The New England Anti-Slavery Society, at its annual meeting held in the spring of that year, resolved, under the auspices of Mr. Garrison and his friends, to hold a series of one hundred conventions. The territory embraced in this plan for creating anti-slavery sentiment included New Hampshire, Vermont, New York, Ohio, Indiana, and Pennsylvania. I had the honor to be chosen one of the agents to assist in these proposed conventions, and I never entered upon any work with more heart and hope. All that the American people needed, I thought, was light. Could they know slavery as I knew it, they would hasten to the work of its extinction. The corps of speakers who were to be associated with me in carrying on these conventions was Messrs. George Bradburn, John A. Collins, James Monroe, William A. White, Charles L. Remond,* and Sydney Howard Gay.* They were all masters of the subject, and some of them able and eloquent orators. It was a piece of great good fortune to me, only a few years from slavery as I was, to be brought into contact with such men. It was a real campaign, and required nearly six months for its accomplishment.

Those who only know the State of Vermont as it is today can hardly understand, and must wonder that there was forty years ago need for anti-slavery effort within its borders. Our first convention was held in Middlebury, its chief seat of learning and the home of William Slade,* who was for years the co-worker with John Quincy Adams* in Congress; and yet in this town the opposition to our anti-slavery convention was intensely bitter and violent. The only man of note in the town whom I now remember as giving us sympathy or welcome was Mr. Edward Barber, who was a man of courage as well as ability, and did his best to make our convention a success. In advance of our arrival the college students had very industriously and mischievously placarded the town with violent aspersions of our characters and the grossest misrepresentations of our principles, measures, and objects. I was described as an escaped convict from the State prison, and the other speakers were assailed not less slanderously. Few people attended our meeting, and apparently little was accomplished by it. In the neighboring town of Ferrisburgh the case was different and more favorable. The way had been prepared for us by such stalwart anti-slavery workers as Orson S. Murray, Charles C. Burleigh, Rowland T. Robinson, and others. Upon the whole, however, the several towns visited showed that Vermont was surprisingly under the influence of the slave power. Her proud boast that within her borders no slave had ever been delivered up to his master, did not hinder her hatred to *anti*-slavery. What was in this respect true of the Green Mountain State was most discouragingly true of New York, the State next visited. All along the Erie canal, from Albany to Buffalo, there was evinced apathy, indifference, aversion, and sometimes a mobocratic spirit. Even Syracuse, afterward the home of the humane Samuel J. May* and the scene of the 'Jerry rescue;'* where Gerrit Smith, Beriah Greene, William Goodell, Alvin Stewart, and other able men taught their noblest lessons, would not at that time furnish us with church, market, house, or hall in which to hold our meetings. Discovering this state of things, some of our number were disposed to turn our backs upon the town and to shake its dust from our feet, but of these, I am glad to say, I was not one. I had somewhere read of a command to go into the hedges and highways and compel men to come in. Mr. Stephen Smith, under whose hospitable roof we were made at home, thought as I did. It would be easy to silence anti-slavery agitation if refusing its agents the use of halls and churches could affect that result. The house of our friend Smith stood on the southwest corner of the park, which was well covered with young trees too small to furnish shade or shelter, but better than none. Taking my stand under a small tree in the southeast corner of this park I began to speak in the morning to an audience of five persons, and before the close of my afternoon meeting I had before me not less than five hundred. In the evening I was waited upon by officers of the Congregational church and tendered the use of an old wooden building which they had deserted for a better, but still owned, and here our convention was continued during three days. I believe there has been no trouble to find places in Syracuse in which to hold anti-slavery meetings since. I never go there without endeavoring to see that tree, which, like the cause it sheltered, has grown large and strong and imposing.

I believe my first offense against our Anti-Slavery Israel was committed during these Syracuse meetings. It was on this wise: Our general agent, John A. Collins, had recently returned from England full of communistic ideas, which ideas would do away with individual property, and have all things in common. He had arranged a corps of speakers of his communistic persuasion, consisting of John O. Wattles, Nathaniel Whiting, and John Orvis, to follow our anti-slavery conventions, and, while our meeting was in progress in Syracuse, a meeting, as the reader will observe, obtained under much difficulty, Mr. Collins came in with his new friends and doctrines and proposed to adjourn our anti-slavery discussions and take up the subject of communism. To this I ventured to object. I held that it was imposing an additional burden of unpopularity on our cause, and an act of bad faith with the people, who paid the salary of Mr. Collins, and were responsible for these hundred conventions. Strange to say, my course in this matter did not meet the approval of Mrs. M. W. Chapman,* an influential member of the board of managers of the Massachusetts Anti-Slavery Society, and called out a sharp reprimand from her, for insubordination to my superiors. This was a strange and distressing revelation to me, and one of which I was not soon relieved. I thought I had only done my duty, and I think so still. The chief reason for the reprimand was the use which the liberty party-papers* would make of my seeming rebellion against the commanders of our anti-slavery army.

In the growing city of Rochester we had in every way a better reception. Abolitionists of all shades of opinion were broad enough to give the Garrisonians (for such we were) a hearing. Samuel D. Porter and the Avery family, though they belonged to the Gerrit Smith, Myron Holly, and William Goodell school, were not so narrow as to refuse us the use of their church for the convention. They heard our moral suasion arguments, and in a manly way met us in debate. We were opposed to carrying the anti-slavery cause to the ballot-box, and they believed in carrying it there. They looked at slavery as a creature of *law*; we regarded it as a creature of public opinion. It is surprising how small the difference appears as I look back to it, over the space of forty years; yet at the time of it this difference was immense.

During our stay at Rochester we were hospitably entertained by Isaac and Amy Post,* two people of all-abounding benevolence, the truest and best of Long Island and Elias Hicks Quakers. They were not more amiable than brave, for they never seemed to ask, What will the world say? but walked straight forward in what seemed to them the line of duty, please or offend whomsoever it might. Many a poor fugitive slave found shelter under their roof when such shelter was hard to find elsewhere, and I mention them here in the warmth and fullness of earnest gratitude.

Pleased with our success in Rochester, we—that is, Mr. Bradburn and myself—made our way to Buffalo, then a rising city of steamboats, bustle, and business. Buffalo was too busy to attend to such matters as we had in hand. Our friend, Mr. Marsh, had been able to secure for our convention only an old dilapidated and deserted room, formerly used as a post-office. We went at the time appointed, and found seated a few cabmen in their coarse, every-day clothes, whips in hand, while their teams were standing on the street waiting for a job. Friend Bradburn looked around upon this unpromising audience, and turned upon his heel, saying he would not speak to 'such a set of ragamuffins,' and took the first steamer to Cleveland, the home of his brother Charles, and left me to 'do' Buffalo alone. For nearly a week I spoke every day in this old post-office to audiences constantly increasing in numbers and respectability, till the Baptist church was thrown open to me; and when this became too small I went on Sunday into the open Park and addressed an assembly of four or five thousand persons. After this my colored friends, Charles L. Remond, Henry Highland Garnett,* Theodore S. Wright, Amos G. Beaman, Charles M. Ray, and other well-known colored men held a convention here, and then Remond and myself left for our next meeting in Clinton county, Ohio. This was held under a great shed, built for this special purpose by the abolitionists, of whom Dr. Abram Brook and Valentine Nicholson were the most noted. Thousands gathered here and were addressed by Bradburn, White, Monroe, Remond, Gay, and myself. The influence of this meeting was deep and widespread. It would be tedious to tell of all, or a small part of all that was interesting and illustrative of the difficulties encountered by the early advocates of anti-slavery in connection with this campaign, and hence I leave this part of it at once.

From Ohio we divided our forces and went into Indiana. At our first meeting we were mobbed, and some of us had our good clothes spoiled by evil-smelling eggs. This was at Richmond, where Henry Clay had been recently invited to the high seat of the Quaker meeting-house just after his gross abuse of Mr. Mendenhall, because of the latter presenting to him a respectful petition, asking him to emancipate his slaves.* At Pendleton this mobocratic spirit was even more pronounced. It was found impossible to obtain a building in which to hold our convention, and our friends, Dr. Fussell and others, erected a platform in the woods, where quite a large audience assembled. Mr. Bradburn, Mr. White and myself were in attendance. As soon as we began to speak a mob of about sixty of the roughest characters I ever looked upon ordered us, through its leaders, to 'be silent,' threatening us, if we were not, with violence. We attempted to dissuade them, but they had not come to parley but to fight, and were well armed. They tore down the platform on which we stood, assaulted Mr. White and knocked out several of his teeth, dealt a heavy blow on William A. White, striking him on the back part of the head, badly cutting his scalp and felling him to the ground. Undertaking to fight my way through the crowd with a stick which I caught up in the mêlée, I attracted the fury of the mob, which laid me prostrate on the ground under a torrent of blows. Leaving me thus, with my right hand broken, and in a state of unconsciousness, the mobocrats hastily mounted their horses and rode to Andersonville, where most of them resided. I was soon raised up and revived by Neal Hardy, a kind-hearted member of the Society of Friends, and carried by him in his wagon about three miles in the country to his home, where I was tenderly nursed and bandaged by good Mrs. Hardy till I was again on my feet; but, as the bones broken were not properly set, my hand has never recovered its natural strength and dexterity. We lingered long in Indiana, and the good effects of our labors there are felt at this day. I have lately visited Pendleton, now one of the best republican towns in the State, and looked again upon the spot where I was beaten down, and have again taken by the hand some of the witnesses of that scene, amongst whom was the kind, good lady—Mrs. Hardy—who, so like the good Samaritan of old, bound up my wounds, and cared for me so kindly. A complete history of these hundred conventions would fill a volume far larger than the one in which this simple reference is to find a place. It would be a grateful duty to speak of the noble young men who forsook ease and pleasure, as did White, Gay, and Monroe, and endured all manner of privations in the cause of the enslaved and down-trodden of my race. Gay, Monroe, and myself are the only ones of those who now survive who participated as agents in the one hundred conventions. Mr. Monroe was for many years consul to Brazil, and has since been a faithful member of Congress from the Oberlin District, Ohio, and has filled other important positions in his State. Mr. Gay was managing editor of the *National Anti-Slavery Standard*, and afterwards of the New York *Tribune*, and still later of the New York *Evening Post*.

# CHAPTER VI.

## IMPRESSIONS ABROAD.

*Danger to be averted—A refuge sought abroad—Voyage on the
steamship Cambria—Refusal of first-class passage—Attractions of the
forecastle-deck—Hutchinson family—Invited to make a speech—
Southerners feel insulted—Captain threatens to put them in irons—
Experiences abroad—Attentions received—Impressions of different
members of Parliament and of other public men—Contrast with life
in America—Kindness of friends—Their purchase of my person and
the gift of the same to myself—My return.*

As I have before intimated, the publishing of my 'Narrative' was
regarded by my friends with mingled feelings of satisfaction and apprehension. They were glad to have the doubts and insinuations which the
advocates and apologists of slavery had made against me proved to the
world to be false, but they had many fears lest this very proof would
endanger my safety, and make it necessary for me to leave a position
which in a signal manner had opened before me, and one in which I had
thus far been efficient in assisting to arouse the moral sentiment of the
community against a system which had deprived me, in common with
my fellow-slaves, of all the attributes of manhood.

I became myself painfully alive to the liability which surrounded me,
and which might at any moment scatter all my proud hopes and return
me to a doom worse than death. It was thus I was led to seek a refuge in
monarchical England from the dangers of republican slavery. A rude,
uncultivated fugitive slave, I was driven to that country to which
American young gentlemen go to increase their stock of knowledge, to
seek pleasure, and to have their rough democratic manners softened by
contact with English aristocratic refinement.

My friend James N. Buffum of Lynn, Mass., who was to accompany
me, applied on board the steamer Cambria of the Cunard line for
tickets, and was told that I could not be received as a cabin passenger.
American prejudice against color had triumphed over British liberality
and civilization, and had erected a color test as a condition for crossing
the sea in the cabin of a British vessel.

The insult was keenly felt by my white friends, but to me such insults
were so frequent and expected that it was of no great consequence
whether I went in the cabin or in the steerage. Moreover, I felt that if
I could not go in the first cabin, first cabin passengers could come in the

second cabin, and in this thought I was not mistaken, as I soon found myself an object of more general interest than I wished to be, and, so far from being degraded by being placed in the second cabin, that part of the ship became the scene of as much pleasure and refinement as the cabin itself. The Hutchinson family from New Hampshire—the sweet singers of anti-slavery and the 'good time coming'—were fellow-passengers, and often came to my rude forecastle-deck and sang their sweetest songs, making the place eloquent with music and alive with spirited conversation. They not only visited me, but invited me to visit them, and in two or three days after leaving Boston one part of the ship was about as free to me as another. My visits there, however, were but seldom. I preferred to live within my privileges and keep upon my own premises. This course was quite as much in accord with good policy as with my own feelings. The effect was that with the majority of the passengers all color distinctions were flung to the winds, and I found myself treated with every mark of respect from the beginning to the end of the voyage, except in one single instance, and in that I came near being mobbed for complying with an invitation given me by the passengers and the captain of the Cambria to deliver a lecture on slavery. There were several young men, passengers from Georgia and New Orleans, and they were pleased to regard my lecture as an insult offered to them, and swore I should not speak. They went so far as to threaten to throw me overboard, and but for the firmness of Captain Judkins they would probably, under the inspiration of slavery and brandy, have attempted to put their threats into execution. I have no space to describe this scene, although its tragic and comic features are well worth describing. An end was put to the *mêlée* by the captain's call to the ship's company to put the salt-water mobocrats in irons, at which determined order the gentlemen of the lash scampered, and for the remainder of the voyage conducted themselves very decorously.

This incident of the voyage brought me within two days after landing at Liverpool before the British public. The gentlemen so promptly withheld in their attempted violence toward me flew to the press to justify their conduct and to denounce me as a worthless and insolent negro. This course was even less wise than the conduct it was intended to sustain, for, besides awakening something like a national interest in me, and securing me an audience, it brought out counter statements and threw upon themselves the blame which they had sought to fasten upon me and upon the gallant captain of the ship.

My visit to England did much for me every way. Not the least among the many advantages derived from it was the opportunity it afforded me of becoming acquainted with educated people and of seeing and hearing many of the most distinguished men of that country. My friend Mr. Wendell Phillips, knowing something of my appreciation of orators and oratory, had said to me before leaving Boston: 'Although Americans are generally better speakers than Englishmen, you will find in England individual orators superior to the best of ours.' I do not know that Mr. Phillips was quite just to himself in this remark, for I found few, if any, superior to him in the gift of speech. When I went to England that country was in the midst of a tremendous agitation. The people were divided by two great questions of 'Repeal'—the repeal of the corn laws* and the repeal of the union between England and Ireland.*

Debate ran high in Parliament and among the people everywhere, especially concerning the corn laws. Two powerful interests of the country confronted each other—one venerable from age, and the other young, stalwart, and growing. Both strove for ascendancy. Conservatism united for retaining the corn laws, while the rising power of commerce and manufactures demanded repeal. It was interest against interest, but something more and deeper, for while there was aggrandizement of the landed aristocracy on the one side, there was famine and pestilence on the other. Of the anti-corn-law movement, Richard Cobden* and John Bright,* both then members of Parliament, were the leaders. They were the rising statesmen of England, and possessed a very friendly disposition toward America. Mr. Bright, who is now Right Honorable John Bright, and occupies a high place in the British cabinet, was friendly to the loyal and progressive spirit which abolished our slavery and saved our country from dismemberment. I have seen and heard both of these men, and, if I may be allowed so much egotism, I may say I was acquainted with both of them. I was, besides, a welcome guest at the house of Mr. Bright in Rochdale, and treated as a friend and brother among his brothers and sisters. Messrs. Cobden and Bright were well-matched leaders. One was in large measure the complement of the other. They were spoken of usually as Cobden and Bright, but there was no reason, except that Cobden was the elder of the two, why their names might not have been reversed.

They were about equally fitted for their respective parts in the great movement of which they were the distinguished leaders, and neither was likely to encroach upon the work of the other. The contrast was quite marked in their persons as well as in their oratory. The powerful speeches of the one, as they traveled together over the country, heightened the effect of the speeches of the other, so that their difference was about as effective for good as was their agreement.

Mr. Cobden—for an Englishman—was lean, tall, and slightly sallow, and might have been taken for an American or Frenchman. Mr. Bright was, in the broadest sense, an Englishman, abounding in all the physical perfections peculiar to his countrymen—full, round and ruddy. Cobden had dark eyes and hair, a well-formed head high above his shoulders, and, when sitting quiet, a look of sadness and fatigue. In the House of Commons he often sat with one hand supporting his head. Bright appeared the very opposite in this and other respects. His eyes were blue, his hair light, his head massive and firmly set upon his shoulders, suggesting immense energy and determination. In his oratory Mr. Cobden was cool, candid, deliberate, straightforward, yet at times slightly hesitating. Bright, on the other hand, was fervid, fluent, rapid; always ready in thought or word. Mr. Cobden was full of facts and figures, dealing in statistics by the hour. Mr. Bright was full of wit, knowledge, and pathos, and possessed amazing power of expression. One spoke to the cold, calculating side of the British nation, which asks 'if the new idea will pay?' The other spoke to the infinite side of human nature—the side which asks, first of all, 'Is it right? is it just? is it humane?' Wherever these two great men appeared, the people assembled in thousands. They could, at an hour's notice, pack the Town Hall of Birmingham, which would hold seven thousand persons, or the Free Trade Hall in Manchester, and Covent Garden theater, London, each of which was capable of holding eight thousand.

One of the first attentions shown me by these gentlemen was to make me welcome at the Free-Trade Club, in London.

I was not long in England before a crisis was reached in the anti-corn-law movement. The announcement that Sir Robert Peel,* then prime minister of England, had become a convert to the views of Messrs. Cobden and Bright, came upon the country with startling effect, and formed the turning-point in the anti-corn-law question. Sir Robert had been the strong defense of the landed aristocracy of England, and his defection left them without a competent leader; and just here came the opportunity for Mr. Benjamin Disraeli,* the Hebrew, since Lord Beaconsfield. To him it was in public affairs the 'tide which led on to fortune.'* With a bitterness unsurpassed he had been denounced, by reason of his being a Jew, as a lineal descendant of the thief on the cross. But now his time had come, and he was not the man to permit it to pass unimproved. For the first time, it seems, he conceived the idea of placing himself at the head of a great party, and thus become the chief defender of the landed aristocracy. The way was plain. He was to transcend all others in effective denunciation of Sir Robert

Peel, and surpass all others in zeal. His ability was equal to the situation, and the world knows the result of his ambition. I watched him narrowly when I saw him in the House of Commons, but I saw and heard nothing there that foreshadowed the immense space he at last came to fill in the mind of his country and the world. He had nothing of the grace and warmth of Peel in debate, and his speeches were better in print than when listened to; yet when he spoke all eyes were fixed and all ears attent. Despite all his ability and power, however, as the defender of the landed interests of England, his cause was already lost. The increasing power of the anti-corn-law league, the burden of the tax upon bread, the cry of distress coming from famine-stricken Ireland, and the adhesion of Peel to the views of Cobden and Bright, made the repeal of the corn laws speedy and certain.

The repeal of the union between England and Ireland was not so fortunate. It is still, under one name or another, the cherished hope and inspiration of her sons. It stands little better or stronger than it did six and thirty years ago, when its greatest advocate, Daniel O'Connell, welcomed me to Ireland and to 'Conciliation Hall,'* and where I first had a specimen of his truly wondrous eloquence. Until I heard this man I had thought that the story of his oratory and power were greatly exaggerated. I did not see how a man could speak to twenty or thirty thousand people at one time and be heard by any considerable portion of them, but the mystery was solved when I saw his ample person and heard his musical voice. His eloquence came down upon the vast assembly like a summer thunder-shower upon a dusty road. He could at will stir the multitude to a tempest of wrath or reduce it to the silence with which a mother leaves the cradle-side of her sleeping babe. Such tenderness, such pathos, such world-embracing love!—and, on the other hand, such indignation, such fiery and thunderous denunciation, such wit and humor, I never heard surpassed, if equaled, at home or abroad. He held Ireland within the grasp of his strong hand, and could lead it whithersoever he would, for Ireland believed in him and loved him as she has loved and believed in no leader since. In Dublin, when he had been absent from that city a few weeks, I saw him followed through Sackville street by a multitude of little boys and girls, shouting in loving accents, 'There goes Dan! there goes Dan!' while he looked at the ragged and shoeless crowd with the kindly air of a loving parent returning to his gleeful children. He was called 'The Liberator,' and not without cause, for, though he failed to effect the repeal of the union between England and Ireland, he fought out the battle of Catholic emancipation, and was clearly the friend of liberty the world over. In introducing me to an immense audience in Conciliation Hall he playfully called me the 'Black O'Connell of the United States.' Nor did he let the occasion pass without his usual word of denunciation of our slave system. O. A. Brownson* had then recently become a Catholic, and taking advantage of his new Catholic audience in 'Brownson's *Review*,' had charged O'Connell with attacking American institutions. In reply Mr. O'Connell said: 'I am charged with attacking American institutions, as slavery is called; I am not ashamed of this attack. My sympathy is not confined to the narrow limits of my own green Ireland; my spirit walks abroad upon sea and land, and wherever there is oppression I hate the oppressor, and wherever the tyrant rears his head I will deal my bolts upon it, and wherever there is sorrow and suffering, there is my spirit to succor and relieve.' No transatlantic statesman bore a testimony more marked and telling against the crime and curse of slavery than did Daniel O'Connell. He would shake the hand of no slaveholder, nor allow himself to be introduced to one if he knew him to be such. When the friends of repeal in the Southern States sent him money with which to carry on his work, he, with ineffable scorn, refused the bribe and sent back what he considered the blood-stained offering, saying he would 'never purchase the freedom of Ireland with the price of slaves.'

It was not long after my seeing Mr. O'Connell that his health broke down, and his career ended in death. I felt that a great champion of freedom had fallen, and that the cause of the American slave, not less than the cause of his country, had met with a great loss. All the more was this felt when I saw the kind of men who came to the front when the voice of O'Connell was no longer heard in Ireland. He was succeeded by the Duffys, Mitchells, Meaghers, and others,—men who loved liberty for themselves and their country, but were utterly destitute of sympathy with the cause of liberty in countries other than their own. One of the first utterances of John Mitchell on reaching this country, from his exile and bondage, was a wish for a 'slave plantation, well stocked with slaves.'

Besides hearing Cobden, Bright, Peel, Disraeli, O'Connell, Lord John Russell, and other Parliamentary debaters, it was my good fortune to hear Lord Brougham* when nearly at his best. He was then a little over sixty, and that for a British statesman is not considered old; and in his case there were thirty years of life still before him. He struck me as the most wonderful speaker of them all. How he was ever reported I cannot imagine. Listening to him was like standing near the track of a railway train, drawn by a locomotive at the rate of forty miles an hour. You are riveted to the spot, charmed with the sublime spectacle of speed and power, but can give no description of the carriages, or of the passengers at the windows. There was so much to see and hear, and so little time left the beholder and hearer to note particulars, that when this strange man sat down you felt like one who had hastily passed through the bewildering wonders of a world's exhibition. On the occasion of my listening to him, his speech was on the postal relations of England with the outside world, and he seemed to have a perfect knowledge of the postal arrangements of every nation in Europe, and, indeed, in the whole universe. He possessed the great advantage, so valuable to a Parliamentary debater, of being able to make all interruptions serve the purpose of his thought and speech, and to carry on a dialogue with several persons without interrupting the rapid current of his reasoning. I had more curiosity to see and hear this man than any other in England, and he more than fulfilled my expectations.

While in England, I saw few literary celebrities, except William and Mary Howitt,* and Sir John Bowering.* I was invited to breakfast by the latter in company with Wm. Lloyd Garrison, and spent a delightful morning with him, chiefly as a listener to their conversation. Sir John was a poet, a statesman, and a diplomat, and had represented England as minister to China. He was full of interesting information, and had a charming way of imparting his knowledge. The conversation was about slavery and about China, and as my knowledge was very slender about the 'Flowery Kingdom' and its people, I was greatly interested in Sir John's description of the ideas and manners prevailing among them. According to him, the doctrine of substitution was in that country carried so far that men sometimes procured others to suffer even the penalty of death in their stead. Justice seemed not intent upon the punishment of the actual criminal, if only somebody was punished when the law was violated.

William and Mary Howitt were among the kindliest people I ever met. Their interest in America, and their well-known testimonies against slavery, made me feel much at home with them at their house in that part of London known as Clapham. Whilst stopping here, I met the Swedish poet and author—Hans Christian Andersen.* He, like myself, was a guest, spending a few days. I saw but little of him though under the same roof. He was singular in his appearance, and equally singular in his silence. His mind seemed to me all the while turned inwardly. He walked about the beautiful garden as one might in a dream. The Howitts had translated his works into English, and could of course address him in his own language. Possibly his bad English, and my destitution of Swedish, may account for the fact of our mutual silence, and yet I observed he was much the same towards every one. Mr. and Mrs. Howitt were indefatigable writers. Two more industrious and kind-hearted people did not breathe. With all their literary work, they always had time to devote to strangers, and to all benevolent efforts to ameliorate the condition of the poor and needy. Quakers though they were, they took deep interest in the Hutchinsons—Judson, John, Asa, and Abby—who were much at their house during my stay there. Mrs. Howitt not inaptly styled them a '*Band of young apostles.*' They sang for the oppressed and the poor—for liberty and humanity.

Whilst in Edinburgh, so famous for its beauty, its educational institutions, its literary men, and its history, I had a very intense desire gratified—and that was to see and converse with George Combe,* the eminent mental philosopher, and author of 'Combe's Constitution of Man,' a book which had been placed in my hands a few years before, by Doctor Peleg Clark of Rhode Island, the reading of which had relieved my path of many shadows. In company with George Thompson, James N. Buffum, and William L. Garrison, I had the honor to be invited by Mr. Combe to breakfast, and the occasion was one of the most delightful I met in dear old Scotland. Of course, in the presence of such men, my part was a very subordinate one. I was a listener. Mr. Combe did the most of the talking, and did it so well that nobody felt like interposing a word, except so far as to draw him on. He discussed the corn laws, and the proposal to reduce the hours of labor. He looked at all political and social questions through his peculiar mental science. His manner was remarkably quiet, and he spoke as not expecting opposition to his views. Phrenology explained everything to him, from the finite to the infinite. I look back with much satisfaction to the morning spent with this singularly clearheaded man.

It would detain the reader too long, and make this volume too large, to tell of the many kindnesses shown me while abroad, or even to mention all the great and noteworthy persons who gave me a friendly hand and a cordial welcome; but there is one other, now long gone to his rest, of whom a few words must be spoken, and that one was Thomas Clarkson*—the last of the noble line of Englishmen who inaugurated the anti-slavery movement for England and the civilized world—the life-long friend and co-worker with Granville Sharpe, William Wilberforce, Thomas Fowell Buxton, and other leaders in that great reform which nearly put an end to slavery in all parts of the globe. As in the case of George Combe, I went to see Mr. Clarkson in company with Messrs. Garrison and Thompson. They had by note advised him of our coming, and had received one in reply, bidding us welcome. We found the venerable object of our visit seated at a table where he had been busily writing a letter to America against slavery; for though in his eighty-seventh year, he continued to write. When we were presented to him, he rose to receive us. The scene was impressive. It was the meeting of two centuries. Garrison, Thompson, and myself were young men. After shaking hands with my two distinguished friends, and giving them welcome, he took one of my hands in both of his, and, in a tremulous voice, said, 'God bless you, Frederick Douglass! I have given sixty years of my life to the emancipation of your people, and if I had sixty years more they should all be given to the same cause.' Our stay with this great-hearted old man was short. He was feeble, and our presence greatly excited him, and we left the house with something of the feeling with which a man takes final leave of a beloved friend at the edge of the grave.

Some notion may be formed of the difference in my feelings and circumstances while abroad, from an extract from one of a series of letters addressed by me to Mr. Garrison, and published in the *Liberator*. It was written on the 1st day of January, 1846:

'My Dear Friend Garrison:

'Up to this time, I have given no direct expression of the views, feelings, and opinions which I have formed respecting the character and condition of the people of this land. I have refrained thus purposely. I wish to speak advisedly, and in order to do this, I have waited till, I trust, experience has brought my opinion to an intelligent maturity. I have been thus careful, not because I think what I say will have much effect in shaping the opinions of the world, but because what influence I may possess, whether little or much, I wish to go in the right direction, and according to truth. I hardly need say that in speaking of Ireland I shall be influenced by no prejudices in favor of America. I think my circumstances all forbid that. I have no end to serve, no creed to uphold, no government to defend; and as to nation, I belong to none. I have no protection at home, or resting-place abroad. The land of my birth welcomes me to her shores only as a slave, and spurns with contempt the idea of treating me differently; so that I am an outcast from the society of my childhood, and an outlaw in the land of my birth. "I am a stranger with thee and a sojourner, as all my fathers were." That men should be patriotic; is to me perfectly natural; and as a philosophical fact, I am able to give it an intellectual recognition. But no further can I go. If ever I had any patriotism, or any capacity for the feeling, it was whipped out of me long since by the lash of the American soul-drivers. In thinking of America, I sometimes find myself admiring her bright blue sky, her grand old woods, her fertile fields, her beautiful rivers, her mighty lakes, and star-crowned mountains. But my rapture is soon checked—my joy is soon turned to mourning. When I remember that all is cursed with the infernal spirit of slaveholding, robbery, and wrong; when I remember that with the waters of her noblest rivers the tears of my brethren are borne to the ocean, disregarded and forgotten, and that her most fertile fields drink daily of the warm blood of my outraged sisters, I am filled with unutterable loathing, and led to reproach myself that anything could fall from my lips in praise of such a land. America will not allow her children to love her. She seems bent on compelling those who would be her warmest friends to be her worst enemies. May God give her repentance before it is too late, is the ardent prayer of my heart. I will continue to pray, labor, and wait, believing that she cannot always be insensible to the dictates of justice, or deaf to the voice of humanity. My opportunities for learning the character and condition of the people of this land have been very great. I have traveled from the Hill of Howth to the Giant's Causeway, and from the Giant's Cause-way to Cape Clear. During these travels I have met with much in the character and condition of the people to approve, and much to condemn; much that has thrilled me with pleasure, and much that has filled me with pain. I will not, in this letter, attempt to give any description of those scenes which give me pain. This I will do hereafter. I have said enough, and more than your subscribers will be disposed to read at one time, of the bright side of the picture. I can truly say I have spent some of the happiest days of my life since landing in this country. I seem to have undergone a transformation. I live a new life. The warm and generous coöperation extended to me by the friends of my despised race; the prompt and liberal manner with which the press has rendered me its aid; the glorious enthusiasm with which thousands have flocked to hear the cruel wrongs of my down-trodden and long-enslaved fellow-countrymen portrayed; the deep sympathy for the slave, and the strong abhorrence of the slaveholder, everywhere evinced; the cordiality with which members and ministers of various religious bodies, and of various shades of religious opinion, have embraced me and lent me their aid; the kind hospitality constantly proffered me by persons of the highest rank in society; the spirit of freedom that seems to animate all with whom I come in contact, and the entire absence of everything that looks like prejudice against me, on account of the color of my skin, contrasts so strongly with my long and bitter experience in the United States, that I look with wonder and amazement on the transition. In the southern part of the United States, I was a slave—thought of and spoken of as property; in the language of law, "held, taken, reputed, and adjudged to be a chattel in the hands of my owners and possessors, and their executors, administrators, and assigns, to all intents, constructions, and purposes, whatsoever." (Brev. Digest.,* 224.) In the Northern States, a fugitive slave, liable to be hunted at any moment like a felon, and to be hurled into the terrible jaws of slavery—doomed, by an inveterate prejudice against color, to insult and outrage on every hand (Massachusetts out of the question)—denied the privileges and courtesies common to others in the use of the most humble means of conveyance—shut out from the cabins on steamboats, refused admission to respectable hotels, caricatured, scorned, scoffed, mocked and maltreated with impunity by any one, no matter how black his heart, so he has a white skin. But now behold the change! Eleven days and a half gone, and I have crossed three thousand miles of perilous deep. Instead of a democratic government, I am under a monarchial government. Instead of the bright, blue sky of America, I am covered with the soft, gray fog of the Emerald Isle. I breathe, and lo! the chattel becomes a man! I gaze around in vain for one who will question my equal humanity, claim me as a slave, or offer me an insult. I employ a cab—I am seated beside white people—I reach the hotel—I enter the same door—I am shown into the same parlor—I dine at the same table—and no one is offended. No delicate nose grows deformed in my presence. I find no difficulty here in obtaining admission into any place of worship, instruction or amusement, on equal terms with people as white as any I ever saw in the United States. I meet nothing to remind me of my complexion. I find myself regarded and treated at every turn with the kindness and deference paid to white people. When I go to church I am met by no upturned nose and scornful lip, to tell me—"We don't allow niggers in here." '

I remember about two years ago there was in Boston, near the southwest corner of Boston Common, a menagerie. I had long desired to see such a collection as I understood was being exhibited there. Never having had an opportunity while a slave, I resolved to seize this, and as I approached the entrance to gain admission, I was told by the doorkeeper, in a harsh and contemptuous tone, '*We don't allow niggers in here.*' I also remember attending a revival meeting in the Rev. Henry Jackson's meeting-house, at New Bedford, and going up the broad aisle for a seat, I was met by a good deacon, who told me, in a pious tone, '*We don't allow niggers in here.*' Soon after my arrival in New Bedford from the South, I had a strong desire to attend the lyceum, but was told, '*They don't allow niggers there.*' While passing from New York to Boston on the steamer Massachusetts, on the night of the 9th of December, 1843, when chilled almost through with the cold, I went into the cabin to get a little warm. I was soon touched upon the shoulder, and told, '*We don't allow niggers in here.*' A week or two before leaving the United States, I had a meeting appointed at Weymouth, the house of that glorious band of true abolitionists—the Weston family and others. On attempting to take a seat in the omnibus to that place, I was told by the driver (and I never shall forget his fiendish hate), 'I don't allow niggers in here.' Thank Heaven for the respite I now enjoy! I had been in Dublin but a few days when a gentleman of great respectability kindly offered to conduct me through all the public buildings of that beautiful city, and soon afterward I was invited by the lord mayor to dine with him. What a pity there was not some democratic Christian at the door of his splendid mansion to bark out at my approach, 'They don't allow niggers in here!' The truth is, the people here knew nothing of the republican negro-hate prevalent in our glorious land. They measure and esteem men according to their moral and intellectual worth, and not according to the color of their skin. Whatever may be said of the aristocracies here, there is none based on the color of a man's skin. This species of aristocracy belongs preëminently to 'the land of the free, and the home of the brave.'* I have never found it abroad in any but Americans. It sticks to them wherever they go. They find it almost as hard to get rid of as to get rid of their skins.

The second day after my arrival in Liverpool, in company with my friend Buffum, and several other friends, I went to Eaton Hall, the residence of the Marquis of Westminster, one of the most splendid buildings in England. On approaching the door, I found several of our American passengers who came out with us in the Cambria, waiting for admission, as but one party was allowed in the house at a time. We all had to wait till the company within came out, and of all the faces expressive of chagrin, those of the Americans were preëminent. They looked as sour as vinegar, and as bitter as gall, when they found I was to be admitted on equal terms with themselves. When the door was opened, I walked in on a footing with my white fellow-citizens, and, from all I could see, I had as much attention paid me by the servants who showed us through the house as any with a paler skin. As I walked through the building the statuary did not fall down, the pictures did not leap from their places, the doors did not refuse to open, and the servants did not say, '*We don't allow niggers in here.*'

My time and labors while abroad were divided between England, Ireland, Scotland, and Wales. Upon this experience alone I might fill a volume. Amongst the few incidents which space will permit me to mention, and one which attracted much attention and provoked much discussion in America, was a brief statement made by me in the World's Temperance Convention, held in Covent Garden theatre, London, August 7, 1846. The United States was largely represented in this convention by eminent divines, mostly doctors of divinity. They had come to England for the double purpose of attending the World's Evangelical Alliance, and the World's Temperance Convention. In the former these ministers were endeavoring to procure endorsement for the Christian character of slaveholders; and, naturally enough, they were adverse to the exposure of slaveholding practices. It was not pleasant to them to see one of the slaves running at large in England, and telling the other side of the story. The Rev. Samuel Hanson Cox,* D. D., of Brooklyn, N. Y., was especially disturbed at my presence and speech in the Temperance Convention. I will give here, first, the reverend gentleman's version of the occasion in a letter from him as it appeared in the New York *Evangelist*, the organ of his denomination. After a description of the place (Covent Garden theatre) and the speakers, he says:

'They all advocated the same cause, showed a glorious unity of thought and feeling, and the effect was constantly raised—the moral scene was superb and glorious—when Frederick Douglass, the colored abolition agitator and ultra-ist, came to the platform and so spake, *à la mode*, as to ruin the influence almost of all that preceded! He lugged in anti-slavery, or abolition, no doubt prompted to it by some of the politic ones who can use him to do what they would not themselves adventure to do in person. He is supposed to have been well paid for the abomination.

'What a perversion, an abuse, an iniquity against the law of reciprocal right-eousness, to call thousands together and get them, some certain ones, to seem conspicuous and devoted for one sole and grand object, and then all at once, with obliquity, open an avalanche on them for some imputed evil or monstros-ity, for which, whatever be the wound or injury inflicted, they were both too fatigued and hurried with surprise, and too straightened for time, to be prop-erly prepared. I say it is a streak of meanness. It is abominable. On this occasion Mr. Douglass allowed himself to denounce America and all its temperance societies together as a grinding community of the enemies of his people; said evil with no alloy of good concerning the whole of us; was perfectly indiscrim-inate in his severities; talked of the American delegates and to them as if he had been our schoolmaster and we his docile and devoted pupils; and launched his revengeful missiles at our country without one palliative, and as if not a Christian or a true anti-slavery man lived in the whole of the United States. The fact is, the man has been petted and flattered and used and paid by certain abolitionists, not unknown to us, of the ne plus ultra stamp, till he forgets him-self, and though he may gratify his own impulses and those of old Adam in others, yet I am sure that all this is just the way to ruin his own influence, to defeat his own object, and to do mischief, not good, to the very cause he pro-fesses to love. With the single exception of one coldhearted parricide, whose character I abhor, and whom I will not name, and who has, I fear, no feeling of true patriotism or piety within him, all the delegates from our country were together wounded and indignant. No wonder at it. I write freely. It was not done in a corner. It was inspired, I believe, from beneath, and not from above. It was adapted to rekindle on both sides of the Atlantic the flames of national exasperation and war. And this is the game which Mr. Frederick Douglass and his silly patrons are playing in England and in Scotland, and wherever they can find "some mischief still for idle hands to do." I came here his sympathizing friend; I am such no more, as I know him. My own opinion is increasingly that this spirit must be exorcised out of England and America before any substantial good can be effected for the cause of the slave. It is adapted only to make bad worse and to inflame the passions of indignant millions to an incurable resent-ment. None but an ignoramus or a mad-man could think that this way was that of the inspired apostles of the Son of God. It may gratify the feelings of a self-deceived and malignant few, but it will do no good in any direction; least of all to the poor slave. It is short-sighted, impulsive, partisan, reckless, and tending only to sanguinary ends. None of this with men of sense and principle.

'We all wanted to reply, but it was too late. The whole theater seemed taken with the spirit of the Ephesian uproar; they were furious and boisterous in the extreme, and Mr. Kirk could hardly obtain a moment, though many were desirous in his behalf, to say a few words as he did, very calm and properly, that the cause of temperance was not at all responsible for slavery, and had no connection with it.'

Now, to show the reader what ground there was for this tirade from the pen of this eminent divine, and how easily Americans parted with their candor and self-possession when slavery was mentioned adversely, I will give here the head and front of my offense. Let it be borne in mind that this was a *world's* convention of the friends of temperance. It was not an American or a white man's convention, but one composed of men of all nations and races; and as such the convention had the right to know all about the temperance cause in every part of the world, and especially to know what hindrances were interposed in any part of the world to its progress. I was perfectly in order in speaking precisely as I did. I was neither an 'intruder' nor 'out of order.' I had been invited and advertised to speak by the same committee that invited Doctors Beecher, Cox, Patton, Kirk, Marsh, and others, and my speech was perfectly within the limits of good order, as the following report will show:

*'Mr. Chairman—Ladies and Gentlemen:*
    'I am not a delegate to this convention. Those who would have been most likely to elect me as a delegate could not, because they are to-night held in abject slavery in the United States. Sir, I regret that I cannot fully unite with the American delegates in their patriotic eulogies of America and American temperance societies. I cannot do so for this good reason: there are at this moment three millions of the American population by slavery and prejudice placed entirely beyond the pale of American temperance societies. The three million slaves are completely excluded by slavery, and four hundred thousand free colored people are almost as completely excluded by an inveterate prejudice against them on account of their color. [Cries of "Shame! shame!"]
    'I do not say these things to wound the feelings of the American delegates. I simply mention them in their presence and before this audience that, seeing how you regard this hatred and neglect of the colored people, they may be inclined on their return home to enlarge the field of their temperance operations and embrace within the scope of their influence my long-neglected race. [Great cheering, and some confusion on the platform.] Sir, to give you some idea of the difficulties and obstacles in the way of the temperance reformation of the colored population in the United States, allow me to state a few facts.
    'About the year 1840, a few intelligent, sober, and benevolent colored gentlemen in Philadelphia, being acquainted with the appalling ravages of intemperance among a numerous class of colored people in that city, and finding themselves neglected and excluded from white societies, organized societies among themselves, appointed committees, sent out agents, built temperance halls, and were earnestly and successfully rescuing many from the fangs of intemperance.

'The cause went on nobly till August 1, 1842, the day when England gave liberty to eight hundred thousand souls in the West Indies. The colored temperance societies selected this day to march in procession through the city, in the hope that such a demonstration would have the effect of bringing others into their ranks. They formed their procession, unfurled their teetotal banners, and proceeded to the accomplishment of their purpose. It was a delightful sight. But, sir, they had not proceeded down two streets before they were brutally assailed by a ruthless mob; their banner was torn down and trampled in the dust, their ranks broken up, their persons beaten and pelted with stones and brickbats. One of their churches was burned to the ground, and their best temperance hall utterly demolished. ["Shame! shame! shame!" from the audience, great confusion, and cries of "Sit down" from the American delegates on the platform.]'

In the midst of this commotion the chairman tapped me on the shoulder, and, whispering, informed me that the fifteen minutes allotted to each speaker had expired; whereupon the vast audience simultaneously shouted: 'Don't interrupt!' 'Don't dictate!' 'Go on!' 'Go on!' 'Douglass!' 'Douglass!' This continued several minutes, when I proceeded as follows: 'Kind friends, I beg to assure you that the chairman has not in the slightest degree sought to alter any sentiment which I am anxious to express on this occasion. He was simply reminding me that the time allotted for me to speak had expired. I do not wish to occupy one moment more than is allotted to other speakers. Thanking you for your kind indulgence, I will take my seat.' Proceeding to do so again, there were loud cries of 'Go on!' 'Go on!' with which I complied for a few moments, but without saying anything more that particularly related to the colored people in America. I did not allow the letter of Dr. Cox to go unanswered through the American journals, but promptly exposed its unfairness. That letter is too long for insertion here. A part of it was published in the *Evangelist* and in many other papers, both in this country and in England. Our eminent divine made no rejoinder, and his silence was regarded at the time as an admission of defeat.

Another interesting circumstance connected with my visit to England was the position of the Free Church of Scotland,* with the great Doctors Chalmers, Cunningham, and Candish at its head. That Church had settled for itself the question which was frequently asked by the opponents of abolition at home, '*What have we to do with slavery?*' by accepting contributions from slaveholders; *i. e.*, receiving the price of blood into its treasury with which to build churches and pay ministers for preaching the gospel; and worse than this, when honest John Murray of Bowlein Bay, with William Smeal, Andrew Paton, Frederick Card, and other sterling anti-slavery men in Glasgow, denounced the transaction as disgraceful, and shocking to the religious sentiment of

Scotland, this church, through its leading divines, instead of repenting and seeking to amend the mistake into which it had fallen, caused that *mistake* to become a flagrant sin by undertaking to defend, in the name of God and the Bible, the principle not only of taking the money of slave-dealers to build churches and thus extend the gospel, but of holding fellowship with the traffickers in human flesh. This, the reader will see, brought up the whole question of slavery, and opened the way to its full discussion. I have never seen a people more deeply moved than were the people of Scotland on this very question. Public meeting succeeded public meeting, speech after speech, pamphlet after pamphlet, editorial after editorial, sermon after sermon; lashed the conscientious Scotch people into a perfect furore. 'SEND BACK THE MONEY!' was indignantly shouted from Greenock to Edinburgh, and from Edinburgh to Aberdeen. George Thompson* of London, Henry C. Wright, J. N. Buffum and myself from America, were of course on the anti-slavery side, and Chalmers, Cunningham, and Candlish on the other. Dr. Cunningham* was the most powerful debater on the slavery side of the question, Mr. Thompson the ablest on the anti-slavery side. A scene occurred between these two men, a parallel to which I think I have never witnessed before or since. It was caused by a single exclamation on the part of Mr. Thompson, and was on this wise:

The general assembly of the Free Church was in progress at Cannon Mills, Edinburgh. The building would hold twenty-five hundred persons, and on this occasion was densely packed, notice having been given that Doctors Cunningham and Candlish would speak that day in defense of the relations of the Free Church of Scotland to slavery in America. Messrs. Thompson, Buffum, myself and a few other anti-slavery friends attended, but sat at such distance and in such position as not to be observed from the platform. The excitement was intense, having been greatly increased by a series of meetings held by myself and friends, in the most splendid hall in that most beautiful city, just previous to this meeting of the general assembly. 'SEND BACK THE MONEY!' in large capitals stared from every street corner; 'SEND BACK THE MONEY!' adorned the broad flags of the pavement; 'SEND BACK THE MONEY!' was the chorus of the popular street-song; 'SEND BACK THE MONEY!' was the heading of leading editorials in the daily newspapers. This day, at Cannon Mills, the great doctors of the church were to give an answer to this loud and stern demand. Men of all parties and sects were most eager to hear. Something great was expected. The occasion was great, the men were great, and great speeches were expected from them.

In addition to the outward pressure there was wavering within. The conscience of the church itself was not at ease. A dissatisfaction with the position of the church touching slavery was sensibly manifest among the members, and something must be done to counteract this untoward influence. The great Dr. Chalmers was in feeble health at the time, so his most potent eloquence could not now be summoned to Cannon Mills, as formerly. He whose voice had been so powerful as to rend asunder and dash down the granite walls of the Established Church of Scotland, and to lead a host in solemn procession from it as from a doomed city, was now old and enfeebled. Besides, he had said his word on this very question, and it had not silenced the clamor without nor stilled the anxious heavings within. The occasion was momentous, and felt to be so. The church was in a perilous condition. A change of some sort must take place, or she must go to pieces. To stand where she did was impossible. The whole weight of the matter fell on Cunningham and Candlish. No shoulders in the church were broader than theirs; and I must say, badly as I detested the principles laid down and defended by them, I was compelled to acknowledge the vast mental endowments of the men.

Cunningham rose, and his rising was the signal for tumultuous applause. It may be said that this was scarcely in keeping with the solemnity of the occasion, but to me it served to increase its grandeur and gravity. The applause, though tumultuous, was not joyous. It seemed to me, as it thundered up from the vast audience, like the fall of an immense shaft, flung from shoulders already galled by its crushing weight. It was like saying 'Doctor, we have borne this burden long enough, and willingly fling it upon you. Since it was you who brought it upon us, take it now and do what you will with it, for we are too weary to bear it.'

The Doctor proceeded with his speech—abounding in logic, learning, and eloquence, and apparently bearing down all opposition; but at the moment—the fatal moment—when he was just bringing all his arguments to a point, and that point being that 'neither Jesus Christ nor his holy apostles regarded slaveholding as a sin,' George Thompson, in a clear, sonorous, but rebuking voice, broke the deep stillness of the audience, exclaiming, 'HEAR! HEAR! HEAR!' The effect of this simple and common exclamation is almost incredible. It was as if a granite wall had been suddenly flung up against the advancing current of a mighty river. For a moment speaker and audience were brought to a dead silence. Both the Doctor and his hearers seemed appalled by the audacity, as well as the fitness of the rebuke. At length a shout went up to the cry of '*Put him out!*' Happily no one attempted to execute this cowardly order, and the discourse went on; but not as before. The exclamation of Thompson must have re-echoed a thousand times in his memory, for the Doctor, during the remainder of his speech, was utterly unable to recover from the blow. The deed was done, however; the pillars of the church—*the proud Free Church of Scotland*—were committed, and the humility of repentance was absent. The Free Church held on to the blood-stained money, and continued to justify itself in its position.

One good result followed the conduct of the Free Church; it furnished an occasion for making the people thoroughly acquainted with the character of slavery and for arraying against it the moral and religious sentiment of that country; therefore, while we did not procure the sending back of the money, we were amply justified by the good which really did result from our labors.

I must add one word in regard to the Evangelical Alliance. This was an attempt to form a union of all Evangelical Christians throughout the world, and which held its first session in London, in the year 1846, at the time of the World's Temperance Convention there. Some sixty or seventy ministers from America attended this convention, the object of some of them being to weave a world wide garment with which to clothe evangelical slaveholders; and in this they partially succeeded. But the question of slavery was too large a question to be finally disposed of by the Evangelical Alliance, and from its judgment we appealed to the judgment of the people of Great Britain, with the happiest effect—this effort of our countrymen to shield the character of slaveholders serving to open a way to the British ear for anti-slavery discussion.

I may mention here an incident somewhat amusing and instructive, as it serves to illustrate how easily Americans could set aside their notoriously inveterate prejudice against color, when it stood in the way of their wishes, or when in an atmosphere which made that prejudice unpopular and unchristian.

At the entrance to the House of Commons I had one day been conversing for a few moments with Lord Morpeth, and just as I was parting from him I felt an emphatic push against my arm, and, looking around, I saw at my elbow Rev. Dr. Kirk of Boston. 'Introduce me to Lord Morpeth,' he said. 'Certainly,' said I, and introduced him; not without remembering, however, that at home the amiable Doctor would scarcely have asked such a favor of a colored man.

The object of my labors in Great Britain was the concentration of the moral and religious sentiment of its people against American slavery.

To this end I visited and lectured in nearly all the large towns and cities in the United Kingdom, and enjoyed many favorable opportunities for observation and information. I should like to write a book on those countries, if for nothing else, to make grateful mention of the many dear friends whose benevolent actions toward me are ineffaceably stamped upon my memory and warmly treasured in my heart. To these friends I owe my freedom in the United States.

Miss Ellen Richardson, an excellent member of the society of Friends, assisted by her sister-in-law, Mrs. Henry Richardson,* a lady devoted to every good word and work, the friend of the Indian and the African, conceived the plan of raising a fund to effect my ransom from slavery. They corresponded with Hon. Walter Forward of Pennsylvania, and through him ascertained that Captain Auld would take one hundred and fifty pounds sterling for me; and this sum they promptly raised and paid for my liberation, placing the papers of my manumission into my hands before they would tolerate the idea of my return to my native land. To this commercial transaction, to this blood-money, I owe my immunity from the operation of the fugitive slave law of 1793, and also from that of 1850.* The whole affair speaks for itself, and needs no comment, now that slavery has ceased to exist in this country, and is not likely ever again to be revived.

Some of my uncompromising anti-slavery friends in this country failed to see the wisdom of this commercial transaction, and were not pleased that I consented to it, even by my silence. They thought it a violation of anti-slavery principles, conceding the right of property in man, and a wasteful expenditure of money. For myself, viewing it simply in the light of a ransom, or as money extorted by a robber, and my liberty of more value than one hundred and fifty pounds sterling, I could not see either a violation of the laws of morality or of economy. It is true I was not in the possession of my claimants, and could have remained in England, for my friends would have generously assisted me in establishing myself there. To this I could not consent. I felt it my duty to labor and suffer with my oppressed people in my native land. Considering all the circumstances, the fugitive bill included, I think now as then, that the very best thing was done in letting Master Hugh have the money, and thus leave me free to return to my appropriate field of labor. Had I been a private person, with no relations or duties other than those of a personal and family nature, I should not have consented to the payment of so large a sum for the privilege of living securely under our glorious republican (?) form of government. I could have lived elsewhere, or perhaps might have been unobserved even here, but I had become somewhat notorious, and withal quite as unpopular in some directions as notorious, and I was therefore much exposed to arrest and capture.[1]

Having remained abroad nearly two years, and being about to return to America, not as I left it, a slave, but a freeman, prominent friends of the cause of emancipation intimated their intention to make me a testimonial, both on grounds of personal regard to me and also to the cause to which they were so ardently devoted. How such a project would have succeeded I do not know, but many reasons led me to prefer that my friends should simply give me the means of obtaining a printing-press and materials to enable me to start a paper advocating the interests of my enslaved and oppressed people. I told them that perhaps the greatest hindrance to the adoption of abolition principles by the people of

---

[1] The following is a copy of these curious papers, both of my transfer from Thomas to Hugh Auld and from Hugh to myself:

'Know all men by these presents: That I, Thomas Auld, of Talbot county and State of Maryland, for and in consideration of the sum of one hundred dollars, current money, to me paid by Hugh Auld of the city of Baltimore, in the said State, at and before the sealing and delivery of these presents, the receipt whereof I, the said Thomas Auld, do hereby acknowledge, have granted, bargained, and sold, and by these presents do grant, bargain, and sell unto the said Hugh Auld, his executors, administrators, and assigns, ONE NEGRO MAN, by the name of FREDERICK BAILEY, or DOUGLASS, as he calls himself—he is now about twenty-eight years of age—to have and to hold the said negro man for life. And I, the said Thomas Auld, for myself, my heirs, executors, and administrators, all and singular, the said FREDERICK BAILEY, alias DOUGLASS, unto the said Hugh Auld, his executors and administrators, and against all and every other person or persons whatsoever, shall and will warrant and forever defend by these presents. In witness whereof, I set my hand and seal this thirteenth day of November, eighteen hundred and forty-six (1846).

'THOMAS AULD.

'Signed, sealed, and delivered in presence of Wrightson Jones, John C. Lear.'

The authenticity of this bill of sale is attested by N. Harrington, a justice of the peace of the State of Maryland and for the county of Talbot, dated same day as above.

'To all whom it may concern: Be it known that I, Hugh Auld of the city of Baltimore, in Baltimore county in the State of Maryland, for divers good causes and considerations me thereunto moving, have released from slavery, liberated, manumitted, and set free, and by these presents do hereby release from slavery, liberate, manumit, and set free, MY NEGRO MAN named FREDERICK BAILEY, otherwise called DOUGLASS, being of the age of twenty-eight years or thereabouts, and able to work and gain a sufficient livelihood and maintenance; and him, the said negro man named FREDERICK DOUGLASS, I do declare to be henceforth free, manumitted, and discharged from all manner of servitude to me, my executors and administrators forever.

'In witness thereof, I, the said Hugh Auld, have hereunto set my hand and seal the fifth of December, in the year one thousand eight hundred and forty-six.

'HUGH AULD.

'Sealed and delivered in presence of T. Hanson Bell, James N. S. T. Wright.'

the United States was the low estimate everywhere in that country placed upon the negro as a man; that because of his assumed natural inferiority people reconciled themselves to his enslavement and oppression as being inevitable, if not desirable. The grand thing to be done, therefore, was to change this estimation by disproving his inferiority and demonstrating his capacity for a more exalted civilization than slavery and prejudice had assigned him. In my judgement, a tolerably well-conducted press in the hands of persons of the despised race would, by calling out and making them acquainted with their own latent powers, by enkindling their hope of a future and developing their moral force, prove a most powerful means of removing prejudice and awakening an interest in them. At that time there was not a single newspaper in the country, regularly published by the colored people, though many attempts had been made to establish such, and had from one cause or another failed. These views I laid before my friends. The result was that nearly two thousand five hundred dollars were speedily raised toward my establishing such a paper as I had indicated. For this prompt and generous assistance, rendered upon my bare suggestion, without any personal effort on my part, I shall never cease to feel deeply grateful, and the thought of fulfilling the expectations of the dear friends who had given me this evidence of their confidence was an abiding inspiration for persevering exertion.

Proposing to leave England and turning my face toward America in the spring of 1847, I was painfully reminded of the kind of life which awaited me on my arrival. For the first time in the many months spent abroad I was met with proscription on account of my color. While in London I had purchased a ticket and secured a berth for returning home in the Cambria—the steamer in which I had come from thence—and paid therefor the round sum of forty pounds nineteen shillings sterling. This was first-cabin fare; but on going on board I found that the Liverpool agent had ordered my berth to be given to another, and forbidden my entering the saloon. It was rather hard, after having enjoyed for so long a time equal social privileges, after dining with persons of great literary, social, political, and religious eminence, and never, during the whole time, having met with a single word, look, or gesture which gave me the slightest reason to think my color was an offense to any body, now to be cooped up in the stern of the Cambria and denied the right to enter the saloon, lest my presence should disturb some democratic fellow-passenger. The reader can easily imagine what must have been my feelings under such an indignity.

This contemptible conduct met with stern rebuke from the British press.* The London *Times* and other leading journals throughout the United Kingdom held up the outrage to unmitigated condemnation. So good an opportunity for calling out British sentiment on the subject had not before occurred, and it was fully embraced. The result was that Mr. Cunard came out in a letter expressive of his regret, and promising that the like indignity should never occur again on his steamers, which promise I believe has been faithfully kept.

# CHAPTER VII.

## TRIUMPHS AND TRIALS.

*New Experiences—Painful Disagreement of Opinion with old Friends—Final Decision to publish my Paper in Rochester—Its Fortunes and its Friends—Change in my own Views Regarding the Constitution of the United States—Fidelity to Conviction—Loss of Old Friends—Support of New Ones—Loss of House, etc., by Fire—Triumphs and Trials—Underground Railroad—Incidents.*

PREPARED as I was to meet with many trials and perplexities on reaching home, one of which I little dreamed was awaiting me. My plans for future usefulness, as indicated in the last chapter, were all settled, and in imagination I already saw myself wielding my pen as well as my voice in the great work of renovating the public mind, and building up a public sentiment, which should send slavery to the grave, and restore to 'liberty and the pursuit of happiness' the people with whom I had suffered.

My friends in Boston had been informed of what I was intending, and I expected to find them favorably disposed toward my cherished enterprise. In this I was mistaken. They had many reasons against it. First, no such paper was needed; secondly, it would interfere with my usefulness as a lecturer; thirdly, I was better fitted to speak than to write; fourthly, the paper could not succeed. This opposition from a quarter so highly esteemed, and to which I had been accustomed to look for advice and direction, caused me not only to hesitate, but inclined me to abandon the undertaking. All previous attempts to establish such a journal having failed, I feared lest I should but add another to the list, and thus contribute another proof of the mental deficiencies of my race. Very much that was said to me in respect to my imperfect literary attainments I felt to be most painfully true. The unsuccessful projectors of all former attempts had been my superiors in point of education, and if *they* had failed how could I hope for success? Yet I did hope for success, and persisted in the undertaking, encouraged by my English friends to go forward.

I can easily pardon those who saw in my persistence an unwarrantable ambition and presumption. I was but nine years from slavery. In many phases of mental experience I was but nine years old. That one under such circumstances and surrounded by an educated people, should aspire to establish a printing-press, might well be considered unpractical, if not ambitious. My American friends looked at me with astonishment. 'A wood-sawyer' offering himself to the public as an editor! A slave, brought up in the depths of ignorance, assuming to instruct the highly civilized people of the north in the principles of liberty, justice, and humanity! The thing looked absurd. Nevertheless, I persevered. I felt that the want of education, great as it was, could be overcome by study, and that wisdom would come by experience; and further (which was perhaps the most controlling consideration) I thought that an intelligent public, knowing my early history, would easily pardon the many deficiencies which I well knew that my paper must exhibit. The most distressing part of it all was the offense which I saw I must give my friends of the old anti-slavery organization, by what seemed to them a reckless disregard of their opinion and advice. I am not sure that I was not under the influence of something like a slavish adoration of these good people, and I labored hard to convince them that my way of thinking about the matter was the right one, but without success.

From motives of peace, instead of issuing my paper in Boston, among New England friends, I went to Rochester, N. Y., among strangers, where the local circulation of my paper—'THE NORTH STAR'*—would not interfere with that of the *Liberator* or the *Anti-Slavery Standard*, for I was then a faithful disciple of Wm. Lloyd Garrison, and fully committed to his doctrine touching the pro-slavery character of the Constitution of the United States, also the *non-voting principle* of which he was the known and distinguished advocate. With him, I held it to be the first duty of the non-slaveholding States to dissolve the union with the slaveholding States, and hence my cry, like his, was 'No union with slaveholders.' With these views I went into western New York, and during the first four years of my labors there I advocated them with pen and tongue to the best of my ability. After a time, a careful reconsideration of the subject convinced me that there was no necessity for dissolving the 'union between the northern and southern States'; that to seek this dissolution was no part of my duty as an abolitionist; that to abstain from voting was to refuse to exercise a legitimate and powerful means for abolishing slavery; and that the Constitution of the United States not only contained no guarantees in favor of slavery, but, on the contrary, was in its letter and spirit an anti-slavery instrument, demanding the abolition of slavery as a condition of its own existence as the supreme law of the land.

This radical change in my opinions produced a corresponding change in my action. To those with whom I had been in agreement and in sympathy, I came to be in opposition. What they held to be a great and important truth I now looked upon as a dangerous error. A very natural, but to me a very painful thing, now happened. Those who could not see any honest reasons for changing their views, as I had done, could not easily see any such reasons for my change, and the common punishment of apostates was mine.

My first opinions were naturally derived and honestly entertained. Brought directly, when I escaped from slavery, into contact with abolitionists who regarded the Constitution as a slaveholding instrument, and finding their views supported by the united and entire history of every department of the government, it is not strange that I assumed the Constitution to be just what these friends made it seem to be. I was bound, not only by their superior knowledge, to take their opinions in respect to this subject, as the true ones, but also because I had no means of showing the unsoundness of these opinions. But for the responsibility of conducting a public journal, and the necessity imposed upon me of meeting opposite views from abolitionists outside of New England, I should in all probability have remained firm in my disunion views. My new circumstances compelled me to re-think the whole subject, and to study with some care not only the just and proper rules of legal interpretation, but the origin, design, nature, rights, powers, and duties of civil governments, and also the relations which human beings sustain to it. By such a course of thought and reading I was conducted to the conclusion that the Constitution of the United States—inaugurated to 'form a more perfect union, establish justice, insure domestic tranquility, provide for the common defense, promote the general welfare, and secure the blessings of liberty'—could not well have been designed at the same time to maintain and perpetuate a system of rapine and murder like slavery, especially as not one word can be found in the Constitution to authorize such a belief. Then, again, if the declared purposes of an instrument are to govern the meaning of all its parts and details, as they clearly should, the Constitution of our country is our warrant for the abolition of slavery in every State of the Union. It would require much time and space to set forth the arguments which demonstrated to my mind the unconstitutionality of slavery; but being convinced of the fact my duty upon this point in the further conduct of my paper was plain. *The North Star* was a large sheet, published weekly, at a cost of $80 per week, and an average circulation of 3,000 subscribers. There were many times when, in my experience as editor and publisher, I was very hard pressed for money, but by one means or another I succeeded so well as to keep my pecuniary engagements, and to keep my anti-slavery banner steadily flying during all the conflict from the autumn of 1847 till the union of the States was assured and emancipation was a fact accomplished. I had friends abroad as well as at home who helped me liberally. I can never be too grateful to Rev. Russell Lant Carpenter* and to Mrs. Carpenter for the moral and material aid they tendered me through all the vicissitudes of my paper enterprise. But to no one person was I more indebted for substantial assistance than to Mrs. Julia Griffiths Crofts.* She came to my relief when my paper had nearly absorbed all my means, and I was heavily in debt, and when I had mortgaged my house to raise money to meet current expenses; and in a single year by her energetic and effective management enabled me to extend the circulation of my paper from 2,000 to 4,000 copies, pay off the debts and lift the mortgage from my house. Her industry was equal to her devotion. She seemed to rise with every emergency, and her resources appeared inexhaustible. I shall never cease to remember with sincere gratitude the assistance rendered me by this noble lady, and I mention her here in the desire in some humble measure to 'give honor to whom honor is due.' During the first three or four years my paper was published under the name of the *North Star*. It was subsequently changed to *Frederick Douglass's Paper*, in order to distinguish it from the many papers with 'Stars' in their titles. There were 'North Stars,' 'Morning Stars,' 'Evening Stars,' and I know not how many other stars in the newspaper firmament, and naturally enough some confusion arose in distinguishing between them; for this reason, and also because some of these stars were older than my star, I felt that mine, not theirs, ought to be the one to 'go out.'

Among my friends in this country, who helped me in my earlier efforts to maintain my paper, I may proudly count such men as the late Hon. Gerrit Smith, and Chief-Justice Chase, Hon. Horace Mann, Hon. Joshua R. Giddings, Hon. Charles Sumner, Hon. John G. Palfry, Hon. Wm. H. Seward, Rev. Samuel J. May, and many others, who though of lesser note were equally devoted to my cause. Among these latter ones were Isaac and Amy Post, William and Mary Hallowell, Asa and Hulda Anthony, and indeed all the committee of the Western New York Anti-Slavery Society. They held festivals and fairs to raise money, and assisted me in every other possible way to keep my paper in circulation, while I was a nonvoting abolitionist, but withdrew from me when I became a voting abolitionist. For a time the withdrawal of their coöperation embarrassed me very much, but soon another class of friends was raised up for me, chief amongst whom were the Porter family of Rochester. The late Samuel D. Porter and his wife Susan F. Porter, and his sisters, Maria and Elmira Porter, deserve grateful mention as among my steadfast friends, who did much in the way of supplying pecuniary aid.

Of course there were moral forces operating against me in Rochester, as well as material ones. There were those who regarded the publication of a 'Negro paper' in that beautiful city as a blemish and a misfortune. The New York *Herald*, true to the spirit of the times, counselled the people of the place to throw my printing-press into Lake Ontario and to banish me to Canada, and, while they were not quite prepared for this violence, it was plain that many of them did not well relish my presence amongst them. This feeling, however, wore away gradually, as the people knew more of me and my works. I lectured every Sunday evening during an entire winter in the beautiful Corinthian Hall, then owned by Wm. R. Reynolds, Esq., who, though he was not an abolitionist, was a lover of fair play, and was willing to allow me to be heard. If in these lectures I did not make abolitionists, I did succeed in making tolerant the moral atmosphere in Rochester; so much so, indeed, that I came to feel as much at home there as I had ever done in the most friendly parts of New England. I had been at work there with my paper but a few years before colored travelers told me that they felt the influence of my labors when they came within fifty miles. I did not rely alone upon what I could do by the paper, but would write all day, then take a train to Victor, Farmington, Canandaigua, Geneva, Waterloo, Batavia, or Buffalo, or elsewhere, and speak in the evening, returning home afterwards or early in the morning, to be again at my desk writing or mailing papers. There were times when I almost thought my Boston friends were right in dissuading me from my newspaper project. But looking back to those nights and days of toil and thought, compelled often to do work for which I had no educational preparation, I have come to think that, under the circumstances, it was the best school possible for me. It obliged me to think and read, it taught me to express my thoughts clearly, and was perhaps better than any other course I could have adopted. Besides, it made it necessary for me to lean upon myself, and not upon the heads of our Anti-Slavery church, to be a principal, and not an agent. I had an audience to speak to every week, and must say something worth their hearing, or cease to speak altogether. There is nothing like the lash and sting of necessity to make a man work, and my paper furnished this motive power. More than one gentleman from the South, when stopping at Niagara, came to see me, that they might know for themselves if I could indeed write, having, as they said, believed it impossible that an uneducated fugitive slave could write the articles attributed to me. I found it hard to get credit in some quarters either for what I wrote or what I said. While there was nothing very profound or learned in either, the low estimate of Negro possibilities induced the belief that both my editorials and my speeches were written by white persons. I doubt if this scepticism does not still linger in the minds of some of my democratic fellow citizens.

The 2d of June, 1872, brought me a very grievous loss. My house in Rochester was burnt to the ground, and among other things of value, twelve volumes of my paper, covering the period from 1848 to 1860, were devoured by the flames. I have never been able to replace them, and the loss is immeasurable. Only a few weeks before, I had been invited to send these bound volumes to the library of Harvard University, where they would have been preserved in a fire-proof building, and the result of my procrastination attests the wisdom of more than one proverb. Outside the years embraced in the late tremendous war, there had been no period more pregnant with great events, or better suited to call out the best mental and moral energies of men, than that covered by these lost volumes. If I have at any time said or written that which is worth remembering or repeating, I must have said such things between the years 1848 and 1860, and my paper was a chronicle of most of what I said during that time. Within that space we had the great Free-Soil Convention at Buffalo,* the Nomination of Martin Van Buren,* the Fugitive-Slave Law, the 7th of March Speech by Daniel Webster,* the Dred Scott decision,* the repeal of the Missouri Compromise, the Kansas Nebraska bill,* the Border war in Kansas,* the John Brown raid upon Harper's Ferry,* and a part of the War against the Rebellion, with much else, well calculated to fire the souls of men having one spark of liberty and patriotism within them. I have only fragments now of all the work accomplished during these twelve years, and must cover this chasm as best I can from memory, and the incidental items which I am able to glean from various sources. Two volumes of the *North Star* have been kindly supplied me, by my friend, Marshall Pierce, of Saco, Me. He had these carefully preserved and bound in one cover and sent to me in Washington. He was one of the most systematically careful men of all my anti-slavery friends, for I doubt if another entire volume of the paper exists.

One important branch of my anti-slavery work in Rochester, in addition to that of speaking and writing against slavery, must not be forgotten or omitted. My position gave me the chance of hitting that old enemy some telling blows, in another direction than these. I was on the southern border of Lake Ontario, and the Queen's dominions were right over the way—and my prominence as an abolitionist, and as the editor of an anti-slavery paper, naturally made me the station-master and conductor of the underground railroad passing through this goodly city. Secrecy and concealment were necessary conditions to the successful operation of this railroad, and hence its prefix 'underground.' My agency was all the more exciting and interesting, because not altogether free from danger. I could take no step in it without exposing myself to fine and imprisonment, for these were the penalties imposed by the fugitive-slave law for feeding, harboring, or otherwise assisting a slave to escape from his master; but, in face of this fact, I can say I never did more congenial, attractive, fascinating, and satisfactory work. True, as a means of destroying slavery, it was like an attempt to bail out the ocean with a teaspoon, but the thought that there was one less slave, and one more freeman—having myself been a slave, and a fugitive slave—brought to my heart unspeakable joy. On one occasion I had eleven fugitives at the same time under my roof, and it was necessary for them to remain with me until I could collect sufficient money to get them on to Canada. It was the largest number I ever had at any one time, and I had some difficulty in providing so many with food and shelter, but, as may well be imagined, they were not very fastidious in either direction, and were well content with very plain food, and a strip of carpet on the floor for a bed, or a place on the straw in the barn-loft.

The underground railroad had many branches; but that one with which I was connected had its main stations in Baltimore, Wilmington, Philadelphia, New York, Albany, Syracuse, Rochester, and St. Catharines (Canada). It is not necessary to tell who were the principal agents in Baltimore; Thomas Garrett was the agent in Wilmington; Melloe McKim, William Still, Robert Purvis, Edward M. Davis, and others did the work in Philadelphia; David Ruggles, Isaac T. Hopper, Napolian, and others, in New York city; the Misses Mott and Stephen Myers were forwarders from Albany; Revs. Samuel J. May and J. W. Loguen were the agents in Syracuse; and J. P. Morris and myself received and dispatched passengers from Rochester to Canada, where they were received by Rev. Hiram Wilson. When a party arrived in Rochester it was the business of Mr. Morris and myself to raise funds with which to pay their passage to St. Catharines, and it is due to truth to state that we seldom called in vain upon whig or democrat for help. Men were better than their theology, and truer to humanity than to their politics, or their offices.

On one occasion while a slave master was in the office of a United States commissioner, procuring the papers necessary for the arrest and rendition of three young men who had escaped from Maryland (one of whom was under my roof at the time, another at Farmington, and the other at work on the farm of Asa Anthony, just a little outside the city limits), the law partner of the commissioner, then a distinguished democrat, sought me out, and told me what was going on in his office, and urged me by all means to get these young men out of the way of their pursuers and claimants. Of course no time was to be lost. A swift horseman was dispatched to Farmington, eighteen miles distant, another to Asa Anthony's farm, about three miles, and another to my house on the south side of the city, and before the papers could be served all three of the young men were on the free waves of Lake Ontario, bound to Canada. In writing to their old master, they had dated their letter at Rochester, though they had taken the precaution to send it to Canada to be mailed, but this blunder in the date had betrayed their whereabouts, so that the hunters were at once on their tracks.

So numerous were the fugitives passing through Rochester that I was obliged at last to appeal to my British friends for the means of sending them on their way, and when Mr. and Mrs. Carpenter and Mrs. Croffts took the matter in hand, I had never any further trouble in that respect. When slavery was abolished I wrote to Mrs. Carpenter, congratulating her that she was relieved of the work of raising funds for such purposes, and the characteristic reply of that lady was that she had been very glad to do what she had done, and had no wish for relief.

My pathway was not entirely free from thorns in Rochester, and the wounds and pains inflicted by them were perhaps much less easily borne, because of my exemption from such annoyances while in England. Men can in time become accustomed to almost anything, even to being insulted and ostracised, but such treatment comes hard at first, and when to some extent unlooked for. The vulgar prejudice against color, so common to Americans, met me in several disagreeable forms. A seminary for young ladies and misses, under the auspices of Miss Tracy, was near my house on Alexander street, and desirous of having my daughter educated like the daughters of other men, I applied to Miss Tracy for her admission to her school. All seemed fair, and the child was duly sent to 'Tracy Seminary,' and I went about my business happy in the thought that she was in the way of a refined and Christian education. Several weeks elapsed before I knew how completely I was mistaken. The little girl came home to me one day and told me she was lonely in that school; that she was in fact kept in solitary confinement; that she was not allowed in the room with the other girls, nor to go into the yard when they went out; that she was kept in a room by herself and not permitted to be seen or heard by the others. No man with the feeling of a parent could be less than moved by such a revelation, and I confess that I was shocked, grieved, and indignant. I went at once to Miss Tracy to ascertain if what I had heard was true, and was coolly told it was, and the miserable plea was offered that it would have injured her school if she had done otherwise. I told her she should have told me so at the beginning, but I did not believe that any girl in the school would be opposed to the presence of my daughter, and that I should be glad to have the question submitted to them. She consented to this, and to the credit of the young ladies not one made objection. Not satisfied with this verdict of the natural and uncorrupted sense of justice and humanity of these young ladies, Miss Tracy insisted that the parents must be consulted, and if one of them objected she should not admit my child to the same apartment and privileges of the other pupils. One parent only had the cruelty to object, and he was Mr. Horatio G. Warner, a democratic editor, and upon his adverse conclusion my daughter was excluded from 'Tracy Seminary.' Of course Miss Tracy was a devout Christian lady after the fashion of the time and locality, in good and regular standing in the church.

My troubles attending the education of my children were not to end here. They were not allowed in the public school in the district in which I lived, owned property, and paid taxes, but were compelled, if they went to a public school, to go over to the other side of the city to an inferior colored school. I hardly need say that I was not prepared to submit tamely to this proscription, any more than I had been to submit to slavery, so I had them taught at home for a while by Miss Thayer. Meanwhile I went to the people with the question, and created considerable agitation. I sought and obtained a hearing before the Board of Education, and after repeated efforts with voice and pen the doors of the public schools were opened and colored children were permitted to attend them in common with others.

There were barriers erected against colored people in most other places of instruction and amusement in the city, and until I went there they were imposed without any apparent sense of injustice and wrong, and submitted to in silence; but one by one they have gradually been removed, and colored people now enter freely, without hindrance or observation, all places of public resort. This change has not been wholly effected by me. From the first I was cheered on and supported in my demands for equal rights by such respectable citizens as Isaac Post, Wm. Hallowell, Samuel D. Porter, Wm. C. Bloss, Benj. Fish, Asa Anthony, and many other good and true men of Rochester.

Notwithstanding what I have said of the adverse feeling exhibited by some of its citizens at my selection of Rochester as the place in which to establish my paper, and the trouble in educational matters just referred to, that selection was in many respects very fortunate. The city was and still is the center of a virtuous, intelligent, enterprising, liberal, and growing population. The surrounding country is remarkable for its fertility, and the city itself possesses one of the finest water-powers in the world. It is on the line of the New York Central railroad—a line that, with its connections, spans the whole country. Its people were industrious and in comfortable circumstances—not so rich as to be indifferent to the claims of humanity, and not so poor as to be unable to help any good cause which commanded the approval of their judgment.

The ground had been measurably prepared for me by the labors of others—notably by Hon. Myron Holley, whose monument of enduring marble now stands in the beautiful cemetery at Mount Hope upon an eminence befitting his noble character. I know of no place in the Union where I could have located at the time with less resistance, or received a larger measure of sympathy and coöperation, and I now look back to my life and labors there with unalloyed satisfaction, and having spent a quarter of a century among its people, I shall always feel more at home there than anywhere else in this country.

# CHAPTER VIII.

## JOHN BROWN AND MRS. STOWE.

*My first meeting with Capt. John Brown—The Free-Soil movement—
Colored Convention—Uncle Tom's Cabin—Industrial School for
colored people—Letter to Mrs. H. B. Stowe.*

ABOUT the time I began my enterprise in Rochester I chanced to
spend a night and a day under the roof of a man whose character and
conversation, and whose objects and aims in life, made a very deep
impression upon my mind and heart. His name had been mentioned to
me by several prominent colored men, among whom were the Rev.
Henry Highland Garnet and J. W. Loguen.* In speaking of him their
voices would drop to a whisper, and what they said of him made me
very eager to see and to know him. Fortunately, I was invited to see him
in his own house. At the time to which I now refer this man was
a respectable merchant in a populous and thriving city, and our first
place of meeting was at his store. This was a substantial brick building
on a prominent, busy street. A glance at the interior, as well as at the
massive walls without, gave me the impression that the owner must be
a man of considerable wealth. My welcome was all that I could have
asked. Every member of the family, young and old, seemed glad to see
me, and I was made much at home in a very little while. I was, however,
a little disappointed with the appearance of the house and its location.
After seeing the fine store I was prepared to see a fine residence in an
eligible locality, but this conclusion was completely dispelled by actual
observation. In fact, the house was neither commodious nor elegant,
nor its situation desirable. It was a small wooden building on a back
street, in a neighborhood chiefly occupied by laboring men and
mechanics; respectable enough, to be sure, but not quite the place,
I thought, where one would look for the residence of a flourishing and
successful merchant. Plain as was the outside of this man's house, the
inside was plainer. Its furniture would have satisfied a Spartan. It would
take longer to tell what was not in this house than what was in it. There
was an air of plainness about it which almost suggested destitution. My
first meal passed under the misnomer of tea, though there was nothing
about it resembling the usual significance of that term. It consisted of
beef-soup, cabbage, and potatoes—a meal such as a man might relish
after following the plow all day or performing a forced march of a dozen
miles over a rough road in frosty weather. Innocent of paint, veneering,

varnish, or table-cloth, the table announced itself unmistakably of pine and of the plainest workmanship. There was no hired help visible. The mother, daughters, and sons did the serving, and did it well. They were evidently used to it, and had no thought of any impropriety or degradation in being their own servants. It is said that a house in some measure reflects the character of its occupants; this one certainly did. In it there were no disguises, no illusions, no make-believes. Everything implied stern truth, solid purpose, and rigid economy. I was not long in company with the master of this house before I discovered that he was indeed the master of it, and was likely to become mine too if I stayed long enough with him. He fulfilled St. Paul's idea of the head of the family. His wife believed in him, and his children observed him with reverence. Whenever he spoke his words commanded earnest attention. His arguments, which I ventured at some points to oppose, seemed to convince all; his appeals touched all, and his will impressed all. Certainly I never felt myself in the presence of a stronger religious influence than while in this man's house.

In person he was lean, strong, and sinewy, of the best New England mold, built for times of trouble and fitted to grapple with the flintiest hardships. Clad in plain American woolen, shod in boots of cowhide leather, and wearing a cravat of the same substantial material, under six feet high, less than 150 pounds in weight, aged about fifty, he presented a figure straight and symmetrical as a mountain pine. His bearing was singularly impressive. His head was not large, but compact and high. His hair was coarse, strong, slightly gray and closely trimmed, and grew low on his forehead. His face was smoothly shaved, and revealed a strong, square mouth, supported by a broad and prominent chin. His eyes were bluish-gray, and in conversation they were full of light and fire. When on the street, he moved with a long, springing, race-horse step, absorbed by his own reflections, neither seeking nor shunning observation. Such was the man whose name I had heard in whispers; such was the spirit of his house and family; such was the house in which he lived; and such was Captain John Brown, whose name has now passed into history, as that of one of the most marked characters and greatest heroes known to American fame.

After the strong meal already described, Captain Brown cautiously approached the subject which he wished to bring to my attention; for he seemed to apprehend opposition to his views. He denounced slavery in look and language fierce and bitter, thought that slaveholders had forfeited their right to live, that the slaves had the right to gain their liberty in any way they could, did not believe that moral suasion would ever liberate the slave, or that political action would abolish the system. He said that he had long had a plan which could accomplish this end, and he had invited me to his house to lay that plan before me. He said he had been for some time looking for colored men to whom he could safely reveal his secret, and at times he had almost despaired of finding such men; but that now he was encouraged, for he saw heads of such rising up in all directions. He had observed my course at home and abroad, and he wanted my coöperation. His plan as it then lay in his mind had much to commend it. It did not, as some suppose, contemplate a general rising among the slaves, and a general slaughter of the slave-masters. An insurrection, he thought, would only defeat the object; but his plan did contemplate the creating of an armed force which should act in the very heart of the South. He was not averse to the shedding of blood, and thought the practice of carrying arms would be a good one for the colored people to adopt, as it would give them a sense of their manhood. No people, he said, could have self-respect, or be respected, who would not fight for their freedom. He called my attention to a map of the United States, and pointed out to me the far-reaching Alleghanies, which stretch away from the borders of New York into the Southern States. 'These mountains,' he said, 'are the basis of my plan. God has given the strength of the hills to freedom; they were placed here for the emancipation of the negro race; they are full of natural forts, where one man for defense will be equal to a hundred for attack; they are full also of good hiding-places, where large numbers of brave men could be concealed, and baffle and elude pursuit for a long time. I know these mountains well, and could take a body of men into them and keep them there despite of all the efforts of Virginia to dislodge them. The true object to be sought is first of all to destroy the money value of slave property; and that can only be done by rendering such property insecure. My plan, then, is to take at first about twenty-five picked men, and begin on a small scale; supply them with arms and ammunition and post them in squads of fives on a line of twenty-five miles. The most persuasive and judicious of these shall go down to the fields from time to time, as opportunity offers, and induce the slaves to join them, seeking and selecting the most restless and daring.'

He saw that in this part of the work the utmost care must be used to avoid treachery and disclosure. Only the most conscientious and skillful should be sent on this perilous duty. With care and enterprise he thought he could soon gather a force of one hundred hardy men, men who would be content to lead the free and adventurous life to which he proposed to train them; when these were properly drilled, and each man had found the place for which he was best suited, they would begin work in earnest; they would run off the slaves in large numbers, retain the brave and strong ones in the mountains, and send the weak and timid to the north by the underground railroad. His operations would be enlarged with increasing numbers and would not be confined to one locality.

When I asked him how he would support these men, he said emphatically that he would subsist them upon the enemy. Slavery was a state of war, and the slave had a right to anything necessary to his freedom. 'But,' said I, 'suppose you succeed in running off a few slaves, and thus impress the Virginia slaveholders with a sense of insecurity in their slaves, the effect will be only to make them sell their slaves further south.' 'That,' said he, 'will be what I want first to do; then I would follow them up. If we could drive slavery out of *one county*, it would be a great gain; it would weaken the system throughout the State.' 'But they would employ bloodhounds to hunt you out of the mountains.' 'That they might attempt,' said he, 'but the chances are, we should whip them, and when we should have whipped one squad, they would be careful how they pursued.' 'But you might be surrounded and cut off from your provisions or means of subsistence.' He thought that this could not be done so they could not cut their way out, but even if the worst came he could but be killed, and he had no better use for his life than to lay it down in the cause of the slave. When I suggested that we might convert the slaveholders, he became much excited, and said that could never be, 'he knew their proud hearts and that they would never be induced to give up their slaves, until they felt a big stick about their heads.' He observed that I might have noticed the simple manner in which he lived, adding that he had adopted this method in order to save money to carry out his purposes. This was said in no boastful tone, for he felt that he had delayed already too long, and had no room to boast either his zeal or his self-denial. Had some men made such display of rigid virtue, I should have rejected it, as affected, false, and hypocritical, but in John Brown, I felt it to be real as iron or granite. From this night spent with John Brown in Springfield, Mass., 1847, while I continued to write and speak against slavery, I became all the same less hopeful of its peaceful abolition. My utterances became more and more tinged by the color of this man's strong impressions. Speaking at an anti-slavery convention in Salem, Ohio, I expressed this apprehension that slavery could only be destroyed by blood-shed, when I was suddenly and sharply interrupted by my good old friend Sojourner Truth* with the question, 'Frederick, is God dead?' 'No,' I answered, 'and because God is not dead slavery can only end in blood.' My quaint old sister was of the Garrison school of non-resistants, and was shocked at my sanguinary doctrine, but she too became an advocate of the sword, when the war for the maintenance of the Union was declared.

In 1848 it was my privilege to attend, and in some measure to participate in the famous Free-Soil Convention held in Buffalo, New York.* It was a vast and variegated assemblage, composed of persons from all sections of the North, and may be said to have formed a new departure in the history of forces organized to resist the growing and aggressive demands of slavery and the slave power. Until this Buffalo convention, anti-slavery agencies had been mainly directed to the work of changing public sentiment by exposing through the press and on the platform the nature of the slave system. Anti-slavery thus far had only been sheet-lightning; the Buffalo convention sought to make it a thunderbolt. It is true the Liberty party,* a political organization, had been in existence since 1840, when it cast seven thousand votes for James G. Birney,* a former slaveholder, but who, in obedience to an enlightened conscience, had nobly emancipated his slaves, and was now devoting his time and talents to the overthrow of slavery. It is true that this little party of brave men had increased their numbers at one time to sixty thousand voters. It, however, had now apparently reached its culminating point, and was no longer able to attract to itself and combine all the available elements at the North capable of being marshaled against the growing and aggressive measures and aims of the slave power. There were many in the old Whig party known as Conscience-Whigs,* and in the Democratic party known as Barn-burners* and Free Democrats, who were anti-slavery in sentiment and utterly opposed to the extension of the slave system to territory hitherto uncursed by its presence, but who, nevertheless, were not willing to join the Liberty party. It was held to be deficient in numbers and wanting in prestige. Its fate was the fate of all pioneers. The work it had been required to perform had exposed it to assaults from all sides, and it wore on its front the ugly marks of conflict. It was unpopular for its very fidelity to the cause of liberty and justice. No wonder that some of its members, such as Gerrit Smith, William Goodell, Beriah Green, and Julius Lemoyne, refused to quit the old for the new. They felt that the Free-Soil party was a step backward, a lowering of the standard; that the people should come to them, not they to the people. The party which had been good enough for them ought to be good enough for all others. Events, however, overruled this reasoning. The conviction became general that the time had come for a new organization which should embrace all who were in any manner opposed to slavery and the slave power, and this Buffalo Free-Soil convention was the result of that conviction. It is easy to say that this or that measure would have been wiser and better than the one adopted. But any measure is vindicated by its necessity and good results. It was impossible for the mountain to go to Mahomet, or for the Free-Soil element to go to the old Liberty party; so the latter went to the former. 'All is well that ends well.' This Buffalo convention of free-soilers, however low was their standard, did lay the foundation of a grand superstructure. It was a powerful link in the chain of events by which the slave system has been abolished, the slave emancipated and the country saved from dismemberment.

It is nothing against the actors in this new movement that they did not see the end from the beginning; that they did not at first take the high ground that further on in the conflict their successors felt themselves called upon to take, or that their Free-Soil party, like the old Liberty party, was ultimately required to step aside and make room for the great Republican party. In all this and more it illustrates the experience of reform in all ages, and conforms to the laws of human progress. Measures change, principles never.

I was not the only colored man well known to the country who was present at this convention. Samuel Ringold Ward, Henry Highland Garnet, Charles L. Remond, and Henry Bibb were there and made speeches which were received with surprise and gratification by the thousands there assembled. As a colored man I felt greatly encouraged and strengthened for my cause while listening to these men, in the presence of the ablest men of the Caucasian race. Mr. Ward* especially attracted attention at that convention. As an orator and thinker he was vastly superior, I thought, to any of us, and being perfectly black and of unmixed African descent, the splendors of his intellect went directly to the glory of race. In depth of thought, fluency of speech, readiness of wit, logical exactness, and general intelligence, Samuel R. Ward has left no successor among the colored men amongst us, and it was a sad day for our cause when he was laid low in the soil of a foreign country.

After the Free-Soil party, with 'Free Soil,' 'Free Labor,' 'Free States,' 'Free Speech,' and 'Free Men' on its banner, had defeated the almost permanently victorious Democratic party under the leadership of so able and popular a standard-bearer as General Lewis Cass,* Mr. Calhoun* and other southern statesmen were more than ever alarmed at the rapid increase of anti-slavery feeling in the North, and devoted their energies more and more to the work of devising means to stay the torrents and tie up the storm. They were not ignorant of whereunto this sentiment would grow if unsubjected and unextinguished. Hence they became fierce and furious in debate, and more extravagant than ever in their demands for additional safeguards for their system of robbery and murder. Assuming that the Constitution guaranteed their rights of property in their fellow-men, they held it to be in open violation of the Constitution for any American citizen in any part of the United States to speak, write, or act against this right. But this shallow logic they plainly saw could do them no good unless they could obtain further safe-guards for slavery. In order to effect this the idea of so changing the Constitution was suggested that there should be two instead of one President of the United States—one from the North and the other from the South—and that no measure should become a law without the assent of both.\* But this device was so utterly impracticable that it soon dropped out of sight, and it is mentioned here only to show the desperation of slaveholders to prop up their system of barbarism against which the sentiment of the North was being directed with destructive skill and effect. They clamored for more slave States, more power in the Senate and House of Representatives, and insisted upon the suppression of free speech. At the end of two years, in 1850, when Clay and Calhoun, two of the ablest leaders the South ever had, were still in the Senate, we had an attempt at a settlement of differences between the North and South which our legislators meant to be final. What those measures were I need not here enumerate, except to say that chief among them was the Fugitive Slave Bill, framed by James M. Mason of Virginia and supported by Daniel Webster of Massachusetts—a bill undoubtedly more designed to involve the North in complicity with slavery and deaden its moral sentiment than to procure the return of fugitives to their so-called owners. For a time this design did not altogether fail. Letters, speeches, and pamphlets literally rained down upon the people of the North, reminding them of their constitutional duty to hunt down and return to bondage runaway slaves. In this the preachers were not much behind the press and the politicians, especially that class of preachers known as Doctors of Divinity. A long list of these came forward with their Bibles to show that neither Christ nor his holy apostles objected to returning fugitives to slavery. Now that that evil day is past, a sight of those sermons would, I doubt not, bring the red blush of shame to the cheeks of many.

Living, as I then did, in Rochester, on the border of Canada, I was compelled to see the terribly distressing effects of this cruel enactment. Fugitive slaves who had lived for many years safely and securely in western New York and elsewhere, some of whom had by industry and economy saved money and bought little homes for themselves and their children, were suddenly alarmed and compelled to flee to Canada for safety as from an enemy's land—a doomed city—and take up a dismal march to a new abode, empty-handed, among strangers. My old friend Ward, of whom I have just now spoken, found it necessary to give up the contest and flee to Canada, and thousands followed his example. Bishop Daniel A. Payne of the African Methodist Episcopal Church came to me about this time to consult me as to whether it was best to stand our ground or flee to Canada. When I told him I could not desert my post until I saw I could not hold it, adding that I did not wish to leave while Garnet and Ward remained, 'Why,' said he, 'Ward? Ward, he is already gone. I saw him crossing from Detroit to Windsor.' I asked him if he were going to stay, and he answered: 'Yes; we are whipped, we are whipped, and we might as well retreat in order.' This was indeed a stunning blow. This man had power to do more to defeat this inhuman enactment than any other colored man in the land, for no other could bring such brain power to bear against it. I felt like a besieged city at news that its defenders had fallen at its gates. The hardships imposed by this atrocious and shameless law were cruel and shocking, and yet only a few of all the fugitives of the Northern States were returned to slavery under its infamously wicked provisions. As a means of recapturing their runaway property in human flesh the law was an utter failure. Its efficiency was destroyed by its enormity. Its chief effect was to produce alarm and terror among the class subject to its operation, and this it did most effectually and distressingly. Even colored people who had been free all their lives felt themselves very insecure in their freedom, for under this law the oaths of any two villains were sufficient to consign a free man to slavery for life. While the law was a terror to the free, it was a still greater terror to the escaped bondman. To him there was no peace. Asleep or awake, at work or at rest, in church or market, he was liable to surprise and capture. By the law the judge got ten dollars a head for all he could consign to slavery, and only five dollars apiece for any which he might adjudge free. Although I was now myself free, I was not without apprehension. My purchase was of doubtful validity, having been bought when out of the possession of my owner and when he must take what was given or take nothing. It was a question whether my claimant could be estopped by such a sale from asserting certain or supposable equitable rights in my body and soul. From rumors that reached me my house was guarded by my friends several nights, when kidnappers, had they come, would have got anything but a cool reception, for there would have been 'blows to take as well as blows to give.' Happily this reign of terror did not continue long. Despite the efforts of Daniel Webster and Millard Fillmore and our Doctors of Divinity, the law fell rapidly into disrepute. The rescue of Shadrack* resulting in the death of one of the kidnappers, in Boston, the cases of Simms and Anthony Burns,* in the same place, created the deepest feeling against the law and its upholders. But the thing which more than all else destroyed the fugitive slave law was the resistance made to it by the fugitives themselves. A decided check was given to the execution of the law at Christiana, Penn., where three colored men, being pursued by Mr. Gorsuch and his son, slew the father, wounded the son, and drove away the officers, and made their escape to my house in Rochester. The work of getting these men safely into Canada was a delicate one. They were not only fugitives from slavery but charged with murder, and officers were in pursuit of them. There was no time for delay. I could not look upon them as murderers. To me, they were heroic defenders of the just rights of man against manstealers and murderers. So I fed them, and sheltered them in my house. Had they been pursued then and there, my home would have been stained with blood, for these men who had already tasted blood were well armed and prepared to sell their lives at any expense to the lives and limbs of their probable assailants. What they had already done at Christiana and the cool determination which showed very plainly especially in Parker, (for that was the name of the leader,) left no doubt on my mind that their courage was genuine and that their deeds would equal their words. The situation was critical and dangerous. The telegraph had that day announced their deeds at Christiana, their escape, and that the mountains of Pennsylvania were being searched for the murderers. These men had reached me simultaneously with this news in the New York papers. Immediately after the occurrence at Christiana, they, instead of going into the mountains, were placed on a train which brought them to Rochester. They were thus almost in advance of the lightning, and much in advance of probable pursuit, unless the telegraph had raised agents already here. The hours they spent at my house were therefore hours of anxiety as well as activity. I dispatched my friend Miss Julia Griffiths to the landing three miles away on the Genesee River to ascertain if a steamer would leave that night for any port in Canada, and remained at home myself to guard my tired, dust-covered, and sleeping guests, for they had been harassed and traveling for two days and nights, and needed rest. Happily for us the suspense was not long, for it turned out that that very night a steamer was to leave for Toronto, Canada.

This fact, however, did not end my anxiety. There was danger that between my house and the landing or at the landing itself we might meet with trouble. Indeed the landing was the place where trouble was likely to occur if at all. As patiently as I could, I waited for the shades of night to come on, and then put the men in my 'Democrat carriage,' and started for the landing on the Genesee. It was an exciting ride, and somewhat speedy withal. We reached the boat at least fifteen minutes before the time of its departure, and that without remark or molestation. But those fifteen minutes seemed much longer than usual. I remained on board till the order to haul in the gang-plank was given; I shook hands with my friends, received from Parker the revolver that fell from the hand of Gorsuch when he died, presented now as a token of gratitude and a memento of the battle for Liberty at Christiana, and I returned to my home with a sense of relief which I cannot stop here to describe. This affair, at Christiana, and the Jerry rescue at Syracuse, inflicted fatal wounds on the fugitive slave bill. It became thereafter almost a dead letter, for slaveholders found that not only did it fail to put them in possession of their slaves, but that the attempt to enforce it brought odium upon themselves and weakened the slave system.

In the midst of these fugitive slave troubles came the book known as Uncle Tom's Cabin,* a work of marvelous depth and power. Nothing could have better suited the moral and humane requirements of the hour. Its effect was amazing, instantaneous, and universal. No book on the subject of slavery had so generally and favorably touched the American heart. It combined all the power and pathos of preceding publications of the kind, and was hailed by many as an inspired production. Mrs. Stowe at once became an object of interest and admiration. She had made fortune and fame at home, and had awakened a deep interest abroad. Eminent persons in England, roused to anti-slavery enthusiasm by her 'Uncle Tom's Cabin,' invited her to visit that country, and promised to give her a testimonial. Mrs. Stowe accepted the invitation and the proffered testimonial. Before sailing for England, however, she invited me from Rochester, N. Y., to spend a day at her house in Andover, Mass. Delighted with an opportunity to become personally acquainted with the gifted authoress, I lost no time in making my way to Andover. I was received at her home with genuine cordiality. There was no contradiction between the author and her book. Mrs. Stowe appeared in conversation equally as well as she appeared in her writing. She made to me a nice little speech in announcing her object in sending for me. 'I have invited you here,' she said, 'because I wish to confer with you as to what can be done for the free colored people of the country. I am going to England and expect to have a considerable sum of money placed in my hands, and I intend to use it in some way for the permanent improvement of the free colored people, and especially for that class which has become free by their own exertions. In what way I can do this most successfully is the subject about which I wish to talk with you. In any event I desire to have some monument rise after Uncle Tom's Cabin, which shall show that it produced more than a transient influence.' She said several plans had been suggested, among others an educational institution pure and simple, but that she thought favorably of the establishment of an industrial school; and she desired me to express my views as to what I thought would be the best plan by which to help the free colored people. I was not slow to tell Mrs. Stowe all I knew and had thought on the subject. As to a purely educational institution, I agreed with her that it did not meet our necessities. I argued against expending money in that way. I was also opposed to an ordinary industrial school where pupils should merely earn the means of obtaining an education in books. There were such schools, already. What I thought of as best was rather a series of workshops, where colored people could learn some of the handicrafts, learn to work in iron, wood, and leather, and where a plain English education could also be taught. I argued that the want of money was the root of all evil to the colored people. They were shut out from all lucrative employments and compelled to be merely barbers, waiters, coachmen, and the like, at wages so low that they could lay up little or nothing. Their poverty kept them ignorant and their ignorance kept them degraded. We needed more to learn how to make a good living than to learn Latin and Greek. After listening to me at considerable length, she was good enough to tell me that she favored my views, and would devote the money she expected to receive abroad to meeting the want I had described as the most important; by establishing an institution in which colored youth should learn trades as well as to read, write, and count. When about to leave Andover, Mrs. Stowe asked me to put my views on the subject in the form of a letter, so that she could take it to England with her and show it to her friends there, that they might see to what their contributions were to be devoted. I acceded to her request and wrote her the following letter for the purpose named:

ROCHESTER, March 8, 1853.
MY DEAR MRS. STOWE:
You kindly informed me, when at your house a fortnight ago, that you designed to do something which should permanently contribute to the improvement and elevation of the free colored people in the United States. You especially expressed an interest in such of this class as had become free by their own exertions, and desired most of all to be of service to them. In what manner

and by what means you can assist this class most successfully, is the subject upon which you have done me the honor to ask my opinion. . . . I assert, then, that *poverty*, *ignorance*, and *degradation* are the combined evils; or in other words, these constitute the social disease of the free colored people of the United States.

To deliver them from this triple malady is to improve and elevate them, by which I mean simply to put them on an equal footing with their white fellow-countrymen in the sacred right to 'Life, *Liberty*, and the pursuit of happiness.' I am for no fancied or artificial elevation, but only ask fair play. How shall this be obtained? I answer, first, not by establishing for our use high schools and colleges. Such institutions are, in my judgment, beyond our immediate occasions and are not adapted to our present most pressing wants. High schools and colleges are excellent institutions, and will in due season be greatly subservient to our progress; but they are the result, as well as they are the demand, of a point of progress which we as a people have not yet attained. Accustomed as we have been to the rougher and harder modes of living, and of gaining a livelihood, we cannot and we ought not to hope that in a single leap from our low condition, we can reach that of *Ministers, Lawyers, Doctors, Editors, Merchants*, etc. These will doubtless be attained by us; but this will only be when we have patiently and laboriously, and I may add successfully, mastered and passed through the intermediate gradations of agriculture and the mechanic arts. Besides, there are (and perhaps this is a better reason for my view of the case) numerous institutions of learning in this country, already thrown open to colored youth. To my thinking, there are quite as many facilities now afforded to the colored people as they can spare the time, from the sterner duties of life, to judiciously appropriate. In their present condition of poverty, they cannot spare their sons and daughters two or three years at boarding-schools or colleges, to say nothing of finding the means to sustain them while at such institutions. I take it, therefore, that we are well provided for in this respect; and that it may be fairly inferred from the fact, that the facilities for our education, so far as schools and colleges in the Free States are concerned, will increase quite in proportion with our future wants. Colleges have been open to colored youth in this country during the last dozen years. Yet few, comparatively, have acquired a classical education; and even this few have found themselves educated far above a living condition there being no methods by which they could turn their learning to account. Several of this latter class have entered the ministry; but you need not be told that an educated people is needed to sustain an educated ministry. There must be a certain amount of cultivation among the people, to sustain such a ministry. At present we have not that cultivation amongst us; and, therefore, we value in the preacher strong lungs rather than high learning. I do not say that educated ministers are not needed amongst us, far from it! I wish there were more of them! but to increase their number is not the largest benefit you can bestow upon us.

We have two or three colored lawyers in this country; and I rejoice in the fact; for it affords very gratifying evidence of our progress. Yet it must be confessed that, in point of success, our lawyers are as great failures as our ministers. White people will not employ them to the obvious embarrassment of their causes, and the blacks, taking their cue from the whites, have not sufficient confidence in their abilities to employ them. Hence educated colored men, among the colored people, are at a very great discount. It would seem that education and emigration go together with us, for as soon as a man rises amongst us, capable, by his genius and learning, to do us great service, just so soon he finds that he can serve himself better by going elsewhere. In proof of this, I might instance the Russwurms, the Garnetts, the Wards, the Crummells, and others, all men of superior ability and attainments, and capable of removing mountains of prejudice against their race, by their simple presence in the country; but these gentlemen, finding themselves embarrassed here by the peculiar disadvantages to which I have referred, disadvantages in part growing out of their education, being repelled by ignorance on the one hand, and prejudice on the other, and having no taste to continue a contest against such odds, have sought more congenial climes, where they can live more peaceable and quiet lives. I regret their election, but I cannot blame them; for with an equal amount of education, and the hard lot which was theirs, I might follow their example. . . .

There is little reason to hope that any considerable number of the free colored people will ever be induced to leave this country, even if such a thing were desirable. The black man (*un*like the Indian) loves civilization. He does not make very great progress in civilization himself, but he likes to be in the midst of it, and prefers to share its most galling evils, to encountering barbarism. Then the love of country, the dread of isolation, the lack of adventurous spirit, and the thought of seeming to desert their 'brethren in bonds,' are a powerful check upon all schemes of colonization, which look to the removal of the colored people, without the slaves. The truth is, dear madam, we are here, and here we are likely to remain. Individuals emigrate—nations never. We have grown up with this republic, and I see nothing in her character, or even in the character of the American people, as yet, which compels the belief that we must leave the United States. If, then, we are to remain here, the question for the wise and good is precisely that which you have submitted to me—namely: What can be done to improve the condition of the free people of color in the United States? The plan which I humbly submit in answer to this inquiry (and in the hope that it may find favor with you, and with the many friends of humanity who honor, love and coöporate with you) is the establishment in Rochester, N. Y., or in some other part of the United States equally favorable to such an enterprise, of an INDUSTRIAL COLLEGE in which shall be taught several important branches of the mechanic arts. This college shall be open to colored youth. I will pass over the details of such an institution as I propose. . . . Never having had a day's schooling in all my life, I may not be expected to map out the details of a plan so comprehensive as that involved in the idea of a college. I repeat, then, that I leave the organization and administration of the institution to the superior wisdom of yourself and the friends who second your noble efforts. The argument in favor of an Industrial College (a college to be conducted by the best men, and the best workmen which the mechanic arts can afford; a college where colored youth can be instructed to use their hands, as well as their heads; where they can be put in possession of the means of getting a living whether their lot in after life may be cast among civilized or uncivilized men; whether they choose to stay here, or prefer to return to the land of their fathers) is briefly this: Prejudice against the free colored people in the United States has shown itself nowhere so invincible as among mechanics. The farmer and the professional man cherish no feeling so bitter as that cherished by these. The latter would starve us out of the country entirely. At this moment I can more easily get my son into a lawyer's office to study law than I can into a blacksmith's shop to blow the bellows and to wield the sledge-hammer. Denied the means of learning useful trades, we are pressed into the narrowest limits to obtain a livelihood; in times past we have been the hewers of wood and drawers of water for American society, and we once enjoyed a monopoly in menial employments, but this is so no longer. Even these employments are rapidly passing away out of our hands. The fact is (every day begins with the lesson, and ends with the lesson) that colored men must learn trades; must find new employments; new modes of usefulness to society, or that they must decay under the pressing wants to which their condition is rapidly bringing them.

We must become mechanics; we must build as well as live in houses; we must make as well as use furniture; we must construct bridges as well as pass over them, before we can properly live or be respected by our fellow men. We need mechanics as well as ministers. We need workers in iron, clay, and leather. We have orators, authors, and other professional men, but these reach only a certain class, and get respect for our race in certain select circles. To live here as we ought we must fasten ourselves to our countrymen through their every-day, cardinal wants. We must not only be able to *black* boots, but to *make* them. At present we are, in the northern States, unknown as mechanics. We give no proof of genius or skill at the county, State, or national fairs. We are unknown at any of the great exhibitions of the industry of our fellow-citizens, and being unknown, we are unconsidered.

The fact that we make no show of our ability is held conclusive of our inability to make any, hence all the indifference and contempt with which incapacity is regarded fall upon us, and that too when we have had no means of disproving the infamous opinion of our natural inferiority. I have, during the last dozen years, denied before the Americans that we are an inferior race; but this has been done by arguments based upon admitted principles rather than by the presentation of facts. Now, firmly believing, as I do, that there are skill, invention, power, industry, and real mechanical genius among the colored people, which will bear favorable testimony for them, and which only need the means to develop them, I am decidedly in favor of the establishment of such a college as I have mentioned. The benefits of such an institution would not be confined to the Northern States, nor to the free colored people. They would extend over the whole Union. The slave not less than the freeman would be benefited by such an institution. It must be confessed that the most powerful argument now used by the southern slaveholder, and the one most soothing to his conscience, is that derived from the low condition of the free colored people of the North. I have long felt that too little attention has been given by our truest friends in this country to removing this stumbling-block out of the way of the slave's liberation.

The most telling, the most killing refutation of slavery is the presentation of an industrious, enterprising, thrifty, and intelligent free black population. Such a population I believe would rise in the Northern States under the fostering care of such a college as that supposed.

To show that we are capable of becoming mechanics I might adduce any amount of testimony; but, dear madam, I need not ring the changes on such a proposition. There is no question in the mind of any unprejudiced person that the Negro is capable of making a good mechanic. Indeed, even those who cherish the bitterest feelings toward us have admitted that the apprehension that negroes might be employed in their stead dictated the policy of excluding them from trades altogether. But I will not dwell upon this point, as I fear I have already trespassed too long upon your precious time, and written more than I ought to expect you to read. Allow me to say in conclusion that I believe every intelligent colored man in America will approve and rejoice at the establishment of some such institution as that now suggested. There are many respectable colored men, fathers of large families, having boys nearly grown up, whose minds are tossed by day and by night with the anxious inquiry, What shall I do with my boys? Such an institution would meet the wants of such persons. Then, too, the establishment of such an institution would be in character with the eminently practical philanthropy of your transatlantic friends. America could scarcely object to it as an attempt to agitate the public mind on the subject of slavery, or to dissolve the Union. It could not be tortured into a cause for hard words by the American people, but the noble and good of all classes would see in the effort an excellent motive, a benevolent object, temperately, wisely, and practically manifested.

Wishing you, dear madam, renewed health, a pleasant passage and safe return to your native land.

I am, most truly, your grateful friend,

FREDERICK DOUGLASS.

*Mrs. H. B. Stowe.*

I was not only requested to write the foregoing letter for the purpose indicated, but I was also asked, with admirable foresight, to see and ascertain, as far as possible, the views of the free colored people themselves in respect to the proposed measure for their benefit. This I was enabled to do in July, 1853, at the largest and most enlightened colored convention* that, up to that time, had ever assembled in this country. This convention warmly approved the plan of a manual labor school, as already described, and expressed high appreciation of the wisdom and benevolence of Mrs. Stowe. This convention was held in Rochester, N. Y., and will long be remembered there for the surprise and gratification it caused our friends in that city. They were not looking for such exhibitions of enlightened zeal and ability as were there displayed in speeches, addresses, and resolutions, and in the conduct of the business for which it had assembled. Its proceedings attracted widespread attention at home and abroad.

While Mrs. Stowe was abroad she was, by the pro-slavery press of our country, so persistently and vigorously attacked for receiving money for her own private use, that the Rev. Henry Ward Beecher* felt called upon to notice and reply to it in the columns of the New York *Independent*,* of which he was then the editor. He denied that Mrs. Stowe was gathering British gold for herself and referred her assailants to me if they would learn what she intended to do with the money. In answer to her maligners, I denounced their accusations as groundless and through the columns of my paper, assured the public that the testimonial then being raised in England by Mrs. Stowe would be sacredly devoted to the establishment of an industrial school for colored youth. This announcement was circulated by other journals, and the attacks ceased. Nobody could well object to such application of the money received from any source, at home or abroad. After her return to this country I called again on Mrs. Stowe, and was much disappointed to learn from her that she had reconsidered her plan for the industrial school. I have never been able to see any force in the reasons for this change. It is enough, however, to say that they were sufficient for her, and that she no doubt acted conscientiously, though her change of purpose was a great disappointment, and placed me in an awkward position before the colored people of this country, as well as to friends abroad, to whom I had given assurances that the money would be appropriated in the manner I have described.

# CHAPTER IX.

## INCREASING DEMANDS OF THE SLAVE POWER.

*Increased demands of slavery—War in Kansas—John Brown's raid—His capture and execution—My escape to England from United States marshals.*

NOTWITHSTANDING the natural tendency of the human mind to weary of an old story, and to turn away from chronic abuses for which it sees no remedy, the anti-slavery agitation for thirty long years (from 1830 to 1860) was sustained with ever-increasing intensity and power. This was not entirely due to the extraordinary zeal and ability of the anti-slavery agitators themselves, for, with all their admitted ardor and eloquence, they could have done very little without the aid rendered them unwittingly by the aggressive character of slavery itself. It was in the nature of the system never to rest in obscurity, although that condition was in a high degree essential to its security. It was forever forcing itself into prominence. Unconscious, apparently, of its own deformity, it omitted no occasion for inviting disgust by seeking approval and admiration. It was noisiest when it should have been most silent and unobtrusive. One of its defenders, when asked what would satisfy him as a slaveholder, said he 'never would be satisfied until he could call the roll of his slaves in the shadow of Bunker Hill monument.'* Every effort made to put down agitation only served to impart to it new strength and vigor. Of this class was the 'gag rule' attempted and partially enforced in Congress; the attempted suppression of the right of petition; the mobocratic demonstrations against the exercise of free speech; the display of pistols, bludgeons, and plantation manners in the Congress of the nation; the demand shamelessly made by our government upon England for the return of slaves who had won their liberty by their valor on the high seas; the bill for the recapture of runaway slaves: the annexation of Texas* for the avowed purpose of increasing the number of slave States, and thus increasing the power of slavery in the Union; the war with Mexico;* the filibustering expeditions against Cuba and Central America; the cold-blooded decision of Chief Justice Taney in the Dred Scott case,* wherein he states, as it were, a historical fact that 'negroes are deemed to have no rights which white men are bound to respect'; the perfidious repeal of the Missouri compromise when all its advantages to the South had been gained and appropriated, and when nothing had been gained by the North;* the armed and bloody attempt to force slavery upon the virgin soil of Kansas;* the efforts of both of the great political parties to drive from place and power every man suspected of ideas and principles hostile to slavery; the rude attacks made upon Giddings, Hale, Chase, Wilson, Wm. H. Seward, and Charles Sumner; the effort to degrade these brave men and to drive them from positions of prominence; the summary manner in which Virginia hanged John Brown; in a word, whatever was done or attempted with a view to the support and security of slavery, only served as fuel to the fire, and heated the furnace of agitation to a higher degree than any before attained. This was true up to the moment when the nation found it necessary to gird on the sword for the salvation of the country and the destruction of slavery.

At no time during all the ten years preceding the war was the public mind at rest. Mr. Clay's compromise measures in 1850, whereby all the troubles of the country about slavery were to be 'in the deep bosom of the ocean buried,'* were hardly dry on the pages of the statute book before the whole land was rocked with rumored agitation, and for one I did my best by pen and voice and by ceaseless activity to keep it alive and vigorous. Later on, in 1854, we had the Missouri compromise, which removed the only grand legal barrier against the spread of slavery over all the territory of the United States. From this time there was no pause, no repose. Everybody, however dull, could see that this was a phase of the slavery question which was not to be slighted or ignored. The people of the North had been accustomed to ask, in a tone of cruel indifference, 'What have we to do with slavery?' and now no labored speech was required in answer. Slaveholding aggression settled this question for us. The presence of slavery in a territory would certainly exclude the sons and daughters of the free States more effectually than statutes or yellow fever. Those who cared nothing for the slave, and were willing to tolerate slavery inside the slave States, were nevertheless not quite prepared to find themselves and their children excluded from the common inheritance of the nation. It is not surprising, therefore, that the public mind of the North was easily kept intensely alive on this subject, or that in 1856 an alarming expression of feeling on this point was seen in the large vote given for John C. Fremont and William L. Dayton for President and Vice-President of the United States.* Until this last uprising of the North against the slave power the anti-slavery movement was largely retained in the hands of the original abolitionists, whose most prominent leaders have already been mentioned elsewhere in this volume. After 1856 a mightier arm and a more numerous host was raised against it, the agitation becoming broader and deeper. The times at this point illustrated the principle of tension and compression, action and reaction. The more open, flagrant, and impudent the slave power, the more firmly it was confronted by the rising anti-slavery spirit of the North. No one act did more to rouse the North to a comprehension of the infernal and barbarous spirit of slavery and its determination to 'rule or ruin,'* than the cowardly and brutal assault made in the American Senate upon Charles Sumner, by Preston S. Brooks, a member of Congress from South Carolina.* Shocking and scandalous as was this attack, the spirit in which the deed was received and commended by the community was still more disgraceful. Southern ladies even applauded the armed bully for his murderous assault upon an unarmed northern Senator, because of words spoken in debate! This more than all else told the thoughtful people of the North the kind of civilization to which they were linked, and how plainly it foreshadowed a conflict on a larger scale.

As a measure of agitation, the repeal of the Missouri Compromise alluded to was perhaps the most effective. It was that which brought Abraham Lincoln into prominence, and into conflict with Stephen A. Douglas* (who was the author of that measure) and compelled the Western States to take a deeper interest than they ever had done before in the whole question. Pregnant words were now spoken on the side of freedom, words which went straight to the heart of the nation. It was Mr. Lincoln who told the American people at this crisis that the 'Union could not long endure half slave and half free; that they must be all one or the other, and that the public mind could find no resting place but in the belief in the ultimate extinction of slavery.'* These were not the words of an abolitionist—branded a fanatic, and carried away by an enthusiastic devotion to the Negro—but the calm, cool, deliberate utterance of a statesman, comprehensive enough to take in the welfare of the whole country. No wonder that the friends of freedom saw in this plain man of Illinois the proper standard-bearer of all the moral and political forces which could be united and wielded against the slave power. In a few simple words he had embodied the thought of the loyal nation, and indicated the character fit to lead and guide the country amid perils present and to come.

The South was not far behind the North in recognizing Abraham Lincoln as the natural leader of the rising political sentiment of the country against slavery, and it was equally quick in its efforts to counteract and destroy his influence. Its papers teemed with the bitterest invectives against the 'backwoodsman of Illinois,' the 'flat-boatman,' the 'rail-splitter,' the 'third-rate lawyer,' and much else and worse.

Preceding the repeal of the Missouri Compromise I gave, at the anniversary of the American and Foreign Anti-Slavery Society in New York, the following picture of the state of the anti-slavery conflict as it then existed:

'It is evident that there is in this country a purely slavery party, a party which exists for no other earthly purpose but to promote the interest of slavery. It is known by no particular name, and has assumed no definite shape, but its branches reach far and wide in church and state. This shapeless and nameless party is not intangible in other and more important respects. It has a fixed, definite, and comprehensive policy towards the whole free colored population of the United States. I understand that policy to comprehend: First, the complete suppression of all anti-slavery discussion; second, the expulsion of the entire free people of the United States; third, the nationalization of slavery; fourth, guarantees for the endless perpetuation of slavery and its extension over Mexico and Central America. Sir, these objects are forcibly presented to us in the stern logic of passing events, and in all the facts that have been before us during the last three years. The country has been and is dividing on these grand issues. Old party ties are broken. Like is finding its like on both sides of these issues, and the great battle is at hand. For the present the best representative of the slavery party is the Democratic party. Its great head for the president is President Pierce, whose boast it was before his election, that his whole life had been consistent with the interests of slavery—that he is above reproach on that score. In his inaugural address he reassures the South on this point, so there shall be no misapprehension. Well, the head of the slave power being in power, it is natural that the pro-slavery elements should be clustered around his admission, and that is rapidly being done. The stringent protectionist and the free-trader strike hands. The supporters of Fillmore are becoming the supporters of Pierce. Silver Gray Whigs shake hands with Hunker Democrats, the former only differing from the latter in name. They are in fact of one heart and one mind, and the union is natural and perhaps inevitable. Pilate and Herod made friends.* The key-stone to the arch of this grand union of forces of the slave party is the so-called Compromise of 1850. In that measure we have all the objects of our slaveholding policy specified. It is, sir, favorable to this view of the situation, that the whig party and the democratic party bent lower, sunk deeper, and strained harder in their conventions, preparatory to the late presidential election, to meet the demands of slavery. Never did parties come before the northern people with propositions of such undisguised contempt for the moral sentiment and religious ideas of that people. They dared to ask them to unite with them in a war upon free speech, upon conscience, and to drive the Almighty presence from the councils of the nation. Resting their platforms upon the fugitive slave bill, they have boldly asked this people for political power to execute its horrible and hell-black provisions. The history of that election reveals with great clearness the extent to which slavery has "shot its leprous distilment"* through the life blood of the nation. The party most thoroughly opposed to the cause of justice and humanity triumphed, while the party only suspected of a leaning toward those principles was overwhelmingly defeated, and, some say, annihilated. But here is a still more important fact, and still better discloses the designs of the slave power. It is a fact full of meaning, that no sooner did the democratic party come into power than a system of legislation was presented to all the legislatures of the Northern States designed to put those States in harmony with the fugitive slave law, and with the malignant spirit evinced by the national government towards the free colored inhabitants of the country. The whole movement on the part of the States bears unmistakable evidence of having one origin of emanating from one head, and urged forward by one power. It was simultaneous, uniform, and general, and looked only to one end. It was intended to put thorns under feet already bleeding; to crush a people already bowed down; to enslave a people already but half free: in a word, it was intended and well calculated to discourage, dishearten, and if possible to drive the whole free colored people out of the country. In looking at the black law then recently enacted in the State of Illinois one is struck dumb by its enormity. It would seem that the men who passed that law had not only successfully banished from their minds all sense of justice, but all sense of shame as well; these law codes propose to sell the bodies and souls of the blacks to provide the means of intelligence and refinement for the whites; to rob every black stranger who ventures among them to increase their educational fund.

'While this kind of legislation is going on in the States, a pro-slavery political board of health is being established at Washington. Senators Hale, Chase, and Sumner are robbed of their senatorial rights and dignity as representatives of sovereign States, because they have refused to be inoculated with the pro-slavery virus of the times. Among the services that a senator is expected to perform are many that can only be done efficiently by those acting as members of important committees, and the slave power in the Senate, in saying to these honorable senators, you shall not serve on the committees of this body, took the responsibility of insulting and robbing the States which have sent them there. It is an attempt at Washington to decide for the States who the States shall send to the Senate. Sir, it strikes me that this aggression on the part of the slave power did not meet at the hands of the proscribed and insulted senators the rebuke which we had a right to expect from them. It seems to me that a great opportunity was lost, that the great principle of senatorial equality was left undefended at a time when its vindication was sternly demanded. But it is not to the purpose of my present statement to criticize the conduct of friends. Much should be left to the discretion of anti-slavery men in Congress. Charges of recreancy should never be made but on the most sufficient grounds. For of all places in the world where an antislavery man needs the confidence and encouragement of his friends, I take Washington—the citadel of slavery—to be that place.

'Let attention now be called to the social influences operating and cooperating with the slave power of the time and designed to promote all its malign objects. We see here the black man attacked in his most vital interests: prejudice and hate are systematically excited against him. The wrath of other laborers is stirred up against him. The Irish, who, at home, readily sympathize with the oppressed everywhere, are instantly taught when they step upon our soil to hate and despise the negro. They are taught to believe that he eats the bread that belongs to them. The cruel lie is told them, that we deprive them of labor and receive the money which would otherwise make its way into their pockets. Sir, the Irish-American will one day find out his mistake. He will find that in assuming our avocation, he has also assumed our degradation. But for the present we are the sufferers. Our old employments by which we have been accustomed to gain a livelihood are gradually slipping from our hands. Every hour sees us elbowed out of some employment to make room for some newly-arrived emigrant from the Emerald Isle, whose hunger and color entitle him to special favor. These white men are becoming house-servants, cooks, stewards, waiters, and flunkies. For aught I see they adjust themselves to their stations with all proper humility. If they cannot rise to the dignity of white men, they show that they can fall to the degradation of black men. But now, sir, look once more! While the colored people are thus elbowed out of employment; while a ceaseless enmity in the Irish is excited against us; while State after State enacts laws against us; while we are being hunted down like wild beasts; while we are oppressed with a sense of increasing insecurity, the American Colonization Society, with hypocrisy written on its brow, comes to the front, awakens to new life, and vigorously presses its scheme for our expatriation upon the attention of the American people. Papers have been started in the North and the South to promote this long-cherished object—to get rid of the negro, who is presumed to be a standing menace to slavery. Each of these papers is adapted to the latitude in which it is published, but each and all are united in calling upon the government for appropriations to enable the Colonization Society to send us out of the country by steam. Evidently this society looks upon our extremity as its opportunity, and whenever the elements are stirred against us it is stimulated to unusual activity. It does not deplore our misfortunes, but rather rejoices in them, since they prove that the two races cannot flourish on the same soil. But, sir, I must hasten. I have thus briefly given my view of one aspect of the present condition and future prospects of the colored people of the United States. What I have said is far from encouraging to my afflicted people. I have seen the cloud gather upon the sable brows of some who hear me. I confess the case looks to be bad enough. Sir, I am not a hopeful man. I think I am apt to undercalculate the benefits of the future. Yet, sir, in this seemingly desperate case, I do not despair for my people. There is a bright side to almost every picture, and ours is no exception to the general rule. If the influences against us are strong, those for us are also strong. To the inquiry, will our enemies prevail in the execution of their designs—in my God, and in my soul, I believe they will not. Let us look at the first object sought for by the slavery party of the country, viz., the suppression of the anti-slavery discussion. They desire to suppress discussion on this subject, with a view to the peace of the slaveholder and the security of slavery. Now, sir, neither the principle nor the subordinate objects, here declared, can be at all gained by the slave power, and for this reason: it involves the proposition to padlock the lips of the whites, in order to secure the fetters on the limbs of the blacks. The right of speech, precious and priceless, cannot—will not—be surrendered to slavery. Its suppression is asked for, as I have said, to give peace and security to slaveholders. Sir, that thing cannot be done. God has interposed an insuperable obstacle to any such result. "There can be no peace, saith my God, to the wicked."* Suppose it were possible to put down this discussion, what would it avail the guilty slaveholder, pillowed as he is upon the heaving bosoms of ruined souls? He could not have a peaceful spirit. If every anti-slavery tongue in the nation were silent—every anti-slavery organization dissolved—every antislavery periodical, paper, pamphlet, book, or what not, searched out, burned to ashes, and their ashes given to the four winds of heaven, still, still the slaveholder could have no peace. In every pulsation of his heart, in every throb of his life, in every glance of his eye, in the breeze that soothes, and in the thunder that startles, would be waked up an accuser, whose cause is, "thou art verily guilty concerning thy brother." '*

This is no fancy sketch of the times indicated. The situation during all the administration of President Pierce* was only less threatening and stormy than that under the administration of James Buchanan.* One sowed, the other reaped. One was the wind, the other was the whirlwind. Intoxicated by their success in repealing the Missouri compromise—in divesting the native-born colored man of American citizenship—in harnessing both the Whig and Democratic parties to the car of slavery, and in holding continued possession of the national government, the propagandists of slavery threw off all disguises, abandoned all semblance of moderation, and very naturally and inevitably proceeded, under Mr. Buchanan, to avail themselves of all the advantages of their victories. Having legislated out of existence the great national wall, erected, in the better days of the republic, against the spread of slavery, and against the increase of its power—having blotted out all distinction, as they thought, between freedom and slavery in the law, theretofore, governing the Territories of the United States, and having left the whole question of the legislation or prohibition of slavery to be decided by the people of a Territory, the next thing in order was to fill up the Territory of Kansas—the one likely to be first organized—with a people friendly to slavery, and to keep out all such as were opposed to making that Territory a free State. Here was an open invitation to a fierce and bitter strife; and the history of the times shows how promptly that invitation was accepted by both classes to which it was given, and shows also the scenes of lawless violence and blood that followed.

All advantages were at first on the side of those who were for making Kansas a slave State. The moral force of the repeal of the Missouri compromise was with them; the strength of the triumphant Democratic party was with them; the power and patronage of the federal government was with them; the various governors, sent out under the Territorial government, were with them; and, above all, the proximity of the Territory to the slave State of Missouri favored them and all their designs. Those who opposed the making Kansas a slave State, for the most part were far away from the battle-ground, residing chiefly in New England, more than a thousand miles from the eastern border of the Territory, and their direct way of entering it was through a country violently hostile to them. With such odds against them, and only an idea—though a grand one—to support them, it will ever be a wonder that they succeeded in making Kansas a free State. It is not my purpose to write particularly of this or of any other phase of the conflict with slavery, but simply to indicate the nature of the struggle, and the successive steps leading to the final result. The important point to me, as one desiring to see the slave power crippled, slavery limited and abolished, was the effect of this Kansas battle upon the moral sentiment of the North: how it made abolitionists of people before they themselves became aware of it, and how it rekindled the zeal, stimulated the activity, and strengthened the faith of our old anti-slavery forces. 'Draw on me for $1,000 per month while the conflict lasts,' said the great-hearted Gerrit Smith. George L. Stearns poured out his thousands, and anti-slavery men of smaller means were proportionally liberal. H. W. Beecher shouted the right word at the head of a mighty column; Sumner in the Senate spoke as no man had ever spoken there before. Lewis Tappan, representing one class of the old opponents of slavery, and William L. Garrison the other, lost sight of their former differences, and bent all their energies to the freedom of Kansas. But these and others were merely generators of anti-slavery force. The men who went to Kansas with the purpose of making it a free State were the heroes and martyrs. One of the leaders in this holy crusade for freedom, with whom I was brought into near relations, was John Brown, whose person, house, and purposes I have already described. This brave old man and his sons were amongst the first to hear and heed the trumpet of freedom calling them to battle. What they did and suffered, what they sought and gained, and by what means, are matters of history, and need not be repeated here.

When it became evident, as it soon did, that the war for and against slavery in Kansas was not to be decided by the peaceful means of words and ballots, but that swords and bullets were to be employed on both sides, Captain John Brown felt that now, after long years of waiting, his hour had come, and never did man meet the perilous requirements of any occasion more cheerfully, courageously, and disinterestedly than he. I met him often during this struggle, and saw deeper into his soul than when I met him in Springfield seven or eight years before, and all

I saw of him gave me a more favorable impression of the man, and inspired me with a higher respect for his character. In his repeated visits to the East to obtain necessary arms and supplies, he often did me the honor of spending hours and days with me at Rochester. On more than one occasion I got up meetings and solicited aid to be used by him for the cause, and I may say without boasting that my efforts in this respect were not entirely fruitless. Deeply interested as 'Ossawatomie Brown' was in Kansas, he never lost sight of what he called his greater work—the liberation of all the slaves in the United States. But for the then present he saw his way to the great end through Kansas. It would be a grateful task to tell of his exploits in the border struggle—how he met persecution with persecution, war with war, strategy with strategy, assassination and house-burning with signal and terrible retaliation, till even the bloodthirsty propagandists of slavery were compelled to cry for quarter. The horrors wrought by his iron hand cannot be contemplated without a shudder, but it is the shudder which one feels at the execution of a murderer. The amputation of a limb is a severe trial to feeling, but necessity is a full justification of it to reason. To call out a murderer at midnight, and without note or warning, judge or jury, run him through with a sword, was a terrible remedy for a terrible malady.

The question was not merely which class should prevail in Kansas, but whether free-State men should live there at all. The border ruffians from Missouri had openly declared their purpose not only to make Kansas a slave State, but that they would make it impossible for free-State men to live there. They burned their towns, burned their farmhouses, and by assassination spread terror among them, until many of the free-State settlers were compelled to escape for their lives. John Brown was therefore the logical result of slaveholding persecutions. Until the lives of tyrants and murderers shall become more precious in the sight of men than justice and liberty, John Brown will need no defender. In dealing with the ferocious enemies of the free-State cause in Kansas, he not only showed boundless courage but eminent military skill. With men so few, and odds against him so great, few captains ever surpassed him in achievements, some of which seem too disproportionate for belief, and yet no voice has yet called them in question. With only eight men he met, fought, whipped, and captured Henry Clay Pate* with twenty-five well-armed and well-mounted men. In this battle he selected his ground so wisely, handled his men so skillfully, and attacked his enemies so vigorously, that they could neither run nor fight, and were therefore compelled to surrender to a force less than one-third their own. With just thirty men on another memorable occasion he met and vanquished 400 Missourians under the command of General Read.* These men had come into the territory under an oath never to return to their homes in Missouri till they had stamped out the last vestige of the free-State spirit in Kansas. But a brush with old Brown instantly took this high conceit out of them, and they were glad to get home upon any terms, without stopping to stipulate. With less than 100 men to defend the town of Lawrence, he offered to lead them and give battle to 1,400 men on the banks of the Waukerusia river, and was much vexed when his offer was refused by General Jim Lane and others, to whom the defense of the place was committed. Before leaving Kansas he went into the border of Missouri and liberated a dozen slaves in a single night, and despite of slave laws and marshals he brought these people through half a dozen States and landed them safe in Canada. The successful efforts of the North in making Kansas a free State, despite all the sophistical doctrines and sanguinary measures of the South to make it a slave State, exercised a potent influence upon subsequent political forces and events in the then-near future.

It is interesting to note the facility with which the statesmanship of a section of the country adapted its convictions to changed conditions. When it was found that the doctrine of popular sovereignty (first, I think, invented by General Cass and afterward adopted by Stephen A. Douglas) failed to make Kansas a slave State, and could not be safely trusted in other emergencies, Southern statesmen promptly abandoned and reprobated that doctrine, and took what they considered firmer ground. They lost faith in the rights, powers, and wisdom of the people and took refuge in the Constitution. Henceforth the favorite doctrine of the South was that the people of a territory had no voice in the matter of slavery whatever; and that the Constitution of the United States, of its own force and effect, carried slavery safely into any territory of the United States and protected the system there until it ceased to be a territory and became a State. The practical operation of this doctrine would be to make all the future new States slaveholding States, for slavery once planted and nursed for years in a territory would easily strengthen itself against the evil day and defy eradication. This doctrine was in some sense supported by Chief-Justice Taney in the infamous Dred Scott decision. This new ground, however, was destined to bring misfortune to its inventors, for it divided for a time the Democratic party, one faction of it going with John C. Breckenridge* and the other espousing the cause of Stephen A. Douglas; the one held firmly to the doctrine that the United States Constitution, without any legislation, territorial, national, or otherwise, by its own force and effect, carried slavery into all the territories of the United States; the other held that the people of a territory had the right to admit slavery or reject slavery, as in their judgment they might deem best.

Now, while this war of words—this conflict of doctrines—was in progress, the portentous shadow of a stupendous civil war became more and more visible. Bitter complaints were raised by the slaveholders that they were about to be despoiled of their proper share in territory won by a common valor or bought by a common treasure. The North, on the other hand, or rather a large and growing party at the North, insisted that the complaint was unreasonable and groundless; that nothing properly considered as property was excluded or intended to be excluded from the territories; that Southern men could settle in any territory of the United States with some kinds of property, and on the same footing and with the same protection as citizens of the North; that men and women are not property in the same sense as houses, lands, horses, sheep and swine are property; that the fathers of the Republic neither intended the extension nor the perpetuity of slavery and that liberty is national and slavery is sectional. From 1856 to 1860 the whole land rocked with this great controversy. When the explosive force of this controversy had already weakened the bolts of the American Union; when the agitation of the public mind was at its topmost height; when the two sections were at their extreme points of difference; when, comprehending the perilous situation, such statesmen of the North as William H. Seward* sought to allay the rising storm by soft, persuasive speech, and when all hope of compromise had nearly vanished, as if to banish even the last glimmer of hope for peace between the sections, John Brown came upon the scene. On the night of the 16th of October, 1859, there appeared near the confluence of the Potomac and Shenandoah rivers a party of nineteen men—fourteen white and five colored. They were not only armed themselves, but they brought with them a large supply of arms for such persons as might join them. These men invaded the town of Harper's Ferry, disarmed the watchman, took possession of the arsenal, rifle factory, armory, and other government property at that place, arrested and made prisoners of nearly all the prominent citizens in the neighborhood, collected about fifty slaves, put bayonets into the hands of such as were able and willing to fight for their liberty, killed three men, proclaimed general emancipation, held the ground more than thirty hours, and were subsequently overpowered and nearly all killed, wounded, or captured by a body of United States troops under command of Col. Robert E. Lee, since famous as the rebel General Lee. Three out of the nineteen invaders were captured while fighting, and one of them was Capt. John Brown, the man who originated, planned, and commanded the expedition. At the time of his capture Capt. Brown was supposed to be mortally wounded, as he had several ugly gashes and bayonet wounds on his head and body, and, apprehending that he might speedily die, or that he might be rescued by his friends, and thus the opportunity to make him a signal example of slaveholding vengeance would be lost, his captors hurried him to Charlestown, 10 miles further within the border of Virginia, placed him in prison strongly guarded by troops, and, before his wounds were healed, he was brought into court, subjected to a nominal trial, convicted of high treason and inciting slaves to insurrection, and was executed.

His corpse was given up to his woe-stricken widow, and she, assisted by anti-slavery friends, caused it to be borne to North Elba, Essex county, N. Y., and there his dust now reposes amid the silent, solemn, and snowy grandeurs of the Adirondacks. This raid upon Harper's Ferry was as the last straw to the camel's back. What in the tone of Southern sentiment had been fierce before, became furious and uncontrollable now. A scream for vengeance came up from all sections of the slave States and from great multitudes in the North. All who were supposed to have been any way connected with John Brown were to be hunted down and surrendered to the tender mercies of slaveholding and panic-stricken Virginia, and there to be tried after the fashion of John Brown's trial, and, of course, to be summarily executed.

On the evening when the news came that John Brown had taken and was then holding the town of Harper's Ferry, it so happened that I was speaking to a large audience in National Hall, Philadelphia. The announcement came upon us with the startling effect of an earthquake. It was something to make the boldest hold his breath. I saw at once that my old friend had attempted what he had long ago resolved to do, and I felt certain that the result must be his capture and destruction. As I expected, the next day brought the news that with two or three men he had fortified and was holding a small engine-house, but that he was surrounded by a body of Virginia militia, who, thus far, had not ventured to capture the insurgents, but that escape was impossible. A few hours later and word came that Colonel Robert E. Lee* with a company of United States troops had made a breach in Capt. Brown's fort, and had captured him alive, though mortally wounded. His carpet-bag had been secured by Governor Wise,* and it was found to contain numerous letters and documents which directly implicated Gerritt Smith, Joshua R. Giddings, Samuel G. Howe,* Frank P. Sanborn,* and myself.

This intelligence was soon followed by a telegram saying that we were all to be arrested. Knowing that I was then in Philadelphia, stopping with my friend Thomas J. Dorsey,* Mr. John Hern, the telegraph operator, came to me and, with others, urged me to leave the city by the first train, as it was known through the newspapers that I was then in Philadelphia, and officers might even then be on my track. To me there was nothing improbable in all this. My friends for the most part were appalled at the thought of my being arrested then or there, or while on my way across the ferry from Walnut street wharf to Camden, for there was where I felt sure the arrest would be made, and asked some of them to go so far as this with me merely to see what might occur; but, upon one ground or another, they all thought it best not to be found in my company at such a time, except dear old Franklin Turner—a true man. The truth is, that in the excitement which prevailed my friends had reason to fear that the very fact that they were with me would be a sufficient reason for their arrest with me. The delay in the departure of the steamer seemed unusually long to me, for I confess I was seized with a desire to reach a more northern latitude. My friend Frank did not leave my side till 'all ashore' was ordered and the paddles began to move. I reached New York at night, still under the apprehension of arrest at any moment, but no signs of such an event being made, I went at once to the Barclay street ferry, took the boat across the river, and went direct to Washington street, Hoboken, the home of Mrs. Marks, where I spent the night, and I may add without undue profession of timidity, an anxious night. The morning papers brought no relief, for they announced that the government would spare no pains in ferreting out and bringing to punishment all who were connected with the Harper's Ferry outrage, and that search would be made for papers as well as persons. I was now somewhat uneasy from the fact that sundry letters and a constitution written by John Brown were locked up in my desk in Rochester. In order to prevent these papers from falling into the hands of the government of Virginia, I got my friend, Miss Ottilia Assing,* to write at my dictation the following telegram to B. F. Blackall, the telegraph operator in Rochester, a friend and frequent visitor at my house, who would readily understand the meaning of the dispatch:

'B. F. BLACKALL, Esq.:
'Tell Lewis (my oldest son) to secure all the important papers in my high desk.'

I did not sign my name, and the result showed that I had rightly judged that Mr. Blackall would understand and promptly attend to the request. The mark of the chisel with which the desk was opened is still on the drawer, and is one of the traces of the John Brown raid. Having taken measures to secure my papers, the trouble was to know just what to do with myself. To stay in Hoboken was out of the question, and to go to Rochester was to all appearance to go into the hands of the hunters, for they would naturally seek me at my home if they sought me at all. I, however, resolved to go home and risk my safety there. I felt sure that, once in the city, I could not be easily taken from there without a preliminary hearing upon the requisition, and not then if the people could be made aware of what was in progress. But how to get to Rochester was a serious question. It would not do to go to New York city and take the train, for that city was not less incensed against John Brown conspirators than many parts of the South. The course hit upon by my friends, Mr. Johnston and Miss Assing, was, to take me at night in a private conveyance from Hoboken to Paterson, where I could take the Erie railroad for home. This plan was carried out, and I reached home in safety, but had been there but a few moments when I was called upon by Samuel D. Porter, Esq., and my neighbor, Lieutenant-Governor Selden, who informed me that the governor of the State would certainly surrender me on a proper requisition from the governor of Virginia, and that while the people of Rochester would not permit me to be taken South, yet, in order to avoid collision with the government and consequent bloodshed, they advised me to quit the country, which I did—going to Canada. Governor Wise, in the meantime, being advised that I had left Rochester for the State of Michigan, made requisition on the governor of that State for my surrender to Virginia.

The following letter from Governor Wise to President James Buchanan (which since the war was sent me by B. F. Lossing, the historian), will show by what means the governor of Virginia meant to get me into his power, and that my apprehensions of arrest were not altogether groundless:

[Confidential.]
RICHMOND, VA., NOV. 13, 1859.
   *To His Excellency James Buchanan, President of the United States, and to the Honorable Postmaster-General of the United States*:

GENTLEMEN—I have information such as has caused me, upon proper affidavits, to make requisition upon the Executive of Michigan for the delivery up of the person of Frederick Douglass, a negro man, supposed now to be in Michigan, charged with murder, robbery, and inciting servile insurrection in the State of Virginia. My agents for the arrest and reclamation of the person so charged are Benjamin M. Morris and William N. Kelly. The latter has the requisition, and will wait on you to the end of obtaining nominal authority as post-office agents. They need be very secretive in this matter, and some pretext for traveling through the dangerous section for the execution of the laws in this behalf, and some protection against obtrusive, unruly, or lawless violence. If it be proper so to do, will the postmaster-general be pleased to give to Mr. Kelly, for each of these men, a permit and authority to act as detectives for the post-office department, without pay, but to pass and repass without question, delay, or hindrance?

Respectfully submitted by your obedient servant,
HENRY A. WISE.

There is no reason to doubt that James Buchanan afforded Governor Wise all the aid and coöperation for which he was asked. I have been informed that several United States marshals were in Rochester in search of me within six hours after my departure. I do not know that I can do better at this stage of my story than to insert the following letter, written by me to the Rochester *Democrat and American*:

CANADA WEST, Oct. 31, 1859.
MR. EDITOR:
I notice that the telegraph makes Mr. Cook* (one of the unfortunate insurgents at Harper's Ferry, and now a prisoner in the hands of the thing calling itself the Government of Virginia, but which in fact is but an organized conspiracy by one part of the people against another and weaker) denounce me as a coward, and assert that I promised to be present in person at the Harper's Ferry insurrection. This is certainly a very grave impeachment, whether viewed in its bearings upon friends or upon foes, and you will not think it strange that I should take a somewhat serious notice of it. Having no acquaintance whatever with Mr. Cook, and never having exchanged a word with him about the Harper's Ferry insurrection, I am disposed to doubt if he could have used the language concerning me which the wires attribute to him. The lightning, when speaking for itself, is among the most direct, reliable, and truthful of things; but when speaking of the terror-stricken slaveholders at Harper's Ferry, it has been made the swiftest of liars. Under its nimble and trembling fingers it magnifies 17 men into 700, and has since filled the columns of the New York *Herald* for days with its interminable contradictions. But assuming that it has told only the simple truth as to the sayings of Mr. Cook in this instance, I have this answer to make to my accuser: Mr. Cook may be perfectly right in denouncing me as a coward; I have not one word to say in defense or vindication of my character for courage; I have always been more distinguished for running than fighting, and, tried by the Harper's-Ferry-insurrection-test, I am most miserably deficient in courage, even more so than Cook when he deserted his brave old captain and fled to the mountains. To this extent Mr. Cook is entirely right, and will meet no contradiction from me, or from anybody else. But wholly, grievously, and most unaccountably wrong is Mr. Cook when he asserts that I promised to be present in person at the Harper's Ferry insurrection. Of whatever other imprudence and indiscretion I may have been guilty, I have never made a promise so rash and wild as this. The taking of Harper's Ferry was a measure never encouraged by my word or by my vote. At

any time or place, my wisdom or my cowardice has not only kept me from Harper's Ferry, but has equally kept me from making any promise to go there. I desire to be quite emphatic here, for of all guilty men, he is the guiltiest who lures his fellow-men to an undertaking of this sort, under promise of assistance which he afterwards fails to render. I therefore declare that there is no man living, and no man dead, who, if living, could truthfully say that I ever promised him, or anybody else, either conditionally, or otherwise, that I would be present in person at the Harper's Ferry insurrection. My field of labor for the abolition of slavery has not extended to an attack upon the United States arsenal. In the teeth of the documents already published and of those which may hereafter be published, I affirm that no man connected with that insurrection, from its noble and heroic leader down, can connect my name with a single broken promise of any sort whatever. So much I deem it proper to say negatively. The time for a full statement of what I know and of ALL I know of this desperate but sublimely disinterested effort to emancipate the slaves of Maryland and Virginia from their cruel task-masters, has not yet come, and may never come. In the denial which I have now made, my motive is more a respectful consideration for the opinions of the slaves' friends than from my fear of being made an accomplice in the general conspiracy against slavery, when there is a reasonable hope for success. Men who live by robbing their fellow-men of their labor and liberty have forfeited their right to know anything of the thoughts, feelings, or purposes of those whom they rob and plunder. They have by the single act of slaveholding voluntarily placed themselves beyond the laws of justice and honor, and have become only fitted for companionship with thieves and pirates—the common enemies of God and of all mankind. While it shall be considered right to protect one's self against thieves, burglars, robbers, and assassins, and to slay a wild beast in the act of devouring his human prey, it can never be wrong for the imbruted and whip-scarred slaves, or their friends, to hunt, harass, and even strike down the traffickers in human flesh. If anybody is disposed to think less of me on account of this sentiment, or because I may have had a knowledge of what was about to occur, and did not assume the base and detestable character of an informer, he is a man whose good or bad opinion of me may be equally repugnant and despicable.

Entertaining these sentiments, I may be asked why I did not join John Brown—the noble old hero whose one right hand had shaken the foundation of the American Union, and whose ghost will haunt the bed-chambers of all the born and unborn slaveholders of Virginia through all their generations, filling them with alarm and consternation. My answer to this has already been given; at least impliedly given—'The tools to those who can use them!' Let every man work for the abolition of slavery in his own way. I would help all and hinder none. My position in regard to the Harper's Ferry insurrection may be easily inferred from these remarks, and I shall be glad if those papers which have spoken of me in connection with it would find room for this brief statement. I have no apology for keeping out of the way of those gentlemanly United States marshals, who are said to have paid Rochester a somewhat protracted visit lately, with a view to an interview with me. A government recognizing the validity of the *Dred Scott* decision at such a time as this, is not likely to have any very charitable feelings towards me, and if I am to meet its representatives I prefer to do so at least upon equal terms. If I have committed any offense against society I have done so on the soil of the State of New York, and I should be perfectly willing to be arraigned there before an impartial jury; but I have quite insuperable objections to being caught by the hounds of Mr. Buchanan, and '*bagged*' by Gov. Wise. For this appears to be the arrangement. Buchanan does the fighting and hunting, and Wise '*bags*' the game. Some reflections may be made upon my leaving on a tour to England just at this time. I have only to say that my going to that country has been rather delayed than hastened by the insurrection at Harper's Ferry. All know that I had intended to leave here in the first week of November.

FREDERICK DOUGLASS.

# CHAPTER X.

## THE BEGINNING OF THE END.

*My connection with John Brown—To and from England—*
*Presidential contest—Election of Abraham Lincoln.*

WHAT was my connection with John Brown, and what I knew of his
scheme for the capture of Harper's Ferry, I may now proceed to state.
From the time of my visit to him in Springfield, Mass., in 1847, our
relations were friendly and confidential. I never passed through
Springfield without calling on him, and he never came to Rochester
without calling on me. He often stopped over night with me, when we
talked over the feasibility of his plan for destroying the value of slave
property, and the motive for holding slaves in the border States. That
plan, as already intimated elsewhere, was to take twenty or twenty-five
discreet and trustworthy men into the mountains of Virginia and
Maryland, and station them in squads of five, about five miles apart, on
a line of twenty-five miles; each squad to co-operate with all, and all
with each. They were to have selected for them secure and comfortable
retreats in the fastnesses of the mountains, where they could easily
defend themselves in case of attack. They were to subsist upon the
country roundabout. They were to be well armed, but were to avoid
battle or violence, unless compelled by pursuit or in self-defence. In
that case, they were to make it as costly as possible to the assailing party,
whether that party should be soldiers or citizens. He further proposed
to have a number of stations from the line of Pennsylvania to the
Canada border, where such slaves as he might, through his men, induce
to run away, should be supplied with food and shelter and be forwarded
from one station to another till they should reach a place of safety either
in Canada or the Northern States. He proposed to add to his force in
the mountains any courageous and intelligent fugitives who might be
willing to remain and endure the hardships and brave the dangers of
this mountain life. These, he thought, if properly selected, could, on
account of their knowledge of the surrounding country, be made valuable auxiliaries. The work of going into the valley of Virginia and persuading the slaves to flee to the mountains was to be committed to the
most courageous and judicious man connected with each squad.

Hating slavery as I did, and making its abolition the object of my life,
I was ready to welcome any new mode of attack upon the slave system

which gave any promise of success. I readily saw that this plan could be made very effective in rendering slave property in Maryland and Virginia valueless by rendering it insecure. Men do not like to buy runaway horses, or to invest their money in a species of property likely to take legs and walk off with itself. In the worse case, too, if the plan should fail, and John Brown should be driven from the mountains, a new fact would be developed by which the nation would be kept awake to the existence of slavery. Hence, I assented to this, John Brown's scheme or plan for running off slaves.

To set this plan in operation, money and men, arms and ammunition, food and clothing, were needed; and these, from the nature of the enterprise, were not easily obtained, and nothing was immediately done. Captain Brown, too, notwithstanding his rigid economy, was poor, and was unable to arm and equip men for the dangerous life he had mapped out. So the work lingered till after the Kansas trouble was over and freedom in that Territory was an accomplished fact. This left him with arms and men, for the men who had been with him in Kansas believed in him, and would follow him in any humane though dangerous enterprise he might undertake.

After the close of his Kansas work, Captain Brown came to my house in Rochester, and said he desired to stop with me several weeks; 'but,' he added, 'I will not stay unless you will allow me to pay board.' Knowing that he was no trifler and meant all he said, and desirous of retaining him under my roof, I charged three dollars a week. While here, he spent most of his time in correspondence. He wrote often to George L. Stearns of Boston, Gerritt Smith of Peterboro, N. Y., and many others, and received many letters in return. When he was not writing letters, he was writing and revising a constitution which he meant to put in operation by means of the men who should go with him into the mountains. He said that, to avoid anarchy and confusion, there should be a regularly-constituted government, which each man who came with him should be sworn to honor and support. I have a copy of this constitution in Captain Brown's own handwriting, as prepared by himself at my house.

He called his friends from Chatham (Canada) to come together, that he might lay his constitution before them for their approval and adoption. His whole time and thought were given to this subject. It was the first thing in the morning and the last thing at night, till I confess it began to be something of a bore to me. Once in a while he would say he could, with a few resolute men, capture Harper's Ferry, and supply himself with arms belonging to the government at that place; but he never announced his intention to do so. It was, however, very evidently passing in his mind as a thing he might do. I paid but little attention to such remarks, though I never doubted that he thought just what he said. Soon after his coming to me, he asked me to get for him two smoothly-planed boards, upon which he could illustrate, with a pair of dividers, by a drawing, the plan of fortification which he meant to adopt in the mountains.

These forts were to be so arranged as to connect one with the other, by secret passages, so that if one was carried another could easily be fallen back upon, and be the means of dealing death to the enemy at the very moment when he might think himself victorious. I was less interested in these drawings than my children were, but they showed that the old man had an eye to the means as well as to the end, and was giving his best thought to the work he was about to take in hand.

It was his intention to begin this work in '58 instead of '59. Why he did not will appear from the following circumstances.

While in Kansas, he made the acquaintance of one Colonel Forbes,* an Englishman, who had figured somewhat in revolutionary movements in Europe, and, as it turned out, had become an adventurer—a soldier of fortune in this country. This Forbes professed to be an expert in military matters, and easily fastened upon John Brown, and, becoming master of his scheme of liberation, professed great interest in it, and offered his services to him in the preparation of his men for the work before them. After remaining with Brown a short time, he came to me in Rochester, with a letter from him, asking me to receive and assist him. I was not favorably impressed with Colonel Forbes at first, but I 'conquered my prejudice,' took him to a hotel and paid his board while he remained. Just before leaving, he spoke of his family in Europe as in destitute circumstances, and of his desire to send them some money. I gave him a little—I forget how much—and through Miss Assing, a German lady, deeply interested in the John Brown scheme, he was introduced to several of my German friends in New York. But he soon wore them out by his endless begging; and when he could make no more money by professing to advance the John Brown project he threatened to expose it, and all connected with it. I think I was the first to be informed of his tactics, and I promptly communicated them to Captain Brown. Through my friend Miss Assing, I found that Forbes had told of Brown's designs to Horace Greeley,* and to the government officials at Washington, of which I informed Captain Brown, and this led to the postponement of the enterprise another year. It was hoped that by this delay the story of Forbes would be discredited, and this calculation was correct, for nobody believed the scoundrel, though in this he told the truth.

While at my house, John Brown made the acquaintance of a colored man who called himself by different names—sometimes 'Emperor,' at other times, 'Shields Green.'* He was a fugitive slave, who had made his escape from Charleston, South Carolina; a State from which a slave found it no easy matter to run away. But Shields Green was not one to shrink from hardships or dangers. He was a man of few words, and his speech was singularly broken; but his courage and self-respect made him quite a dignified character. John Brown saw at once what 'stuff' Green 'was made of,' and confided to him his plans and purposes. Green easily believed in Brown, and promised to go with him whenever he should be ready to move. About three weeks before the raid on Harper's Ferry, John Brown wrote to me, informing me that a beginning in his work would soon be made, and that before going forward he wanted to see me, and appointed an old stone-quarry near Chambersburg, Penn., as our place of meeting. Mr. Kagi, his secretary, would be there, and they wished me to bring any money I could command, and Shields Green along with me. In the same letter, he said that his 'mining tools' and stores were then at Chambersburg, and that he would be there to remove them. I obeyed the old man's summons. Taking Shields, we passed through New York city, where we called upon Rev. James Glocester and his wife, and told them where and for what we were going, and that our old friend needed money. Mrs. Glocester gave me ten dollars, and asked me to hand the same to John Brown, with her best wishes.

When I reached Chambersburg, a good deal of surprise was expressed (for I was instantly recognized) that I should come there unannounced, and I was pressed to make a speech to them, with which invitation I readily complied. Meanwhile, I called upon Mr. Henry Watson, a simple-minded and warm-hearted man, to whom Capt. Brown had imparted the secret of my visit, to show me the road to the appointed rendezvous. Watson was very busy in his barber's shop, but he dropped all and put me on the right track. I approached the old quarry very cautiously, for John Brown was generally well armed, and regarded strangers with suspicion. He was then under the ban of the government, and heavy rewards were offered for his arrest, for offenses said to have been committed in Kansas. He was passing under the name of John Smith. As I came near, he regarded me rather suspiciously, but soon recognized me, and received me cordially. He had in his hand when I met him a fishing-tackle, with which he had apparently been fishing in a stream hard by; but I saw no fish, and did not suppose that he cared much for his 'fisherman's luck.' The fishing was simply a disguise, and was certainly a good one. He looked every way like a man of the neighborhood, and as much at home as any of the farmers around there. His hat was old and storm-beaten, and his clothing was about the color of the stone-quarry itself—his then present dwelling-place.

His face wore an anxious expression, and he was much worn by thought and exposure. I felt that I was on a dangerous mission, and was as little desirous of discovery as himself, though no reward had been offered for me.

We—Mr. Kagi, Captain Brown, Shields Green, and myself—sat down among the rocks and talked over the enterprise which was about to be undertaken. The taking of Harper's Ferry, of which Captain Brown had merely hinted before, was now declared as his settled purpose, and he wanted to know what I thought of it. I at once opposed the measure with all the arguments at my command. To me such a measure would be fatal to running off slaves (as was the original plan), and fatal to all engaged in doing so. It would be an attack upon the federal government, and would array the whole country against us. Captain Brown did most of the talking on the other side of the question. He did not at all object to rousing the nation; it seemed to him that something startling was just what the nation needed. He had completely renounced his old plan, and thought that the capture of Harper's Ferry would serve as notice to the slaves that their friends had come, and as a trumpet to rally them to his standard. He described the place as to its means of defense, and how impossible it would be to dislodge him if once in possession. Of course I was no match for him in such matters, but I told him, and these were my words, that all his arguments, and all his descriptions of the place, convinced me that he was going into a perfect steel-trap, and that once in he would never get out alive; that he would be surrounded at once and escape would be impossible. He was not to be shaken by anything I could say, but treated my views respectfully, replying that even if surrounded he would find means for cutting his way out; but that would not be forced upon him; he should, at the start, have a number of the best citizens of the neighborhood as his prisoners and that holding them as hostages he should be able, if worse came to worse, to dictate terms of egress from the town. I looked at him with some astonishment, that he could rest upon a reed so weak and broken, and told him that Virginia would blow him and his hostages sky-high, rather than that he should hold Harper's Ferry an hour. Our talk was long and earnest; we spent the most of Saturday and a part of Sunday

in this debate—Brown for Harper's Ferry, and I against it; he for striking a blow which should instantly rouse the country, and I for the policy
of gradually and unaccountably drawing off the slaves to the mountains, as at first suggested and proposed by him. When I found that he
had fully made up his mind and could not be dissuaded, I turned to
Shields Green and told him he heard what Captain Brown had said; his
old plan was changed, and that I should return home, and if he wished
to go with me he could do so. Captain Brown urged us both to go with
him, but I could not do so, and could but feel that he was about to rivet
the fetters more firmly than ever on the limbs of the enslaved. In parting he put his arms around me in a manner more than friendly, and
said: 'Come with me, Douglass; I will defend you with my life. I want
you for a special purpose. When I strike, the bees will begin to swarm,
and I shall want you to help hive them.' But my discretion or my cowardice made me proof against the dear old man's eloquence—perhaps
it was something of both which determined my course. When about to
leave I asked Green what he had decided to do, and was surprised by his
coolly saying, in his broken way, 'I b'leve I'll go wid de ole man.' Here
we separated; they to go to Harper's Ferry, I to Rochester. There has
been some difference of opinion as to the propriety of my course in
thus leaving my friend. Some have thought that I ought to have gone
with him; but I have no reproaches for myself at this point, and since
I have been assailed only by colored men who kept even farther from
this brave and heroic man than I did, I shall not trouble myself much
about their criticisms. They compliment me in assuming that I should
perform greater deeds than themselves.

Such then was my connection with John Brown, and it may be asked,
if this is all, why I should have objected to being sent to Virginia to be
tried for the offense charged. The explanation is not difficult. I knew
that if my enemies could not prove me guilty of the offense of being
with John Brown, they could prove that I was Frederick Douglass; they
could prove that I was in correspondence and conspiracy with Brown
against slavery; they could prove that I brought Shields Green, one of
the bravest of his soldiers, all the way from Rochester to him at
Chambersburg; they could prove that I brought money to aid him, and
in what was then the state of the public mind I could not hope to make
a jury of Virginia believe I did not go the whole length he went, or that
I was not one of his supporters; and I knew that all Virginia, were I once
in her clutches, would say 'Let him be hanged.' Before I had left
Canada for England, Jeremiah Anderson,* one of Brown's men, who
was present and took part in the raid, but escaped by the mountains,

joined me, and he told me that he and Shields Green were sent out on special duty as soon as the capture of the arsenal, etc., was effected. Their business was to bring in the slaves from the surrounding country, and hence they were on the outside when Brown was surrounded. I said to him, 'Why then did not Shields come with you?' 'Well,' he said, 'I told him to come; that we could do nothing more, but he simply said he must go down to de ole man.' Anderson further told me that Captain Brown was careful to keep his plans from his men, and that there was much opposition among them when they found what were the precise movements determined upon; but they were an oath-bound company, and like good soldiers were agreed to follow their captain wherever he might lead.

On the 12th of November, 1859, I took passage from Quebec on board the steamer Scotia, Captain Thompson, of the Allan line. My going to England was not at first suggested by my connection with John Brown, but the fact that I was now in danger of arrest on the ground of complicity with him made what I had intended a pleasure a necessity, for though in Canada, and under British law, it was not impossible that I might be kidnapped and taken to Virginia. England had given me shelter and protection when the slave-hounds were on my track four-teen years before, and her gates were still open to me now that I was pursued in the name of Virginia justice. I could but feel that I was going into exile, perhaps for life. Slavery seemed to be at the very top of its power; the national government, with all its powers and appliances, was in its hands, and it bade fair to wield them for many years to come. Nobody could then see that in the short space of four years this power would be broken and the slave system destroyed. So I started on my voyage with feelings far from cheerful. No one who has not himself been compelled to leave his home and country and go into permanent banishment can well imagine the state of mind and heart which such a condition brings. The voyage out was by the north passage, and at this season, as usual, it was cold, dark, and stormy. Before quitting the coast of Labrador we had four degrees below zero. Although I had crossed the Atlantic twice before, I had not experienced such unfriendly weather as during the most of this voyage. Our great ship was dashed about upon the surface of the sea as though she had been the smallest 'dug-out.' It seemed to tax all the seamanship of our captain to keep her in manageable condition; but after battling with the waves on an angry ocean during fourteen long days I gratefully found myself upon the soil of Great Britain, beyond the reach of Buchanan's power and Virginia's prisons. Upon reaching Liverpool I learned that England was nearly as much alive to what had happened at Harper's Ferry as was the United States, and I was immediately called upon in different parts of the country to speak on the subject of slavery, and especially to give some account of the men who had thus flung away their lives in a desperate attempt to free the slaves. My own relation to the affair was a subject of much interest, as was the fact of my presence there being in some sense to elude the demands of Governor Wise, who, having learned that I was not in Michigan, but was on a British steamer bound for England, publicly declared that 'could he overtake that vessel he would take me from her deck at any cost.'

While in England, wishing to visit France, I wrote to Mr. George M. Dallas, the American minister at the British court, to obtain a passport. The attempt upon the life of Napoleon III* about that time, and the suspicion that the conspiracy against him had been hatched in England, made the French government very strict in the enforcement of its passport system. I might possibly have been permitted to visit that country without a certificate of my citizenship, but wishing to leave nothing to chance, I applied to the only competent authority; but, true to the traditions of the Democratic party, true to the slaveholding policy of his country, true to the decision of the United States Supreme Court, and true, perhaps, to the petty meanness of his own nature, Mr. George M. Dallas, the Democratic American minister, refused to grant me a passport, on the ground that I was not a citizen of the United States. I did not beg or remonstrate with this dignitary further, but simply addressed a note to the French minister in London asking for a permit to visit France, and that paper came without delay. I mention this not to belittle the civilization of my native country, but as a part of the story of my life. I could have borne this denial with more serenity could I have foreseen what has since happened, but under the circumstances it was a galling disappointment.

I had at this time been about six months out of the United States. My time had been chiefly occupied in different parts of England and Scotland, in speaking on slavery and other subjects, meeting and enjoying the while the society of many of the kind friends whose acquaintance I had made during my visit, fourteen years before, to those countries. Much of the excitement caused by the Harper's Ferry insurrection had subsided, both at home and abroad, and I should have now gratified a long-cherished desire to visit France, and availed myself for that purpose of the permit so promptly and civilly given by the French minister, had not news reached me from home of the death of my beloved daughter Annie,* the light and life of my house. Deeply distressed by this bereavement, and acting upon the impulse of the moment, regardless of the peril, I at once resolved to return home, and took the first outgoing steamer for Portland, Maine. After a rough passage of seventeen days I reached home by way of Canada, and remained in my house nearly a month before the knowledge got abroad that I was again in this country. Great changes had now taken place in the public mind touching the John Brown raid. Virginia had satisfied her thirst for blood. She had executed all the raiders who had fallen into her hands. She had not given Captain Brown the benefit of a reasonable doubt, but hurried him to the scaffold in panic-stricken haste. She had made herself ridiculous by her fright and despicable by her fury. Emerson's prediction that Brown's gallows would become like the cross was already being fulfilled.* The old hero, in the trial hour, had behaved so grandly that men regarded him not as a murderer but as a martyr. All over the North men were singing the John Brown song.* His body was in the dust, but his soul was marching on. His defeat was already assuming the form and pressure of victory, and his death was giving new life and power to the principles of justice and liberty. He had spoken great words in the face of death and the champions of slavery. He had quailed before neither. What he had lost by the sword he had more than gained by the truth. Had he wavered, had he retreated or apologized, the case had been different. He did not even ask that the cup of death might pass from him. To his own soul he was right, and neither 'principalities nor powers, life nor death, things present nor things to come,'* could shake his dauntless spirit or move him from his ground. He may not have stooped on his way to the gallows to kiss a little colored child, as it is reported he did, but the act would have been in keeping with the tender heart, as well as with the heroic spirit of the man. Those who looked for confession heard only the voice of rebuke and warning.

Early after the insurrection at Harper's Ferry an investigating committee was appointed by Congress, and a 'drag net' was spread all over the country in the hope of inculpating many distinguished persons. They had imprisoned Thaddeus Hyatt, who denied their right to interrogate him, and had called many witnesses before them, as if the judicial power of the nation had been confided to their committee and not to the Supreme Court of the United States. But Captain Brown implicated nobody. Upon his own head he invited all the bolts of slaveholding vengeance. He said that he, and he alone, was responsible for all that had happened. He had many friends, but no instigators. In all their efforts this committee signally failed, and soon after my arrival home they gave up the search and asked to be discharged, not having half fulfilled the duty for which they were appointed.

I have never been able to account satisfactorily for the sudden abandonment of this investigation on any other ground than that the men engaged in it expected soon to be in rebellion themselves, and that, not a rebellion for liberty, like that of John Brown, but a rebellion for slavery, and that they saw that by using their senatorial power in search of rebels they might be whetting a knife for their own throats. At any rate the country was soon relieved of the congressional drag-net and was now engaged in the heat and turmoil of a presidential canvass—a canvass which had no parallel, involving as it did the question of peace or war, the integrity or the dismemberment of the Republic, and, I may add, the maintenance or destruction of slavery. In some of the Southern States the people were already organizing and arming to be ready for an apprehended contest, and with this work on their hands they had no time to spare to those they had wished to convict as instigators of the raid, however desirous they might have been to do so under other circumstances, for they had parted with none of their hate. As showing their feeling toward me, I may state that a colored man appeared about this time in Knoxville, Tenn., and was beset by a furious crowd with knives and bludgeons because he was supposed to be Fred. Douglass. But, however perilous it would have been for me to have shown myself in any Southern State, there was no especial danger for me at the North.

Though disappointed in my tour on the Continent, and called home by one of the saddest events that can afflict the domestic circle, my presence here was fortunate, since it enabled me to participate in the most important and memorable presidential canvass ever witnessed in the United States, and to labor for the election of a man who in the order of events was destined to do a greater service to his country and to mankind than any man who had gone before him in the presidential office. It is something to couple one's name with great occasions, and it was a great thing to me to be permitted to bear some humble part in this, the greatest that had thus far come to the American people. It was a great thing to achieve American independence when we numbered three millions, but it was a greater thing to save this country from dismemberment and ruin when it numbered thirty millions. He alone of all our Presidents was to have the opportunity to destroy slavery, and to lift into manhood millions of his countrymen hitherto held as chattels and numbered with the beasts of the field.

The presidential canvass of 1860 was three-sided, and each side had its distinctive doctrine as to the question of slavery and slavery extension.

We had three candidates in the field. Stephen A. Douglas was the standard-bearer of what may be called the western faction of the old divided democratic party, and John C. Breckenridge was the standard-bearer of the southern or slaveholding faction of that party. Abraham Lincoln represented the then young, growing, and united republican party. The lines between these parties and candidates were about as distinctly and clearly drawn as political lines are capable of being drawn. The name of Douglas stood for territorial sovereignty, or, in other words, for the right of the people of a territory to admit or exclude, to establish or abolish, slavery, as to them might seem best. The doctrine of Breckenridge was that slaveholders were entitled to carry their slaves into any territory of the United States and to hold them there, with or without the consent of the people of the territory; that the Constitution of its own force carried slavery into any territory open for settlement in the United States, and protected it there. To both these parties, factions, and doctrines, Abraham Lincoln and the republican party stood opposed. They held that the Federal Government had the right and the power to exclude slavery from the territories of the United States, and that that right and power ought to be exercised to the extent of confining slavery inside the slave States, with a view to its ultimate extinction. The position of Mr. Douglas gave him a splendid pretext for the display of a species of oratory of which he was a distinguished master. He alone of the three candidates took the stump as the preacher of popular sovereignty, called in derision at the time, 'Squatter' Sovereignty. This doctrine, if not the times, gave him a chance to play fast and loose, blow hot and cold, as occasion might require. In the South and among slaveholders he could say, 'My great principle of popular sovereignty does not and was not intended by me to prevent the extension of slavery; on the contrary, it gives you the right to take your slaves into the territories and secure legislation legalizing slavery; it denies to the Federal Government all right of interference against you, and hence is eminently favorable to your interests.' When among people known to be indifferent he could say, 'I do not care whether slavery is voted up or down in the territory,' but when addressing the known opponents of the extension of slavery, he could say that the people of the territories were in no danger of having slavery forced upon them, since they could keep it out by adverse legislation. Had he made these representations before railroads, electric wires, phonography, and newspapers had become the powerful auxiliaries they have done, Mr. Douglas might have gained many votes, but they were of little avail now. The South was too sagacious to leave slavery to the chance of defeat in a fair vote by the people of a territory. Of all property none could less afford to take such a risk, for no property can require more strongly favoring conditions for its existence. Not only the intelligence of the slave, but the instincts of humanity, must be barred by positive law, hence Breckenridge and his friends erected the flinty walls of the Constitution and the Supreme Court for the protection of slavery at the outset. Against both Douglas and Breckenridge Abraham Lincoln proposed his grand historic doctrine of the power and duty of the National Government to prevent the spread and perpetuity of slavery. Into this contest I threw myself, with firmer faith and more ardent hope than ever before, and what I could do by pen or voice was done with a will. The most remarkable and memorable feature of this canvass was, that it was prosecuted under the portentous shadow of a threat: leading public men of the South had, with the vehemence of fiery purpose, given it out in advance that in case of their failure to elect their candidate (Mr. John C. Breckenridge) they would proceed to take the slaveholding States out of the Union, and that, in no event whatever, would they submit to the rule of Abraham Lincoln. To many of the peace-loving friends of the Union, this was a fearful announcement, and it doubtless cost the Republican candidates many votes. To many others, however, it was deemed a mere bravado—sound and fury signifying nothing. With a third class its effect was very different. They were tired of the rule-or-ruin intimidation adopted by the South, and felt then, if never before, that they had quailed before it too often and too long. It came as an insult and a challenge in one, and imperatively called upon them for independence, self-assertion, and resentment. Had southern men puzzled their brains to find the most effective means to array against slavery and slaveholding manners the solid opposition of the North, they could not have hit upon any expedient better suited to that end than was this threat. It was not only unfair, but insolent, and more like an address to cowardly slaves than one to independent freemen. It had in it the meanness of the horse-jockey who, on entering a race, proposes, if beaten, to run off with the stakes. In all my speeches made during this canvass, I did not fail to take advantage of this southern bluster and bullying.

As I have said, this southern threat lost many votes, but it gained more than would cover the lost. It frightened the timid, but stimulated the brave; and the result was—the triumphant election of Abraham Lincoln.*

Then came the question. What will the South do about it? Will she eat her bold words, and submit to the verdict of the people, or proceed to the execution of the programme she had marked out for herself prior to the election? The inquiry was an anxious one, and the blood of the North stood still, waiting for the response. It had not to wait long, for the trumpet of war was soon sounded, and the tramp of armed men was heard in that region. During all the winter of 1860 notes of preparation for a tremendous conflict came to us from that quarter on every wind. Still the warning was not taken. Few of the North could really believe that this insolent display of arms would end in anything more substantial than dust and smoke.

The shameful and shocking course of President Buchanan and his cabinet towards this rising rebellion against the government which each and all of them had solemnly sworn to 'support, defend and maintain'—the facts that the treasury was emptied; that the army was scattered; that our ships of war were sent out of the way; that our forts and arsenals in the South were weakened and crippled,—purposely left an easy prey to the prospective insurgents,—that one after another the States were allowed to secede; that these rebel measures were largely encouraged by the doctrine of Mr. Buchanan, that he found no power in the Constitution to coerce a State, are all matters of history, and need only the briefest mention here.

To arrest this tide of secession and revolution, which was sweeping over the South, the southern papers, which still had some dread of the consequences likely to ensue from the course marked out before the election, proposed as a means for promoting conciliation and satisfaction that 'each northern State, through her legislature, or in convention assembled, should repeal all laws passed for the injury of the constitutional rights of the South (meaning thereby all laws passed for the protection of personal liberty); that they should pass laws for the easy and prompt execution of the fugitive-slave law; that they should pass other laws imposing penalties on all malefactors who should hereafter assist or encourage the escape of fugitive slaves; also, laws declaring and protecting the right of slaveholders to travel and sojourn in northern States, accompanied by their slaves; also, that they should instruct their representatives and senators in Congress to repeal the law prohibiting the sale of slaves in the District of Columbia, and pass laws sufficient for the full protection of slave property in the Territories of the Union.'

It may indeed be well regretted that there was a class of men in the North willing to patch up a peace with this rampant spirit of disunion by compliance with these offensive, scandalous, and humiliating terms, and to do so without any guarantee that the South would then be pacified; rather with the certainty, learned by past experience, that it would by no means promote this end. I confess to a feeling allied to satisfaction at the prospect of a conflict between the North and the South. Standing outside the pale of American humanity, denied citizenship, unable to call the land of my birth my country, and adjudged by the supreme court of the United States to have no rights which white men were bound to respect, and longing for the end of the bondage of my people, I was ready for any political upheaval which should bring about a change in the existing condition of things. Whether the war of words would or would not end in blows was for a time a matter of doubt; and when it became certain that the South was wholly in earnest, and meant at all hazards to execute its threats of disruption, a visible change in the sentiment of the North was apparent.

The reaction from the glorious assertion of freedom and independence on the part of the North in the triumphant election of Abraham Lincoln, was a painful and humiliating development of its weakness. It seemed as if all that had been gained in the canvass was about to be surrendered to the vanquished, and that the South, though beaten at the polls, was to be victorious and have everything its own way in the final result. During all the intervening months, from November to the ensuing March, the drift of Northern sentiment was towards compromise. To smooth the way for this, most of the Northern legislatures repealed their personal liberty bills, as they were supposed to embarrass the surrender of fugitive slaves to their claimants. The feeling everywhere seemed to be that something must be done to convince the South that the election of Mr. Lincoln meant no harm to slavery or the slave power, and that the North was sound on the question of the right of the master to hold and hunt his slave as long as he pleased, and that even the right to hold slaves in the Territories should be submitted to the supreme court, which would probably decide in favor of the most extravagant demands of the slave States. The Northern press took on a more conservative tone towards the slavery propagandists, and a corresponding tone of bitterness towards anti-slavery men and measures. It came to be a no uncommon thing to hear men denouncing South Carolina and Massachusetts in the same breath, and in the same measure of disapproval. The old pro-slavery spirit which, in 1835, mobbed anti-slavery prayer-meetings, and dragged William Lloyd Garrison through the streets of Boston with a halter about his neck, was revived.* From Massachusetts to Missouri, anti-slavery meetings were ruthlessly assailed and broken up. With others, I was roughly handled in Tremont Temple, Boston, by a mob headed by one of the wealthiest men of that city. The talk was that the blood of some abolitionist must be shed to appease the wrath of the offended South, and to restore peaceful relations between the two sections of the country. A howling mob followed Wendell Phillips for three days whenever he appeared on the pavements of his native city, because of his ability and prominence in the propagation of anti-slavery opinions.

While this humiliating reaction was going on at the North, various devices to bring about peace and reconciliation were suggested and pressed at Washington. Committees were appointed to listen to southern grievances, and, if possible, devise means of redress for such as might be alleged. Some of these peace propositions would have been shocking to the last degree to the moral sense of the North, had not fear for the safety of the Union overwhelmed all moral conviction. Such men as William H. Seward, Charles Francis Adams, Henry B. Anthony, Joshua R. Giddings, and others—men whose courage had been equal to all other emergencies—bent before this southern storm, and were ready to purchase peace at any price. Those who had stimulated the courage of the North before the election, and had shouted 'Who's afraid?' were now shaking in their shoes with apprehension and dread. One was for passing laws in the northern States for the better protection of slave-hunters, and for the greater efficiency of the fugitive-slave bill. Another was for enacting laws to punish the invasion of the slave States, and others were for so altering the Constitution of the United States that the federal government should never abolish slavery while any one State should object to such a measure.[1] Everything that could be demanded by insatiable pride and selfishness on the part of the slave-holding South, or could be surrendered by abject fear and servility on the part of the North, had able and eloquent advocates.

Happily for the cause of human freedom, and for the final unity of the American nation, the South was mad, and would listen to no concessions. It would neither accept the terms offered, nor offer others to be accepted. It had made up its mind that under a given contingency it would secede from the Union and thus dismember the Republic. That contingency had happened, and it should execute its threat. Mr. Ireson of Georgia* expressed the ruling sentiment of his section when he told the northern peacemakers that if the people of the South were given a blank sheet of paper upon which to write their own terms on which they would remain in the Union, they would not stay. They had come to hate everything which had the prefix 'Free'—free soil, free States, free territories, free schools, free speech, and freedom generally, and they would have no more such prefixes. This haughty and unreasonable

[1] See History of American Conflict, Vol. II, by Horace Greeley.

and unreasoning attitude of the imperious South saved the slave and saved the nation. Had the South accepted our concessions and remained in the Union, the slave power would in all probability have continued to rule; the North would have become utterly demoralized; the hands on the dial-plate of American civilization would have been reversed, and the slave would have been dragging his hateful chains to-day wherever the American flag floats to the breeze. Those who may wish to see to what depths of humility and self-abasement a noble people can be brought under the sentiment of fear, will find no chapter of history more instructive than that which treats of the events in official circles in Washington during the space between the months of November, 1859, and March, 1860.

# CHAPTER XI.

## SECESSION AND WAR.

*Recruiting of the 54th and 55th Colored Regiments—Visit to President Lincoln and Secretary Stanton—Promised a Commission as Adjutant-General to General Thomas—Disappointment.*

THE cowardly and disgraceful reaction from a courageous and manly assertion of right principles, as described in the foregoing pages, continued surprisingly long after secession and war were commenced. The patience and forbearance of the loyal people of the North were amazing. Speaking of this feature of the situation in Corinthian Hall, Rochester, at the time, I said:

'We (the people of the North) are a charitable people, and, in the excess of this feeling, we were disposed to put the very best construction upon the strange behavior of our southern brethren. We hoped that all would yet go well. We thought that South Carolina might secede. It was entirely like her to do so. she had talked extravagantly about going out of the Union, and it was natural that she should do something extravagant and startling, if for nothing else, to make a show of consistency. Georgia, too, we thought might possibly secede. But, strangely enough, we thought and felt quite sure that these twin rebellious States would stand alone and unsupported in their infamy and their impotency, that they would soon tire of their isolation, repent of their folly, and come back to their places in the Union. Traitors withdrew from the Cabinet, from the House of Representatives, and from the Senate, and hastened to their several States to "fire the Southern heart," and to fan the hot flames of treason at home. Still we doubted if anything serious would come of it. We treated it as a bubble on the wave—a nine-days' wonder. Calm and thoughtful men ourselves, we relied upon the sober second thought of the southern people. Even the capture of a fort, a shot at one of our ships—an insult to the national flag—caused only a momentary feeling of indignation and resentment. We could not but believe that there existed at the South a latent and powerful Union sentiment which would assert itself at last. Though loyal soldiers had been fired upon in the streets of Baltimore, though loyal blood had stained the pavements of that beautiful city, and the national government was warned to send no troops through Baltimore to the defense of the National Capital, we could not be made to believe that the border States would plunge madly into the bloody vortex of rebellion.

'But this confidence, patience, and forbearance could not last forever. These blissful illusions of hope were, in a measure, dispelled when the batteries of Charleston harbor were opened upon the starving garrison at Fort Sumter. For the moment the northern lamb was transformed into a lion, and his roar was terrible. But he only showed his teeth, and clearly had no wish to use them. We preferred to fight with dollars, and not daggers. "The fewer battles the better," was the hopeful motto at Washington. "Peace in sixty days" was held out by the astute Secretary of State. In fact, there was at the North no disposition to fight, no spirit of hate, no comprehension of the stupendous character and dimensions of the rebellion, and no proper appreciation of its inherent wickedness. Treason had shot its poisonous roots deeper and had spread its death-dealing branches further than any northern calculation had covered. Thus, while rebels were waging a barbarous war, marshaling savage Indians to join them in the slaughter, while rifled cannon-balls were battering down the walls of our forts, and the iron-clad hand of monarchical power was being invoked to assist in the destruction of our government and the dismemberment of our country, while a tremendous rebel ram was sinking our fleet and threatening the cities of our coast, we were still dreaming of peace. This infatuation, this blindness to the significance of passing events, can only be accounted for by the rapid passage of these events and by the fact of the habitual leniency and good will cherished by the North towards the South. Our very lack of preparation for the conflict disposes us to look for some other than the way of blood out of the difficulty. Treason had largely infected both army and navy. Floyd had scattered our arms, Cobb had depleted our treasury, and Buchanan had poisoned the political thought of the times by his doctrines of anti-coercion. It was in such a condition of things as this that Abraham Lincoln (compelled from fear of assassination to enter the capital in disguise) was inaugurated and issued his proclamation for the "repossession of the forts, places, and property which had been seized from the Union," and his call upon the militia of the several States to the number of 75,000 men—a paper which showed how little even he comprehended the work then before the loyal nation. It was perhaps better for the country and for mankind that the good man could not know the end from the beginning. Had he foreseen the thousands who must sink into bloody graves, the mountains of debt to be laid on the breast of the nation, the terrible hardships and sufferings involved in the contest, and his own death by an assassin's hand, he too might have adopted the weak sentiment of those who said "Erring sisters, depart in peace." *

From the first, I, for one, saw in this war the end of slavery; and truth requires me to say that my interest in the success of the North was largely due to this belief. True it is that this faith was many times shaken by passing events, but never destroyed. When Secretary Seward instructed our ministers to say to the governments to which they were accredited that, 'terminate however it might, the status of no class of the people of the United States would be changed by the rebellion—that the slaves would be slaves still, and that the masters would be masters still'—when General McClellan* and General Butler* warned the slaves in advance that, 'if any attempt was made by them to gain their freedom it would be suppressed with an iron hand'—when the government persistently refused to employ colored troops—when the emancipation proclamation of General John C. Fremont, in Missouri, was withdrawn*—when slaves were being returned from our lines to their masters—when Union soldiers were stationed about the farm-houses of Virginia to guard and protect the master in holding his slaves—when Union soldiers made themselves more active in kicking colored men out of their camps than in shooting rebels—when even Mr. Lincoln could tell the poor negro that 'he was the cause of the war,' I still believed, and spoke as I believed, all over the North, that the mission of the war was the liberation of the slave, as well as the salvation of the Union; and hence from the first I reproached the North that they fought the rebels with only one hand, when they might strike effectually with two—that they fought with their soft white hand, while they kept their black iron hand chained and helpless behind them—that they fought the effect, while they protected the cause, and that the Union cause would never prosper till the war assumed an anti-slavery attitude, and the negro was enlisted on the loyal side. In every way possible—in the columns of my paper and on the platform, by letters to friends, at home and abroad, I did all that I could to impress this conviction upon this country. But nations seldom listen to advice from individuals, however reasonable. They are taught less by theories than by facts and events. There was much that could be said against making the war an abolition war—much that seemed wise and patriotic. 'Make the war an abolition war,' we were told, 'and you drive the border States into the rebellion, and thus add power to the enemy and increase the number you will have to meet on the battle-field. You will exasperate and intensify southern feeling, making it more desperate, and put far away the day of peace between the two sections.' 'Employ the arm of the negro, and the loyal men of the North will throw down their arms and go home.' 'This is the white man's country and the white man's war.' 'It would inflict an intolerable wound upon the pride and spirit of white soldiers of the Union to see the negro in the United States uniform. Besides, if you make the negro a soldier, you cannot depend on his courage; a crack of his old master's whip will send him scampering in terror from the field.' And so it was that custom, pride, prejudice, and the old-time respect for southern feeling, held back the government from an anti-slavery policy and from arming the negro. Meanwhile the rebellion availed itself of the negro most effectively. He was not only the stomach of the rebellion, by supplying its commissary department, but he built its forts, dug its intrenchments and performed other duties of the camp which left the rebel soldier more free to fight the loyal army than he could otherwise have been. It was the cotton and corn of the negro that made the rebellion sack stand on end and caused a continuance of the war. 'Destroy these,' was the burden of all my utterances during this part of the struggle, 'and you cripple and destroy the rebellion.' It is surprising how long and bitterly the government resisted and rejected this view of the situation. The abolition heart of the North ached over the delay, and uttered its bitter complaints, but the administration remained blind and dumb. Bull Run, Ball's Bluff, Big Bethel, Fredericksburg, and the Peninsula disasters were the only teachers whose authority was of sufficient importance to excite the attention or respect of our rulers, and they were even slow in being taught by these. An important point was gained, however, when General B. F. Butler, at Fortress Monroe, announced the policy of treating the slaves as 'contrabands,' to be made useful to the Union cause, and was sustained therein at Washington, and sentiments of a similar nature were expressed on the floor of Congress by Hon. A. G. Riddle of Ohio. A grand accession was made to this view of the case when Hon. Simon Cameron, then secretary of war, gave it his earnest support, and General David Hunter put the measure into practical operation in South Carolina. General Phelps from Vermont, in command at Carrollton, La., also advocated the same plan, though under discouragements which cost him his command. And many and grievous disasters on flood and field were needed to educate the loyal nation and President Lincoln up to the realization of the necessity, not to say justice, of this position, and many devices, intermediate steps, and make-shifts were suggested to smooth the way to the ultimate policy of freeing the slave, and arming the freedmen.

When at last the truth began to dawn upon the administration that the negro might be made useful to loyalty, as well as to treason, to the Union as well as to the Confederacy, it began to consider in what way it could employ him which would the least shock and offend the popular prejudice against him. He was already in the army as a waiter, and in that capacity there was no objection to him; and so it was thought that as this was the case, the feeling which tolerated him as a waiter would not seriously object if he should be admitted to the army as a laborer, especially as no one under a southern sun cared to have a monopoly of digging and toiling in trenches. This was the first step in employing negroes in the United States service. The second step was to give them a peculiar costume which should distinguish them from soldiers, and yet mark them as a part of the loyal force. As the eyes of the loyal administration still further opened, it was proposed to give these laborers something better than spades and shovels with which to defend themselves in cases of emergency. Still later it was proposed to make them soldiers, but soldiers without the blue uniform, soldiers with a mark upon them to show that they were inferior to other soldiers; soldiers with a badge of degradation upon them. However, once in the army as a laborer, once there with a red shirt on his back and a pistol in his belt, the negro was not long in appearing on the field as a soldier. But still, he was not to be a soldier in the sense, and on an equal footing, with white soldiers. It was given out that he was not to be employed in the open field with white troops, under the inspiration of doing battle and winning victories for the Union cause, and in the face and teeth of his old masters, but that he should be made to garrison forts in yellow-fever and otherwise unhealthy localities of the South, to save the health of white soldiers; and, in order to keep up the distinction further, the black soldiers were to have only half the wages of the white soldiers, and were to be commanded entirely by white commissioned officers. While of course I was deeply pained and saddened by the estimate thus put upon my race, and grieved at the slowness of heart which marked the conduct of the loyal government, I was not discouraged, and urged every man who could, to enlist; to get an eagle on his button, a musket on his shoulder, and the star-spangled banner over his head. Hence, as soon as Governor Andrew of Massachusetts received permission from Mr. Lincoln to raise two colored regiments, the 54th and 55th,* I made the following address to the colored citizens of the North through my paper, then being published in Rochester, which was copied in the leading journals:

'MEN OF COLOR, TO ARMS!

'When first the rebel cannon shattered the walls of Sumter and drove away its starving garrison, I predicted that the war then and there inaugurated would not be fought out entirely by white men. Every month's experience during these dreary years has confirmed that opinion. A war undertaken and brazenly carried on for the perpetual enslavement of colored men, calls logically and loudly for colored men to help suppress it. Only a moderate share of sagacity was needed to see that the arm of the slave was the best defense against the arm of the slave-holder. Hence, with every reverse to the national arms, with every exulting shout of victory raised by the slaveholding rebels, I have implored the imperiled nation to unchain against her foes her powerful black hand. Slowly and reluctantly that appeal is beginning to be heeded. Stop not now to complain that it was not heeded sooner. That it should not may or may not have been best. This is not the time to discuss that question. Leave it to the future. When the war is over, the country saved, peace established and the black man's rights are secured, as they will be, history with an impartial hand will dispose of that and sundry other questions. Action! action! not criticism, is the plain duty of this hour. Words are now useful only as they stimulate to blows. The office of speech now is only to point out when, where, and how to strike to the best advantage. There is no time to delay. The tide is at its flood that leads on to fortune. From East to West, from North to South, the sky is written all over, "Now OR NEVER." Liberty won by white men would lose half its luster. "Who would be free themselves must strike the blow." "Better even die free, than to live slaves." This is the sentiment of every brave colored man amongst us. There are weak and cowardly men in all nations. We have them amongst us. They tell you this is the "white man's war"; that you "will be no better off after than before the war"; that the getting of you into the army is to "sacrifice you on the first opportunity." Believe them not; cowards themselves, they do not wish to have their cowardice shamed by your brave example. Leave them to their timidity, or to whatever motive may hold them back. I have not thought lightly of the words I am now addressing you. The counsel I give comes of close observation of the great struggle now in progress, and of the deep conviction that this is your hour and mine. In good earnest, then, and after the best deliberation, I now, for the first time during this war, feel at liberty to call and counsel you to arms. By every consideration which binds you to your enslaved fellow-country-men and to the peace and welfare of your country; by every aspiration which you cherish for the freedom and equality of yourselves and your children; by all the ties of blood and identity which make us one with the brave black men now fighting our battles in Louisiana and in South Carolina. I urge you to fly to arms, and smite with death the power that would bury the government and your liberty in the same hopeless grave. I wish I could tell you that the State of New York calls you to this high honor. For the moment her constituted authorities are silent on the subject. They will speak by and by, and doubtless on the right side: but we are not compelled to wait for her. We can get at the throat of treason and slavery through the State of Massachusetts. She was first in the War of Independence; first to break the chains of her slaves; first to make the black man equal before the law; first to admit colored children to her common schools, and she was first to answer with her blood the alarm-cry of the nation, when its capital was menaced by rebels. You know her patriotic governor, and you know Charles Sumner. I need not add more.

Massachusetts now welcomes you to arms as soldiers. She has but a small colored population from which to recruit. She has full leave of the general government to send one regiment to the war, and she has undertaken to do it. Go quickly and help fill up the first colored regiment from the North. I am authorized to assure you that you will receive the same wages, the same rations, the same equipments, the same protection, the same treatment, and the same bounty, secured to white soldiers. You will be led by able and skillful officers, men who will take especial pride in your efficiency and success. They will be quick to accord to you all the honor you shall merit by your valor, and to see that your rights and feelings are respected by other soldiers. I have assured myself on these points, and can speak with authority. More than twenty years of unswerving devotion to our common cause may give me some humble claim to be trusted at this momentous crisis. I will not argue. To do so implies hesitation and doubt, and you do not hesitate. You do not doubt. The day dawns; the morning star is bright upon the horizon! The iron gate of our prison stands half open. One gallant rush from the North will fling it wide open, while four millions of our brothers and sisters shall march out into liberty. The chance is now given you to end in a day the bondage of centuries, and to rise in one bound from social degradation to the place of common equality with all other varieties of men. Remember Denmark Vessey* of Charleston; remember Nathaniel Turner of South Hampton; remember Shields Green and Copeland*, who followed noble John Brown, and fell as glorious martyrs for the cause of the slave. Remember that in a contest with oppression, the Almighty has no attribute which can take sides with oppressors. The case is before you. This is our golden opportunity. Let us accept it, and forever wipe out the dark reproaches unsparingly hurled against us by our enemies. Let us win for ourselves the gratitude of our country, and the best blessings of our posterity through all time. The nucleus of this first regiment is now in camp at Readville, a short distance from Boston. I will undertake to forward to Boston all persons adjudged fit to be mustered into the regiment, who shall apply to me at any time within the next two weeks.

'ROCHESTER, March 2, 1863.'

Immediately after authority had been given by President Lincoln to Governor John A. Andrew of Massachusetts, to raise and equip two regiments of colored men for the war, I received a letter from George L. Stearns of Boston, a noble worker for freedom in Kansas, and a warm friend of John Brown, earnestly entreating me to assist in raising the required number of men. It was presumed that by my labors in the anti-slavery cause, I had gained some influence with the colored men of the country, and that they would listen to me in this emergency; which supposition, I am happy to say, was supported by the results. There were fewer colored people in Massachusetts then than now, and it was necessary, in order to make up the full quota of these regiments, to recruit for them in other Northern States. The nominal conditions upon which colored men were asked to enlist were not satisfactory to me or to them; but assurances from Governor Andrew that they would in the end be made just and equal, together with my faith in the logic of events and my conviction that the wise thing for the colored man to do was to get into the army by any door open to him, no matter how narrow, made me accept with alacrity the work to which I was invited. The raising of these two regiments—the 54th and 55th—and their splendid behavior in South and North Carolina, was the beginning of great things for the colored people of the whole country; and not the least satisfaction I now have in contemplating my humble part in raising them, is the fact that my two sons, Charles and Lewis,* were the first two in the State of New York to enlist in them. The 54th was not long in the field before it proved itself gallant and strong, worthy to rank with the most courageous of its white companions in arms. Its assault upon Fort Wagner, in which it was so fearfully cut to pieces, and lost nearly half its officers, including its beloved and trusted commander, Col. Shaw,* at once gave it a name and a fame throughout the country. In that terrible battle, under the wing of night, more cavils in respect of the quality of negro manhood were set at rest than could have been during a century of ordinary life and observation. After that assault we heard no more of sending negroes to garrison forts and arsenals, to fight miasma, yellow-fever, and small-pox. Talk of his ability to meet the foe in the open field, and of his equal fitness with the white man to stop a bullet, then began to prevail. From this time (and the fact ought to be remembered) the colored troops were called upon to occupy positions which required the courage, steadiness, and endurance of veterans, and even their enemies were obliged to admit that they proved themselves worthy the confidence reposed in them. After the 54th and 55th Massachusetts colored regiments were placed in the field, and one of them had distinguished itself with so much credit in the hour of trial, the desire to send more such troops to the front became pretty general. Pennsylvania proposed to raise ten regiments. I was again called by my friend Mr. Stearns to assist in raising these regiments, and I set about the work with full purpose of heart, using every argument of which I was capable, to persuade every colored man able to bear arms to rally around the flag and help to save the country and the race. It was during this time that the attitude of the government at Washington caused me deep sadness and discouragement, and forced me in a measure to suspend my efforts in that direction. I had assured colored men that, once in the Union army, they would be put upon an equal footing with other soldiers; that they would be paid, promoted, and exchanged as prisoners of war, Jeff Davis's threat that they would be treated as felons, to the contrary notwithstanding. But thus far, the government had not kept its promise, or the promise made for it. The following letter which I find published in my paper of the same date will show the course I felt it my duty to take under the circumstances:

'ROCHESTER, August 1st, 1863.

'MAJOR GEORGE L. STEARNS:

'*My Dear Sir*,—Having declined to attend the meeting to promote enlistments, appointed for me at Pittsburgh, in present circumstances, I owe you a word of explanation. I have hitherto deemed it a duty, as it certainly has been a pleasure, to cooperate with you in the work of raising colored troops in the free States to fight the battles of the Republic against slaveholding rebels and traitors. Upon the first call you gave me to this work I responded with alacrity. I saw, or thought I saw, a ray of light, brightening the future of my whole race, as well as that of our war-troubled country, in arousing colored men to fight for the nation's life. I continue to believe in the black man's arm, and still have some hope in the integrity of our rulers. Nevertheless, I must for the present leave to others the work of persuading colored men to join the Union army. I owe it to my long-abused people, and especially to those already in the army, to expose their wrongs and plead their cause. I cannot do that in connection with recruiting. When I plead for recruits I want to do it with all my heart, without qualification. I cannot do that now. The impression settles upon me that colored men have much over-rated the enlightenment, justice, and generosity of our rulers at Washington. In my humble way I have contributed somewhat to that false estimate. You know that when the idea of raising colored troops was first suggested, the special duty to be assigned them was the garrisoning of forts and arsenals in certain warm, unhealthy, and miasmatic localities in the South. They were thought to be better adapted to that service than white troops. White troops trained to war, brave and daring, were to take fortifications, and the blacks were to hold them from falling again into the hands of the rebels. Three advantages were to arise out of this wise division of labor: 1st, The spirit and pride of white troops was not to waste itself in dull, monotonous inactivity in fort life; their arms were to be kept bright by constant use. 2d, The health of white troops was to be preserved. 3d, Black troops were to have the advantage of sound military training and to be otherwise useful, at the same time that they should be tolerably secure from capture by the rebels, who early avowed their determination to enslave and slaughter them in defiance of the laws of war. Two out of the three advantages were to accrue to the white troops. Thus far, however, I believe that no such duty as holding fortifications has been committed to colored troops. They have done far other and more important work than holding fortifications. I have no special complaint to make at this point, and I simply mention it to strengthen the statement that, from the beginning of this business, it was the confident belief among both the colored and white friends of colored enlistments that President Lincoln, as commander-in-chief of the army and navy, would certainly see to it that his colored troops should be so handled and disposed of as to be but little exposed to capture by the rebels, and that, if so exposed, as they have repeatedly been from the first, the President possessed both the disposition and the means for compelling the rebels to respect the rights of such as might fall into their hands. The piratical proclamation of Jefferson Davis,* announcing slavery and assassination to colored prisoners, was before the country and the world. But men had faith in Mr. Lincoln and his advisers. He was silent, to be sure, but charity suggested that being a man of action rather than words he only waited for a case in which he should be required to act. This faith in the man enabled us to speak with warmth and effect in urging enlistments among colored men. That faith, my dear sir, is now nearly gone. Various occasions have arisen during the last six months for the exercise of his power in behalf of the colored men in his service. But no word comes to us from the war department, sternly assuring the rebel chief that inquisition shall yet be made for innocent blood. No word of retaliation when a black man is slain by a rebel in cold blood. No word was said when free men from Massachusetts were caught and sold into slavery in Texas. No word is said when brave black men, according to the testimony of both friend and foe, fought like heroes to plant the star-spangled banner on the blazing parapets of Fort Wagner and in so doing were captured, mutilated, killed, and sold into slavery. The same crushing silence reigns over this scandalous outrage as over that of the slaughtered teamsters at Murfreesboro; the same as over that at Milliken's Bend and Vicksburg. I am free to say, my dear sir, that the case looks as if the confiding colored soldiers had been betrayed into bloody hands by the very government in whose defense they were heroically fighting. I know what you will say to this; you will say "Wait a little longer, and, after all, the best way to have justice done to your people is to get them into the army as fast as you can." You may be right in this; my argument has been the same; but have we not already waited, and have we not already shown the highest qualities of soldiers, and on this account deserve the protection of the government for which we are fighting? Can any case stronger than that before Charleston ever arise? If the President is ever to demand justice and humanity for black soldiers, is not this the time for him to do it? How many 54ths must be cut to pieces, its mutilated prisoners killed, and its living sold into slavery, to be tortured to death by inches, before Mr. Lincoln shall say, "Hold, enough!"*

'You know the 54th. To you, more than to any one man, belongs the credit of raising that regiment. Think of its noble and brave officers literally hacked to pieces, while many of its rank and file have been sold into slavery worse than death; and pardon me if I hesitate about assisting in raising a fourth regiment until the President shall give the same protection to them as to white soldiers.

With warm and sincere regards,
FREDERICK DOUGLASS.'

'Since writing the foregoing letter, which we have now put upon record, we have received assurances from Major Stearns that the government of the United States is already taking measures which will secure the captured colored soldiers at Charleston and elsewhere the same protection against slavery and cruelty that is extended to white soldiers. What ought to have been done at the beginning comes late, but it comes. The poor colored soldiers have purchased interference dearly. It really seems that nothing of justice, liberty, or humanity can come to us except through tears and blood.'

## THE BLACK MAN AT THE WHITE HOUSE.*

My efforts to secure just and fair treatment for the colored soldiers did not stop at letters and speeches. At the suggestion of my friend, Major Stearns, to whom the foregoing letter was addressed, I was induced to go to Washington and lay the complaints of my people before President Lincoln and the Secretary of War and to urge upon them such action as should secure to the colored troops then fighting for the country a reasonable degree of fair play. I need not say that at the time I undertook this mission it required much more nerve than a similar one would require now. The distance then between the black man and the white American citizen was immeasurable. I was an ex-slave, identified with a despised race, and yet I was to meet the most exalted person in this great republic. It was altogether an unwelcome duty, and one from which I would gladly have been excused. I could not know what kind of a reception would be accorded me. I might be told to go home and mind my business, and leave such questions as I had come to discuss to be managed by the men wisely chosen by the American people to deal with them. Or I might be refused an interview altogether. Nevertheless, I felt bound to go, and my acquaintance with Senators Charles Sumner, Henry Wilson, Samuel Pomeroy, Secretary Salmon P. Chase, Secretary William H. Seward, and Assistant Secretary of War Charles A. Dana encouraged me to hope at least for a civil reception. My confidence was fully justified in the result. I shall never forget my first interview with this great man. I was accompanied to the executive mansion and introduced to President Lincoln by Senator Pomeroy. The room in which he received visitors was the one now used by the President's secretaries. I entered it with a moderate estimate of my own consequence, and yet there I was to talk with, and even to advise, the head man of a great nation. Happily for me, there was no vain pomp and ceremony about him. I was never more quickly or more completely put at ease in the presence of a great man than in that of Abraham Lincoln. He was seated, when I entered, in a low armchair with his feet extended on the floor, surrounded by a large number of documents and several busy secretaries. The room bore the marks of business, and the persons in it, the President included, appeared to be much over-worked and tired. Long lines of care were already deeply written on Mr. Lincoln's brow, and his strong face, full of earnestness, lighted up as soon as my name was mentioned. As I approached and was introduced to him he arose and extended his hand, and bade me welcome. I at once felt myself in the presence of an honest man—one whom I could love, honor, and trust without reserve or doubt. Proceeding to tell him who I was and what I was doing, he promptly, but kindly, stopped me, saying: 'I know who you are, Mr. Douglass; Mr. Seward has told me all about you. Sit down. I am glad to see you.' I then told him the object of my visit: that I was assisting to raise colored troops; that several months before I had been very successful in getting men to enlist, but that now it was not easy to induce the colored men to enter the service, because there was a feeling among them that the government did not, in several respects, deal fairly with them. Mr. Lincoln asked me to state particulars. I replied that there were three particulars which I wished to bring to his attention. First, that colored soldiers ought to receive the same wages as those paid to white soldiers. Second, that colored soldiers ought to receive the same protection when taken prisoners, and be exchanged as readily and on the same terms as any other prisoners, and if Jefferson Davis should shoot or hang colored soldiers in cold blood the United States government should, without delay, retaliate in kind and degree upon Confederate prisoners in its hands. Third, when colored soldiers, seeking 'the bubble reputation at the cannon's mouth,'* performed great and uncommon service on the battle-field, they should be rewarded by distinction and promotion precisely as white soldiers are rewarded for like services.

Mr. Lincoln listened with patience and silence to all I had to say. He was serious and even troubled by what I had said and by what he himself had evidently before thought upon the same points. He, by his silent listening not less than by his earnest reply to my words, impressed me with the solid gravity of his character.

He began by saying that the employment of colored troops at all was a great gain to the colored people; that the measure could not have been successfully adopted at the beginning of the war; that the wisdom of making colored men soldiers was still doubted; that their enlistment was a serious offense to popular prejudice; that they had larger motives for being soldiers than white men; that they ought to be willing to enter the service upon any condition; that the fact that they were not to receive the same pay as white soldiers seemed a necessary concession to smooth the way to their employment at all as soldiers, but that ultimately they would receive the same. On the second point, in respect to equal protection, he said the case was more difficult. Retaliation was a terrible remedy, and one which it was very difficult to apply; that, if once begun, there was no telling where it would end; that if he could get hold of the Confederate soldiers who had been guilty of treating colored soldiers as felons he could easily retaliate, but the thought of hanging men for a crime perpetrated by others was revolting to his feelings. He thought that the rebels themselves would stop such barbarous warfare; that less evil would be done if retaliation were not resorted to and that he had already received information that colored soldiers were being treated as prisoners of war. In all this I saw the tender heart of the man rather than the stern warrior and commander-in-chief of the American army and navy, and, while I could not agree with him, I could but respect his humane spirit.

On the third point he appeared to have less difficulty, though he did not absolutely commit himself. He simply said that he would sign any commission to colored soldiers whom his Secretary of War should commend to him. Though I was not entirely satisfied with his views, I was so well satisfied with the man and with the educating tendency of the conflict that I determined to go on with the recruiting.

From the President I went to see Secretary Stanton.* The manner of no two men could be more widely different. I was introduced by

Assistant Secretary Dana, whom I had known many years before at 'Brook Farm,' Mass., and afterward as managing editor of the New York *Tribune*.* Every line in Mr. Stanton's face told me that my communication with him must be brief, clear, and to the point; that he might turn his back upon me as a bore at any moment; that politeness was not one of his weaknesses. His first glance was that of a man who says: 'Well, what do you want? I have no time to waste upon you or anybody else, and I shall waste none. Speak quick, or I shall leave you.' The man and the place seemed alike busy. Seeing I had no time to lose, I hastily went over the ground I had gone over to President Lincoln. As I ended I was surprised by seeing a changed man before me. Contempt and suspicion and brusqueness had all disappeared from his face and manner, and for a few minutes he made the best defense that I had then heard from anybody of the treatment of colored soldiers by the government. I was not satisfied, yet I left in the full belief that the true course to the black man's freedom and citizenship was over the battle-field, and that my business was to get every black man I could into the Union armies. Both the President and Secretary of War assured me that justice would ultimately be done my race, and I gave full faith and credit to their promise. On assuring Mr. Stanton of my willingness to take a commission, he said he would make me assistant adjutant to General Thomas, who was then recruiting and organizing troops in the Mississippi valley. He asked me how soon I could be ready. I told him in two weeks, and that my commission might be sent to me at Rochester. For some reason, however, my commission never came. The government, I fear, was still clinging to the idea that positions of honor in the service should be occupied by white men, and that it would not do to inaugurate just then the policy of perfect equality. I wrote to the department for my commission, but was simply told to report to General Thomas. This was so different from what I expected and from what I had been promised that I wrote to Secretary Stanton that I would report to General Thomas on receipt of my commission, but it did not come, and I did not go to the Mississippi valley as I had fondly hoped. I knew too much of camp life and the value of shoulder straps in the army to go into the service without some visible mark of my rank. I have no doubt that Mr. Stanton in the moment of our meeting meant all he said, but thinking the matter over he felt that the time had not then come for a step so radical and aggressive. Meanwhile my three sons were in the service, Lewis and Charles, as already named, in the Massachusetts regiments, and Frederick* recruiting colored troops in the Mississippi valley.

# CHAPTER XII.

## HOPE FOR THE NATION.

*Proclamation of emancipation—Its reception in Boston—Objections brought against it—Its effect on the country—Interview with President Lincoln—New York riots—Re-election of Mr. Lincoln—His inauguration, and inaugural—Vice-President Johnson—Presidential reception—The fall of Richmond—Faneuil Hall—The assassination—Condolence.*

THE first of January, 1863, was a memorable day in the progress of American liberty and civilization. It was the turning-point in the conflict between freedom and slavery. A death-blow was given to the slave-holding rebellion. Until then the federal arm had been more than tolerant to that relic of barbarism. It had defended it inside the slave States; it had countermanded the emancipation policy of John C. Fremont in Missouri; it had returned slaves to their so-called owners; it had threatened that any attempt on the part of the slaves to gain their freedom by insurrection, or otherwise, should be put down with an iron hand; it had even refused to allow the Hutchinson family to sing their anti-slavery songs in the camps of the Army of the Potomac; it had surrounded the houses of slaveholders with bayonets for their protection; and through its secretary of war, William H. Seward, had given notice to the world that, 'however the war for the Union might terminate, no change would be made in the relation of master and slave.' Upon this pro-slavery platform the war against the rebellion had been waged during more than two years. It had not been a war of conquest, but rather a war of conciliation. McClellan, in command of the army, had been trying, apparently, to put down the rebellion without hurting the rebels, certainly without hurting slavery, and the government had seemed to coöperate with him in both respects. Charles Sumner, William Lloyd Garrison, Wendell Phillips, Gerrit Smith and the whole anti-slavery phalanx at the North, had denounced this policy, and had besought Mr. Lincoln to adopt an opposite one, but in vain. Generals in the field, and councils in the Cabinet, had persisted in advancing this policy through defeats and disasters, even to the verge of ruin. We fought the rebellion, but not its cause. The key to the situation was the four millions of slaves; yet the slave who loved us, was hated, and the slaveholder who hated us, was loved. We kissed the hand that smote us, and spurned the hand that helped us. When the means of victory were before us,—within our grasp,—we went in search of the means of defeat. And now, on this day of January 1st, 1863, the formal and solemn announcement was made that thereafter the government would be found on the side of emancipation. This proclamation changed everything. It gave a new direction to the councils of the Cabinet, and to the conduct of the national arms. I shall leave to the statesman, the philosopher and the historian, the more comprehensive discussion of this document, and only tell how it touched me, and those in like condition with me at the time. I was in Boston, and its reception there may indicate the importance attached to it elsewhere. An immense assembly convened in Tremont Temple to await the first flash of the electric wires announcing the 'new departure.' Two years of war, prosecuted in the interests of slavery, had made free speech possible in Boston, and we were now met together to receive and celebrate the first utterance of the long-hoped-for proclamation, if it came, and, if it did not come, to speak our minds freely; for, in view of the past, it was by no means certain that it would come. The occasion, therefore, was one of both hope and fear. Our ship was on the open sea, tossed by a terrible storm; wave after wave was passing over us, and every hour was fraught with increasing peril. Whether we should survive or perish depended in large measure upon the coming of this proclamation. At least so we felt. Although the conditions on which Mr. Lincoln had promised to withhold it had not been complied with, yet, from many considerations, there was room to doubt and fear. Mr. Lincoln was known to be a man of tender heart, and boundless patience: no man could tell to what length he might go, or might refrain from going, in the direction of peace and reconciliation. Hitherto, he had not shown himself a man of heroic measures, and, properly enough, this step belonged to that class. It must be the end of all compromises with slavery—a declaration that thereafter the war was to be conducted on a new principle, with a new aim. It would be a full and fair assertion that the government would neither trifle, or be trifled with, any longer. But would it come? On the side of doubt, it was said that Mr. Lincoln's kindly nature might cause him to relent at the last moment; that Mrs. Lincoln, coming from an old slaveholding family, would influence him to delay, and to give the slaveholders one other chance.[1] Every moment of waiting chilled our hopes, and strengthened our fears. A line of messengers was established between the telegraph office and the platform of Tremont Temple, and the time was occupied with brief speeches from Hon. Thomas Russell of

---

[1] I have reason to know that this supposition did Mrs. Lincoln great injustice.

Plymouth, Miss Anna E. Dickinson* (a lady of marvelous eloquence), Rev. Mr. Grimes, J. Sella Martin,* William Wells Brown,* and myself. But speaking or listening to speeches was not the thing for which the people had come together. The time for argument was passed. It was not logic, but the trump of jubilee, which everybody wanted to hear. We were waiting and listening as for a bolt from the sky, which should rend the fetters of four millions of slaves; we were watching, as it were, by the dim light of the stars, for the dawn of a new day; we were longing for the answer to the agonizing prayers of centuries. Remembering those in bonds as bound with them,* we wanted to join in the shout for freedom, and in the anthem of the redeemed.

Eight, nine, ten o'clock came and went, and still no word. A visible shadow seemed falling on the expecting throng, which the confident utterances of the speakers sought in vain to dispel. At last, when patience was well-nigh exhausted, and suspense was becoming agony, a man (I think it was Judge Russell) with hasty step advanced through the crowd, and with a face fairly illumined with the news he bore, exclaimed in tones that thrilled all hearts, 'It is coming!' 'It is on the wires!!' The effect of this announcement was startling beyond description, and the scene was wild and grand. Joy and gladness exhausted all forms of expression, from shouts of praise to sobs and tears. My old friend Rue, a colored preacher, a man of wonderful vocal power, expressed the heartfelt emotion of the hour, when he led all voices in the anthem, 'Sound the loud timbrel o'er Egypt's dark sea, Jehovah hath triumphed, his people are free.'*

About twelve o'clock, seeing there was no disposition to retire from the hall, which must be vacated, my friend Grimes (of blessed memory), rose and moved that the meeting adjourn to the Twelfth Baptist church, of which he was pastor, and soon that church was packed from doors to pulpit, and this meeting did not break up till near the dawn of day. It was one of the most affecting and thrilling occasions I ever witnessed, and a worthy celebration of the first step on the part of the nation in its departure from the thraldom of ages.

There was evidently no disposition on the part of this meeting to criticise the proclamation; nor was there with any one at first. At the moment we saw only its antislavery side. But further and more critical examination showed it to be extremely defective. It was not a proclamation of 'liberty throughout all the land, unto all the inhabitants thereof,'* such as we had hoped it would be, but was one marked by discriminations and reservations. Its operation was confined within certain geographical and military lines. It only abolished slavery where it did not exist, and left it intact where it did exist. It was a measure apparently inspired by the low motive of military necessity, and by so far as it was so, it would become inoperative and useless when military necessity should cease. There was much said in this line, and much that was narrow and erroneous. For my own part, I took the proclamation, first and last, for a little more than it purported, and saw in its spirit a life and power far beyond its letter. Its meaning to me was the entire abolition of slavery, wherever the evil could be reached by the Federal arm, and I saw that its moral power would extend much further. It was, in my estimation, an immense gain to have the war for the Union committed to the extinction of slavery, even from a military necessity. It is not a bad thing to have individuals or nations do right, though they do so from selfish motives. I approved the one-spur-wisdom of 'Paddy,' who thought if he could get one side of his horse to go, he could trust the speed of the other side.

The effect of the proclamation abroad was highly beneficial to the loyal cause. Disinterested parties could now see in it a benevolent character. It was no longer a mere strife for territory and dominion, but a contest of civilization against barbarism.

The proclamation itself was throughout like Mr. Lincoln. It was framed with a view to the least harm and the most good possible in the circumstances, and with especial consideration of the latter. It was thoughtful, cautious, and well guarded at all points. While he hated slavery, and really desired its destruction, he always proceeded against it in a manner the least likely to shock or drive from him any who were truly in sympathy with the preservation of the Union, but who were not friendly to emancipation. For this he kept up the distinction between loyal and disloyal slaveholders, and discriminated in favor of the one, as against the other. In a word, in all that he did, or attempted, he made it manifest that the one great and all-commanding object with him was the peace and preservation of the Union, and that this was the motive and main-spring of all his measures. His wisdom and moderation at this point were for a season useful to the loyal cause in the border States, but it may be fairly questioned whether it did not chill the union ardor of the loyal people of the North in some degree, and diminish rather than increase the sum of our power against the rebellion; for moderate, cautious, and guarded as was this proclamation, it created a howl of indignation and wrath amongst the rebels and their allies. The old cry was raised by the copperhead organs of 'an abolition war,' and a pretext was thus found for an excuse for refusing to enlist, and for marshaling all the negro prejudice of the North on the rebel side. Men could say they were willing to fight for the Union, but that they were not willing to fight for the freedom of the negroes; and thus it was made difficult to procure enlistments or to enforce the draft. This was especially true of New York, where there was a large Irish population. The attempt to enforce the draft in that city was met by mobs, riot, and bloodshed. There is perhaps no darker chapter in the whole history of the war than this cowardly and bloody uprising in July, 1863.* For three days and nights New York was in the hands of a ferocious mob, and there was not sufficient power in the government of the country or of the city itself to stay the hand of violence and the effusion of blood. Though this mob was nominally against the draft which had been ordered, it poured out its fiercest wrath upon the colored people and their friends. It spared neither age nor sex; it hanged negroes simply because they were negroes; it murdered women in their homes, and burnt their homes over their heads; it dashed out the brains of young children against the lamp-posts; it burned the colored orphan asylum, a noble charity on the corner of Fifth avenue, and, scarce allowing time for the helpless two hundred children to make good their escape, plundered the building of every valuable piece of furniture; and forced colored men, women and children to seek concealment in cellars or garrets or wheresoever else it could be found, until this high carnival of crime and reign of terror should pass away.

In connection with George L. Stearns, Thomas Webster, and Col. Wagner, I had been at Camp William Penn, Philadelphia, assisting in the work of filling up the colored regiments, and was on my way home from there just as these events were transpiring in New York. I was met by a friend at Newark, who informed me of this condition of things. I, however, pressed on my way to the Chambers street station of the Hudson River Railroad in safety, the mob, fortunately for me, being in the upper part of the city, for not only my color, but my known activity in procuring enlistments, would have made me especially obnoxious to its murderous spirit. This was not the first time I had been in imminent peril in New York city. My first arrival there, after my escape from slavery, was full of danger. My passage through its borders after the attack of John Brown on Harper's Ferry was scarcely less safe. I had encountered Isaiah Rynders and his gang of ruffians in the old Broadway Tabernacle at our anti-slavery anniversary meeting, and I knew something of the crazy temper of such crowds; but this anti-draft, anti-negro mob, was something more and something worse—it was a part of the rebel force, without the rebel uniform, but with all its deadly hate; it was the fire of the enemy opened in the rear of the loyal army. Such men as Franklin Pierce and Horatio Seymour had done much in their utterances to encourage resistance to the drafts. Seymour was then Governor of the State of New York, and while the mob was doing its deadly work he addressed them as 'My friends,' telling them to desist then, while he could arrange at Washington to have the draft arrested. Had Governor Seymour been loyal to his country, and to his country's cause, in this her moment of need, he would have burned his tongue with a red hot iron sooner than allow it to call these thugs, thieves, and murderers his 'friends.'

My interviews with President Lincoln and his able Secretary, before narrated, greatly increased my confidence in the anti-slavery integrity of the government, although I confess I was greatly disappointed at my failure to receive the commission promised me by Secretary Stanton. I, however, faithfully believed, and loudly proclaimed my belief, that the rebellion would be suppressed, the Union preserved, the slaves emancipated and that the colored soldiers would in the end have justice done them. This confidence was immeasurably strengthened when I saw Gen. George B. McClellan relieved from the command of the army of the Potomac and Gen. U. S. Grant* placed at its head, and in command of all the armies of the United States. My confidence in Gen. Grant was not entirely due to his brilliant military successes, but there was a moral as well as military basis for my faith in him. He had shown his single-mindedness and superiority to popular prejudice by his prompt coöperation with President Lincoln in his policy of employing colored troops and by his order commanding his soldiers to treat such troops with due respect. In this way he proved himself to be not only a wise general, but a great man—one who could adjust himself to new conditions, and adopt the lessons taught by the events of the hour. This quality in General Grant was and is made all the more conspicuous and striking in contrast with his West Point education and his former political associations; for neither West Point nor the Democratic party have been good schools in which to learn justice and fair play to the negro.

It was when General Grant was fighting his way through the Wilderness to Richmond, on the 'line' he meant to pursue 'if it took all summer,' and every reverse to his arms was made the occasion for a fresh demand for peace without emancipation, that President Lincoln did me the honor to invite me to the Executive Mansion for a conference on the situation.* I need not say I went most gladly. The main subject on which he wished to confer with me was as to the means most desirable to be employed outside the army to induce the slaves in the rebel States to come within the Federal lines. The increasing opposition to the war, in the North, and the mad cry against it, because it was being made an abolition war, alarmed Mr. Lincoln, and made him apprehensive that a peace might be forced upon him which would leave still in slavery all who had not come within our lines. What he wanted was to make his proclamation as effective as possible in the event of such a peace. He said, in a regretful tone, 'The slaves are not coming so rapidly and so numerously to us as I had hoped.' I replied that the slaveholders knew how to keep such things from their slaves, and probably very few knew of his proclamation. 'Well,' he said, 'I want you to set about devising some means of making them acquainted with it, and for bringing them into our lines.' He spoke with great earnestness and much solicitude, and seemed troubled by the attitude of Mr. Greeley and by the growing impatience at the war that was being manifested throughout the North. He said he was being accused of protracting the war beyond its legitimate object and of failing to make peace when he might have done so to advantage. He was afraid of what might come of all these complaints, but was persuaded that no solid and lasting peace could come short of absolute submission on the part of the rebels, and he was not for giving them rest by futile conferences with unauthorized persons, at Niagara Falls, or elsewhere. He saw the danger of premature peace, and, like a thoughtful and sagacious man as he was, wished to provide means of rendering such consummation as harmless as possible. I was the more impressed by this benevolent consideration because he before said, in answer to the peace clamor, that his object was to *save the Union*, and to do so with or without slavery. What he said on this day showed a deeper moral conviction against slavery than I had ever seen before in anything spoken or written by him. I listened with the deepest interest and profoundest satisfaction, and, at his suggestion, agreed to undertake the organizing a band of scouts, composed of colored men, whose business should be somewhat after the original plan of John Brown, to go into the rebel States, beyond the lines of our armies, and carry the news of emancipation, and urge the slaves to come within our boundaries.

This plan, however, was very soon rendered unnecessary, by the success of the war in the Wilderness and elsewhere, and by its termination in the complete abolition of slavery.

I refer to this conversation because I think that, on Mr. Lincoln's part, it is evidence conclusive that the proclamation, so far at least as he was concerned, was not effected merely as a 'necessity.'

An incident occurred during this interview which illustrates the character of this great man, though the mention of it may savor a little of vanity on my part. While in conversation with him his Secretary twice announced 'Governor Buckingham of Connecticut,' one of the noblest and most patriotic of the loyal governors. Mr. Lincoln said, 'Tell Governor Buckingham to wait, for I want to have a long talk with my friend Frederick Douglass.' I interposed, and begged him to see the Governor at once, as I could wait; but no, he persisted that he wanted to talk with me and that Governor Buckingham could wait. This was probably the first time in the history of this Republic when its chief magistrate had found an occasion or shown a disposition to exercise such an act of impartiality between persons so widely different in their positions and supposed claims upon his attention. From the manner of the Governor, when he was finally admitted, I inferred that he was as well satisfied with what Mr. Lincoln had done, or had omitted to do, as I was.

I have often said elsewhere what I wish to repeat here, that Mr. Lincoln was not only a great President, but a GREAT MAN—too great to be small in anything. In his company I was never in any way reminded of my humble origin, or of my unpopular color. While I am, as it may seem, boasting of the kind consideration which I have reason to believe that Mr. Lincoln entertained towards me, I may mention one thing more. At the door of my friend John A. Gray, where I was stopping in Washington, I found one afternoon the carriage of Secretary Dole, and a messenger from President Lincoln with an invitation for me to take tea with him at the Soldiers' Home, where he then passed his nights, riding out after the business of the day was over at the Executive Mansion. Unfortunately, I had an engagement to speak that evening, and having made it one of the rules of my conduct in life never to break an engagement if possible to keep it, I felt obliged to decline the honor. I have often regretted that I did not make this an exception to my general rule. Could I have known that no such opportunity could come to me again, I should have justified myself in disappointing a large audience for the sake of such a visit with Abraham Lincoln.

It is due perhaps to myself to say here that I did not take Mr. Lincoln's attentions as due to my merits or personal qualities. While I have no doubt that Messrs. Seward and Chase had spoken well of me to him, and that the fact of my having been a slave and gained my freedom and of having picked up some sort of an education, and being in some sense a 'self-made man,' and having made myself useful as an advocate of the claims of my people, gave me favor in his eyes; yet I am quite sure that the main thing which gave me consideration with him was my well-known relation to the colored people of the Republic, and especially the help which that relation enabled me to give to the work of suppressing the rebellion and of placing the Union on a firmer basis than it ever had or could have sustained in the days of slavery.

So long as there was any hope whatsoever of the success of Rebellion, there was of course a corresponding fear that a new lease of life would be granted to slavery. The proclamation of Fremont in Missouri, the letter of Phelps in the Department of the Gulf, the enlistment of colored troops by Gen. Hunter, the 'Contraband' letter of Gen. B. F. Butler, the soldierly qualities surprisingly displayed by colored soldiers in the terrific battles of Port Hudson, Vicksburg, Morris Island and elsewhere and the Emancipation proclamation by Abraham Lincoln, had given slavery many and deadly wounds, yet it was in fact only wounded and crippled, not disabled and killed. With this condition of national affairs came the summer of 1864, and with it the revived Democratic party with the story in its mouth that the war was a failure, and with it Gen. George B. McClellan, the greatest failure of the war, as its candidate for the presidency. It is needless to say that the success of such a party, on such a platform, with such a candidate, at such a time, would have been a fatal calamity. All that had been done toward suppressing the rebellion and abolishing slavery would have proved of no avail, and the final settlement between the two sections of the Republic touching slavery and the right of secession would have been left to tear and rend the country again at no distant future.

It was said that this Democratic party, which under Mr. Buchanan had betrayed the government into the hands of secession and treason, was the only party which could restore the country to peace and union. No doubt it would have 'patched up' a peace, but it would have been a peace more to be dreaded than war. So at least I felt and worked. When we were thus asked to exchange Abraham Lincoln for George B. McClellan—a successful Union President for an unsuccessful Union general—a party earnestly endeavoring to save the Union, torn and rent by a gigantic rebellion, I thought with Mr. Lincoln that it was not wise to 'swap horses while crossing a stream.' Regarding, as I did, the continuance of the war to the complete suppression of the rebellion and the retention in office of President Lincoln as essential to the total destruction of slavery, I certainly exerted myself to the uttermost in my small way to secure his reelection. This most important object was not attained, however, by speeches, letters, or other electioneering appliances. The staggering blows dealt upon the rebellion that year by the armies under Grant and Sherman, and his own great character, ground all opposition to dust and made his election sure even before the question reached the polls. Since William the Silent,* who was the soul of the mighty war for religious liberty against Spain and the Spanish inquisition, no leader of men has been loved and trusted in such generous measures as was Abraham Lincoln. His election silenced in a good degree the discontent felt at the length of the war and the complaints of its being an abolition war. Every victory of our arms on flood and field was a rebuke to McClellan and the Democratic party, and an indorsement of Abraham Lincoln for President and of his new policy. It was my good fortune to be present at his inauguration in March, and to hear on that occasion his remarkable inaugural address. On the night previous I took tea with Chief Justice Chase* and assisted his beloved daughter, Mrs. Sprague, in placing over her honored father's shoulders the new robe then being made, in which he was to administer the oath of office to the reëlected President. There was a dignity and grandeur about the Chief Justice which marked him as one born great. He had known me in early anti-slavery days and had welcomed me to his home and his table when to do so was a strange thing in Washington, and the fact was by no means an insignificant one.

The inauguration, like the election, was a most important event. Four years before, after Mr. Lincoln's first election, the pro-slavery spirit determined against his inauguration, and it no doubt would have accomplished its purpose had he attempted to pass openly and recognized through Baltimore. There was murder in the air then, and there was murder in the air now. His first inauguration arrested the fall of the Republic, and the second was to restore it to enduring foundations. At the time of the second inauguration the rebellion was apparently vigorous, defiant, and formidable, but in reality, weak, dejected, and desperate. It had reached that verge of madness when it had called upon the negro for help to fight against the freedom which he so longed to find, for the bondage he would escape—against Lincoln the emancipator for Davis the enslaver. But desperation discards logic as well as law, and the South was desperate. Sherman was marching to the sea, and Virginia with its rebel capital was in the firm grasp of Ulysses S. Grant. To those who knew the situation it was evident that unless some startling change was made the Confederacy had but a short time to live, and that time full of misery. This condition of things made the air at Washington dark and lowering. The friends of the Confederate cause here were neither few nor insignificant. They were among the rich and influential. A wink or a nod from such men might unchain the hand of violence and set order and law at defiance. To those who saw beneath the surface it was clearly perceived that there was danger abroad, and as the procession

passed down Pennsylvania avenue I for one felt an instinctive apprehension that at any moment a shot from some assassin in the crowd
might end the glittering pageant and throw the country into the depths
of anarchy. I did not then know, what has since become history, that the
plot was already formed and its execution which, though several weeks
delayed, at last accomplished its deadly work was contemplated for that
very day. Reaching the Capitol, I took my place in the crowd where
I could see the presidential procession as it came upon the east portico,
and where I could hear and see all that took place. There was no such
throng as that which celebrated the inauguration of President Garfield
nor that of President Rutherford B. Hayes. The whole proceeding was
wonderfully quiet, earnest, and solemn. From the oath as administered
by Chief Justice Chase, to the brief but weighty address delivered by
Mr. Lincoln, there was a leaden stillness about the crowd. The address
sounded more like a sermon than like a state paper. In the fewest words
possible he referred to the condition of the country four years before on
his first accession to the presidency, to the causes of the war, and the
reasons on both sides for which it had been waged. 'Neither party,' he
said, 'expected for the war the magnitude or the duration which it had
already attained. Neither anticipated that the cause of the conflict
might cease with or even before the conflict itself should cease. Each
looked for an easier triumph and a result less fundamental and astound-
ing.' Then in a few short sentences admitting the conviction that slavery had been the 'offense which in the providence of God must needs
come, and the war as the woe due to those by whom the offense came,'
he asks if there can be 'discerned in this any departure from those
Divine attributes which the believers in a loving God always ascribe to
him? Fondly do we hope,' he continued, 'fervently do we pray, that this
mighty scourge of war may speedily pass away. Yet if God wills that it
continue until all the wealth piled by the bondman's two hundred and
fifty years of unrequited toil shall be sunk, and until every drop of
blood drawn with the lash shall be paid for by another drawn with the
sword, as was said three thousand years ago, so still it must be said,
'The judgments of the Lord are true and righteous altogether.'*

'With malice toward none, with charity for all, with firmness in the right
as God gives us to see the right, let us strive to finish the work we
are in, to bind up the nation's wounds, to care for him who shall have borne
the battle, and for his widow and his orphans, to do all which may achieve
and cherish a just and lasting peace among ourselves and with all nations.'

I know not how many times and before how many people I have
quoted these solemn words of our martyred President. They struck me

at the time, and have seemed to me ever since to contain more vital substance than I have ever seen compressed in a space so narrow; yet on this memorable occasion, when I clapped my hands in gladness and thanksgiving at their utterance, I saw in the faces of many about me expressions of widely different emotion.

On this inauguration day, while waiting for the opening of the ceremonies, I made a discovery in regard to the Vice President, Andrew Johnson.* There are moments in the lives of most men when the doors of their souls are open, and, unconsciously to themselves, their true characters may be read by the observant eye. It was at such an instant that I caught a glimpse of the real nature of this man, which all subsequent developments proved true. I was standing in the crowd by the side of Mrs. Thomas J. Dorsey, when Mr. Lincoln touched Mr. Johnson and pointed me out to him. The first expression which came to his face, and which I think was the true index of his heart, was one of bitter contempt and aversion. Seeing that I observed him, he tried to assume a more friendly appearance, but it was too late; it is useless to close the door when all within has been seen. His first glance was the frown of the man; the second was the bland and sickly smile of the demagogue. I turned to Mrs. Dorsey and said, 'Whatever Andrew Johnson may be, he certainly is no friend of our race.'

No stronger contrast between two men could well be presented than the one exhibited on this day between President Lincoln and Vice-President Johnson. Mr. Lincoln was like one who was treading the hard and thorny path of duty and self-denial; Mr. Johnson was like one just from a drunken debauch. The face of the one was full of manly humility, although at the topmost height of power and pride; that of the other was full of pomp and swaggering vanity. The fact was, though it was yet early in the day, Mr. Johnson was drunk.

In the evening of the day of the inauguration, another new experience awaited me. The usual reception was given at the executive mansion, and though no colored persons had ever ventured to present themselves on such occasions, it seemed, now that freedom had become the law of the republic, and colored men were on the battle-field mingling their blood with that of white men in one common effort to save the country, that it was not too great an assumption for a colored man to offer his congratulations to the President with those of other citizens. I decided to go, and sought in vain for some one of my own color to accompany me. It is never an agreeable experience to go where there can be any doubt of welcome, and my colored friends had too often realized discomfiture from this cause to be willing to subject themselves to such unhappiness; they wished me to go, as my New England colored friends in the long-ago liked very well to have me take passage on the first-class cars, and be hauled out and pounded by rough-handed brakemen, to make way for them. It was plain, then, that some one must lead the way, and that if the colored man would have his rights, he must take them; and now, though it was plainly quite the thing for me to attend President Lincoln's reception, 'they all with one accord began to make excuse.'* It was finally arranged that Mrs. Dorsey should bear me company, so together we joined in the grand procession of citizens from all parts of the country, and moved slowly towards the executive mansion. I had for some time looked upon myself as a man, but now in this multitude of the élite of the land, I felt myself a man among men. I regret to be obliged to say, however, that this comfortable assurance was not of long duration, for on reaching the door, two policemen stationed there took me rudely by the arm and ordered me to stand back, for their directions were to admit no persons of my color. The reader need not be told that this was a disagreeable set-back. But once in the battle, I did not think it well to submit to repulse. I told the officers I was quite sure there must be some mistake, for no such order could have emanated from President Lincoln; and that if he knew I was at the door he would desire my admission. They then, to put an end to the parley, as I suppose, for we were obstructing the doorway, and were not easily pushed aside, assumed an air of politeness, and offered to conduct me in. We followed their lead, and soon found ourselves walking some planks out of a window, which had been arranged as a temporary passage for the exit of visitors. We halted so soon as we saw the trick, and I said to the officers: 'You have deceived me. I shall not go out of this building till I see President Lincoln.' At this moment a gentleman who was passing in recognized me, and I said to him: 'Be so kind as to say to Mr. Lincoln that Frederick Douglass is detained by officers at the door.' It was not long before Mrs. Dorsey and I walked into the spacious East Room, amid a scene of elegance such as in this country I had never before witnessed. Like a mountain pine high above all others, Mr. Lincoln stood, in his grand simplicity, and *home-like beauty*. Recognizing me, even before I reached him, he exclaimed. so that all around could hear him, 'Here comes my friend Douglass.' Taking me by the hand, he said, 'I am glad to see you. I saw you in the crowd to-day, listening to my inaugural address; how did you like it?' I said, 'Mr. Lincoln, I must not detain you with my poor opinion, when there are thousands waiting to shake hands with you.' 'No, no,' he said, 'you must stop a little, Douglass; there is no man in the country whose opinion

I value more than yours. I want to know what you think of it?' I replied, 'Mr. Lincoln, that was a sacred effort.' 'I am glad you liked it!' he said; and I passed on, feeling that any man, however distinguished, might well regard himself honored by such expressions, from such a man.

It came out that the officers at the White House had received no orders from Mr. Lincoln, or from any one else. They were simply complying with an old custom, the outgrowth of slavery, as dogs will sometimes rub their necks, long after their collars are removed, thinking they are still there. My colored friends were well pleased with what had seemed to them a doubtful experiment, and I believe were encouraged by its success to follow my example. I have found in my experience that the way to break down an unreasonable custom, is to contradict it in practice. To be sure in pursuing this course I have had to contend not merely with the white race, but with the black. The one has condemned me for my presumption in daring to associate with it, and the other for pushing myself where it takes it for granted I am not wanted. I am pained to think that the latter objection springs largely from a consciousness of inferiority, for as colors alone can have nothing against each other, and the conditions of human association are founded upon character rather than color, and character depends upon mind and morals, there can be nothing blameworthy in people thus equal meeting each other on the plane of civil or social rights.

A series of important events followed soon after the second inauguration of Mr. Lincoln, conspicuous amongst which was the fall of Richmond. The strongest endeavor, and the best generalship of the Rebellion, was employed to hold that place, and when it fell, the pride, prestige, and power of the rebellion fell with it, never to rise again. The news of this great event found me again in Boston. The enthusiasm of that loyal city cannot be easily described. As usual when anything touches the great heart of Boston, Faneuil Hall became vocal and eloquent. This hall is an immense building, and its history is correspondingly great. It has been the theater of much patriotic declamation from the days of the 'Revolution,' and before; as it has since my day been the scene where the strongest efforts of the most popular orators of Massachusetts have been made. Here Webster, the great 'expounder,' addressed the 'sea of upturned faces.' Here Choate, the wonderful Boston barrister, by his weird, electric eloquence, enchained his thousands; here Everett charmed with his classic periods the flower of Boston aristocracy; and here, too, Charles Sumner, Horace Mann, John A. Andrew, and Wendell Phillips, the last equal to most, and superior to many, have for forty years spoken their great words of justice, liberty, and humanity, sometimes in the calm and sunshine of unruffled peace, but oftener in the tempest and whirlwind of mobocratic violence. It was here that Mr. Phillips made his famous speech in denunciation of the murder of Elijah P. Lovejoy* in 1837, which changed the whole current of his life, and made him pre-eminently the leader of anti-slavery thought in New England. Here, too, Theodore Parker, whose early death not only Boston, but the lovers of liberty throughout the world, still mourn, gave utterance to his deep and life-giving thoughts in words of fullness and powers. But I set out to speak of the meeting which was held there, in celebration of the fall of Richmond, for it was a meeting as remarkable for its composition as for its occasion. Among the speakers by whom it was addressed and who gave voice to the patriotic sentiments which filled and overflowed each loyal heart, were Hon. Henry Wilson,* and Hon. Robert C. Winthrop.* It would be difficult to find two public men more distinctly opposite than these. If any one may properly boast an aristocratic descent, or if there be any value or worth in that boast, Robert C. Winthrop may, without undue presumption, avail himself of it. He was born in the midst of wealth and luxury, and never felt the flint of hardship or the grip of poverty. Just the opposite to this was the experience of Henry Wilson. The son of common people, wealth and education had done little for him; but he had in him a true heart, and a world of common sense; and these, with industry, good habits, and perseverance, had carried him further and lifted him higher than the brilliant man with whom he formed such striking contrast. Winthrop, before the war, like many others of his class, had resisted the anti-slavery current of his state, had sided largely with the demands of the slave power, had abandoned many of his old Whig friends, when they went for free soil and free men in 1848, and gone into the Democratic party.

During the war he was too good to be a rebel sympathizer, and not quite good enough to become as Wilson was—a power in the union cause. Wilson had risen to eminence by his devotion to liberal ideas, while Winthrop had sunken almost to obscurity from his indifference to such ideas. But now either himself or his friends, most likely the latter, thought that the time had come when some word implying interest in the loyal cause should fall from his lips. It was not so much the need of the union, as the need of himself, that he should speak; the time when the union needed him, and all others, was when the slave-holding rebellion raised its defiant head, not when, as now, that head was in the dust and ashes of defeat and destruction. But the beloved Winthrop, the proud representative of what Daniel Webster once called the 'solid

men of Boston,' had great need to speak now. It had been no fault of the
loyal cause that he had not spoken sooner. Its 'gates, like those of
Heaven, stood open night and day.'* If he did not come in, it was his
own fault. Regiment after regiment, brigade after brigade, had passed
over Boston Common to endure the perils and hardships of war;
Governor Andrew had poured out his soul, had exhausted his wonderful powers of speech in patriotic words to the brave departing sons of
old Massachusetts, and a word from Winthrop would have gone far to
nerve up those young soldiers going forth to lay down their lives for the
life of the republic; but no word came. Yet now, in the last quarter of the
eleventh hour, when the day's work was nearly done, Robert C. Winthrop
was seen standing upon the same platform with the veteran Henry
Wilson. He was there in all his native grace and dignity, elegantly and
aristocratically clothed, his whole bearing marking his social sphere as
widely different from many present. Happily for his good name, and for
those who shall bear it when he is no longer among the living, that he
was found, even at the last hour, in the right place—in old Faneuil
Hall—side by side with plain Henry Wilson—the shoemaker senator.
But this was not the only contrast on that platform on that day. It was
my strange fortune to follow Mr. Winthrop on this interesting occasion. I remember him as the guest of John H. Clifford of New Bedford,
afterwards Governor of Massachusetts, when twenty-five years before,
I had been only a few months from slavery—I was behind his chair as
waiter, and was even then charmed by his elegant conversation—and
now, after this lapse of time, I found myself no longer behind the chair
of this princely man, but announced to succeed him in the order of
speakers, before that brilliant audience. I was not insensible to the contrast in our history and positions, and was curious to observe if it
affected him, and how. To his credit, I am happy to say he bore himself
grandly throughout. His speech was fully up to the enthusiasm of the
hour, and the great audience greeted his utterances with merited
applause. I need not speak of the speeches of Henry Wilson and others,
or of my own. The meeting was every way a remarkable expression of
popular feeling, created by a great and important event.

After the fall of Richmond the collapse of the rebellion was not long
delayed, though it did not perish without adding to its long list of atrocities one which sent a thrill of horror throughout the civilized world,
in the assassination of Abraham Lincoln; a man so amiable, so kind,
humane, and honest, that one is at a loss to know how he could have had
an enemy on earth. The details of his 'taking off' are too familiar to be
more than mentioned here. The recently-attempted assassination of

James Abraham Garfield* has made us all too painfully familiar with the shock and sensation produced by the hell-black crime to make any description necessary. The curious will note that the Christian name of both men is the same, and that both were remarkable for their kind qualities and for having risen by their own energies from among the people, and that both were victims of assassins at the beginning of a presidential term.

Mr. Lincoln had reason to look forward to a peaceful and happy term of office. To all appearance, we were on the eve of a restoration of the union and of a solid and lasting peace. He had served one term as President of the Disunited States, he was now for the first time to be President of the United States. Heavy had been his burden, hard had been his toil, bitter had been his trials, and terrible had been his anxiety; but the future seemed now bright and full of hope. Richmond had fallen, Grant had General Lee and the army of Virginia firmly in his clutch; Sherman had fought and found his way from the banks of the great river to the shores of the sea, leaving the two ends of the rebellion squirming and twisting in agony, like the severed parts of a serpent, doomed to inevitable death; and now there was but a little time longer for the good President to bear his burden, and be the target of reproach. His accusers, in whose opinion he was always too fast or too slow, too weak or too strong, too conciliatory or too aggressive, would soon become his admirers; it was soon to be seen that he had conducted the affairs of the nation with singular wisdom, and with absolute fidelity to the great trust confided in him. A country redeemed and regenerated from the foulest crime against human nature that ever saw the sun! What a bright vision of peace, prosperity, and happiness must have come to that tired and over-worked brain, and weary spirit. Men used to talk of his jokes, and he no doubt indulged in them; but I seemed never to have the faculty of calling them to the surface. I saw him oftener than many who have reported him, but I never saw any levity in him. He always impressed me as a strong, earnest man, having no time or disposition to trifle; grappling with all his might the work he had in hand. The expression of his face was a blending of suffering with patience and fortitude. Men called him homely, and homely he was; but it was manifestly a human homeliness, for there was nothing of the tiger or other wild animal about him. His eyes had in them the tenderness of motherhood, and his mouth and other features the highest perfection of a genuine manhood. His picture, by Marshall, now before me in my study, corresponds well with the impression I have of him. But, alas! what are all good and great qualities; what are human hopes and human happiness to the revengeful hand of an assassin? What are sweet dreams of peace; what are visions of the future? A simple leaden bullet and a few grains of powder are sufficient in the shortest limit of time to blast and ruin all that is precious in human existence, not alone of the murdered, but of the murderer. I write this in the deep gloom flung over my spirit by the cruel, wanton, and cold-blooded attempted assassination of Abraham Garfield, as well as that of Abraham Lincoln.

I was in Rochester, N. Y., where I then resided, when news of the death of Mr. Lincoln was received. Our citizens, not knowing what else to do in the agony of the hour, betook themselves to the city hall. Though all hearts ached for utterance, few felt like speaking. We were stunned and overwhelmed by a crime and calamity hitherto unknown to our country and our government. The hour was hardly one for speech, for no speech could rise to the level of feeling. Doctor Robinson, then of Rochester University, but now of Brown University, Providence, R. I., was prevailed upon to take the stand, and made one of the most touching and eloquent speeches I ever heard. At the close of his address, I was called upon, and spoke out of the fullness of my heart, and, happily, gave expression to so much of the soul of the people present that my voice was several times utterly silenced by the sympathetic tumult of the great audience. I had resided long in Rochester, and had made many speeches there which had more or less touched the hearts of my hearers, but never till this day was I brought into such close accord with them. We shared in common a terrible calamity, and this 'touch of nature made us'* more than countrymen, it made us 'kin.'[1]

[1] I sincerely regret that I have done Mr. Winthrop great injustice. This Faneuil Hall speech of his was not the first manifestation of his zealous interest in the loyal cause during the late war. While it is quite true that Mr. Winthrop was strongly against the anti-slavery movement at the North, his addresses and speeches delivered during the war, as they have come to my knowledge since writing the foregoing chapter, prove him to have been among the most earnest in his support of the National Government in its efforts to suppress the rebellion and to restore the Union.

FREDERICK DOUGLASS

# CHAPTER XIII.

## VAST CHANGES.

WHEN the war for the Union was substantially ended, and peace had dawned upon the land, as was the case almost immediately after the tragic death of President Lincoln; when the gigantic system of American slavery which had defied the march of time and resisted all the appeals and arguments of the abolitionists and the humane testimonies of good men of every generation during two hundred and fifty years, was finally abolished and forever prohibited by the organic law of the land,* a strange and, perhaps, perverse feeling came over me. My great and exceeding joy over these stupendous achievements, especially over the abolition of slavery (which had been the deepest desire and the great labor of my life), was slightly tinged with a feeling of sadness.

I felt that I had reached the end of the noblest and best part of my life; my school was broken up, my church disbanded, and the beloved congregation dispersed, never to come together again. The anti-slavery platform had performed its work, and my voice was no longer needed. 'Othello's occupation was gone.'* The great happiness of meeting with my fellow-workers was now to be among the things of memory. Then, too, some thought of my personal future came in. Like Daniel Webster, when asked by his friends to leave John Tyler's cabinet,* I naturally inquired: 'Where shall I go?' I was still in the midst of my years, and had something of life before me, and as the minister (urged by my old friend George Bradburn to preach anti-slavery, when to do so was unpopular) said, 'It is necessary for ministers to live,' I felt it was necessary for me to live, and to live honestly. But where should I go, and what should I do? I could not now take hold of life as I did when I first landed in New Bedford, twenty-five years before; I could not go to the wharf of either Gideon or George Howland, to Richmond's brass foundry, or Richetson's candle and oil works, load and unload vessels, or even ask

Governor Clifford for a place as a servant. Rolling oil-casks and shoveling coal were all well enough when I was younger, immediately after getting out of slavery. Doing this was a step up, rather than a step down; but all these avocations had had their day for me, and I had had my day for them. My public life and labors had unfitted me for the pursuits of my earlier years, and yet had not prepared me for more congenial and higher employment. Outside the question of slavery my thoughts had not been much directed, and I could hardly hope to make myself useful in any other cause than that to which I had given the best twenty-five years of my life. A man in the situation in which I found myself has not only to divest himself of the old, which is never easily done, but to adjust himself to the new, which is still more difficult. Delivering lectures under various names, John B. Gough says, 'Whatever may be the title, my lecture is always on Temperance'; and such is apt to be the case with any man who has devoted his time and thoughts to one subject for any considerable length of time. But what should I do, was the question. I had a few thousand dollars (a great convenience, and one not generally so highly prized by my people as it ought to be) saved from the sale of 'My Bondage and My Freedom,' and the proceeds of my lectures at home and abroad, and with this sum I thought of following the noble example of my old friends Stephen and Abby Kelley Foster, purchase a little farm and settle myself down to earn an honest living by tilling the soil. My children were grown and ought to be able to take care of themselves. This question, however, was soon decided for me. I had after all acquired (a very unusual thing) a little more knowledge and aptitude fitting me for the new condition of things than I knew, and had a deeper hold upon public attention than I had supposed. Invitations began to pour in upon me from colleges, lyceums, and literary societies, offering me one hundred, and even two hundred dollars for a single lecture.

I had, some time before, prepared a lecture on 'Self-made Men,' and also one upon Ethnology, with special reference to Africa. The latter had cost me much labor, though, as I now look back upon it, it was a very defective production. I wrote it at the instance of my friend Doctor M. B. Anderson, President of Rochester University, himself a distinguished ethnologist, a deep thinker and scholar. I had been invited by one of the literary societies of Western Reserve College (then at Hudson, but recently removed to Cleveland, Ohio), to address it on Commencement day; and never having spoken on such an occasion, never, indeed, having been myself inside of a school-house for the purpose of an education, I hesitated about accepting the invitation, and finally called upon Prof. Henry Wayland, son of the great Doctor Wayland of Brown University, and on Doctor Anderson, and asked their advice whether I ought to accept. Both gentlemen advised me to do so. They knew me, and evidently thought well of my ability. But the puzzling question now was, what shall I say if I do go there? It won't do to give them an old-fashioned anti-slavery discourse. (I learned afterwards that such a discourse was precisely what they needed, though not what they wished; for the faculty, including the President, was in great distress because I, a colored man, had been invited, and because of the reproach this circumstance might bring upon the College.) But what shall I talk about? became the difficult question. I finally hit upon the one before mentioned. I had read, with great interest, when in England a few years before, parts of Doctor Pritchard's 'Natural History of Man,'* a large volume marvelously calm and philosophical in its discussion of the science of the origin of the races, and was thus in the line of my then convictions. I at once sought in our bookstores for this valuable book, but could not obtain it anywhere in this country. I sent to England, where I paid the sum of seven and a half dollars for it. In addition to this valuable work President Anderson kindly gave me a little book entitled 'Man and His Migrations,' by Dr. R. G. Latham,* and loaned me the large work of Dr. Morton, the famous archæologist,* and that of Messrs. Nott and Glidden,* the latter written evidently to degrade the Negro and support the then-prevalent Calhoun doctrine of the rightfulness of slavery. With these books and occasional suggestions from Dr. Anderson and Prof. Wayland I set about preparing my commencement address. For many days and nights I toiled, and succeeded at last in getting something together in due form. Written orations had not been in my line. I had usually depended upon my unsystematized knowledge and the inspiration of the hour and the occasion, but I had now got the 'scholar bee in my bonnet,' and supposed that inasmuch as I was to speak to college professors and students I must at least make a show of some familiarity with letters. It proved as to its immediate effect, a great mistake, for my carefully-studied and written address, full of learned quotations, fell dead at my feet, while a few remarks I made extemporaneously at collation were enthusiastically received. Nevertheless, the reading and labor expended were of much value to me. They were needed steps preparatory to the work upon which I was about to enter. If they failed at the beginning, they helped to success in the end. My lecture on 'The Races of Men' was seldom called for, but that on 'Self-made Men'* was in great demand, especially through the West. I found that the success of a lecturer depends more upon the quality of his stock in store than the amount. My friend Wendell Phillips (for such I esteem him), who has said more cheering words to me and in vindication of my race than any man now living, has delivered his famous lecture on the 'Lost Arts' during the last forty years; and I doubt if among all his lectures, and he has many, there is one in such requisition as this. When Daniel O'Connell was asked why he did not make a new speech he playfully replied that 'it would take Ireland twenty years to learn his old ones.' Upon some such consideration as this I adhered pretty closely to my old lecture on 'Self-made Men,' retouching and shading it a little from time to time as occasion seemed to require.

Here, then, was a new vocation before me, full of advantages mentally and pecuniarily. When in the employment of the American Anti-Slavery Society my salary was about four hundred and fifty dollars a year, and I felt I was well paid for my services; but I could now make from fifty to a hundred dollars a night, and have the satisfaction, too, that I was in some small measure helping to lift my race into consideration, for no man who lives at all lives unto himself—he either helps or hinders all who are in any wise connected with him. I never rise to speak before an American audience without something of the feeling that my failure or success will bring blame or benefit to my whole race. But my activities were not now confined entirely to lectures before lyceums. Though slavery was abolished, the wrongs of my people were not ended. Though they were not slaves, they were not yet quite free. No man can be truly free whose liberty is dependent upon the thought, feeling, and action of others, and who has himself no means in his own hands for guarding, protecting, defending, and maintaining that liberty. Yet the Negro, after his emancipation, was precisely in this state of destitution. The law on the side of freedom is of great advantage only where there is power to make that law respected. I know no class of my fellow-men, however just, enlightened, and humane, which can be wisely and safely trusted absolutely with the liberties of any other class. Protestants are excellent people, but it would not be wise for Catholics to depend entirely upon them to look after their rights and interests. Catholics are a pretty good sort of people (though there is a soul-shuddering history behind them), yet no enlightened Protestants would commit their liberty to their care and keeping. And yet the government had left the freedmen in a worse condition than either of these. It felt that it had done enough for him. It had made him free, and henceforth he must make his own way in the world. Yet he had none of the conditions for self-preservation or self-protection. He was free from the individual master, but the slave of society. He had neither money, property, nor friends. He was free from the old plantation, but he had nothing but the dusty road under his feet. He was free from the old quarter that once gave him shelter, but a slave to the rains of summer and to the frosts of winter. He was, in a word, literally turned loose, naked, hungry, and destitute, to the open sky. The first feeling toward him by the old master classes was full of bitterness and wrath. They resented his emancipation as an act of hostility toward them, and, since they could not punish the emancipator, they felt like punishing the object which that act had emancipated. Hence they drove him off the old plantation, and told him he was no longer wanted there. They not only hated him because he had been freed as a punishment to them, but because they felt that they had been robbed of his labor. An element of greater bitterness still came into their hearts; the freedman had been the friend of the government, and many of his class had borne arms against them during the war. The thought of paying cash for labor that they could formerly extort by the lash did not in any wise improve their disposition to the emancipated slave, or improve his own condition. Now, since poverty has, and can have, no chance against wealth, the landless against the landowner, the ignorant against the intelligent, the freedman was powerless. He had nothing left him with which to fight the battle of life, but a slavery-distorted and diseased body and lame and twisted limbs. I therefore soon found that the Negro had still a cause, and that he needed my voice and pen with others to plead for it. The American Anti-Slavery Society under the lead of Mr. Garrison had disbanded, its newspapers were discontinued, its agents were withdrawn from the field, and all systematic efforts by abolitionists were abandoned. Many of the society, Mr. Phillips and myself amongst the number, differed from Mr. Garrison as to the wisdom of this course. I felt that the work of the society was not done and that it had not fulfilled its mission, which was, not merely to emancipate, but to elevate the enslaved class. But against Mr. Garrison's leadership, and the surprise and joy occasioned by the emancipation, it was impossible to keep the association alive, and the cause of the freedmen was left mainly to individual effort and to hastily-extemporized societies of an ephemeral character; brought together under benevolent impulse, but having no history behind them, and, being new to the work, they were not as effective for good as the old society would have been had it followed up its work and kept its old instrumentalities in operation.

From the first I saw no chance of bettering the condition of the freedman until he should cease to be merely a freedman and should become a citizen. I insisted that there was no safety for him or for any-body else in America outside the American government; that to guard, protect, and maintain his liberty the freedman should have the ballot; that the liberties of the American people were dependent upon the ballot-box, the jury-box, and the cartridge-box; that without these no class of people could live and flourish in this country; and this was now the word for the hour with me, and the word to which the people of the North willingly listened when I spoke. Hence, regarding as I did the elective franchise as the one great power by which all civil rights are obtained, enjoyed, and maintained under our form of government, and the one without which freedom to any class is delusive if not impos-sible, I set myself to work with whatever force and energy I possessed to secure this power for the recently-emancipated millions.

The demand for the ballot was such a vast advance upon the former objects proclaimed by the friends of the colored race, that it startled and struck men as preposterous and wholly inadmissible. Anti-slavery men themselves were not united as to the wisdom of such demand. Mr. Garrison himself, though foremost for the abolition of slavery, was not yet quite ready to join this advanced movement. In this respect he was in the rear of Mr. Phillips, who saw not only the justice, but the wisdom and necessity of the measure. To his credit it may be said, that he gave the full strength of his character and eloquence to its adoption. While Mr. Garrison thought it too much to ask, Mr. Phillips thought it too little. While the one thought it might be postponed to the future, the other thought it ought to be done at once. But Mr. Garrison was not a man to lag far in the rear of truth and right, and he soon came to see with the rest of us that the ballot was essential to the freedom of the freedman. A man's head will not long remain wrong, when his heart is right. The applause awarded to Mr. Garrison by the conservatives, for his moderation both in respect of his views on this question, and the disbandment of the American Anti-Slavery Society must have dis-turbed him. He was at any rate soon found on the right side of the suffrage question.

The enfranchisement of the freedmen was resisted on many grounds, but mainly on these two: first, the tendency of the measure to bring the freedmen into conflict with the old master-class and the white people of the South generally; secondly, their unfitness, by reason of their ignor-ance, servility and degradation, to exercise over the destinies of this great nation so great a power as the ballot.

These reasons against the measure which were supposed to be unanswerable, were in some sense the most powerful arguments in its favor. The argument that the possession of suffrage would be likely to bring the negro into conflict with the old master-class at the South, had its main force in the admission that the interests of the two classes antagonized each other and that the maintenance of the one would prove inimical to the other. It resolved itself into this, that, if the negro had the means of protecting his civil rights, those who had formerly denied him these rights would be offended and make war upon him. Experience has shown in a measure the correctness of this position. The old master was offended to find the negro whom he lately possessed the right to enslave and flog to toil, casting a ballot equal to his own, and resorted to all sorts of meanness, violence, and crime, to dispossess him of the enjoyment of this point of equality. In this respect the exercise of the right of suffrage by the negro has been attended with the evil, which the opponents of the measure predicted, and they could say 'I've told you so,' but immeasurably and intolerably greater would have been the evil consequences resulting from the denial to one class of this natural means of protection, and granting it to the other, and hostile class. It would have been, to have committed the lamb to the care of the wolf—the arming of one class and disarming the other—protecting one interest, and destroying the other, making the rich strong, and the poor weak—the white man a tyrant, and the black man a slave. The very fact therefore that the old master-classes of the South felt that their interests were opposed to those of the freedmen, instead of being a reason against their enfranchisement, was the most powerful one in its favor. Until it shall be safe to leave the lamb in the hold of the lion, the laborer in the power of the capitalist, the poor in the hands of the rich, it will not be safe to leave a newly emancipated people completely in the power of their former masters, especially when such masters have not ceased to be such from enlightened moral convictions but by irresistible force. Then on the part of the government itself, had it denied this great right to the freedmen, it would have been another proof that 'Republics are ungrateful.' It would have been rewarding its enemies, and punishing its friends—embracing its foes, and spurning its allies,—setting a premium on treason, and degrading loyalty. As to the second point, viz.: the negro's ignorance and degradation, there was no disputing either. It was the nature of slavery, from whose depths he had arisen, to make him so, and it would have kept him so. It was the policy of the system to keep him both ignorant and degraded, the better and more safely to defraud him of his hard earnings. This argument never staggered me. The ballot in the hands of the negro was necessary to open the door of the school-house and to unlock to him the treasures of its knowledge. Granting all that was said of his ignorance, I used to say, 'if the negro knows enough to fight for his country he knows enough to vote; if he knows enough to pay taxes for the support of the government, he knows enough to vote; if he knows as much when sober, as an Irishman knows when drunk, he knows enough to vote.'

And now while I am not blind to the evils which have thus far attended the enfranchisement of the colored people, I hold that the evils from which we escaped, and the good we have derived from that act, amply vindicate its wisdom. The evils it brought are in their nature temporary, and the good is permanent. The one is comparatively small, the other absolutely great. The young child has staggered on his little legs, and he has sometimes fallen and hurt his head in the fall, but then he has learned to walk. The boy in the water came near drowning, but then he has learned to swim. Great changes in the relations of mankind can never come, without evils analogous to those which have attended the emancipation and enfranchisement of the colored people of the United States. I am less amazed at these evils, than by the rapidity with which they are subsiding, and not more astonished at the facility with which the former slave has become a free man, than at the rapid adjustment of the master-class to the new situation.

Unlike the movement for the abolition of slavery, the success of the effort for the enfranchisement of the freedmen was not long delayed. It is another illustration of how any advance in pursuance of a right principle prepares and makes easy the way to another. The way of transgression is a bottomless pit, one step in that direction invites the next, and the end is never reached; and it is the same with the path of righteous obedience. Two hundred years ago, the pious Doctor Godwin dared affirm that it was 'not a sin to baptize a negro,'* and won for him the rite of baptism. It was a small concession to his manhood; but it was strongly resisted by the slave-holders of Jamaica and Virginia. In this they were logical in their argument, but they were not logical in their object. They saw plainly that to concede the negro's right to baptism was to receive him into the Christian Church, and make him a brother in Christ; and hence they opposed the first step sternly and bitterly. So long as they could keep him beyond the circle of human brotherhood, they could scourge him to toil, as a beast of burden, with a good Christian conscience, and without reproach. 'What!' said they, 'baptize a negro? preposterous!' Nevertheless the negro was baptized and admitted to church fellowship; and though for a long time his soul belonged to God, his body to his master, and he, poor fellow, had nothing left for himself, he is at last not only baptized, but emancipated and enfranchised.

In this achievement, an interview with President Andrew Johnson, on the 7th of February, 1866, by a delegation consisting of George T. Downing, Lewis H. Douglass, Wm. E. Matthews, John Jones, John F. Cook, Joseph E. Otis, A. W. Ross, William Whipper, John M. Brown, Alexander Dunlop, and myself, will take its place in history as one of the first steps. What was said on that occasion brought the whole question virtually before the American people. Until that interview the country was not fully aware of the intentions and policy of President Johnson on the subject of reconstruction, especially in respect of the newly emancipated class of the South. After having heard the brief addresses made to him by Mr. Downing and myself, he occupied at least three-quarters of an hour in what seemed a set speech, and refused to listen to any reply on our part, although solicited to grant a few moments for that purpose. Seeing the advantage that Mr. Johnson would have over us in getting his speech paraded before the country in the morning papers, the members of the delegation met on the evening of that day, and instructed me to prepare a brief reply, which should go out to the country simultaneously with the President's speech to us. Since this reply indicates the points of difference between the President and ourselves, I produce it here as a part of the history of the times, it being concurred in by all the members of the delegation.

Both the speech and the reply were commented upon very extensively.

MR. PRESIDENT: In consideration of a delicate sense of propriety as well as of your own repeated intimations of indisposition to discuss or listen to a reply to the views and opinions you were pleased to express to us in your elaborate speech to-day, the undersigned would respectfully take this method of replying thereto. Believing as we do that the views and opinions you expressed in that address are entirely unsound and prejudicial to the highest interests of our race as well as to our country at large, we cannot do other than expose the same and, as far as may be in our power, arrest their dangerous influence. It is not necessary at this time to call attention to more than two or three features of your remarkable address:

1. The first point to which we feel especially bound to take exception, is your attempt to found a policy opposed to our enfranchisement, upon the alleged ground of an existing hostility on the part of the former slaves toward the poor white people of the South. We admit the existence of this hostility, and hold that it is entirely reciprocal. But you obviously commit an error by drawing an argument from an incident of slavery, and making it a basis for a policy adapted to a state of freedom. The hostility between the whites and blacks of the South is easily explained. It has its root and sap in the relation of slavery, and was incited on both sides by the cunning of the slave masters. Those masters secured their ascendency over both the poor whites and blacks by putting enmity between them.

They divided both to conquer each. There was no earthly reason why the blacks should not hate and dread the poor whites when in a state of slavery, for it was from this class that their masters received their slave catchers, slave drivers, and overseers. They were the men called in upon all occasions by the masters whenever any fiendish outrage was to be committed upon the slave. Now, sir, you cannot but perceive, that the cause of this hatred removed, the effect must be removed also. Slavery is abolished. The cause of this antagonism is removed, and you must see that it is altogether illogical (and 'putting new wine into old bottles') to legislate from slaveholding and slave-driving premises for a people whom you have repeatedly declared it your purpose to maintain in freedom.

2. Besides, even if it were true, as you allege, that the hostility of the blacks toward the poor whites must necessarily project itself into a state of freedom, and that this enmity between the two races is even more intense in a state of freedom than in a state of slavery, in the name of heaven, we reverently ask how can you, in view of your professed desire to promote the welfare of the black man, deprive him of all means of defence, and clothe him whom you regard as his enemy in the panoply of political power? Can it be that you recommend a policy which would arm the strong and cast down the defenceless? Can you, by any possibility of reasoning, regard this as just, fair, or wise? Experience proves that those are most abused who can be abused with the greatest impunity. Men are whipped oftenest who are whipped easiest. Peace between races is not to be secured by degrading one race and exalting another; by giving power to one race and withholding it from another; but by maintaining a state of equal justice between all classes. First pure, then peaceable.

3. On the colonization theory you were pleased to broach, very much could be said. It is impossible to suppose, in view of the usefulness of the black man in time of peace as a laborer in the South, and in time of war as a soldier at the North, and the growing respect for his rights among the people and his increasing adaptation to a high state of civilization in his native land, that there can ever come a time when he can be removed from this country without a terrible shock to its prosperity and peace. Besides, the worst enemy of the nation could not cast upon its fair name a greater infamy than to admit that negroes could be tolerated among them in a state of the most degrading slavery and oppression, and must be cast away, driven into exile, for no other cause than having been freed from their chains.

WASHINGTON, February 7, 1866.

From this time onward the question of suffrage for the freedmen was not allowed to rest. The rapidity with which it gained strength was something quite marvelous and surprising even to its advocates. Senator Charles Sumner soon took up the subject in the Senate, and treated it in his usually able and exhaustive manner. It was a great treat to listen to his argument running through two days, abounding as it did in eloquence, learning, and conclusive reasoning. A committee of the Senate had reported a proposition giving to the States lately in rebellion, in so many words, complete option as to the enfranchisement of their colored citizens; only coupling with that proposition the condition that, to such States as chose to enfranchise such citizens, the basis of their representation in Congress should be proportionately increased; or, in other words, that only three-fifths of the colored citizens should be counted in the basis of representation in States where colored citizens were not allowed to vote, while in the States granting suffrage to colored citizens, the entire colored people should be counted in the basis of representation. Against this proposition myself and associates addressed to the Senate of the United States the following memorial:

'To the Honorable the Senate of the United States:

'The undersigned, being a delegation representing the colored people of the several States, and now sojourning in Washington, charged with the duty to look after the best interests of the recently emancipated, would most respectfully, but earnestly, pray your honorable body to favor no amendment of the Constitution of the United States which will grant any one or all of the States of this Union to disfranchise any class of citizens on the ground of race or color, for any consideration whatever. They would further respectfully represent that the Constitution as adopted by the fathers of the Republic in 1789, evidently contemplated the result which has now happened, to wit, the abolition of slavery. The men who framed it, and those who adopted it, framed and adopted it for the people, and the whole people—colored men being at that time legal voters in most of the States. In that instrument, as it now stands, there is not a sentence or a syllable conveying any shadow of right or authority by which any State may make color or race a disqualification for the exercise of the right of suffrage; and the undersigned will regard as a real calamity the introduction of any words, expressly or by implication, giving any State or States such power; and we respectfully submit that if the amendment now pending before your honorable body shall be adopted, it will enable any State to deprive any class of citizens of the elective franchise, notwithstanding it was obviously framed with a view to affect the question of negro suffrage only.

'For these and other reasons the undersigned respectfully pray that the amendment to the Constitution, recently passed by the House and now before your body, be not adopted. And as in duty bound, etc.'

It was the opinion of Senator Wm. Pitt Fessenden, Senator Henry Wilson, and many others, that the measure here memorialized against would, if incorporated into the Constitution, certainly bring about the enfranchisement of the whole colored population of the South. It was held by them to be an inducement to the States to make suffrage universal, since the basis of representation would be enlarged or contracted according as suffrage should be extended or limited; but the judgment of these leaders was not the judgment of Senator Sumner, Senators Wade, Yates, Howe and others, or of the colored people. Yet, weak as this measure was, it encountered the united opposition of democratic senators. On that side the Hon. Thomas H. Hendricks,* of Indiana, took the lead in appealing to popular prejudice against the negro. He contended that among other objectionable and insufferable results that would flow from its adoption, would be, that a negro would ultimately be a member of the United States Senate. I never shall forget the ineffable scorn and indignation with which Mr. Hendricks deplored the possibility of such an event. In less, however, than a decade from that debate, Senators Revels and Bruce,* both colored men, had fulfilled the startling prophecy of the Indiana senator. It was not, however, by the half-way measure, which he was opposing for its radicalism, but by the fourteenth and fifteenth amendments, that these gentlemen reached their honorable positions.

In defeating the option proposed to be given to the States to extend or deny suffrage to their colored population, much credit is due to the delegation already named as visiting President Johnson. That delegation made it their business to personally see and urge upon leading republican statesmen the wisdom and duty of impartial suffrage. Day after day Mr. Downing and myself saw and conversed with those members of the Senate whose advocacy of suffrage would be likely to insure its success.

The second marked step in effecting the enfranchisement of the negro was made at the 'National Loyalist's Convention,' held at Philadelphia, in September, 1866. This body was composed of delegates from the South, North, and West. Its object was to diffuse clear views of the situation of affairs at the South and to indicate the principles by it deemed advisable to be observed in the reconstruction of society in the Southern States.

This convention was, as its history shows, numerously attended by the ablest and most influential men from all sections of the country, and its deliberations participated in by them.

The policy foreshadowed by Andrew Johnson (who, by the grace of the assassin's bullet, was then in Abraham Lincoln's seat)—a policy based upon the idea that the rebel States were never out of the Union, and hence had forfeited no rights which his pardon could not restore—gave importance to this convention, more than anything which was then occurring at the South; for through the treachery of this bold, bad man, we seemed then about to lose nearly all that had been gained by the war.

I was at the time residing in Rochester and was duly elected as a delegate from that city to attend this convention. The honor was a surprise and a gratification to me. It was unprecedented for a city of over sixty thousand white citizens and only about two hundred colored residents, to elect a colored man to represent them in a national political convention, and the announcement of it gave a shock of no inconsiderable violence to the country. Many Republicans, with every respect for me personally, were unable to see the wisdom of such a course. They dreaded the clamor of social equality and amalgamation which would be raised against the party, in consequence of this startling innovation. They, dear fellows, found it much more agreeable to talk of the principles of liberty as glittering generalities, than to reduce those principles to practice.

When the train on which I was going to the convention reached Harrisburg, it met and was attached to another from the West crowded with Western and Southern delegates on the way to the convention, and among them were several loyal Governors, chief among whom was the loyal Governor of Indiana, Oliver P. Morton,* a man of Websterian mould in all that appertained to mental power. When my presence became known to these gentlemen, a consultation was immediately held among them, upon the question as to what was best to do with me. It seems strange now, in view of all the progress which had been made, that such a question could arise. But the circumstances of the times made me the Jonah of the Republican ship, and responsible for the contrary winds and misbehaving weather. Before we reached Lancaster, on our eastward bound trip, I was duly waited upon by a committee of my brother delegates, which had been appointed by other honorable delegates, to represent to me the undesirableness of my attendance upon the National Loyalist's Convention. The spokesman of these sub-delegates was a gentleman from New Orleans with a very French name, which has now escaped me, but which I wish I could recall, that I might credit him with a high degree of politeness and the gift of eloquence. He began by telling me that he knew my history and my works, and that he entertained a very high respect for me, that both himself and the gentlemen who sent him, as well as those who accompanied him, regarded me with admiration; that there was not among them the remotest objection to sitting in the convention with me, but their personal wishes in the matter they felt should be set aside for the sake of our common cause; that whether I should or should not go into the convention was purely a matter of expediency; that I must know that there was a very strong and bitter prejudice against my race in the North as well as at the South; and that the cry of social and political equality would not fail to be raised against the Republican party if

I should attend this loyal national convention. He insisted that it was a time for the sacrifice of my own personal feeling, for the good of the Republican cause; that there were several districts in the State of Indiana so evenly balanced that a very slight circumstance would be likely to turn the scale against us, and defeat our Congressional candidates, and thus leave Congress without a two-thirds vote to control the headstrong and treacherous man then in the presidential chair. It was urged that this was a terrible responsibility for me or any other man to take.

I listened very attentively to this address, uttering no word during its delivery; but when it was finished, I said to the speaker and the committee, with all the emphasis I could throw into my voice and manner: 'Gentlemen, with all respect, you might as well ask me to put a loaded pistol to my head and blow my brains out, as to ask me to keep out of this convention, to which I have been duly elected. Then, gentlemen, what would you gain by this exclusion? Would not the charge of cowardice, certain to be brought against you, prove more damaging than that of amalgamation? Would you not be branded all over the land as dastardly hypocrites, professing principles which you have no wish or intention of carrying out? As a matter of policy or expediency, you will be wise to let me in. Everybody knows that I have been duly elected by the city of Rochester as a delegate. The fact has been broadly announced and commented upon all over the country. If I am not admitted, the public will ask, 'Where is Douglass? Why is he not seen in the convention?' and you would find that enquiry more difficult to answer than any charge brought against you for favoring political or social equality; but, ignoring the question of policy altogether, and looking at it as one of right and wrong, I am bound to go into that convention; not to do so, would contradict the principle and practice of my life.' With this answer, the committee retired from the car in which I was seated, and did not again approach me on the subject; but I saw plainly enough then, as well as on the morning when the loyalist procession was to march through the streets of Philadelphia, that while I was not to be formally excluded, I was to be ignored by the Convention.

I was the ugly and deformed child of the family, and to be kept out of sight as much as possible while there was company in the house. Especially was it the purpose to offer me no inducement to be present in the ranks of the procession of its members and friends, which was to start from Independence Hall on the first morning of its meeting.

In good season, however, I was present at this grand starting point. My reception there confirmed my impression as to the policy intended to be pursued towards me. Few of the many I knew were prepared to give me a cordial recognition, and among these few I may mention Gen. Benj. F. Butler, who, whatever others may say of him, has always shown a courage equal to his convictions. Almost everybody else on the ground whom I met seemed to be ashamed or afraid of me. On the previous night I had been warned that I should not be allowed to walk through the city in the procession; fears had been expressed that my presence in it would so shock the prejudices of the people of Philadelphia, as to cause the procession to be mobbed.

The members of the convention were to walk two abreast, and as I was the only colored member of the convention, the question was, as to who of my brother members would consent to walk with me? The answer was not long in coming. There was *one man* present who was broad enough to take in the whole situation, and brave enough to meet the duty of the hour; one who was neither afraid nor ashamed to own me as a man and a brother; one man of the purest Caucasian type, a poet and a scholar, brilliant as a writer, eloquent as a speaker, and holding a high and influential position—the editor of a weekly journal having the largest circulation of any weekly paper in the city or State of New York—and that man was *Mr. Theodore Tilton.** He came to me in my isolation, seized me by the hand in a most brotherly way, and pro-posed to walk with me in the procession.

I have in my life been in many awkward and disagreeable positions when the presence of a friend would have been highly valued, but I think I never appreciated an act of courage and generous sentiment more highly than I did that of this brave young man when we marched through the streets of Philadelphia on this memorable day.

Well! what came of all these dark forebodings of timid men? How was my presence regarded by the populace? and what effect did it pro-duce? I will tell you. The fears of the loyal governors who wished me excluded to propitiate the favor of the crowd, met with a signal reproof. Their apprehensions were shown to be groundless, and they were com-pelled, as many of them confessed to me afterwards, to own themselves entirely mistaken. The people were more enlightened and had made more progress than their leaders had supposed. An act for which those leaders expected to be pelted with stones, only brought to them unmeasured applause. Along the whole line of march my presence was cheered repeatedly and enthusiastically. I was myself utterly surprised by the heartiness and unanimity of the popular approval. We were marching through a city remarkable for the depth and bitterness of its hatred of the abolition movement; a city whose populace had mobbed

anti-slavery meetings, burned temperance halls and churches owned
by colored people and burned down Pennsylvania Hall because it had
opened its doors upon terms of equality to people of different colors.
But now the children of those who had committed these outrages and
follies were applauding the very principles which their fathers had condemned. After the demonstrations of this first day, I found myself
a welcome member of the convention, and cordial greeting took the
place of cold aversion. The victory was short, signal, and complete.

During the passage of the procession, as we were marching through
Chestnut street, an incident occurred which excited some interest in
the crowd, and was noticed by the press at the time, and may perhaps
be properly related here as a part of the story of my eventful life. It was
my meeting Mrs. Amanda Sears,* the daughter of my old mistress,
Miss Lucretia Auld, the same Lucretia to whom I was indebted for so
many acts of kindness when under the rough treatment of Aunt Katy,
at the 'old plantation home' of Col. Edward Lloyd. Mrs. Sears now
resided in Baltimore, and as I saw her on the corner of Ninth and
Chestnut streets, I hastily ran to her, and expressed my surprise and joy
at meeting her. 'But what brought you to Philadelphia at this time?'
I asked. She replied, with animated voice and countenance, 'I heard you
were to be here, and I came to see you walk in this procession.' The dear
lady, with her two children, had been following us for hours. Here was
the daughter of the owner of a slave, following with enthusiasm that
slave as a free man, and listening with joy to the plaudits he received as
he marched along through the crowded streets of the great city. And
here I may relate another circumstance which should have found place
earlier in this story, which will further explain the feeling subsisting
between Mrs. Sears and myself.

Seven years prior to our meeting, as just described, I delivered a lecture in National Hall, Philadelphia, and at its close a gentleman
approached me and said, 'Mr. Douglass, do you know that your once
mistress has been listening to you to-night?' I replied that I did not, nor
was I inclined to believe it. I had four or five times before had a similar
statement made to me by different individuals in different States and
this made me skeptical in this instance. The next morning, however,
I received from a Mr. Wm. Needles a very elegantly written note, which
stated that she who was Amanda Auld, daughter of Thomas and
Lucretia Auld, and grand daughter to my old master, Capt. Aaron
Anthony, was now married to Mr. John L. Sears, a coal merchant in
West Philadelphia. The street and number of Mr. Sears's office was
given, so that I might, by seeing him, assure myself of the facts in the

case, and perhaps learn something of the relatives whom I left in slavery. This note, with the intimation given me the night before, convinced me there was something in it, and I resolved to know the truth. I had now been out of slavery twenty years, and no word had come to me from my sisters, or my brother Perry, or my grandmother. My separation had been as complete as if I had been an inhabitant of another planet. A law of Maryland at that time visited with heavy fine and imprisonment any colored person who should come into the State; so I could not go to them any more than they could come to me.

Eager to know if my kinsfolk still lived, and what was their condition, I made my way to the office of Mr. Sears, found him in, and handed him the note I had received from Mr. Needles, and asked him to be so kind as to read it and to tell me if the facts were as there stated. After reading the note, he said it was true but he must decline any conversation with me, since not to do so would be a sacrifice to the feelings of his father-in-law. I deeply regretted his decision, spoke of my long separation from my relations and appealed to him to give me some information concerning them. I saw that my words were not without their effect. Presently he said, 'You publish a newspaper, I believe?' 'I do,' I said, 'but if that is your objection to speaking with me, no word of our conversation shall go into its columns.' To make a long story short, we had then quite a long conversation, during which Mr. Sears said that in my 'Narrative' I had done his father-in-law injustice, for he was really a kind-hearted man, and a good master. I replied that there must be two sides to the relation of master and slave, and what was deemed kind and just to the one was the opposite to the other. Mr. Sears was not disposed to be unreasonable and the longer we talked the nearer we came together. I finally asked permission to see Mrs. Sears, the little girl of seven or eight years when I left the eastern shore of Maryland. This request was at first a little too much for him, and he put me off by saying that she was a mere child when I last saw her and that she was now the mother of a large family of children and I would not know her. He, as well as she, could tell me everything about my people. I pressed my suit, however, insisting that I could select Miss Amanda out of a thousand other ladies, my recollection of her was so perfect, and begged him to test my memory at this point. After much parley of this nature, he at length consented to my wishes, giving me the number of his house and name of street, with permission to call at three o'clock P. M. on the next day. I left him, delighted, and prompt to the hour was ready for my visit. I dressed myself in my best, and hired the finest carriage I could get to take me, partly because of the distance, and partly to make the contrast between the slave and the free man as striking as possible. Mr. Sears had been equally thoughtful. He had invited to his house a number of friends to witness the meeting between Mrs. Sears and myself.

I was somewhat disconcerted when I was ushered into the large parlors occupied by about thirty ladies and gentlemen, to all of whom I was a perfect stranger. I saw the design to test my memory by making it difficult for me to guess who of the company was 'Miss Amanda.' In her girlhood she was small and slender, and hence a thin and delicately-formed lady was seated in a rocking-chair near the center of the room with a little girl by her side. The device was good, but it did not succeed. Glancing around the room, I saw in an instant the lady who was a child twenty-five years before, and the wife and mother now. Satisfied of this, I said, 'Mr. Sears, if you will allow me, I will select Miss Amanda from this company.' I started towards her, and she, seeing that I recognized her, bounded to me with joy in every feature, and expressed her great happiness at seeing me. All thought of slavery, color, or what might seem to belong to the dignity of her position vanished, and the meeting was as the meeting of friends long separated, yet still present in each other's memory and affection.

Amanda made haste to tell me that she agreed with me about slavery, and that she had freed all her slaves as they had become of age. She brought her children to me, and I took them in my arms, with sensations which I could not if I would stop here to describe. One explanation of the feeling of this lady towards me was, that her mother, who died when she was yet a tender child, had been briefly described by me in a little 'Narrative of my life,' published many years before our meeting, and when I could have had no motive but the highest for what I said of her. She had read my story and had through me learned something of the amiable qualities of her mother. She also recollected that as I had had trials as a slave she had had her trials under the care of a step-mother, and that when she was harshly spoken to by her father's second wife she could always read in my dark face the sympathy of one who had often received kind words from the lips of her beloved mother. Mrs. Sears died three years ago in Baltimore, but she did not depart without calling me to her bedside, that I might tell her as much as I could about her mother, whom she was firm in the faith that she should meet in another and better world. She especially wished me to describe to her the personal appearance of her mother, and desired to know if any of her own children then present resembled her. I told her that the young lady standing in the corner of the room was the image of her mother in form and features. She looked at her daughter and said,

'Her name is Lucretia—after my mother.' After telling me that her life had been a happy one, and thanking me for coming to see her on her death-bed, she said she was ready to die. We parted to meet no more in life. The interview touched me deeply, and was, I could not help thinking, a strange one—another proof that 'truth is often stranger than fiction.'

If any reader of this part of my life shall see in it the evidence of a want of manly resentment for wrongs inflicted by slavery upon myself and race, and by the ancestors of this lady, so it must be. No man can be stronger than nature, one touch of which, we are told, makes all the world akin. I esteem myself a good, persistent hater of injustice and oppression, but my resentment ceases when they cease, and I have no heart to visit upon children the sins of their fathers.

It will be noticed that when I first met Mr. Sears in Philadelphia he declined to talk with me, on the ground that I had been unjust to Captain Auld, his father-in-law. Soon after that meeting Captain Auld had occasion to go to Philadelphia, and, as usual, went straight to the house of his son-in-law. He had hardly finished the ordinary salutations when he said: 'Sears, I see by the papers that Frederick has recently been in Philadelphia. Did you go to hear him?' 'Yes, sir,' was the reply. After asking something about my lecture he said, 'Well, Sears, did Frederick come to see you?' 'Yes, sir,' said Sears. 'Well, how did you receive him?' Mr. Sears then told him all about my visit, and had the satisfaction of hearing the old man say that he had done right in giving me welcome to his house. This last fact I have from Rev. J. D. Long, who, with his wife, was one of the party invited to meet me at the house of Mr. Sears on the occasion of my visit to Mrs. Sears.

But I must now return from this digression and further relate my experience in the loyalist national convention, and how, from that time, there was an impetus given to the enfranchisement of the freedmen which culminated in the fifteenth amendment to the Constitution of the United States. From the first the members of the convention were divided in their views of the proper measures of reconstruction, and this division was in some sense sectional. The men from the far South, strangely enough, were quite radical, while those from the border States were mostly conservative, and unhappily, these last had from the first the control of the convention. A Kentucky gentleman was made president. Its other officers were for the most part Kentuckians and all were in sentiment opposed to colored suffrage. There was a 'whole heap' (to use a Kentucky phrase) of 'halfness' in that State during the war for the Union, and there was much more there after the war. The

Maryland delegates, with the exception of Hon. John L. Thomas, were in sympathy with Kentucky. Those from Virginia, except Hon. John Minor Botts, were unwilling to entertain the question. The result was that the convention was broken square in two. The Kentucky president declared it adjourned, and left the chair, against the earnest protests of the friends of manhood suffrage.

But the friends of this measure were not to be out-generaled and suppressed in this way, and instantly reorganized, elected Hon. John M. Botts of Virginia president, discussed and passed resolutions in favor of enfranchising the freedmen, and thus placed the question before the country in such a manner that it could not be ignored. The delegates from the Southern States were quite in earnest, and bore themselves grandly in support of the measure; but the chief speakers and advocates of suffrage on that occasion were Mr. Theodore Tilton and Miss Anna E. Dickinson. Of course, on such a question, I could not be expected to be silent. I was called forward and responded with all the energy of my soul, for I looked upon suffrage to the Negro as the only measure which could prevent him from being thrust back into slavery.

From this time onward the question of suffrage had no rest. The rapidity with which it gained strength was more than surprising to me.

In addition to the justice of the measure, it was soon commended by events, as a political necessity. As in the case of the abolition of slavery, the white people of the rebellious States have themselves to thank for its adoption. Had they accepted with moderate grace the decision of the court to which they appealed, and the liberal conditions of peace offered to them, and united heartily with the national government in its efforts to reconstruct their shattered institutions, instead of sullenly refusing as they did their counsel and their votes to that end, they might easily have defeated the argument based upon the necessity for the measure. As it was, the question was speedily taken out of the hands of colored delegations and mere individual efforts and became a part of the policy of the Republican party, and President U. S. Grant, with his characteristic nerve and clear perception of justice, promptly recommended the great amendment to the Constitution* by which colored men are to-day invested with complete citizenship—the right to vote and to be voted for in the American Republic.

# CHAPTER XIV.

## LIVING AND LEARNING.

*Inducements to a political career—Objections—A newspaper enter-
prise—The new National Era—Its abandonment—The Freedmen's
Savings and Trust Company—Sad experience—Vindication.*

THE adoption of the fourteenth and fifteenth amendments and their
incorporation into the Constitution of the United States opened a very
tempting field to my ambition, and one to which I should probably have
yielded had I been a younger man. I was earnestly urged by many of my
respected fellow-citizens, both colored and white, and from all sections
of the country, to take up my abode in some one of the many districts of
the South where there was a large colored vote and get myself elected,
as they were sure I easily could do, to a seat in Congress—possibly in
the Senate. That I did not yield to this temptation was not entirely due
to my age, for the idea did not square well with my better judgment and
sense of propriety. The thought of going to live among a people in order
to gain their votes and acquire official honors was repugnant to my self-
respect, and I had not lived long enough in the political atmosphere of
Washington to have this sentiment sufficiently blunted to make me
indifferent to its suggestions. I do not deny that the arguments of my
friends had some weight in them, and from their standpoint it was all
right; but I was better known to myself than to them. I had small faith
in my aptitude as a politician, and could not hope to cope with rival
aspirants. My life and labors in the North had in a measure unfitted me
for such work, and I could not have readily adapted myself to the peculiar oratory found to be most effective with the newly-enfranchised
class. In the New England and Northern atmosphere I had acquired
a style of speaking which in the South would have been considered
tame and spiritless, and consequently he who 'could tear a passion to
tatters and split the ear of groundlings'* had far better chance of success with the masses there than one so little boisterous as myself.

Upon the whole I have never regretted that I did not enter the arena
of Congressional honors to which I was invited.

Outside of mere personal considerations I saw, or thought I saw, that
in the nature of the case the sceptre of power had passed from the old
slave and rebellious States to the free and loyal States, and that hereafter, at least for some time to come, the loyal North, with its advanced
civilization, must dictate the policy and control the destiny of the

republic. I had an audience ready-made in the free States; one which the labors of thirty years had prepared for me, and before this audience the freedmen of the South needed an advocate as much as they needed a member of Congress. I think in this I was right; for thus far our colored members of Congress have not largely made themselves felt in the legislation of the country; and I have little reason to think I could have done any better than they.

I was not, however, to remain long in my retired home in Rochester, where I had planted my trees and was reposing under their shadows. An effort was being made about this time to establish a large weekly news-paper* in the city of Washington, which should be devoted to the defence and enlightenment of the newly-emancipated and enfranchised people; and I was urged by such men as George T. Downing, J. H. Hawes, J. Sella Martin, and others, to become its editor-in-chief. My sixteen years' experience as editor and publisher of my own paper, and the knowledge of the toil and anxiety which such a relation to a public jour-nal must impose, caused me much reluctance and hesitation; neverthe-less, I yielded to the wishes of my friends and counsellors, went to Washington, threw myself into the work, hoping to be able to lift up a standard at the national capital for my people which should cheer and strengthen them in the work of their own improvement and elevation.

I was not long connected with this enterprise before I discovered my mistake. The coöperation so liberally promised, and the support which had been assured, were not very largely realized. By a series of circum-stances, a little bewildering as I now look back upon them, I found myself alone, under the mental and pecuniary burden involved in the prosecution of the enterprise. I had been misled by loud talk of a grand incorporated publishing company, in which I should have shares if I wished, and in any case a fixed salary for my services; and after all these fair-seeming conditions I had not been connected with the paper one year before its affairs had been so managed by the agent appointed by this invisible company, or corporate body, as to compel me to bear the burden alone, and to become the sole owner of the printing estab-lishment. Having become publicly associated with the enterprise, I was unwilling to have it prove a failure, and had allowed it to become in debt to me, both for money loaned and for services, and at last it seemed wise that I should purchase the whole concern, which I did, and turned it over to my sons Lewis and Frederic, who were practical printers, and who, after a few years, were compelled to discontinue its publication. This paper was the *New National Era*,* to the columns of which the colored people are indebted for some of the best things ever uttered in behalf of their cause; for, aside from its editorials and selections, many of the ablest colored men of the country made it the medium through which to convey their thoughts to the public. A misadventure though it was, which cost me from nine to ten thousand dollars, over it I have no tears to shed. The journal was valuable while it lasted, and the experiment was to me full of instruction, which has to some extent been heeded, for I have kept well out of newspaper undertakings since.

Some one has said that 'experience is the best teacher.' Unfortunately the wisdom acquired in one experience seems not to serve for another and new one; at any rate, my first lesson at the national capital, bought rather dearly as it was, did not preclude the necessity of a second whetstone to sharpen my wits in this, my new home and new surroundings. It is not altogether without a feeling of humiliation that I must narrate my connection with the 'Freedmen's Savings and Trust Company.'*

This was an institution designed to furnish a place of security and profit for the hard earnings of the colored people, especially at the South. Though its title was 'The Freedmen's Savings and Trust Company,' it is known generally as the 'Freedmen's Bank.' According to its managers it was to be this and something more. There was something missionary in its composition, and it dealt largely in exhortations as well as promises. The men connected with its management were generally church members, and reputed eminent for their piety. Some of its agents had been preachers of the 'Word.' Their aim was now to instil into the minds of the untutored Africans lessons of sobriety, wisdom, and economy, and to show them how to rise in the world. Like snowflakes in winter, circulars, tracts and other papers were, by this benevolent institution, scattered among the sable millions, and they were told to 'look' to the Freedman's Bank and 'live.' Branches were established in all the Southern States, and as a result, money to the amount of millions flowed into its vaults. With the usual effect of sudden wealth, the managers felt like making a little display of their prosperity. They accordingly erected on one of the most desirable and expensive sites in the national capital, one of the most costly and splendid buildings of the time, finished on the inside with black walnut and furnished with marble counters and all the modern improvements. The magnificent dimensions of the building bore testimony to its flourishing condition. In passing it on the street I often peeped into its spacious windows, and looked down the row of its gentlemanly and elegantly dressed colored clerks, with their pens behind their ears and button-hole bouquets in their coat-fronts, and felt my very eyes enriched. It was a sight I had never expected to see. I was amazed with the facility with which they counted the money. They threw off the thousands with the dexterity, if not the accuracy, of old and experienced clerks. The whole thing was beautiful. I had read of this bank when I lived in Rochester, and had indeed been solicited to become one of its trustees, and had reluctantly consented to do so; but when I came to Washington and saw its magnificent brown stone front, its towering height, its perfect appointments and the fine display it made in the transaction of its business, I felt like the Queen of Sheba when she saw the riches of Solomon, that 'the half had not been told me.'*

After settling myself down in Washington in the office of the *New Era*, I could and did occasionally attend the meetings of the Board of Trustees, and had the pleasure of listening to the rapid reports of the condition of the institution, which were generally of a most encouraging character. My confidence in the integrity and wisdom of the management was such that at one time I had entrusted to its vaults about twelve thousand dollars. It seemed fitting to me to cast in my lot with my brother freedmen and to help build up an institution which represented their thrift and economy to so striking advantage; for the more millions accumulated there, I thought, the more consideration and respect would be shown to the colored people of the whole country.

About four months before this splendid institution was compelled to close its doors in the starved and deluded faces of its depositors, and while I was assured by its President and by its Actuary of its sound condition, I was solicited by some of its trustees to allow them to use my name in the board as a candidate for its presidency. So I waked up one morning to find myself seated in a comfortable arm chair, with gold spectacles on my nose, and to hear myself addressed as President of the Freedmen's Bank. I could not help reflecting on the contrast between Frederick the slave boy, running about at Col. Lloyd's with only a tow linen shirt to cover him, and Frederick—President of a bank counting its assets by millions. I had heard of golden dreams, but such dreams had no comparison with this reality. And yet this seeming reality was scarcely more substantial than a dream. My term of service on this golden height covered only the brief space of three months, and these three months were divided into two parts, during the first part of which I was quietly employed in an effort to find out the real condition of the bank and its numerous branches. This was no easy task. On paper, and from the representations of its management, its assets amounted to three millions of dollars, and its liabilities were about equal to its assets. With such a showing I was encouraged in the belief that by curtailing the expenses, and doing away with non-paying branches, which policy the trustees had now adopted, we could be carried safely through the financial distress then upon the country. So confident was I of this, that in order to meet what was said to be a temporary emergency, I was induced to loan the bank ten thousand dollars of my own money, to be held by it until it could realize on a part of its abundant securities. This money, though it was repaid, was not done so as promptly as, under the supposed circumstances, I thought it should be, and these circumstances increased my fears lest the chasm was not so easily bridged as the actuary of the institution had assured me it could be. The more I observed and learned the more my confidence diminished. I found that those trustees who wished to issue cards and publish addresses professing the utmost confidence in the bank, had themselves not one dollar deposited there. Some of them, while strongly assuring me of its soundness, had withdrawn their money and opened accounts elsewhere. Gradually I discovered that the bank had, through dishonest agents, sustained heavy losses at the South; that there was a discrepancy on the books of forty thousand dollars for which no account could be given, and that, instead of our assets being equal to our liabilities, we could not in all likelihoods of the case pay seventy-two cents on the dollar. There was an air of mystery, too, about the spacious and elegant apartments of the bank building, which greatly troubled me, and which I have only been able to explain to myself on the supposition that the employees, from the actuary and the inspector down to the messengers, were (perhaps) naturally anxious to hold their places, and consequently have the business continued. I am not a violent advocate of the doctrine of the total depravity of human nature. I am inclined, on the whole, to believe it a tolerably good nature, yet instances do occur which oblige me to concede that men can and do act from mere personal and selfish motives. In this case, at any rate, it seemed not unreasonable to conclude that the finely dressed young gentlemen, adorned with pens and bouquets, the most fashionable and genteel of all our colored youth, stationed behind those marble counters, should desire to retain their places as long as there was money in the vaults to pay them their salaries.

Standing on the platform of this large and complicated establishment, with its thirty-four branches, extending from New Orleans to Philadelphia, its machinery in full operation, its correspondence carried on in cipher, its actuary dashing in and out of the bank with an air of pressing business, if not of bewilderment, I found the path of enquiry I was pursuing an exceedingly difficult one. I knew there had been very lately several runs on the bank, and that there had been a heavy draft made upon its reserve fund, but I did not know, what

I should have been told before being allowed to enter upon the duties of my office, that this reserve, which the bank by its charter was required to keep, had been entirely exhausted, and that hence there was nothing left to meet any future emergency. Not to make too long a story, I was, in six weeks after my election as president of this bank, convinced that it was no longer a safe custodian of the hard earnings of my confiding people. This conclusion once reached, I could not hesitate as to my duty in the premises, and this was, to save as much as possible of the assets held by the bank for the benefit of the depositors; and to prevent their being further squandered in keeping up appearances, and in paying the salaries of myself and other officers in the bank. Fortunately, Congress, from which we held our charter, was then in session, and its committees on finance were in daily session. I felt it my duty to make known as speedily as possible to Hon. John Sherman, Chairman of the Senate Committee on Finance, and to Senator Scott of Pennsylvania, also of the same committee, that I regarded the institution as insolvent and irrecoverable, and that I could no longer ask my people to deposit their money in it. This representation to the finance committee subjected me to very bitter opposition on the part of the officers of the bank. Its actuary, Mr. Stickney, immediately summoned some of the trustees, a dozen or so of them, to go before the finance committee and make a counter statement to that made by me; and this they did. Some of them who had assisted me by giving me facts showing the insolvency of the bank, now made haste to contradict that conclusion and to assure the committee that it was, if allowed to go on, abundantly able to weather the financial storm and pay dollar for dollar to its depositors.

I was not exactly thunderstruck, but I was much amazed by this contradiction. I, however, adhered to my statement that the bank ought to stop. The finance committee substantially agreed with me and in a few weeks so legislated, by appointing three commissioners to take charge of its affairs, as to bring this imposing banking business to a close.

This is a fair and unvarnished narration of my connection with the Freedmen's Savings and Trust Company, otherwise known as the Freedmen's Savings Bank, a connection which has brought upon my head an amount of abuse and detraction greater than any encountered in any other part of my life.

Before leaving the subject I ought in justice to myself to state that, when I found that the affairs of the bank were to be closed up, I did not, as I might easily have done, and as others did, make myself a preferred creditor and take my money out of the bank, but on the contrary,

I determined to take my chances with the other depositors, and left my money, to the amount of two thousand dollars, to be divided with the assets among the creditors of the bank. And now, after seven years have been allowed for the value of the securities to appreciate and the loss of interests on the deposits for that length of time, the depositors may deem themselves fortunate if they receive sixty cents on the dollar of what they placed in the care of this fine savings institution.

It is also due to myself to state, especially since I have seen myself accused of bringing the Freedmen's Bank into ruin, and squandering in senseless loans on bad security the hardly-earned moneys of my race, that all the loans ever made by the bank were made prior to my connection with it as its president. Not a dollar, not a dime of its millions were loaned by me, or with my approval. The fact is, and all investigation shows it, that I was married to a corpse. The fine building, with its marble counters and black walnut finishings, was there, as were the affable and agile clerks and the discreet and colored cashier: but the LIFE, which was the money, was gone, and I found that I had been placed there with the hope that by 'some drugs, some charms, some conjuration, or some mighty magic,'* I would bring it back.

When I became connected with the bank I had a tolerably fair name for honest dealing; I had expended in the publication of my paper in Rochester thousands of dollars annually, and had often to depend upon my credit to bridge over immediate wants, but no man there or elsewhere can say I ever wronged him out of a cent; and I could, to-day, with the confidence of the converted centurion, offer 'to restore fourfold to any from whom I have unjustly taken aught.'* I say this, not for the benefit of those who know me, but for the thousands of my own race who hear of me mostly through the malicious and envious assaults of unscrupulous aspirants who vainly fancy that they lift themselves into consideration by wanton attacks upon the characters of men who receive a larger share of respect and esteem than themselves.

# CHAPTER XV.

## WEIGHED IN THE BALANCE.

*The Santo Domingo controversy—Decoration Day at Arlington, 1871—Speech delivered there—National colored convention at New Orleans, 1872—Elector at large for the State of New York—Death of Hon. Henry Wilson.*

THE most of my story is now before the reader. Whatever of good or ill the future may have in store for me, the past at least is secure. As I review the last decade up to the present writing, I am impressed with a sense of completeness; a sort of rounding up of the arch to the point where the keystone may be inserted, the scaffolding removed, and the work, with all its perfections or faults, left to speak for itself. This decade, from 1871 to 1881, has been crowded, if time is capable of being thus described, with incidents and events which may well enough be accounted remarkable. To me they certainly appear strange, if not wonderful. My early life not only gave no visible promise, but no hint of such experience. On the contrary, that life seemed to render it, in part at least, impossible. In addition to what is narrated in the foregoing chapter, I have, as belonging to this decade, to speak of my mission to Santo Domingo; of my appointment as a member of the council for the government of the District of Columbia; of my election as elector at large for the State of New York; of my invitation to speak at the monument of the unknown loyal dead, at Arlington, on Decoration day; of my address on the unveiling of Lincoln monument, at Lincoln Park, Washington; of my appointment to bring the electoral vote from New York to the national capital; of my invitation to speak near the statue of Abraham Lincoln, Madison Square, New York; of my accompanying the body of Vice-President Wilson from Washington to Boston; of my conversations with Senator Sumner and President Grant; of my welcome to the receptions of Secretary Hamilton Fish; of my appointment by President R. B. Hayes to the office of Marshal of the District of Columbia; of my visit to Thomas Auld, the man who claimed me as his slave, and from whom I was purchased by my English friends; of my visit, after an absence of fifty-six years, to Lloyd's plantation, the home of my childhood; and of my appointment by President James A. Garfield to the office of Recorder of Deeds of the District of Columbia.

Those who knew of my more than friendly relations with Hon. Charles Sumner, and of his determined opposition to the annexation of

Santo Domingo to the United States, were surprised to find me earnestly taking sides with General Grant upon that question.* Some of my
white friends, and a few of those of my own color—who, unfortunately,
allow themselves to look at public questions more through the medium
of feeling than of reason, and who follow the line of what is grateful to
their friends rather than what is consistent with their own convictions—thought my course was an ungrateful return for the eminent
services of the Massachusetts senator. I am free to say that, had I been
guided only by the promptings of my heart, I should in this controversy have followed the lead of Charles Sumner. He was not only the
most clear-sighted, brave, and uncompromising friend of my race who
had ever stood upon the floor of the Senate, but was to me a loved,
honored, and precious personal friend; a man possessing the exalted
and matured intellect of a statesman, with the pure and artless heart of
a child. Upon any issue, as between him and others, when the right
seemed in anywise doubtful, I should have followed his counsel and
advice. But the annexation of Santo Domingo, to my understanding,
did not seem to be any such question. The reasons in its favor were
many and obvious; and those against it, as I thought, were easily
answered. To Mr. Sumner, annexation was a measure to extinguish
a colored nation, and to do so by dishonorable means and for selfish
motives. To me it meant the alliance of a weak and defenceless people,
having few or none of the attributes of a nation, torn and rent by
internal feuds and unable to maintain order at home or command
respect abroad, to a government which would give it peace, stability,
prosperity, and civilization, and make it helpful to both countries. To
favor annexation at the time when Santo Domingo asked for a place in
our union, was a very different thing from what it was when Cuba and
Central America were sought by fillibustering expeditions.* When the
slave power bore rule, and a spirit of injustice and oppression animated
and controlled every part of our government, I was for limiting our
dominion to the smallest possible margin; but since liberty and equality
have become the law of our land, I am for extending our dominion
whenever and wherever such extension can peaceably and honorably,
and with the approval and desire of all the parties concerned, be accomplished. Santo Domingo wanted to come under our government upon
the terms thus described; and for more reasons than I can stop here to
give, I then believed, and do now believe, it would have been wise to
have received her into our sisterhood of States.

   The idea that annexation meant degradation to a colored nation was
altogether fanciful; there was no more dishonor to Santo Domingo in

making her a State of the American Union, than in making Kansas, Nebraska, or any other territory such a State. It was giving to a part the strength of the whole, and lifting what must be despised for its isolation into an organization and relationship which would compel consideration and respect.

Although I differed from Mr. Sumner in respect of this measure and although I told him that I thought he was unjust to President Grant, it never disturbed our friendship. After his great speech against annexation, which occupied six hours in its delivery, and in which he arraigned the President in a most bitter and fierce manner, being at the White House one day, I was asked by President Grant what I 'now thought of my friend, Mr. Sumner'? I replied that I believed Mr. Sumner sincerely thought, that in opposing annexation, he was defending the cause of the colored race as he always had done, but that I thought he was mistaken. I saw that my reply was not very satisfactory, and said: 'What do you, Mr. President, think of Senator Sumner'? He answered, with some feeling: 'I think he is mad.'

The difference in opinion on this question between these two great men was the cause of bitter personal estrangement, and one which I intensely regretted. The truth is, that neither one was entirely just to the other, because neither saw the other in his true character; and having once fallen asunder, the occasion never came when they could be brought together.

Variance between great men finds no healing influence in the atmosphere of Washington. Interested parties are ever ready to fan the flame of animosity and magnify the grounds of hostility in order to gain the favor of one or the other. This is perhaps true in some degree in every community; but it is especially so of the national capital, and this for the reason that there is ever a large class of people here dependent for their daily bread upon the influence and favor of powerful public men.

My selection to visit Santo Domingo with the commission sent thither, was another point indicating the difference between the OLD TIME and the NEW. It placed me on the deck of an American man-of-war, manned by one hundred marines and five hundred men-of-wars-men, under the national flag, which I could now call mine, in common with other American citizens, and gave me a place not in the fore-castle, among the hands, nor in the caboose with the cooks, but in the captain's saloon and in the society of gentlemen, scientists and statesmen. It would be a pleasing task to narrate the varied experiences and the distinguished persons encountered in this Santo Domingo tour, but the material is too boundless for the limits of these pages. I can only say that it was highly interesting and instructive. The conversations at the Captain's table (at which I had the honor of a seat) were usually led by Messrs. Wade, Howe and White*—the three commissioners; and by Mr. Hurlburt of the New York World. The last-named gentleman impressed me as one remarkable for knowledge and refinement, in which he was no whit behind Messrs. Howe and White. As for Hon. Benj. F. Wade, he was there, as everywhere, abundant in knowledge and experience, fully able to take care of himself in the discussion of any subject in which he chose to take a part. In a circle so brilliant, it is no affectation of modesty to say that I was for the most part a listener and a learner. The commander of our good ship on this voyage, Capt. Temple, now promoted to the position of Commodore, was a very imposing man, and deported himself with much dignity towards us all. For his treatment to me I am especially grateful. A son of the United States navy as he was—a department of our service considerably distinguished for its aristocratic tendencies—I expected to find something a little forbidding in his manner; but I am bound to say that in this I was agreeably disappointed. Both the commander and the officers under him bore themselves in a friendly manner towards me during all the voyage; and this is saying a great thing for them, for the spectacle presented by a colored man seated at the captain's table was not only unusual, but had never before occurred in the history of the United States navy. If, during this voyage, there was anything to complain of, it was not in the men in authority, or in the conduct of the thirty gentlemen who went out as the honored guests of the expedition, but in the colored waiters. My presence and position seemed to trouble them for its incomprehensibility, and they did not know exactly how to deport themselves towards me. Possibly they may have detected in me something of the same sort in respect of themselves; at any rate, we seemed awkwardly related to each other during several weeks of the voyage. In their eyes I was Fred. Douglass, suddenly, and possibly undeservedly, lifted above them. The fact that I was colored and they were colored had so long made us equal, that the contradiction now presented was too much for them. After all, I have no blame for Sam and Garrett. They were trained in the school of servility to believe that white men alone were entitled to be waited upon by colored men; and the lesson taught by my presence on the 'Tennessee' was not to be learned upon the instant, without thought and experience. I refer to the matter simply as an incident quite commonly met with in the lives of colored men who, by their own exertions or otherwise, have happened to occupy positions of respectability and honor. While the rank and file of our race quote, with much vehemence, the doctrine of human equality, they are often among the first to deny and denounce it in practice. Of course this is true only of the more ignorant. Intelligence is a great leveler here as elsewhere. It sees plainly the real worth of men and things, and is not easily imposed upon by the dressed-up emptiness of human pride.

With a colored man on a sleeping-car as its conductor, the last to have his bed made up at night, and the last to have his boots blacked in the morning, and the last to be served in any way, is the colored passenger. This conduct is the homage which the black man pays to the white man's prejudice, whose wishes, like a well-trained servant, he is taught to anticipate and obey. Time, education, and circumstances are rapidly destroying these mere color distinctions, and men will be valued in this country, as well as in others, for what they are and for what they can do.

My appointment at the hands of President Grant to a seat in the council—by way of eminence sometimes called the upper house of the territorial legislature of the District of Columbia*—must be taken as, at the time it was made, a signal evidence of his high sense of justice, fairness, and impartiality. The colored people of the district constituted then, as now, about one-third of the whole population. They were given by Gen. Grant, three members of this legislative council—a representation more proportionate than any that has existed since the government has passed into the hands of commissioners, for they have all been white men.

It has sometimes been asked why I am called 'Honorable.' My appointment to this council must explain this, as it explains the impartiality of Gen. Grant, though I fear it will hardly sustain this prodigious handle to my name, as well as it does the former part of this proposition. The members of this district council were required to be appointed by the President, with the advice and consent of the United States Senate. This is the ground, and only ground that I know of, upon which anybody has claimed this title for me. I do not pretend that the foundation is a very good one, but as I have generally allowed people to call me what they have pleased, and as there is nothing necessarily dishonorable in this, I have never taken the pains to dispute its application and propriety; and yet I confess that I am never so spoken of without feeling a trifle uncomfortable—about as much so as when I am called, as I sometimes am, the *Rev.* Frederick Douglass. My stay in this legislative body was of short duration. My vocation abroad left me little time to study the many matters of local legislation; hence my resignation, and the appointment of my son Lewis to fill out my term.

I have thus far told my story without copious quotations from my letters, speeches, or other writings, and shall not depart from this rule in what remains to be told, except to insert here my speech, delivered at Arlington, near the monument to the 'Unknown Loyal Dead,' on Decoration Day, 1871. It was delivered under impressive circumstances, in presence of President Grant, his Cabinet, and a great multitude of distinguished people, and expresses, as I think, the true view which should be taken of the great conflict between slavery and freedom to which it refers.

'Friends and Fellow Citizens: Tarry here for a moment. My words shall be few and simple. The solemn rites of this hour and place call for no lengthened speech. There is, in the very air of this resting ground of the unknown dead a silent, subtle and all-pervading eloquence, far more touching, impressive, and thrilling than living lips have ever uttered. Into the measureless depths of every loyal soul it is now whispering lessons of all that is precious, priceless, holiest, and most enduring in human existence.

'Dark and sad will be the hour to this nation when it forgets to pay grateful homage to its greatest benefactors. The offering we bring to-day is due alike to the patriot soldiers dead and their noble comrades who still live; for, whether living or dead, whether in time or eternity, the loyal soldiers who imperiled all for country and freedom are one and inseparable.

'Those unknown heroes whose whitened bones have been piously gathered here, and whose green graves we now strew with sweet and beautiful flowers choice emblems alike of pure hearts and brave spirits, reached, in their glorious career that last highest point of nobleness beyond which human power cannot go. They died for their country.

'No loftier tribute can be paid to the most illustrious of all the benefactors of mankind than we pay to these unrecognized soldiers when we write above their graves this shining epitaph.

'When the dark and vengeful spirit of slavery, always ambitious, preferring to rule in hell than to serve in heaven, fired the Southern heart and stirred all the malign elements of discord, when our great Republic, the hope of freedom and self-government throughout the world, had reached the point of supreme peril, when the Union of these States was torn and rent asunder at the center, and the armies of a gigantic rebellion came forth with broad blades and bloody hands to destroy the very foundation of American society, the unknown braves who flung themselves into the yawning chasm, where cannon roared and bullets whistled, fought and fell. They died for their country.

'We are sometimes asked, in the name of patriotism, to forget the merits of this fearful struggle, and to remember with equal admiration those who struck at the nation's life and those who struck to save it, those who fought for slavery and those who fought for liberty and justice.

'I am no minister of malice. I would not strike the fallen. I would not repel the repentant; but may my "right hand forget her cunning and my tongue cleave to the roof of my mouth,"* if I forget the difference between the parties to that terrible, protracted, and bloody conflict.

'If we ought to forget a war which has filled our land with widows and orphans; which has made stumps of men of the very flower of our youth; which has sent them on the journey of life armless, legless, maimed and mutilated; which has piled up a debt heavier than a mountain of gold, swept uncounted thousands of men into bloody graves and planted agony at a million hearthstones—I say, if this war is to be forgotten, I ask, in the name of all things sacred, what shall men remember?

'The essence and significance of our devotions here to-day are not to be found in the fact that the men whose remains fill these graves were brave in battle. If we met simply to show our sense of bravery, we should find enough on both sides to kindle admiration. In the raging storm of fire and blood, in the fierce torrent of shot and shell, of sword and bayonet, whether on foot or on horse, unflinching courage marked the rebel not less than the loyal soldier.

'But we are not here to applaud manly courage, save as it has been displayed in a noble cause. We must never forget that victory to the rebellion meant death to the republic. We must never forget that the loyal soldiers who rest beneath this sod flung themselves between the nation and the nation's destroyers. If to-day we have a country not boiling in an agony of blood, like France,* if now we have a united country, no longer cursed by the hell-black system of human bondage, if the American name is no longer a by-word and a hissing to a mocking earth, if the star-spangled banner floats only over free American citizens in every quarter of the land, and our country has before it a long and glorious career of justice, liberty, and civilization, we are indebted to the unselfish devotion of the noble army who rest in these honored graves all around us.'

In the month of April, 1872, I had the honor to attend and preside over a national convention of colored citizens held in New Orleans.* It was a critical period in the history of the Republican party, as well as in that of the country. Eminent men who had hitherto been looked upon as the pillars of republicanism had become dissatisfied with President Grant's administration, and determined to defeat his nomination for a second term. The leaders in this unfortunate revolt were Messrs. Trumbull, Schurz, Greeley, and Sumner. Mr. Schurz* had already succeeded in destroying the Republican party in the State of Missouri. It seemed to be his ambition to be the founder of a new party; and to him more than to any other man belongs the credit of what was once known as the Liberal-Republican party, which made Horace Greeley* its standard-bearer in the campaign of that year.

At the time of the convention in New Orleans the elements of this new combination were just coming together. The division in the Republican ranks seemed to be growing deeper and broader every day. The colored people of the country were much affected by the threatened disruption, and their leaders were much divided as to the side upon which they should give their voice and their votes. The names of Greeley and Sumner, on account of their long and earnest advocacy of justice and liberty to the blacks, had powerful attractions for the newly-enfranchised class, and there was in this convention at New Orleans naturally enough a strong disposition to fraternize with the new party and follow the lead of their old friends. Against this policy I exerted whatever influence I possessed, and, I think, succeeded in holding back that convention from what I felt sure then would have been a fatal political blunder, and time has proved the correctness of that position. My speech on taking the chair on that occasion was telegraphed in full from New Orleans to the New York *Herald*, and the key-note of it was that there was no path out of the Republican party that did not lead directly into the Democratic party—away from our friends and directly to our enemies. Happily this convention pretty largely agreed with me, and its members have not since regretted that agreement.

From this convention onward, until the nomination and election of Grant and Wilson, I was actively engaged on the stump, a part of the time in Virginia with Hon. Henry Wilson, in North Carolina with John M. Langston and John H. Smyth, and in the State of Maine with Senator Hamlin, Gen. B. F. Butler, Gen. Woodford, and Hon. James G. Blaine.

Since 1872 I have been regularly what my old friend Parker Pillsbury would call a 'field hand' in every important political campaign, and at each national convention have sided with what has been called the stalwart element of the Republican party. It was in the Grant presidential campaign that New York took an advanced step in the renunciation of a timid policy. The Republicans of that State, not having the fear of popular prejudice before their eyes, placed my name as an elector at large at the head of their presidential ticket. Considering the deep-rooted sentiment of the masses against Negroes, the noise and tumult likely to be raised, especially among our adopted citizens of Irish descent, this was a bold and manly proceeding, and one for which the Republicans of the State of New York deserve the gratitude of every colored citizen of the Republic, for it was a blow at popular prejudice in a quarter where it was capable of making the strongest resistance. The result proved not only the justice and generosity of the measure, but its wisdom. The

Republicans carried the State by a majority of fifty thousand over the heads of the Liberal-Republican and Democratic parties combined.

Equally significant of the turn now taken in the political sentiment of the country was the action of the Republican electoral college at its meeting in Albany, when it committed to my custody the sealed-up electoral vote of the great State of New York and commissioned me to bring that vote to the national capital. Only a few years before this any colored man was forbidden by law to carry a United States mail bag from one post-office to another. He was not allowed to touch the sacred leather, though locked in 'triple steel,'* but now not a mail bag, but a document which was to decide the presidential question with all its momentous interests, was committed to the hands of one of this despised class, and around him, in the execution of his high trust, was thrown all the safeguards provided by the Constitution and the laws of the land. Though I worked hard and long to secure the nomination and election of Gen. Grant in 1872, I neither received nor sought office from him. He was my choice upon grounds altogether free from selfish or personal considerations. I supported him because he had done all, and would do all, he could to save not only the country from ruin but the emancipated class from oppression and ultimate destruction, and because Mr. Greeley, with the Democratic party behind him, would not have the power, even if he had the disposition, to afford us the needed protection which our peculiar condition required. I could easily have secured the appointment as minister to Hayti, but preferred to urge the claims of my friend Ebenezer Bassett,* a gentleman and a scholar, and a man well fitted by his good sense and amiable qualities to fill the position with credit to himself and his country. It is with a certain degree of pride that I am able to say that my opinion of the wisdom of sending Mr. Bassett to Hayti has been fully justified by the creditable manner in which, for eight years, he discharged the difficult duties of that position, for I have the assurance of Hon. Hamilton Fish, Secretary of State of the United States, that Mr. Bassett was a good minister. In so many words the ex-Secretary told me that he 'wished that one-half of his ministers abroad performed their duties as well as Mr. Bassett.' To those who know Hon. Hamilton Fish this compliment will not be deemed slight, for few men are less given to exaggeration and are more scrupulously exact in the observance of law and in the use of language than is that gentleman. While speaking in this strain of complacency in reference to Mr. Bassett, I take pleasure also in bearing my testimony, based upon knowledge obtained at the State Department, that Mr. John Mercer Langston,* the present minister to Hayti, has acquitted himself with equal wisdom and ability to that of Mr. Bassett in the same position. Having known both these gentlemen in their youth, when the one was at Yale and the other at Oberlin College, and witnessed their efforts to qualify themselves for positions of usefulness, it has afforded me no limited satisfaction to see them rise in the world. Such men increase the faith of all in the possibilities of their race, and make it easier for those who are to come after them.

The unveiling of Lincoln monument* in Lincoln Park, Washington, April 14, 1876, and the part taken by me in the ceremonies of that grand occasion, takes rank among the most interesting incidents of my life, since it brought me into mental communication with a greater number of the influential and distinguished men of the country than any I had before known. There were present the President of the United States and his Cabinet, judges of the Supreme Court, the Senate and House of Representatives, and many thousands of citizens to listen to my address upon the illustrious man to whose memory the colored people of the United States had, as a mark of their gratitude, erected that impressive monument. Occasions like this have done wonders in the removal of popular prejudice and lifting into consideration the colored race, and I reckon it one of the high privileges of my life that I was permitted to have a share in this and several other like celebrations.

The progress of a nation is sometimes indicated by small things. When Henry Wilson, an honored Senator and Vice-President of the United States, died in the Capitol of the nation, it was a significant and telling indication of national advance, that three colored citizens, Mr. Robert Purvis, Mr. James Wormley and myself, were selected with the Senate Committee, to accompany his honored remains from Washington to the grand old commonwealth he loved so well, and whom in turn she had so greatly loved and honored. It was meet and right that we should be represented in the long procession that met those remains in every State between here and Massachusetts, for Henry Wilson was among the foremost friends of the colored race in this country, and this was the first time in its history that a colored man had been made a pall-bearer at the funeral, as I was in this instance, of a Vice-President of the United States.

An appointment to any important and lucrative office under the United States government usually brings its recipient a large measure of praise and congratulation on the one hand, and much abuse and disparagement on the other; and he may think himself singularly fortunate if the censure does not exceed the praise. I need not dwell upon the causes of this extravagance, but I may say that there is no office of any value in the country which is not desired and sought by many persons equally meritorious and equally deserving. But as only one person can be appointed to any one office, only one can be pleased, while many are offended. Unhappily, resentment follows disappointment, and this resentment often finds expression in disparagement and abuse of the successful man. As in most else that I have said, I borrow this reflection from my own experience.

My appointment as United States Marshal of the District of Columbia,* was in keeping with the rest of my life, as a freeman. It was an innovation upon long established usage, and opposed to the general current of sentiment in the community. It came upon the people of the District as a gross surprise, and almost a punishment; and provoked something like a scream—I will not say a *yell*—of popular displeasure. As soon as I was named by President Hayes for the place, efforts were made by members of the bar to defeat my confirmation before the Senate. All sorts of reasons against my appointment, but the true one, were given, and that was withheld more from a sense of shame, than from a sense of justice. The apprehension doubtless was, that if appointed marshal, I would surround myself with colored deputies, colored bailiffs and colored messengers and pack the jury-box with colored jurors; in a word, Africanize the courts. But the most dreadful thing threatened, was a colored man at the *Executive Mansion* in white kid gloves, sparrow-tailed coat, patent-leather boots, and alabaster cravat, performing the ceremony—a very empty one—of introducing the aristocratic citizens of the republic to the President of the United States. This was something entirely too much to be borne; and men asked themselves in view of it. To what is the world coming? and where will these things stop? Dreadful! Dreadful!

It is creditable to the manliness of the American Senate, that it was moved by none of these things, and that it lost no time in the matter of my confirmation. I learn, and believe my information correct, that foremost among those who supported my confirmation against the objections made to it, was Hon. Roscoe Conkling* of New York. His speech in executive session is said by the senators who heard it, to have been one of the most masterly and eloquent ever delivered on the floor of the Senate; and this too I readily believe, for Mr. Conkling possesses the ardor and fire of Henry Clay, the subtlety of Calhoun, and the massive grandeur of Daniel Webster.

The effort to prevent my confirmation having failed, nothing could be done but to wait for some overt act to justify my removal; and for this my unfriends had not long to wait. In the course of one or two months I was invited by a number of citizens of Baltimore to deliver a lecture in that city, in Douglass Hall—a building named in honor of myself, and devoted to educational purposes. With this invitation I complied, giving the same lecture which I had two years before delivered in the city of Washington, and which was at the time published in full in the newspapers, and very highly commended by them. The subject of the lecture was, 'Our National Capital.' and in it I said many complimentary things of the city, which were as true as they were complimentary. I spoke of what it had been in the past, what it was at that time, and what I thought it destined to become in the future; giving it all credit for its good points, and calling attention to some of its ridiculous features.* For this I got myself pretty roughly handled. The newspapers worked themselves up to a frenzy of passion, and committees were appointed to procure names to a petition to President Hayes demanding my removal. The tide of popular feeling was so violent, that I deemed it necessary to depart from my usual custom when assailed, so far as to write the following explanatory letter, from which the reader will be able to measure the extent and quality of my offense:

'To the Editor of the Washington Evening *Star*:
'Sir:—You were mistaken in representing me as being off on a lecturing tour, and, by implication, neglecting my duties as United States Marshal of the District of Columbia. My absence from Washington during two days was due to an invitation by the managers to be present on the occasion of the inauguration of the International Exhibition in Philadelphia.*

'In complying with this invitation, I found myself in company with other members of the government who went thither in obedience to the call of patriotism and civilization. No one interest of the Marshal's office suffered by my temporary absence, as I had seen to it that those upon whom the duties of the office devolved were honest, capable, industrious, painstaking, and faithful. My Deputy Marshal is a man every way qualified for his position, and the citizens of Washington may rest assured that no unfaithful man will be retained in any position under me. Of course I can have nothing to say as to my own fitness for the position I hold. You have a right to say what you please on that point; yet I think it would be only fair and generous to wait for some dereliction of duty on my part before I shall be adjudged as incompetent to fill the place.

'You will allow me to say also that the attacks upon me on account of the remarks alleged to have been made by me in Baltimore, strike me as both malicious and silly. Washington is a great city, not a village nor a hamlet, but the capital of a great nation, and the manners and habits of its various classes are proper subjects for presentation and criticism, and I very much mistake if this great city can be thrown into a tempest of passion by any humorous reflections I may take the liberty to utter. The city is too great to be small, and I think it will laugh at the ridiculous attempt to rouse it to a point of furious hostility to me for anything said in my Baltimore lecture.

'Had the reporters of that lecture been as careful to note what I said in praise of Washington as what I said, if you please, in disparagement of it, it would have been impossible to awaken any feeling against me in this community for what I said. It is the easiest thing in the world, as all editors know, to pervert the meaning and give a one-sided impression of a whole speech by simply giving isolated passages from the speech itself, without any qualifying connections. It would hardly be imagined from anything that has appeared here that I had said one word in that lecture in honor of Washington, and yet the lecture itself, as a whole, was decidedly in the interest of the national capital. I am not such a fool as to decry a city in which I have invested my money and made my permanent residence.

'After speaking of the power of the sentiment of patriotism I held this language: "In the spirit of this noble sentiment I would have the American people view the national capital. It is our national center. It belongs to us; and whether it is mean or majestic, whether arrayed in glory or covered with shame, we cannot but share its character and its destiny. In the remotest section of the republic, in the most distant parts of the globe, amid the splendors of Europe or the wilds of Africa, we are still held and firmly bound to this common center. Under the shadow of Bunker Hill monument, in the peerless eloquence of his diction, I once heard the great Daniel Webster give welcome to all American citizens, assuring them that whereever else they might be strangers, they were all at home there.* The same boundless welcome is given to all American citizens by Washington. Elsewhere we may belong to individual States, but here we belong to the whole United States. Elsewhere we may belong to a section, but here we belong to a whole country, and the whole country belongs to us. It is national territory, and the one place where no American is an intruder or a carpet-bagger. The new comer is not less at home than the old resident. Under its lofty domes and stately pillars, as under the broad blue sky, all races and colors of men stand upon a footing of common equality.

' "The wealth and magnificence which elsewhere might oppress the humble citizen has an opposite effect here. They are felt to be a part of himself and serve to ennoble him in his own eyes. He is an owner of the marble grandeur which he beholds about him,—as much so as any of the forty millions of this great nation. Once in his life every American who can should visit Washington: not as the Mohametan to Mecca; not as the Catholic to Rome: not as the Hebrew to Jerusalem, nor as the Chinaman to the Flowery kingdom, but in the spirit of enlightened patriotism, knowing the value of free institutions and how to perpetuate and maintain them.

' "Washington should be contemplated not merely as an assemblage of fine buildings; not merely as the chosen resort of the wealth and fashion of the country; not merely as the honored place where the statesmen of the nation assemble to shape the policy and frame the laws; not merely as the point at which we are most visibly touched by the outside world, and where the diplomatic skill and talent of the old continent meet and match themselves against those of the new, but as the national flag itself—a glorious symbol of civil and religious liberty, leading the world in the race of social science, civilization, and renown."

'My lecture in Baltimore required more than an hour and a half for its delivery, and every intelligent reader will see the difficulty of doing justice to such a speech when it is abbreviated and compressed into a half or three-quarters of a column. Such abbreviation and condensation has been resorted to in this instance. A few stray sentences, culled out from their connections, would be deprived of much of their harshness if presented in the form and connection in which they were uttered; but I am taking up too much space, and will close with the last paragraph of the lecture, as delivered in Baltimore. "No city in the broad world has a higher or more beneficent mission. Among all the great capitals of the world it is pre-eminently the capital of free institutions. Its fall would be a blow to freedom and progress throughout the world. Let it stand then where it does now stand—where the father of his country planted it, and where it has stood for more than half a century; no longer sandwiched between two slave States; no longer a contradiction to human progress; no longer the hot-bed of slavery and the slave trade; no longer the home of the duelist, the gambler, and the assassin; no longer the frantic partisan of one section of the country against the other; no longer anchored to a dark and semi-barbarous past, but a redeemed city, beautiful to the eye and attractive to the heart, a bond of perpetual union, an angel of peace on earth and good will to men, a common ground upon which Americans of all races and colors, all sections, North and South, may meet and shake hands, not over a chasm of blood, but over a free, united, and progressive republic." '

I have already alluded to the fact that much of the opposition to my appointment to the office of United States Marshal of the District of Columbia was due to the possibility of my being called to attend President Hayes at the Executive Mansion upon state occasions, and having the honor to introduce the guests on such occasions. I now wish to refer to the reproaches liberally showered upon me for holding the office of Marshal while denied this distinguished honor, and to show that the complaint against me at this point is not a well founded complaint.

1st. Because the office of United States Marshal is distinct and separate and complete in itself, and must be accepted or refused upon its own merits. If, when offered to any person, its duties are such as he can properly fulfill, he may very properly accept it; or, if otherwise, he may as properly refuse it.

2d. Because the duties of the office are clearly and strictly defined in the law by which it was created; and because nowhere among these duties is there any mention or intermention that the Marshal may or shall attend upon the President of the United States at the Executive Mansion on state occasions.

3d. Because the choice as to who shall have the honor and privilege of such attendance upon the President belongs exclusively and reasonably to the President himself, and that therefore no one, however distinguished, or in whatever office, has any just cause to complain of the exercise by the President of this right of choice, or because he is not himself chosen.

In view of these propositions, which I hold to be indisputable, I should have presented to the country a most foolish and ridiculous figure had I, as absurdly counseled by some of my colored friends, resigned the office of Marshal of the District of Columbia, because President Rutherford B. Hayes, for reasons that must have been satisfactory to his judgment, preferred some person other than myself to attend upon him at the Executive Mansion and perform the ceremony of introducing on state occasions. But it was said, that this statement did not cover the whole ground; that it was customary for the United States Marshal of the District of Columbia to perform this social office; and that the usage had come to have almost the force of law. I met this at the time, and I meet it now by denying the binding force of this custom. No President has any right or power to make his example the rule for his successor. The custom of inviting the Marshal to perform the duty mentioned was made by a President and could be as properly unmade by a President. Besides, the usage is altogether a modern one and had its origin in peculiar circumstances and was justified by those circumstances. It was introduced by President Lincoln in the time of war when he made his old law partner and intimate acquaintance Marshal of the District, and was continued by Gen. Grant when he appointed a relative of his, Gen. Sharp, to the same office. But again, it was said that President Hayes only departed from this custom because the Marshal in my case was a colored man. The answer I made to this, and now make to it, is, that it is a gratuitous assumption and entirely begs the question. It may or may not be true that my complexion was the cause of this departure, but no man has any right to assume that position in advance of a plain declaration to that effect by President Hayes himself. Never have I heard from him any such declaration or intimation. In so far as my intercourse with him is concerned, I can say that I at no time discovered in him a feeling of aversion to me on account of my complexion, or on any other account, and, unless I am greatly deceived, I was ever a welcome visitor at the

Executive Mansion on state occasions and all others, while Rutherford B. Hayes was President of the United States. I have further to say that I have many times during his administration had the honor to introduce distinguished strangers to him, both of native and foreign birth, and never had reason to feel myself slighted by himself or his amiable wife; and I think he would be a very unreasonable man who could desire for himself, or for any other, a larger measure of respect and consideration than this at the hands of a man and woman occupying the exalted positions of Mr. and Mrs. Hayes.

I should not do entire justice to the Honorable ex-President if I did not bear additional testimony to his noble and generous spirit. When all Washington was in an uproar, and a wild clamor rent the air for my removal from the office of Marshal on account of the lecture delivered by me in Baltimore and when petitions were flowing in upon him demanding my degradation, he nobly rebuked the mad spirit of persecution by openly declaring his purpose to retain me in my place.

One other word. During the tumult raised against me in consequence of this lecture on the 'National Capital,' Mr. Columbus Alexander, one of the old and wealthy citizens of Washington, who was on my bond for twenty thousand dollars, was repeatedly besought to withdraw his name, and thus leave me disqualified; but like the President, both he and my other bondsman, Mr. George Hill, Jr., were steadfast and immovable. I was not surprised that Mr. Hill stood bravely by me, for he was a Republican; but I was surprised and gratified that Mr. Alexander, a Democrat, and, I believe, once a slaveholder, had not only the courage, but the magnanimity to give me fair play in this fight. What I have said of these gentlemen, can be extended to very few others in this community, during that period of excitement, among either the white or colored citizens, for, with the exception of Dr. Charles B. Purvis,* no colored man in the city uttered one public word in defence or extenuation of me or of my Baltimore speech.

This violent hostility kindled against me was singularly evanescent. It came like a whirlwind, and like a whirlwind departed. I soon saw nothing of it, either in the courts among the lawyers, or on the streets among the people; for it was discovered that there was really in my speech at Baltimore nothing which made me 'worthy of stripes or of bonds.'*

I can say of my experience in the office of United States Marshal of the District of Columbia that it was every way agreeable. When it was an open question whether I should take the office or not, it was apprehended and predicted that, if I should accept it in face of the opposition of the lawyers and judges of the courts, I should be subjected to numberless suits for damages and so vexed and worried that the office would be rendered valueless to me and that it would not only eat up my salary, but possibly endanger what little I might have laid up for a rainy day. I have now to report that this apprehension was in no sense realized. What might have happened had the members of the District bar been half as malicious and spiteful as they had been industriously represented as being, or if I had not secured as my assistant a man so capable, industrious, vigilant, and careful as Mr. L. P. Williams, of course I cannot know. But I am bound to praise the bridge that carries me safely over it. I think it will ever stand as a witness to my fitness for the position of Marshal, that I had the wisdom to select for my assistant a gentleman so well instructed and competent. I also take pleasure in bearing testimony to the generosity of Mr. Phillips, the Assistant Marshal who preceded Mr. Williams in that office, in giving the new assistant valuable information as to the various duties he would be called upon to perform. I have further to say of my experience in the Marshal's office, that while I have reason to know that the eminent Chief Justice of the District of Columbia and some of his associates were not well pleased with my appointment, I was always treated by them, as well as by the chief clerk of the courts, Hon. J. R. Meigs, and the subordinates of the latter (with a single exception), with the respect and consideration due to my office. Among the eminent lawyers of the District I believe I had many friends, and there were those of them to whom I could always go with confidence in an emergency for sound advice and direction, and this fact, after all the hostility felt in consequence of my appointment, and revived by my speech at Baltimore, is another proof of the vincibility of all feelings arising out of popular prejudices.

In all my forty years of thought and labor to promote the freedom and welfare of my race, I never found myself more widely and painfully at variance with leading colored men of the country than when I opposed the effort to set in motion a wholesale exodus of colored people of the South to the Northern States;* and yet I never took a position in which I felt myself better fortified by reason and necessity. It was said of me, that I had deserted to the old master class, and that I was a traitor to my race; that I had run away from slavery myself, and yet I was opposing others in doing the same. When my opponents condescended to argue, they took the ground that the colored people of the South needed to be brought into contact with the freedom and civilization of the North; that no emancipated and persecuted people ever had or ever could rise in the presence of the people by whom they had been enslaved, and that the true remedy for the ills which the freedmen were suffering, was to initiate the Israelitish departure from our modern Egypt to a land abounding, if not in 'milk and honey,'* certainly in pork and hominy.

Influenced, no doubt, by the dazzling prospects held out to them by the advocates of the exodus movement, thousands of poor, hungry, naked and destitute colored people were induced to quit the South amid the frosts and snows of a dreadful winter in search of a better country. I regret to say that there was something sinister in this so-called exodus, for it transpired that some of the agents most active in promoting it had an understanding with certain railroad companies, by which they were to receive one dollar per head upon all such passengers. Thousands of these poor people, traveling only so far as they had money to bear their expenses, were dropped in the extremest destitution on the levees of St. Louis, and their tales of woe were such as to move a heart much less sensitive to human suffering than mine. But while I felt for these poor deluded people, and did what I could to put a stop to their ill-advised and ill-arranged stampede, I also did what I could to assist such of them as were within my reach, who were on their way to this land of promise. Hundreds of these people came to Washington, and at one time there were from two to three hundred lodges here unable to get further for the want of money. I lost no time in appealing to my friends for the means of assisting them. Conspicuous among these friends was Mrs. Elizabeth Thompson* of New York city—the lady who, several years ago, made the nation a present of Carpenter's great historical picture of the 'Signing of the Emancipation Proclamation,'* and who had expended large sums of her money in investigating the causes of yellow-fever, and in endeavors to discover means for preventing its ravages in New Orleans and elsewhere. I found Mrs. Thompson consistently alive to the claims of humanity in this, as in other instances, for she sent me, without delay, a draft for two hundred and fifty dollars, and in doing so expressed the wish that I would promptly inform her of any other opportunity of doing good. How little justice was done me by those who accused me of indifference to the welfare of the colored people of the South on account of my opposition to the so-called exodus will be seen by the following extracts from a paper on that subject laid before the Social Science Congress at Saratoga,* when the question was before the country:

'Important as manual labor everywhere is, it is nowhere more important and absolutely indispensable to the existence of society than in the more southern of the United States. Machinery may continue to do, as it has done, much of the work of the North, but the work of the South requires for its performance bone, sinew and muscle of the strongest and most enduring kind. Labor in that section must know no pause. Her soil is pregnant and prolific with life and energy. All the forces of nature within her borders are wonderfully vigorous, persistent, and active. Aided by an almost perpetual summer, abundantly supplied with heat and moisture, her soil readily and rapidly covers itself with noxious weeds, dense forests, and impenetrable jungles. Only a few years of non-tillage would be needed to give the sunny and fruitful South to the bats and owls of a desolate wilderness. From this condition, shocking for a southern man to contemplate, it is now seen that nothing less powerful than the naked iron arm of the negro can save her. For him, as a Southern laborer there is no competitor or substitute. The thought of filling his place by any other variety of the human family, will be found delusive and utterly practicable. Neither Chinaman, German. Norwegian, nor Swede can drive him from the sugar and cotton fields of Louisiana and Mississippi. They would certainly perish in the black bottoms of these States if they could be induced, which they cannot, to try the experiment.

'Nature itself, in those States, comes to the rescue of the negro, fights his battles, and enables him to exact conditions from those who would unfairly treat and oppress him. Besides being dependent upon the roughest and flintiest kind of labor, the climate of the South makes such labor uninviting and harshly repulsive to the white man. He dreads it, shrinks from it, and refuses it. He shuns the burning sun of the fields, and seeks the shade of the verandas. On the contrary, the negro walks, labors, and sleeps in the sunlight unharmed. The standing apology for slavery was based upon a knowledge of this fact. It was said that the world must have cotton and sugar, and that only the negro could supply this want; and that he could be induced to do it only under the "beneficent whip" of some bloodthirsty *Legree*.* The last part of this argument has been happily disproved by the large crops of these productions since Emancipation; but the first part of it stands firm, unassailed, and unassailable.

'Even if climate and other natural causes did not protect the negro from all competition in the labor market of the South. Inevitable social causes would probably effect the same result. The slave system of that section has left behind it, as in the nature of the case it must, manners, customs, and conditions to which free white laboring men will be in no haste to submit themselves and their families. They do not emigrate from the free North, where labor is respected, to a lately enslaved South, where labor has for centuries been whipped, chained and degraded. Naturally enough such emigration follows the lines of latitude in which they who compose it were born. Not from South to North, but from East to West "the Star of Empire takes its way."*

'Hence it is seen that the dependence upon the negro of the planters, landowners, and the old master-class of the South, however galling and humiliating to Southern pride and power, is nearly complete and perfect. There is only one mode of escape for them, and that mode they will certainly not adopt. It is to take off their own coats, cease to whittle sticks and talk politics at cross-roads, and go themselves to work in their broad and sunny fields of cotton and sugar. An invitation to do this is about as harsh and distasteful to all their inclinations as would be an invitation to step down into their graves. With the negro all this is different. Neither natural, artificial nor traditional causes stand in the way of the freedman's laboring in the South. Neither the heat nor the fever-demon which lurks in her tangled and oozy swamps affrights him, and he stands to-day the admitted author of whatever prosperity, beauty, and civilization are now possessed by the South, and the admitted arbiter of her destiny.

'This, then, is the high vantage ground of the negro; he has labor; the South wants it, and must have it or perish. Since he is free he can now give it or withhold it; use it where he is, or take it elsewhere as he pleases. His labor made him a slave, and his labor can, if he will, make him free, comfortable, and independent. It is more to him than fire, swords, ballot-boxes, or bayonets. It touches the heart of the South through its pocket. This power served him well years ago, when in the bitterest extremity of destitution. But for it he would have perished when he dropped out of slavery. It saved him then, and it will save him again. Emancipation came to him surrounded by extremely unfriendly circumstances. It was not the choice or consent of the people among whom he lived, but against their will and a death struggle on their part to prevent it. His chains were broken in the tempest and whirlwind of civil war. Without food, without shelter, without land, without money, and without friends, he, with his children, his sick, his aged and helpless ones, were turned loose and naked to the open sky. The announcement of his freedom was instantly followed by an order from his master to quit his old quarters, and to seek bread thereafter from the hands of those who had given him his freedom. A desperate extremity was thus forced upon him at the outset of his freedom, and the world watched with humane anxiety to see what would become of him. His peril was imminent. Starvation and death stared him in the face and marked him for their victim.

'It will not soon be forgotten that, at the close of a five-hours' speech by the late Senator Sumner, in which he advocated, with unequaled learning and eloquence, the enfranchisement of the freed men, the best argument with which he was met in the Senate was, that legislation at that point would be utterly superfluous, that the negro was rapidly dying out, and must inevitably and speedily disappear and become extinct.

'Inhuman and shocking as was this consignment of millions of human beings to extinction, the extremity of the negro at that date did not contradict, but favored, the prophecy. The policy of the old master-class, dictated by passion, pride and revenge, was to make the freedom of the negro a greater calamity to him, if possible, than had been his slavery. But happily, both for the old master-class and for the recently emancipated, there came then, as there will come now, the sober second thought. The old master-class then found it had made a great mistake. It had driven away the means of its own support. It had destroyed the hands, and left the mouths. It had starved the negro and starved itself. Not even to gratify its own anger and resentment could it afford to allow its fields to go uncultivated and its tables unsupplied with food. Hence the freedman, less from humanity than cupidity, less from choice than necessity, was speedily called back to labor and life.

'But now, after fourteen years of service and fourteen years of separation from the visible presence of slavery, during which he has shown both disposition and ability to supply the labor-market of the South, and that he could do so far better as a freedman than he even did as a slave, that more cotton and sugar can be raised by the same hands under the inspiration of liberty and hope than can be raised under the influence of bondage and the whip, he is again, alas! in the deepest trouble, again without a home, out under the open sky with his wife and little ones. He lines the sunny banks of the Mississippi, fluttering in rags and wretchedness, mournfully imploring hard-hearted steamboat captains to take him on board, while the friends of the emigration movement are diligently soliciting funds all over the North to help him away from his old home to the new Canaan of Kansas.'

I am sorry to be obliged to omit the statement which here follows, of the reasons given for the Exodus movement, and my explanation of them, but from want of space I can present only such portions of the paper as express most vividly and in fewest words my position in regard to the question. I go on to say:

'Bad as is the condition of the negro to-day at the South, there was a time when it was flagrantly and incomparably worse. A few years ago he had nothing—he had not even himself. He belonged to somebody else, who could dispose of his person and his labor as he pleased. Now he has himself, his labor, and his right to dispose of one and the other as shall best suit his own happiness. He has more. He has a standing in the supreme law of the land—in the Constitution of the United States—not to be changed or affected by any conjunction of circumstances likely to occur in the immediate or remote future. The Fourteenth Amendment makes him a citizen, and the Fifteenth makes him a voter. With power behind him, at work for him, and which cannot be taken from him, the negro of the South may wisely bide his time. The situation at the moment is exceptional and transient. The permanent powers of the government are all on his side. What though for the moment the hand of violence strikes down the negro's rights in the South, those rights will revive, survive, and flourish again. They are not the only people who have been, in a moment of popular passion, maltreated and driven from the polls. The Irish and Dutch have frequently been so treated. Boston, Baltimore, and New York have been the scenes of lawless violence; but those scenes have now disappeared. . . . . Without abating one jot of our horror and indignation at the outrages committed in some parts of the Southern States against the negro, we cannot but regard the present agitation of an African exodus from the South as ill-timed and, in some respects, hurtful. We stand to-day at the beginning of a grand and beneficent reaction. There is a growing recognition of the duty and obligation of the American people to guard, protect, and defend the personal and political rights of all the people of all the States, and to uphold the principles upon which rebellion was suppressed, slavery abolished, and the country saved from dismemberment and ruin.

'We see and feel to-day, as we have not seen and felt before, that the time for conciliation and trusting to the honor of the late rebels and slaveholders has passed. The President of the United States himself, while still liberal, just, and generous toward the South, has yet sounded a halt in that direction, and has bravely, firmly, and ably asserted the constitutional authority to maintain the public peace in every State in the Union and upon every day in the year, and has maintained this ground against all the powers of House and Senate.

'We stand at the gateway of a marked and decided change in the statesmanship of our rulers. Every day brings fresh and increasing evidence that we are, and of right ought to be, a nation, that Confederate notions of the nature and powers of our government ought to have perished in the rebellion which they supported, that they are anachronisms and superstitions, and no longer fit to be above ground. . . . .

'At a time like this, so full of hope and courage, it is unfortunate that a cry of despair should be raised in behalf of the colored people of the South, unfortunate that men are going over the country begging in the name of the poor colored man of the South, and telling the people that the government has no power to enforce the Constitution and laws in that section, and that there is no hope for the poor negro but to plant him in the new soil of Kansas or Nebraska.

'These men do the colored people of the South a real damage. They give their enemies an advantage in the argument for their manhood and freedom. They assume their inability to take care of themselves. The country will be told of the hundreds who go to Kansas, but not of the thousands who stay in Mississippi and Louisiana.

'It will be told of the destitute who require material aid, but not of the multitude who are bravely sustaining themselves where they are.

'In Georgia the negroes are paying taxes upon six millions of dollars, in Louisiana upon forty or fifty millions, and upon unascertained sums elsewhere in the Southern States.

'Why should people who have made such progress in the course of a few years be humiliated and scandalized by exodus agents, begging money to remove them from their homes, especially at a time when every indication favors the position that the wrongs and hardships which they suffer are soon to be redressed?

'Besides the objection thus stated, it is manifest that the public and noisy advocacy of a general stampede of the colored people from the South to the North is necessarily an abandonment of the great and paramount principle of protection to person and property in every State in the Union. It is an evasion of a solemn obligation and duty. The business of this nation is to protect its citizens where they are, not to transport them where they will not need protection. The best that can be said of this exodus in this respect is, that it is an attempt to climb up some other way—it is an expedient, a half-way measure, and tends to weaken in the public mind a sense of the absolute right, power and duty of the government, inasmuch as it concedes, by implication at least, that on the soil of the South the law of the land cannot command obedience, the ballot-box cannot be kept pure, peaceable elections cannot be held, the Constitution cannot be enforced, and the lives and liberties of loyal and peaceable citizens cannot be protected. It is a surrender, a premature disheartening surrender, since it would secure freedom and free institutions by migration rather than by protection, by flight rather than by right, by going into a strange land rather than by staying in one's own. It leaves the whole question of equal rights on the soil of the South open and still to be settled, with the moral influence of the exodus against us, since it is a confession of the utter impracticability of equal rights and equal protection in any State where those rights may be struck down by violence.

'It does not appear that the friends of freedom should spend either time or talent in furtherance of this exodus as a desirable measure, either for the North or the South. If the people of this country cannot be protected in every State of the Union, the government of the United States is shorn of its rightful dignity and power, the late rebellion has triumphed, the sovereignty of the nation is an empty name, and the power and authority in individual States is greater than the power and authority of the United States. . . . . .

'The colored people of the South, just beginning to accumulate a little property, and to lay the foundation of family, should not be in haste to sell that little and be off to the banks of the Mississippi. The habit of roaming from place to place in pursuit of better conditions of existence is never a good one. A man should never leave his home for a new one till he has earnestly endeavored to make his immediate surroundings accord with his wishes. The time and energy expended in wandering from place to place, if employed in making him a comfortable home where he is, will, in nine cases out of ten, prove the best investment. No people ever did much for themselves or for the world without the sense and inspiration of native land, of a fixed home, of familiar neighborhood, and common associations. The fact of being to the manor born has an elevating power upon the mind and heart of a man. It is a more cheerful thing to be able to say, I was born here and know all the people, than to say, I am a stranger here and know none of the people.

'It cannot be doubted that, in so far as this exodus tends to promote restlessness in the colored people of the South, to unsettle their feeling of home, and to sacrifice positive advantages where they are for fancied ones in Kansas or elsewhere, it is an evil. Some have sold their little homes, their chickens, mules, and pigs, at a sacrifice, to follow the exodus. Let it be understood that you are going, and you advertise the fact that your mule has lost half its value, for your staying with him makes half his value. Let the colored people of Georgia offer their six millions' worth of property for sale, with the purpose to leave Georgia, and they will not realize half its value. Land is not worth much where there are no people to occupy it, and a mule is not worth much where there is no one to drive him.

'It may be safely asserted that, whether advocated and commended to favor on the ground that it will increase the political power of the Republican party, and thus help to make a solid North against a solid South, or upon the ground that it will increase the power and influence of the colored people as a political element, and enable them the better to protect their rights, and insure their moral and social elevation, the exodus will prove a disappointment, a mistake, and a failure; because, as to strengthening the Republican party, the emigrants will go only to those States where the Republican party is strong and solid enough already with their votes; and in respect to the other part of the argument, it will fail because it takes colored voters from a section of the country where they are sufficiently numerous to elect some of their number to places of honor and profit, and places them in a country where their proportion to other classes will be so small as not to be recognized as a political element or entitled to be represented by one of themselves. And further, because go where they will, they must for a time inevitably carry with them poverty, ignorance, and other repulsive incidents inherited from their former condition of slaves—a circumstance which is about as likely to make votes for Democrats as for Republicans, and as likely to raise up bitter prejudice against them as to raise up friends for them. . . .

'Plainly enough, the exodus is less harmful as a measure than are the arguments by which it is supported. The one is the result of a feeling of outrage and despair, but the other comes of cool, selfish calculation. One is the result of honest despair, and appeals powerfully to the sympathies of men; the other is an appeal to our selfishness, which shrinks from doing right because the way is difficult.

'Not only is the South the best locality for the Negro, on the ground of his political powers and possibilities, but it is best for him as a field of labor. He is there, as he is nowhere else, an absolute necessity. He has a monopoly of the labor market. His labor is the only labor which can successfully offer itself for sale in that market. This fact, with a little wisdom and firmness, will enable him to sell his labor there on terms more favorable to himself than he can elsewhere. As there are no competitors or substitutes he can demand living prices with the certainty that the demand will be complied with. Exodus would deprive him of this advantage.

'The Negro, as already intimated, is preeminently a Southern man. He is so both in constitution and habits, in body as well as mind. He will not only take with him to the North southern modes of labor but southern modes of life. The careless and improvident habits of the South cannot be set aside in a generation. If they are adhered to in the North, in the fierce winds and snows of Kansas and Nebraska, the emigration must be large to keep up their numbers.

'As an assertion of power by a people hitherto held in bitter contempt, as an emphatic and stinging protest against high-handed, greedy, and shameless injustice to the weak and defenseless, as a means of opening the blind eyes of oppressors to their folly and peril, the exodus has done valuable service. Whether it has accomplished all of which for the present it is capable in this direction is a question which may well be considered. With a moderate degree of intelligent leadership among the laboring class of the South properly handling the justice of its cause and wisely using the exodus example, it can easily exact better terms for its labor than ever before. Exodus is a medicine, not food; it is for disease, not health; it is not to be taken from choice, but from necessity. In anything like a normal condition of things the South is the best place for the Negro. Nowhere else is there for him a promise of a happier future. Let him stay there if he can, and save both the South and himself to civilization. While, however, it may be the highest wisdom in the circumstances for the freedmen to stay where they are, no encouragement should be given to any measures of coercion to keep them there. The American people are bound, if they are or can be bound to anything, to keep the north gate of the South open to black and white and to all the people. The time to assert a right, Webster says, is when it is called in question. If it is attempted by force or fraud to compel the colored people to stay there, they should by all means go—go quickly and die, if need be, in the attempt.'

# CHAPTER XVI.

## 'TIME MAKES ALL THINGS EVEN.'

*Return to the 'old master'—A last interview—Capt. Auld's admission, 'had I been in your place, I should have done as you did'—Speech at Easton—The old jail there—Invited to a sail on the revenue cutter Guthrie—Hon. John L. Thomas—Visit to the old plantation—Home of Col. Lloyd—Kind reception and attentions—Familiar scenes—Old memories—Burial ground—Hospitality—Gracious reception from Mrs. Buchanan—A little girl's floral gift—A promise of a 'good time coming'—Speech at Harper's Ferry, Decoration day, 1881—Storer College—Hon. A. J. Hunter.*

THE leading incidents to which it is my purpose to call attention and make prominent in the present chapter will, I think, address the imagination of the reader with peculiar and poetic force, and might well enough be dramatized for the stage. They certainly afford another striking illustration of the trite saying that 'truth is stranger than fiction.'

The first of these events occurred four years ago, when, after a period of more than forty years, I visited and had an interview with Captain Thomas Auld at St. Michaels, Talbot county, Maryland. It will be remembered by those who have followed the thread of my story that St. Michaels was at one time the place of my home and the scene of some of my saddest experiences of slave life, and that I left there, or rather was compelled to leave there, because it was believed that I had written passes for several slaves to enable them to escape from slavery, and that prominent slaveholders in that neighborhood had, for this alleged offense, threatened to shoot me on sight, and to prevent the execution of this threat my master had sent me to Baltimore.

My return, therefore, in peace, to this place and among the same people, was strange enough in itself; but that I should, when there, be formally invited by Captain Thomas Auld, then over eighty years old, to come to the side of his dying bed,* evidently with a view to a friendly talk over our past relations, was a fact still more strange, and one which, until its occurrence, I could never have thought possible. To me Captain Auld had sustained the relation of master—a relation which I had held in extremest abhorrence, and which for forty years I had denounced in all bitterness of spirit and fierceness of speech. He had struck down my personality, had subjected me to his will, made property of my body and soul, reduced me to a chattel, hired me out to a noted slave breaker to be worked like a beast and flogged into submission, taken my hard earnings, sent me to prison, offered me for sale, broken up my Sunday-school, forbidden me to teach my fellow-slaves to read on pain of nine and thirty lashes on my bare back and had, without any apparent disturbance of his conscience, sold my body to his brother Hugh and pocketed the price of my flesh and blood. I, on my part, had traveled through the length and breadth of this country and of England, holding up this conduct of his, in common with that of other slaveholders, to the reprobation of all men who would listen to my words. I had by my writings made his name and his deeds familiar to the world in four different languages,* yet here we were, after four decades, once more face to face—he on his bed, aged and tremulous, drawing near the sunset of life, and I, his former slave, United States Marshal of the district of Columbia, holding his hand and in friendly conversation with him in a sort of final settlement of past differences preparatory to his stepping into his grave, where all distinctions are at an end, and where the great and the small, the slave and his master, are reduced to the same level. Had I been asked in the days of slavery to visit this man I should have regarded the invitation as one to put fetters on my ankles and handcuffs on my wrists. It would have been an invitation to the auction-block and the slave-whip. I had no business with this man under the old regime but to keep out of his way. But now that slavery was destroyed, and the slave and the master stood upon equal ground, I was not only willing to meet him, but was very glad to do so. The conditions were favorable for remembrance of all his good deeds, and generous extenuation of all his evil ones. He was to me no longer a slaveholder either in fact or in spirit, and I regarded him as I did myself, a victim of the circumstances of birth, education, law, and custom.

Our courses had been determined for us, not by us. We had both been flung, by powers that did not ask our consent, upon a mighty current of life, which we could neither resist nor control. By this current he was a master, and I a slave; but now our lives were verging towards a point where differences disappear, where even the constancy of hate breaks down and where the clouds of pride, passion and selfishness vanish before the brightness of infinite light. At such a time, and in such a place, when a man is about closing his eyes on this world and ready to step into the eternal unknown, no word of reproach or bitterness should reach him or fall from his lips; and on this occasion there was to this rule no transgression on either side.

As this visit to Capt. Auld has been made the subject of mirth by heartless triflers, and by serious-minded men regretted as a weakening of my life-long testimony against slavery, and as the report of it, published in the papers immediately after it occurred, was in some respects defective and colored, it may be proper to state exactly what was said and done at this interview.

It should in the first place be understood that I did not go to St. Michaels upon Capt. Auld's invitation, but upon that of my colored friend, Charles Caldwell; but when once there, Capt. Auld sent Mr. Green, a man in constant attendance upon him during his sickness, to tell me he would be very glad to see me, and wished me to accompany Green to his house, with which request I complied. On reaching the house I was met by Mr. Wm. H. Bruff, a son-in-law of Capt. Auld, and Mrs. Louisa Bruff, his daughter, and was conducted by them immediately to the bed-room of Capt. Auld. We addressed each other simultaneously, he calling me 'Marshal Douglass,' and I, as I had always called him, 'Captain Auld.' Hearing myself called by him 'Marshal Douglass,' I instantly broke up the formal nature of the meeting by saying, 'not *Marshal*, but Frederick to you as formerly.' We shook hands cordially, and in the act of doing so, he, having been long stricken with palsy, shed tears as men thus afflicted will do when excited by any deep emotion. The sight of him, the changes which time had wrought in him, his tremulous hands constantly in motion, and all the circumstances of his condition affected me deeply, and for a time choked my voice and made me speechless. We both, however, got the better of our feelings, and conversed freely about the past.

Though broken by age and palsy, the mind of Capt. Auld was remarkably clear and strong. After he had become composed I asked him what he thought of my conduct in running away and going to the north. He hesitated a moment as if to properly formulate his reply, and said: 'Frederick, I always knew you were too smart to be a slave, and had I been in your place, I should have done as you did.' I said, 'Capt. Auld, I am glad to hear you say this. I did not run away from *you*, but from *slavery*; it was not that I loved Caesar less, but Rome more.'* I told him that I had made a mistake in my narrative, a copy of which I had sent him, in attributing to him ungrateful and cruel treatment of my grandmother; that I had done so on the supposition that in the division of the property of my old master, Mr. Aaron Anthony, my grandmother had fallen to him, and that he had left her in her old age, when she could be no longer of service to him, to pick up her living in solitude with none to help her, or, in other words, had turned her out to die like an old horse. 'Ah!' he said, 'that was a mistake, I never owned your grandmother; she in the division of the slaves was awarded to my brother-in-law,

Andrew Anthony; but,' he added quickly, 'I brought her down here and took care of her as long as she lived.' The fact is, that, after writing my narrative describing the condition of my grandmother, Capt. Auld's attention being thus called to it, he rescued her from her destitution. I told him that this mistake of mine was corrected as soon as I discovered it, and that I had at no time any wish to do him injustice; that I regarded both of us as victims of a system. 'Oh, I never liked slavery,' he said, 'and I meant to emancipate all of my slaves when they reached the age of twenty-five years.' I told him I had always been curious to know how old I was and that it had been a serious trouble to me, not to know when was my birthday. He said he could not tell me that, but he thought I was born in February, 1818. This date made me one year younger than I had supposed myself from what was told me by Mistress Lucretia, Captain Auld's former wife, when I left Lloyd's for Baltimore in the Spring of 1825;* she having then said that I was eight, going on nine. I know that it was in the year 1825 that I went to Baltimore, because it was in that year that Mr. James Beacham built a large frigate* at the foot of Alliceana street, for one of the South American Governments. Judging from this, and from certain events which transpired at Col. Lloyd's such as a boy under eight years old, without any knowledge of books, would hardly take cognizance of, I am led to believe that Mrs. Lucretia was nearer right as to my age than her husband.

Before I left his bedside Captain Auld spoke with a cheerful confidence of the great change that awaited him, and felt himself about to depart in peace. Seeing his extreme weakness I did not protract my visit. The whole interview did not last more than twenty minutes, and we parted to meet no more. His death was soon after announced in the papers,* and the fact that he had once owned me as a slave was cited as rendering that event noteworthy.

It may not, perhaps, be quite artistic to speak in this connection of another incident of something of the same nature as that which I have just narrated, and yet it quite naturally finds place here; and that is, my visit to the town of Easton, county seat of Talbot County, two years later, to deliver an address in the Court House, for the benefit of some association in that place. The visit was made interesting to me, by the fact that forty-five years before I had, in company with Henry and John Harris, been dragged behind horses to Easton, with my hands tied, put in jail and offered for sale, for the offense of intending to run away from slavery.

It may easily be seen that this visit, after this lapse of time, brought with it feelings and reflections such as only unusual circumstances can awaken. There stood the old jail, with its white-washed walls and iron gratings, as when in my youth I heard its heavy locks and bolts clank behind me.

Strange too, Mr. Joseph Graham, who was then sheriff of the County, and who locked me in this gloomy place, was still living, though verging towards eighty, and was one of the gentlemen who now gave me a warm and friendly welcome, and was among my hearers when I delivered my address at the Court House. There too in the same old place stood Sol. Law's Tavern, where once the slave traders were wont to congregate, and where I now took up my abode and was treated with a hospitality and consideration undreamed of by me in the olden time as possible.

When one has advanced far in the journey of life, when he has seen and traveled over much of this great world, and has had many and strange experiences of shadow and sunshine, when long distances of time and space have come between him and his point of departure, it is natural that his thoughts should return to the place of his beginning, and that he should be seized with a strong desire to revisit the scenes of his early recollection, and live over in memory the incidents of his childhood. At least such for several years had been my thoughts and feeling in respect of Col. Lloyd's plantation on Wye River, Talbot County, Maryland; for I had never been there since I left it, when eight years old, in 1825.

While slavery continued, of course this very natural desire could not be safely gratified; for my presence among slaves was dangerous to the public peace, and could no more be tolerated than could a wolf among sheep, or fire in a magazine. But now that the results of the war had changed all this, I had for several years determined to return, upon the first opportunity, to my old home. Speaking of this desire of mine last winter, to Hon. John L. Thomas, the efficient collector at the port of Baltimore, and a leading republican of the State of Maryland, he urged me very much to go, and added that he often took a trip to the eastern shore in his revenue cutter Guthrie, (otherwise known in time of war as the Ewing,) and would be much pleased to have me accompany him on one of these trips. I expressed some doubt as to how such a visit would be received by the present Col. Edward Lloyd, now proprietor of the old place, and grandson of Governor Ed. Lloyd, whom I remembered. Mr. Thomas promptly assured me that from his own knowledge I need have no trouble on that score. Mr. Lloyd was a liberal-minded gentleman, and he had no doubt would take a visit from me very kindly. I was very glad to accept the offer. The opportunity for the trip however did not occur till the 12th of June,* and on that day, in company with

Messrs. Thomas, Thompson, and Chamberlain, on board the cutter, we started for the contemplated visit. In four hours after leaving Baltimore we were anchored in the river off the Lloyd estate, and from the deck of our vessel I saw once more the stately chimneys of the grand old mansion which I had last seen from the deck of the Sallie Lloyd when a boy. I left there as a slave, and returned as a freeman; I left there unknown to the outside world, and returned well known; I left there on a freight boat, and returned on a revenue cutter; I left on a vessel belonging to Col. Edward Lloyd, and returned on one belonging to the United States.

As soon as we had come to anchor, Mr. Thomas dispatched a note to Col. Edward Lloyd, announcing my presence on board his cutter, and inviting him to meet me, informing him it was my desire, if agreeable to him, to revisit my old home. In response to this note, Mr. Howard Lloyd, a son of Col. Lloyd, a young gentleman of very pleasant address, came on board the cutter, and was introduced to the several gentlemen and myself.

He told us that his father had gone to Easton on business, expressed his regret at his absence, hoped he would return before we should leave, and in the meantime received us cordially, and invited us ashore, escorted us over the grounds, and gave us as hearty a welcome as we could have wished. I hope I shall be pardoned for speaking with much complacency of this incident. It was one which could happen to but few men, and only once in the life time of any. The span of human life is too short for the repetition of events which occur at the distance of fifty years. That I was deeply moved and greatly affected by it can be easily imagined. Here I was, being welcomed and escorted by the great grand-son of Colonel Edward Lloyd—a gentleman I had known well fifty-six years before, and whose form and features were as vividly depicted on my memory as if I had seen him but yesterday. He was a gentleman of the olden time, elegant in his apparel, dignified in his deportment, a man of few words and of weighty presence; and I can easily conceive that no Governor of the State of Maryland ever commanded a larger measure of respect than did this great-grandfather of the young gentle-man now before me. In company with Mr. Howard was his little brother Decosa, a bright boy of eight or nine years, disclosing his aristocratic descent in the lineaments of his face, and in all his modest and graceful movements. As I looked at him I could not help the reflections naturally arising from having seen so many generations of the same family on the same estate. I had seen the elder Lloyd, and was now walking around with the youngest member of that name. In respect to the place itself,

I was most agreeably surprised to find that time had dealt so gently with it, and that in all its appointments it was so little changed from what it was when I left it, and from what I have elsewhere described it. Very little was missing except the squads of little black children which were once seen in all directions, and the great number of slaves in its fields. Col. Lloyd's estate comprised twenty-seven thousand acres, and the home-farm seven thousand. In my boyhood sixty men were employed in cultivating the home farm alone. Now, by the aid of machinery, the work is accomplished by ten men. I found the buildings, which gave it the appearance of a village, nearly all standing, and I was astonished to find that I had carried their appearance and location so accurately in my mind during so many years. There was the long quarter, the quarter on the hill, the dwelling-house of my old master Aaron Anthony, and the overseer's house, once occupied by William Sevier, Austin Gore, James Hopkins, and other overseers. In connection with my old master's house was the kitchen where Aunt Katy presided, and where my head had received many a thump from her unfriendly hand. I looked into this kitchen with peculiar interest, and remembered that it was there I last saw my mother. I went round to the window at which Miss Lucretia used to sit with her sewing, and at which I used to sing when hungry, a signal which she well understood, and to which she readily responded with bread. The little closet in which I slept in a bag had been taken into the room; the dirt floor, too, had disappeared under plank. But upon the whole the house is very much as it was in the old time. Not far from it was the stable formerly in charge of old Barney. The store-house at the end of it, of which my master carried the keys, had been removed. The large carriage house, too, which in my boyhood days contained two or three fine coaches, several phaetons, gigs, and a large sleigh, (for the latter there was seldom any use) was gone. This carriage house was of much interest to me, because Col. Lloyd some-times allowed his servants the use of it for festal occasions, and in it there was at such times music and dancing. With these two exceptions the houses of the estate remained. There was the shoemaker's shop, where Uncle Abe made and mended shoes; and there the blacksmith's shop, where Uncle Tony hammered iron, and the weekly closing of which first taught me to distinguish Sundays from other days. The old barn, too, was there—time-worn, to be sure, but still in good condi-tion—a place of wonderful interest to me in my childhood, for there I often repaired to listen to the chatter and watch the flight of swallows among its lofty beams, and under its ample roof. Time had wrought some changes in the trees and foliage. The Lombardy poplars, in the branches of which the red-winged black birds used to congregate and sing, and whose music awakened in my young heart sensations and aspirations deep and undefinable, were gone; but the oaks and elms, where young Daniel (the uncle of the present Edward Lloyd) used to divide with me his cakes and biscuits, were there as umbrageous and beautiful as ever. I expressed a wish to Mr. Howard to be shown into the family burial ground, and thither we made our way. It is a remarkable spot—the resting place for all the deceased Lloyds for two hundred years, for the family have been in possession of the estate since the settlement of the Maryland colony.

The tombs there remind one of what may be seen in the grounds of moss-covered churches in England. The very names of those who sleep within the oldest of them are crumbled away and become undecipherable. Everything about it is impressive, and suggestive of the transient character of human life and glory. No one could stand under its weeping willows, amidst its creeping ivy and myrtle, and look through its somber shadows, without a feeling of unusual solemnity. The first interment I ever witnessed was in this place. It was the great-great-grandmother, brought from Annapolis in a mahogany coffin, and quietly, without ceremony, deposited in this ground.

While here Mr. Howard gathered for me a bouquet of flowers and evergreens from the different graves around us, and which I carefully brought to my home for preservation.

Notable among the tombs were those of Admiral Buchanan, who commanded the Merrimac in the action at Hampton Roads with the Monitor, March 8, 1862, and that of General Winder of the Confederate army, both sons-in-law of the elder Lloyd. There was also pointed out to me the grave of a Massachusetts man, a Mr. Page, a teacher in the family, whom I had often seen and wondered what he could be thinking about as he silently paced up and down the garden walks, always alone, for he associated neither with Captain Anthony, Mr. McDermot, nor the overseers. He seemed to be one by himself. I believe he originated somewhere near Greenfield, Massachusetts, and members of his family will perhaps learn for the first time, from these lines, the place of his burial; for I have had intimation that they knew little about him after he once left home.

We then visited the garden, still kept in fine condition, but not as in the days of the elder Lloyd, for then it was tended constantly by Mr. McDermot, a scientific gardener, and four experienced hands, and formed, perhaps, the most beautiful feature of the place. From this we were invited to what was called by the slaves the Great House—the mansion of the Lloyds, and were helped to chairs upon its stately veranda, where we could have full view of its garden, with its broad walks, hedged with box and adorned with fruit trees and flowers of almost every variety. A more tranquil and tranquilizing scene I have seldom met in this or any other country.

We were soon invited from this delightful outlook into the large dining-room, with its old-fashioned furniture, its mahogany side-board, its cut-glass chandeliers, decanters, tumblers, and wine-glasses, and cordially invited to refresh ourselves with wine of most excellent quality.

To say that our reception was every way gratifying is but a feeble expression of the feeling of each and all of us.

Leaving the Great House, my presence became known to the colored people, some of whom were children of those I had known when a boy. They all seemed delighted to see me, and were pleased when I called over the names of many of the old servants, and pointed out the cabin where Dr. Copper, an old slave, used, with a hickory stick in hand, to teach us to say the 'Lord's Prayer.' After spending a little time with these, we bade good-bye to Mr. Howard Lloyd, with many thanks for his kind attentions, and steamed away to St. Michael's, a place of which I have already spoken.

The next part of this memorable trip took us to the home of Mrs. Buchanan, the widow of Admiral Buchanan,* one of the two only living daughters of old Governor Lloyd, and here my reception was as kindly as that received at the Great House, where I had often seen her when a slender young lady of eighteen. She is now about seventy-four years of age but marvelously well preserved. She invited me to a seat by her side, introduced me to her grandchildren and conversed with me as freely and with as little embarrassment as if I had been an old acquaintance and occupied an equal station with the most aristocratic of the Caucasian race. I saw in her much of the quiet dignity as well as the features of her father. I spent an hour or so in conversation with Mrs. Buchanan, and when I left a beautiful little grand-daughter of hers, with a pleasant smile on her face, handed me a bouquet of many-colored flowers. I never accepted such a gift with a sweeter sentiment of gratitude than from the hand of this lovely child. It told me many things, and among them that a new dispensation of justice, kindness, and human brotherhood was dawning not only in the North, but in the South; that the war and the slavery that caused the war were things of the past, and that the rising generation are turning their eyes from the sunset of decayed institutions to the grand possibilities of a glorious future.

The next, and last noteworthy incident in my experience, and one which further and strikingly illustrates the idea with which this chapter sets out, is my visit to Harper's Ferry on the 30th of May, of this year, and my address on John Brown, delivered in that place before Storer College,* an Institution established for the education of the children of those whom John Brown endeavored to liberate. It is only a little more than twenty years ago when the subject of my discourse (as will be seen elsewhere in this volume) made a raid upon Harper's Ferry; when its people, and we may say the whole nation were filled with astonishment, horror, and indignation at the mention of his name; when the government of the United States coöperated with the State of Virginia in efforts to arrest and bring to capital punishment all persons in any way connected with John Brown and his enterprise; when United States Marshals visited Rochester and elsewhere in search of me, with a view to my apprehension and execution, for my supposed complicity with Brown; when many prominent citizens of the North were compelled to leave the country to avoid arrest, and men were mobbed, even in Boston, for daring to speak a word in vindication or extenuation of what was considered Brown's stupendous crime; and yet here, upon the very soil he had stained with blood and among the very people he had startled and outraged and who a few years ago would have hanged me in open daylight to the first tree, I was, after two decades, allowed to deliver an address, not merely defending John Brown, but extolling him as a hero and martyr to the cause of liberty, and doing it with scarcely a murmur of disapprobation. I confess that as I looked out upon the scene before me and the towering heights around me, and remembered the bloody drama there enacted; as I saw the log-house in the distance where John Brown collected his men and saw the little engine-house where the brave old Puritan fortified himself against a dozen companies of Virginia Militia, and the place where he was finally captured by the United States troops under Col. Robert E. Lee, I was a little shocked at my own boldness in attempting to deliver in such presence an address of the character advertised in advance of my coming. But there was no cause of apprehension. The people of Harper's Ferry have made wondrous progress in their ideas of free-dom, of thought and speech. The abolition of slavery has not merely emancipated the negro, but liberated the whites. It has taken the lock from their tongues and the fetters from their press. On the platform from which I spoke, sat Hon. Andrew J. Hunter,* the prosecuting attor-ney for the State of Virginia, who conducted against John Brown, the cause of the State that consigned him to the gallows. This man, now well stricken in years, greeted me cordially and in conversation with me after the address, bore testimony to the manliness and courage of John Brown, and though he still disapproved of the raid made by him upon Harper's Ferry, commended me for my address and gave me a pressing invitation to visit Charlestown, where he lives, and offered to give me some facts which might prove interesting to me, as to the sayings and conduct of Captain Brown while in prison and on trial, up to the time of his execution. I regret that my engagements and duties were such that I could not then and there accept his invitation, for I could not doubt the sincerity with which it was given, or fail to see the value of compliance. Mr. Hunter not only congratulated me upon my speech, but at parting, gave me a friendly grip, and added that if Robert E. Lee were alive and present, he knew he would give me his hand also.

This man, by his frequent interruptions, added much to the interest of the occasion, approving and condemning my sentiments as they were uttered. I only regret that he did not undertake a formal reply to my speech, but this, though invited, he declined to do. It would have given me an opportunity of fortifying certain positions in my address which were perhaps insufficiently defended. Upon the whole, taking the visit to Capt. Auld, to Easton with its old jail, to the home of my old master at Col. Lloyd's, and this visit to Harper's Ferry, with all their associations, they fulfill the expectation created at the beginning of this chapter.

# CHAPTER XVII.

## INCIDENTS AND EVENTS.

*Hon. Gerrit Smith and Mr. E. C. Delevan—Experiences at hotels and on steamboats and other modes of travel—Hon. Edward Marshall—Grace Greenwood—Hon. Moses Norris—Robert G. Ingersoll—Reflections and conclusions—Compensations.*

IN escaping from the South, the reader will have observed that I did not escape from its widespread influence in the North. That influence met me almost everywhere outside of pronounced anti-slavery circles, and sometimes even within them. It was in the air, and men breathed it and were permeated by it often when they were quite unconscious of its presence.

I might recount many occasions when I have encountered this feeling, some painful and melancholy, some ridiculous and amusing. It has been a part of my mission to expose the absurdity of this spirit of caste and in some measure help to emancipate men from its control.

Invited to accompany Hon. Gerrit Smith to dine with Mr. E. C. Delevan at Albany many years ago, I expressed to Mr. Smith my awkwardness and embarrassment in the society I was likely to meet there. 'Ah!' said that good man, 'you must go, Douglass; it is your mission to break down the walls of separation between the two races.' I went with Mr. Smith, and was soon made at ease by Mr. Delevan and the ladies and gentlemen there. They were among the most refined and brilliant people I had ever met. I felt somewhat surprised that I could be so much at ease in such company, but I found it then, as I have since, that the higher the gradation in intelligence and refinement the farther removed are all artificial distinctions and restraints of mere caste or color.

In one of my anti-slavery campaigns in New York five and thirty years ago I had an appointment at Victor, a town in Ontario county. I was compelled to stop at the hotel. It was the custom at that time to seat the guests at a long table running the length of the dining-room. When I entered I was shown a little table off in a corner. I knew what it meant, but took my dinner all the same. When I went to the desk to pay my bill I said, 'Now, landlord, be good enough to tell me just why you gave me my dinner at the little table in the corner by myself.' He was equal to the occasion, and quickly replied, 'Because, you see, I wished to give you something better than the others.' The cool reply staggered me, and I gathered up my change, muttering only that I did not want to be treated better than other people, and bade him good morning.

On an anti-slavery tour through the West, in company with H. Ford Douglas, a young colored man of fine intellect and much promise, and my old friend John Jones (both now deceased), we stopped at a hotel in Janesville, and were seated by ourselves to take our meals where all the bar-room loafers of the town could stare at us. Thus seated, I took occasion to say loud enough for the crowd to hear me, that I had just been out to the stable, and had made a great discovery. Asked by Mr. Jones what my discovery was, I said that I saw there black horses and white horses eating together in peace from the same trough, from which I inferred that the horses of Janesville were more civilized than its people. The crowd saw the hit, and broke out into a good-natured laugh. We were afterward entertained at the same table with other guests.

Many years ago, on my way from Cleveland to Buffalo on one of the lake steamers, the gong sounded for supper. There was a rough element on board, such as at that time might be found anywhere between Buffalo and Chicago. It was not to be trifled with, especially when hungry. At the first sound of the gong there was a furious rush for the table. From prudence, more than from lack of appetite, I waited for the second table, as did several others. At this second table I took a seat far apart from the few gentlemen scattered along its side, but directly opposite a well-dressed, fine-featured man of the fairest complexion, high forehead, golden hair, and light beard. His whole appearance told me he was somebody. I had been seated but a minute or two when the steward came to me and roughly ordered me away. I paid no attention to him, but proceeded to take my supper, determined not to leave unless compelled to do so by superior force, and, being young and strong, I was not entirely unwilling to risk the consequences of such a contest. A few moments passed, when on each side of my chair there appeared a stalwart of my own race. I glanced at the gentleman opposite. His brow was knit, his color changed from white to scarlet, and his eyes were full of fire. I saw the lightning flash, but I could not tell where it would strike. Before my sable brethren could execute their captain's order, and just as they were about to lay violent hands upon me, a voice from that man of golden hair and fiery eyes resounded like a clap of summer thunder. 'Let the gentleman alone! I am not ashamed to take my tea with Mr. Douglass.' His was a voice to be obeyed, and my right to my seat and my supper was no more disputed.

I bowed my acknowledgment to the gentleman and thanked him for his chivalrous interference, and, as modestly as I could, asked him his name. 'I am Edward Marshall of Kentucky, now of California,' he said. 'Sir, I am very glad to know you; I have just been reading your speech in Congress,' I said. Supper over, we passed several hours in conversation with each other, during which he told me of his political career in California, of his election to Congress, and that he was a Democrat, but had no prejudice against color. He was then just coming from Kentucky, where he had been in part to see his black mammy, for, said he, 'I nursed at the breasts of a colored mother.'

I asked him if he knew my old friend John A. Collins in California. 'Oh, yes,' he replied; 'he is a smart fellow. He ran against me for Congress. I charged him with being an abolitionist, but he denied it; so I sent off and got the evidence of his having been general agent of the Massachusetts Anti-Slavery Society, and that settled him.'

During the passage Mr. Marshall invited me into the bar-room to take a drink. I excused myself from drinking, but went down with him. There were a number of thirsty-looking individuals standing around, to whom Mr. Marshall said, 'Come, boys, take a drink.' When the drinking was over he threw down upon the counter a twenty-dollar gold piece, at which the barkeeper made large eyes and said he could not change it. 'Well, keep it,' said the gallant Marshall; 'it will all be gone before morning.' After this we naturally fell apart, and he was monopolized by other company; but I shall never fail to bear willing testimony to the generous and manly qualities of this brother of the gifted and eloquent Thomas Marshall of Kentucky.

In 1842 I was sent by the Massachusetts Anti-Slavery Society to hold a Sunday meeting in Pittsfield, N. H., and was given the name of Mr. Hilles, a subscriber to the *Liberator*. It was supposed that any man who had the courage to take and read the *Liberator*, edited by William Lloyd Garrison, or the *Herald of Freedom*,* edited by Nathaniel P. Rodgers, would gladly receive and give food and shelter to any colored brother laboring in the cause of the slave. As a general rule this was very true.

There were no railroads in New Hampshire in those days, so I reached Pittsfield by stage, glad to be permitted to ride upon the top thereof, for no colored person could be allowed inside. This was many years before the days of civil rights bills, black Congressmen, colored United States Marshals, and such like.

Arriving at Pittsfield, I was asked by the driver where I would stop. I gave him the name of my subscriber to the *Liberator*. 'That is two miles beyond,' he said. So, after landing his other passengers, he took me on to the house of Mr. Hilles.

I confess I did not seem a very desirable visitor. The day had been warm and the road dusty. I was covered with dust, and then I was not of the color fashionable in that neighborhood, for colored people were scarce in that part of the old Granite State. I saw in an instant that, though the weather was warm, I was to have a cool reception; but, cool or warm, there was no alternative left me but to stay and take what I could get.

Mr. Hilles scarcely spoke to me, and, from the moment he saw me jump down from the top of the stage, carpet-bag in hand, his face wore a troubled look. His good wife took the matter more philosophically, and evidently thought my presence there for a day or two could do the family no especial harm; but her manner was restrained, silent, and formal, wholly unlike that of anti-slavery ladies I had met in Massachusetts and Rhode Island.

When tea-time came, I found that Mr. Hilles had lost his appetite and could not come to the table. I suspected his trouble was colorphobia, and, though I regretted his malady, I knew his case was not necessarily dangerous; and I was not without some confidence in my skill and ability in healing diseases of that type. I was, however, so affected by his condition, that I could not eat much of the pie and cake before me, and felt so little in harmony with things about me that I was, for me, remarkably reticent during the evening, both before and after the family worship, for Mr. Hilles was a pious man.

Sunday morning came, and in due season the hour for meeting. I had arranged a good supply of work for the day. I was to speak four times: at ten o'clock A. M., at one P. M., at five, and again at half-past seven in the evening.

When meeting-time came, Mr. Hilles brought his fine phaeton to the door, assisted his wife in, and, although there were two vacant seats in his carriage, there was no room in it for me. On driving off from his door, he merely said, addressing me, 'You can find your way to the town hall, I suppose?' 'I suppose I can,' I replied, and started along behind his carriage on the dusty road toward the village. I found the hall, and was very glad to see in my small audience the face of good Mrs. Hilles. Her husband was not there, but had gone to his church. There was no one to introduce me, and I proceeded with my discourse without introduction. I held my audience till twelve o'clock—noon—and then took the usual recess of Sunday meetings in country towns, to allow the people to take their lunch. No one invited me to lunch, so I remained in the town hall till the audience assembled again, when I spoke till nearly three o'clock, when the people again dispersed, and left me as before. By this time I began to be hungry, and, seeing a small hotel near, I went into it and offered to buy a meal; but I was told 'they did not entertain niggers there.' I went back to the old town hall hungry and cold, for an infant 'New England northeaster' was beginning to chill the air, and a drizzling rain to fall. I saw that my movements were being observed from the comfortable homes around, with apparently something of the feeling that children might experience in seeing a bear prowling about town. There was a graveyard near the town hall, and, attracted thither, I felt some relief in contemplating the resting-places of the dead, where there was an end to all distinctions between rich and poor, white and colored, high and low.

While thus meditating on the vanities of the world and my own loneliness and destitution, and recalling the sublime pathos of the saying of Jesus, 'The foxes have holes, and the birds of the air have nests, but the Son of Man hath not where to lay His head,'* I was approached rather hesitatingly by a gentleman, who inquired my name. 'My name is Douglass,' I replied. 'You do not seem to have any place to stay while in town.' I told him I had not. 'Well,' said he, 'I am no abolitionist, but if you will go with me I will take care of you.' I thanked him, and turned with him toward his fine residence. On the way I asked him his name. 'Moses Norris,'* he said. 'What! Hon. Moses Norris?' I asked. 'Yes,' he answered. I did not, for a moment, know what to do, for I had read that this same man had literally dragged the Reverend George Storrs* from the pulpit, for preaching abolitionism. I, however, walked along with him, and was invited into his house, when I heard the children running and screaming, 'Mother, mother, there is a nigger in the house! There's a nigger in the house!' and it was with some difficulty that Mr. Norris succeeded in quieting the tumult. I saw that Mrs. Norris, too, was much disturbed by my presence, and I thought for a moment of beating a retreat; but the kind assurances of Mr. Norris decided me to stay. When quiet was restored, I ventured the experiment of asking Mrs. Norris to do me a kindness. I said, 'Mrs. Norris, I have taken cold, and am hoarse from speaking, and I have found that nothing relieves me so readily as a little loaf sugar and cold water.' The lady's manner changed, and with her own hands she brought me the water and sugar. I thanked her with genuine earnestness; and from that moment I could see that her prejudices were more than half gone, and that I was more than half welcome at the fireside of this Democratic senator. I spoke again in the evening, and at the close of the meeting there was quite a contest between Mrs. Norris and Mrs. Hilles as to which one I should see home. I considered Mrs. Hilles' kindness to me, though her manner had been formal. I knew the cause, and I thought, especially as my carpet-bag was there, I would go with her. So giving Mr. and Mrs. Norris many thanks, I bade them good-bye, and went home with Mr. and Mrs. Hilles, where I found the atmosphere wondrously and most agreeably changed. Next day, Mr. Hilles took me, in the same carriage in which I did not ride on Sunday, to my next appointment, and on the way told me he felt more honored by having me in it than he would be if he had the President of the United States. This compliment would have been a little more flattering to my self-esteem had not John Tyler then occupied the Presidential chair.

In those unhappy days of the Republic, when all presumptions were in favor of slavery, and a colored man as a slave met less resistance in the use of public conveyances than a colored man as a freeman, I happened to be in Philadelphia, and was afforded an opportunity to witness this preference. I took a seat in a street car, by the side of my friend, Mrs. Amy Post, of Rochester, New York, who, like myself, had come to Philadelphia to attend an anti-slavery meeting. I had no sooner seated myself, than the conductor hastened to remove me from the car. My friend remonstrated, and the amazed conductor said, 'Lady, does he belong to you?' 'He does,' said Mrs. Post, and there the matter ended. I was allowed to ride in peace, not because I was a man and had paid my fare, but because I belonged to somebody. My color was no longer offensive when it was supposed that I was not a person, but a piece of property.

Another time, in the same city, I took a seat, unobserved, far up in the street car, among the white passengers. All at once I heard the conductor, in an angry tone, order another colored man, who was modestly standing on the platform of the rear end of the car, to get off, and actually stopped the car to push him off, when I, from within, with all the emphasis I could throw into my voice, in imitation of my chivalrous friend Marshall, of Kentucky, sung out, 'Go on! Let the gentleman alone! No one here objects to his riding.' Unhappily, the fellow saw where the voice came from, and turned his wrathful attention to me, and said, 'You shall get out also!' I told him I would do no such thing, and if he attempted to remove me by force he would do it at his peril. Whether the young man was afraid to tackle me, or did not wish to disturb the passengers, I do not know. At any rate, he did not attempt to execute his threat, and I rode on in peace till I reached Chestnut street, when I got off and went about my business.

On my way down the Hudson river, from Albany to New York, at one time, on the steamer Alida, in company with some English ladies who had seen me in their own country, received and treated as a gentleman, I ventured, like any other passenger, to go, at the call of the dinner bell, into the cabin and take a seat at the table; but I was forcibly taken from it and compelled to leave the cabin. My friends, who wished to enjoy a day's trip on the beautiful Hudson, left the table with me, and went to New York hungry and not a little indignant and disgusted at such barbarism. There were influential persons on board the Alida, on this occasion, a word from whom might have spared me this indignity; but there was no Edward Marshall among them to defend the weak and rebuke the strong.

When Miss Sarah Jane Clark,* one of America's brilliant literary ladies, known to the world under the *nom de plume* of Grace Greenwood, was young and as brave as she was beautiful, I encountered, on one of the Ohio river steamers, an experience similar to that on the Alida, and that lady, being on board, arose from her seat at the table, expressed her disapprobation and, with her sister, moved majestically away to the upper deck. Her conduct seemed to amaze the lookers on, but it filled me with grateful admiration.

When on my way, in 1852, to attend at Pittsburg the great Free Soil Convention which nominated John P. Hale* for President and George W. Julian for Vice-President, the train stopped for dinner at Alliance, Ohio, and I attempted to enter the hotel with the other delegates, but was rudely repulsed, when many of them, learning of it, rose from the table, denounced the outrage and refused to finish their dinners.

In anticipation of our return, at the close of the convention, Mr. Sam. Beck, the proprietor of the hotel, prepared dinner for three hundred guests, but when the train arrived not one of the large company went into his place, and his dinner was left to spoil.

A dozen years ago, or more, on one of the frostiest and coldest nights I ever experienced, I delivered a lecture in the town of Elmwood, Illinois, twenty miles distant from Peoria. It was one of those bleak and flinty nights, when prairie winds pierce like needles, and a step on the snow sounds like a file on the steel teeth of a saw. My next appointment after Elmwood was on Monday night, and in order to reach it in time, it was necessary to go to Peoria the night previous, so as to take an early morning train, and I could only accomplish this by leaving Elmwood after my lecture at midnight, for there was no Sunday train. So a little before the hour at which my train was expected at Elmwood, I started for the station with my friend Mr. Brown, the gentleman who had kindly entertained me during my stay. On the way I said to him, 'I am going to Peoria with something like a real dread of the place. I expect to be compelled to walk the streets of that city all night to keep from freezing.' I told him that 'the last time I was there I could obtain no shelter at any hotel and I fear I shall meet a similar exclusion to-night.' Mr. Brown was visibly affected by the statement and for some time was silent. At last, as if suddenly discovering a way out of a painful situation, he said, 'I know a man in Peoria, should the hotels be closed against you there, who would gladly open his doors to you—a man who will receive you at any hour of the night, and in any weather, and that man is Robert G. Ingersoll.'* 'Why,' said I, 'it would not do to disturb a family at such a time as I shall arrive there, on a night so cold as this.' 'No matter about the hour,' he said; 'neither he nor his family would be happy if they thought you were shelterless on such a night. I know Mr. Ingersoll, and that he will be glad to welcome you at midnight or at cock-crow.' I became much interested by this description of Mr. Ingersoll. Fortunately I had no occasion for disturbing him or his family. I found quarters for the night at the best hotel in the city. In the morning I resolved to know more of this now famous and noted 'infidel.' I gave him an early call, for I was not so abundant in cash as to refuse hospitality in a strange city when on a mission of 'good will to men.' The experiment worked admirably. Mr. Ingersoll was at home, and if I have ever met a man with real living human sunshine in his face, and honest, manly kindness in his voice, I met one who possessed these qualities that morning. I received a welcome from Mr. Ingersoll and his family which would have been a cordial to the bruised heart of any proscribed and storm-beaten stranger, and one which I can never forget or fail to appreciate. Perhaps there were Christian ministers and Christian families in Peoria at that time by whom I might have been received in the same gracious manner. In charity I am bound to say there probably were such ministers and such families, but I am equally bound to say that in my former visits to this place I had failed to find them. Incidents of this character have greatly tended to liberalize my views as to the value of creeds in estimating the character of men. They have brought me to the conclusion that genuine goodness is the same, whether found inside or outside the church, and that to be an 'infidel' no more proves a man to be selfish, mean, and wicked. than to be evangelical proves him to be honest, just, and humane.

It may possibly be inferred from what I have said of the prevalence of prejudice, and the practice of proscription, that I have had a very miserable sort of life, or that I must be remarkably insensible to public aversion. Neither inference is true. I have neither been miserable because of the ill-feeling of those about me, nor indifferent to popular approval; and I think, upon the whole, I have passed a tolerably cheerful and even joyful life. I have never felt myself isolated since I entered the field to plead the cause of the slave, and demand equal rights for all. In every town and city where it has been my lot to speak, there have been raised up for me friends of both colors to cheer and strengthen me in my work. I have always felt, too, that I had on my side all the invisible forces of the moral government of the universe. Happily for me I have had the wit to distinguish between what is merely artificial and transient and what is fundamental and permanent; and resting on the latter, I could cheerfully encounter the former. 'How do you feel,' said a friend to me, 'when you are hooted and jeered on the street on account of your color?' 'I feel as if an ass had kicked, but had hit nobody,' was my answer.

I have been greatly helped to bear up under unfriendly conditions, too, by a constitutional tendency to see the funny sides of things, which has enabled me to laugh at follies that others would soberly resent. Besides, there were compensations as well as drawbacks in my relations to the white race. A passenger on the deck of a Hudson river steamer, covered with a shawl, well-worn and dingy, I was addressed by a remarkably-religiously-missionary-looking man in black coat and white cravat, who took me for one of the noble red men of the far West, with 'From away back?' I was silent, and he added, 'Indian, Indian?' 'No, no,' I said; 'I am a negro.' The dear man seemed to have no missionary work with me, and retreated with evident marks of disgust.

On another occasion, traveling by a night train on the New York Central railroad, when the cars were crowded and seats were scarce, and I was occupying a whole seat, the only luxury my color afforded me in traveling, I had laid down, with my head partly covered, thinking myself secure in my possession, when a well dressed man approached and wished to share the seat with me. Slightly rising, I said, 'Don't sit down here, my friend, I am a nigger.' 'I don't care who the devil you are,' he said, 'I mean to sit with you.' 'Well, if it must be so,' I said, 'I can stand it if you can,' and we at once fell into a very pleasant conversation, and passed the hours on the road very happily together. These two incidents illustrate my career in respect of popular prejudice. If I have had kicks, I have also had kindness. If cast down, I have been exalted; and the latter experience has, after all, far exceeded the former.

During a quarter of a century I resided in the city of Rochester, N. Y. When I removed from there, my friends caused a marble bust to be made from me, and have since honored it with a place in Sibley Hall, of Rochester University. Less in a spirit of vanity than that of gratitude,

I copy here the remarks of the Rochester *Democrat and Chronicle* on the occasion, and on my letter of thanks for the honor done me by my friends and fellow-citizens of that beautiful city:

ROCHESTER, June 28, 1879.
FREDERICK DOUGLASS.

'It will be remembered that a bust of Frederick Douglass was recently placed in Sibley Hall of the University of Rochester. The ceremonies were quite informal, too informal, we think, as commemorating a deserved tribute from the people of Rochester to one who will always rank as among her most distinguished citizens. Mr. Douglass himself was not notified officially of the event, and therefore could, in no public manner, take notice of it. He was, however, informed privately of it by the gentlemen whose address is given below, and responded to it most happily, as will be seen by the following letter which we are permitted to publish.' Then follows the letter which I omit, and add the further comments of the *Chronicle*. 'It were alone worth all the efforts of the gentlemen who united in the fitting recognition of the public services and the private worth of Frederick Douglass, to have inspired a letter thus tender in its sentiment, and so suggestive of the various phases of a career than which the republic has witnessed none more strange or more noble. Frederick Douglass can hardly be said to have risen to greatness on account of the opportunities which the republic offers to self-made men, and concerning which we are apt to talk with an abundance of self-gratulation. It sought to fetter his mind equally with his body. For him it builded no school-house, and for him it erected no church. So far as he was concerned freedom was a mockery, and law was the instrument of tyranny. In spite of law and gospel, despite of statutes which thralled him and opportunities which jeered at him, he made himself by trampling on the law and breaking through the thick darkness that encompassed him. There is no sadder commentary upon American slavery than the life of Frederick Douglass. He put it under his feet and stood erect in the majesty of his intellect; but how many intellects as brilliant and as powerful as his it stamped upon and crushed, no mortal can tell until the secrets of its terrible despotism are fully revealed. Thanks to the conquering might of American freemen, such sad beginnings of such illustrious lives as that of Frederick Douglass are no longer possible; and that they are no longer possible, is largely due to him who, when his lips were unlocked, became a deliverer of his people. Not alone did his voice proclaim emancipation. Eloquent as was that voice, his life in its pathos and its grandeur, was more eloquent still; and where shall be found, in the annals of humanity, a sweeter rendering of poetic justice than that he, who has passed through such vicissitudes of degradation and exaltation, has been permitted to behold the redemption of his race?

'Rochester is proud to remember that Frederick Douglass was, for many years, one of her citizens. He who pointed out the house where Douglass lived, hardly exaggerated when he called it the residence of the greatest of our citizens; for Douglass must rank as among the greatest men, not only of this city, but of the nation as well—great in gifts, greater in utilizing them, great in his inspiration, greater in his efforts for humanity, great in the persuasion of his speech, greater in the purpose that informed it.

'Rochester could do nothing more graceful than to perpetuate in marble the features of this citizen in her hall of learning; and it is pleasant for her to know that he so well appreciates the esteem in which he is held here. It was a thoughtful thing for Rochester to do, and the response is as heartfelt as the tribute is appropriate.'

# CHAPTER XVIII.

## 'HONOR TO WHOM HONOR.'

*Grateful recognition—Friends in need—Lucretia Mott—Lydia Maria Child—Sarah and Angelina Grimke—Abby Kelley—H. Beecher Stowe—Other Friends—Woman Suffrage.*

GRATITUDE to benefactors is a well recognized virtue, and to express it in some form or other, however imperfectly, is a duty to ourselves as well as to those who have helped us. Never reluctant or tardy, I trust, in the discharge of this duty, I have seldom been satisfied with the manner of its performance. When I have made my best effort in this line, my words have done small justice to my feelings. And now, in mentioning my obligations to my special friends, and acknowledging the help I received from them in the days of my need, I can hope to do no better than give a faint hint of my sense of the value of their friendship and assistance. I have sometimes been credited with having been the architect of my own fortune, and have pretty generally received the title of a 'self-made man;' and while I cannot altogether disclaim this title, when I look back over the facts of my life, and consider the helpful influences exerted upon me, by friends more fortunately born and educated than myself, I am compelled to give them at least an equal measure of credit, with myself, for the success which has attended my labors in life. The little energy, industry, and perseverance which have been mine, would hardly have availed me, in the absence of thoughtful friends, and highly favoring circumstances. Without these, the last forty years of my life might have been spent on the wharves of New Bedford, rolling oil casks, loading ships for whaling voyages, sawing wood, putting in coal, picking up a job here and there, wherever I could find one, and in the race for life and bread, holding my own with difficulty against gauntsided poverty. I never see one of my old companions of the lower strata, begrimed by toil, hard handed and dust covered, receiving for wages scarcely enough to keep the 'wolf' at a respectful distance from his door and hearthstone, without a fellow feeling and the thought that I have been separated from him only by circumstances other than those of my own making. Much to be thankful for, I find here but little room for boasting. It was mine to take the 'Tide at its flood.'* It was my good fortune to get out of slavery at the right time, and to be speedily brought into contact with that circle of highly cultivated men and women, banded together for the overthrow of slavery, of which Wm. Lloyd Garrison was the acknowledged leader. To these friends, earnest, courageous, inflexible, ready to own me as a man and brother, against all the scorn, contempt, and derision of a slavery-polluted atmosphere, I owe my success in life. The story is simple, and the truth plain. They thought that I possessed qualities that might be made useful to my race, and through them I was brought to the notice of the world, and gained a hold upon the attention of the American people, which I hope remains unbroken to this day. The list of these friends is too long certainly to be inserted here, but I cannot forbear to recall in this connection the names of Francis Jackson, Joseph Southwick, Samuel E. Sewell, Samuel J. May, John Pierpont, Henry I. Bowditch, Theodore Parker, Wendell Phillips, Edmund Quincy, Isaac T. Hopper, James N. Buffum, Ellis Gray Loring, Andrew Robeson, Seth Hunt, Arnold Buffum, Nathaniel B. Borden, Boone Spooner, William Thomas, John Milton Earle, John Curtis, George Foster, Clother Gifford, John Bailey, Nathaniel P. Rodgers, Stephen S. Foster, Parker Pillsbury, the Hutchinson family, Dr. Peleg Clark, the Burleigh brothers, William Chase, Samuel and Harvey Chase, John Brown, C. C. Eldredge, Daniel Mitchell, William Adams, Isaac Kenyon, Joseph Sisson, Daniel Goold, Kelton brothers, Geo. James Adams, Martin Cheeney, Edward Harris, Robert Shove, Alpheus Jones, Asa Fairbanks, Gen. Sam'l Fessenden, William Aplin, John Clark, Thomas Davis, George L. Clark; these all took me to their hearts and homes, and inspired me with an incentive which a confiding and helpful friendship can alone impart.

Nor were my influential friends all of the Caucasian race. While many of my own people thought me unwise and somewhat fanatical in announcing myself a fugitive slave, and in practically asserting the rights of my people, on all occasions, in season and out of season, there were brave and intelligent men of color all over the United States who gave me their cordial sympathy and support. Among these, and foremost, I place the name of Doctor James McCune Smith;* educated in Scotland, and breathing the free air of that country, he came back to his native land with ideas of liberty which placed him in advance of most of his fellow citizens of African descent. He was not only a learned and skillful physician, but an effective speaker, and a keen and polished writer. In my newspaper enterprise, I found in him an earnest and effective helper. The cause of his people lost an able advocate when he died. He was never among the timid who thought me too aggressive and wished me to tone down my testimony to suit the times. A brave man himself, he knew how to esteem courage in others.

Of David Ruggles I have already spoken. He gave me my send off from New York to New Bedford, and when I came into public life, he was among the first with words of cheer. Jehiel C. Beman too, a noble man, kindly took me by the hand. Thomas Van Ranselear was among my fast friends. No young man, starting in an untried field of usefulness, and needing support, could find that support in larger measure than I found it, in William Whipper, Robert Purvis, William P. Powell, Nathan Johnson, Charles B. Ray, Thomas Downing, Theodore S. Wright or Charles L. Reason. Notwithstanding what I have said of my treatment, at times, by people of my own color, when traveling, I am bound to say that there is another and brighter side to that picture. Among the waiters and attendants on public conveyances, I have often found real gentlemen; intelligent, aspiring, and who fully appreciated all my efforts in behalf of our common cause. Especially have I found this to be the case in the East. A more gentlemanly and self-respecting class of men it would be difficult to find, than those to be met on the various lines between New York and Boston. I have never wanted for kind attention, or any effort they could make to render my journeying with them smooth and pleasant. I owe this solely to my work in our common cause, and to their intelligent estimate of the value of that work. Republics are said to be ungrateful, but ingratitude is not among the weaknesses of my people. No people ever had a more lively sense of the value of faithful endeavor to serve their interests than they. But for this feeling towards me on their part, I might have passed many nights hungry and cold, and without any place to lay my head. I need not name my colored friends to whom I am thus indebted. They do not desire such mention, but I wish any who have shown me kindness, even so much as to give me a cup of cold water, to feel themselves included in my thanks.

It is also due to myself, to make some more emphatic mention than I have yet done, of the honorable women, who have not only assisted me, but who according to their opportunity and ability, have generously contributed to the abolition of slavery, and the recognition of the equal manhood of the colored race. When the true history of the anti-slavery cause shall be written, women will occupy a large space in its pages; for the cause of the slave has been peculiarly woman's cause. Her heart and her conscience have supplied in large degree its motive and mainspring. Her skill, industry, patience, and perseverance have been wonderfully manifest in every trial hour. Not only did her feet run on 'willing errands,' and her fingers do the work which in large degree supplied the sinews of war, but her deep moral convictions, and her tender human sensibilities, found convincing and persuasive expression by her pen and her voice. Foremost among these noble American women, in point of clearness of vision, breadth of understanding, fullness of knowledge, catholicity of spirit, weight of character, and widespread influence, was Lucretia Mott* of Philadelphia. Great as this woman was in speech, and persuasive as she was in her writings, she was incomparably greater in her presence. She spoke to the world through every line of her countenance. In her there was no lack of symmetry—no contradiction between her thought and act. Seated in an anti-slavery meeting, looking benignantly around upon the assembly, her silent presence made others eloquent, and carried the argument home to the heart of the audience.

The known approval of such a woman, in any cause, went far to commend it.

I shall never forget the first time I ever saw and heard Lucretia Mott. It was in the town of Lynn, Massachusetts. It was not in a magnificent hall, where such as she seemed to belong, but in a little hall over Jonathan Buffum's store, the only place then open, even in that so-called radical anti-slavery town, for an anti-slavery meeting on Sunday. But in this day of small things, the smallness of the place was no mater of complaint or murmuring. It was a cause of rejoicing that any kind of place could be had for such a purpose. But Jonathan Buffum's courage was equal to this and more.

The speaker was attired in the usual Quaker dress, free from startling colors, plain, rich, elegant, and without superfluity—the very sight of her, a sermon. In a few moments after she began to speak, I saw before me no more a woman, but a glorified presence, bearing a message of light and love from the Infinite to a benighted and strangely wandering world, straying away from the paths of truth and justice into the wilderness of pride and selfishness, where peace is lost and true happiness is sought in vain. I heard Mrs. Mott thus, when she was comparatively young. I have often heard her since, sometimes in the solemn temple, and sometimes under the open sky, but whenever and wherever I have listened to her, my heart has always been made better and my spirit raised by her words; and in speaking thus for myself I am sure I am expressing the experience of thousands.

Kindred in spirit with Mrs. Mott was Lydia Maria Child.* They both exerted an influence with a class of the American people which neither Garrison, Phillips nor Gerrit Smith could reach. Sympathetic in her nature, it was easy for Mrs. Child to 'remember those in bonds as bound with them;' and her 'appeal for that class of Americans called Africans,' issued, as it was, at an early stage in the anti-slavery conflict, was one of the most effective agencies in arousing attention to the cruelty and injustice of slavery. When, with her husband, David Lee Child, she edited the *National Anti-Slavery Standard*, that paper was made attractive to a broad circle of readers, from the circumstance that each issue contained a 'Letter from New York,' written by her on some passing subject of the day, in which she always managed to infuse a spirit of brotherly love and good will, with an abhorrence of all that was unjust, selfish and mean, and in this way won to anti-slavery many hearts which else would have remained cold and indifferent.

Of Sarah and Angelina Grimke* I knew but little personally. These brave sisters from Charleston, South Carolina, had inherited slaves, but in their conversion from Episcopacy to Quakerism, in 1828, they became convinced that they had no right to such inheritance. They emancipated their slaves and came North and entered at once upon pioneer work in advancing the education of woman, though they saw then in their course only their duty to the slave. They had 'fought the good fight' before I came into the ranks, but by their unflinching testimony and unwavering courage, they had opened the way and made it possible, if not easy, for other women to follow their example.

It is memorable of them that their public advocacy of anti-slavery was made the occasion of the issuing by the evangelical clergy of Boston, of a papal bull, in the form of a 'pastoral letter,' in which the churches and all God-fearing people were warned against their influence.

For solid, persistent, indefatigable work for the slave Abby Kelley was without a rival. In the 'History of Woman Suffrage,' just published by Mrs. Stanton, Miss Anthony, and Mrs. Joseph Gage, there is this fitting tribute to her: 'Abby Kelley was the most untiring and most persecuted of all the women who labored throughout the anti-slavery struggle. She traveled up and down, alike in winter's cold and summer's heat, with scorn, ridicule, violence and mobs accompanying her, suffering all kinds of persecutions, still speaking whenever and whereever she gained an audience—in the open air, in school house, barn, depot, church, or public hall, on week day or Sunday, as she found opportunity.' And, incredible as it will soon seem, if it does not appear so already, 'for listening to her on Sunday many men and women were expelled from their churches.'

When the abolitionists of Rhode Island were seeking to defeat the restricted constitution of the Dorr party, already referred to in this volume, Abby Kelley was more than once mobbed in the old town hall in the city of Providence, and pelted with bad eggs.

And what can be said of the gifted authoress of 'Uncle Tom's Cabin,' Harriet Beecher Stowe? Happy woman must she be that to her was given the power in such unstinted measure to touch and move the popular heart! More than to reason or religion are we indebted to the influence which this wonderful delineation of American chattel slavery produced on the public mind.

Nor must I omit to name the daughter of the excellent Myron Holly,* who in her youth and beauty espoused the cause of the slave, nor of Lucy Stone* and Antoinette Brown,* for when the slave had few friends and advocates they were noble enough to speak their best word in his behalf.

Others there were who, though they were not known on the platform, were none the less earnest and effective for anti-slavery in their more retired lives. There were many such to greet me and welcome me to my newly-found heritage of freedom. They met me as a brother, and by their kind consideration did much to make endurable the rebuffs I encountered elsewhere. At the antislavery office in Providence, Rhode Island, I remember with a peculiar interest Lucinda Wilmarth, whose acceptance of life's duties and labors, and whose heroic struggle with sickness and death, taught me more than one lesson; and Amorancy Paine, who was never weary in performing any service, however arduous, which fidelity to the slave demanded of her. Then there were Phebe Jackson, Elizabeth Chace, the Sisson sisters, the Chases, the Greenes, the Browns, the Goolds, the Shoves, the Anthonys, the Roses, the Fayerweathers, the Motts, the Earles, the Spooners, the Southwicks, the Buffums, the Fords, the Wilburs, the Henshaws, the Burgesses, and others whose names are lost, but whose deeds are living yet in the regenerated life of our new republic cleansed from the curse and sin of slavery.

Observing woman's agency, devotion, and efficiency in pleading the cause of the slave, gratitude for this high service early moved me to give favorable attention to the subject of what is called 'woman's rights' and caused me to be denominated a woman's-rights man. I am glad to say that I have never been ashamed to be thus designated. Recognizing not sex nor physical strength, but moral intelligence and the ability to discern right from wrong, good from evil, and the power to choose between them, as the true basis of republican government, to which all are alike subject and all bound alike to obey, I was not long in reaching the conclusion that there was no foundation in reason or justice for woman's exclusion from the right of choice in the selection of the persons who should frame the laws, and thus shape the destiny of all the people, irrespective of sex.

In a conversation with Mrs. Elizabeth Cady Stanton* when she was yet a young lady and an earnest abolitionist, she was at the pains of setting before me in a very strong light the wrong and injustice of this exclusion. I could not meet her arguments except with the shallow plea of 'custom,' 'natural division of duties,' 'indelicacy of woman's taking part in politics,' the common talk of 'woman's sphere,' and the like, all of which that able woman, who was then no less logical than now, brushed away by those arguments which she has so often and effectively used since, and which no man has yet successfully refuted. If intelligence is the only true and rational basis of government, it follows that that is the best government which draws its life and power from the largest sources of wisdom, energy, and goodness at its command. The force of this reasoning would be easily comprehended and readily assented to in any case involving the employment of physical strength. We should all see the folly and madness of attempting to accomplish with a part what could only be done with the united strength of the whole. Though his folly may be less apparent, it is just as real when one-half of the moral and intellectual power of the world is excluded from any voice or vote in civil government. In this denial of the right to participate in government, not merely the degradation of woman and the perpetuation of a great injustice happens, but the maiming and repudiation of one-half of the moral and intellectual power of the government of the world. Thus far all human governments have been failures, for none have secured, except in a partial degree, the ends for which governments are instituted.

War, slavery, injustice and oppression, and the idea that might makes right have been uppermost in all such governments, and the weak, for whose protection governments are ostensibly created, have had practically no rights which the strong have felt bound to respect. The slayers of thousands have been exalted into heroes, and the worship of mere physical force has been considered glorious. Nations have been and still are but armed camps, expending their wealth and strength and ingenuity in forging weapons of destruction against each other; and while it may not be contended that the introduction of the feminine element in government would entirely cure this tendency to exalt woman's influence over right, many reasons can be given to show that woman's influence would greatly tend to check and modify this barbarous and destructive tendency. At any rate, seeing that the male governments of the world have failed, it can do no harm to try the experiment of a government by man and woman united. But it is not my purpose to argue the question here, but simply to state in a brief way the ground of my espousal of the cause of woman's suffrage. I believed that the exclusion of my race from participation in government was not only a wrong, but a great mistake, because it took from that race motives for high thought and endeavor and degraded them in the eyes of the world around them. Man derives a sense of his consequence in the world not merely subjectively, but objectively. If from the cradle through life the outside world brands a class as unfit for this or that work, the character of the class will come to resemble and conform to the character described. To find valuable qualities in our fellows, such qualities must be presumed and expected. I would give woman a vote, give her a motive to qualify herself to vote, precisely as I insisted upon giving the colored man the right to vote; in order that she shall have the same motives for making herself a useful citizen as those in force in the case of other citizens. In a word, I have never yet been able to find one consideration, one argument, or suggestion in favor of man's right to participate in civil government which did not equally apply to the right of woman.

# CHAPTER XIX.

## RETROSPECTION.

*Meeting of colored citizens in Washington to express their sympathy at the great national bereavement, the death of President Garfield—Concluding reflections and convictions.*

ON the day of the interment of the late James A. Garfield, at Lake View cemetery, Cleveland, Ohio, a day of gloom long to be remembered as the closing scene in one of the most tragic and startling dramas ever witnessed in this or in any other country, the colored people of the District of Columbia assembled in the Fifteenth street Presbyterian church, and expressed by appropriate addresses and resolutions their respect for the character and memory of the illustrious deceased. On that occasion I was called on to preside, and by way of introducing the subsequent proceedings (leaving to others the grateful office of delivering eulogies), made the following brief reference to the solemn and touching event:

'*Friends and fellow citizens:*

'To-day our common mother Earth has closed over the mortal remains of James A. Garfield, at Cleveland, Ohio. The light of no day in our national history has brought to the American people a more intense bereavement, a deeper sorrow, or a more profound sense of humiliation. It seems only as yesterday, that in my quality as United States Marshal of the District of Columbia, it was made my duty and privilege to walk at the head of the column in advance of this our President-elect, from the crowded Senate Chamber of the national capitol, through the long corridors and the grand rotunda, beneath the majestic dome, to the platform on the portico, where, amid a sea of transcendent pomp and glory, he who is now dead was hailed with tumultuous applause from uncounted thousands of his fellow citizens, and was inaugurated Chief Magistrate of the United States. The scene was one never to be forgotten by those who beheld it. It was a great day for the nation, glad and proud to do honor to their chosen ruler. It was a glad day for James A. Garfield. It was a glad day for me, that I—one of the proscribed race—was permitted to bear so prominent a part in its august ceremonies. Mr. Garfield was then in the midst of his years, in the fulness and vigor of his manhood, covered with honors beyond the reach of princes, entering upon a career more abundant in promise than ever before invited president or potentate.

'Alas, what a contrast as he lay in state under the same broad dome, viewed by sorrowful thousands day after day! What is the life of man? What are all his plans, purposes and hopes? What are the shouts of the multitude, or the pride and pomp of this world? How vain and unsubstantial, in the light of this sad and shocking experience, do they all appear! Who can tell what a day or an hour will bring forth? Such reflections inevitably present themselves as most natural and fitting on an occasion like this.

'Fellow citizens, we are here to take suitable notice of the sad and appalling event of the hour. We are here, not merely as American citizens, but as colored American citizens. Although our hearts have gone along with those of the nation at large, in every expression, in every token and demonstration of honor to the dead, of sympathy with the living, and abhorrence for the horrible deed which has at last done its final work; though we have watched with beating hearts the long and heroic struggle for life, and endured all the agony of suspense and fear; we have felt that something more, something more specific and distinctive, was due from us. Our relation to the American people makes us in some sense a peculiar class, and unless we speak separately, our voice is not heard. We therefore propose to put on record tonight our sense of the worth of President Garfield, and of the calamity involved in his death. Called to preside on this occasion, my part in the speaking shall be brief. I cannot claim to have been on intimate terms with the late President. There are other gentlemen here who are better qualified than myself to speak of his character. I may say, however, that soon after he came to Washington I had a conversation with him of much interest to the colored people, since it indicated his just and generous intentions towards them, and goes far to present him in the light of a wise and patriotic statesman, and a friend of our race.

'I called at the executive mansion, and was received very kindly by Mr. Garfield, who, in the course of the conversation, said, that he felt the time had come when a step should be taken in advance, in recognition of the claims of colored citizens, and expressed his intention of sending some colored representatives abroad to other than colored nations. He enquired of me how I thought such representations would be received? I assured him that I thought they would be well received; that in my own experience abroad I had observed that the higher we go in the gradations of human society, the farther we get from prejudice of race or color. I was greatly pleased with the assurance of his liberal policy towards us. I remarked to him, that no part of the American people would be treated with respect if systematically ignored by the government and denied all participation in its honors and emoluments. To this he assented, and went so far as to propose my going in a representative capacity to an important post abroad—a compliment which I gratefully acknowledged, but respectfully declined. I wished to remain at home and to retain the office of United States Marshal of the District of Columbia.

'It is a great thing for Hon. John Mercer Langston to represent this republic at Port au Prince, and for Henry Highland Garnet to represent us in Liberia, but it would be indeed a step in advance to have some colored men sent to represent us in white nationalities, and we have reason for profound regret that Mr. Garfield could not have lived to carry out his just and wise intentions towards us. I might say more of this conversation, but I will not detain you except to say that America has had many great men, but no man among them all has had better things said of him than has he who has been reverently committed to the dust in Cleveland to-day.'

Mr. Douglass then called upon Professor Greener,* who read a series of resolutions eloquently expressive of their sense of the great loss that had been sustained and of their sympathy with the family of the late President. Prof. Greener then spoke briefly, and was followed by Prof. John M. Langston and Rev. W. W. Hicks. All the speakers expressed their confidence in President Arthur,* and in his ability to give the country a wise and beneficial administration.

# CONCLUSION.

As far as this volume can reach that point I have now brought my readers to the end of my story. What may remain of life to me, through what experiences I may pass, what heights I may attain, into what depths I may fall, what good or ill may come to me, or proceed from me in this breathing world where all is change and uncertainty and largely at the mercy of powers over which the individual man has no absolute control; all this, if thought worthy and useful, will probably be told by others when I have passed from the busy stage of life. I am not looking for any great changes in my fortunes or achievements in the future. The most of the space of life is behind me and the sun of my day is nearing the horizon. Notwithstanding all that is contained in this book my day has been a pleasant one. My joys have far exceeded my sorrows and my friends have brought me far more than my enemies have taken from me. I have written out my experience here, not in order to exhibit my wounds and bruises and to awaken and attract sympathy to myself personally, but as a part of the history of a profoundly interesting period in American life and progress. I have meant it to be a small individual contribution to the sum of knowledge of this special period, to be handed down to after-coming generations which may want to know what things were allowed and what prohibited; what moral, social and political relations subsisted between the different varieties of the American people down to the last quarter of the nineteenth century and by what means they were modified and changed. The time is at hand when the last American slave and the last American slaveholder will disappear behind the curtain which separates the living from the dead and when neither master nor slave will be left to tell the story of their respective relations or what happened to either in those relations. My part has been to tell the story of the slave. The story of the master never wanted for narrators. The masters, to tell their story, had at call all the talent and genius that wealth and influence could command. They have had their full day in court. Literature, theology, philosophy, law and learning have come willingly to their service, and, if condemned, they have not been condemned unheard.

It will be seen in these pages that I have lived several lives in one: first, the life of slavery; secondly, the life of a fugitive from slavery; thirdly, the life of comparative freedom; fourthly, the life of conflict and battle; and, fifthly, the life of victory, if not complete, at least assured. To those who have suffered in slavery I can say, I, too, have suffered. To those who have taken some risks and encountered hardships in the flight from bondage I can say, I, too, have endured and risked. To those who have battled for liberty, brotherhood, and citizenship I can say, I, too, have battled. And to those who have lived to enjoy the fruits of victory I can say, I, too, live and rejoice. If I have pushed my example too prominently for the good taste of my Caucasian readers, I beg them to remember that I have written in part for the encouragement of a class whose aspirations need the stimulus of success.

I have aimed to assure them that knowledge can be obtained under difficulties; that poverty may give place to competency; that obscurity is not an absolute bar to distinction, and that a way is open to welfare and happiness to all who will resolutely and wisely pursue that way; that neither slavery, stripes, imprisonment nor proscription need extinguish self-respect, crush manly ambition, or paralyze effort; that no power outside of himself can prevent a man from sustaining an honorable character and a useful relation to his day and generation; that neither institutions nor friends can make a race to stand unless it has strength in its own legs; that there is no power in the world which can be relied upon to help the weak against the strong or the simple against the wise; that races, like individuals, must stand or fall by their own merits; that all the prayers of Christendom cannot stop the force of a single bullet, divest arsenic of poison, or suspend any law of nature. In my communication with the colored people I have endeavored to deliver them from the power of superstition, bigotry, and priest-craft. In theology I have found them strutting about in the old clothes of the masters, just as the masters strut about in the old clothes of the past. The falling power remains among them long since it has ceased to be the religious fashion in our refined and elegant white churches. I have taught that the 'fault is not in our stars, but in ourselves, that we are underlings,'* that 'who would be free, themselves must strike the blow.'* I have urged upon them self-reliance, self-respect, industry, perseverance, and economy, to make the best of both worlds, but to make the best of this world first because it comes first, and that he who does not improve himself by the motives and opportunities afforded by this world gives the best evidence that he would not improve in any other world. Schooled as I have been among the abolitionists of New England, I recognize that the universe is governed by laws which are unchangeable and eternal, that what men sow they will reap, and that there is no way to dodge or circumvent the consequences of any act or deed. My views at this point receive but limited endorsement among my people. They, for the most part, think they have means of procuring special favor and help from the Almighty; and, as their 'faith is the substance of things hoped for and the evidence of things not seen,'* they find much in this expression which is true to faith, but utterly false to fact. But I meant here only to say a word in conclusion. Forty years of my life have been given to the cause of my people, and if I had forty years more they should all be sacredly given to the same great cause. If I have done something for that cause, I am, after all, more a debtor to it than it is debtor to me.

# APPENDIX.

ORATION BY FREDERICK DOUGLASS, DELIVERED ON THE OCCASION OF THE UNVEILING OF THE FREEDMEN's MONUMENT, IN MEMORY OF ABRAHAM LINCOLN, IN LINCOLN PARK, WASHINGTON, D.C., APRIL 14, 1876.

*Friends and Fellow Citizens*:

I warmly congratulate you upon the highly interesting object which has caused you to assemble in such numbers and spirit as you have to-day. This occasion is, in some respects, remarkable. Wise and thoughtful men of our race who shall come after us and study the lesson of our history in the United States, who shall survey the long and dreary spaces over which we have traveled and who shall count the links in the great chain of events by which we have reached our present position, will make a note of this occasion. They will think of it and speak of it with a sense of manly pride and complacency.

I congratulate you, also, upon the very favorable circumstances in which we meet to-day. They are high, inspiring, and uncommon. They lend grace, glory, and significance to the object for which we have met. Nowhere else in this great country, with its uncounted towns and cities, unlimited wealth, and immeasurable territory extending from sea to sea, could conditions be found more favorable to the success of this occasion than are found here.

We stand to-day at the national center to perform something like a national act—an act which is to go into history; and we are here where every pulsation of the national heart can be heard, felt, and reciprocated. A thousand wires, fed with thought and winged with lightning, put us in instantaneous communication with the loyal and true men all over this country.

Few facts could better illustrate the vast and wonderful change which has taken place in our condition as a people than the fact of our assembling here to-day for the purpose which has called us together. Harmless, beautiful, proper and praiseworthy as this demonstration is, I cannot forget that no such demonstration would have been tolerated here twenty years ago. The spirit of slavery and barbarism which, in some dark and distant parts of our country, still lingers to blight and to destroy, would have made our assembling here the signal and excuse for opening upon us all the flood-gates of wrath and violence. That we are here in peace to-day is a compliment and a credit to American civilization and a prophecy of still greater national enlightenment and progress in the future. I refer to the past, not in malice, for this is no day for malice, but simply to place more distinctly in front the gratifying and glorious change which has come both to our white fellow-citizens and to ourselves, and to congratulate all upon the contrast between now and then—between the new dispensation of freedom with its thousand blessings to both races, and the old dispensation of slavery with its ten thousand evils to both races, white and black. In view, then, of the past, the present, and the future, with the long and dark history of our bondage behind us, and with liberty, progress, and enlightenment before us, I again congratulate you upon this auspicious day and hour.

Friends and fellow citizens, the story of our presence here is soon and easily told. We are here in the District of Columbia, here in the city of Washington, the most luminous point of American territory, a city recently transformed and made beautiful in its body and in its spirit. We are here in the place where the ablest and best men of the country are sent to devise the policy, enact the laws, and shape the destiny of the Republic. We are here, with the stately pillars and majestic dome of the Capitol of the nation looking down upon us; we are here, with the broad earth freshly adorned with the foliage and flowers of spring for our church, and all races, colors, and conditions of men for our congregation—in a word, we are here to express, as best we may, by appropriate forms and ceremonies, our grateful sense of the vast, high and preëminent services rendered by Abraham Lincoln to ourselves, to our race, to our country and to the whole world.

The sentiment that brings us here to-day is one of the noblest that can stir and thrill the human heart. It has crowned the high places of all civilized nations and made them glorious with the grandest and most enduring works of art, designed to illustrate the characters and perpetuate the memories of great public men. It is the sentiment which from year to year adorns with fragrant and beautiful flowers the graves of our loyal, brave, and patriotic soldiers who fell in defence of the Union and liberty. It is the sentiment of gratitude and appreciation, which has, in the presence of many who hear me, often filled yonder heights of Arlington with the eloquence of eulogy and the sublime enthusiasm of poetry and song; a sentiment which can never die while the Republic lives.

For the first time in the history of our people, and in the history of the whole American people, we join in this high worship, and march conspicuously in the line of this time-honored custom. First things are always interesting, and this is one of our first things. It is the first time that, in this form and manner, we have sought to do honor to an American great man, however deserving and illustrious. I commend the fact to notice. Let it be told in every part of the Republic. Let men of all parties and opinions hear it. Let those who despise us, not less than those who respect us, know it and that now and here, in the spirit of liberty, loyalty and gratitude, we unite in this act of reverent homage. Let it be known every where, and by everybody who takes an interest in human progress and in the amelioration of the condition of mankind, that, in the presence and with the approval of the members of the American House of Representatives, reflecting the general sentiment of the country: that in the presence of that august body, the American Senate, representing the highest intelligence and the calmest judgment in the country; in the presence of the Supreme Court and Chief-Justice of the United States, to whose decisions we all patriotically bow; in the presence and under the steady eye of the honored and trusted President of the United States, with the members of his wise and patriotic Cabinet, we, the colored people, newly emancipated and rejoicing in our blood-bought freedom, near the close of the first century in the life of this Republic, have now and here unveiled, set apart, and dedicated a monument of enduring granite and bronze, in every line, feature, and figure of which the men of this generation may read, and those of after-coming generations may read, something of the exalted character and great works of Abraham Lincoln, the first martyr President of the United States.

Fellow citizens, in what we have said and done to-day, and in what we may say and do hereafter, we disclaim everything like arrogance and assumption. We claim for ourselves no superior devotion to the character, history, and memory of the illustrious name whose monument we have here this day dedicated. We fully comprehend the relation of Abraham Lincoln both to ourselves and to the white people of the United States. Truth is proper and beautiful at all times and in all places and it is never in any case more proper and beautiful than when one is speaking of a great public man whose example is likely to be commended for honor and imitation long after his departure to the solemn shades,—the silent continents of eternity. It must be admitted, truth compels me to admit, even here in the presence of the monument we have erected to his memory, that Abraham Lincoln was not, in the fullest sense of the word, either our man or our model. In his interests, in his associations, in his habits of thought and in his prejudices, he was a white man.

He was preëminently the white man's President, entirely devoted to the welfare of white men. He was ready and willing at any time during the first years of his administration to deny, postpone and sacrifice the rights of humanity in the colored people in order to promote the welfare of the white people of this country. In all his education and feeling he was an American of the Americans. He came into the Presidential chair upon one principle alone, namely, opposition to the extension of slavery. His arguments in furtherance of this policy had their motive and mainspring in his patriotic devotion to the interests of his own race. To protect, defend, and perpetuate slavery in the States where it existed Abraham Lincoln was not less ready than any other President to draw the sword of the nation. He was ready to execute all the supposed constitutional guarantees of the United States Constitution in favor of the slave system anywhere inside the slave States. He was willing to pursue, recapture, and send back the fugitive slave to his master, and to suppress a slave rising for liberty, though the guilty master were already in arms against the Government. The race to which we belong were not the special objects of his consideration. Knowing this, I concede to you, my white fellow citizens, a preëminence in this worship at once full and supreme. First, midst, and last, you and yours were the objects of his deepest affection and his most earnest solicitude. You are the children of Abraham Lincoln. We are at best only his step-children; children by adoption, children by force of circumstances and necessity. To you it especially belongs to sound his praises, to preserve and perpetuate his memory, to multiply his statues, to hang his pictures high upon your walls, and to commend his example; for to you he was a great and glorious friend and benefactor. Instead of supplanting you at this altar, we would exhort you to build high his monuments; let them be of the most costly material, of the most cunning workmanship. Let their forms be symmetrical, beautiful and perfect. Let their bases be upon the solid rocks and let their summits lean against the unchanging, blue, overhanging sky, and let them endure forever! But while in the abundance of your wealth, and in the fullness of your just and patriotic devotion, you do all this, we entreat you to despise not the humble offering we this day unveil to view; for while Abraham Lincoln saved for you a country, he delivered us from a bondage, one hour of which, according to Jefferson, was worse than ages of the oppression your fathers rose in rebellion to oppose.

Fellow citizens, ours is no new-born zeal and devotion—merely a thing of this moment. The name of Abraham Lincoln was near and dear to our hearts in the darkest and most perilous hours of the

Republic. We were no more ashamed of him when shrouded in clouds of darkness, of doubt, and defeat than when we saw him crowned with victory, honor, and glory. Our faith in him was often taxed and strained to the uttermost, but it never failed. When he tarried long in the mountain; when he strangely told us that we were the cause of the war; when he still more strangely told us to leave the land in which we were born; when he refused to employ our arms in defence of the Union; when, after accepting our services as colored soldiers, he refused to retaliate our murder and torture as colored prisoners; when he told us he would save the Union if he could with slavery; when he revoked the Proclamation of Emancipation of General Frémont; when he refused, in the days of the inaction and defeat of the Army of the Potomac, to remove its popular commander who was more zealous in his efforts to protect slavery than to suppress rebellion; when we saw all this, and more, we were at times grieved, stunned, and greatly bewildered; but our hearts believed while they ached and bled. Nor was this, even at that time, a blind and unreasoning superstition. Despite the mist and haze that surround him; despite the tumult, the hurry, and confusion of the hour, we were able to take a comprehensive view of Abraham Lincoln, and to make reasonable allowance for the circumstances of his position. We saw him, measured him, and estimated him; not by stray utterances to injudicious and tedious delegations, who often tried his patience; not by isolated facts torn from their connection; not by any partial and imperfect glimpses, caught at inopportune moments; but by a broad survey, in the light of the stern logic of great events, and in view of that 'divinity which shapes our ends, rough hew them how we will.'* We came to the conclusion that the hour and the man of our redemption had somehow met in the person of Abraham Lincoln. It mattered little to us what language he might employ on special occasions; it mattered little to us, when we fully knew him, whether he was swift or slow in his movements; it was enough for us that Abraham Lincoln was at the head of a great movement, and was in living and earnest sympathy with that movement, which, in the nature of things, must go on until slavery should be utterly and forever abolished in the United States.

When, therefore, it shall be asked what we have to do with the memory of Abraham Lincoln, or what Abraham Lincoln had to do with us, the answer is ready, full, and complete. Though he loved Cæsar less than Rome, though the Union was more to him than our freedom or our future, under his wise and beneficent rule we saw ourselves gradually lifted from the depths of slavery to the heights of liberty and manhood; and his wise and beneficent rule, and by measures approved and vigorously pressed by him, we saw that the handwriting of ages, in the form of prejudice and proscription, was rapidly fading from the face of our whole country; under his rule, and in due time, about as soon after all as the country could tolerate the strange spectacle, we saw our brave sons and brothers laying off the rags of bondage, and being clothed all over in the blue uniforms of the soldiers of the United States; under his rule we saw two hundred thousand of our dark and dusky people responding to the call of Abraham Lincoln, and with muskets on their shoulders, and eagles on their buttons, timing their high footsteps to liberty and union under the national flag; under his rule we saw the independence of the black republic of Hayti, the special object of slave-holding aversion and horror, fully recognized, and her minister, a colored gentleman, duly received here in the city of Washington; under his rule we saw the internal slave-trade, which had so long disgraced the nation, abolished, and slavery abolished in the District of Columbia; under his rule we saw for the first time the law enforced against the foreign slave-trade and for the first time a slave-trader hanged like any other pirate or murderer; under his rule, assisted by the greatest captain of our age and his inspiration, we saw the Confederate States, based upon the idea that our race must be slaves and slaves forever, battered to pieces and scattered to the four winds; under his rule, and in the fullness of time, we saw Abraham Lincoln, after giving the slaveholders three months' grace in which to save their hateful slave system, penning the immortal paper, which, special in its language, but general in its principles and effect, makes slavery forever impossible in the United States. Though we waited long, we saw all this and more.

Can any colored man, or any white man friendly to the freedom of all men, ever forget the night which followed the first day of January, 1863, when the world was to see if Abraham Lincoln would prove to be as good as his word? I shall never forget that memorable night, when at a public meeting, in a distant city, with three thousand others not less anxious than myself, I waited and watched for the word of deliverance which we have heard read today. Nor shall I ever forget the outburst of joy and thanksgiving that rent the air when the lightning brought to us the emancipation proclamation. In that happy hour we forgot all delay and forgot all tardiness; forgot that the President, by a promise to withhold the bolt which would smite the slave system with destruction, had bribed the rebels to lay down their arms; and we were thenceforward willing to allow the President all the latitude of time, phraseology and every honorable device that statesmanship might require for the achievement of a great and beneficent measure of liberty and progress.

Fellow citizens, there is little necessity on this occasion to speak critically and at length of this great and good man and of his high mission in the world. That ground has been fully occupied and completely covered both here and elsewhere. The whole field of fact and fancy has been gleaned and garnered. Any man can say things that are true of Abraham Lincoln, but no man can say anything that is new of Abraham Lincoln. His personal traits and public acts are better known to the American people than are those of any other man of his age. He was a mystery to no man who saw him and heard him. Though high in position, the humblest could approach him and feel at home in his presence. Though deep, he was transparent; though strong, he was gentle; though decided and pronounced in his convictions, he was tolerant towards those who differed from him, and patient under reproaches. Even those who only knew him through his public utterances obtained a tolerably clear idea of his character and his personality. The image of the man went out with his words, and those who read them, knew him.

I have said that President Lincoln was a white man and shared towards the colored race the prejudices common to his countrymen. Looking back to his times and to the condition of his country, we are compelled to admit that this unfriendly feeling on his part may be safely set down as one element of his wonderful success in organizing the loyal American people for the tremendous conflict before them, and bringing them safely through that conflict. His great mission was to accomplish two things: first, to save his country from dismemberment and ruin; and second, to free his country from the great crime of slavery. To do one or the other, or both, he must have the earnest sympathy and the powerful coöperation of his loyal fellow-countrymen. Without this primary and essential condition to success his efforts must have been vain and utterly fruitless. Had he put the abolition of slavery before the salvation of the Union, he would have inevitably driven from him a powerful class of the American people and rendered resistance to rebellion impossible. Viewed from the genuine abolition ground, Mr. Lincoln seemed tardy, cold, dull, and indifferent; but measuring him by the sentiment of his country, a sentiment he was bound as a statesman to consult, he was swift, zealous, radical, and determined.

Though Mr. Lincoln shared the prejudices of his white fellow-countrymen against the negro, it is hardly necessary to say that in his heart of hearts he loathed and hated slavery.[1] The man who could say, 'Fondly do we hope, fervently do we pray, that this mighty scourge of war shall soon pass away, yet if God wills it continue till all the wealth piled by two hundred years of bondage shall have been wasted, and each drop of blood drawn by the lash shall have been paid for by one drawn by the sword, the judgments of the Lord are true and righteous altogether,' gives all needed proof of his feeling on the subject of slavery. He was willing, while the South was loyal, that it should have its pound of flesh, because he thought it was so nominated in the bond; but farther than this no earthly power could make him go.

Fellow-citizens, whatever else in the world may be partial, unjust and uncertain, time, time! is impartial, just and certain in its action. In the realm of mind, as well as in the realm of matter, it is a great worker, and often works wonders. The honest and comprehensive statesman, clearly discerning the needs of his country, and earnestly endeavoring to do his whole duty, though covered and blistered with reproaches, may safely leave his course to the silent judgment of time. Few great public men have ever been the victims of fiercer denunciation than was Abraham Lincoln during his administration. He was often wounded in the house of his friends. Reproaches came thick and fast upon him from within and from without, and from opposite quarters. He was assailed by abolitionists; he was assailed by slaveholders; he was assailed by the men who were for peace at any price; he was assailed by those who were for a more vigorous prosecution of the war; he was assailed for not making the war an abolition war; and he was most bitterly assailed for making the war an abolition war.

But now behold the change: the judgment of the present hour is, that, taking him for all in all; measuring the tremendous magnitude of the work before him; considering the necessary means to ends, and surveying the end from the beginning, infinite wisdom has seldom sent any man into the world better fitted for his mission than was Abraham Lincoln. His birth, his training and his natural endowments, both mental and physical, were strongly in his favor. Born and reared among the lowly; a stranger to wealth and luxury; compelled from tender youth to sturdy manhood to grapple single-handed with the flintiest hardships of life, he grew strong in the manly and heroic qualities demanded by the great mission to which he was called by the votes of

---

[1] 'I am naturally anti-slavery. If slavery is not wrong, nothing is wrong. I cannot remember when I did not so think and feel.'—*Letter of Mr. Lincoln to Mr. Hodges, of Kentucky, April 4, 1864.*

his countrymen. The hard condition of his early life, which would have depressed and broken down weaker men, only gave greater life, vigor, and buoyancy to the heroic spirit of Abraham Lincoln. He was ready for any kind and quality of work. What other young men dreaded in the shape of toil he took hold of with the utmost cheerfulness.

> A spade, a rake, a hoe,
> A pick-ax, or a bill;
> A hook to reap, a scythe to mow,
> A flail, or what you will.*

All day long he could split heavy rails in the woods, and half the night long he could study his English grammar by the uncertain flare and glare of the light made by a pine knot. He was at home on the land with his axe, with his maul, with gluts, and his wedges; and he was equally at home on the water with his oars, with his poles, with his planks, and with his boat-hooks. And whether in his flat-boat on the Mississippi river, or at the fireside of his frontier cabin, he was a man of work. A son of toil himself, he was linked in brotherly sympathy with the sons of toil in every loyal part of the republic. This very fact gave him tremendous power with the American people, and materially contributed not only to selecting him to the presidency, but in sustaining his administration of the government.

Upon his inauguration as President of the United States, an office fitted to tax and strain the largest abilities, even when it is assumed under the most favorable conditions, Abraham Lincoln was met by a tremendous crisis. He was called upon not merely to administer the government, but to decide in the face of terrible odds the fate of the republic.

A formidable rebellion rose in his path before him. The Union was practically dissolved. His country was torn and rent asunder at the center. Hostile armies, armed with the munitions of war which the republic had provided for its own defense, were already organized against the republic. The tremendous question for him to decide was whether his country should survive the crisis and flourish, or be dismembered and perish. His predecessor in office had already decided the question in favor of national dismemberment by denying to it the right of self-defense and self-preservation—a right which belongs to the meanest insect.

Happily for the country, happily for you and for me, the judgment of James Buchanan, the patrician, was not the judgment of Abraham Lincoln, the plebeian. He brought his strong common sense, sharpened in the school of adversity, to bear upon the question. He did not hesitate, he did not doubt, he did not falter; but at once resolved that, at whatever peril, at whatever cost, the union of the States should be preserved. A patriot himself, his faith was strong and unwavering in the patriotism of his countrymen. Timid men said before Mr. Lincoln's inauguration that we had seen the last President of the United States. A voice in influential quarters said, 'Let the Union slide.'* Some said that a Union maintained by the sword was worthless. Others said a rebellion of eight millions cannot be suppressed. But in the midst of all this tumult and timidity, and against all this Abraham Lincoln was clear in his duty, and had an oath in heaven. He calmly and bravely heard the voice of doubt and fear all around him, but he had an oath in heaven, and there was not power enough on earth to make this honest boatman, backwoodsman, and broad-handed splitter of rails evade or violate that sacred oath. He had not been schooled in the ethics of slavery; his plain life had favored his love of truth. He had not been taught that treason and perjury were the proof of honor and honesty. His moral training was against his saying one thing when he meant another. The trust which Abraham Lincoln had in himself and in the people was surprising and grand, but it was also enlightened and well founded. He knew the American people better than they knew themselves and his truth was based upon this knowledge.

Fellow-citizens, the fourteenth day of April, 1866,* of which this is the eleventh anniversary, is now and will ever remain a memorable day in the annals of this republic. It was on the evening of this day, while a fierce and sanguinary rebellion was in the last stages of its desolating power, while its armies were broken and scattered before the invincible armies of Grant and Sherman, while a great nation, torn and rent by war, was already beginning to raise to the skies loud anthems of joy at the dawn of peace, that it was startled, amazed, and overwhelmed by the crowning crime of slavery—the assassination of Abraham Lincoln. It was a new crime—a pure act of malice. No purpose of the rebellion was to be served by it. It was the simple gratification of a hell-black spirit of revenge. But it has done good after all. It has filled the country with a deeper abhorrence of slavery and a deeper love for the great liberator.

Had Abraham Lincoln died from any of the numerous ills to which flesh is heir; had he reached that good old age of which his vigorous constitution and his temperate habits gave promise; had he been permitted to see the end of his great work; had the solemn curtain of death come down but gradually, we should still have been smitten with a heavy grief, and treasured his name lovingly. But, dying as he did die, by the red hand of violence, killed, assassinated, taken off without warning, not because of personal hate—for no man who knew Abraham

Lincoln could hate him—but because of his fidelity to union and liberty, he is doubly dear to us, and his memory will be precious forever.

Fellow-citizens, I end as I began, with congratulations. We have done a good work for our race to-day. In doing honor to the memory of our friend and liberator we have been doing highest honors to ourselves and to those who come after us. We have been attaching to ourselves a name and fame imperishable and immortal; we have also been defending ourselves from a blighting scandal. When now it shall be said that the colored man is soulless, that he has no appreciation of benefits or benefactors; when the foul reproach of ingratitude is hurled at us, and it is attempted to scourge us beyond the range of human brotherhood, we may calmly point to the monument we have this day erected to the memory of Abraham Lincoln.

SPEECH AT ELMIRA.
WEST INDIA EMANCIPATION.

Extract from a speech delivered by Frederick Douglass in Elmira, N. Y., August 1, 1880, at a great meeting of colored people met to celebrate West India emancipation, and where he was received with marked respect and approval by the president of the day and the immense crowd there assembled. It is placed in this book partly as a grateful tribute to the noble transatlantic men and women through whose unwearied exertions the system of negro slavery was finally abolished in all the British Isles:

*Mr. President*:—I thank you sincerely for this cordial greeting. I hear in your speech something like a welcome home after a long absence. More years of my life and labors have been spent in this than in any other State of the Union. Anywhere within a hundred miles of the goodly city of Rochester I feel myself at home and among friends. Within that circumference there resides a people which have no superiors in point of enlightenment, liberality and civilization. Allow me to thank you also for your generous words of sympathy and approval. In respect to this important support to a public man, I have been unusually fortunate. My forty years of work in the cause of the oppressed and enslaved has been well noted, well appreciated and well rewarded. All classes and colors of men, at home and abroad, have in this way assisted in holding up my hands. Looking back through these long years of toil and conflict, during which I have had blows to take as well as blows to give, and have sometimes received wounds and bruises, both in body and in mind, my only regret is that I have been enabled to do so little to lift up and strengthen our long-enslaved and still oppressed people.

My apology for these remarks personal to myself is in the fact that I am now standing mainly in the presence of a new generation. Most of the men with whom I lived and labored in the early years of the abolition movement, have passed beyond the borders of this life. Scarcely any of the colored men who advocated our cause, and who started when I did, are now numbered among the living, and I begin to feel somewhat lonely. But while I have the sympathy and approval of men and women like these before me, I shall give with joy my latest breath in support of your claim to justice, liberty and equality among men. The day we celebrate is preëminently the colored man's day. The great event by which it is distinguished, and by which it will forever be distinguished from all other days of the year, has justly claimed thoughtful attention among statesmen and social reformers throughout the world. While to them it is a luminous point in human history, and worthy of thought in the colored man, it addresses not merely the intelligence, but the feeling. The emancipation of our brothers in the West Indies comes home to us and stirs our hearts and fills our souls with those grateful sentiments which link mankind in a common brotherhood.

In the history of the American conflict with slavery, the day we celebrate has played an important part. Emancipation in the West Indies was the first bright star in a stormy sky; the first smile after a long providential frown; the first ray of hope; the first tangible fact demonstrating the possibility of a peaceable transition from slavery to freedom, of the negro race. Whoever else may forget or slight the claims of this day, it can never be to us other than memorable and glorious. The story of it shall be brief and soon told. Six-and-forty years ago,* on the day we now celebrate, there went forth over the blue waters of the Carribean Sea a great message from the British throne, hailed with startling shouts of joy and thrilling songs of praise. That message liberated, set free, and brought within the pale of civilization eight hundred thousand people, who, till then, had been esteemed as beasts of burden. How vast, sudden, and startling was this transformation! In one moment, a mere tick of a watch, the twinkle of an eye, the glance of the morning sun, saw a bondage which had resisted the humanity of ages, defied earth and heaven, instantly ended; saw the slave-whip burnt to ashes; saw the slave's chains melted; saw his fetters broken and the irresponsible power of the slave-master over his victim forever destroyed.

I have been told by eye-witnesses of the scene, that, in the first moment of it, the emancipated hesitated to accept it for what it was. They did not know whether to receive it as a reality, a dream, or a vision of the fancy.

No wonder they were thus amazed and doubtful, after their terrible years of darkness and sorrow, which seemed to have no end. Like much other good news, it was thought too good to be true. But the silence and hesitation they observed was only momentary. When fully assured that the good tidings which had come across the sea to them were not only good, but true; that they were indeed no longer slaves, but free; that the lash of the slave-driver was no longer in the air, but buried in the earth; that their limbs were no longer chained, but subject to their own will, the manifestations of their joy and gratitude knew no bounds, and sought expression in the loudest and wildest possible forms. They ran about, they danced, they sang, they gazed into the blue sky, bounded into the air, kneeled, prayed, shouted, rolled upon the ground and embraced each other. They laughed and wept for joy. Those who witnessed the scene say that they never before saw anything like it.

We are sometimes asked why we American citizens annually celebrate West India emancipation when we might celebrate American emancipation. Why go abroad, say they, when we might as well stay at home?

The answer is easily given. Human liberty excludes all idea of home and abroad. It is universal and spurns localization.

> 'When a deed is done for freedom,
>    Through the broad earth's aching breast
> Runs a thrill of joy prophetic,
>    Trembling on from East to West.'*

It is bounded by no geographical lines and knows no national limitations. Like the glorious sun of the heavens, its light shines for all. But besides this general consideration, this boundless power and glory of liberty, West India emancipation has claims upon us as an event in this nineteenth century in which we live; for, rich as this century is in moral and material achievements, in progress and civilization, it can claim nothing for itself greater and grander than this act of the West India emancipation.

Whether we consider the matter or the manner of it, the tree or its fruit, it is noteworthy, memorable, and sublime. Especially is the manner of its accomplishment worthy of consideration. Its best lesson to the world, its most encouraging word to all who toil and trust in the cause of justice and liberty, to all who oppose oppression and slavery, is a word of sublime faith and courage—faith in the truth and courage in the expression.

Great and valuable concessions have in different ages been made to the liberties of mankind. They have, however, come not at the command of reason and persuasion, but by the sharp and terrible edge of the sword. To this rule West India emancipation is a splendid exception. It came, not by the sword, but by the word; not by the brute force of numbers, but by the still small voice of truth; not by barricades, bayonets, and bloody revolution, but by peaceful agitation; not by divine interference, but by the exercise of simple, human reason and feeling. I repeat, that, in this peculiarity, we have what is most valuable to the human race generally.

It is a revelation of a power inherent in human society. It shows what can be done against wrong in the world, without the aid of armies on the earth or of angels in the sky. It shows that men have in their own hands the peaceful means of putting all their moral and political enemies under their feet and of making this world a healthy and happy dwelling-place, if they will but faithfully and courageously use these means.

The world needed just such a revelation of the power of conscience and of human brotherhood, one that overleaped the accident of color and of race, and set at naught the whisperings of prejudice. The friends of freedom in England saw in the negro a man, a moral and responsible being. Having settled this in their own minds, they, in the name of humanity, denounced the crime of his enslavement. It was the faithful, persistent, and enduring enthusiam of Thomas Clarkson, William Wilberforce, Granville Sharpe, William Knibb, Henry Brougham, Thomas Fowell Buxton, Daniel O'Connell, George Thompson, and their noble co-workers, that finally thawed the British heart into sympathy for the slave, and moved the strong arm of that government in mercy to put an end to his bondage.

Let no American, especially no colored American, withhold a generous recognition of this stupendous achievement. What though it was not American, but British; what though it was not Republican, but Monarchical; what though it was not from the American Congress, but from the British Parliament; what though it was not from the chair of a President, but from the throne of a Queen, it was none the less a triumph of right over wrong, of good over evil, and a victory for the whole human race.

Besides: We may properly celebrate this day because of its special relation to our American Emancipation. In doing this we do not sacrifice the general to the special, or the universal to the local. The cause of human liberty is one the whole world over. The downfall of slavery under British power meant the downfall of slavery, ultimately, under American power, and the downfall of negro slavery everywhere. But the effect of this great and philanthropic measure, naturally enough, was greater here than elsewhere. Outside the British empire no other nation was in a position to feel it as much as we. The stimulus it gave to the American antislavery movement was immediate, pronounced, and powerful. British example became a tremendous lever in the hands of American abolitionists. It did much to shame and discourage the spirit of caste and the advocacy of slavery in church and state. It could not well have been otherwise. No man liveth unto himself.

What is true in this respect of individual men, is equally true of nations. Both impart good or ill to their age and generation. But putting aside this consideration, so worthy of thought, we have special reasons for claiming the First of August as the birth-day of negro emancipation, not only in the West Indies, but in the United States. Spite of our national independence, a common language, a common literature, a common history, and a common civilization makes us and keeps us still a part of the British nation, if not a part of the British empire. England can take no step forward in the pathway of a higher civilization without drawing us in the same direction. She is still the mother country, and the mother, too, of our abolition movement. Though her emancipation came in peace, and ours in war; though hers cost treasure, and ours blood; though hers was the result of a sacred preference, and ours resulted in part from necessity, the motive and mainspring of the respective measures were the same in both.

The abolitionists of this country have been charged with bringing on the war between the North and South, and in one sense this is true. Had there been no anti-slavery agitation at the North, there would have been no active anti-slavery anywhere to resist the demands of the slave-power at the South, and where there is no resistance there can be no war. Slavery would then have been nationalized, and the whole country would then have been subjected to its power. Resistance to slavery and the extension of slavery invited and provoked secession and war to perpetuate and extend the slave system. Thus, in the same sense, England is responsible for our civil war. The abolition of slavery in the West Indies gave life and vigor to the abolition movement in America. Clarkson of England gave us Garrison of America; Granville Sharpe of England gave us our Wendell Phillips; and Wilberforce of England gave us our peerless Charles Sumner.

These grand men and their brave co-workers here took up the moral thunder-bolts which had struck down slavery in the West Indies, and hurled them with increased zeal and power against the gigantic system of slavery here, till, goaded to madness, the traffickers in the souls and bodies of men flew to arms, rent asunder the Union at the center, and filled the land with hostile armies and the ten thousand horrors of war. Out of this tempest, out of this whirlwind and earthquake of war, came the abolition of slavery, came the employment of colored troops, came colored citizens, came colored jurymen, came colored congressmen, came colored schools in the South, and came the great amendments of our national constitution.

We celebrate this day, too, for the very good reason that we have no other to celebrate. English emancipation has one advantage over American emancipation. Hers has a definite anniversary. Ours has none. Like our slaves, the freedom of the negro has no birthday. No man can tell the day of the month, or the month of the year, upon which slavery was abolished in the United States. We cannot even tell when it began to be abolished. Like the movement of the sea, no man can tell where one wave begins and another ends. The chains of slavery with us were loosened by degrees. First, we had the struggle in Kansas with border ruffians; next, we had John Brown at Harper's Ferry; next the firing upon Fort Sumter; a little while after, we had Fremont's order, freeing the slaves of the rebels in Missouri. Then we had General Butler declaring and treating the slaves of rebels as contraband of war; next we had the proposition to arm colored men and make them soldiers for the Union. In 1862 we had the conditional promise of a proclamation of emancipation from President Lincoln, and, finally, on the 1st of January, 1863, we had the proclamation itself—and still the end was not yet. Slavery was bleeding and dying, but it was not dead, and no man can tell just when its foul spirit departed from our land, if, indeed, it has yet departed, and hence we do not know what day we may properly celebrate as coupled with this great American event.

When England, during our late civil war, behaved so badly, I, for one, felt like giving up these 1st of August celebrations. But I remembered that during that war, there were two Englands, as there were two Americas, and that one was true to liberty while the other was true to slavery. It was not the England which gave us West India emancipation that took sides with the slaveholder's rebellion. It was not the England of John Bright and William Edward Forster* that permitted Alabamas to escape from British ports,* and prey upon our commerce, or that otherwise favored slaveholding in the South, but it was the England which had done what it could to prevent West India emancipation.

It was the tory party in England that fought the abolition party at home, and the same party it was that favored our slaveholding rebellion.

Under a different name, we had the same, or a similar party, here; a party which despised the negro and consigned him to perpetual slavery; a party which was willing to allow the American Union to be shivered into fragments, rather than that one hair of the head of slavery should be injured.

But, fellow-citizens, I should but very imperfectly fulfil the duty of this hour if I confined myself to a merely historical or philosophical discussion of West India emancipation. The story of the 1st of August has been told a thousand times over, and may be told a thousand times more. The cause of freedom and humanity has a history and a destiny nearer home.

How stands the case with the recently-emancipated millions of colored people in our own country? What is their condition to-day? What is their relation to the people who formerly held them as slaves? These are important questions, and they are such as trouble the minds of thoughtful men of all colors, at home and abroad. By law, by the constitution of the United States, slavery has no existence in our country. The legal form has been abolished. By the law and the constitution, the negro is a man and a citizen, and has all the rights and liberties guaranteed to any other variety of the human family, residing in the United States.

He has a country, a flag, and a government, and may legally claim full and complete protection under the laws. It was the ruling wish, intention, and purpose of the loyal people, after rebellion was suppressed, to have an end to the entire cause of that calamity by forever putting away the system of slavery and all its incidents. In pursuance of this idea, the negro was made free, made a citizen, made eligible to hold office, to be a juryman, a legislator, and a magistrate. To this end, several amendments to the constitution were proposed, recommended, and adopted. They are now a part of the supreme law of the land, binding alike upon every State and Territory of the United States, North and South. Briefly, this is our legal and theoretical condition. This is our condition on paper and parchment. If only from the national statute book we were left to learn the true condition of the colored race, the result would be altogether creditable to the American people. It would give them a clear title to a place among the most enlightened and liberal nations of the world. We could say of our country, as Curran once said of England, 'The spirit of British law makes liberty commensurate with and inseparable from the British soil.' Now I say that this eloquent tribute to England, if only we looked into our constitution, might apply to us. In that instrument we have laid down the law, now and forever, that there shall be no slavery or involuntary servitude in this republic, except for crime.

We have gone still further. We have laid the heavy hand of the constitution upon the matchless meanness of caste, as well as upon the hell-black crime of slavery. We have declared before all the world that there shall be no denial of rights on account of race, color, or previous condition of servitude. The advantage gained in this respect is immense.

It is a great thing to have the supreme law of the land on the side of justice and liberty. It is the line up to which the nation is destined to march—the law to which the nation's life must ultimately conform. It is a great principle, up to which we may educate the people, and to this extent its value exceeds all speech.

But to-day, in most of the Southern States, the fourteenth and fifteenth amendments are virtually nullified.

The rights which they were intended to guarantee are denied and held in contempt. The citizenship granted in the fourteenth amendment is practically a mockery, and the right to vote, provided for in the fifteenth amendment, is literally stamped out in face of government. The old master class is to-day triumphant, and the newly-enfranchised class in a condition but little above that in which they were found before the rebellion.

Do you ask me how, after all that has been done, this state of things has been made possible? I will tell you. Our reconstruction measures were radically defective. They left the former slave completely in the power of the old master, the loyal citizen in the hands of the disloyal rebel against the government. Wise, grand, and comprehensive in scope and design as were the reconstruction measures, high and honorable as were the intentions of the statesmen by whom they were framed and adopted, time and experience, which try all things, have demonstrated that they did not successfully meet the case.

In the hurry and confusion of the hour, and the eager desire to have the Union restored, there was more care for the sublime superstructure of the republic than for the solid foundation upon which it could alone be upheld. To the freedmen was given the machinery of liberty, but there was denied to them the steam to put it in motion. They were given the uniform of soldiers, but no arms; they were called citizens, but left subjects; they were called free, but left almost slaves. The old master class was not deprived of the power of life and death, which was the soul of the relation of master and slave. They could not, of course, sell their former slaves, but they retained the power to starve them to death, and wherever this power is held there is the power of slavery. He who can say to his fellow-man, 'You shall serve me or starve,' is a master and his subject is a slave. This was seen and felt by Thaddeus Stevens, Charles Sumner, and leading stalwart Republicans; and had their counsels prevailed the terrible evils from which we now suffer would have been averted. The negro to-day would not be on his knees, as he is, abjectly supplicating the old master class to give him leave to toil. Nor would he now be leaving the South as from a doomed city, and seeking a home in the uncongenial North, but tilling his native soil in comparative independence. Though no longer a slave, he is in a thralldom grievous and intolerable, compelled to work for whatever his employer is pleased to pay him, swindled out of his hard earnings by money orders redeemed in stores, compelled to pay the price of an acre of ground for its use during a single year, to pay four times more than a fair price for a pound of bacon and to be kept upon the narrowest margin between life and starvation. Much complaint has been made that the freedmen have shown so little ability to take care of themselves since their emancipation. Men have marvelled that they have made so little progress. I question the justice of this complaint. It is neither reasonable, nor in any sense just. To me the wonder is, not that the freedmen have made so little progress, but, rather, that they have made so much; not that they have been standing still, but that they have been able to stand at all.

We have only to reflect for a moment upon the situation in which these people found themselves when liberated. Consider their ignorance, their poverty, their destitution, and their absolute dependence upon the very class by which they had been held in bondage for centuries, a class whose every sentiment was averse to their freedom, and we shall be prepared to marvel that they have, under the circumstances, done so well.

History does not furnish an example of emancipation under conditions less friendly to the emancipated class than this American example. Liberty came to the freedmen of the United States not in mercy, but in wrath, not by moral choice but by military necessity, not by the generous action of the people among whom they were to live, and whose good-will was essential to the success of the measure, but by strangers, foreigners, invaders, trespassers, aliens, and enemies. The very manner of their emancipation invited to the heads of the freedmen the bitterest hostility of race and class. They were hated because they had been slaves, hated because they were now free, and hated because of those who had freed them. Nothing was to have been expected other than what has happened, and he is a poor student of the human heart who does not see that the old master class would naturally employ every power and means in their reach to make the great measure of emancipation unsuccessful and utterly odious. It was born in the tempest and whirlwind of war, and has lived in a storm of violence and blood. When the Hebrews were emancipated, they were told to take spoil from the Egyptians. When the serfs of Russia were emancipated, they were given three acres of ground upon which they could live and make a living. But not so when our slaves were emancipated. They were sent away empty-handed, without money, without friends and without a foot of land upon which to stand. Old and young, sick and well, were turned loose to the open sky, naked to their enemies. The old slave quarter that had before sheltered them and the fields that had yielded them corn were now denied them. The old master class, in its wrath, said, 'Clear out! The Yankees have freed you, now let them feed and shelter you!'

Inhuman as was this treatment, it was the natural result of the bitter resentment felt by the old master class; and, in view of it, the wonder is, not that the colored people of the South have done so little in the way of acquiring a comfortable living, but that they live at all.

Taking all the circumstances into consideration, the colored people have no reason to despair. We still live, and while there is life there is hope. The fact that we have endured wrongs and hardships which would have destroyed any other race, and have increased in numbers and public consideration, ought to strengthen our faith in ourselves and our future. Let us, then, wherever we are, whether at the North or at the South, resolutely struggle on in the belief that there is a better day coming, and that we, by patience, industry, uprightness, and economy may hasten that better day. I will not listen, myself, and I would not have you listen to the nonsense, that no people can succeed in life among a people by whom they have been despised and oppressed.

The statement is erroneous and contradicted by the whole history of human progress. A few centuries ago, all Europe was cursed with serfdom, or slavery. Traces of this bondage still remain, but are not easily visible.

The Jews, only a century ago, were despised, hated, and oppressed, but they have defied, met, and vanquished the hard conditions imposed upon them, and are now opulent and powerful, and compel respect in all countries.

Take courage from the example of all religious denominations that have sprung up since Martin Luther. Each in its turn has been oppressed and persecuted.

Methodists, Baptists, and Quakers have all been compelled to feel the lash and sting of popular disfavor—yet all in turn have conquered the prejudice and hate of their surroundings.

Greatness does not come on flowery beds of ease to any people. We must fight to win the prize. No people to whom liberty is given, can hold it as firmly and wear it as grandly as those who wrench their liberty from the iron hand of the tyrant. The hardships and dangers involved in the struggle give strength and toughness to the character, and enable it to stand firm in storm as well as in sunshine.

One thought more before I leave this subject, and it is a thought I wish you all to lay to heart. Practice it yourselves and teach it to your children. It is this: neither we, nor any other people, will ever be respected till we respect ourselves, and we will never respect ourselves till we have the means to live respectably. An exceptionally poor and dependent people will be despised by the opulent and despise themselves.

You cannot make an empty sack stand on end. A race which cannot save its earnings, which spends all it makes and goes in debt when it is sick, can never rise in the scale of civilization, no matter under what laws it may chance to be. Put us in Kansas or in Africa, and until we learn to save more than we spend, we are sure to sink and perish. It is not in the nature of things that we should be equally rich in this world's goods. Some will be more successful than others and poverty, in many cases, is the result of misfortune rather than of crime; but no race can afford to have all its members the victims of this misfortune, without being considered a worthless race. Pardon me, therefore, for urging upon you, my people, the importance of saving your earnings; of denying yourselves in the present, that you may have something in the future, of consuming less for yourselves that your children may have a start in life when you are gone.

With money and property comes the means of knowledge and power. A poverty-stricken class will be an ignorant and despised class, and no amount of sentiment can make it otherwise. This part of our destiny is in our own hands. Every dollar you lay up represents one day's independence, one day of rest and security in the future. If the time shall ever come when we shall possess in the colored people of the United States, a class of men noted for enterprise, industry, economy, and success, we shall no longer have any trouble in the matter of civil and political rights. The battle against popular prejudice will have been fought and won, and, in common with all other races and colors, we shall have an equal chance in the race for life.

Do I hear you ask in a tone of despair if this time will ever come to our people in America? The question is not new to me. I have tried to answer it many times and in many places, when the outlook was less encouraging than now. There was a time when we were compelled to walk by faith in this matter, but now, I think, we may walk by sight. Notwithstanding the great and all-abounding darkness of our social past; notwithstanding the clouds that still overhang us in the moral and social sky and the defects inherited from a bygone condition of servitude, it is the faith of my soul that this brighter and better day will yet come. But whether it shall come late or come soon will depend mainly upon ourselves.

The laws which determine the destinies of individuals and nations are impartial and eternal. We shall reap as we sow. There is no escape. The conditions of success are universal and unchangeable. The nation or people which shall comply with them will rise, and those which violate them will fall, and will perhaps, disappear altogether. No power beneath the sky can make an ignorant, wasteful, and idle people prosperous, or a licentious people happy.

One ground of hope for my people is founded upon the returns of the last census. One of the most disheartening ethnological speculations concerning us has been that we shall die out; that, like the Indian, we shall perish in the blaze of Caucasian civilization. The census sets to rest that heresy concerning us. We are more than holding our own in all the Southern States. We are no longer four millions of slaves, but six millions of freemen.

Another ground of hope for our race is in the progress of education. Everywhere in the South the colored man is learning to read. None now denies the ability of the colored race to acquire knowledge of anything which can be communicated to the human understanding by letters. Our colored schools in the city of Washington compare favorably with the white schools, and what is true of Washington is equally true of other cities and towns of the South. Still another ground of hope I find in the fact that colored men are strong in their gratitude to benefactors, and firm in their political convictions. They cannot be coaxed or driven to vote with their enemies against their friends.

Nothing but the shot-gun or the bull-dozer's whip can keep them from voting their convictions. Then another ground of hope is that as a general rule we are an industrious people. I have traveled extensively over the South, and almost the only people I saw at work there were the colored people. In any fair condition of things the men who till the soil will become proprietors of the soil. Only arbitrary conditions can prevent this. To-day the negro, starting from nothing, pays taxes upon six millions in Georgia, and forty millions in Louisiana. Not less encouraging than this, is the political situation at the South.

The vote of the colored man, formerly beaten down and stamped out by intimidation, is now revived, sought, and defended by powerful allies, and this from no transient sentiment of the moment, but from the permanent laws controlling the action of political parties.

While the Constitution of the United States shall guarantee the colored man's right to vote, somebody in the South will want that vote and will offer the terms upon which that vote can be obtained.

Thus the forces against us are passion and prejudice, which are transient, and those for us are principles, self-acting, self-sustaining, and permanent. My hope for the future of my race is further supported by the rapid decline of an emotional, shouting, and thoughtless religion. Scarcely in any direction can there be found a less favorable field for mind or morals than where such a religion prevails. It abounds in the wildest hopes and fears, and in blind unreasoning faith. Instead of adding to faith virtue, its tendency is to substitute faith for virtue, and is a deadly enemy to our progress. There is still another ground for hope. It arises out of a comparison of our past condition with our present one,—the immeasurable depths from which we have come, and the point of progress already attained. We shall look over the world, and survey the history of any other oppressed and enslaved people in vain, to find one which has made more progress within the same length of time, than have the colored people of the United States. These, and many other considerations which I might name, give brightness and fervor to my hopes that that better day for which the more thoughtful amongst us have long labored, and the millions of our people have sighed for centuries, is near at hand.

# THIRD PART.

# CHAPTER I.

## LATER LIFE.

*Again summoned to the defense of his people—The difficulties of the task—The race problem—His life work—The anti-slavery movement.*

TEN years ago* when the preceding chapters of this book were written, having then reached in the journey of life the middle of the decade beginning at sixty and ending at seventy, and naturally reminded that I was no longer young, I laid aside my pen with some such sense of relief as might be felt by a weary and over-burdened traveler when arrived at the desired end of a long journey, or as an honest debtor wishing to be square with all the world might feel when the last dollar of an old debt was paid off. Not that I wished to be discharged from labor and service in the cause to which I have devoted my life, but from this peculiar kind of labor and service. I hardly need say to those who know me, that writing for the public eye never came quite as easily to me as speaking to the public ear. It is a marvel to me that under the circumstances I learned to write at all. It has been a still greater marvel that in the brief working period in which they lived and wrought, such men as Dickens,* Dumas, Carlyle* and Sir Walter Scott could have produced the works ascribed to them. But many have been the impediments with which I have had to struggle. I have, too, been embarrassed by the thought of writing so much about myself when there was so much else of which to write. It is far easier to write about others than about one's self. I write freely of myself, not from choice, but because I have, by my cause, been morally forced into thus writing. Time and events have summoned me to stand forth both as a witness and an advocate for a people long dumb, not allowed to speak for themselves, yet much misunderstood and deeply wronged. In the earlier days of my freedom, I was called upon to expose the direful nature of the slave system, by telling my own experience while a slave, and to do what I could thereby to make slavery odious and thus to hasten the day of emancipation. It was no time to mince matters or to stand upon a delicate sense of propriety, in the presence of a crime so gigantic as our slavery was, and the duty to oppose it so imperative. I was called upon to expose even my stripes, and with many misgivings obeyed the summons and tried thus to do my whole duty in this my first public work and what I may say proved to be the best work of my life.

Fifty years have passed since I entered upon that work, and now that it is ended, I find myself summoned again by the popular voice and by what is called the negro problem, to come a second time upon the witness stand and give evidence upon disputed points concerning myself and my emancipated brothers and sisters who, though free, are yet oppressed and are in as much need of an advocate as before they were set free. Though this is not altogether as agreeable to me as was my first mission, it is one that comes with such commanding authority as to compel me to accept it as a present duty. In it I am pelted with all sorts of knotty questions, some of which might be difficult even for Humboldt,* Cuvier* or Darwin,* were they alive, to answer. They are questions which range over the whole field of science, learning and philosophy, and some descend to the depths of impertinent, unmannerly and vulgar curiosity. To be able to answer the higher range of these questions I should be profoundly versed in psychology, anthropology, ethnology, sociology, theology, biology, and all the other ologies, philosophies and sciences. There is no disguising the fact that the American people are much interested and mystified about the mere matter of color as connected with manhood. It seems to them that color has some moral or immoral qualities and especially the latter. They do not feel quite reconciled to the idea that a man of different color from themselves should have all the human rights claimed by themselves. When an unknown man is spoken of in their presence, the first question that arises in the average American mind concerning him and which must be answered is, Of what color is he? and he rises or falls in estimation by the answer given. It is not whether he is a good man or a bad man. That does not seem of primary importance. Hence I have often been bluntly and sometimes very rudely asked, of what color my mother was, and of what color was my father? In what proportion does the blood of the various races mingle in my veins, especially how much white blood and how much black blood entered into my composition? Whether I was not part Indian as well as African and Caucasian? Whether I considered myself more African than Caucasian, or the reverse? Whether I derived my intelligence from my father, or from my mother, from my white, or from my black blood? Whether persons of mixed blood are as strong and healthy as persons of either of the races whose blood they inherit? Whether persons of mixed blood do permanently remain of the mixed complexion or finally take on the complexion of one or the other of the two or more races of which they may be composed? Whether they live as long and raise as large families as other people? Whether they inherit only evil from both parents and good from neither? Whether evil dispositions are more transmissible than good? Why did I marry a person of my father's complexion instead of marrying one of my mother's complexion?* How is the race problem to be solved in this country? Will the negro go back to Africa or remain here? Under this shower of purely American questions, more or less personal, I have endeavored to possess my soul in patience and get as much good out of life as was possible with so much to occupy my time; and, though often perplexed, seldom losing my temper, or abating heart or hope for the future of my people. Though I cannot say I have satisfied the curiosity of my countrymen on all the questions raised by them, I have, like all honest men on the witness stand, answered to the best of my knowledge and belief, and I hope I have never answered in such wise as to increase the hardships of any human being of whatever race or color.

When the first part of this book was written, I was, as before intimated, already looking toward the sunset of human life and thinking that my children would probably finish the recital of my life, or that possibly some other persons outside of family ties to whom I am known might think it worth while to tell what he or she might know of the remainder of my story. I considered, as I have said, that my work was done. But friends and publishers concur in the opinion that the unity and completeness of the work require that it shall be finished by the hand by which it was begun.

Many things touched me and employed my thoughts and activities between the years 1881 and 1891. I am willing to speak of them. Like most men who give the world their autobiographies I wish my story to be told as favorably towards myself as it can be with a due regard to truth. I do not wish it to be imagined by any that I am insensible to the singularity of my career, or to the peculiar relation I sustain to the history of my time and country. I know and feel that it is something to have lived at all in this Republic during the latter part of this eventful century, but I know it is more to have had some small share in the great events which have distinguished it from the experience of all other centuries. No man liveth unto himself, or ought to live unto himself.* My life has conformed to this Bible saying, for, more than most men, I have been the thin edge of the wedge to open for my people a way in many directions and places never before occupied by them. It has been mine, in some degree, to stand as their defense in moral battle against the shafts of detraction, calumny and persecution, and to labor in removing and overcoming those obstacles which, in the shape of erroneous ideas and customs, have blocked the way to their progress. I have found this to be no hardship, but the natural and congenial vocation of my life. I had hardly become a thinking being when I first learned to hate slavery, and hence I was no sooner free than I joined the noble band of Abolitionists in Massachusetts, headed by William Lloyd Garrison and Wendell Phillips. Afterward, by voice and pen, in season and out of season, it was mine to stand for the freedom of people of all colors, until in our land the last yoke was broken and the last bondsman was set free. In the war for the Union I persuaded the colored man to become a soldier. In the peace that followed, I asked the Government to make him a citizen. In the construction of the rebellious States I urged his enfranchisement.

Much has been written and published during the last ten years purporting to be a history of the anti-slavery movement and of the part taken by the men and women engaged in it, myself among the number. In some of these narrations I have received more consideration and higher estimation than I perhaps deserved. In others I have not escaped undeserved disparagement, which I may leave to the reader and to the judgment of those who shall come after me to reply to and to set right.

The anti-slavery movement, that truly great moral conflict which rocked the land during thirty years, and the part taken by the men and women engaged in it, are not quite far enough removed from us in point of time to admit at present of an impartial history. Some of the sects and parties that took part in it still linger with us and are zealous for distinction, for priority and superiority. There is also the disposition to unduly magnify the importance of some men and to diminish the importance of others. While over all this I spread the mantle of charity, it may in a measure explain whatever may seem like prejudice, bigotry and partiality in some attempts already made at the history of the anti-slavery movement. As in a great war, amid the roar of cannon, the smoke of powder, the rising dust and the blinding blaze of fire and counter-fire of battle, no one participant may be blamed for not being able to see and correctly to measure and report the efficiency of the different forces engaged, and to render honor where honor is due; so we may say of the late historians who have essayed to write the history of the anti-slavery movement. It is not strange that those who write in New England from the stand occupied by William Lloyd Garrison and his friends, should fail to appreciate the services of the political abolitionists and of the Free Soil and Republican parties. Perhaps a political abolitionist would equally misjudge and underrate the value of the non-voting and moral-suasion party, of which Mr. Garrison was the admitted leader; while in fact the two were the halves necessary to make the whole. Without Adams, Giddings, Hale, Chase, Wade, Seward, Wilson and Sumner to plead our cause in the councils of the nation, the taskmasters would have remained the contented and undisturbed rulers of the Union, and no condition of things would have been brought about authorizing the Federal Government to abolish slavery in the country's defense. As one of those whose bonds have been broken, I cannot see without pain any attempt to disparage and under-value any man's work in this cause.

Hereafter, when we get a little farther away from the conflict, some brave and truth-loving man, with all the facts before him, uninfluenced by filial love and veneration for men, or party associations, or pride of name, will gather from here and there the scattered fragments, my small contribution perhaps among the number, and give to those who shall come after us an impartial history of this the grandest moral con-flict of the century. Truth is patient and time is just. With these and like reflections, which have often brought consolation to better men than myself, when upon them has fallen the keen edge of censure, and with the scrupulous justice done me in the biography of myself lately writ-ten by Mr. Frederick May Holland* of Concord, Massachusetts, I can easily rest contented.

# CHAPTER II.

## A GRAND OCCASION.

*Inauguration of President Garfield—A valuable precedent—An affecting scene—The greed of the office-seekers—Conference with President Garfield—Distrust of the Vice-President.*

IN the first part of this remarkable decade of American life and history, we had the election and grand inauguration of James A. Garfield as President of the United States, and in a few months thereafter we had his tragic death by the hand of a desperate assassin. On the 4th of March in that year, I happened to be United States Marshal of the District of Columbia, having been appointed to that office four years previous to that date by President Rutherford B. Hayes. This official position placed me in touch with both the outgoing President and the President elect. By the unwritten law of long-established usage, the United States Marshal of the District of Columbia is accorded a conspicuous position on the occasion of the inauguration of a new President of the United States. He has the honor of escorting both the outgoing and the incoming President, from the imposing ceremonies in the U. S. Senate Chamber to the east front of the Capitol, where, on a capacious platform erected for the purpose, before uncounted thousands and in the presence of grave Senators, Members of Congress and representatives of all the civilized nations of the world, the presidential oath is solemnly administered to the President elect, who proceeds to deliver his inaugural address, a copy of which has already been given to the press. In the procession from the Senate I had the honor, in the presence of all the many thousands of the dignitaries there assembled, of holding the right and marching close by the side of both Presidents. The grandeur and solemnity of the occasion appeared to me no less great and uncommon because of the honorable and responsible position I that day held. I was a part of a great national event and one which would pass into American history, but at the moment I had no intimation or foreshadowing of how dark, dreadful and bloody would be the contents of the chapter. I have sometimes had what seemed to me startling presentiments of coming evil, but there were none on this grand inaugural day. The moral and political sky was calmly blue, bright and beautiful, and full of hope for the new President and for the nation. I felt myself standing on new ground, on a height never before trodden by any of my people; one heretofore occupied only by members of the Caucasian race. I do not doubt that this sudden elevation and distinction made upon me a decided impression. But I knew that my elevation was temporary; that it was brilliant but not lasting; and that like many others tossed by the late war to the surface, I should soon be reduced to the ranks of my common people. However, I deemed the event highly important as a new circumstance in my career, as a new recognition of my class, and as a new step in the progress of the nation. Personally it was a striking contrast to my early condition. Yonder I was an unlettered slave toiling under the lash of Covey, the negro breaker; here I was the United States Marshal of the capital of the nation, having under my care and guidance the sacred persons of an ex-President and of the President elect of a nation of sixty millions, and was armed with a nation's power to arrest any arm raised against them. While I was not insensible or indifferent to the fact that I was treading the high places of the land, I was not conscious of any unsteadiness of head or heart. I was United States Marshal by accident. I was no less Frederick Douglass, identified with a proscribed class whose perfect and practical equality with other American citizens was yet far down the steps of time. Yet I was not sorry to have this brief authority, for I rejoiced in the fact that a colored man could occupy this height. The precedent was valuable. Though the tide that carried me there might not soon again rise so high, it was something that it had once so risen and had remained up long enough to leave its mark on the point it touched and that not even the hoary locks of Time could remove it or conceal it from the eyes of mankind. The incident was valuable as showing that the sentiment of the nation was more liberal towards the colored man in proportion to its proximity, in point of time, to the war and to the period when his services were fresh in its memory, for his condition is affected by his nearness to or remoteness from the time when his services were rendered. The imperfections of memory, the multitudinous throngs of events, the fading effects of time upon the national mind, and the growing affection of the loyal nation for the late rebels, will, on the page of our national history, obscure the negro's part, though they can never blot it out entirely, nor can it be entirely forgotten.

The inauguration of President Garfield was exceptional in its surroundings. The coronation of a king could hardly have been characterized by more display of joy and satisfaction. The delight and enthusiasm of the President's friends knew no bounds. The pageant was to the last degree brilliant and memorable, and the scene became sublime when, after his grand inaugural address, the soldier, the orator, the statesman, the President elect of this great nation, stepped aside, bowed his splendid form, and, in sight of all the people, kissed his mother. It was a reminder to the dear mother that, though her son was President of the United States, he was still her son, and that none of the honors he that day received could make him forget for a moment the debt of love due to that mother whose hand had guided his infancy. Some thought that this act was somewhat theatrical and wanting in dignity, but as a near spectator of the scene, I thought it touching and beautiful. Nothing so unaffected and spontaneous and sacred could awaken in the heart of a true man other than sentiments of respect and admiration. On that day of glory, and amid demonstrations so sublime, no thought of the tragic death that awaited the illustrious object of this grand ovation could have intruded itself. It is not to be supposed that, even in the mind of the mad assassin Guiteau, the thought of murdering the President had yet dawned. I heard at his trial this demon-possessed man talk, and came to the conclusion that this deed was the result of madness for office, and that this madness carried the assassin beyond the limit to which the same madness sometimes carries other men. Others conspire, intrigue, lie and slander in order to get office, but this crazy creature thought that he could get office by killing a President. He thought that if he gave the Presidency to Mr. Arthur, the latter would serve him a similar good turn, and not only protect him from punishment, but give him an office. No better evidence of insanity could be wanted than this mode of reasoning. Guiteau may have been in some measure responsible, but I have always thought him hopelessly insane.

No doubt there were many present at this inauguration who, like the assassin, thought that in the bestowment of patronage, the new President would not forget them. It is painful to think that to this selfish feeling we may rightfully ascribe much of the display and seeming enthusiasm on such occasions; that because of it, banners wave, men march, rockets cleave the air, and cannon pour out their thunders. Only the common people, animated by patriotism, and without hope of reward, know on such occasions the thrill of a pure enthusiasm. To the office-seeker the whole is gone through with as a mere hollow, dumb show. It is not uncommon to hear men boast of how much they did for the victorious party; how much marching and counter-marching they did, and how much influence they brought to the successful candidates, and on the strength of it threaten that they will never do the like again if their services shall fail to get them office. The madness of Guiteau was but the exaggerated madness of other men. It is impossible to measure the evil which this craving madness may yet bring upon the country. Any civil-service reform which will diminish it, even if it does not entirely banish it from the minds of Americans, should be supported by every patriotic citizen.

Few men in the country felt more than I the shock caused by the assassination of President Garfield, and few men had better reason for thus feeling. I not only shared with the nation its great common sorrow because a good man had been cruelly and madly slain in the midst of his years and in the morning of his highest honors and usefulness, but because of the loss which I thought his death had entailed upon the colored people of the country. For though I at one time had my fears as to the course Mr. Garfield would pursue towards us, my hopes were stronger than my fears, and my faith stronger than my doubts. Only a few weeks before his tragic death, he invited me to the executive mansion to talk over matters pertaining to the cause of my people, and here came up the subject of his foreign appointments. In this conversation he referred to the fact that his Republican predecessors in office had never sent colored men to any of the white nations. He said that he meant to depart from this usage; that he had made up his mind to send some colored men abroad to some of the white nationalities, and he wanted to know of me if such persons would be acceptable to some such nations. I, of course, thought the way clear to this new departure, and encouraged the President in his proposed advanced step. At the time this promise was made and this hope was held out, I had little doubt of its perfect fulfilment. There was in the President's manner the appearance of a well-matured, fixed, and resolute purpose to try the experiment. Hence his sudden and violent death came to me, not only with the crushing significance of a great crime against the nation and against mankind, but as a killing blow to my newly awakened hopes for my struggling people. I thought that could this new departure in the policy of our Government be carried out, a death wound would be given to American prejudice, and a new and much needed assurance would be given to the colored citizen. Thereafter he would be more respected at home and abroad than he had ever before been. It would be conclusive evidence that the American people and Government were in earnest, and that they were not trifling and deceiving him when they clothed him with American citizenship. It would say to the country and to the civilized world that the great Republican party of the American Union, which carried the nation through the war, saved the country from dismemberment, reconstructed the Government on the basis of liberty, emancipated the slave and made him a citizen, was an honest party, and meant all it had said, and was determined hereafter to take no step backward. Cherishing, as I did, this view of what was promised and should be expected from the continued life of Mr. Garfield, his death appeared to me as among the gloomiest calamities that could have come to my people. The hopes awakened by the kind-hearted President had no support in my knowledge of the character of the self-indulgent man who was elected, in the contingency of death, to succeed him. The announcement, at the Chicago Convention, of this man's name as that of the candidate for the Vice-Presidency, strangely enough brought over me a shudder such as one might feel in coming upon an armed murderer or a poisonous reptile. For some occult and mysterious cause, I know not what, I felt the hand of death upon me. I do not say or intimate that Mr. Arthur had anything to do with the taking off of the President. I might have had the same shudder had any other man been named, but I state the simple fact precisely as it was.

# CHAPTER III.

## DOUBTS AS TO GARFIELD'S COURSE.

*Garfield not a stalwart—Encounter of Garfield with Tucker—Hope in promises of a new departure—The sorrow-stricken nation.*

WHETHER President Garfield would have confirmed or disappointed my hopes had his life been spared by the assassin's bullet can, of course, never be known. His promise to break the record of former Presidents was plain, emphatic and hearty. Considering the strength of popular prejudice against the negro, the proposition to send a colored man to an admitted post of honor in a white nation was a bold one. While there was much in the history and generous nature of Mr. Garfield to justify hope, I must say that there was also something in his temperament and character to cause doubt and fear that his resolution in the end might be sicklied over with the pale cast of thought. Mr. Garfield, though a good man, was not my man for the Presidency. For that place I wanted a man of sterner stuff. I was for General Grant, and for him with all the embarrassment and burden of a 'third term' attaching to his candidacy. I held that even defeat with Grant was better than success with a temporizer. I knew both men personally and valued the qualities of both. In the Senate Mr. Garfield was in his place. He was able in debate, amiable in disposition, and lovable in character, and when surrounded by the right influences would be sure to go right; but he did not, to my mind, have in his moral make-up sufficient 'backbone' to fit him for the chief magistracy of the nation at such a time as was then upon the country. In this place, a clear head, quick decision and firm purpose are required. The conditions demanded stalwart qualities and he was not a stalwart. The country had not quite survived the effects and influence of its great war for existence. The serpent had been wounded but not killed. Under the disguise of meekly accepting the results and decisions of the war, the rebels had come back to Congress more with the pride of conquerors than with the repentant humility of defeated traitors. Their heads were high in the air. It was not they but the loyal men who were at fault. Under the fair-seeming name of local self-government, they were shooting to death just as many of the newly made citizens of the South as was necessary to put the individual States of the Union entirely into their power. The object which through violence and bloodshed they had accomplished in the several States, they were already aiming to accomplish in the United

States by address and political strategy. They had captured the individual States and meant now to capture the United States. The moral difference between those who fought for the Union and liberty, and those who had fought for slavery and the dismemberment of the Union, was fast fading away. The language of a sickly conciliation, inherited from the administration of President Hayes, was abroad. Insolency born of slave mastery had begun to exhibit itself in the House and Senate of the nation. The recent amendments of the Constitution, adopted to secure the results of the war for the Union, were beginning to be despised and scouted, and the ship of state seemed fast returning to her ancient moorings. It was therefore no blind partiality that led me to prefer General Grant to General Garfield. The one might arrest the reaction and stay the hand of violence and bloodshed at the South; the other held out little promise of such a result. I had once seen the mettle of Mr. Garfield tried when it seemed to me he did not exhibit the pure gold of moral courage; when, in fact, he quailed under the fierce glance of Randolph Tucker,* a returned slave-holding rebel. I can never forget the scene. Mr. Garfield had used the phrase 'perjured traitors' as descriptive of those who had been educated by the Government and sworn to support and defend the Constitution and yet had betaken themselves to the battlefield and fought to destroy it. Mr. Tucker had resented these terms as thus applied, and the only defense Mr. Garfield made to this brazen insolence of Mr. Tucker was that he did not make the dictionary. This was perhaps the soft answer that turneth away wrath, but it is not the answer with which to rebuke effrontery, haughtiness and presumption. It is not the answer that Charles Sumner or Benjamin F. Wade or Owen Lovejoy* would have given. Neither of these brave men would in such a case have sheltered himself behind the dictionary. In nature exuberant, readily responsive in sympathy, shrinking from conflict with his immediate surroundings, abounding in love of approbation, Mr. Garfield himself admitted that he had made promises that he could not fulfill. His amiable disposition to make himself agreeable to those with whom he came in contact made him weak and led him to create false hopes in those who approached him for favors. This was shown in a case to which I was a party. Prior to his inauguration he solemnly promised Senator Roscoe Conkling that he would appoint me United States Marshal for the District of Columbia. He not only promised, but did so with emphasis. He slapped the table with his hand when he made the promise. When I apologized to Mr. Conkling for the failure of Mr. Garfield to fulfill his promise, that gentleman silenced me by repeating with increasing emphasis, 'But he told me he would appoint you United States marshal of the District of Columbia.' To all I could say in defense of Mr. Garfield, Mr. Conkling repeated this promise with increasing solemnity till it seemed to reproach me not less than Mr. Garfield; he for failing to keep his word and I for defending him. It need not be said to those who knew the character and composition of Senator Conkling that it was impossible for him to tolerate or excuse a broken promise. No man more than he considered a man's word his bond. The difference between the two men is the difference between one guided by principle and one controlled by sentiment.

Although Mr. Garfield had given me this cause to doubt his word, I still had faith in his promised new departure. I believed in it all the more because Mr. Blaine,* then Secretary of State and known to have great influence with the President, was with him in this new measure. Mr. Blaine went so far as to ask me to give him the names of several colored men who could fill such places with credit to the Government and to themselves. All this was ended by the accursed bullet of the assassin. I therefore not only shared the general sorrow of the woe-smitten nation, but lamented the loss of a great benefactor. Nothing could be more sad and pathetic than the death of this lovable man. It was his lot while in full health standing at the gateway of a great office armed with power and supplied with opportunity, with high and pure purposes in life and with heart and mind cheerfully surveying the broad field of duty outstretched before him, to be suddenly and without warning cut down in an instant, in the midst of his years and in the fulness of his honors. There was no true man in the land who did not share the pain of the illustrious sufferer while he lingered in life, or who could refuse a tear when the final hour came when his life and suffering ended.

# CHAPTER IV.

## RECORDER OF DEEDS.

*Activity in behalf of his people—Income of the Recorder of Deeds—False impressions as to his wealth—Appeals for assistance—Persistent beggars.*

ALTHOUGH I was not reappointed to the office of Marshal of the District of Columbia as I had reason to expect and to believe that I should be, not only because under me the office had been conducted blamelessly, but because President Garfield had solemnly promised Senator Conkling that I should be so appointed, I was given the office of Recorder of Deeds for the District of Columbia.* This office was, in many respects, more congenial to my feelings than was that of United States Marshal of the District which made me the daily witness in the criminal court of a side of the District life to me most painful and repulsive. Happily, I was never required personally to superintend or witness an execution or to take any part in one. That sad and solemn business had, prior to my appointment, been committed to the warden of the jail, but the contact with the criminal class and the responsibility of watching and taking care of criminals were in every way distasteful to me, and hence I would, under any circumstances, have preferred the office of Recorder of Deeds to that of Marshal. The duties of Recorder, though specific, exacting, and imperative, are easily performed. The office is one that imposes no social duties whatever, and therefore neither fettered my pen nor silenced my voice in the cause of my people. I wrote much and spoke often, and perhaps because of this activity gave to envious tongues a pretext against me. I think that I was not, while in this office or in that of Marshal, less outspoken against what I considered the errors of rulers, than while outside of the office. My cause first, midst, last, and always, whether in office or out of office, was and is that of the black man; not because he is black, but because he is a man, and a man subjected in this country to peculiar wrongs and hardships.

As in the case of United States Marshal, so in that of Recorder of Deeds, I was the first colored man who held the office, and like all innovations on established usage, my appointment did not meet with the approval of the conservatives and old-time rulers of the country, but, on the contrary, met with resistance from both these and the press as well as from the street corners. Happily for me the American people possess in large measure a proneness to acquiescence. They readily submit to the 'powers that be' and to the rule of the majority. This sheet anchor of our national stability, prosperity and peace served me in good stead in this crisis in my career, as indeed it had done in many others.

I held the office of Recorder of Deeds of the District of Columbia for nearly five years. Having, so to speak, broken the ice by giving to the country the example of a colored man at the head of that office, it has become the one special office to which, since that time, colored men have aspired. Much that is sheep-like is illustrated in the colored race, and perhaps the same is true in all races. Where one goes the others are apt to follow. The office has, ever since I left it, been sought for and occupied by colored men. In this, if not in anything else, I have opened the gate and led the way upward for the people with whom I am identified. The office of Recorder was far less remunerative when I held it than it has since become. With the almost wonderful increase of population, after long years of stationary condition due to the existence of slavery, and with the vast improvements in its sanitary conditions, there has come to Washington a surprising activity in the real estate business. As the office of Recorder is supported by fees, and every transfer of property and every deed of trust and every mortgage executed must be recorded, the income of this office has risen to a larger sum than that of any office of the National Government except that of the President of the United States.

In my experience in public life I have learned that there are many ways by which confidence in public men may be undermined and destroyed, and against which they are comparatively helpless. One of the most successful methods is to start the rumor that a man has made a large fortune out of the Government and is rich. This method of political warfare, I will hardly say assassination, has not escaped the vigilant eye of the Afro-American press or of the aspirant and office-seeker, who, when he has found a public man supposed to be in the way of his ambition, has resorted to this device. In my case this method has not only been well studied but diligently and vigorously employed. The surprising feature is that at this point no amount of testimony and denial has any effect. It is only necessary to get the rumor well started to have it roll on and increase like a ball in adhesive snow. I have, for instance, seen myself described, in some of our Afro-American newspapers, as a man of large fortune, worth half a million of dollars, and the impression was given by the writer that I had made this large fortune out of the Government. The absurdity of all this would readily assert itself to the thoughtful readers of these papers, if they would only stop to think; but, unfortunately, all the readers of Afro-American or other newspapers are not very thoughtful or painstaking in such investigations, but usually accept a 'rumor' or an 'It is said' as law and gospel. The rumors of my wealth are not only not true, but in the nature of my work and history could not be true. A half a million indeed! The fact is, I never was worth one-fifth of that sum and never expect to be. The offices held by me during the eleven years of my official life never brought me over three thousand dollars a year above the current expenses of living, and during some of the years my income was much less than this sum.

While I hold it to be no sin to be rich, but, on the contrary, wish there were many rich men among American citizens of color, the notoriety foolishly or maliciously given me has, in some measure, placed me unfavorably before the people I have most endeavored to serve, and has naturally enough subjected me to some annoyances which I might otherwise have escaped. Aside from the envy and prejudice excited by seeing one man in better circumstances than another, it has overwhelmed me with applications to travel and lecture at my own expense for this and that good object. It has also brought me much correspondence to occupy and consume the time and attention which perhaps might be more usefully employed in other directions. Numerous pressing and pathetic appeals for assistance, written under the delusion of my great wealth, have come to me from colored people from all parts of the country, with heart-rending tales of destitution and misery, such as I would gladly relieve did my circumstances admit of it. This confidence in my benevolent disposition has been flattering enough and gratefully appreciated by me, but I have found it difficult to make the applicants believe that I have no power to justify it. While some of these applications for aid have been distressing, others have been simply amusing in their absurdity. One person wholly unknown to me besought me for the modest sum of four thousand dollars. She had seen a house that would exactly suit herself and daughter for a home. It could be purchased for that amount, and she implored me to send her the money. Another wrote me setting forth the goodness of divine providence in blessing me with great riches, and beseeching me to forward to her the price of a piano, assuring me that she had never before troubled me for money. She knew that her daughter was remarkably gifted in music, and could make her way in the world if to start with she could only have a piano. These were no doubt honest people, and applied to me confidently expecting to get the money for which they asked. They were not of that class of professional beggars who hide away in garrets, cellars, and other out-of-the-way places, and load the mails with ingeniously framed begging letters to persons known to have means and supposed to be benevolent, and upon whom they think they can impose. They are, however, of that large class of persons who are perfectly willing to subsist at other people's expense. Happily, the speculators in human credulity generally reveal the presence of fraud by their elaborate and overdrawn tales of woe and suffering, and thus defeat themselves. The witness who gives evidence merely from memory, and not from the knowledge of the case then present to his mind, may tell a straight story, but one not so straight will often better secure belief. The skilful lawyer can generally detect in the perfection of the story the vice of the evidence.

Among the numerous and persistent beggars whom I have to encounter in this class are those who come in the character of creditors to demand from me the payment of a debt which I especially owe them for the great services which they or their fathers or grandfathers have rendered to the cause of emancipation. 'They have assisted slaves in their flight from bondage.' 'They have traveled miles to hear me lecture.' 'They remember some things which they heard me say.' 'They read everything that I ever wrote.' 'Their fathers kept stations on the underground railroad.' 'They voted the Liberty party ticket many years ago, when no one else did.' And much else of the same sort, but always concluding with a solid demand for money or for my influence to get positions under the Government for themselves or for their friends. Though I could not exactly see how or why I should be called upon to pay the debt of emancipation for the whole four millions of liberated people, I have always tried to do my part as opportunity has offered. At the same time it has seemed to me incomprehensible that they did not see that the real debtors in this woeful account are themselves, and that the absurdity of their posing as creditors did not occur to them.

# CHAPTER V.

## PRESIDENT CLEVELAND'S ADMINISTRATION.

*Circumstances of Cleveland's election—Political standing of the District of Columbia—Estimate of Cleveland's character—Respect for Mr. Cleveland—Decline of strength in the Republican Party—Time of gloom for the colored people—Reason for the defeat of Blaine.*

THE last year of my service in the comfortable office of Recorder of Deeds for the District of Columbia, to which aspirants have never been few in number or wanting in zeal, was under the early part of the remarkable administration of President Grover Cleveland.* It was thought by some of my friends, and especially by my Afro-American critics, that I ought instantly to have resigned this office upon the incoming of the new administration. I do not know how much the desirableness of the office influenced my opinion in an opposite direction, for the human heart is very deceitful, but I took a different view in this respect from my colored critics. The office of Recorder, like that of the Register of Wills, is a purely local office, though held at the pleasure of the President, and it is in no sense a federal or political office. The Federal Government provides no salary for it. It is supported solely by fees paid for work actually done by its employees for the citizens of the District of Columbia. While these citizens, outside the eager applicants for the place, made no complaint of my continuance in the office, I saw no reason to retire from it. Then, too, President Cleveland did not appear to be in haste or to desire my resignation half as much as some of my Afro-American brethren desired me to make room for them. Besides, he owed his election to a peculiar combination of circumstances favorable to my remaining where I was. He had been supported by Republican votes as well as by Democratic votes. He had been the candidate of civil-service reformers, the fundamental idea of whom is that there should be no removal from an office the duties of which have been fully and faithfully performed by the incumbent. Being elected by the votes of civil-service reformers, there was an implied political obligation imposed upon Mr. Cleveland to respect the idea represented by the votes of these reformers. During the first part of his administration, the time in which I held office under him, the disposition on the part of the President to fulfil that obligation was quite manifest, and the feeling at the time was that we were entering upon a new era of American politics, in which there would be no removals from office on the ground of party politics. It seemed that for better or for worse we had reversed the practice of both parties in our political history, and that the old formula, 'To the victor belong the spoils,' was no longer to be the approved rule in politics. Then again I saw that there was less reason for resigning because of the election of a President of a different party from my own, when the political status of the people of the District of Columbia was considered. These people are outside of the United States. They occupy neutral ground and have no political existence. They have neither voice nor vote in all the practical politics of the United States. They are hardly to be called citizens of the United States. Practically they are aliens; not citizens, but subjects. The District of Columbia is the one spot where there is no government for the people, of the people, and by the people. Its citizens submit to rulers whom they have had no choice in selecting. They obey laws which they had no voice in making. They have a plenty of taxation, but no representation. In the great questions of politics in the country they can march with neither army, but are relegated to the position of neuters.

I have nothing to say in favor of this anomalous condition of the people of the District of Columbia, and hardly think that it ought to be or will be much longer endured; but while it exists it does not appear that the election of a President of the United States should make it the duty of a purely local officer, holding an office supported, not by the United States, but by the disfranchised people of the District of Columbia, to resign such office. For these reasons I rested securely in the Recorder's office until the President, whether intentionally or not, had excited the admiration of the civil-service reformers by whom he was elected, after which he vigorously endeavored to conform his policy to the opposing ideas of the Democratic party. Having received all possible applause from the reformers, and thus made it difficult for them to contradict their approval and return to the Republican party, he went to work in earnest at the removal from office of all those whom he regarded as offensive partisans, myself among the number. Seldom has a political device worked better. In face of all the facts, the civil-service reformers adhered to their President. He had not done all they had hoped for, but he had done what they insisted was the best that he could do under the circumstances.

In parting with President Grover Cleveland, it is due to state that, personally, I have no cause of complaint against him. On the contrary, there is much for which I have reason to commend him. I found him a robust, manly man, one having the courage to act upon his convictions, and to bear with equanimity the reproaches of those who differed from him. When President Cleveland came to Washington, I was under a considerable cloud not altogether free from angry lightning. False friends of both colors were loading me with reproaches. No man, perhaps, had ever more offended popular prejudice than I had then lately done. I had married a wife. People who had remained silent over the unlawful relations of the white slave masters with their colored slave women loudly condemned me for marrying a wife a few shades lighter than myself. They would have had no objection to my marrying a person much darker in complexion than myself, but to marry one much lighter, and of the complexion of my father rather than of that of my mother, was, in the popular eye, a shocking offense, and one for which I was to be ostracized by white and black alike. Mr. Cleveland found me covered with these unjust, inconsistent, and foolish reproaches, and instead of joining in with them or acting in accordance with them, or in anywise giving them countenance as a cowardly and political trickster might and probably would have done, he, in the face of all vulgar criticism, paid me all the social consideration due to the office of Recorder of Deeds of the District of Columbia. He never failed, while I held office under him, to invite myself and wife to his grand receptions, and we never failed to attend them. Surrounded by distinguished men and women from all parts of the country and by diplomatic representatives from all parts of the world, and under the gaze of the late slaveholders, there was nothing in the bearing of Mr. and Mrs. Cleveland toward Mrs. Douglass and myself less cordial and courteous than that extended to the other ladies and gentlemen present. This manly defiance, by a Democratic President, of a malignant and time-honored prejudice, won my respect for the courage of Mr. Cleveland. We were in politics separated from each other by a space ocean wide. I had done all that I could to defeat his election and to elect Mr. James G. Blaine, but this made no apparent difference with Mr. Cleveland. He found me in office when he came into the Presidency, and he was too noble to refuse me the recognition and hospitalities that my official position gave me the right to claim. Though this conduct drew upon him fierce and bitter reproaches from members of his own party in the South, he never faltered or flinched, and continued to invite Mrs. Douglass and myself to his receptions during all the time that I was in office under his administration, and often wrote the invitations with his own hand. Among my friends in Europe, a fact like this will excite no comment. There, color does not decide the civil and social position of a man. Here, a white scoundrel, because he is white, is preferred to an honest and educated black man. A white man of the baser sort can ride in first-class carriages on railroads, attend the theaters and enter the hotels and restaurants of our cities, and be accommodated, while a man with the least drop of African blood in his veins would be refused and insulted. Nowhere in the world are the worth and dignity of manhood more exalted in speech and press than they are here, and nowhere is manhood pure and simple more despised than here. We affect contempt for the castes and aristocracies of the old world and laugh at their assumptions, but at home foster pretensions far less rational and much more ridiculous.

I have spoken freely of the sensible and manly course of Mr. Cleveland, and shall perhaps, for this reason, be thought and described as having a leaning towards the Democratic party. No greater mistake could be made. No such inference should be drawn from anything that I have said. I am a Republican and am likely to remain a Republican, but I was never such a partisan that I could not commend a noble action performed by any man of whatever party or sect.

During the administration of Chester A. Arthur, as also during that of Rutherford B. Hayes, the spirit of slavery and rebellion increased in power and advanced towards ascendency. At the same time, the spirit which had abolished slavery and saved the Union steadily and proportionately declined, and with it the strength and unity of the Republican party also declined. The dawn of this deplorable action became visible when the Republican Speaker of the House of Representatives defeated the bill to protect colored citizens of the South from rapine and murder.* Under President Hayes it took organic, chronic form, and rapidly grew in bulk and force. This well-meaning President turned his back upon the loyal state governments of the South, gave the powerful Post-Office Department into the hands of a Southern Democrat, filled the Southern States with rebel postmasters, went South, praised the honesty and bravery of the rebels, preached pacification, and persuaded himself and others to believe that this conciliation policy would arrest the hand of violence, put a stop to outrage and murder, and restore peace and prosperity to the rebel States. The results of this policy were no less ruinous and damning because of the good intention of President Hayes. Its effect upon the Republican spirit of the country was like the withering blast of the sirocco upon all vegetation within its reach. The sentiment that gave us a reconstructed Union on a basis of liberty for all people was blasted as a flower is blasted by a killing frost. The whole four years of this administration were, to the loyal colored citizen, full of darkness and dismal terror. The only gleam of hope afforded him was that the empty form, at least, of the Republican party was still in power, and that it would yet regain something of the strength and vitality that characterized it in the days of Grant, Sumner, and Conkling and the period of reconstruction. How vain was this hope I need not here stop to describe. Fate was against us. The death of Mr. Garfield placed in the Presidential chair Chester A. Arthur, who did nothing to correct the errors of President Hayes, or to arrest the decline and fall of the Republican party, but, on the contrary, by his self-indulgence, indifference and neglect of opportunity, allowed the country to drift (like an oarless boat in the rapids) towards the howling chasm of the slaveholding Democracy.

It was not 'Rum, Romanism, and Rebellion'* that defeated Mr. James G. Blaine, but it was Mr. Blaine who defeated himself. The foundation of his defeat was laid by his own hand in the defeat of the bill to protect the lives and political rights of Southern Republicans. Up to that hour the Republican party was courageous, confident and strong, and able to elect any candidate it might deem it wise to put in nomination for the Presidency; but from that hour it was smitten with moral decay; its courage quailed, its confidence vanished, and it has since hardly lived at all, but has been suspended, and has, comparatively, only lingered between life and death. The lesson taught by its example and its warning is, that political parties, like individual men, are only strong while they are consistent and honest, and that treachery and deception are only the sand on which political fools vainly endeavor to build. When the Republican party ceased to care for and protect its Southern allies, and sought the smiles of the Southern negro murderers, it shocked, disgusted, and drove away its best friends. The scepter of power could no longer be held by it, and it opened the way for the defeat of Mr. Blaine and the election of Mr. Cleveland.

Clinging in hope to the Republican party, thinking it would cease its backsliding and resume its old character as the party of progress, justice and freedom, I regretted its defeat and shared in some measure the painful apprehension and distress felt by my people at the South from the return to power of the old Democratic and slavery party. To many of them it seemed that they were left naked to their enemies; in fact, lost; that Mr. Cleveland's election meant the revival of the slave power, and that they would now be again reduced to slavery and the lash. The misery brought to the South by this widespread alarm can hardly be described or measured. The wail of despair from the late bondsmen was for a time deep, bitter and heartrending. Illiterate and unable to learn to read or to learn of any limit to the power of the party now in the ascendant, their fears were unmitigated and intolerable, and their out-cry of alarm was like the cry of dismay uttered by an army when its champion has fallen and no one appears to take his place. It was well for the poor people in this condition that Mr. Cleveland himself kindly sent word South to allay their fears and to remove their agony. In this trepidation of the unlettered negro something is apparent aside from his ignorance. If he knew nothing of letters, he knew something of events and of the history of parties to them. He knew that the Republican party was the party hated by the old master class, and that the Democratic party was the party beloved of the old master class.

# CHAPTER VI.

## THE SUPREME COURT DECISION.

*Action of the Supreme Court—Its effect on the colored people—Address at Lincoln Hall.*

IN further illustration of the reactionary tendencies of public opinion against the black man and of the increasing decline, since the war for the Union, in the power of resistance to the onward march of the rebel States to their former control and ascendency in the councils of the nation, the decision of the United States Supreme Court, declaring the Civil Rights law of 1875* unconstitutional, is striking and convincing. The strength and activities of the malign elements of the country against equal rights and equality before the law seem to increase in proportion to the increasing distance between that time and the time of the war. When the black man's arm was needed to defend the country; when the North and the South were in arms against each other and the country was in danger of dismemberment, his rights were well considered. That the reverse is now true, is a proof of the fading and defacing effect of time and the transient character of Republican gratitude. From the hour that the loyal North began to fraternize with the disloyal and slaveholding South; from the hour that they began to 'shake hands over the bloody chasm;'* from that hour the cause of justice to the black man began to decline and lose its hold upon the public mind, and it has lost ground ever since.

The future historian will turn to the year 1883 to find the most flagrant example of this national deterioration. Here he will find the Supreme Court of the nation reversing the action of the Government, defeating the manifest purpose of the Constitution, nullifying the Fourteenth Amendment, and placing itself on the side of prejudice, proscription, and persecution.

Whatever this Supreme Court may have been in the past, or may by the Constitution have been intended to be, it has, since the days of the Dred Scott decision, been wholly under the influence of the slave power, and its decisions have been dictated by that power rather than by what seemed to be sound and established rules of legal interpretation.

Although we had, in other days, seen this court bend and twist the law to the will and interest of the slave power, it was supposed that by the late war and the great fact that slavery was abolished, and the further fact that the members of the bench were now appointed by a Republican administration, the spirit as well as the body had been exorcised. Hence the decision in question came to the black man as a painful and bewildering surprise. It was a blow from an unsuspected quarter. The surrender of the national capital to Jefferson Davis in time of the war could hardly have caused a greater shock. For the moment the colored citizen felt as if the earth was opened beneath him. He was wounded in the house of his friends. He felt that this decision drove him from the doors of the great temple of American Justice. The nation that he had served against its enemies had thus turned him over naked to those enemies. His trouble was without any immediate remedy. The decision must stand until the gates of death could prevail against it.

The colored men in the capital of the nation where the deed was done were quick to perceive its disastrous significance, and in the helpless horror of the moment they called upon myself and others to express their grief and indignation. In obedience to that call a meeting was assembled in Lincoln Hall, the largest hall in the city, which was packed by an audience of all colors, to hear what might be said to this new and startling event. Though we were powerless to arrest the wrong or modify the consequences of this extraordinary decision, we could, at least, cry out against its absurdity and injustice.

On that occasion our cause was ably and eloquently presented by that distinguished lawyer and eminent philanthropist, Robert G. Ingersoll. For my own part I felt it to be a serious thing to contradict the judgment of the highest court in the land, especially in view of the danger of being betrayed into unwise and extravagant language by the wild excitement of the moment. As the first speaker on that memorable occasion, I present here as a part of my 'Life and Times' what I there said.

I have only a few words to say to you this evening. . . . It may be, after all, that the hour calls more loudly for silence than for speech. Later on in this discussion, when we shall have before us the full text of the Supreme Court and the dissenting opinion of Judge Harlan,* who must have weighty reasons for separating from his associates and incurring thereby, as he must, an amount of criticism from which even the bravest man might shrink, we may be in a better frame of mind, better supplied with facts, and better prepared to speak calmly, correctly and wisely than now. The temptation at this time is to speak more from feeling than reason, more from impulse than reflection.

We have been, as a class, grievously wounded, wounded in the house of our friends, and this wound is too deep and too painful for ordinary and measured speech.

'When a deed is done for freedom,
    Through the broad earth's aching breast
Runs a thrill of joy prophetic,
    Trembling on from east to west.'*

But when a deed is done for slavery, caste and oppression, and a blow is struck at human progress, whether so intended or not, the heart of humanity sickens in sorrow and writhes in pain. It makes us feel as if some one were stamping upon the graves of our mothers, or desecrating our sacred temples. Only base men and oppressors can rejoice in a triumph of injustice over the weak and defenseless; for weakness ought itself to protect from assaults of pride, prejudice and power.

The cause which has brought us here to-night is neither common nor trivial. Few events in our national history have surpassed it in magnitude, importance and significance. It has swept over the land like a cyclone, leaving moral desolation in its track. This decision belongs with a class of judicial and legislative wrongs by which we have been oppressed.

We feel it as we felt years ago the furious attempt to force the accursed system of slavery upon the soil of Kansas; as we felt the enactment of the Fugitive Slave Bill, the repeal of the Missouri Compromise, and the Dred Scott decision. I look upon it as one more shocking development of that moral weakness in high places which has attended the conflict between the spirit of liberty and the spirit of slavery, and I venture to predict that it will be so regarded by aftercoming generations. Far down the ages, when men shall wish to inform themselves as to the real state of liberty, law, religion, and civilization in the United States at this juncture of our history, they will overhaul the proceedings of the Supreme Court, and read this strange decision declaring the Civil Rights Bill unconstitutional and void.

From this more than from many volumes they will learn how far we had advanced, in this year of grace, from the barbarism of slavery toward civilization and the rights of man.

Fellow-citizens! Among the great evils which now stalk abroad in our land, the one, I think, which most threatens to undermine and destroy the foundations of our free institutions in this country is the great and apparently increasing want of respect entertained for those to whom are committed the responsibility and the duty of administering our government. On this point I think all good men must agree, and against the evil I trust you feel the deepest repugnance, and that we will, neither here nor elsewhere, give it the least breath of sympathy or encouragement. We should never forget, whatever may be the incidental mistakes or misconduct of rulers, that government is better than anarchy, and that patient reform is better than violent revolution.

But while I would increase this feeling and give it the emphasis of a voice from heaven, it must not be allowed to interfere with free speech, honest expression of opinion, and fair criticism. To give up this would be to give up progress, and to consign the nation to moral stagnation, putrefaction and death.

In the matter of respect for dignitaries, it should, however, never be forgotten that duties are reciprocal, and that while the people should frown down every manifestation of levity and contempt for those in power, it is the duty of the possessors of power so to use it as to deserve and insure respect and reverence.

To come a little nearer to the case now before us. The Supreme Court of the United States, in the exercise of its high and vast constitutional power, has suddenly and unexpectedly decided that the law intended to secure to colored people the civil rights guaranteed to them by the following provision of the Constitution of the United States, is unconstitional and void. Here it is:—

'No state,' says the Fourteenth Amendment, 'shall make or enforce any law which shall abridge the privileges or immunities of citizens of the United States; nor shall any state deprive any person of life, liberty, or property, without due process of the law; or deny any person within its jurisdiction the equal protection of the laws.'

Now, when a bill has been discussed for weeks and months and even years, in the press and on the platform, in Congress and out of Congress; when it has been calmly debated by the clearest heads and the most skillful and learned lawyers in the land; when every argument against it has been over and over again carefully considered and fairly answered; when its constitutionality has been especially discussed, pro and con.; when it has passed the United States House of Representatives and has been solemnly enacted by the United States Senate (perhaps the most imposing legislative body in the world); when such a bill has been submitted to the cabinet of the nation, composed of the ablest men in the land; when it has passed under the scrutinizing eye of the Attorney-General of the United States; when the Executive of the nation has given to it his name and formal approval; when it has taken its place upon the statute-book and has remained there for nearly a decade, and the country has largely assented to it, you will agree with me that the reasons for declaring such a law unconstitutional and void should be strong, irresistible, and absolutely conclusive.

Inasmuch as the law in question is a law in favor of liberty and justice, it ought to have had the benefit of any doubt which could arise as to its strict constitutionality. This, I believe, will be the view taken of it, not only by laymen like myself, but by eminent lawyers as well.

All men who have given any thought to the machinery, structure, and practical operation of our government, must have recognized the importance of absolute harmony between its various departments and their respective powers and duties. They must have seen clearly the mischievous tendency and danger to the body politic of any antagonisms between any of its various branches. To feel the force of this thought, we have only to remember the history of the administration of President Johnson, and the conflict which took place between the national Executive and the national Congress, when the will of the people was again and again met by the Executive veto, and when the country seemed upon the verge of another revolution. No patriot, however bold, can wish for his country a repetition of those gloomy days.

Now let me say here, before I go on a step or two further in this discussion, that if any man has come here to-night with his breast heaving with passion, his heart flooded with acrimony, and wishing and expecting to hear violent denunciation of the Supreme Court on account of this decision, he has mistaken the object of this meeting and the character of the men by whom it is called.

We neither come to bury Cæsar nor to praise him. The Supreme Court is the autocratic point in our government. No monarch in Europe has a power more absolute over the laws, lives, and liberties of his people than that court has over our laws, lives and liberties. Its judges live, and ought to live, an eagle's flight beyond the reach of fear or favor, praise or blame, profit or loss. No vulgar prejudice should touch the members of that court anywhere. Their decisions should come down to us like the calm, clear light of infinite justice. We should be able to think of them and to speak of them with profoundest respect for their wisdom and deepest reverence for their virtue; for what his Holiness the Pope is to the Roman Catholic Church, the Supreme Court is to the American state. Its members are men, to be sure, and may not, like the Pope, claim infallibility, and they are not infallible, but they are the supreme law-giving power of the nation, and their decisions are law until changed by that court.

What will be said here to-night will be spoken, I trust, more in sorrow than in anger; more in a tone of regret than in bitterness and reproach, and more to promote sound views than to find bad motives for unsound views.

We cannot, however, overlook the fact that though not so intended, this decision has inflicted a heavy calamity upon seven millions of the people of this country, and left them naked and defenseless against the action of a malignant, vulgar and pitiless prejudice from which the Constitution plainly intended to shield them.

It presents the United States before the world as a nation utterly destitute of power to protect the constitutional rights of its own citizens upon its own soil.

It can claim service and allegiance, loyalty and life from them, but it cannot protect them against the most palpable violation of the rights of human nature; rights to secure which governments are established. It can tax their bread and tax their blood, but it has no protecting power for their persons. Its national power extends only to the District of Columbia and the Territories—to where the people have no votes, and to where the land has no people. All else is subject to the States. In the name of common sense, I ask what right have we to call ourselves a nation, in view of this decision and of this utter destitution of power?

In humiliating the colored people of this country, this decision has humbled the nation. It gives to the railroad conductor in South Carolina or Mississippi more power than it gives to the National Government. He may order the wife of the Chief Justice of the United States into a smoking-car full of hirsute men, and compel her to go and to listen to the coarse jests and inhale the foul smoke of a vulgar crowd. It gives to hotel-keepers who may, from a prejudice born of the Rebellion, wish to turn her out at midnight into the storm and darkness, power to compel her to go. In such a case, according to this decision of the Supreme Court, the National Government has no right to interfere. She must take her claim for protection and redress, not to the nation, but to the State; and when the State, as I understand it, declares that there is upon its statute-book no law for her protection, and that the State has made no law against her, the function and power of the National Government are exhausted and she is utterly without any redress.

Bad, therefore, as our case is, under this decision, the evil principle affirmed by the court is not wholly confined to or spent upon persons of color. The wife of Chief-Justice Waite—I speak it respectfully—is protected to-day, not by the law, but solely by the accident of her color. So far as the law of the land is concerned, she is in the same condition as that of the humblest colored woman in the Republic. The difference between colored and white here is that the one, by reason of color, does not need protection. It is nevertheless true that manhood is insulted in both cases. 'No man can put a chain about the ankle of his fellow-man, without at last finding the other end of it about his own neck.'

The lesson of all the ages upon this point is, that a wrong done to one man is a wrong done to all men. It may not be felt at the moment, and the evil may be long delayed, but so sure as there is a moral government of the universe, so sure as there is a God of the universe, so sure will the harvest of evil come.

Color prejudice is not the only prejudice against which a Republic like ours should guard. The spirit of caste is malignant and dangerous everywhere. There is the prejudice of the rich against the poor, the pride and prejudice of the idle dandy against the hard-handed workingman. There is, worst of all, religious prejudice, a prejudice which has stained whole continents with blood. It is, in fact, a spirit infernal, against which every enlightened man should wage perpetual war. Perhaps no class of our fellow-citizens has carried this prejudice against color to a point more extreme and dangerous than have our Catholic Irish fellow-citizens, and yet no people on the face of the earth have been more relentlessly persecuted and oppressed on account of race and religion than have this same Irish people.

But in Ireland persecution has at last reached a point where it reacts terribly upon her persecutors. England is to-day reaping the bitter consequences of her own injustice and oppression. Ask any man of intelligence, 'What is the chief source of England's weakness? What has reduced her to the rank of a second-class power?' and if truly answered, the answer will be 'Ireland!' But poor, ragged, hungry, starving, and oppressed as Ireland is, she is strong enough to be a standing menace to the power and glory of England.

Fellow-citizens! We want no black Ireland in America. We want no aggrieved class in America. Strong as we are without the negro, we are stronger with him than without him. The power and friendship of seven millions of people, however humble and scattered all over the country, are not to be despised.

To-day our Republic sits as a queen among the nations of the earth. Peace is within her walls and plenteousness within her palaces, but he is bolder and a far more hopeful man than I am who will affirm that this peace and prosperity will always last. History repeats itself. What has happened once may happen again.

The negro, in the Revolution, fought for us and with us. In the war of 1812 General Jackson, at New Orleans, found it necessary to call upon the colored people to assist in its defense against England. Abraham Lincoln found it necessary to call upon the negro to defend the Union against rebellion. In all cases the negro responded gallantly.

Our legislators, our Presidents, and our judges should have a care, lest, by forcing these people outside of law, they destroy that love of country which in the day of trouble is needful to the nation's defense.

I am not here in this presence to discuss the constitutionality or the unconstitutionality of this decision of the Supreme Court. The decision may or may not be constitutional. That is a question for lawyers and not for laymen; and there are lawyers on this platform as learned, able and eloquent as any who have appeared in this case before the Supreme Court, or as any in the land. To these I leave the exposition of the Constitution; but I claim the right to remark upon a strange and glaring inconsistency of this decision with former decisions, where the rules of law apply. It is a new departure, entirely out of the line of precedents and decisions of the Supreme Court at other times and in other directions where the rights of colored men were concerned. It has utterly ignored and rejected the force and application of the object and intention of the adoption of the Fourteenth Amendment. It has made no account whatever of the intention and purpose of Congress and the President in putting the Civil Rights Bill upon the statute book of the nation. It has seen fit in this case affecting a weak and much persecuted people, to be guided by the narrowest and most restricted rules of legal interpretation. It has viewed both the Constitution and the law with a strict regard to their letter, but without any generous recognition and application of their broad and liberal spirit. Upon those narrow principles the decision is logical and legal of course. But what I complain of, and what every lover of liberty in the United States has a right to complain of, is this sudden and causeless reversal of all the great rules of legal interpretation by which this court was once governed in the construction of the Constitution and of laws respecting colored people.

In the dark days of slavery this court on all occasions gave the greatest importance to intention as a guide to interpretation. The object and intention of the law, it was said, must prevail. Everything in favor of slavery and against the negro was settled by this object and intention rule. We were over and over again referred to what the framers meant, and plain language itself was sacrificed and perverted from its natural and obvious meaning that the so affirmed intention of these framers might be positively asserted and given the force of law. When we said in behalf of the negro that the Constitution of the United States was intended to establish justice and to secure the blessings of liberty to ourselves and our posterity, we were told that the words said so, but that

that was obviously not its intention; that it was intended to apply only to white people, and that the intention must govern.

When we came to the clause of the Constitution* which declares that the immigration or importation of such persons as any of the States may see fit to admit shall not be prohibited, and the friends of liberty declared that this provision of the Constitution did not describe the slave-trade, they were told that while its language applied not to the slaves but to persons, still the object and intention of that clause of the Constitution was plainly to protect the slave-trade, and that that intention was the law and must prevail. When we came to that clause of the Constitution which declares that 'No person held to labor or service in one State under the laws thereof, escaping into another, shall in consequence of any law or regulation therein be discharged from such labor or service, but shall be delivered up on claim of the party to whom such labor or service may be due,' we insisted that it neither described nor applied to slaves; that it applied only to persons owing service and labor; that slaves did not and could not owe service and labor; that this clause of the Constitution said nothing of slaves or of the masters of slaves; that it was silent as to slave States or free States; that it was simply a provision to enforce a contract and not to force any man into slavery, for the slave could not owe service or make a contract.

We affirmed that it gave no warrant for what was called 'The Fugitive Slave Bill,' and we contended that the bill was therefore unconstitutional; but our arguments were laughed to scorn by that court and by all the courts of the country. We were told that the intention of the Constitution was to enable masters to recapture slaves, and that the law of '93 and the Fugitive Slave Law of 1850 were constitutional, binding not only on the State but upon each citizen of a State.

Fellow-citizens! While slavery was the base line of American society, while it ruled the church and state; while it was the interpreter of our law and the exponent of our religion, it admitted no quibbling, no narrow rules of legal or scriptural interpretations of the Bible or of the Constitution. It sternly demanded its pound of flesh, no matter how the scale turned or how much blood was shed in the taking of it. It was enough for it to be able to show the intention to get all it asked in the courts or out of the courts. But now slavery is abolished. Its reign was long, dark and bloody. Liberty is now the base line of the Republic. Liberty has supplanted slavery, but I fear it has not supplanted the spirit or power of slavery. Where slavery was strong, liberty is now weak.

Oh, for a Supreme Court of the United States which shall be as true to the claims of humanity as the Supreme Court formerly was to the demands of slavery! When that day comes, as come it will, a Civil Rights Bill will not be declared unconstitutional and void, in utter and flagrant disregard of the objects and intentions of the national legislature by which it was enacted and of the rights plainly secured by the Constitution.

This decision of the Supreme Court admits that the Fourteenth Amendment is a prohibition on the States. It admits that a State shall not abridge the privileges or immunities of citizens of the United States, but commits the seeming absurdity of allowing the people of a State to do what it prohibits the State itself from doing.

It used to be thought that the whole was more than a part; that the greater included the less, and that what was unconstitutional for a State to do was equally unconstitutional for an individual member of a State to do. What is a State, in the absence of the people who compose it? Land, air and water. That is all. Land and water do not discriminate. All are equal before them. This law was made for people. As individuals, the people of the State of South Carolina may stamp out the rights of the negro wherever they please, so long as they do not do so as a State, and this absurd conclusion is to be called a law. All the parts can violate the Constitution, but the whole cannot. It is not the act itself, according to this decision, that is unconstitutional. The unconstitutionality of the case depends wholly upon the party committing the act. If the State commits it, the act is wrong; if the citizen of the State commits it, the act is right.

O consistency, thou art indeed a jewel! What does it matter to a colored citizen that a State may not insult and outrage him, if the citizen of the State may? The effect upon him is the same, and it was just this effect that the framers of the Fourteenth Amendment plainly intended by that article to prevent.

It was the act, not the instrument; it was the murder, not the pistol or dagger, which was prohibited. It meant to protect the newly enfranchised citizen from injustice and wrong, not merely from a State, but from the individual members of a State. It meant to give the protection to which his citizenship, his loyalty, his allegiance, and his services entitled him; and this meaning and this purpose and this intention are now declared by the Supreme Court of the United States to be unconstitutional and void.

I say again, fellow-citizens, Oh, for a Supreme Court which shall be as true, as vigilant, as active and exacting in maintaining laws enacted for the protection of human rights, as in other days was that court for the destruction of human rights!

It is said that this decision will make no difference in the treatment of colored people; that the Civil Rights Bill was a dead letter and could not be enforced. There may be some truth in all this, but it is not the whole truth. That bill, like all advance legislation, was a banner on the outer wall of American liberty; a noble moral standard uplifted for the education of the American people. There are tongues in trees, sermons in stones, and books in the running brooks. This law, though dead, did speak. It expressed the sentiment of justice and fair play common to every honest heart. Its voice was against popular prejudice and meanness. It appealed to all the noble and patriotic instincts of the American people. It told the American people that they were all equal before the law; that they belonged to a common country and were equal citizens. The Supreme Court has hauled down this broad and glorious flag of liberty in open day and before all the people, and has thereby given joy to the heart of every man in the land who wishes to deny to others the rights he claims for himself. It is a concession to race pride, selfishness, and meanness, and will be received with joy by every upholder of caste in the land, and for this I deplore and denounce this decision.

It is a frequent and favorite device of an indefensible cause to misstate and pervert the views of those who advocate a good cause, and I have never seen this device more generally resorted to than in the case of the late decision on the Civil Rights Bill. When we dissent from the opinion of the Supreme Court and give the reasons why we think the opinion unsound, we are straightway charged in the papers with denouncing the court itself, and thus put in the attitude of bad citizens. Now, I utterly deny that there has ever been any denunciation of the Supreme Court by the speakers on this platform, and I defy any man to point out one sentence or one syllable of any speech of mine in denunciation of that court.

Another illustration of this tendency to put opponents in a false position, is seen in the persistent effort to stigmatize the Civil Rights Bill as a Social Rights Bill. Now, where under the whole heavens, outside of the United States, could any such perversion of truth have any chance of success? No man in Europe would ever dream that because he has a right to ride on a railway, or stop at a hotel, he therefore has the right to enter into social relations with anybody. No one has a right to speak to another without that other's permission. Social equality and civil equality rest upon an entirely different basis, and well enough the American people know it; yet, in order to inflame a popular prejudice, respectable papers like the New York *Times* and the Chicago *Tribune* persist in describing the Civil Rights Bill as a Social Rights Bill.

When a colored man is in the same room or in the same carriage with white people, as a servant, there is no talk of social equality, but if he is there as a man and a gentleman, he is an offense. What makes the difference? It is not color, for his color is unchanged. The whole essence of the thing is in its purpose to degrade and stamp out the liberties of the race. It is the old spirit of slavery and nothing else. To say that because a man rides in the same car with another, he is therefore socially equal, is one of the wildest absurdities.

When I was in England, some years ago, I rode upon highways, byways, steamboats, stage-coaches and omnibuses. I was in the House of Commons, in the House of Lords, in the British Museum, in the Coliseum, in the National Gallery, everywhere; sleeping in rooms where lords and dukes had slept; sitting at tables where lords and dukes were sitting; but I never thought that those circumstances made me socially the equal of these lords and dukes. I hardly think that some of our Democratic friends would be regarded among those lords as their equals. If riding in the same car makes one equal, I think that the little poodle dog I saw one day sitting in the lap of a lady was made equal by riding in the same car with her. Equality, social equality, is a matter between individuals. It is a reciprocal understanding. I do not think that when I ride with an educated, polished rascal he is thereby made my equal, or that when I ride with a numskull it makes him my equal. Social equality does not necessarily follow from civil equality, and yet for the purpose of a hell-black and damning prejudice, our papers still insist that the Civil Rights Bill is a bill to establish social equality.

If it is a bill for social equality, so is the Declaration of Independence, which declares that all men have equal rights; so is the Sermon on the Mount; so is the golden rule that commands us to do to others as we would that others should do to us; so is the teaching of the Apostle that of one blood God has made all nations to dwell on the face of the earth; so is the Constitution of the United States, and so are the laws and customs of every civilized country in the world; for nowhere, outside of the United States, is any man denied civil rights on account of his color.

# CHAPTER VII.

## DEFEAT OF JAMES G. BLAINE.

*Causes of the Republican defeat—Tariff and free trade—No confidence in the Democratic party.*

THE next event worthy of remark after the decision of the Supreme Court against the validity of the Civil Rights Law, and one which strikingly illustrated the reaction of public sentiment and the steady march of the slave power toward national supremacy since the agonies of the war, was the defeat in 1884 of Mr. James G. Blaine, the Republican candidate for the presidency, and the election of Mr. Grover Cleveland, the Democratic candidate for that office. This result, in view of the men and the parties represented, was a marked surprise. Mr. Blaine was supposed to be the most popular statesman in the country, while his opponent was little known outside of his own State. Besides, the attitude and behavior of the Democratic party during the war had been such as to induce belief that many years must elapse before it could again be trusted with the reins of the National Government. Events show that little dependence can be wisely placed upon the political stability of the masses. Popularity to-day is, with them, no guaranty of popularity to-morrow. Offenses and services are alike easily and speedily forgotten by them. They change front at the command of the moment. Yet it is never difficult to account for a change after that change has taken place.

The defeat of the Republican party in 1884 was due rather to its own folly than to the wisdom of the Democratic party. It despised and rejected the hand that had raised it to power, and it paid the penalty of its own folly. The life of the Republican party lay in its devotion to justice, liberty and humanity. When it abandoned or slighted these great moral ideas and devoted itself to materialistic measures, it no longer appealed to the heart of the nation, but to its pocket. It became a Samson shorn of its locks. The leader in this new and downward departure of the party was the first to feel its fatal consequences. It was he, more than any other man, who defeated the policy of Grant, Conkling, Gen. Butler, and other true men, in favor of extending national protection to colored citizens in their right to vote. His mistake became sensible even to him in the hour of his defeat. It was all plain then. He made, at Augusta, at the close of the campaign, the speech which he should have made at its beginning. In that speech he showed plainly that the hand which struck down the negro voter was the same hand by which he himself was politically slain.

This degeneracy in the Republican party began to manifest itself when the voices of Sumner, Wade, Morton, Conkling, Stevens, and Logan were no longer controlling in its councils; when Morton was laughed at for 'waving the bloody shirt'* and for exposing the bloody crimes and outrages against the Republican voters of the South; when the talk of unloading the negro waxed louder and louder; when Southern men pretended to be aching for a favorable moment for deserting the Democratic party and joining the Republican party, and when it was thought that the white vote of the South could be secured if the black vote was abandoned. Then came along the old issues of tariff and free trade, and kindred questions of material interests, to the exclusion of the more vital principles for which the Republican party stood in the days of its purity and power. But the expected accessions to its ranks from the white voters of the South did not take place. If anything, the South became, with every concession made by the Republicans to win its white vote, more solidly Democratic. There never was yet, and there never will be, an instance of permanent success where a party abandons its righteous principles to win favor of the opposing party. Mankind abhors the idea of abandoning friends in order to win the support of enemies. Considering that the Republican party had fallen away from the grand ideas of liberty, progress, and national unity in which it had originated, and no longer felt that it should protect the rights it had recognized in the Constitution, some of its foremost men lost their interest in its success, and others deserted outright, claiming that as there was now, on the Southern question, no difference between the two parties, there was therefore no choice. Even colored voters in the North, where in doubtful Republican States their votes are most important and can turn the scale for or against one or the other of the parties, began to advocate the withdrawal of their support from the old party by which they were made citizens and to join the Democratic party. Of this class I was not one. I knew that however bad the Republican party was, the Democratic party was much worse. The elements of which the Republican party was composed gave better ground for the ultimate hope of the success of the colored man's cause than those of the Democratic party. The Democratic party was the party of reaction and the chosen party of the old master class. It was true to that class in the darkest hours of the Rebellion, and was true to the same in its resistance of all the measures intended to secure to the nation the blood-bought results of the war. I was convinced that it was not wise to cast in my lot with that party. Considerations of gratitude as well as of wisdom bound me to the Republican party. If men in either party could be induced to extend the arm of the nation for the protection of the negro voter I believed that the Republican party would be that party.

# CHAPTER VIII.

## EUROPEAN TOUR.

*Revisits Parliament—Changes in Parliament—Recollections of Lord Broughan—Listens to Gladstone—Meeting with old friends.*

SEPTEMBER, 1886, was quite a milestone in my experience and journey of life. I had long desired to make a brief tour through several countries in Europe and especially to revisit England, Ireland and Scotland, and to meet once more the friends I met with in those countries more than forty years before. I had twice visited England, but I had never been on the continent of Europe, and this time I was accompanied by my wife.

I shall attempt here no ample description of our travels abroad. For this more space would be required than the limits of this volume will permit. Besides, with such details the book-shelves are already crowded. To revisit places, scenes, and friends after forty years is not a very common occurrence in the lives of men; and while the desire to do so may be intense, the realization has to it a sad side as well as a cheerful one. The old people first met there have passed away, the middle-aged have grown old, and the young have only heard their fathers and mothers speak of you. The places are there, but the people are gone. I felt this when looking upon the members of the House of Commons. When I was there forty-five years before, I saw many of England's great men; men whom I had much desired to see and hear and was much gratified by being able to see and hear. There were Sir Robert Peel, Daniel O'Connell, Richard Cobden, John Bright, Lord John Russell, Sir James Graham, Benjamin Disraeli, Lord Morpeth, and others, but except Mr. Gladstone, not one who was there then is there now. Mr. Bright was alive, but ill health kept him out of Parliament. Five and forty years before, I saw him there, young, robust and strong; a rising British statesman representing a new element of power in his country, and battling as the co-worker of Richard Cobden, against the corn-laws which kept bread from the mouths of the hungry. His voice and eloquence were then a power in Parliament. At that time the question which most deeply interested and agitated England was the repeal of the corn-laws. Of this agitation Mr. Richard Cobden and Mr. Bright, backed by the anti-corn-law league, were the leaders. The landed aristocracy of England, represented by the Tory party, opposed the repeal with intense zeal and bitterness. But the circumstances were against that interest and against that party. The famine of 1845 was doing its ghastly work, and the people not only of Ireland, but of England and Scotland, were asking for bread, more bread, and cheaper bread; and this was a petition to which resistance was vain. The facts and figures of Cobden and the eloquence of Mr. Bright, supported by the needs of the people, bore down the powerful opposition of the aristocracy, and finally won over to repeal the great Tory leader in the person of Sir Robert Peel, one of the most graceful debaters and ablest parliamentarians that England ever had. A more fascinating man than he I never saw or heard in any legislative body. But able and skillful leader as he was, he could not carry his party with him. The landed proprietors opposed him to the last. Their cause was espoused by Lord George Bentinck and Mr. Benjamin Disraeli. The philippics of the latter against Sir Robert were among the most scathing and torturing of anything in their line to which I ever listened. His invectives were all the more burning and blistering because delivered with the utmost coolness and studied deliberation. But he too was gone when I looked into the House of Commons this time. The grand form and powerful presence of Daniel O'Connell was no longer there. The diminutive but dignified figure of Lord John Russell, that great Whig leader, was absent. In the House of Lords, where, five and forty years before, I saw and heard Lord Brougham, all were gone, and he with the rest. He was the most remarkable speaker I ever heard. Such a flow of language; such a wealth of knowledge; such an aptitude of repartee; such quickness in reply to difficult questions suddenly sprung upon him, I think I never saw equaled in any other speaker. In his attitudes and gestures he was in all respects original, and just the opposite of Daniel Webster. As he spoke, his tall frame reeled to and fro like a reed in a gale, and his arms were everywhere, down by his sides, extended in front and over his head; always in action and never at rest. He was discussing when I heard him the postal relations of England, and he seemed to know the postal arrangements of every civilized people in the world. He was often interrupted by 'the noble Lords,' but he very simply disposed of them with a word or two that made them objects of pity and sometimes of ridicule. I wondered how they dared to expose their lordly heads to the heels of such a perfect race-horse in debate as he seemed to be. He simply played with them. When they came too near he gave them a kick and scampered away over the field of his subject without looking back to see if his victims were living, wounded, or dead. But this marvelous man, though he lived long, was now gone, and I saw in England no man like him filling his place or likely to fill his place.

While in England during this last visit I had the good fortune to see and hear Mr. William E. Gladstone,* the great Liberal leader, and, since Sir Robert Peel, the acknowledged prince of parliamentary debaters. He was said by those who had often heard him to be on this occasion in one of his happiest speaking moods, and he made one of his best speeches. I went early. The House was already crowded with members and spectators when Mr. Gladstone came in and took his seat opposite Mr. Balfour,* the Tory leader. Though seventy-seven years had passed over him his step was firm and his bearing confident and vigorous. Expectation had been raised by the announcement in advance that Mr. Gladstone would that day move for the indefinite postponement of the Irish Force Bill,* the measure of all others to which the Government was committed as a remedy for the ills of Ireland. As he sat in front of the Government leader, an able debater awaiting the moment to begin his speech, I saw in the face of Mr. Gladstone a blending of opposite qualities. There were the peace and gentleness of the lamb, with the strength and determination of the lion. Deep earnestness was expressed in all his features. He began his speech in a tone conciliatory and persuasive. His argument against the bill was based upon statistics which he handled with marvelous facility. He showed that the amount of crimes in Ireland for which the Force Bill was claimed as a remedy by the Government was not greater than the great class of crimes in England; and that therefore there was no reason for a Force Bill in one country more than in the other. After marshaling his facts and figures to this point, in a masterly and convincing manner, raising his voice and pointing his finger directly at Mr. Balfour, he exclaimed, in a tone almost menacing and tragic, 'What are you fighting for?' The effect was thrilling. His peroration was a splendid appeal to English love of liberty. When he sat down the House was instantly thinned out. There seemed neither in members nor spectators any desire to hear another voice after hearing Mr. Gladstone's, and I shared this feeling with the rest. A few words were said in reply by Mr. Balfour, who, though an able debater, was no match for the aged Liberal leader.

Leaving public persons, of whom many more could be mentioned, I turned to the precious friends from whom I parted at the end of my first visit to Great Britain and Ireland. In Dublin, the first city I then visited, I was kindly received by Mr. Richard Webb,* Richard Allen,* James Haughton,* and others. They were now all gone, and except some of their children, I was among strangers. These received me in the same cordial spirit that distinguished their fathers and mothers. I did not visit dear old Cork, where in 1845 I was made welcome by the Jennings, the

Warings, the Wrights, and their circle of friends, most of whom I learned had passed away. The same was true of the Neals, the Workmans, the McIntyres, and the Nelsons at Belfast. I had friends in Limerick, in Waterford, in Eniscorthy, and other towns of Ireland, but I saw none of them during this visit. What was true of the mortality of my friends in Ireland, was equally true of those in England. Few who first received me in that country are now among the living. It was, however, my good fortune to meet once more Mrs. Anna Richardson and Miss Ellen Richardson, the two members of the Society of Friends, both beyond three-score and ten, who, forty-five years before, opened a correspondence with my old master and raised seven hundred and fifty dollars with which to purchase my freedom. Mrs. Anna Richardson, having reached the good old age of eighty-six years, her life marvelously filled up with good works, for her hand was never idle and her heart and brain were always active in the cause of peace and benevolence, a few days before this writing passed away. Miss Ellen Richardson, now over eighty, still lives and continues to take a lively interest in the career of the man whose freedom she was instrumental in procuring. It was a great privilege once more to look into the faces and hear the voices of these noble and benevolent women. I saw in England, too, Mr. and Mrs. Russell Lant Carpenter, two friends who were helpful to me when in England, and, until within a few days, helpful to me still. During all the time that I edited and published my paper in Rochester, New York, I had the material and moral support of Rev. Russell Lant Carpenter and that of his excellent wife. But now he too has passed away, covered with honors. He was one of the purest spirits and most impartial minds I ever met. Though a man of slender frame, his life was one of earnest work, and he reached the age of seventy-five. He was the son of Rev. Lant Carpenter, who for a long time was an honored pastor in Bristol. He was also the brother of Philip and Mary Carpenter, and one of a family distinguished for every moral and intellectual excellence.

I missed the presence of George Thompson, one of the most eloquent men who ever advocated the cause of the colored man, either in England or America. Joseph Sturge and most of his family had also passed away. But I will pursue this melancholy enumeration no further, except to say that, in meeting with the descendants of anti-slavery friends in England, Ireland and Scotland, it was good to have confirmed the scriptural saying, 'Train up a child in the way he should go and when he is old he will not depart from it.'*

# CHAPTER IX.

## CONTINUATION OF EUROPEAN TOUR.

*Through France—Dijon and Lyons—The palace of the Popes—The
Amphitheater at Arles—Visits Nice—Pisa and its leaning
tower—The Pantheon—Modern Rome—Religion at Rome—Rome
of the Past—Vesuvius and Naples—Through the Suez Canal—Life
in the East—The Nile—The religion of Mahomet—At the graves of
Theodore Parker and Mrs. Browning—The mountains of the Tyrol.*

ASIDE from the great cities of London and Paris, with their varied and
brilliant attractions, the American tourist will find no part of a European
tour more interesting than the country lying between Paris and Rome.
Here was the cradle in which the civilization of Western Europe and
our own country was rocked and developed. The whole journey between
these two great cities is deeply interesting and thought-suggesting. It
was the battle-ground and the scene of heroic endeavor, where every
inch of the field was sternly disputed; where the helmet, shield, and
spear of Eastern civilization met the sling and arrow and desperate
courage of determined barbarism. Nor was the tide of battle always in
one direction. Indications of the sternness and duration of the conflict
are still visible all along the line. These are seen in walled and fortified
towns, in grim and solemn convents, in old monasteries and castles, in
massive walls and gates, in huge iron bolts and heavily barred windows,
and fortifications built after the wisdom of the wary eagle on lofty crags
and clefts of rocks and mountain fastnesses, hard to assault and easy to
defend. These all tell of the troublous times in which they were erected,
when homes were castles, palaces were prisons, and men held their lives
and property by the might of the strongest. Here met the old and the
new, and here was fought out the irrepressible conflict between
European civilization and barbarism.

As the traveler moves eastward and southward between those two
great cities, he will observe an increase of black hair, black eyes, full
lips, and dark complexions. He will observe a Southern and Eastern
style of dress; gay colors, startling jewelry, and an outdoor free-and-
easy movement of the people.

I have seen it alleged that the habit of carrying the burdens on the
head is a mark of inferiority peculiar to the negro. It was not necessary
that I should go to Europe to be able to refute this allegation, yet I was
glad to see, both in Italy and the south of France, that this custom is

about as common there as it is among the dusky daughters of the Nile. Even if originated by the negro, it has been well copied by some of the best types of the Caucasian. In any case it may be welcomed as a proof of a common brotherhood.

In other respects I saw in France and Italy evidences of a common identity with the African. In Africa the people congregate at night in their towns and villages, while their living is made by tilling the soil outside. We saw few farm-houses in the south of France. Beautiful fields and vineyards are there, but few farmhouses. The village has taken the place of the farmhouse, and the peasants sometimes go several miles from their villages to work their vineyards. They may be seen in gangs in the morning going to their work, and returning in gangs in the evening from their work. Men and women share this toil alike, and one of the pleasantest sights to be seen in passing along are the groups of these people, seated along the roadside and taking their frugal meal of brown bread and sour wine, as cheerful and happy as if their fare was sumptuous and their raiment purple and fine linen. This sight, like many others, is a gratifying evidence that the poor often get as much happiness out of life as do the rich and great, and perhaps more. American ideas, however, would be unreconciled and shocked by the part borne by the women in the labors of the field. If an equal share in the hardships of life is desired by women, the battle for it has been already fought and won by the women of the Old World. Like men they go to the field, bright and early in the morning, and like the men they return to their villages late in the somber shades of evening, with faces browned by the sun and hands hardened by the hoe.

Leaving Paris and passing the famous grounds of Fontainebleau,* one is reminded that they are no longer, as of yore, the proud abode of royalty. Like all else of imperial and monarchical possessions, the palace here has, under the Republic,* passed from the hands of princes to the possession of the people. It is still kept in excellent condition. Its grounds conform in the strictest sense to French taste and skill, the main feature of which is perfect uniformity. Its trees and its walks conform to straight lines. The plummet and pruning-hook are employed with remorseless severity. No branch of a tree is permitted to be found longer than another, and the hedge seems to be trimmed by rule, compass, and square. But little liberty is allowed to nature in direction. Her crooked ways must be made straight, her bent forms made vertical, high must be made low, and all be cut down to a dead level. The houses, gardens, roads and bridges are all more or less subject to this rule. As you see them in one part of the country so you see them in another.

Dijon, so closely associated with the names of Bossuet* and St. Bernard,* the center, also, of the finest vineyards and the finest wines in France, and the ancient seat of the great dukes of Burgundy, traces of whose wealth and power are still visible in what remains of the ducal palace and the ancient castle, whose walls when a prison inclosed the restless Mirabeau, takes a deep hold upon the interest of the traveler. Its venerable and picturesque churches, in a chapel of one of which is a black image of the Virgin Mary about which one might philosophize, leave upon the mind an impression very different from the one felt on reaching Lyons, that center of the greatest silk industry in France. The main feature of our interest in the latter town, aside from its historical associations, was the Heights of Fourvières, from which one of the grandest views of the surrounding country can in clear weather be had. We were conducted to this immense height by a kind-hearted woman who seemed to know at once that we were strangers and in need of a guide. She volunteered to serve without promise of reward. She would not touch a penny for her service. She was evidently a good Catholic, and her kindness made even more impression upon us than the sonorous bells of her city. We saw in Lyons, too, a grand French military display, twenty thousand men in procession, rank upon rank with their glittering steel and splendid uniform, with all the pomp and circumstance of glorious war, a spectacle at once brilliant and sad to behold. Soldiers and slaughter go together.

Avignon, more than seventy years the home of the popes and the scene of pontifical magnificence, powerfully impresses the mind. Five ecclesiastical dignitaries at the least, according to history, were here consecrated to the service of the church. Avignon especially illustrates what I have said of the general character of the country through which we passed on our way to the Eternal City. It is surrounded by a wall flanked by thirty-nine towers and is entered through four great gates. Though this wall is twelve feet high and is thus flanked by towers, and though it was doubtless at one time a means of defense, it would be nothing against the projectiles of modern warfare. Like many other things, it has survived the use for which it was erected. The object of chief interest in Avignon, its palace of the popes, is certainly a very striking feature. In its appointments it justifies the German proverb, 'They who have the cross will bless themselves.' Situated on an eminence proudly overlooking the city and its surroundings, the grounds large and beautiful, the popes who resided there no doubt found it a very pleasant abode. In looking at the situation of the palace, it was evident to me that Catholics have long known how to select locations for their churches and other buildings. They are masters of geographical and topographical conditions as well as of things ecclesiastical. This famous old building was not only a palace, or a strictly religious institution, but it was at once a palace and a prison. Many a poor soul is said to have endured within its walls the agony of a trial and the still greater one of torture for opinion's sake. If it was a place of prayer, it was also a place of punishment. The holy men who ruled at that day could be lions as well as lambs. In this building were many halls,—halls of judgment, halls of inquisition, halls of torture, and halls of banqueting. In the day of its palatial glory, religion stood no such nonsense as freedom of thought. Believe with the church or else be accursed; accept our faith or be hurled among the damned, was the stern voice of religion at that time. Men like Robert G. Ingersoll would then have had short lives. Until the days of Louis Napoleon, the implements of torture in this old building were exhibited to travelers, but not so now. Cold and cruel as was this Napoleon, he was ashamed to have these terrible instruments exhibited to the eye of modern civilization. Guilty as he was of stamping out the liberties of the Republic which he betrayed, he had too much consideration for the humanity of the nineteenth century to give it the shock of a sight of these fiendish instruments. There are, however, to be seen within these walls dark rooms, narrow passages, huge locks, heavy bars and bolts; enough of the ghosts of dead and buried fanaticism, superstition and bigotry to cause a man of modern times to shudder. Looking into the open and stony mouth of the dungeon into which heretics were hurled and out of which none were allowed to come alive, it required no effort of the imagination to create visions of the Inquisition, to see the terror-stricken faces, the tottering forms, and pleading tears of the accused, and the saintly satisfaction of the inquisitors while ridding the world of the representatives of unbelief and misbelief.

It is hard to think that men could from innocent motives thus punish their fellows, but such is, no doubt, the fact. They were conscientious, and felt that they were doing righteous service unto the Lord. They believed literally in cutting off right hands and plucking out right eyes. Heaven and hell were alike under their control. They believed that they had the keys, and they lived up to their convictions. They could smile when they heard bones crack in the stocks and saw the maiden's flesh torn from her bones. It is only the best things that serve the worst perversions. Many pious souls to-day hate the negro while they think they love the Lord. A difference of religion in the days of this old palace did for a man what a difference of color does for him in some quarters at this day; and though light has not dawned upon the color question as upon freedom of thought, it is to be hoped that it soon will. This old palace is no longer the home of saints, but the home of soldiers. It is no longer the stronghold of the church, but the stronghold of the state. The roll of the drum has taken the place of the bell for prayer. Martial law has taken the place of ecclesiastical law, and there is no doubt which is the more merciful.

Though Avignon awakened in us a train of gloomy thoughts, we still think of it as a charming old city. We went there with much curiosity and left it with much reluctance. It would be a pleasure to visit the old city again. No American tourist should go through the south of France without tarrying awhile within the walls of Avignon, and no one should visit that city without going through the old papal palace.

One of the oldest and most fascinating old towns met with in a trip from Paris to Marseilles is that of Arles. Its streets are the narrowest, queerest and crookedest of any yet seen in our journey. It speaks of Greek as well as of Roman civilization. The bits of marble picked up in the streets show that they have been under the skillful hands either of the Greek or Roman workmen. The old Amphitheater, a miniature Coliseum, where men fought with wild beasts amid the applauding shouts of ladies and gentlemen of the period, though used no longer for its old-time purposes, is in good condition and may yet stand for a thousand years. We were shown through its various apartments where the lions were kept, and the dens out of which they came to the arena, where, lashed to fury, they waged their bloody contests with men. A sight of this old theater of horrors, once strangely enough the place of amusement to thousands, makes one thankful that his lot is cast in our humane and enlightened age. There is, however, enough of the wild beast left in our modern human life to modify the pride of our enlightenment and humanity, and to remind us of our kinship with the people who once delighted in the brutality and cruelty practiced in this amphitheater. In this respect our newspapers tell us a sad story. They would not be filled with the details of prize-fights, and discussions of the brutal perfections of prize-fighters, if such things did not please the brutal proclivities of a large class of readers.

Another interesting object in Arles is a long line of granite coffins, buried here for ages and discovered at last by excavations for a railroad just outside of the town. These houses of the dead are well preserved, but the dust and ashes once their tenants are lost and scattered to the winds.

An hour or two after leaving this quaint and sinuous old town, we were confronted at Marseilles by the blue and tideless waters of the

Mediterranean, a sea charming in itself and made more charming by the poetry and eloquence it has inspired. Its deep blue waters sparkling under a summer sun and a half tropical sky, fanned by balmy breezes from Afric's golden sand, was in fine contrast with the snow-covered mountains and plains we had just left behind us. Only a few hours before reaching Marseilles we were in mid-winter; but now all at once we were greeted with the lemon and the orange, the olive and the oleander, all flourishing under the open sky. The transition was so sudden and so agreeable and so completely in contrast, that it seemed more like magic than reality. Not only was the climate different, but the people and everything else seemed different. There was a visible blending of the orient with the occident. The sails of the ships, the rigging of the smaller vessels, the jib-like mainsails, and the general appearance of all, resembled the marine pictures of the East and made the whole scene novel, picturesque and attractive. A general view of that far-famed city made plainly visible in Marseilles the results of large wealth and active commerce as expressed in the far-reaching streets, large warehouses, and fine residences. We, however, cared less for all this than for Château D'If,* the old prison anchored in the sea and around which the genius of Alexander Dumas has woven such a network of enchantment that a desire to visit it is irresistible; hence, the first morning after our arrival Mrs. Douglass and myself hired one of the numerous boats in the harbor and employed an old man to row us out to the enchanted scene. The morning was clear, bright and balmy. The distance was so great and the air so warm that the old man of the sea was quite ready to have me take a hand at the oars. After a long pull and a strong pull, as the sailors say, we reached the weird old rock from which Edmond Dantes was hurled. The reality of the scene was not of course up to the point as painted by Dumas. But we were glad to have seen it disrobed of the enchantment that distance and genius have thrown around it. It is a queer old place, surrounded by the sea, lone and desolate, standing boldly and high against the horizon, and the blue waves coming from afar dashing themselves against its sharp and flinty sides, made for us a picture most striking and not soon to be forgotten.

On our way along the far-famed Riviera to Genoa, once the city of sea-kings and merchant princes, we, like most travelers, tarried awhile at Nice, that favorite resort of health and pleasure and one beautiful for situation. The outlook from it on the sea is enchanting, but no one should visit Nice with a lean purse, and a man with a full one will be wise not to tarry long. It was the most expensive place we found abroad.

Genoa, the birthplace of Christopher Columbus, the man who saw by an eye of faith the things hoped for and the evidence of things not seen, is a grand old city with its multitude of churches, numerous narrow streets, many-colored buildings, and splendid palaces. Looking out upon the sea I recalled to mind one of the finest pieces of word painting I ever heard from the lips of the late Wendell Phillips. He visited this city fifty years ago. He was then a young man fresh from his marriage tour of the continent of Europe. He was speaking on the platform of the old tabernacle in Broadway, New York, and criticising the conduct of our Government in refusing to unite with England and France to suppress the African slave-trade. While in Genoa, the correspondence between our Government and that of France and England was going on. General Cass, who represented us at the court of Louis Philippe, had placed our Government on the wrong side of this question. In this very city, standing perhaps on these very heights upon which I stood looking off to sea, Mr. Phillips saw our well-known ship of war, the Ohio, lying in the harbor, and thus describes the feeling with which he contemplated that ship in view of our attitude towards other nations in regard to the slave-trade. With a face expressive of indignation, shame and scorn, Phillips said, 'As I stood upon the shores of Genoa, and saw floating upon the placid waters of the Mediterranean our beautiful American ship, the Ohio, with masts tapering proportionately aloft and an Eastern sun reflecting her graceful form upon the waters, attracting the view of the multitude upon the shore, it was enough to pride any American heart to think himself an American; but when I thought that in all probability the first time that gallant ship would gird on her gorgeous apparel and wake from her sides her dormant thunders it would be in defense of the African slave-trade, I could but blush and hang my head to think myself an American.'

This fine passage in the speech of Wendell Phillips, uttered when I was new from slavery, was one element in my desire to see Genoa and to look out upon the sea from the same height upon which he stood. At the time of hearing it I had no idea that I should ever realize this desire.

Like most Italian cities, Genoa upholds the reputation of its country in respect of art. The old masters in painting and sculpture—and their name is legion—are still largely represented in the palaces of the merchant princes of this city. One of its singular features is the abundance of fresco work seen on both the inside and the outside of buildings. One feels emphatically the presence and power of the Roman Catholic Church in the multitude of shrines seen everywhere and containing pictures of apostles or saints, or the Virgin Mother and the infant Jesus. But of all the interesting objects collected in the Museum of Genoa, the one that touched me most was the violin that had belonged to and been played upon by Paganini,* the greatest musical genius of his time. This violin is treasured in a glass case and beyond the touch of careless fingers, a thing to be seen and not handled. There are some things and places made sacred by their uses and by the events with which they are associated, especially those which have in any measure changed the current of human taste, thought, and life, or which have revealed new powers and triumphs of the human soul. The pen with which Lincoln wrote the emancipation proclamation, the sword worn by Washington through the war of the Revolution, though of the same material and form of other pens and swords, have an individual character, and stir in the minds of men peculiar sensations. So this old violin, made after the pattern of others and perhaps not more perfect in its construction and tone than hundreds seen elsewhere, detained me longer and interested me more than anything else in the Museum of Genoa. Emerson says, 'It is not the thing said, but the man behind it, that is important.'* So it was not this old violin, but the marvelous man behind it, the man who had played on it and played as never man played before, and thrilled the hearts of thousands by his playing, that made it a precious object in my eyes. Owing perhaps to my love of music and of the violin in particular, I would have given more for that old violin of wood, horse-hair, and catgut than for any one of the long line of pictures I saw before me. I desired it on account of the man who had played upon it—the man who revealed its powers and possibilities as they were never known before. This was his old violin, his favorite instrument, the companion of his toils and triumphs, the solace of his private hours, the minister to his soul in his battles with sin and sorrow. It had delighted thousands. Men had listened to it with admiration and wonder. It had filled the largest halls of Europe with a concord of sweet sounds. It had even stirred the dull hearts of courts, kings and princes, and revealed to them their kinship to common mortals as perhaps had been done by no other instrument. It was with some difficulty that I moved away from this old violin of Paginini.

Never to be forgotten by one who has enjoyed it is a morning at Pisa, the city of the leaning tower; a city renowned in Italian history. Though still possessing many imposing buildings, like many other once famous places its glory has departed. Its grand old cathedral, baptistery, and leaning tower are the features that most attract the attention of the tourist. The baptistery is especially interesting for its acoustic properties. The human voice heard here has imparted to it the richest notes of the organ, and goes on repeating and prolonging itself, increasing in volume and ranging higher and higher in ascent till lost in whispers almost divine at the very top of the dome.

But no American sensitive and responsive to what is old, grand and historic, with his face towards the East and the city of Rome only a few hours away, will tarry long even in this fine old city of Pisa. Like the mysterious loadstone to steel, he is attracted by an invisible power, and the attraction increases with every step of his approach. All that one has ever read, heard, felt, thought, or imagined concerning Rome comes thronging upon mind and heart and makes one eager and impatient to be there. The privilege of daylight was denied us on our arrival, and our first glimpse of Rome was by the light of moon and stars. More unfortunate still, we were landed in the new part of the city, which contradicted all our dreams of the Eternal City. To all appearances we might have been dropped down at any railway station in Paris, London or New York, or at some of the grand hotels at Saratoga or Coney Island. At this station were long rows of carriages, coaches, omnibuses and other vehicles, with their usual accompaniment of drivers, porters and runners, clamorous for passengers for their several hotels. All was more like an American town of the latest pattern than a city whose foundations were laid nearly a thousand years before the flight of Joseph and Mary into Egypt. We were disappointed by this intensely modern aspect, it was not the Rome we came to see. But the disappointment was temporary, and happily enough the first impression heightened the effect of the subsequent happy realization of what we had expected. With the light of day, the Eternal City, seated on its throne of seven hills, fully gave us all it had promised, banished every feeling of disappointment, and filled our minds with ever-increasing wonder and amazement. In all directions were disclosed those indications of her ancient greatness for which we were looking, and of her fitness to be the seat of the most powerful empire that man had ever seen—truly the mistress of the known world and for a thousand years the recognized metropolis of the Christian faith and the head still of the largest organized church in the world. Here can be seen together the symbols of both Christian and pagan Rome; the temples of discarded gods and those of the accepted Saviour of the world, the Son of the Virgin Mary. Empires, principalities, powers, and dominions have perished; altars and their gods have mingled with the dust; a religion which made men virtuous in peace and invincible in war has perished or been supplanted, yet the Eternal City itself remains. It speaks from the spacious Forum,* yet studded with graceful but time-worn columns, where Cicero poured out his burning eloquence against Catiline and against Antony,* for which latter speech he lost his head; from the Palatine,* from whose summit the palaces of the Cæsars overlooked a large part of the ancient city; and from the Pantheon,* built twenty-seven years before the songs of the angels were heard on the plains of Bethlehem, and of which Byron says:—

> 'Simple, erect, severe, austere, sublime,
> Shrine of all saints and temple of all gods,
> . . . spared and blessed by time;
> Looking tranquillity, while falls or nods
> Arch, empire, each thing round thee, and man plods
> His way through thorns to ashes—glorious dome!
> Shalt thou not last? Time's scythe and tyrant's rods
> Shiver upon thee—sanctuary and home
> Of art and piety—Pantheon!—pride of Rome!'*

Though two thousand years have rolled over it, and though the beautiful marble which once adorned and protected its exterior has been torn off and made to serve other and inferior purposes, there, speaking to us of ages past, it stands, erect and strong, and may stand yet a thousand years longer. Its walls, twenty feet thick, give few signs of decay. More than any building I saw in Rome, it tells of the thoroughness of the Romans in everything they thought it worth their while to undertake to be or to do.

Hardly less indicative of their character did we find the remains of the stupendous Baths of Titus, Diocletian, and Caracalla, among the ruins of whose spacious apartments, designed to fulfill every conceivable condition of ease and luxury, one needs not to consult Gibbon* for the causes of the decline and fall of the Roman Empire. The lap of luxury and the pursuit of ease and pleasure are death to manly courage, energy, will, and enterprise.

None of the splendid arches, recalling as they do the glories of Rome's triumphs, can, by the reflective mind, be contemplated with a deeper, sadder interest than is indelibly associated with that of Titus,* commemorating the destruction of the unhappy Jews and making public to a pagan city the desecration of all that was most sacred to the religion of that despised people. This arch is an object which must forever be a painful one to every Jew, since it reminds him of the loss of his beloved Jerusalem. Surely none who have never suffered a like scorn can adequately feel for their humiliation, as they, for their abasement, were forced to pass beneath that arch whose sculptured sides portrayed the sacred vessels torn, in the profanation of their Temple, from its Holy of Holies.

Among other objects calling up ancient events in the history of Rome, stands the Column of Trajan,* after which Napoleon's monument in Paris was modeled. It tells of the many battles fought and won by Trajan, and is a beautiful column. Though now slowly yielding to the wasting touch of Time, we may still say of it as was once said by the great Daniel Webster of Bunker Hill Monument: 'It looks, it speaks, it acts.'* It certainly is a memorial of the past, a monitor of the present, though it may not be a hope of the future. In sight of the palaces of the Cæsars and the Temple of the Vestal Virgins and the Capitoline Hill, darkening the horizon with its somber and time-defying walls, rises the immense and towering form of the Coliseum,—an ancient hell of human horrors,—where the *élite* of Rome enjoyed the sport of seeing men torn to pieces by hungry and infuriated lions and tigers and by each other. No building more elaborate, vast and wonderful than this has risen since the Tower of Babel.

While the old part of Rome has antiquities of its own, the new part has antiquities from abroad. There are here fourteen obelisks from Egypt, one of the finest of which adorns the square in front of St. Peter's.

The streets of Rome, except in the newest part, are generally very narrow, and the houses on either side of them being very high, there is much more shade than sunshine in them, and hence the remarkably chilly atmosphere of which strangers complain. Yet the city is not without redeeming and compensating features. It has many fine open spaces and public squares, supplied with large flowing fountains, and adorned with various attractive devices, where the people have abundant pure water, fresh air, and bright, health-giving sunlight.

Of street life in Rome I must not speak except to mention one feature of it which overtops all others, and that is the part taken both consciously and unconsciously by members of various bodies of the church. All that we see and hear impresses us with the gigantic, all-pervading, complicated, accumulated and mysterious power of this great religious and political organization. Wherever else the Roman Church may question its own strength and practice a modest reserve, here she is open, free, self-asserting and bold in her largest assumptions. She writes indulgences* over her gateways as boldly to-day as if Luther* had never lived, and she jingles the keys of heaven and hell as confidently as if her right to do so had never been called into question. About every fifth man met with holds some official relation to this stupendous and far-reaching body and is at work in some way to maintain its power, ascendancy and glory. Religion seems to be in Rome the chief business by which men live. Throngs of young students of all lands and languages march through the streets at all hours of the day, but never unattended. Experienced, well-dressed, discreet and dignified ecclesiastics attend them everywhere. On the surface these dear young people, so pure and in the full fresh bloom of youth, are beautiful to look upon; but when you reflect that they are being trained to defend dogmas and superstitions contrary to the progress and enlightenment of the age, the spectacle becomes sad indeed.

In contrast to them are other specimens of religious zeal, neither pleasant to the eye, to the touch nor even to the thought. They are the vacant-faced, bare-legged, grimy monks, who have taken a vow neither to marry, nor to work, nor to wash, and who live by prayer; who beg and pay for what they get by praying for the donors. It is strange that such fanaticism is encouraged by a church so worldly-wise as that of Rome; and yet in this I may be less wise than the church. She may have a use for them too occult for my dim vision.

The two best points from which to view the exterior of Rome are the Pincian Hill* and the Janiculum.* Of the seven hills these are not the least interesting, and from their summits can be taken in its full magnificence a general view of the Eternal City. Once seen from these points it will never be forgotten, but will dwell in the mind forever. A glance reveals all the great features of the city, with its grand and impressive surroundings. Here begins the far-reaching and much-dreaded Campagna,* and at one's feet lies a whole forest of grand historical churches, which with their domes, towers and turrets rising skyward, and their deep sonorous bells, form a combination of sight and sound to be seen and heard nowhere in the world outside of Rome. From one of these points, the Pincian, can be enjoyed the finest view perhaps to be had of the far-famed dome of St. Peter's.* It is difficult to imagine any structure built by human hands more grand and imposing than this dome as seen from the Pincian Hill, especially near the sunset hour. Towering high above the ample body of the great cathedral and the world-famed Vatican, it is bathed in a sea of ethereal glory. Its magnificence and impressiveness gain by distance. When you move away from it, it seems to follow you, and though you travel fast and far, when you look back it will be there and more impressive than ever.

The outside of St. Peter's and her three hundred sister churches and the many-storied Vatican give no hint of the wealth and grandeur within them. As in its day pagan Rome drew tribute from all the known world, so the Church of Rome to-day receives gifts from all the Christian world, our own republican country included, and the end is not yet. Even a President of the United States sends his presents to his Holiness the Pope. A look into some of these Romish churches will show that even Solomon in all his glory was not arrayed like one of these. All that architecture, sculpture, and fine colors can do, all that art and skill can do to render them beautiful and imposing, has been done in these magnificent edifices. St. Peter's, by its vastness, wealth, splendor, and architectural perfections, acts upon us like some great and overpowering natural wonder. It awes us into silent, speechless admiration. One is at a loss to know how the amplitudinous and multitudinous whole that is there displayed to view has been brought together. The more one sees of it the more impressive and wonderful it becomes. Several other churches are very little inferior to St. Peter's in this wealth and splendor. For one, however, I was much more interested in the Rome of the past than in the Rome of the present; in the banks of its Tiber with their history than in the images, angles and pictures on the walls of its splendid churches; in the preaching of Paul eighteen hundred years ago than in the preaching of the priests and popes of to-day. The fine silks and costly jewels and vestments of the priests of the present could hardly have been dreamed of by the first great preacher of Christianity at Rome, who lived in his own hired house, and whose hands ministered to his own necessities. It was something to feel ourselves standing where this brave man stood, looking on the place where he lived, and walking on the same Appian Way where he walked, when, having appealed to Cæsar, he was bravely on the way to this same Rome to meet his fate, whether that should be life or death. This was more to me than being shown, as we were, under the dome of St. Peter's, the head of St. Luke in a casket, a piece of the true cross, a lock of the Virgin Mary's hair, and the leg-bone of Lazarus; or any of the wonderful things in that line palmed off on a credulous and superstitious people. In one of these churches we were shown a great doll, covered with silks and jewels and all manner of strange devices, and this wooden baby was solemnly credited with miraculous power in healing the sick and averting many of the evils to which flesh is heir. In the same church we were, with equal solemnity, shown a print of the devil's cloven foot in the hard stone. I could but ask myself what the devil could a devil be doing in such a holy place. I had some curiosity in seeing devout people going up to the black statue of St. Peter—I was glad to find him black; I have no prejudice against his color—and kissing the old fellow's big toe, one side of which has been nearly worn away by these devout and tender salutes of which it has been the cold subject. In seeing these, one may well ask himself, What will not men believe? Crowds of men and women going up a stairway on their knees; monks making ornaments of dead men's bones; others refusing to wash themselves,—and all in order to secure the favor of God,—give a degrading idea of man's relation to the Infinite Author of the universe. But there is no reasoning with faith. It is doubtless a great comfort to these people, after all, to have kissed the great toe of the black image of the Apostle Peter, and to have bruised their knees in substituting them for feet in ascending a stairway, called the Scala Santa. I felt, in looking upon these religious shows in Rome, as the late Benjamin Wade said he felt at a negro camp-meeting, where there were much howling, shouting, and jumping: 'This is nothing to me, but it surely must be something to them.'

The railway south from Rome, through the Campagna, gives a splendid view of miles of Roman arches over which water was formerly brought to the city. Few works better illustrate the spirit and power of the Roman people than do these miles of masonry. Humanly speaking, there was nothing requiring thought, skill, energy and determination which these people could not and did not do. The ride from Rome to Naples in winter is delightful. A beautiful valley diversified on either side by mountain peaks capped with snow, is a perpetual entertainment to the eye of the traveler. Only a few hours' ride and behold a scene of startling sublimity! It is a broad column of white vapor from the summit of Vesuvius, slowly and majestically rising against the blue Italian sky and before gentle northern and land breezes grandly moving off to sea, a thing of wonder. For more than seventeen hundred years this vapor, sometimes mingled with the lurid light of red-hot lava, has been rising thus from the open mouth of this mountain, and its fires are still burning and its vapor still ascending, and no man can tell when they will cease, or when in floods of burning lava it will again burst forth and overwhelm unsuspecting thousands in the fate that befell Pompeii and Herculaneum, cities so long buried from the world by its ashes. It is a grand spectacle to see this vapor silently and peacefully rolling up the sky and moving off to sea, but we shudder at the thought of what may yet befall the populous towns and villages that still hover so daringly about its dangerous base.

Naples is a great city, and its bay is all that its fame has taught us to expect. Its beautiful surroundings rich with historical associations would easily keep one lingering for months. Pompeii, Herculaneum, Puteoli where St. Paul landed from his perilous voyage to Rome; the tomb of Virgil; the spot still traceable where stood one of the villas of Cicero; the islands of Capri and Ischia, and a thousand other objects full of worthy interest, afford constant activity to both reflection and imagination. Mrs. Douglass and myself were much indebted to the kindness of Rev. J. C. Fletcher and wife during our stay in this celebrated city.

When once an American tourist has quitted Rome and has felt the balmy breezes of the Mediterranean; has seen the beautiful Bay of Naples; reveled in the wonders of its neighborhood; stood at the base of Vesuvius; surveyed the narrow streets, the majestic halls, and the luxurious houses of long-buried Pompeii; stood upon the spot where the great apostle Paul first landed at Puteoli after his eventful and perilous voyage on his way to Rome,—he is generally seized with an ardent desire to wander still farther eastward and southward. Sicily will tempt him, and once there, and his face turned towards the rising sun, he will want to see Egypt, the Suez Canal, the Libyan desert, the wondrous Nile—land of obelisks and hieroglyphys which men are so well learning to read; land of sphinxes and mummies many thousand years old, of great pyramids and colossal ruins that speak to us of a civilization which extends back into the misty shadows of the past, far beyond the reach and grasp of authentic history. The more he has seen of modern civilization in England, France and Italy, the more he will want to see the traces of that civilization which existed when these countries of Europe were inhabited by barbarians. When once so near to this more renowned and ancient abode of civilization, the scene of so many Bible events and wonders, the desire to see it becomes almost irresistible.

I confess, however, that my desire to visit Egypt did not rest entirely upon the basis thus foreshadowed. I had a motive far less enthusiastic and sentimental; an ethnological purpose in the pursuit of which I hoped to turn my visit to some account in combating American prejudice against the darker colored races of mankind, and at the same time to raise colored people somewhat in their own estimation and thus stimulate them to higher endeavors. I had a theory for which I wanted the support of facts in the range of my own knowledge. But more of this in another place.

The voyage from Naples to Port Said on a good steamer is accomplished in four days, and in fine weather it is a very delightful one. In our case, air, sea and sky assumed their most amiable behavior, and early dawn found us face to face with old Stromboli, whose cone-shaped summit seems to rise almost perpendicularly from the sea. We pass through the straits of Messina, leave behind us the smoke and vapor of Mount Etna, and in three days are safely anchored in front of Port Said, the west end of the Suez Canal, that stupendous work which has brought the occident face to face with the orient and changed the route taken by the commerce of the world; which has brought Australia within forty days of England, and saved the men who go down to the sea in ships much of the time and danger once their lot in finding their way to the East around the Cape of Good Hope.

At Port Said, where we entered the Suez Canal, the vessels of all nations halt. The few houses that make up the town look white, new and temporary, reminding one of some of the hastily built wooden towns of the American frontier, where there is much space outside and little within. Here our good ship, the Ormuz, the largest vessel that had then ever floated through the Suez Canal, stopped to take in a large supply of coal prior to proceeding on her long voyage to Australia. Great barges loaded with this fuel stored there from England for the purpose of coaling her eastern-bound vessels, were brought alongside of our steamer and their contents soon put on board by a small army of Arabs. It was something to see these men of the desert at work. As I looked at them and listened to their fun and frolic while bearing their heavy burdens, I said to myself: 'You fellows are, at least in your disposition, half brothers to the negro.' The negro works best and hardest when it is no longer work, but becomes play with joyous singing. These children of the desert performed their task in like manner, amid shouts of laughter and tricks of fun, as if their hard work were the veriest sport. In color these Arabs are something between two riding-saddles, the one old and the other new. They are a little lighter than the one and a little darker than the other. I did not see a single fat man among them. They were erect and strong, lean and sinewy. Their strength and fleetness were truly remarkable. They tossed the heavy bags of coal on their shoulders and trotted on board our ship with them for hours without halt or weariness. Lank in body, slender in limb, full of spirit, they reminded one of blooded horses. It was the month of February, and the water by no means warm, but these people seemed about as much at home in the water as on the land, and gave us some fine specimens of their swimming and diving ability. Passengers would throw small coins into the water for the interest of seeing them dive for them; and this they did with almost fish-like swiftness, and never failed to bring from the bottom the coveted sixpence or franc, as the case might be, and to show it between their white teeth as they came to the surface.

Slowly and carefully moving through the canal an impressive scene was presented to the eye. Nothing in my American experience ever gave me such a deep sense of unearthly silence, such a sense of vast, profound, unbroken sameness and solitude, as did this passage through the Suez Canal, moving smoothly and noiselessly between two spade-built banks of yellow sand, watched over by the jealous care of England and France, two rival powers each jealous of the other. We find here, too, the motive and mainspring of English Egyptian occupation and of English policy.* On either side stretches a sandy desert, to which the eye, even with the aid of the strongest field-glass, can find no limit but the horizon; land where neither tree, shrub nor vegetation of any kind, nor human habitation breaks the view. All is flat, broad, silent, dreamy and unending solitude. There appears occasionally away in the distance a white line of life which only makes the silence and solitude more pronounced. It is a line of flamingoes, the only bird to be seen in the desert, making us wonder what they find upon which to subsist. But here, too, is another sign of life, wholly unlooked for, and for which it is hard to account. It is the half-naked, hungry form of a human being, a young Arab, who seems to have started up out of the yellow sand under his feet, for no town, village, house or shelter is seen from which he could have emerged; but here he is, and he is as lively as a cricket, running by the ship's side up and down the sandy banks for miles and for hours with the speed of a horse and the endurance of a hound, plaintively shouting as he runs: 'Backsheesh! Backsheesh! Backsheesh!'* and only stopping in the race to pick up the pieces of bread and meat thrown to him from the ship. Far away in the distance, through the quivering air and sunlight, a mirage appears. Now it is a splendid forest and now a refreshing lake. The illusion is perfect. It is a forest without trees and a lake without water. As one travels on, the mirage travels also, but its distance from the observer remains ever the same.

After more than a day and a night on this weird, silent, and dreamy canal, under a cloudless sky, almost unconscious of motion, yet moving on and on without pause and without haste, through a noiseless, treeless, houseless, and seemingly endless wilderness of sand, where not even the crowing of a cock or the barking of a dog is heard, we were transferred to a smart little French steamer and landed at Ismalia, where, since leaving the new and shambling town of Port Said, we see the first sign of civilization and begin to realize that we are entering the land of the Pharaohs.

Here the Khedive* has one of his many palaces, and here and there are a few moderately comfortable dwellings with two or three hotels and a railroad station. How and by what means the people in this place live is a mystery. For miles around there is no sign of grain or grass or vegetation of any kind. Here we first caught sight of the living locomotive of the East, that marvelous embodiment of strength, docility, and obedience, of patient endurance of hunger and thirst—the camel. I have large sympathy with all burden-bearers, whether they be men or beasts, and having read of the gentle submission of the camel to hardships and abuse, of how he will kneel to receive his heavy burden and groan to have it made lighter, I was glad right here in the edge of Egypt to have a visible illustration of these qualities of the animal. I saw him kneel and saw the heavy load of sand put on his back; I saw him try to rise under its weight and heard his sad moan. I had at the moment much the same feeling as when I first saw a gang of slaves chained together and shipped to a foreign market.

A long line of camels attended by three or four Arabs came slowly moving over the desert. This spectacle, more than the language or customs of the people, gave me a vivid impression of Eastern life; a picture of it as it was in the days of Abraham and Moses. In this wide waste, under this cloudless sky, star-lighted by night and by a fierce blazing sun by day, where even the wind seems voiceless, it was natural for men to look up to the sky and stars and contemplate the universe and infinity above and around them; the signs and wonders in the heavens above and in the earth beneath. In such loneliness, silence and expansiveness, imagination is unchained and man has naturally a deeper sense of the Infinite Presence than is to be felt in the noise and bustle of the towns and men-crowded cities. Religious ideas have come to us from the wilderness, from mountain tops, from dens and caves, and from the vast silent spaces from which come the mirage and other shadowy illusions which create rivers, lakes and forests where there are none. The song of the angels could be better heard by the shepherds on the plains of Bethlehem than by the jostling crowds in the busy streets of Jerusalem. John the Baptist could preach better in the wilderness than in the busy marts of men. Jesus said his best word to the world when on the Mount of Olives. Moses learned more of the laws of God when in the mountains than when down among the people. The Hebrew prophets frequented dens and caves and desert places. John saw his wonderful vision in the Isle of Patmos with naught in sight but the sea and sky. It was in a lonely place that Jacob wrestled with the angel. The Transfiguration was on a mountain. No wonder that Moses wandering in the vast and silent desert, after killing an Egyptian and brooding over the oppressed condition of his people, should hear the voice of Jehovah saying, 'I have seen the affliction of my people.' Paul was not in Damascus, but on his lonely way thither, when he heard a voice from heaven. The heart beats louder and the soul hears quicker in silence and solitude. It was from the vastness and silence of the desert that Mahomet learned his religion, and once he thought he had discovered man's true relation to the Infinite he proclaimed himself a prophet and began to preach with that sort of authority and power which never failed to make converts.

Such speculations were for me ended by the startling whistle of the locomotive and the sound of the rushing train—things which put an end to religious reveries and fix attention upon the things of this busy world. In passing through the land of Goshen I experienced a thrill of satisfaction in viewing the scene of one of the most affecting stories ever written—the story of Jacob; how his sons were compelled by famine to go into Egypt to buy corn; how they sold their young brother Joseph into slavery; how they came home with a lie upon their lips to hide their treachery and cruelty; how the slave boy Joseph gained favor in the eyes of Pharaoh; how these brothers who had sold him were again by famine brought face to face with Joseph who stipulated that the only condition upon which he could again see them was that they should bring their young brother Benjamin with them; how Jacob plaintively appealed against this arrangement by which his gray hair might be brought down in sorrow to the grave, and finally, through the good offices of Joseph, the happy settlement of the whole family in this fertile land of Goshen. Than this simple tale nothing has been written, nothing can be found in literature, more pathetic and touching. Here was the land of Goshen, with fields yet green, its camels still grazing and its corn still growing as when Jacob and his sons with their flocks and herds were settled in it three thousand years ago.

The fertilizing power of the Nile, wherever the land is overflowed by it, is very marked, especially in contrast with the sandy desert. It is seen in the deep black and glossy soil, and in the thick and full growth and deep green color of its vegetation. No fences divide field from field and define the possession of different proprietors. To all appearance the land might belong to one man alone. The overflow of the Nile explains this feature of the country, as its mighty floods would sweep away such barriers. The mode of grazing cattle is to us peculiar. The donkeys, horses, cows and camels are not allowed to roam over the field as with us, but are tethered to stakes driven down in the ground. They eat all before them, leaving the land behind them as though it had been mowed with a scythe or a sickle. They present a pleasant picture, standing in rows like soldiers, with their heads towards the tall vegetation and seemingly as orderly as civilized people at their dining-tables.

Every effort is made to get as much of the Nile water as possible. Ditches are cut, ponds are made, and men are engaged day and night in dipping it up and having it placed where it is most needed. The two processes adopted by which to raise this water are the shâdûf and the sâkiyeh.* Long lines of women are sometimes seen with heavy earthen jars on their heads distributing this precious fertilizing water over the thirsty land. Seeing the value of this water and how completely the life of man and beast is dependent upon it, one cannot wonder at the deep solicitude with which its rise is looked for, watched and measured.

Egypt may have invented the plow, but it has not improved upon the invention. The kind used there is perhaps as old as the time of Moses, and consists of two or three pieces of wood so arranged that the end of one piece turns no furrow, but simply scratches the soil. Still, in the distance, the man who holds this contrivance and the beast that draws it look very much as if they were plowing. I am told, however, that this kind of plow does better service for the peculiar soil of Egypt than ours would do; that the experiment of tilling the ground with our plow has been tried in Egypt and has failed; so that the cultivation of the soil, like many other things, is best where it answers its purposes best and produces the best results.

Cairo with its towers, minarets and mosques presents a strangely fascinating scene, especially from the citadel, where away off in the distance, rising between the yellow desert and the soft blue cloudless sky, we discern the unmistakable forms of those mysterious piles of masonry, the Pyramids. According to one theory they were built for sepulchral purposes; and according to another they were built for a standard of measurement, but neither theory has perhaps entirely set aside the other, and both may be wrong. There they stand, however, grandly, in sight of Cairo, just in the edge of the Libyan desert and overlooking the valley of the Nile, as they have stood during more than three thousand years and are likely to stand as many thousand years longer, for nothing grows old here but time, and that lives on forever.

One of the first exploits a tourist is tempted to perform here is to ascend to the top of the highest Pyramid. The task is by no means an easy one, nor is it entirely free from danger. It is clearly dangerous if undertaken without the assistance of two or more guides. You need them not only to show you where to put your feet, but to lift you over the huge blocks of stone of which the Pyramids are built, for some of these stones are from three to four feet in thickness and height. Neither in ascending nor descending is it safe to look down. One misstep and all is over. I went, with seventy years on my head, to the top of the highest Pyramid, but nothing in the world would tempt me to try the experiment again. I had two Arabs before me pulling, and two at my back pushing, but the main work I had to do myself. I did not recover from the terrible strain in less than two weeks. I paid dearly for the venture. Still, it was worth something to stand for once on such a height and above the work and the world below. Taking the view altogether—the character of the surroundings, the great unexplained and inexplicable Sphinx, the Pyramids and other wonders of Sakkara, the winding river of the valley of the Nile, the silent, solemn and measureless desert, the

seats of ancient Memphis and Heliopolis, the distant mosques, minarets, and stately palaces, the ages and events that have swept over the
scene and the millions on millions that lived, wrought and died
there—there are stirred in the one who beholds it for the first time
thoughts and feelings never thought and felt before. While nothing
could tempt me to climb the rugged jagged, steep and perilous sides of
the Great Pyramid again, yet I am very glad to have had the experience
once, and once is enough for a lifetime.

I have spoken of the prevalence and power at Rome of the Christian
Church and religion and of the strange things believed and practiced
there in the way of religious rites and ceremonies. The religion and
church of Egypt, though denounced as a fraud and their author
branded throughout Christendom as an impostor, are not less believed
in and followed in Egypt than the church and Christianity are believed
in and followed at Rome. Two hundred millions of people follow
Mahomet to-day, and the number is increasing. Annually in Cairo
twelve thousand students study the Koran with a view to preaching its
doctrines in Africa and else-where. So sacred do these people hold their
mosques that a Christian is not allowed to enter them without putting
off his shoes and putting on Mahometan slippers. If Rome has its
unwashed monks, Cairo has its howling and dancing dervishes, and
both seem equally deaf to the dictates of reason. The dancing and howling dervishes often spin around in their religious transports till their
heads lose control and they fall to the floor sighing, groaning, and
foaming at the mouth like madmen, reminding one of scenes that
sometimes occur at our own old-fashioned camp-meetings.

It is not within the scope and purpose of this supplement of my story
to give an extended account of my travels or to tell all I have seen and
heard and felt. I had strange dreams of travel even in my boyhood days.
I thought I should some day see many of the famous places of which
I heard men speak, and of which I read even while a slave. During my
visit to England, as I have before said, I had a strong desire to go to
France, and should have done so but for a Mr. George M. Dallas, who
was then minister to England. He refused to give me a passport on the
ground that I was not and could not be an American citizen. This man
is now dead and generally forgotten, as I shall be; but I have lived to see
myself everywhere recognized as an American citizen. In view of my
disappointment and the repulse I met with at the hands of this American
minister, my gratification was all the more intense that I was not only
permitted to visit France and see something of life in Paris; to walk the
streets of that splendid city and spend days and weeks in her charming

art galleries, but to extend my tour to other lands and visit other cities; to look upon Egypt; to stand on the summit of its highest Pyramid; to walk among the ruins of old Memphis; to gaze into the dead eyes of Pharaoh; to feel the smoothness of granite tombs polished by Egyptian workmen three thousand years ago; to see the last remaining obelisk of Heliopolis; to view the land of Goshen; to sail on the bosom of the Nile; to pass in sight of Crete, looking from the deck of our steamer perhaps as it did when Paul saw it on the voyage to Rome eighteen hundred years ago; to walk among the marble ruins of the Acropolis; to stand upon Mars Hill, where Paul preached; to ascend Lycabettus and overlook the plains of Marathon, the gardens of Plato, and the rock where Demosthenes declaimed against the breezes of the sea; to gaze upon the Parthenon, the Temple of Theseus, the Temple of Wingless Victory, and the Theatre of Dionysius. To think that I, once a slave on the eastern shore of Maryland, was experiencing all this was well calculated to intensify my feeling of good fortune by reason of contrast, if nothing more. A few years back my Sundays were spent on the banks of the Chesapeake Bay, bemoaning my condition and looking out from the farm of Edward Covey, and, with a heart aching to be on their decks, watching the white sails of the ships passing off to sea. Now I was enjoying what the wisest and best of the world have bestowed for the wisest and best to enjoy.

Touching at Naples, we returned to Rome, where the longer one stays the longer one wants to stay. No place is better fitted to withdraw one from the noise and bustle of modern life and fill one's soul with solemn reflections and thrilling sensations. Under one's feet and all around are the ashes of human greatness. Here, according to the age and body of its time, human ambition reached its topmost height and human power its utmost limit. The lesson of the vanity of all things is taught in deeply buried palaces, in fallen columns, in defaced monuments, in decaying arches, and in crumbling walls; all perishing under the silent and destructive force of time and the steady action of the elements, in utter mockery of the pride and power of the great people by whom they were called into existence.

Next to Rome, in point of interest to me, is the classic city of Florence, and thither we went from the Eternal City. One might never tire of what is here to be seen. The first thing Mrs. Douglass and I did, on our arrival in Florence, was to visit the grave of Theodore Parker and at the same time that of Elizabeth Barrett Browning.* The preacher and the poet lie near each other. The soul of each was devoted to liberty. The brave stand taken by Theodore Parker during the anti-slavery conflict endeared him to my heart, and naturally enough the spot made sacred by his ashes was the first to draw me to its side. He had a voice for the slave when nearly all the pulpits of the land were dumb. Looking upon the little mound of earth that covered his dust, I felt the pathos of his simple grave. It did not seem well that the remains of the great American preacher should rest thus in a foreign soil, far away from the hearts and hands which would gladly linger about it and keep it well adorned with flowers. Than Theodore Parker no man was more intensely American. Broad as the land in his sympathy with mankind, he was yet a loving son of New England and thoroughly Bostonian in his thoughts, feelings and activities. The liberal thought which he taught had in his native land its natural home and largest welcome, and I therefore felt that his dust should have been brought here. It was in his pulpit that I made my first anti-slavery speech in Roxbury. That its doors opened to me in that dark period was due to him. I remember, too, his lovingkindness when I was persecuted for my change of opinion as to political action. Theodore Parker never joined that warfare upon me. He loved Mr. Garrison, but was not a Garrisonian. He worked with the sects, but was not a sectarian. His character was cast in a mold too large to be pressed into a form or reform less broad than humanity. He would shed his blood as quickly for a black fugitive slave pursued by human hounds as for a white President of the United States. He was the friend of the non-voting and non-resistant class of Abolitionists, but not less the friend of Henry Wilson, Charles Sumner, Gerrit Smith and John Brown. He was the large and generous brother of all men, honestly endeavoring to bring about the abolition of negro slavery. It has lately been attempted to class him with the contemners of the negro. Could that be established, it would convict him of duplicity and hypocrisy of the most revolting kind. But his whole life and character are in direct contradiction to that assumption.

Its ducal palaces, its grand Duomo, its fine galleries of art, its beautiful Arno, its charming environs, and its many associations of great historical personages, especially of Michel Angelo, Dante and Savonarola, give it a controlling power over mind and heart. I have traveled over no equal space between any two cities in Italy where the scenery was more delightful than that between Florence and Venice. I enjoyed it with the ardor of a boy to whom all the world is new. Born and raised in a flat country without the diversity of hill and valley, mountains have always attracted me. Those in sight on this journey were far away, but lost nothing by the soft haze that blended their dark summits with the clouds and sky. There were, too, the mountains of the

Tyrol, the scene of the patriotic exploits of Hofer and his countrymen. The railway between Florence and Venice is over some of the oldest and best cultivated parts of Italy. The land is rich and fruitful. Every outlook has the appearance of thrift. There is not a single point upon which to hang the reproach of laziness so commonly charged against the Italians. I saw in Italy nothing to justify this unenviable reputation. In city and country alike the people seemed to me remarkably industrious and well provided with food and raiment.

I could tell much of the once famous city of Venice, of Milan, Lucerne, and other points subsequently visited; but it is enough that I have given my readers an idea of the use I made of my time during this absence from the scenes and activities that occupied me at home. I assume that they will rejoice that after my life of hardships in slavery and of conflict with race and color prejudice and proscription at home, there was left to me a space in life when I could and did walk the world unquestioned, a man among men.

# CHAPTER X.

## THE CAMPAIGN OF 1888.

*Preference for John Sherman—Speech at the convention—On the stump—The tariff question.*

RETURNING from Europe in 1887 after a year of sojourn abroad, I found, as is usual when our country is nearing the close of a presidential term, the public mind largely occupied with the question in respect of a successor to the outgoing President. The Democratic party had the advantage of the Republican party in two points: it was already in power, and had its mind fixed upon one candidate, in the person of Grover Cleveland, whose term was then expiring. Although he had not entirely satisfied the Southern section of his party or the civil-service reformers of the North, to whom he owed his election, he had so managed his administration that neither of these factions could afford to oppose his nomination for a second term of the presidency. With the Republican party the case was different. It was not only out of power and deprived of the office-holding influence and machinery to give it unity and force, but its candidates for presidential honors were legion, and there was much doubt as to who would be chosen standard bearer in the impending contest. Among the doubters I was happily not one. From the first my candidate was Senator John Sherman* of Ohio. Not only was he the man fitted for the place by his eminent abilities and tried statesmanship in regard to general matters, but more important still, he was the man whose attitude towards the newly enfranchised colored citizens of the South best fitted him for the place. In the convention at Chicago I did what I could to secure his nomination, as long as there was any ground of hope for success. In every convention of the kind there comes a time when the judgment of factions must yield to the judgment of the majority. Either Russell A. Alger of Michigan, Allison of Iowa, Gresham of Indiana, or Depew of New York, would in my opinion have made an excellent President. But my judgment as to either was not the judgment of the convention, so I went, as in duty bound, with the choice of the majority of my party and have never regretted my course.

Although I was not a delegate to this National Republican Convention, but was, as in previous ones, a spectator, I was early honored by a spontaneous call to the platform to address the convention. It was a call not to be disregarded. It came from ten thousand leading Republicans of the land. It offered me an opportunity to give what I thought ought to be the accepted keynote to the opening campaign. How faithfully I responded will be seen by the brief speech I made in response to this call. It was not a speech to tickle men's ears or to flatter party pride, but to stir men up to the discharge of an imperative duty. It would have been easy on such an occasion to make a speech composed of glittering generalities; but the cause of my outraged people was on my heart, and I spoke out of its fullness; and the response that came back to me showed that the great audience to which I spoke was in sympathy with my sentiments. After thanking the convention for the honor of its hearty call upon me for a speech I said,—

I have only one word to say to this convention and it is this: I hope this convention will make such a record in its proceedings as will entirely put it out of the power of the leaders of the Democratic party and of the leaders of the Mugwump party* to say that they see no difference between the position of the Republican party in respect to the class I represent and that of the Democratic party. I have a great respect for a certain quality for which the Democratic party is distinguished. That quality is fidelity to its friends, its faithfulness to those whom it has acknowledged as its masters during the last forty years. It was faithful to the slave-holding class during the existence of slavery. It was faithful to them before the war. It gave them all the encouragement that it possibly could without drawing its own neck into the halter. It was also faithful during the period of reconstruction, and it has been faithful ever since. It is to-day faithful to the solid South. I hope and believe that the great Republican party will prove itself equally faithful to its friends, those friends with black faces who during the war were eyes to your blind, shelter to your shelterless, when flying from the lines of the enemy. They are as faithful to-day as when the great Republic was in the extremest need; when its fate seemed to tremble in the balance; when the crowned heads of the Old World were gloating over our ruin, saying, 'Aha! aha! the great Republican bubble is about to burst.' When your army was melting away before the fire and pestilence of rebellion; when your star-spangled banner trailed in the dust or, heavy with blood, dropped at the mast head, you called upon the negro. Yes, Abraham Lincoln called upon the negro to reach forth with his iron arm and catch with his steel fingers your faltering flag, and he came, he came full two hundred thousand strong. Let us in the platform we are about to promulgate remember the brave black men, and let us remember that these brave black men are now stripped of their constitutional right to vote. Let this remembrance be embodied in the standard bearer whom you will present to the country. Leave these men no longer compelled to wade to the ballot-box through blood, but extend over them the protecting arm of this government, and make their pathway to the ballot-box as straight and as smooth and as safe as that of any other class of citizens. Be not deterred from this duty by the cry of the bloody shirt. Let that shirt be waved as long as there shall be a drop of innocent blood upon it. A government that can give liberty in its constitution ought to have the power in its administration to protect and defend that liberty. I will not further take up your time. I have spoken for millions, and my thought is now before you.

As soon as the presidential campaign was fairly opened and a request was made for speakers to go before the people and support by the living voice the nominations and principles of the Republican party, though somewhat old for such service and never much of a stump speaker, I obeyed the summons. In company with my young friend Charles S. Morris, a man rarely gifted with eloquence, I made speeches in five different States, indoors and out of doors, in skating-rinks and public halls, day and night, at points where it was thought by the National Republican Committee that my presence and speech would do most to promote success.

While the committee was anxious to have the question of tariff made the prominent topic in the campaign, it did not in words restrict me to that one topic. I could not have gone into the field with any such restriction, had any such been imposed. Hence, I left the discussion of the tariff to my young friend Morris, while I spoke for justice and humanity, as did that noble woman and peerless orator, Miss Anna E. Dickinson, whose heart has ever been true to the oppressed, and who was a speaker in the same campaign. I took it to be the vital and animating principle of the Republican party. I found that people more courageous than their party leaders. What the leaders were afraid to teach, the people were brave enough and glad enough to learn. I held that the soul of the nation was in this question, and that the gain of all the gold in the world would not compensate for the loss of the nation's soul. National honor is the soul of the nation, and when this is lost all is lost. The Republican party and the nation were pledged to the protection of the constitutional rights of the colored citizens. If it refused to perform its promise it would be false to its highest trust. As with an individual, so too with a nation, there is a time when it may properly be asked, 'What doth it profit to gain the whole world and thereby lose one's soul?'*

With such views as these I supported the Republican party in this somewhat remarkable campaign. I based myself upon that part of the

Republican platform which I supported in my speech before the Republican convention at Chicago. No man who knew me could have expected me to pursue any other course. The little I said on the tariff was simply based upon the principle of self-protection taught in every department of nature, whether in men, beasts or plants. It comes with the inherent right to exist. It is in every blade of grass as well as in every man and nation. if foreign manufacturers oppress and cripple ours and serve to retard our natural progress, we have the right to protect ourselves against such efforts. Of course this right of self-protection has its limits, and the thing most important is to discover these limits and to observe them. There is no doubt as to the principle, but like all other principles, it may not justify all the inferences which may be deduced from it. There seems to be no difference between the Republican and Democratic parties as to the principle of protection. They only differ in the inferences drawn from the principle. One is for a tariff for revenue only, and the other is for a tariff not only for revenue, but for protection to such industries as are believed to stand in need of protection. While on this question I have always taken sides with the Republican party, I have always felt that in the presence of the oppression and persecution to which the colored race is subjected in the Southern States, no colored man can consistently base his support of any party upon any other principle than that which looks to the protection of men and women from lynch law and murder.

# CHAPTER XI.

## ADMINISTRATION OF PRESIDENT HARRISON.

*Appointed Minister to Haïti—Unfriendly criticism—Admiral Gherardi.*

My appointment by President Harrison* in 1889 to the office of Minister Resident and Consul General to the Republic of Haïti did not pass without adverse comment at the time it was made; nor did I escape criticism at any time during the two years I had the honor to hold that office. In respect to the unfavorable comments upon my appointment, it may be truly said that they had their origin and inspiration from two very natural sources: first, American race and color prejudice, and second, a desire on the part of certain influential merchants in New York to obtain concessions from Haïti upon grounds that I was not likely to favor. When there is made upon a public man an attack by newspapers differing at all other points and united only in this attack, there is some reason to believe that they are inspired by a common influence. Neither my character nor my color was acceptable to the New York press. The fault of my character was that upon it there could be predicated no well grounded hope that I would allow myself to be used, or allow my office to be used, to further selfish schemes of any sort for the benefit of individuals, either at the expense of Haiti or at the expense of the character of the United States. And the fault of my color was that it was a shade too dark for American taste. It was not charged, as perhaps it well might have been, that I was unfit for the place by reason of inexperience and want of aptitude to perform the duties of the office; but the color argument was relied upon. It was that I was not rightly colored for the place, although I matched well with the color of Haïti. It was held that the office should be given to a white man, both on the ground of fitness and on the ground of efficiency,—on the ground of fitness because it was alleged that Haïti would rather have in her capital a white minister Resident and Consul General than a colored one; and on the ground of efficiency because a white minister by reason of being white, and therefore superior, could obtain from Haïti concessions which a colored minister could not. It was also said that I would not be well received by Haïti because I had at one time advocated the annexation of Santo Domingo to the United States, a measure to which Haïti was strongly opposed. Every occasion was embraced by the New York press to show that my experience in Haïti confirmed their views and predictions. Before I went there they endeavored to show that the captain of the ship designated by the government to take me to my post at Port au Prince had refused to take me on board, and as an excuse for his refusal, had made a false statement concerning the unseaworthiness of his vessel, when the real ground of objection was the color of my skin. When it was known that I had not been fully accredited in due form to the Government of President Hyppolite* and that there was a delay of many weeks in my formal recognition by the Haïtian government, the story was trumpeted abroad that I was 'snubbed' by Haïti, and in truth was having a hard time down there. After I was formally recognized and had entered upon the duties of my office, I was followed by the same unfriendly spirit, and every effort was made to disparage me in the eyes of both the people of the United States and those of Haïti. Strangely enough, much of this unfriendly influence came from officers of the American navy; men in the pay of the government. The appearance in the harbor of Port au Prince of United States ships of war, instead of being a support to the American Minister, was always followed by a heavy broadside against him in the American papers. Our ships seemed to be well supplied with salt water correspondents; men who had studied the science of polite detraction at the public expense and had reached in it a high degree of perfection. The arrival of an American war vessel became a source of apprehension, and an admiral's pennon in the harbor of Port au Prince was a signal of attack upon the United States Minister.

Speaking of the acquisition of the Môle St. Nicolas* as a United States naval station, one of these fruitful correspondents thus exposed the real cause of complaint against me: 'When by the active intervention and material aid of the States, General Hyppolite was placed in power in October, 1889, . . . American influence was paramount, and had a shrewd and capable American then been sent by the United States to conduct the negotiations so ably initiated by Rear-Admiral Gherardi,* there would be a different condition of affairs to report today. At Admiral Gherardi's suggestion a new minister was sent to Port au Prince. . . . The lack of wisdom, however, displayed in the choice . . . has by the result attained become only too apparent.' 'Of the Clyde concession it is perhaps needless to say anything, . . . has failed completely. . . . But with the negotiations in the hands of Rear-Admiral Gherardi a decision must be reached shortly. Admiral Gherardi is sent to resuscitate the negotiations. Admiral Gherardi will succeed eventually.' 'It is recognized that were the United States to possess a coaling-station in Haïti . . . would intervene to end the petty revolutions that distract the country.'

Thus we had Admiral Gherardi at every turn of Haïtian affairs. it was at his suggestion that a new minister was appointed. It was he who made American influence paramount in Haïti. It was he who was to conduct the negotiations for the naval station. It was he who counseled the State Department at Washington. It was he who decided the question of the fitness of the American Minister at Haïti. In all this I am not disclosing Cabinet or State secrets. This and much more was published in the New York papers. The comment that I have to make upon it is, that no better way could have been devised to arouse the suspicion of Haïtian statesmen and lead them to reject our application for a naval station, than to make such representations as these coming from the decks of the flag-ship of Rear-Admiral Gherardi.

# CHAPTER XII.

## MINISTER TO HAÏTI.

*The Môle St. Nicolas—Social Relations—Sympathy for Haïti—*
*The facts about the Môle St. Nicolas—Conference with the Haïtian*
*Government—Negotiations for the Môle St. Nicolas—Close of the*
*interview.*

THE part I bore in the matter of obtaining at the Môle St. Nicolas a naval station for the United States, and the real cause for the failure of the enterprise, are made evident in the following articles from me, published in the *North American Review* for September and October, 1891.*

'I propose to make a plain statement regarding my connection with the late negotiations with the government of Haïti for a United States naval station at the Môle St. Nicolas. Such a statement seems required, not only as a personal vindication from undeserved censure, but as due to the truth of history. Recognizing my duty to be silent while the question of the Môle was pending, I refrained from making any formal reply to the many misstatements and misrepresentations which have burdened the public press unchallenged during the last six months. I have, however, long intended to correct some of the grosser errors contained in these misrepresentations, should the time ever come when I could do so without exposing myself to the charge of undue sensitiveness and without detriment to the public interest. That time has now come, and there is no ground of sentiment, reason, or propriety for a longer silence, especially since, through no fault of mine, the secrets of the negotiations in question have already been paraded before the public, apparently with no other purpose than to make me responsible for their failure.

'There are many reasons why I would be gladly excused from appearing before the public in the attitude of self-defense. But while there are times when such defense is a privilege to be exercised or omitted at the pleasure of the party assailed, there are other times and circumstances when it becomes a duty which cannot be omitted without the imputation of cowardice or of conscious guilt. This is especially true in a case where the charges vitally affect one's standing with the people and government of one's country. In such a case a man must defend himself, if only to demonstrate his fitness to defend anything else. In discharging this duty I shall acknowledge no favoritism to men in high places, no restraint but candor, and no limitation but truth. It is easy to whip a man when his hands are tied. It required little courage for these men of war to assail me while I was in office and known to be forbidden by its rules to write or to speak in my own defense. They had everything their own way.

'Perhaps it was thought that I lacked the spirit or the ability to reply. On no other ground of assurance could there have been such loose and reckless disregard of easily ascertained facts to contradict them. It is also obvious that the respectability of the public journals, rather than the credibility of the writers themselves, was relied upon to give effect to their statements. Had they disclosed their names and their true addresses, the public could have easily divined a motive which would have rendered unnecessary any word of mine in self-defense. It would have become evident in that case that there was a premeditated attempt to make me a scapegoat to bear off the sins of others. It may be noted, too, that prompt advantage has been taken of the fact that falsehood is not easily exposed when it has had an early start in advance of truth. As mindful of some things as they were, however, they forgot that innocence needs no defense until it is accused.

'The charge is, that I have been the means of defeating the acquisition of an important United States naval station at the Môle St. Nicolas. It is said, in general terms, that I wasted the whole of my first year in Haïti in needless parley and delay, and finally reduced the chances of getting the Môle to such a narrow margin as to make it necessary for our government to appoint Rear-Admiral Gherardi as a special commissioner to Haïti to take the whole matter of negotiation for the Môle out of my hands. One of the charitable apologies they are pleased to make for my failure is my color; and the implication is that a white man would have succeeded where I failed. This color argument is not new. It besieged the White House before I was appointed Minister Resident and Consul-General to Haïti. At once and all along the line, the contention was then raised that no man with African blood in his veins should be sent as minister to the Black Republic. White men professed to speak in the interest of black Haïti; and I could have applauded their alacrity in upholding her dignity if I could have respected their sincerity. They thought it monstrous to compel black Haïti to receive a minister as black as herself. They did not see that it would be shockingly inconsistent for Haïti to object to a black minister while she herself is black.

'Prejudice sets all logic at defiance. It takes no account of reason or consistency. One of the duties of minister in a foreign land is to cultivate good social as well as civil relations with the people and government to which he is sent. Would an American white man, imbued with our national sentiments, be more likely than an American colored man to cultivate such relations? Would his American contempt for the colored race at home fit him to win the respect and good-will of colored people abroad? Or would he play the hypocrite and pretend to love negroes in Haïti when he is known to hate negroes in the United States,—aye, so bitterly that he hates to see them occupy even the comparatively humble position of Consul-General to Haïti? Would not the contempt and disgust of Haïti repel such a sham?

'Haïti is no stranger to Americans or to American prejudice. Our white fellow-countrymen have taken little pains to conceal their sentiments. This objection to my color and this demand for a white man to succeed me spring from the very feeling which Haïti herself contradicts and detests. I defy any man to prove, by any word or act of the Haïtian Government, that I was less respected at the capital of Haïti than was any white minister or consul. This clamor for a white minister for Haïti is based upon the idea that a white man is held in higher esteem by her than is a black man, and that he could get more out of her than can one of her own color. It is not so, and the whole free history of Haïti proves it not to be so. Even if it were true that a white man could, by reason of his alleged superiority, gain something extra from the servility of Haïti, it would be the height of meanness for a great nation like the United States to take advantage of such servility on the part of a weak nation. The American people are too great to be small, and they should ask nothing of Haïti on grounds less just and reasonable than those upon which they would ask anything of France or England. Is the weakness of a nation a reason for our robbing it? Are we to take advantage, not only of its weakness, but of its fears? Are we to wring from it by dread of our power what we cannot obtain by appeals to its justice and reason? If this is the policy of this great nation, I own that my assailants were right when they said that I was not the man to represent the United States in Haïti.

'I am charged with sympathy for Haïti. I am not ashamed of that charge; but no man can say with truth that my sympathy with Haïti stood between me and any honorable duty that I owed to the United States or to any citizen of the United States.

'The attempt has been made to prove me indifferent to the acquisition of a naval station in Haïti, and unable to grasp the importance to American commerce and to American influence of such a station in the Caribbean Sea. The fact is, that when some of these writers were in their petticoats, I had comprehended the value of such an acquisition, both in respect to American commerce and to American influence. The policy of obtaining such a station is not new. I supported Gen. Grant's ideas on this subject against the powerful opposition of my honored and revered friend Charles Sumner, more than twenty years ago, and proclaimed it on a hundred platforms and to thousands of my fellow-citizens. I said then that it was a shame to American statesmanship that, while almost every other great nation in the world had secured a foot-hold and had power in the Caribbean Sea, where it could anchor in its own bays and moor in its own harbors, we, who stood at the very gate of that sea, had there no anchoring ground anywhere. I was for the acqui-sition of Samana, and of Santo Domingo herself, if she wished to come to us. While slavery existed, I was opposed to all schemes for the exten-sion of American power and influence. But since its abolition, I have gone with him who goes farthest for such extension.

'But the pivotal and fundamental charge made by my accusers is that I wasted a whole year in fruitless negotiations for a coaling-station at the Môle St. Nicolas, and allowed favorable opportunities for obtaining it to pass unimproved, so that it was necessary at last for the United States Government to take the matter out of my hands, and send a special commissioner to Haïti, in the person of Rear-Admiral Gherardi, to negotiate for the Môle. A statement more false than this never dropped from lip or pen. I here and now declare, without hesi-tation or qualification or fear of contradiction, that there is not one word of truth in this charge. If I do not in this state the truth, I may be easily contradicted and put to open shame. I therefore affirm that at no time during the first year of my residence in Haïti was I charged with the duty or invested with any authority by the President of the United States, or by the Secretary of State, to negotiate with Haïti for a United States naval station at the Môle St. Nicolas, or anywhere else in that country. Where no duty was imposed, no duty was neglected. It is not for a diplomat to run before he is sent, especially in matters involving large consequences like those implied in extending our power into a neighboring country.

'Here, then, let me present the plain facts in the case. They, better than anything else I can say, vindicate my conduct in connection with this question.

'On the 26th of January, 1891, Rear-Admiral Gherardi, having arrived at Port au Prince, sent one of his under-officers on shore to the United States Legation, to invite me on board of his flagship, the Philadelphia. I complied with the invitation, although I knew that, in strict politeness, it would have been more appropriate for Admiral Gherardi himself to come to me. I felt disinclined, however, to stand upon ceremony or to endeavor to correct the manners of an American admiral. Having long since decided to my own satisfaction that no expression of American prejudice or slight on account of my color could diminish my self-respect or disturb my equanimity, I went on board as requested, and there for the first time learned that I was to have some connection with negotiations for a United States coaling-station at the Môle St. Nicolas; and this information was imparted to me by Rear-Admiral Gherardi. He told me in his peculiarly emphatic manner that he had been duly appointed a United States special commissioner; that his mission was to obtain a naval station at the Môle St. Nicolas; and that it was the wish of Mr. Blaine and Mr. Tracy, and also of the President of the United States, that I should earnestly co-operate with him in accomplishing this object. He further made me acquainted with the dignity of his position, and I was not slow in recognizing it.

'In reality, some time before the arrival of Admiral Gherardi on this diplomatic scene, I was made acquainted with the fact of his appointment. There was at Port au Prince an individual, of whom we shall hear more elsewhere, acting as agent of a distinguished firm in New York, who appeared to be more fully initiated into the secrets of the State Department at Washington than I was, and who knew, or said he knew, all about the appointment of Admiral Gherardi, whose arrival he diligently heralded in advance, and carefully made public in all the political and business circles to which he had access. He stated that I was discredited at Washington, had, in fact, been suspended and recalled, and that Admiral Gherardi had been duly commissioned to take my place. This news was sudden and far from flattering. It is unnecessary to say that it placed me in an unenviable position, both before the community of Port au Prince and before the government of Haïti. It had, however, the advantage, so far as I was able to believe anything so anomalous, of preparing me for the advent of my successor, and of softening the shock of my fall from my high estate. My connection with this negotiation, as all may see, was very humble, secondary and subordinate. The glory of success or the shame of defeat was to belong to the new minister. I was made subject to the commissioner. This was not quite so bad as the New York agent had prepared me to expect, but it was not what I thought I deserved and what my position as minister called for at the hands of my government. Strangely enough, all my instructions concerning the Môle came to me through my newly constituted superior. He was fresh from the face of our Secretary of State, knew his most secret intentions and the wants and wishes of the government, and I, naturally enough, received the law from his lips.

'The situation suggested the resignation of my office as due to my honor; but reflection soon convinced me that such a course would subject me to a misconstruction more hurtful than any which, in the circumstances, could justly arise from remaining at my post. The government had decided that a special commissioner was needed in Haïti. No charges were brought against me, and it was not for me to set up my wisdom or my resentment as a safer rule of action than that prescribed by the wisdom of my government. Besides, I did not propose to be pushed out of office in this way. I therefore resolved to co-operate with the special commissioner in good faith and in all earnestness, and did so to the best of my ability.

'It was first necessary, in furtherance of the mission of Admiral Gherardi, to obtain for him as early as possible an interview with Mr. Firmin,* the Haïtian Minister of Foreign Affairs, and with His Excellency Florvil Hyppolite, the President of Haïti. This, by reason of my position as minister and my good relations with the government of Haïti, I accomplished only two days after the arrival of the admiral. Not even my accusers can charge me with tardiness in obeying in this, or in anything else, the orders of my superior. In acting under him I put aside the fact of the awkward position in which the officious agent had placed me, and the still more galling fact that the instructions I received had not reached me from the State Department in the usual and appropriate way, as also the fact that I had been in some degree subjected to the authority of an officer who had not, like myself, been duly appointed by the President and confirmed by the Senate of the United States, and yet one whose name and bearing proclaimed him practically the man having full command. Neither did I allow anything like a feeling of offended dignity to diminish my zeal and alacrity in carrying out his instructions. I consoled myself with the thought that I was acting like a good soldier, promptly and faithfully executing the orders of my superior, and obeying the will of my government. Our first conference with President Hyppolite and his foreign secretary was held at the palace at Port au Prince on the 28th of January, 1891. At this conference, which was, in fact, the real beginning of the negotiations for the Môle St. Nicolas, the wishes of our government were made known to the government of Haïti by Rear-Admiral Gherardi; and I must do him the justice to say that he stated the case with force and ability. If anything was omitted or insisted upon calculated to defeat the object in view, this defect must be looked for in the admiral's address, for he was the principal speaker, as he was also the principal negotiator.

'Admiral Gherardi based our claim for this concession upon the ground of services rendered by the United States to the Hyppolite revolution. He claimed it also on the ground of promises made to our government by Hyppolite and Firmin through their agents while the revolution was in progress, and affirmed that but for the support of our government the revolution would have failed. I supplemented his remarks, not in opposition to his views, but with the intention of impressing the government of Haïti with the idea that the concession asked for was in the line of good neighborhood and advanced civilization and in every way consistent with the autonomy of Haïti; urging that the concession would be a source of strength rather than of weakness to the Haïtian Government; that national isolation was a policy of the past; that the necessity for it in Haïti, for which there was an apology at the commencement of her existence, no longer exists; that her relation to the world and that of the world to her are not what they were when her independence was achieved; that her true policy now is to touch the world at all points that make for civilization and commerce; and that, instead of asking in alarm what will happen if a naval station be conceded to the United States, it should ask, "What will happen if such a naval station be not conceded?" I insisted that there was far more danger to be apprehended to the stability of the existing government from allowing the rumor to float in the air that it was about to sell out the country, than by granting the lease of the Môle and letting the country know precisely what had been done and the reasons in the premises for the same; that a fact accomplished carries with it a power to promote acquiescence; and I besought them to meet the question with courage.

'In replying to us, Mr. Firmin demanded to know on which of the two grounds we based our claim for the possession of this naval station. If it were demanded, he said, upon any pledge made by President Hyppolite and himself, he denied the existence of any such promise or pledge, and insisted that, while the offer of certain advantages had been made to our government, the government at Washington had not at the time accepted them. The letter in proof of the different view was, he said, only a copy of the original letter, and the original letter was never accepted by the American Government.

'This position of Mr. Firmin's was resisted by Admiral Gherardi, who contended with much force that, while there was no formal agreement consummated between the two governments, Haïti was nevertheless bound, since the assistance for which she asked had made Hyppolite President of Haïti. Without intending to break the force of the admiral's contention at this point, I plainly saw the indefensible attitude in which he was placing the government of the United States in representing our government as interfering by its navy with the affairs of a neighboring country, covertly assisting in putting down one government and setting up another; and I therefore adhered to the grounds upon which I based our demand for a coaling-station at the Môle. I spoke in the interest and honor of the United States. It did not strike me that what was claimed by Admiral Gherardi to have been done—though I did not say as much—is the work for which the United States is armed, equipped, manned and supported by the American people. It was alleged that, though our government did not authorize Rear-Admiral Gherardi to overthrow Légitime and to set up Hyppolite as President of Haïti, it gave him the wink, and left him to assume the responsibility. I did not accept this as a foundation upon which I could base my diplomacy. If this was a blunder on my part, it was a blunder of which I am not ashamed, and it was committed in the interest of my country.

'At the close of this conference we were asked by Mr. Firmin to put into writing our request for the Môle, and the terms upon which we asked its concession.

# CHAPTER XIII.

## CONTINUED NEGOTIATIONS FOR THE MÔLE ST. NICOLAS.

*Unfortunate delay—Renewed authority from the United States—
Haïti's refusal—Reasons for the refusal—The Clyde contract—A
dishonest proposition—A strange demand—Haïti's mistake—Bad
effect of the Clyde proposition—Final words.*

'AT a meeting subsequent to the one already described, application for
a United States naval station at the Môle St. Nicolas was made in due
form to Mr. Firmin, the Haïtian Minister of Foreign Affairs. At his
request, as already stated, this application was presented to him in writing. It was prepared on board the Philadelphia, the flagship of Rear-
Admiral Bancroft Gherardi, and bore his signature alone. I neither
signed it nor was asked to sign it, although it met my entire approval.
I make this statement not in the way of complaint or grievance, but
simply to show what, at the time, was my part, and what was not my
part, in this important negotiation, the failure of which has unjustly
been laid to my charge. Had the Môle been acquired, in response to this
paper, the credit of success, according to the record, would have properly belonged to the gallant admiral in whose name it was demanded;
for in it I had neither part nor lot.

'At this point, curiously enough, and unfortunately for the negotiations, the Haïtian Minister, who is an able man and well skilled in the
technicalities of diplomacy, asked to see the commission of Admiral
Gherardi and to read his letter of instructions. When these were presented to Mr. Firmin, he, after carefully reading them, pronounced
them insufficient, and held that by them the government of the United
States would not be bound by any convention which Haïti might make
with the admiral. This position of Mr. Firmin's was earnestly and
stoutly opposed by Admiral Gherardi, who insisted that his instructions were full, complete, and amply sufficient. Unfortunately, however, he did not leave the matter in controversy without intimating that
he thought that Mr. Firmin might be insincere in raising such an
objection, and that he was urging it simply with a view to cause unnecessary delay. This was more like the blunt admiral than the discreet diplomat. Such an imputation was obviously out of place, and not likely
to smooth the way to a successful proceeding; quite the reverse.
Mr. Firmin insisted that his ground was well and honestly taken.

'Here, therefore, the negotiation was brought to a sudden halt, and the question for us then was, What shall be done next? Three ways were open to us: first, to continue to insist upon the completeness of the authority of Admiral Gherardi; second, to abandon the scheme of a naval station altogether; third, to apply to the government at Washington for the required letter of credence. It was my opinion that it was hardly worth while to continue to insist upon the sufficiency of the admiral's papers, since it seemed useless to contend about mere technicalities; more especially as we were now in telegraphic connection with the United States, and could in the course of a few days easily obtain the proper and required papers.

'Besides, I held that a prompt compliance with the demand of the Haïtian Government for a perfect letter of credence would be not only the easiest way out of the difficulty, but the wisest policy by which to accomplish the end we sought, since such compliance on our part with even what might be fairly considered an unreasonable demand would make refusal by Haïti to grant the Môle all the more difficult.

'I did not understand Admiral Gherardi to combat this opinion of mine, for he at once acted upon it, and caused an officer from his flagship to go with me to my house and prepare a telegram to be sent to Washington for the required letter of credence. To this telegram he, two days thereafter, received answer that such a letter would be immediately sent by a Clyde steamer to Gonaïves, and thither the admiral went to receive his expected letter. But, from some unexplained cause, no such letter came by the Clyde steamer at the time appointed, and two months intervened before the desired credentials arrived. This unexpected delay proved to be very mischievous and unfavorable to our getting the Môle, since it gave rise among the Haïtian people to much speculation and many disquieting rumors prejudicial to the project. It was said that Admiral Gherardi had left Port au Prince in anger, and had gone to take possession of the Môle without further parley; that the American flag was already floating over our new naval station; that the United States wanted the Môle as an entering wedge to obtaining possession of the whole island; with much else of like inflammatory nature. Although there was no truth in all this, it had the unhappy effect among the masses of stirring up suspicion and angry feelings towards the United States, and of making it more difficult than it might otherwise have been for the government of Haïti to grant the required concession.

'Finally, after this long interval of waiting, during which the flagship of Admiral Gherardi was reported at different points, sometimes at

Gonaïves, sometimes at the Môle, and sometimes at Kingston, Jamaica, the desired letter of credence arrived. The next day I was again summoned on board the Philadelphia, and there was shown me a paper, signed by the President of the United States and by the Secretary of State, authorizing myself, as Minister Resident to Haïti, and Rear-Admiral Gherardi, as special commissioner, to negotiate with such persons as Haïti might appoint, for the purpose of concluding a convention by which we should obtain a lease of the Môle St. Nicolas as a United States naval station.

'It may be here remarked that the letter of credence signed by President Harrison and by the Secretary of State differed in two respects from the former and rejected letter under which we had previously acted. First, it charged me, equally with Admiral Gherardi, with the duty of negotiation; and secondly, it was an application for a naval station pure and simple, without limitation and without conditions.

'Before presenting to Haïti this new letter, which had the advantage of being free from the conditions specified in the old one, the question arose between the admiral and myself as to whether or not we should begin our new negotiations, under our new commission, separate and entirely apart from all that had been attempted under the instructions contained in the old letter. On this point I differed from the admiral. I took the position that we should ignore the past altogether, and proceed according to the instructions of the new letter alone, unencumbered by any terms or limitations contained in the old letter. I felt sure that there were features in the conditions of the old letter which would be met by the representatives of Haïti with strong objections. But the admiral and his able lieutenant insisted that the present letter did not exclude the conditions of the old one, but was, in its nature, only supplementary to them, and hence that this was simply a continuation of what had gone before. It was therefore decided to proceed with the negotiations on the basis of both the old and the new letter. Under the former letter of instructions, our terms were precise and explicit; under the latter we were left largely to our own discretion: we were simply to secure from the government of Haïti a lease of the Môle St. Nicolas for a naval station.

'The result is known. Haïti refused to grant the lease, and alleged that to do so was impossible under the hard terms imposed in the previous letter of instructions. I do not know that our government would have accepted a naval station from Haïti upon any other or less stringent terms or conditions than those exacted in our first letter of instructions; but I do know that the main grounds alleged by Haïti for its refusal were the conditions set forth in this first letter of instructions, one of which is expressed as follows: "That so long as the United States may be the lessee of the Môle St. Nicolas, the government of Haïti will not lease or otherwise dispose of any port or harbor or other territory in its dominions, or grant any special privileges or rights of use therein, to any other power, state or government." This was not only a comprehensive limitation of the power of Haïti over her own territory, but a denial to all others of that which we claim for ourselves.

'But no one cause fully explains our failure to get a naval station at the Môle. One fundamental element in our non-success was found, not in any aversion to the United States or in any indifference on my part, as has often been charged, but in the government of Haïti itself. It was evidently timid. With every disposition to oblige us, it had not the courage to defy the well-known, deeply rooted, and easily excited prejudices and traditions of the Haïtian people. Nothing is more repugnant to the thoughts and feelings of the masses of that country than the alienation of a single rood of their territory to a foreign power.

'This sentiment originated, very naturally, in the circumstances in which Haïti began her national existence. The whole Christian world was at that time against her. The Caribbean Sea was studded with communities hostile to her. They were slave-holding. She, by her bravery and her blood, was free. Her existence was, therefore, a menace to them, and theirs was a menace to her. France, England, Spain, Portugal and Holland, as well as the United States, were wedded to the slave system, which Haïti had, by arms, thrown off; and hence she was regarded as an outcast, and was outlawed by the Christian world. Though time and events have gone far to change this relation of hers to the outside world, the sentiment that originated in the beginning of her existence continues on both sides until this day. It was this that stood like a wall of granite against our success. Other causes co-operated, but this was the principal cause. Of course our peculiar and intense prejudice against the colored race was not forgotten. Our contrast to other nations, in this respect, is often dwelt upon in Haïti to our disadvantage. In no part of Europe will a Haïtian be insulted because of his color, and Haïtians well know that this is not the case in the United States.

'Another influence unfavorable to our obtaining the coveted naval station at the Môle was the tone of the New York press on the subject. It more than hinted that, once in possession of the Môle, the United States would control the destiny of Haïti. Torn and rent by revolution as she has been and still is, Haïti yet has a large share of national pride, and scorns the idea that she needs or will submit to the rule of a foreign power. Some of her citizens would doubtless be glad of American rule, but the overwhelming majority would burn their towns and freely shed their blood over their ashes to prevent such a consummation.

'Not the least, perhaps, among the collateral causes of our non-success was the minatory attitude assumed by us while conducting the negotiation. What wisdom was there in confronting Haïti at such a moment with a squadron of large ships of war with a hundred canon and two thousand men? This was done, and it was naturally construed into a hint to Haïti that if we could not, by appeals to reason and friendly feeling, obtain what we wanted, we could obtain it by a show of force. We appeared before the Haïtians, and before the world, with the pen in one hand and the sword in the other. This was not a friendly and considerate attitude for a great government like ours to assume when asking a concession from a small and weak nation like Haïti. It was ill timed and out of all proportion to the demands of the occasion. It was also done under a total misapprehension of the character of the people with whom we had to deal. We should have known that, whatever else the Haïtian people may be, they are not cowards, and hence are not easily scared.

'In the face of all these obvious and effective causes of failure, is it not strange that our intelligent editors and our nautical newspaper writers could not have found for the American Government and people a more rational cause for the failure of the negotiations for the Môle St. Nicolas than that of my color, indifference, and incompetency to deal with a question of such a magnitude? Were I disposed to exchange the position of accused for that of accuser, I could find ample material to sustain me in that position. Other persons did much to create conditions unfavorable to our success, but I leave to their friends the employment of such personal assaults.

'On the theory that I was the cause of this failure, we must assume that Haïti was willing to grant the Môle; that the timidity of the Haïtian Government was all right; that the American prejudice was all right; that the seven ships of war in the harbor of Port au Prince were all right; that Rear-Admiral Gherardi was all right, and that I alone was all wrong; and, moreover, that but for me the Môle St. Nicolas, like an over-ripe apple shaken by the wind, would have dropped softly into our national basket. I will not enlarge upon this absurd assumption, but will leave the bare statement of it to the intelligent reader, that it may perish by its flagrant contradiction of well-known facts and by its own absurdity.

'I come now to another cause of complaint against me, scarcely less serious in the minds of those who now assail me than the charge of having defeated the lease of the Môle St. Nicolas; namely, the failure of what is publicly known as the Clyde contract. Soon after my arrival in Haïti I was put in communication with an individual calling himself the agent of the highly respectable mercantile firm of William P. Clyde & Co. of New York. He was endeavoring to obtain a subsidy of a half million dollars from the government of Haïti to enable this firm to ply a line of steamers between New York and Haïti. From the first this agent assumed toward me a dictatorial attitude. He claimed to be a native of South Carolina, and it was impossible for him to conceal his contempt for the people whose good will it was his duty to seek. Between this agent and the United States Government I found myself somewhat in the position of a servant between two masters; either one of them, separately and apart, might be served acceptably; but to serve both satisfactorily at the same time and place might be a difficult task, if not an impossible one. There were times when I was compelled to prefer the requirements of the one to the ardent wishes of the other, and I thought as between this agent and the United States, I chose to serve the latter.

'The trouble between us came about in this way: Mr. Firmin, the Haïtian Minister of Foreign Affairs, had objected to granting the Clyde concession on the ground that, if it were granted and this heavy drain were made upon the treasury of his country, Mr. Douglass stood ready to present and to press upon Haïti the payment of the claims of many other American citizens, and that this would greatly embarrass the newly organized government of President Hyppolite. In view of this objection, the zealous agent in question came to me and proposed that I should go to Mr. Firmin, in my quality of Minister Resident and Consul-General of the United States, and assure him that, if he would only grant the Clyde concession, I, on my part, would withhold and refrain from pressing the claims of other American citizens.

'The proposition shocked me. It sounded like the words of Satan on the mountain, and I thought it time to call a halt. I was in favor of the Clyde contract, but I could not see what I had said or done to make it possible for any man to make to me a proposal so plainly dishonest and scandalous. I refused to do any such thing. Here was my first offense, and it at once stamped me as an unprofitable servant. It did not seem to occur to this agent that he had made to me a shameful, dishonest and shocking proposition. Blinded by zeal or by an influence still more misleading, he seemed to see in it only an innocent proposal. He thereafter looked upon me as an unworthy ally, and duly reported me as such to his master and to other influential persons. He could not understand my conduct as proceeding from other or better motives than that of over-affection for the Haïtians. In his eyes I was, from that time, more a Haïtian than an American, and I soon saw myself so characterized in American journals.

'The refusal to compromise and postpone the just claims of other American citizens for that of his master's contract was not, however, my only offense. On obtaining a leave of absence from my post, in July, 1890, I, of course, as was my duty, called upon President Hyppolite before my departure, for the purpose of paying to him my respects. This agent at once sought me and desired me to make use of this visit of mere ceremony as an occasion to press anew the Clyde contract upon the attention of the President. This I could not properly do, especially as I had on previous occasions repeatedly urged its consideration upon him. The President already knew well enough my sense of the importance to Haïti of this measure, not only as a means of enlarging her commerce and of promoting her civilization, but also as a guaranty of the stability of her government. Nevertheless, my refusal to urge in so unbecoming a manner a demand already repeatedly urged upon the attention of the Haïtian Government was made use of by this agent to my injury, both at the State Department and with Mr. Clyde's firm. I was reported at Washington and to various persons in high places as unfriendly to this concession.

'When at last it appeared to the agent that the government of Haïti was, as he thought, stubbornly blind to its own interests, and that it would not grant the contract in question, he called at the United States Legation and expressed to me his disappointment and disgust at the delay of Haïti in accepting his scheme. He said he did not believe that the government really intended to do anything for his firm; that he himself had spent much time and money in promoting the concession; and as he did not think that Mr. Clyde ought to be made to pay for the time thus lost and the expense incurred by the delay and dallying of the Haïtian Government, he should therefore demand his pay of Haïti. This determination struck me as very odd, and I jocosely replied,—

'"Then, sir, as they will not allow you to put a hot poker down their backs, you mean to make them pay for heating it!"

'This rejoinder was my final destruction in the esteem of this zealous advocate. He saw at once that he could not count upon my assistance in making this new demand. I was both surprised by his proposal and amused by it, and wondered that he could think it possible that he could get this pay. It seemed to me that Haïti would scout the idea at once. She had not sent for him. She had not asked him to stay. He was there for purposes of his own and not for any purpose of hers. I could not see why Haïti should pay him for coming, going or staying. but this gentleman knew better than I the generous character of the people with whom he had to deal, and he followed them up till they actually paid him five thousand dollars in gold.

'But compliance with his demand proved a woeful mistake on the part of Haïti, and, in fact, nonsense. This man, after getting his money, went away, but he did not stay away. He was soon back again to press his scheme with renewed vigor. His demands were now to be complied with or he would make, not Rome, but Haïti, howl. To him it was nothing that Haïti was already wasted by repeated revolutions; nothing that she was already staggering under the weight of a heavy national debt; nothing that she herself ought to be the best judge of her ability to pour out a half million of dollars in this new and, to her, doubtful enterprise; nothing that she had heard his arguments in its favor a hundred times over; nothing that in her judgment she had far more pressing needs for her money than the proposed investment in this steamship subsidy, as recommended by him; nothing that she had told him plainly that she was afraid to add to her pecuniary burdens this new and onerous one; and nothing that she had just paid him five thousand dollars in gold to get rid of his importunities.

'Now, while I was in favor of Haïti's granting the subsidy asked for in the name of Clyde & Co., and thought that it would be in many ways a good thing for Haïti to have the proposed line of steamers for which a subsidy was asked, I had, and I now have, nothing but disgust for the method by which this scheme was pressed upon Haïti.

'I must say in conclusion that, while, as already intimated, it does not appear certain that Haïti would have leased us the Môle on any conditions whatever, it is certain that the application for it was ill timed in more respects than one. It was especially unfortunate for us that the Clyde concession was applied for in advance of our application for a lease of the Môle. Whatever else may be said of the Haïtians, this is true of them: they are quick to detect a fault and to distinguish a trick from an honest proceeding. To them the preference given to the interests of an individual firm over those of the United States seemed to wear a sinister aspect. In the opinion of many intelligent persons in Haïti, had a lease of the Môle been asked for in advance of the concession to Mr. Clyde, the application for it might have been successful. This, however, is not my opinion. I do not now think that any earthly power outside of absolute force could have gotten for us a naval station at the Môle St. Nicolas. Still, to all appearances, the conditions of success were more favorable before than after the Clyde contract was urged upon Haïti. Prior to this, the country, weary of war, was at peace. Ambitious leaders had not begun openly to conspire. The government under Hyppolite was newly organized. Confidence in its stability was unimpaired. It was, naturally enough, reaching out its hand to us for friendly recognition. Our good offices during the war were fresh in its memory. France, England and Germany were not ready to give it recognition. In fact, all the conditions conspired to influence Haïti to listen to our request for a coaling-station at the Môle St. Nicolas, but instead of a proposition for a coaling-station at the Môle St. Nicolas, there was presented one for a subsidy to an individual steamship company. All must see that the effect of this was calculated to weaken our higher claim and to place us at a disadvantage before Haïti and before all the world.

'And now, since the American people have been made thoroughly acquainted with one view of this question, I know of no interest which will suffer and no just obligation which will be impaired by the presentation of such facts as I have here submitted to the public judgment. If in this my course is thought to be unusual, it should be remembered that the course pursued towards me by the press has been unusual, and that they who had no censure for the latter should have none for the former.'

I have nearly reached the end of the period of which, in the beginning, I purposed to write, and should I live to see the end of another decade, it is not at all likely that I shall feel disposed to add another word to this volume. I may therefore make this the concluding chapter of this part of my autobiography. Contemplating my life as a whole, I have to say that, although it has at times been dark and stormy, and I have met with hardships from which other men have been exempted, yet my life has in many respects been remarkably full of sunshine and joy. Servitude, persecution, false friends, desertion and depreciation have not robbed my life of happiness or made it a burden. I have been, and still am, especially fortunate, and may well indulge sentiments of warmest gratitude for the allotments of life that have fallen to me. While I cannot boast of having accomplished great things in the world, I cannot on the other hand feel that I have lived in vain. From first to last I have, in large measure, shared the respect and confidence of my fellow-men. I have had the happiness of possessing many precious and long-enduring friendships with good men and women. I have been the recipient of many honors, among which my unsought appointment by President Benjamin Harrison to the office of Minister Resident and

Consul-General to represent the United States at the capital of Haïti, and my equally unsought appointment by President Florvil Hyppolite to represent Haïti among all the civilized nations of the globe at the World's Columbian Exposition,* are crowning honors to my long career and a fitting and happy close to my whole public life.

# APPENDIX

## FREDERICK DOUGLASS, *Lessons of the Hour*

'I am here to speak for, and to defend, so far as I can do so within the bounds of truth, a long-suffering people, and one just now subject to much misrepresentation and persecution. Charges are at this time preferred against them, more damaging and distressing than any which they have been called upon to meet since their emancipation' (p. 523). So Frederick Douglass declares in *Lessons of the Hour*, an address he delivered in the Metropolitan African Methodist Episcopal Church, in Washington, D.C., on 9 January 1894, just two years after he published his final edition of *Life and Times of Frederick Douglass, Written By Himself*, and over a year before he died on 20 February 1895. In the same year, Douglass arranged for his address to be printed by the Baltimore-based publishers, Thomas and Evans, with an artistic rendering of John Howe Kent's original photograph, the same portrait which he had included as the frontispiece to the 1892 edition of *Life and Times*, reproduced on the front cover. As the full and complete transcription of his speech which Douglass himself commissioned and authorized, we reproduce the pamphlet version of *Lessons of the Hour* in this Oxford World's Classics edition for the first time.

As *Life and Times* is accompanied by a long and complex publishing history, so *Lessons of the Hour* exists in multiple published and unpublished editions. Working tirelessly to author the speech and pamphlet versions of his address, Douglass produced numerous draft manuscripts and typescripts. These surviving works have all been digitized as part of the Frederick Douglass Papers and are available for consultation at the Library of Congress website.[1] As Douglass' *Life and Times* is a powerful memorial to the 'conflict between the spirit of liberty and the spirit of slavery' (p. 451) that had in no way lessened its grip on U.S. society, so *Lessons of the Hour* is a searing indictment of the nefarious rise not only 'of the spirit of bondage' but of the 'spirit of mastery' on the nation in the closing decades of the nineteenth century.[2] Just a year before his death, Douglass predicted the 'damaging and distressing' acts of white supremacist disenfranchisement

---

[1] See Frederick Douglass, 'Lessons of the Hour—8 Folders', Speech, Article and Book File, Frederick Douglass Papers, Manuscripts Division, Library of Congress, Washington, D.C.

[2] In some of the unpublished manuscript and typescript drafts of 'Lessons of the Hour' held in the Frederick Douglass Papers at the Library of Congress, Douglass rephrases his condemnation of 'the spirit of bondage' to his denunciation of the 'spirit of mastery'.

and discrimination, no less than of 'misrepresentation and persecution', that were to continue to be perpetrated against his 'long-suffering people'. A powerful work of protest, *Lessons of the Hour* is Douglass' blistering denunciation of a white racist 'ruling class' that unforgivably and ignorantly believed that the United States was still the 'white man's country' as a nation dominated by a white persecutory government which 'did not consider that the black man had any rights which the white men were bound to respect' (p. 534).

Newly accompanied by the extended title, *Lessons of the Hour In Which He Discusses The Various Aspects of the So-Called, But Mis-Called, Negro Problem*, when this address was published in pamphlet form, Douglass' determination to interrogate white racist constructions of the 'mis-called negro problem' lays bare his self-appointed role as a spokesperson for, and defender of, his misrepresented, persecuted and 'long-suffering people'. He provides hard-hitting confirmation of his powerful realization he had expressed just two years earlier in *Life and Times* that 'I find myself summoned again by the popular voice and by what is called the negro problem, to come a second time upon the witness stand and give evidence upon disputed points concerning myself and my emancipated brothers and sisters who, though free, are yet oppressed and are in as much need of an advocate as before they were set free' (p. 427). A lifelong 'witness' and 'advocate' for the rights of his 'brothers and sisters' who 'though free' were still 'oppressed', Douglass' *Lessons of the Hour* is an unequivocal testament to his determination to speak for and defend the civil rights of 'my emancipated brothers and sisters'. In this emotionally and politically hardhitting social justice address, he proved he had lost none of his powers as an anti-racist activist and anti-discrimination campaigner in his final years.

Ever the 'watchman' on the 'walls' of 'my people' for 'more than fifty years'[3] here he voices his conviction that the 'mis-called, negro problem' is nothing less than the nefarious work of white U.S. supremacist prejudicial and persecutory propagandists. As he had explained in a speech he delivered a year earlier in 1893, 'There is no Negro problem.'[4] Rather, he was under no illusion that the actual and real 'problem is whether the American people have honesty enough, loyalty enough, honor enough, patriotism enough to live up to their Constitution'.[5] While Douglass dedicated his life to the impassioned defense of his 'long-suffering people', he

---

[3] Douglass, 'Blessings of Liberty and Education,' 3 September 1894.

[4] Frederick Douglass, 'Colored People's Day at the World Columbian Exposition', 25 August 1893, *Chicago Tribune*, 26 August 1893. Rpt. John R. McKivigan and Heather L. Kaufman, eds, *In the Words of Frederick Douglass: Quotations from Liberty's Champion* (Ithaca: Cornell University Press, 2012), 65.

[5] Ibid.

remained the unequivocal accuser, denouncer, and interrogator of the immorality, barbarism, and savagery of an ignorant and unjust white 'American people' who refused to 'live up to' the human rights principles of their political 'Constitution'. For Douglass and all Black freedom-fighters and their allies working for equal rights at the turn of the century, the 'lessons of the hour' were the 'lessons' of social justice, equal rights, and a respect for human life that had yet to be learned by a white U.S. 'ruling class' that continued to dedicate itself to supremacist acts of racist torture, abuse, disenfranchisement, and murder against Black lives.

'Not a breeze comes to us now from the late rebellious States that is not tainted and freighted with negro blood' (p. 524), Douglass painfully communicates to his audiences in *Lessons of the Hour*. Condemning the emotionally and physically traumatizing atrocities that were committed against his 'long-suffering people' in every 'hour' of every day, he exposes white supremacist acts of 'mob violence and murder' as 'not only a disgrace and scandal to that particular section but a menace to the peace and security of the people of the whole country' (p. 524). At the heart of Douglass' protest against white acts of barbarity is his condemnation of 'lynch law' (p. 525), an inhumane practice that had become widespread in the U.S. in the decades following the Civil War. A murderous ritual according to which untold numbers of Black people of all ages and genders were tortured and killed by white 'American people', 'lynch law' was illegally instituted and immorally justified by white 'mobocratic murderers' on the 'old thread-bare lie that Negro men rape white women'.[6] Warring against any and all white supremacist racist myths concerning Black manhood, Douglass dismisses these persecutory allegations as nothing more than the reprehensible delusions and criminal lies invented by self-serving white racist mobs as a quick and easy way to defend their monstrous desire for 'negro blood'. 'I reject the charge brought against the negro as a class,' he maintains. He again takes to the 'witness stand' to state that 'all through the late war', Black men were 'never accused of assault, insult, or an attempt to commit an assault upon any white woman in the whole South' (p. 529). For Douglass, whether he was writing in the 1840s or 1890s, Black male innocence was categorical confirmation of white male guilt.

In powerful vindication of the lifelong struggles of his 'brothers and sisters' who were fighting for their rights not only to a life but even to an existence in a white supremacist U.S. society, Douglass was only too well aware that the 'old thread-bare lie that Negro men rape white women' was

[6] Ida B. Wells-Barnett, *Southern Horrors: Lynch Law in All Its Phases* (New York: New York Age Print, 1892), n.p. Available online: https://www.gutenberg.org/files/14975/14975-h/14975-h.htm

an unfounded white racist 'charge' that was 'not so much against the crime itself, as against the color of the man alleged to be guilty of it' (p. 533). In *Lessons of the Hour*, Douglass, a self-liberated freedom-fighter who had been born to an enslaved mother and an unnamed white male enslaver during 'the hell of unending slavery,' dedicated himself to the traumatizing work of exposing the centuries of sexual violence that had been committed against untold generations of enslaved people by untold generations of enslaving white men. 'Slavery itself, you will remember, was a system of legalized outrage upon the black women of the South' (p. 533), he recalls only to remind his audiences of the unforgivable injustice that 'no white man was ever shot, burned, or hanged for availing himself of all the power that slavery gave him at this point' (p. 533). A hard-hitting condemnation of white racist acts of 'legalized outrage' in pre- and post- Civil War eras, Douglass is immovable in his belief that all acts of white male violence signalled no new departure but were in the heartbreaking tradition of hundreds of years of institutionalized rape as committed against the 'black women of the South'. Bearing witness to the centuries-long yet repeatedly hidden, denied, and sanitized history of white 'mobocratic murderers' who had not only raped but had 'shot', 'burned', and 'hung' Black people during and after the legal end of slavery, Douglass assumes the role of social justice educator for his white audiences. According to his human rights philosophy, the one and only 'lesson of the hour' the white 'American people' needed to learn was a lesson in which they faced up to, recognized, took full responsibility for, and personally confessed to their acts of unparalleled barbarity, murderous cruelty, unrivaled savagery, and unimaginable brutality.

'We are not, in this case, dealing with men in their natural condition', Douglass is careful to stipulate in *Lessons of the Hour*, 'but with men brought up in the exercise of arbitrary power' (p. 534). The self-evident antithesis of 'honorable men and good citizens', he condemns the dominant character traits of these white 'mobocratic murderers' by stating, 'We are dealing with men whose ideas, habits and customs are entirely different from those of ordinary men' (p. 534). For all white audiences, north and south, who were, at worst, apologists for, or at best disbelievers of, the acts of 'mob violence and murder' committed by white 'mobocratic murderers', Douglass teaches them a lesson they will never forget. Stating that it is 'quite gratuitous to assume that the principles that apply to other men apply to the Southern murderers of the negro' (p. 534), he cuts to the heart of 'the mistake of the Northern people', by calling them to account for endorsing an unforgivable error. 'They do not see that the rules resting upon the justice and benevolence of human nature do not apply to the mobocrats, or to those who were educated in the habits and customs of a slave-holding community' (p. 534), he urges. In *Lessons of the Hour*,

Douglass holds white northern ignorance to political and moral account when it comes to white southern racists and their acts of lawless torture and murder against innocent Black lives.

As a man who had lived the first two decades of his life in 'the hell black system of slavery' when he was himself personally subjected to repeated acts of persecution, torture, and violence at the hands of white male enslavers, Douglass defies any one to disagree with him by insisting that 'What these habits are I have a right to know, both in theory and in practice' (p. 534). According to his radical philosophy of equal human rights as born of his personal experience as well as his pioneering theoretical formulation, white 'Northern people' who were listening to or reading his address had no choice but to mend the errors of their ways by paying due and careful heed to his incisive assessment that white southerners 'have had among them for centuries a peculiar institution, and that peculiar institution has stamped them as a peculiar people' (p. 534). As a centuries-long institution in which white enslavers possessed every form of power—legal, financial, physical, psychological, sexual, emotional, and spiritual—over enslaved people of all genders and ages, he commands his audiences not only to comprehend but to acknowledge and directly confront the devastating reality that 'Their institutions have taught them no respect for human life and especially the life of the negro' (p. 534). Never one to sanitize or dilute white racist histories of persecution and oppression either during slavery or in its traumatizing aftermath, Douglass exposes the jugular vein of white barbaric cruelty and murderous tyranny by confiding, 'A dead negro is with them a common jest' (p. 534).

In the decades following the end of legal slavery and in the final years before his death, Douglass refused to shy away from the traumatizing reality not only that 'the condition of the emancipated is wretched and deplorable' (p. 542) but that 'the negro is in some respects, and in some localities, in a worse condition today than in the time of slavery' (p. 542). However, he purposefully breaks away from, challenges, and sets at naught any and all white racist assessments as endorsed by an unjust white 'American people' who continued to fail to live up to the egalitarian principles of the Constitution by willfully and ignorantly 'ascrib[ing] this condition to emancipation'. Douglass defies anyone to disagree with him by confirming that for his 'long-suffering people' fighting to survive in a U.S. society politically and legally dominated by white 'mobocratic murderers' for whom 'A dead negro' is a 'common jest', there can be no doubt that 'the blame for this condition does not rest upon emancipation, but upon slavery'. As he had confided in *Life and Times* regarding the unending 'conflict between the spirit of liberty and the spirit of slavery', the persecutions, tortures, and killings endured by his 'brothers and sisters' were 'not the result of emancipation, but the defeat of emancipation'. For the 'peculiar' descendants of a 'peculiar' people who had lived as white enslavers exercising all rights of arbitrary tyranny and abusive power over enslaved Black people over centuries, Douglass was only too well aware that the cause for the ongoing discriminations, disenfranchisements, and murders experienced by Black people was 'not the work of the spirit of liberty, but the work of the spirit of bondage, and of the determination of slavery to perpetuate itself, if not under one form, then under another'. For Douglass campaigning for equal human rights and justice for 'my people' in *Lessons of the Hour* only a year before his death, the war waged on not only to defeat the 'spirit of bondage' but to defend the 'spirit of liberty'.

Working to annihilate all persecutory trace of the 'spirit of bondage' from the prejudiced minds, hearts, behaviors, and politics of white racist audiences living in all areas of the U.S. nation in *Lessons of the Hour*, Douglass sought to inspire them to a shared recognition of the life-giving force of the 'spirit of liberty'. 'Put away your race prejudice,' he commanded his white racist listeners to whom he issued the following social justice demands: 'Banish the idea that one class must rule over another. Recognize the fact that the rights of the humblest citizen are as worthy of protection as are those of the highest' (p. 549). In vindication of his conviction that there was 'no negro problem' but only a white 'American people problem', he counsels his white audiences that it is only by heeding his equal human rights demands that they will 'no longer' be guilty of 'evading the claims of justice' with the immediate result that there will 'be no negro problem to vex the South, or to vex the nation' as 'your problem will be solved' (p. 547). As Douglass argues, it is only when the U.S. nation is no longer the 'white man's country' but is instead a nation with 'no race prejudice' that it will be newly possible to secure the 'protection' of the 'rights' of every 'humble citizen' and to usher in a new egalitarian social order as 'based upon the eternal principles of truth, justice and humanity'. As Douglass confides to his white listeners, it is then and only then, that, 'your Republic will stand and flourish forever' (p. 549). As of writing in the first decades of the twenty-first century, the fate of the 'Republic' remains at risk as a nation that has yet to live up to Douglass' vision of the United States as a country 'based upon the eternal principles of truth, justice and humanity'.

A revolutionary blueprint and human rights manifesto, *Lessons of the Hour* lives on as Douglass' call to arms for all present and future Black freedom-fighters and their allies. To the day that he died, Frederick Douglass battled for all freedoms. He lived his life as a powerful 'memorial' for the inspiration of 'my people' and as a last will and testament to his undying conviction, 'We have a fight on our hands right here, a fight for the whole race' (p. 541).

## Lessons of the Hour

Friends and Fellow Citizens:—

No man should come before an audience like the one by whose presence I am now honored, without a noble object and a fixed and earnest purpose. I think that, in whatever else I may be deficient, I have the qualifications indicated, to speak to you this evening. I am here to speak for, and to defend, so far as I can do so within the bounds of truth, a long-suffering people, and one just now subject to much misrepresentation and persecution. Charges are at this time preferred against them, more damaging and distressing than any which they have been called upon to meet since their emancipation.

I propose to give you a colored man's view of the unhappy relations at present existing between the white and colored people of the Southern States of our union. We have had the Southern white man's view of the subject. It has been presented with abundant repetition and with startling emphasis, colored by his peculiar environments. We have also had the Northern white man's view tempered by time, distance from the scene, and his higher civilization. This kind of evidence may be considered by some as all-sufficient upon which to found an intelligent judgment of the whole matter in controversy, and that therefore my testimony is not needed. But experience has taught us that it is sometimes wise and necessary to have more than the testimony of two witnesses to bring out the whole truth, especially is this the case where one of the witnesses has a powerful motive for concealing or distorting the facts in any given case. You must not, therefore, be surprised if my version of the Southern question shall widely differ from both the North and the South, and yet I shall fearlessly submit my testimony to the candid judgment of all who hear me. I shall do so in the firm belief that my testimony is true. There is one thing, however, in which I think we shall all agree at the start. It is that the so-called, but mis-called, negro problem is one of the most important and urgent subjects that can now engage public attention. It is worthy of the most earnest consideration of every patriotic American citizen. Its solution involves the honor or dishonor, glory or shame, happiness or misery of the whole American people. It involves more. It touches deeply not only the good name and fame of the Republic, but its highest moral welfare and its permanent safety. Plainly enough the peril it involves is great, obvious and increasing, and should be removed without delay.

The presence of eight millions of people in any section of this country constituting an aggrieved class, smarting under terrible wrongs, denied the exercise of the commonest rights of humanity, and regarded by the ruling class in that section, as outside of the government, outside of the law, and outside of society; having nothing in common with the people with whom they live, the sport of mob violence and murder is not only a disgrace and scandal to that particular section but a menace to the peace and security of the people of the whole country.

I have waited patiently but anxiously to see the end of the epidemic of mob law and persecution now prevailing at the South. But the indications are not hopeful, great and terrible as have been its ravages in the past, it now seems to be increasing not only in the number of its victims, but in its frantic rage and savage extravagance. Lawless vengeance is beginning to be visited upon white men as well as black. Our newspapers are daily disfigured by its ghastly horrors. It is no longer local, but national; no longer confined to the South, but has invaded the North. The contagion is spreading, extending and over-leaping geographical lines and state boundaries, and if permitted to go on it threatens to destroy all respect for law and order not only in the South, but in all parts of our country—North as well as South. For certain it is, that crime allowed to go on unresisted and unarrested will breed crime. When the poison of anarchy is once in the air, like the pestilence that walketh in the darkness,* the winds of heaven will take it up and favor its diffusion. Though it may strike down the weak to-day, it will strike down the strong to-morrow.

Not a breeze comes to us now from the late rebellious States that is not tainted and freighted with negro blood. In its thirst for blood and its rage for vengeance, the mob has blindly, boldly and defiantly supplanted sheriffs, constables and police. It has assumed all the functions of civil authority. It laughs at legal processes, courts and juries, and its red-handed murderers range abroad unchecked and unchallenged by law or by public opinion. Prison walls and iron bars are no protection to the innocent or guilty, if the mob is in pursuit of negroes accused of crime. Jail doors are battered down in the presence of unresisting jailors, and the accused, awaiting trial in the courts of law are dragged out and hanged, shot, stabbed or burned to death as the blind and irresponsible mob may elect.

We claim to be a Christian country and a highly civilized nation, yet, I fearlessly affirm that there is nothing in the history of savages to surpass the blood chilling horrors and fiendish excesses perpetrated against the colored people by the so-called enlightened and Christian people of the South. It is commonly thought that only the lowest and most disgusting birds and beasts, such as buzzards, vultures and hyenas, will gloat over and prey upon dead bodies, but the Southern mob in its rage feeds its vengeance by shooting, stabbing and burning when their victims are dead.

Now the special charge against the negro by which this ferocity is justified, and by which mob law is defended by good men North and South, is alleged to be assaults by negroes upon white women. This charge once fairly started, no matter by whom or in what manner, whether well or ill-founded, whether true or false, is certain to subject the accused to immediate death. It is nothing, that in the case there may be a mistake as to identity. It is nothing that the victim pleads 'not guilty'. It is nothing that he only asks for time to establish his innocence. It is nothing that the accused is of fair reputation and his accuser is of an abandoned character. It is nothing that the majesty of the law is defied and insulted; no time is allowed for defence or explanation; he is bound with cords, hurried off amid the frantic yells and cursing of the mob to the scaffold and under its shadow he is tortured till by pain or promises, he is made to think he can possibly gain time or save his life by confession, and then whether innocent or guilty, he is shot, hanged, stabbed or burned to death amid the wild shouts of the mob. When the will of the mob has been accomplished, when its thirst for blood has been quenched, when its victim is speechless, silent and dead, his mobocratic accusers and murderers of course have the ear of the world all to themselves, and the world generally approves their verdict.

Such then is the state of Southern civilization in its relation to the colored citizens of that section and though the picture is dark and terrible I venture to affirm that no man North or South can deny the essential truth of the picture.

Now it is important to know how this state of affairs is viewed by the better classes of the Southern States. I will tell you, and I venture to say if our hearts were not already hardened by familiarity with such crimes against the negro, we should be shocked and astonished by the attitude of these so-called better classes of the Southern people and their lawmakers. With a few noble exceptions the upper classes of the South are in full sympathy with the mob and its deeds. There are few earnest words uttered against the mob or its deeds. Press, platform and pulpit are either generally silent or they openly apologize for the mob. The mobocratic murderers are not only permitted to go free, untried and unpunished, but are lauded and applauded as honorable men and good citizens, the guardians of Southern women. If lynch law is in any case condemned, it is only condemned in one breath, and excused in another.

The great trouble with the negro in the South is, that all presumptions are against him. A white man has but to blacken his face and commit a crime, to have some negro lynched in his stead. An abandoned woman has only to start the cry that she has been insulted by a black man, to have him arrested and summarily murdered by the mob. Frightened and tortured by his captors, confused into telling crooked stories about his whereabouts at the time when the alleged crime was committed and the death penalty is at once inflicted, though his story may be but the incoherency of ignorance or distraction caused by terror.

Now in confirmation of what I have said of the better classes of the South, I have before me the utterances of some of the best people of that section, and also the testimony of one from the North, a lady, from whom, considering her antecedents, we should have expected a more considerate, just and humane utterance.

In a late number of the 'Forum' Bishop Haygood,* author of the 'Brother in Black,' says that 'The most alarming fact is, that execution by lynching has ceased to surprise us. The burning of a human being for any crime, it is thought, is a horror that does not occur outside of the Southern States or the American Union, yet unless assaults by negroes come to an end, there will most probably be still further display of vengeance that will shock the world, and men who are just will consider the provocation.'

In an open letter addressed to me by ex-Governor Chamberlain,* of South Carolina, and published in the 'Charleston News and Courier,' a letter which I have but lately seen, in reply to an article of mine on the subject published in the 'North American Review,'* the ex-Governor says: 'Your denunciation of the South on this point is directed exclusively, or nearly so, against the application of lynch law for the punishment of one crime, or one sort of crime, the existence, I suppose, I might say the prevalence of this crime at the South is undeniable. But I read your (my) article in vain for any special denunciation of the crime itself. As you say your people are lynched, tortured and burned for assault on white women. As you value your own good fame and safety as a race, stamp out the infamous crime.' He further says, the way to stop lynching is to stamp out the crime.

And now comes the sweet voice of a Northern woman, of Southern principles, in the same tone and the same accusation, the good Miss Frances Willard, of the W.C.T.U.* She says in a letter now before me, 'I pity the Southerner. The problem on their hands is immeasurable. The colored race,' she says, 'multiplies like the locusts of Egypt. The safety of woman, of childhood, of the home, is menaced in a thousand localities at this moment, so that men dare not go beyond the sight of their own roof tree.'* Such then is the crushing indictment drawn up against the Southern negroes, drawn up, too, by persons who are perhaps the fairest and most humane of the negro's accusers. But even they paint him as a moral monster ferociously invading the sacred rights of women and endangering the homes of the whites.

The crime they allege against the negro, is the most revolting which men can commit. It is a crime that awakens the intensest abhorrence and invites mankind to kill the criminal on sight. This charge thus brought against the negro, and as constantly reiterated by his enemies, is not merely against the individual culprit, as would be in the case with an individual culprit of any other race, but it is in a large measure a charge against the colored race as such. It throws over every colored man a mantle of odium and sets upon him a mark for popular hate, more distressing than the mark set upon the first murderer. It points him out as an object of suspicion and avoidance. Now it is in this form that you and I, and all of us, are required to meet it and refute it, if that can be done. In the opinion of some of us, it is thought that it were well to say nothing about it, that the least said about it the better. In this opinion I do not concur. Taking this charge in its broad and comprehensive sense in which it is presented, and as now stated, I feel that it ought to be met, and as a colored man, I am grateful for the opportunity now afforded me to meet it. For I believe it can be met and successfully met. I am of opinion that a people too spiritless to defend themselves are not worth defending.

Without boasting, on this broad issue as now presented, I am ready to confront ex-Governor Chamberlain, Bishop Fitzgerald,* Bishop Haygood, and Miss Frances Willard and all others, singly or altogether, without any doubt of the result.

But I want to be understood at the outset. I do not pretend that negroes are saints or angels. I do not deny that they are capable of committing the crime imputed to them, but I utterly deny that they are any more addicted to the commission of that crime than is true of any other variety of the human family. In entering upon my argument, I may be allowed to say, that I appear here this evening not as the defender of any man guilty of this atrocious crime, but as the defender of the colored people as a class.

In answer to the terrible indictment, thus read, and speaking for the colored people as a class, I, in their stead, here and now plead not guilty and shall submit my case with confidence of acquittal by good men and women North and South.

It is the misfortune of the colored people in this country that the sins of the few are visited upon the many, and I am here to speak for the many whose reputation is put in peril by the sweeping charge in question. With General Grant and every other honest man, my motto is, 'Let no guilty man escape.'* But while I am here to say this, I am here also to say, let no innocent man be condemned and killed by the mob, or crushed under the weight of a charge of which he is not guilty.

You will readily see that the cause I have undertaken to support, is not to be maintained by any mere confident assertions or general denials. If I had no better ground to stand upon than this I would leave the field of controversy and give up the colored man's cause at once to his able accusers. I am aware however, that I am here to do in some measure what the masters of logic say cannot be done,—prove a negative.

Of course, I shall not be able to succeed in doing the impossible, but this one thing I can and will do. I can and will show that there are sound reasons for doubting and denying this horrible and hell-black charge of rape as the peculiar crime of the colored people of the South. My doubt and denial are based upon two fundamental and invincible grounds.

The first is, the well established and well tested character of the negro on the very point upon which he is now violently and persistently accused. The second ground for my doubt and denial is based upon what I know of the character and antecedents of the men and women who bring this charge against him. I undertake to say that the strength of this position will become more manifest as I proceed with my argument.

At the outset I deny that a fierce and frenzied mob is or ought to be deemed a competent witness against any man accused of any crime whatever. The ease with which a mob can be collected and the slight causes by which it may be set in motion, and the elements of which it is composed, deprives its testimony of the qualities that should inspire confidence and command belief. It is moved by impulses utterly unfavorable to an impartial statement of the truth. At the outset, therefore, I challenge the credibility of the mob, and as the mob is the main witness in the case against the negro, I appeal to the common sense of mankind in support of my challenge. It is the mob that brings this charge, and it is the mob that arraigns, condemns and executes, and it is the mob that the country has accepted as its witness.

Again, I impeach and discredit the veracity of southern men generally, whether mobocrats or otherwise, who now openly and deliberately nullify and violate the provisions of the constitution of their country, a constitution, which they have solemnly sworn to support and execute. I apply to them the legal maxim, 'False in one, false in all.'*

Again I arraign the negro's accuser on another ground, I have no confidence in the truthfulness of men who justify themselves in cheating the negro out of his constitutional right to vote. The men, who either by false returns, or by taking advantage of his illiteracy or surrounding the ballot-box with obstacles and sinuosities intended to bewilder him and defeat his rightful exercise of the elective franchise, are men who are not to be believed on oath. That this is done in the Southern States is not only admitted, but openly defended and justified by so-called honorable men inside and outside of Congress.

Just this kind of fraud in the South is notorious. I have met it face to face. It was boldly defended and advocated a few weeks ago in a solemn paper by Prof. Weeks,* a learned North Carolinian, in my hearing. His paper was one of the able papers read before one of the World's Auxiliary Congresses at Chicago.

Now men who openly defraud the negro by all manner of artifice and boast of it in the face of the world's civilization, as was done at Chicago,

I affirm that they are not to be depended upon for truth in any case whatever, where the rights of the negro are involved. Their testimony in the case of any other people than the negro, against whom they should thus commit fraud would be instantly and utterly discredited, and why not the same in this case? Every honest man will see that this point is well taken, and I defy any argument that would drive me from this just contention. It has for its support common sense, common justice, common honesty, and the best sentiment of mankind, and has nothing to oppose it but a vulgar popular prejudice against the colored people of our country, which prejudice strikes men with moral blindness and renders them incapable of seeing any distinction between right and wrong.

But I come to a stronger position. I rest my conclusion not merely upon general principles, but upon well known facts. I reject the charge brought against the negro as a class, because all through the late war, while the slave masters of the South were absent from their homes in the field of rebellion, with bullets in their pockets, treason in their hearts, broad blades in their blood stained hands, seeking the life of the nation, with the vile purpose of perpetuating the enslavement of the negro, their wives, their daughters, their sisters and their mothers were left in the absolute custody of these same negroes, and during all those long four years of terrible conflict, when the negro had every opportunity to commit the abominable crime now alleged against him, there was never a single instance of such crime reported or charged against him. He was never accused of assault, insult, or an attempt to commit an assault upon any white woman in the whole South. A fact like this, although negative, speaks volumes and ought to have some weight with the American people.

Then, again on general principles, I do not believe the charge because it implies an improbable, if not an impossible, change in the mental and moral character and composition of the negro. It implies a change wholly inconsistent with well known facts of human nature. It is a contradiction to well known human experience. History does not present an example of such a transformation in the character of any class of men so extreme, so unnatural and so complete as is implied in this charge. The change is too great and the period too brief. Instances may be cited where men fall like stars from heaven, but such is not the usual experience. Decline in the moral character of a people is not sudden, but gradual. The down ward steps are marked at first by degrees and by increasing momentum from bad to worse. Time is an element in such chances, and I contend that the negroes of the South have not had time to experience this great change and reach this lower depth of infamy. On the contrary, in point of fact, they have been and still are, improving and ascending to higher levels of moral and social worth.

Again, I do not believe it and utterly deny it, because those who bring the charge do not, and dare not, give the negro a chance to be heard in his own defence. He is not allowed to explain any part of his alleged offense. He is not allowed to vindicate his own character or to criminate the character and motives of his accusers. Even the mobocrats themselves admit that it would be fatal to their purpose to have the character of his accusers brought into court. They pretend to a delicate regard for the feelings of the parties assaulted, and therefore object to giving a fair trial to the accused. The excuse in this case is contemptible. It is not only mock modesty but mob modesty. Men who can collect hundreds and thousands, if we may believe them, and can spread before them in the tempest and whirlwind of vulgar passion, the most disgusting details of crime with the names of women, with the alleged offense, should not be allowed to shelter themselves under any pretense of modesty. Such a pretense is absurd and shameless. Who does not know that the modesty of womanhood is always an object for protection in a court of law? Who does not know that a lawless mob composed in part of the basest of men can have no such respect for the modesty of women as a court of law? No woman need be ashamed to confront one who has insulted or assaulted her in a court of law. Besides innocence does not hesitate to come to the rescue of justice.

Again, I do not believe it, and deny it because if the evidence were deemed sufficient to bring the accused to the scaffold, through the action of an impartial jury, there could be, and would be, no objection to having the alleged offender tried in conformity to due process of law.

Any pretence that a guilty negro, especially one guilty of the crime now charged, would in any case be permitted to escape condign* punishment, is an insult to common sense. Nobody believes or can believe such a thing as escape possible, in a country like the South, where public opinion, the laws, the courts, the juries, and the advocates are all known to be against him, he could hardly escape if innocent. I repeat, therefore, I do not believe it, because I know, and you know, that a passionate and violent mob bent upon taking life, from the nature of the case, is not a more competent and trustworthy body to determine the guilt or innocence of a negro accused in such a case, than is a court of law. I would not, and you would not, convict a dog on such testimony.

But I come to another fact, and an all-important fact, bearing upon this case. You will remember that during all the first years of re-construction and long after the war when the Southern press and people found it necessary to invent, adopt, and propagate almost every species of falsehood to create sympathy for themselves and to formulate an excuse for gratifying their brutal instincts, there was never a charge then made against a negro involving an assault upon any white woman or upon any little white child.

During all this time the white women and children were absolutely safe. During all this time there was no call for Miss Willard's pity, or Bishop Haygood's defense of burning negroes to death.

You will remember also that during this time the justification for the murder of negroes was said to be negro conspiracies, insurrections, schemes to murder all the white people, to burn the town, and commit violence generally. These were the excuses then depended upon, but never a word was then said or whispered about negro outrages upon white women and children. So far as the history of that time is concerned, white women and children were absolutely safe, and husbands and fathers could leave home without the slightest anxiety on account of their families.

But when events proved that no such conspiracies; no such insurrections as were then pretended to exist and were paraded before the world in glaring head-lines, had ever existed or were even meditated; when these excuses had run their course and served their wicked purpose; when the huts of negroes had been searched, and searched in vain, for guns and ammunition to prove these charges, and no evidence was found, when there was no way open thereafter to prove these charges against the negro and no way to make the North believe in these excuses for murder, they did not even then bring forward the present allegation against the negro. They, however, went on harassing and killing just the same. But this time they based the right thus to kill on the ground that it was necessary to check the domination and supremacy of the negro and to secure the absolute rule of the Anglo-Saxon race.

It is important to notice that there has been three distinct periods of persecution of negroes in the South, and three distinct sets of excuses for persecution. They have come along precisely in the order in which they were most needed. First you remember it was insurrection. When that was worn out, negro supremacy became the excuse. When that is worn out, now it is assault upon defenseless women. I undertake to say, that this order and periodicity is significant and means something and should not be over-looked. And now that negro supremacy and negro domination are no longer defensible as an excuse for negro persecutions, there has come in due course, this heart-rending cry about the white women and little white children of the South.

Now, my friends, I ask what is the rational explanation of this singular omission of this charge in the two periods preceding the present? Why was not the charge made at that time as now? The negro was the same then as to-day. White women and children were the same then as to-day. Temptations to wrong doing were the same then as to-day. Why then was not this dreadful charge brought forward against the negro in war times and why was it not brought forward in reconstruction times?

I will tell you, or you, yourselves, have already answered the question. The only rational answer is that there was no foundation for such a charge or that the charge itself was either not thought of or was not deemed necessary to excuse the lawless violence with which the negro was then pursued and killed. The old charges already enumerated were deemed all sufficient. This new charge has now swallowed up all the old ones and the reason is obvious.

Things have changed since then, old excuses were not available and the negro's accusers have found it necessary to change with them. The old charges are no longer valid. Upon them the good opinion of the North and of mankind cannot be secured. Honest men no longer believe in the worn-out stories of insurrection. They no longer believe that there is just ground to apprehend negro supremacy. Time and events have swept away these old refuges of lies. They did their work in their day, and did it with terrible energy and effect, but they are now cast aside as useless. The altered times and circumstances have made necessary a sterner, stronger, and more effective justification of Southern barbarism, and hence, according to my theory, we now have to look into the face of a more shocking and blasting charge than either negro supremacy or insurrection or that of murder itself.

This new charge has come at the call of new conditions, and nothing could have been hit upon better calculated to accomplish its purpose. It clouds the character of the negro with a crime the most revolting, and is fitted to drive from him all sympathy and all fair play and all mercy. It is a crime that places him outside of the pale of the law, and settles upon his shoulders a mantle of wrath and fire that blisters and burns into his very soul.

It is for this purpose, as I believe, that this new charge unthought of in the times to which I have referred, has been largely invited, if not entirely trumped up. It is for this purpose that it has been constantly reiterated and adopted. It was to blast and ruin the negro's character as a man and a citizen.

I need not tell you how thoroughly it has already done its wonted work. You may feel its malign influence in the very air. You may read it in the faces of men. It has cooled our friends. It has heated our enemies, and arrested in some measure the efforts that good men were wont to make for the colored man's improvement and elevation. It has deceived our friends at the North and many good friends at the South, for nearly all have in some measure accepted the charge as true. Its perpetual reiteration in our newspapers and magazines has led men and women to regard us with averted eyes, increasing hate and dark suspicion.

Some of the Southern papers have denounced me for my unbelief, in their new departure, but I repeat I do not believe it and firmly deny it. I reject it because I see in it, evidence of an invention, called into being by a well defined motive, a motive sufficient to stamp it as a gross expedient to justify murderous assault upon a long enslaved and hence a hated people.

I do not believe it because it bears on its face, the marks of being a make-shift for a malignant purpose. I reject it not only because it was sprung upon the country simultaneously with well-known efforts now being indus-triously made to degrade the negro by legislative enactments, and by repealing all laws for the protection of the ballot, and by drawing the color line in all railroad cars and stations and in all other public places in the South; but because I see in it a means of paving the way for our entire disfranchisement.

Again, I do not believe it, and deny it, because the charge is not so much against the crime itself, as against the color of the man alleged to be guilty of it. Slavery itself, you will remember, was a system of legalized outrage upon the black women of the South, and no white man was ever shot, burned, or hanged for availing himself of all the power that slavery gave him at this point.

Upon these grounds then,—grounds which I believe to be solid and immovable—I dare here and now in the capital of the nation and in the presence of Congress to reject it, and ask you and all just men to reject this horrible charge so frequently made and construed against the negro as a class.

To sum up my argument on this lynching business. It remains to be said that I have shown that the negro's accusers in this case have violated their oaths and have cheated the negro out of his vote; that they have robbed and defrauded the negro systematically and persistently, and have boasted of it. I have shown that when the negro had every opportunity to commit the crime now charged against him he was never accused of it by his bitterest enemies. I have shown that during all the years of reconstruction, when he was being murdered at Hamburg,* Yazoo,* New Orleans,* Copiah* and elsewhere, he was never accused of the crime now charged against him. I have shown that in the nature of things no such change in the character and composition of a people as this charge implies could have taken place in the limited period allowed for it. I have shown that those who accuse him dare not confront him in a court of law and have their witnesses subjected to proper legal inquiry. And in showing all this, and more, I have shown that they who charge him with this foul crime may be justly doubted and deemed unworthy of belief.

But I shall be told by many of my Northern friends that my argument, though plausible, is not conclusive. It will be said that the charges against the negro are specific and positive, and that there must be some foundation for them, because as they allege men in their normal condition do not shoot and hang their fellowmen who are guiltless of crime. Well! This assumption is very just, very charitable. I only ask something like the same justice and charity could be shown to the negro as well as to the mob. It is creditable to the justice and humanity of the good people of the North by whom it is entertained. They rightly assume that men do not shoot and hang their fellowmen without just cause. But the vice of their argument is in their assumption that the lynchers are like other men. The answer to that argument is what may be truly predicated of human nature under one condition is not what may be true of human nature under another. Uncorrupted human nature may shudder at the commission of such crimes as those of which the Southern mob is guilty.

But human nature uncorrupted is one thing and human nature corrupted and perverted by long abuse of irresponsible power, is quite another and different thing. No man can reason correctly on this question who reasons on the assumption that the lynchers are like ordinary men.

We are not, in this case, dealing with men in their natural condition, but with men brought up in the exercise of arbitrary power. We are dealing with men whose ideas, habits and customs are entirely different from those of ordinary men. It is, therefore, quite gratuitous to assume that the principles that apply to other men apply to the Southern murderers of the negro, and just here is the mistake of the Northern people. They do not see that the rules resting upon the justice and benevolence of human nature do not apply to the mobocrats, or to those who were educated in the habits and customs of a slave-holding community. What these habits are I have a right to know, both in theory and in practice.

I repeat: The mistake made by those who on this ground object to my theory of the charge against the negro, is that they overlook the natural effect and influence of the life, education and habits of the lynchers. We must remember that these people have not now and have never had any such respect for human life as is common to other men. They have had among them for centuries a peculiar institution, and that peculiar institution has stamped them as a peculiar people. They were not before the war, they were not during the war and have not been since the war in their spirit or in their civilization, a people in common with the people of the North. I will not here harrow up your feelings by detailing their treatment of Northern prisoners during the war. Their institutions have taught them no respect for human life and especially the life of the negro. It has in fact taught them absolute contempt for his life. The sacredness of life which ordinary men feel does not touch them anywhere. A dead negro is with them a common jest.

They care no more for a negro's right to live than they care for his rights to liberty, or his rights to the ballot. Chief Justice Taney told the exact truth about these people when he said: 'They did not consider that the black man had any rights which the white men were bound to respect.'* No man of the

South ever called in question that statement and they never will. They could always shoot, stab and burn the negro without any such remorse or shame as other men would feel after committing such a crime. Any Southern man who is honest and is frank enough to talk on the subject, will tell you that he has no such idea as we have of the sacredness of human life and especially, as I have said, of the life of the negro. Hence it is absurd to meet my arguments with the facts predicated of our common human nature.

I know I shall be charged with apologizing for criminals. Ex-Governor Chamberlain has already virtually done as much. But there is no foundation for any such charge. I affirm that neither I nor any other colored man of like standing with myself, has ever raised a finger or uttered a word in defense of any one really guilty of the dreadful crime now in question.

But, what I contend for, and what every honest man, black or white should contend for, is that when any man is accused of this or any other crime, of whatever name, nature, or extent, he shall have the benefit of a legal investigation; that he shall be confronted by his accusers; and that he shall through proper counsel, be able to question his accusers in open court and in open day-light so that his guilt or his innocence may be duly proved and established.

If this is to make me liable to the charge of apologizing for crime, I am not ashamed to be so charged. I dare to contend for the colored people of the United States that they are a law-abiding people, and I dare to insist upon it that they or any man, black or white, accused of crime, shall have a fair trial before he is punished.

Again, I cannot dwell too much upon the fact that colored people are much damaged by this charge. As an injured class we have a right to appeal from the judgment of the mob to the judgment of the law and the American people. Our enemies have known well where to strike and how to stab us most fatally. Owing to popular prejudice it has become the misfortune of the colored people of the South and of the North as well, to have as I have said, the sins of the few visited upon the many. When a white man steals, robs or murders, his crime is visited upon his own head alone. But not so with the black man. When he commits a crime the whole race is made to suffer the cause before us is an example. This unfairness confronts us not only here, but it confronts us everywhere else.

Even when American art undertakes to picture the types of the two races it invariably places in comparison not the best of both races as common fairness would dictate, but it puts side by side in glaring contrast the lowest type of the negro with the highest type of the white man and calls upon you to 'look upon this picture then upon that.'

When a black man's language is quoted, in order to belittle and degrade him, his ideas are put into the most grotesque and unreadable English, while the utterances of negro scholars and authors are ignored. A hundred white men will attend a concert of white negro minstrels with faces blackened with burnt cork, to one who will attend a lecture by an intelligent negro.

On this ground I have a criticism to make, even of the late World's Columbian Exposition. While I join with all other men in pronouncing the Exposition itself one of the grandest demonstrations of civilization that the world has ever seen, yet great and glorious as it was, it was made to show just this kind of unfairness and discrimination against the negro.*

As nowhere else in the world it was hoped that here the idea of human brotherhood would have been fully recognized and most gloriously illustrated. It should have been, and would have been, had it been what it professed to be, a World's Exposition. It was, however, in a marked degree an American Exposition. The spirit of American caste made itself conspicuously felt against the educated American negro, and to this extent, the Exposition was made simply an American Exposition and that in one of America's most illiberal features.

Since the day of Pentecost, there has never assembled in any one place or on any one occasion, a larger variety of peoples of all forms, features and colors, and all degrees of civilization, than was assembled at this World's Exposition. It was a grand ethnological lesson, a chance to study all likenesses and differences. Here were Japanese, Soudanese, Chinese, Cingalese, Syrians, Persians, Tunisians, Algerians, Egyptians, East Indians, Laplanders, Esquimaux, and as if to shame the educated negro of America, the Dahomeyans were there to exhibit their barbarism, and increase American contempt for the negro intellect. All classes and conditions were there save the educated American negro. He ought to have been there if only to show what American slavery and freedom have done for him. The fact that all other nations were there and there at their best, made his exclusion the more marked, and the more significant. People from abroad noticed the fact that while we have eight millions of colored people in the United States, many of them gentlemen and scholars, not one of them was deemed worthy to be appointed a Commissioner, or a member of an important committee, or a guide, or a guard on the Exposition grounds. What a commentary is this upon our boasted American liberty and American equality! It is a silence to be sure, but it is a silence that speaks louder than words. It says to the world that the colored people of America are deemed by Americans not within the compass of American law and of American civilization. It says to the lynchers and mobocrats of the South, go on in your hellish work of negro persecution. What you do to their bodies, we do to their souls.

I come now to the question of negro suffrage. It has come to be fashionable of late to ascribe much of the trouble at the South to ignorant negro suffrage. The great measure according suffrage to the negro recommended by General Grant and adopted by the loyal nation is now denounced as a blunder and a failure.* They would, therefore, in some way abridge and limit this right by imposing upon it an educational or some other qualification. Among those who take this view are Mr. John J. Ingalls,* and Mr. John M. Langston. They are both eloquent, both able, and both wrong. Though they are both Johns neither of them is to my mind a 'St. John' and not even a 'John the Baptist.' They have taken up an idea which they seem to think quite new, but which in reality is as old as despotism and about as narrow and selfish. It has been heard and answered a thousand times over. It is the argument of the crowned heads and privileged classes of the world. It is as good against our Republican form of government as it is against the negro. The wonder is that its votaries do not see its consequences. It does away with that noble and just idea of Abraham Lincoln, that our government should be a government of the people, by the people, and for the people, and for *all* the people.*

These gentlemen are very learned, very eloquent and very able, but I cannot follow them. Much learning has made them mad.* Education is great, but manhood is greater. The one is the principle, the other is the accident. Man was not made as an attribute to education, but education is an attribute to man. I say to these gentlemen, first protect the man and you will thereby protect education. I would not make illiteracy a bar to the ballot, but would make the ballot a bar to illiteracy. Take the ballot from the negro and you take from him the means and motives that make for education. Those who are already educated and are vested with political power and have thereby an advantage, will have a strong motive for refusing to divide that advantage with others, and least of all will they divide it with the negro to whom they would deny all right to participate in the government.

I, therefore, cannot follow these gentlemen in their proposition to limit suffrage to the educated alone. I would not make suffrage more exclusive, but more inclusive. I would not have it embrace merely the elite, but would include the lowly. I would not only include the men, I would gladly include the women, and make our government in reality as in name a government of the people and of the whole people.

But manifestly suffrage to the colored people is not the cause of the failure of good government, or the cause of trouble in the Southern States, but it is the lawless limitations of suffrage that makes the trouble.

Much thoughtless speech is heard about the ignorance of the negro in the South. But plainly enough it is not the ignorance of the negro, but the malevolence of his accusers, which is the real cause of Southern disorder.

The illiteracy of the negro has no part or lot in the disturbances there. They who contend for disfranchisement on this ground know, and know very well, that there is no truth whatever in their contention. To make out their case they must show that some oppressive and hurtful measure has been imposed upon the country by negro voters. But they cannot show any such thing.

The negro has never set up a separate party, never adopted a negro platform, never proclaimed or adopted a separate policy for himself or for the country. His assailants know that he has never acted apart from the whole American people. They know that he has never sought to lead, but has always been content to follow. They know that he has not made his ignorance the rule of his political conduct, but the intelligence of white people has always been his guide. They know that he has simply kept pace with the average intelligence of his age and country. They know that he has gone steadily along in the line of his politics with the most enlightened citizens of the country. They know that he has always voted with one or the other of the two great political parties. They know that if the votes of these parties have been guided by intelligence and patriotism, the same may be said for the vote of the negro. They ought to know, therefore, that it is a shame and an outrage upon common sense and common fairness to make the negro responsible, or his ignorance responsible, for any disorder and confusion that may reign in the Southern States. Yet, while any lie may be safely told against the negro and be credited, this lie will find eloquent mouths bold enough to tell it, and pride themselves upon their superior wisdom in denouncing the ignorant negro voter.

It is true that the negro once voted solidly for the candidates of the Republican party, but what if he did? He then only voted with John Mercer Langston, John J. Ingalls, John Sherman,* General Harrison,* Senator Hoar,* Henry Cabot Lodge,* and Governor McKinley,* and many of the most intelligent statesmen and patriots of whom this country can boast. The charge against him at this point is, therefore, utterly groundless. It is a mere pretense, a sham, an excuse for fraud and violence, for persecution and a cloak for popular prejudice.

The proposition to disfranchise the colored voter of the South in order to solve the race problem I hereby denounce as a mean and cowardly proposition, utterly unworthy of an honest, truthful and grateful nation. It is a proposition to sacrifice friends in order to conciliate enemies, to surrender the constitution to the late rebels for the lack of moral courage to execute its provisions. It says to the negro citizens, 'The Southern nullifiers have robbed you of a part of your rights, and as we are powerless and cannot help you, and wish to live on good terms with our Southern brethren, we propose to join your oppressors so that our practice shall be consistent within their theories. Your suffrage has been practically rendered a failure by violence, we now propose to make it a failure by law. Instead of conforming our practice to the theory of our government and the genius of our institutions, we now propose, as means of conciliation, to conform our practice to the theory of your oppressors.'

Than this, was there ever a surrender more complete, more cowardly or more base? Upon the statesman, black or white, who could dare to hint such a scheme of national debasement as a means of settling the race problem, I should inflict no punishment more severe than to keep him at home, and deprived of all legislative trusts forever.

Do not ask me what will be the final result of the so-called negro problem. I cannot tell you. I have sometimes thought that the American people are too great to be small, too just and magnanimous to oppress the weak, too brave to yield up the right to the strong, and too grateful for public services ever to forget them or fail to reward them. I have fondly hoped that this estimate of American character would soon cease to be contradicted or put in doubt. But the favor with which this cowardly proposition of disfranchisement has been received by public men, white and black, by Republicans as well as Democrats, has shaken my faith in the nobility of the nation. I hope and trust all will come out right in the end, but the immediate future looks dark and troubled. I cannot shut my eyes to the ugly facts before me.

Strange things have happened of late and are still happening. Some of these tend to dim the lustre of the American name, and chill the hopes once entertained for the cause of American liberty. He is a wiser man than I am, who can tell how low the moral sentiment of this republic may yet fall. When the moral sense of a nation begins to decline and the wheel of progress to roll backward, there is no telling how low the one will fall or where the other may stop. The downward tendency already manifest has swept away some of the most important safeguards. The Supreme Court has surrendered. State sovereignty is restored. It has destroyed the civil rights Bill, and converted the Republican party into a party of money rather than a party of morals, a party of things rather than a party of humanity and justice. We may well ask what next?

The pit of hell is said to be bottomless.* Principles which we all thought to have been firmly and permanently settled by the late war, have been boldly assaulted and overthrown by the defeated party. Rebel rule is now nearly complete in many States and it is gradually capturing the nation's Congress. The cause lost in the war, is the cause regained in peace, and the cause gained in war, is the cause lost in peace.

There was a threat made long ago by an American statesman, that the whole body of legislation enacted for the protection of American liberty and to secure the results of the war for the Union, should be blotted from the national statute book. That threat is now being sternly pursued, and may yet be fully realized. The repeal of the laws intended to protect the elective franchise has heightened the suspicion that Southern rule may yet become complete, though I trust, not permanent. There is no denying that the trend is in the wrong way at present. The late election, however, gives us hope that the loyal Republican party may return to its first born.*

But I come now to another proposition held up just now as a solution of the race problem, and this I consider equally unworthy with the one just disposed of. The two belong to the same low-bred family of ideas.

This proposition is to colonize the colored people of America in Africa, or somewhere else. Happily this scheme will be defeated, both by its impolicy and its impracticability. It is all nonsense to talk about the removal of eight millions of the American people from their homes in America to Africa. The expense and hardships, to say nothing of the cruelty of such a measure, would make success to such a measure impossible. The American people are wicked, but they are not fools, they will hardly be disposed to incur the expense, to say nothing of the injustice which this measure demands. Nevertheless, this colonizing scheme, unworthy as it is, of American statesmanship and American honor, and though full of mischief of the colored people, seems to have a strong hold on the public mind and at times has shown much life and vigor.

The bad thing about it is that it has now begun to be advocated by colored men of acknowledged ability and learning, and every little while some white statesman becomes its advocate. Those gentlemen will doubtless have their opinion of me; I certainly have mine of them. My opinion of them is that if they are sensible, they are insincere, and if they are sincere they are not sensible. They know, or they ought to know, that it would take more money than the cost of the late war, to transport even one-half of the colored people of the United States to Africa. Whether intentionally or not they are, as I think, simply trifling with an afflicted people. They urge them to look for relief, where they ought to know that relief is impossible. The only excuse they can make is that there is no hope for the negro here and that the colored people in America owe something to Africa.

This last sentimental idea makes colonization very fascinating to dreamers of both colors. But there is really for it no foundation.

They tell us that we owe something to our native land. But when the fact is brought to view, which should never be forgotten, that a man can only have one native land, and that is the land in which he was born, the bottom falls entirely out of this sentimental argument.

Africa, according to her advocates, is by no means modest in her demand upon us. She calls upon us to send her only our best men. She does not want our riff raff, but our best men. But these are just the men we want at home. It is true we have a few preachers and laymen with a missionary turn of mind who might be easily spared. Some who would possibly do as much good by going there as by staying here. But this is not the only colonization idea. Its advocates want not only the best, but millions of the best. They want the money to be voted by the United States Government to send them there.

Now I hold that the American negro owes no more to the negroes in Africa than he owes to the negroes in America. There are millions of needy people over there, but there are also millions of needy people over here as well, and the millions here need intelligent men of their numbers to help them, as much as intelligent men are needed in Africa. We have a fight on our hands right here, a fight for the whole race, and a blow struck for the negro in America is a blow struck for the negro in Africa. For until the negro is respected in America, he need not expect consideration elsewhere. All this native land talk is nonsense. The native land of the American negro is America. His bones, his muscles, his sinews, are all American. His ancestors for two hundred and seventy years have lived, and labored, and died on American soil, and millions of his posterity have inherited Caucasian blood.

It is competent, therefore, to ask, in view of this admixture, as well as in view of other facts, where the people of this mixed race are to go, for their ancestors are white and black, and it will be difficult to find their native land anywhere outside of the United States.

But the worse thing, perhaps, about this colonization nonsense is, that it tends to throw over the negro a mantle of despair. It leads him to doubt the possibility of his progress as an American citizen. It also encourages popular prejudice with the hope that by persecution or persuasion the negro can finally be driven from his natural home, while in the nature of the case, he must stay here, and will stay here and cannot well get away.

It tends to weaken his hold on one country while it can give him no rational hope of another. Its tendency is to make him dispondent and doubtful, where he should be made to feel assured and confident. It forces upon him the idea that he is forever doomed to be a stranger and sojourner in the land of his birth, and that he has no permanent abiding place here.

All this is hurtful, with such ideas constantly flaunted before him he cannot easily set himself to work to better his condition in such ways as are open to him here. It sets him to groping everlastingly after the impossible.

Every man who thinks at all must know that home is the fountain head, the inspiration, the foundation and main support not only of all social virtue, but of all motives to human progress and that no people can prosper or amount to much without a home. To have a home, the negro must have a country, and he is an enemy to the moral progress of the negro, whether he knows it or not, who calls upon him to break up his home in this country for an uncertain home in Africa.

But the agitation of this subject has a darker side still. It has already been given out that we may be forced to go at the point of the bayonet. I cannot say we shall not, but badly as I think of the tendency of our times, I do not think that American sentiment will ever reach a condition which will make the expulsion of the negro from the United States by such means possible.

Colonization is no solution of the race problem. It is an evasion. It is not repenting of wrong but putting out of sight the people upon whom wrong has been inflicted. Its reiteration and agitation only serve to fan the flame of popular prejudice and encourage the hope that in some way or other, in time or in eternity, those who hate the negro will get rid of him.

If the American people could endure the negro's presence while a slave, they certainly can and ought to endure his presence as a free-man. If they could tolerate him when he was a heathen, they might bear with him when he is a Christian, a gentleman and a scholar.

But woe to the South when it no longer has the strong arm of the negro to till its soil! And woe to the nation if it shall ever employ the sword to drive the negro from his native land!

Such a crime against justice, such a crime against gratitude, should it ever be attempted, would certainly bring a national punishment which would cause the earth to shudder. It would bring a stain upon the nation's honor, like the blood on Lady Macbeth's hand.* The waters of all the oceans would not suffice to wash out the infamy that such an act of ingratitude and cruelty would leave on the character of the American people.

Another mode of impeaching the wisdom of emancipation, and one that seems to give pleasure to our enemies, is, as they say, that the condition of the colored people of the South has been made worse; that freedom has made their condition worse.

The champions of this idea are the men who glory in the good old times when the slaves were under the lash and were bought and sold in the market with horses, sheep and swine. It is another way of saying that slavery is better than freedom; that darkness is better than light and that wrong is better than right. It is the American method of reasoning in all matters concerning the negro. It inverts everything; turns truth upside down and puts the case of the unfortunate negro wrong end foremost every time. There is, however, always some truth on their side.

When these false reasoners assert that the condition of the emancipated is wretched and deplorable, they tell in part the truth, and I agree with them. I even concur with them that the negro is in some respects, and in some localities, in a worse condition today than in the time of slavery, but I part with these gentlemen when they ascribe this condition to emancipation.

To my mind, the blame for this condition does not rest upon emancipation, but upon slavery. It is not the result of emancipation, but the defeat of emancipation. It is not the work of the spirit of liberty, but the work of the spirit of bondage, and of the determination of slavery to perpetuate itself, if not under one form, then under another. It is due to the folly of endeavoring to retain the new wine of liberty in the old bottles of slavery.* I concede the evil but deny the alleged cause.

The land owners of the South want the labor of the negro on the hardest possible terms. They once had it for nothing. They now want it for next to nothing and they have contrived three ways of thus obtaining it. The first is to rent their land to the negro at an exorbitant price per annum, and compel him to mortgage his crop in advance. The laws under which this is done are entirely in the interest of the landlord. He has a first claim upon everything produced on the land. The negro can have nothing, can keep nothing, can sell nothing, without the consent of the landlord. As the negro is at the start poor and empty handed, he has to draw on the landlord for meat and bread to feed himself and family while his crop is growing. The landlord keeps books; the negro does not; hence, no matter how hard he may work or how saving he may be, he is, in most cases, brought in debt at the end of the year, and once in debt, he is fastened to the land as by hooks of steel. If he attempts to leave he may be arrested under the law.

Another way, which is still more effective, is the payment of the labor with orders on stores instead of in lawful money. By this means money is kept entirely out of the hands of the negro. He cannot save money because he has no money to save. He cannot seek a better market for his labor because he has no money with which to pay his fare and because he is, by that vicious order system, already in debt, and therefore already in bondage. Thus he is riveted to one place and is, in some sense, a slave; for a man to whom it can be said, 'You shall work for me for what I shall choose to pay you and how I shall choose to pay you,' is in fact a slave though he may be called free man.

We denounce the landlord and tenant system of England, but it can be said of England as cannot be said of our free country, that by law no laborer can be paid for labor in any other than lawful money. England holds any other payment to be a penal offense and punishment by fine and imprisonments. The same should be the case in every State in the Union.

Under the mortgage system, no matter how industrious or economical the negro may be, he finds himself at the end of the year in debt to the landlord, and from year to year he toils on and is tempted to try again and again, seldom with any better result.

With this power over the negro, this possession of his labor, you may easily see why the South sometimes brags that it does not want slavery back. It had the negro's labor heretofore for nothing, and now it has it for next to nothing, and at the same time is freed from the obligation to take care of the young and the aged, the sick and the decrepit.

I now come to the so-called, but miscalled 'Negro Problem,' as a characterization of the relations existing in the Southern States.

I say at once, I do not like or admit the justice or propriety of this formula. Words are things.*They certainly are such in this case, and I may say they are a very bad thing in this case, since they give us a misnomer and one that is misleading. It is a formula of Southern origin, and has a strong bias against the negro. It handicaps his cause with all the prejudice known to exist against him. It has been accepted by the good people of the North, as I think, without investigation. It is a crafty invention and is in every way, worthy of its inventors.

The natural effect and purpose on its face of this formula is to divert attention from the true issue now before the American people. It does this by holding up the preoccupying the public mind with an issue entirely different from the real one in question. That which really is a great national problem and which ought to be so considered, dwarfs into a 'negro problem.'

The device is not new. It is an old trick. It has been oft repeated, and with similar purpose and effect. For truth, it gives us falsehood. For innocence, it gives us guilt. It removes the burden of proof from the old master class, and imposes it upon the negro. It puts upon a race a work which belongs to the nation. It belongs to the craftiness often displayed by disputants, who aim to make the worse appear the better reason. It gives bad names to good things, and good names to bad things.

The negro has often been the victim of this kind of low cunning. You may remember that during the late war, when the South fought for the perpetuity of slavery, it called the slaves 'domestic servants,' and slavery 'a domestic institution.' Harmless names, indeed, but the things they stood for were far from harmless.

The South has always known how to have a dog hanged by giving him a bad name. When it prefixed 'negro' to the national problem, it knew that the device would awaken and increase a deep-seated prejudice at once, and that it would repel fair and candid investigation. As it stands, it implies that the negro is the cause of whatever trouble there is in the South. In old slave times, when a little white child lost his temper, he was given a little whip and told to go and whip 'Jim' or 'Sal' and thus regained his temper. The same is true, to-day on a larger scale.

I repeat, and my contention is, that this negro problem formula lays the fault at the door of the negro, and removes it from the door of the white man, shields the guilty, and blames the innocent. Makes the negro responsible and not the nation.

Now the real problem is, and ought to be regarded by the American people, a great national problem. It involves the question, whether, after all, with our Declaration of Independence, with our glorious free constitution, whether with our sublime Christianity, there is enough of national virtue in this great nation to solve this problem, in accordance with wisdom and justice.

The marvel is that this old trick of misnaming things, so often played by Southern politicians, should have worked so well for the bad cause in which it is now employed—for the northern people have fallen in with it. It is still more surprising that the colored press of the country, and some of the colored orators of the country, insist upon calling it a 'negro problem,' or a Race problem, for by it they mean the negro Race. Now—there is nothing the matter with the negro. He is all right. Learned or ignorant, he is all right. He is neither a Lyncher, a Mobocrat, or an Anarchist. He is now, what he has ever been, a loyal, law-abiding, hard-working, and peaceable man; so much so, that men have thought him cowardly and spiritless. They say that any other people would have found some violent way in which to resent their wrongs. If this problem depended upon *his* character and conduct, there would be no problem to solve; there would be no menace to the peace and good order of Southern society. He makes no unlawful fight between labor and capital. That problem which often makes the American people thoughtful, is not of his bringing—though he may some day be compelled to talk, and on this tremendous problem.

He has as little to do with the cause of Southern trouble as he has with its cure. There is no reason, therefore, in the world, why he should give a name to this problem, and this lie, like all other lies, must eventually come to naught. A lie is worth nothing when it has lost its ability to deceive, and if it is at all in my power, this lie shall lose its power to deceive.

I well remember that this same old falsehood was employed and used against the negro, during the late war. He was then charged and stigmatized with being the cause of the war, on the principle that there would be no highway robbers if there were nobody on the road to be robbed. But as absurd as this pretense was, the color prejudice of the country was stimulated by it and joined in the accusation, and the negro has to bear the brunt of it.

Even at the North, he was hated and hunted on account of it. In the great city of New York, his houses were burned, his children were hunted down like wild beasts, and his people were murdered in the streets, because 'they were the cause of the war.'* Even the noble and good Mr. Lincoln, one of the best men that ever lived, told a committee of negroes who waited upon him at Washington, that 'they were the cause of the war.'* Many were the men who accepted this theory, and wished the negro in Africa, or in a hotter climate, as some do now.

There is nothing to which prejudice is not equal in the way of perverting the truth and inflaming the passions of men.

But call this problem what you may, or will, the all important question is: How can it be solved? How can the peace and tranquility of the South, and of the country, be secured and established?

There is nothing occult or mysterious about the answer to the question. Some things are to be kept in mind when dealing with this subject and never be forgotten. It should be remembered that in the order of Divine Providence the man who puts one end of a chain around the ankle of his fellow man will find the other end around his own neck. And it is the same with a nation. Confirmation of this truth is as strong as thunder. 'As we sow, we shall reap,'* is a lesson to be learned here as elsewhere. We tolerated slavery, and it cost us a million graves, and it may be that lawless murder, if permitted to go on, may yet bring vengeance, not only on the reverend head of age and upon the heads of helpless women, but upon the innocent babe in the cradle.

But how can this problem be solved? I will tell you how it can *not* be solved. It cannot be solved by keeping the negro poor, degraded, ignorant, and half-starved, as I have shown is now being done in the Southern States.

It cannot be solved by keeping the wages of the laborer back by fraud, as is now being done by the landlords of the South.

It cannot be done by ballot-box stuffing, by falsifying election returns, or by confusing the negro voter by cunning devices.

It cannot be done by repealing all federal laws enacted to secure honest elections.

It can, however, be done, and very easily done, for where there's a will, there's a way!

Let the white people of the North and South conquer their prejudices.

Let the great Northern press and pulpit proclaim the gospel of truth and justice against war now being made upon the negro.

Let the American people cultivate kindness and humanity.

Let the South abandon the system of 'mortgage' labor, and cease to make the negro a pauper, by paying him scrip for his labor.

Let them give up the idea that they can be free, while making the negro a slave. Let them give up the idea that to degrade the colored man, is to elevate the white man.

Let them cease putting new wine into old bottles, and mending old garments with new cloth.

They are not required to do much. They are only required to undo the evil that they have done, in order to solve this problem.

In old times when it was asked, 'How can we abolish slavery?' the answer was 'Quit stealing.'

The same is the solution of the Race problem to-day. The whole thing can be done by simply no longer violating the amendments of the Constitution of the United States, and no longer evading the claims of justice. If this were done, there would be no negro problem to vex the South, or to vex the nation.

Let the organic law of the land be honestly sustained and obeyed.

Let the political parties cease to palter in a double sense and live up to the noble declarations we find in their platforms.

Let the statesmen of the country live up to their convictions.

In the language of Senator Ingalls: 'Let the nation try justice and the problem will be solved.'

Two hundred and twenty years ago, the negro was made the subject of a religious problem, one which gave our white forefathers much perplexity and annoyance. At that time the problem was in respect of what relation a negro would sustain to the Christian Church, whether he was a fit subject for baptism, and Dr. Godwin, a celebrated divine of his time, and one far in advance of his brethren, was at the pains of writing a book of two hundred pages, or more, containing an elaborate argument to prove that it was not a sin in the sight of God to baptize a negro.*

His argument was very able, very learned, very long. Plain as the truth may now seem, there were at that time very strong arguments against the position of the learned divine.

As usual, it was not merely the baptism of the negro that gave trouble, but it was what might follow his baptism. The sprinkling him with water was a very simple thing, but the slave holders of that day saw in the innovation something more dangerous than water. They said that to baptize the negro and make him a member of the Church of Christ, was to make him an important person—in fact, to make him an heir of God and a joint heir of Jesus Christ. It was to give him a place at the Lord's supper. It was to take him out the category of heathenism, and make it inconsistent to hold him as a slave; for the Bible made only the heathen a proper subject for slavery.

These were formidable consequences, certainly, and it is not strange that the Christian slave holders of that day viewed these consequences with immeasurable horror. It was something more terrible and dangerous than the fourteenth* and fifteenth amendments to our Constitution. It was a difficult thing, therefore, at that day to get the negro in the water.

Nevertheless, our learned Doctor of Divinity, like many of the same class in our day, was quite equal to the emergency. He was able to satisfy all the important parties to the problem, except the negro, and him it did not seem necessary to satisfy.

The Doctor was [a] skilled dialectician. He did not only divide the word with skill, but he could divide the negro in two parts. He argued that the negro had a soul as well as a body, and insisted that while his body rightfully belonged to his master on earth, his soul belonged to his Master in heaven. By this convenient arrangement, somewhat metaphysical, to be sure, but entirely evangelical and logical, the problem of negro baptism was solved.

But with the negro in the case, as I have said, the argument was not entirely satisfactory. The operation was much like that by which the white man got the turkey and the Indian got the crow. When the negro looked around for his body, that belonged to his earthly master. When he looked around for his soul, that had been appropriated by his Heavenly Master. And when he looked around for something that really belonged to himself, he found nothing but his shadow, and that vanished in the shade.

One thing, however, is to be noticed with satisfaction, it is this: Something was gained to the cause of righteousness by this argument. It was a contribution to the cause of liberty. It was largely in favor of the negro. It was recognition of his manhood, and was calculated to set men to thinking that the negro might have some other important rights, no less than the religious right to baptism.

Thus with all its faults, we are compelled to give the pulpit the credit of furnishing the first important argument in favor of the religious character and manhood rights of the negro. Dr. Godwin was undoubtedly a good man. He wrote at a time of much moral darkness, and property in man was nearly everywhere recognized as a rightful institution. He saw only a part of the truth. He saw that the negro had a right to be baptized, but he could not all at once see that he had a paramount right to himself.

But this was not the only problem slavery had in store for the negro. Time and events brought another and it was this very important one: Can the negro sustain the legal relation of a husband to a wife? Can he make a valid marriage contract in this Christian country.

This problem was solved by the same slave holding authority, entirely against the negro. Such a contract, it was argued, could only be binding upon men providentially enjoying the right to life, liberty, and the pursuit of happiness, and, since the negro is a slave, and slavery a divine institution, legal marriage was wholly inconsistent with the institution of slavery.

When some of us at the North questioned the ethics of this conclusion, we were told to mind our business, and our Southern brethren asserted, as they assert now, that they alone are competent to manage this, and all other questions relating to the negro.

In fact, there has been no end to the problems of some sort or other, involving the negro in difficulty.

Can the negro be a citizen? was the question of the Dred Scott decision.

Can the negro be educated? Can the negro be induced to work for himself, without a master? Can the negro be a soldier? Time and events have answered these and all other like questions. We have amongst us, those who have taken the first prizes as scholars; those who have won distinction for courage and skill on the battlefield; those who have taken rank as lawyers, doctors and ministers of the gospel; those who shine among men in every useful calling; and yet we are called 'a problem;' 'a tremendous problem;' a mountain of difficulty; a constant source of apprehension; a disturbing force, threatening destruction to the holiest and best interest of society. I declare this statement concerning the negro, whether by Miss Willard, Bishop Fitzgerald, Ex-Governor Chamberlain or by any and all others as false and deeply injurious to the colored citizen of the United States.

But, my friends, I must stop. Time and strength are not equal to the task before me. But could I be heard by this great nation, I would call to mind the sublime and glorious truths with which, at its birth, it saluted a listening world. Its voice then, was as the trump of an archangel, summoning hoary forms of oppression and time honored tyranny, to judgement. Crowned heads heard it and shrieked. Toiling millions heard it and clapped their hands for joy. It announced the advent of a nation, based upon human brotherhood and the self-evident truths of liberty and equality. Its mission was the redemption of the world from the bondage of ages. Apply these sublime and glorious truths to the situation now before you. Put away your race prejudice. Banish the idea that one class must rule over another. Recognize the fact that the rights of the humblest citizen are as worthy of protection as are those of the highest, and your problem will be solved; and, whatever may be in store for it in the future, whether prosperity, or adversity; whether it shall have foes without, or foes within, whether there shall be peace, or war; based upon the eternal principles of truth, justice and humanity, and with no class having any cause of complaint or grievance, your Republic will stand and flourish forever.

# EXPLANATORY NOTES

3 *George L. Ruffin*: (1834–86), George Lewis Ruffin, a free-born lawyer and judge, was a social justice campaigner and an inspirational leader in the recruitment of Black combat soldiers during the Civil War. He was the first African American graduate from Harvard Law School, and the first to serve in the Massachusetts state legislature. A heartfelt admirer of his achievements, Frederick Douglass wrote Ruffin personal letters of congratulation.

19 *Horace Walpole's . . . at Boston*: Horace Walpole (1717–97), 4th Earl of Oxford, historian, politician, and man of letters. Ruffin refers to Walpole's letter of 24 November 1774 to Sir Horace Mann: 'The next Augustan age will dawn on the other side of the Atlantic. There will be, perhaps a Thucydides at Boston, a Xenophon at New York, and in time a Virgil at Mexico and a Newton at Peru.'

20 *Garrison . . . have gone*: William Lloyd Garrison (1805–79), foremost white U.S. abolitionist, social justice campaigner, and newspaper editor. He co-founded *The Liberator* newspaper (1831–65) and was leader of the American Anti-Slavery Society. Gerrit Smith (1797–1874), white U.S. radical reformer and philanthropist, who helped with the funding of *Frederick Douglass' Paper*. Joshua Reed Giddings (1795–1864), a white U.S. antislavery congressman from Ohio. Charles Sumner (1811–74), a white U.S. lawyer, senator, antislavery, and civil rights campaigner.

*Emancipation of the slaves*: on 22 September 1862, President Abraham Lincoln confirmed that the Emancipation Proclamation would take legal effect from 1 January 1863. According to this war-time legislation, he declared all enslaved people living in the white enslaving Confederate states in rebellion against the U.S. government were to be legally free. In the October 1862 issue of his newspaper, *Douglass' Monthly*, Frederick Douglass was jubilant: 'Common sense, the necessities of the war, to say nothing of the dictation of justice and humanity have at last prevailed. We shout for joy that we live to record this righteous decree.'

*'lost cause' . . . Appomatox*: white southern Confederate forces officially surrendered at Appomattox, Virginia, on 9 April 1865. Subsequently the 'Lost Cause' philosophy established a white supremacist and white apologist and explicitly racist revisionist view of history that erroneously and unforgivably viewed the Civil War as a noble struggle in defense of states' rights and in support of the U.S. nation as, in Frederick Douglass' words, 'the white man's country' that was for whites only.

*John Brown raid at Harper's Ferry*: See Part 2, Chapter 9.

20 *Roderick Dhus . . . Lady of the Lake*: a reference to Roderick Dhus, Ellen Douglas, and Lord James of Douglas, characters in Walter Scott's poem *The Lady of the Lake* (1810).

*'hair-breadth escapes'*: *Othello* I.iii.138.

21 *'Something attempted . . . a night's repose'*: the final two lines of 'The Village Blacksmith' (1841) by white U.S. poet, Henry Wadsworth Longfellow (1807–82).

22 *Edmund Burke*: (1729–97), Whig politician and political philosopher.

*Everett*: Edward Everett (1794–1865), academic, orator, politician, editor of the *North American Review*.

*Sumner*: see note to p. 20.

*Fox*: Charles James Fox (1749–1806), Whig politician and opponent of the British policy of coercion in the American colonies.

*Henry Clay*: (1777–1852), white U.S. enslaver, pro-slavery politician, and a leading supporter of the American Colonization Society, a white racist organization that was committed to the removal of people of African descent from the U.S. nation. In his article titled 'Colonization', that he published in his newspaper, *The North Star* on 26 January 1849, Frederick Douglass voiced his powerful condemnation of this persecutory and prejudicial organization. 'Our minds are made up to live here if we can, or die here if we must; so every attempt to remove us will be, as it ought to be, labor lost. Here we are, and here we shall remain. While our brethren are in bondage on these shores, it is idle to think of inducing any considerable number of the free colored people to quit this for a foreign land,' he declared.

*Daniel Webster*: (1782–1852), white U.S. lawyer, senator, and Secretary of State, Webster was an outspoken opponent of slavery, though his reputation amongst abolitionists was tarnished by his 7 March 1850 speech in the U.S. senate (see note to p. 289).

25 *John Brown . . . Tremont Temple*: the meeting at Boston Tremont Temple on 3 December 1860 to commemorate the first anniversary of the white revolutionary and radical abolitionist John Brown's execution was disrupted by a white proslavery mob.

*Toussaint L'Overture*: (1743–1803), Toussaint Louverture, self-liberated military general, leader of the Haitian Revolution, and a world-renowned founder of the First Black Republic in the western hemisphere. During his lifetime Frederick Douglass delivered many speeches and authored many essays in which he took inspiration from Louverture as the 'hero of Santo Domingo'. Celebrating his inspirational military prowess, Douglass writes of Louverture, 'His high character, his valor, his wisdom, and his unflinching fidelity to the cause of liberty are an inheritance of which his people should be proud.'

*Alexander Dumas*: (1802–70), Alexandre Dumas, a renowned French novelist whose grandmother, Marie-Cessette Dumas (1714–86), was an enslaved woman of African descent who was born in present-day Haiti.

Frederick Douglass was an avid reader of Dumas' world-renowned novels as he was one of his favorite authors.

29 *February, 1817*: an inventory of enslaved people authored by Douglass' white enslaver, Aaron Anthony, recorded his birth-date as follows: 'Frederick Augustus, son of Harriet, Feby. 1818.'

*Betsey and Isaac Bailey*: Betsey Bailey (1774–1849), Douglass' maternal grandmother; Isaac Bailey (n.d.), his maternal grandfather.

30 *my own mother*: Harriet Bailey (1792–1825).

*Prichard's 'Natural History of Man' . . . page 157*: James Cowles Pritchard (1786–1848), British physician, whose *The Natural History of Man* (1843) argued for a monogenistic theory of racial unity. Douglass refers to a sketch of Ramesses II (1303–1213 BC), an Egyptian pharaoh.

32 *'Old Master'*: Aaron Anthony (1767–1826), Douglass' white enslaver, overseer and manager of the estate belonging to the white enslaving Lloyd family living in Maryland.

33 *Colonel Lloyd*: Edward Lloyd V (1744–1834).

*'toteing'*: an American colloquial word meaning 'to carry as a burden'.

34 *Perry*: Perry Bailey (1813–80), Douglass' brother.

*Sarah and Eliza*: Sarah Bailey (1814–?) and Eliza Bailey (1816–*c*.76), Douglass' sisters.

36 *Aunt Katy*: Kate Emblem (1789–?), daughter of Sarah Emblem, a woman enslaved to white enslaver Aaron Anthony.

39 *Mr. Page*: Joel Page (1784–1832), a white U.S. Yale graduate and tutor for the Lloyd family.

40 *Tilgmans . . . Gibsons*: Douglass lists four of the most prominent white enslaving families on the Eastern Shore of Maryland.

41 *great house*: Wye House, main residence of Edward Lloyd V, and located at the centre of his labour camp of enslaved people.

42 *'none to molest them or make them afraid'*: Micah 4:4, 'But they shall sit every man under his vine and under his fig tree; and none shall make them afraid: for the mouth of the Lord of hosts hath spoken it.'

44 *Andrew and Richard*: Andrew Skinner Anthony (1797–1833) and Richard Lee Anthony (1800–28), sons of Aaron Anthony.

*Lucretia . . . Auld*: Lucretia Planner Anthony Auld (1804–27), daughter of Aaron Anthony, and wife of Thomas Auld (1795–1880), an employee of Edward Lloyd.

*Aunt Esther*: Hester Bailey (n.d.), the sister of Douglass' mother, Harriet Bailey.

45 *Daniel Lloyd*: (1811–?).

*Edward and Murray*: Edward Lloyd VI (1798–1861), eldest child of Edward Lloyd V; and James Murray Lloyd (1803–47), middle son of Edward Lloyd V.

47 *cousin of mine*: Henny Bailey (1816–?).

52 *Rigby Hopkins*: (n.d.), a white U.S. Methodist minister and enslaver.

53 *Ireland*: in the autumn of 1845 a failure in the Irish potato crop led to famine throughout the country, with estimates of 20,000 deaths from starvation between 1846 and 1851.

54 *'I did not . . . ineffable sadness'*: Douglass is here recalling a passage from his *Narrative of the Life of Frederick Douglass, An American Slave* (chapter 2).

56 *'purple and fine linen . . . every day'*: Luke 16:19: 'There was a certain rich man, which was clothed in purple and fine linen, and fared sumptuously every day.'

60 *Austin Woldfolk*: Douglass here means Austin Woolfolk (1796–1847), a Georgia-born white U.S. enslaver whom he condemned for plying his immoral and inhumane trade in enslaved people in Baltimore, Maryland.

62 *Austin Gore*: Orson Gore (Douglass mistakenly identifies him as Austin) (1794–1871), white U.S. overseer of white U.S. enslaver Lloyd's labour camp of enslaved people.

63 *Bill Denby*: (c.1802–23), an enslaved man living on white U.S. enslaver Edward Lloyd V's labour camp of enslaved people, brutally, inhumanely, and horrifically murdered by white U.S. persecutor and killer Gore.

64 *Beal Bondley*: Douglass means John Beale Bordley (1800–82), white U.S. lawyer and portrait painter, who until his mid-twenties lived on his father's estate close to the Lloyd labour camp of enslaved people.

68 *Hugh Auld*: (1799–1861), brother of Thomas Auld and married to Sophia Keithley Auld (1797–1880).

69 *Tom*: Tom Bailey (1814–?).

70 *Annapolis*: capital of the state of Maryland.

*dome of the State house*: the state house at Annapolis, completed in 1797, is topped by a wooden dome.

*Fell's point*: a piece of land extending out into Baltimore's outer harbor; by the time of Douglass' arrival it was a heavily populated centre for shipbuilding.

*Thomas*: Thomas Auld (1824–48).

73 *ell*: an antiquated English unit of measurement, equivalent to 45 inches.

77 *Webster's spelling-book*: white U.S. lexicographer Noah Webster (1758–1843) first published his *A Grammatical Institute of the English Language* in 1783. In 1787 this became *The American Spelling Book*, and the book went through numerous editions in the nineteenth century.

*'The Columbian Orator,'*: *The Columbian Orator* (1797), compiled by white U.S. author and educator, Caleb Bingham (1757–1817), an anthology of texts for reading and citation.

78 *short dialogue . . . his slave*: 'Dialogue between a Master and Slave', an anonymous extract in *The Columbian Orator*.

*Sheridan's . . . Catholic Emancipation*: the attribution of the speech in *The Columbian Orator* on Catholic Emancipation to Richard Sheridan (1751–1816), the Irish politician and playwright, is mistaken. Douglass is more likely to be referring to an excerpt of a speech by Arthur O'Connor (1763–1852), an Irish politician, in support of Catholic rights.

*Lord Chatham's . . . American War*: William Pitt (1708–78), first earl of Chatham, is excerpted four times in *The Columbian Orator*. His parliamentary speeches often opposed British policies in the American colonies.

*William Pitt*: (1759–1806), politician and British Prime Minister (1783–1801; 1804–6), second son of the earl of Chatham.

*Fox*: Charles James Fox (1749–1806), British politician.

80 *like the blows . . . upon his ass*: a reference to the biblical story of Balaam's ass (Numbers 22:21–30).

81 *'Baltimore American'*: the Baltimore *American*, the oldest newspaper in Maryland, first published in 1799.

82 *Nat Turner*: (1800–31), Nathaniel Turner, a preacher, paper-maker, radical revolutionary, political thinker, freedom-fighter, and military leader who was born into slavery and who led a revolution of enslaved people in Southampton County, Virginia, on 21 August 1831. Waging a war for the liberation of all enslaved people, he and the men he had trained as military soldiers succeeded in killing approximately 60 members of local white enslaving families. The horrific vengeance exacted by white U.S. enslaving torturers and murderers not only against Turner and his followers but against untold numbers of innocent enslaved women, children, and men was on an unimaginable scale. In nineteenth-century white U.S. society, Turner is pejoratively dismissed as Nat Turner. As a result, Douglass always referred to him by his full name, Nathaniel Turner, out of respect for his world-renowned status as an inspirational military general and founding father of Black revolutionary U.S. liberation movements.

*Hanson*: the Reverend James M. Hanson (1782–1860), a Baltimore-based white U.S. Methodist Episcopal Church minister.

83 *Charles Lawson*: (n.d.), a free-born member of Baltimore's Bethel African Methodist Church and an inspirational religious leader. For Frederick Douglass he was a surrogate father, a role model, and an inspiration for his future life of authorship and activism.

*'cast all my care upon God'*: Douglass paraphrases 1 Peter 5:7: 'Casting all your care upon him; for he careth for you.'

*Beverly Waugh*: (1789–1858), white U.S. Methodist Episcopal Church preacher in Baltimore, at the church attended by the Hugh Auld family.

84 *"Ask, and it shall be given to you"*: Matthew 7:7.

87 *my old master himself died*: Douglass misremembers the order in which the Anthony/Auld family members died: Aaron Anthony (d. 1826); Lucretia Anthony Auld (d. 1827); and Richard Anthony (d. 1828).

90 *Amanda*: Arianna Amanda Auld (1826–78), the only child of Thomas and Lucretia Auld.

91 *'Gone, gone . . . stolen daughters!'*: the first stanza of 'Of a Virginia Slave Mother to Her Daughters Sold into Bondage', by John Greenleaf Whittier (1807–92), white U.S. poet, politician, and abolitionist.

*Rowena Hamilton*: Douglass means Rowena Hambleton (1812–42), who became the second wife of Thomas Auld in 1829.

*William Hamilton*: William Hambleton (c.1783–1855), father of Rowena.

93 *'Uncle Tom' . . . Mrs. Stowe's Christian hero*: Douglass is referring to Tom, the enslaved protagonist who endorsed a method of Christian self-sacrificial resistance in the bestselling novel, *Uncle Tom's Cabin* (1852) by white U.S. author and abolitionist Harriet Beecher Stowe (1811–96).

95 *'stars shall fall from heaven'*: Matthew 24:29.

96 *'bless them . . . His kingdom'*: a paraphrase of Deuteronomy 28:5: 'Blessed be thy basket and thy store.'

99 *Methodist Discipline*: Douglass is quoting from *The Doctrines and Discipline of the Methodist Episcopal Church* (1832).

100 *George Cookman*: (1800–41), a British-born Methodist minister who migrated to the U.S. in 1825.

*colonization ideas*: some white antislavery advocates were members of the American Colonization Society and regarded the emigration of enslaved people to Africa as a method of eradicating slavery from the U.S.

*Samuel Harrison*: (?–1837), white Maryland-born enslaver who stipulated in his will that all the enslaved people living on his labour camp were to be given their freedom upon his death.

*Mason and Dixon's line*: the topographical line mapped between 1763 and 1767 by British astronomer Charles Mason (1728–86) and surveyor Jeremiah Dixon (1733–79) to establish the precise borders between Pennsylvania in the north and Maryland and Virginia in the south.

101 *'That servant . . . many stripes.'*: Luke 12:47.

102 *Sarah (Mrs. Cline)*: Sarah Auld Cline (1811–?), sister of Hugh and Thomas Auld.

*Edward Covey*: (1806–75), white Maryland-born enslaver, farmer, and racist persecutor and torturer Douglass denounces and condemns as a 'negro-breaker'.

119 *'bind heavy burdens . . . their fingers.'*: Matthew 23:4.

124 *He had more . . . mercifully given.*: Douglass paraphrases Mark 2:27: 'And he said unto them, The sabbath was made for man, and not man for the sabbath.'

128 *'Hereditary bondmen . . . strike the blow?'*: lines from *Childe Harold's Pilgrimage* (1812), canto 2, stanza 76, by George Gordon (Lord Byron) (1788–1824).

130 *'jubilee beating'*: or juba beating, an improvisatory rhythmic dancing.

132 *'trifles light as air'*: *Othello* III.iii.322.

133 *'Howbeit, that . . . is spiritual.'*: 1 Corinthians 15:46.

135 *'search the Scriptures'*: John 5:39.

141 *'O Canaan . . . of Canaan,'*: From 'Sweet Canaan' (n.d.), an African American spiritual.

   *'I thought I heard . . . Much longer here,'*: from 'Run to Jesus' (n.d.), an African American spiritual.

144 *'Rather bear the ills . . . we knew not of.'*: Douglass slightly misquotes *Hamlet* III.i.81–2.

   *Patrick Henry*: (1736–99), white Virginia lawyer, politician, and orator.

   *'Give me . . . or death'*: from a speech made by Patrick Henry to the Second Virginia Convention, 23 March 1775.

157 *bowse*: to haul with tackle.

163 *'East Baltimore Mental Improvement Society'*: a debating club established by free African American men in Baltimore which Douglass joined in the late 1830s and which had a major impact on his life.

169 *'underground railroad'*: a phrase that refers to the clandestine system of liberation routes and safe houses by which enslaved people escaped from slavery into the northern U.S. states and Canada. The account books of the Rochester Female Anti-Slavery Society based in Rochester, New York, confirm that while they were living in the city, Frederick Douglass and his wife, Anna Murray Douglass (1813–82), and his daughters, Rosetta (1839–1906) and Annie (1849–60), and his sons, Lewis Henry (1840–1908), Frederick Jr (1842–92), and Charles Remond Douglass (1844–1920), were leading activists in the Underground Railroad for the two decades before the Civil War. On 27 March 1893, Douglass wrote a letter to white U.S. historian, William H. Seibert, in which he not only confirms, 'My connection with the Underground Railroad began long before I left the South' but states that it 'was continued as long as slavery continued, whether I lived in New Bedford, Lynn, or Rochester, N.Y. In the latter place I had as many as eleven fugitives under my roof at one time.'

173 *Charles T. Torrey*: (1813–46), white U.S. abolitionist and journalist, he established an important route on the Underground Railroad from Washington, D.C., to Albany, N.Y. He was arrested in 1844, and died in prison two years later.

174 *a sailor's protection*: Seamen Protection Certificates, issued to U.S. sailors, guaranteeing citizenship and certifying non-enslaved status.

   *'those who . . . in ships.'*: Psalms 107:23.

175 *'Free trade and sailors' rights'*: a political slogan adopted by the U.S. in the War of 1812 against Great Britain.

177 *'quick round of blood'*: a phrase from *Festus*, an epic poem published in two editions (1839, 1845) by the British writer Philip James Bailey (1816–1902).

177 *'I felt . . . hungry lions'*: An allusion to the biblical story of Daniel in the lions' den (Daniel 6:1–28).

179 *'The Tombs'*: New York City's first prison, built in 1838.

*David Ruggles*: (1810–49), a Black radical abolitionist, Underground Railroad conductor, and member of the New York Vigilance Committee.

*Isaac T. Hopper*: (1771–1852), white U.S. abolitionist, prison reformer, and member of the American Anti-Slavery Society in New York.

*Lewis and Arthur Tappan*: Lewis (1788–1873) and Arthur (1786–1865) Tappan were prominent white U.S. abolitionists, helping to found the American Anti-Slavery Society in 1833.

*Theodore S. Wright*: (1797–1847), a Black Presbyterian minister and founder of the American and Foreign Anti-Slavery Society in 1840.

*Samuel Cornish*: (1795–1858), a Black Presbyterian minister, abolitionist and journalist, and an editor of *Freedom's Journal*, the first Black newspaper in the U.S.

*Thomas Downing*: (1791–1866), Black New York City restaurant owner and advocate for equal rights. His son, George T. Downing (1819–1903), would become a close associate of the Douglass family.

*Philip A. Bell*: (1808–89), Black newspaper editor and abolitionist, founder of *The Weekly Advocate*, later renamed the *Colored American*.

*Elevator*: Black weekly newspaper published between 1865 and 1889.

*my intended wife*: Anna Murray Douglass (1813–82), a free woman born in Denton, Maryland. An inspirational and trailblazing revolutionary political thinker, radical reformer, antislavery activist, Underground Railroad liberator, social justice and human rights campaigner, foodways specialist, and business manager, among any more outstanding accolades, she was married to Frederick Douglass for over forty-four years.

*J. W. C. Pennington*: James William Charles Pennington (1809–71), a self-liberated radical abolitionist, scholar, social justice campaigner, and religious minister living in the northern states who had been born into slavery in Maryland.

180 *Dyer*: Samuel Dyer (1785–1835), British composer of sacred music who moved to the U.S. in 1811.

*Shaw*: Oliver Shaw (1779–1848), a white U.S. composer of sacred music.

*Nathan Johnson*: (*c*.1797–1880) was a renowned Black activist, freedom-fighter, Underground Railroad conductor, antislavery campaigner, scholar, and successful businessman.

*'took me in . . . when hungry,'*: Douglass paraphrases Matthew 25:35.

181 *'Lady of the Lake'*: see note to p. 21.

*'stalwart hand'*: a reference to Walter Scott's *The Lady of the Lake*: ' "I never knew but one," he said, | "Whose stalwart arm might brook to wield | A blad like this in battle-field" ' (Canto 1, stanza 28, lines 565–7).

184 *Rodney French*: (1802–82), white U.S. abolitionist, businessman and politician.

*New Bedford Lyceum*: established in 1828, the Lyceum Society organized public lectures, concerts and performances.

*Chas. Sumner*: see note to p. 20.

*Theodore Parker*: (1810–60), white U.S. Unitarian clergyman and reformer.

*Ralph W. Emerson*: Ralph Waldo Emerson (1803–82), white U.S. philosopher, essayist, poet, and lecturer.

*Horace Mann*: (1796–1859), white U.S. lawyer and radical education reformer.

186 *Liberator*: see note to p. 20.

*Isaac Knapp*: (1804–43), white U.S. abolitionist and co-publisher of the *Liberator* with Garrison (see note to p. 20).

*Liberty Hall*: Liberty Hall in New Bedford, built in 1797, housed the New Bedford Lyceum. Douglass heard Garrison here for the first time on 13 April 1839.

*'on one cheek . . . the other also'*: a paraphrase of Matthew 5:39.

*'father the devil'*: John 8:44.

188 *grand anti-slavery convention*: the Massachusetts Anti-Slavery Society met in Nantucket on 10–12 August 1841.

*William C. Coffin*: (1816–?), white U.S. abolitionist and banker.

*John A. Collins*: (1810–c.79), white U.S. abolitionist and social reformer.

189 *George Foster*: (c.1811–?), white U.S. Quaker, abolitionist, and traveling agent for the *National Anti-Slavery Standard* and the *Liberator*.

*Anti-Slavery Standard*: the *National Anti-Slavery Standard*, weekly newspaper of the American Anti-Slavery Society, was established in 1840 under the editorship of white U.S. reformers Lydia Maria Child and David Lee Child. It ran until 1870.

191 *Mr. Phillips*: Wendell Phillips (1811–84), white U.S. abolitionist, orator, and lawyer.

192 *Thomas W. Dorr*: (1805–54), white Rhode Island politician and reformer. These opening paragraphs describe the Dorr Rebellion (1841–2), an attempt to revise Rhode Island's electoral rules to expand the franchise.

193 *Stephen S. Foster*: (1809–81), white U.S. abolitionist, orator, and conductor on the Underground Railroad, and married to Abby Kelley.

*Parker Pillsbury*: (1809–98), white U.S. abolitionist, clergyman, and editor.

*Abby Kelley*: (1811–87), white U.S. abolitionist, orator, and social reformer, and married to Stephen S. Foster.

*James Monroe*: (1821–98), white U.S. abolitionist, lecturer, and (later) Ohio politician.

194 *spirit of its founder*: a reference to Rhode Island's white founder, the dissenting minister Roger Williams (1603–83).

195 *William White*: (1818–56), white U.S. abolitionist and temperance reformer.

*Jim Crow car*: 'Jim Crow' was originally a white racist fictional character created by white U.S. performer Thomas Dartmouth Rice (1808–60), in the first half of the nineteenth century. In the decades that followed and on through to the present day, the phrase 'Jim Crow' has become synonymous with white persecutory systems of legal racial segregation. Here Douglass includes the phrase 'Jim Crow car' to refer to a segregated train carriage. Due to white U.S. systems of racist persecution and prejudicial exclusion, African American travellers were prohibited from using all carriages apart from the 'Jim Crow car'.

196 *James N. Buffum*: James Needham Buffum (1807–87), white Massachusetts merchant and abolitionist who would later accompany Douglass on a lecture tour of Great Britain (1845–7).

197 *Charles L. Remond*: (1810–73), Charles Lenox Remond, a free-born world-renowned and celebrated abolitionist, activist, orator, and political thinker. A close Douglass family friend, Anna Murray and Frederick Douglass decided to name their youngest son, Charles Remond Douglass, after their inspirational friend and activist collaborator.

*Sydney Howard Gay*: (1814–88), white U.S. lawyer, journalist, and abolitionist, editor of the *National Anti-Slavery Standard* from 1844 to 1854.

*William Slade*: (1786–1859), white U.S. representative for Vermont (1831–43) and opponent of slavery.

*John Quincy Adams*: (1767–1848), white, sixth U.S. President (1825–9) and representative for Massachusetts (1831–48).

198 *Samuel J. May*: (1797–1871), white U.S. Unitarian minister, abolitionist, and activist.

*'Jerry rescue'*: Douglass refers to the rescue of a self-liberated enslaved man, William 'Jerry' Henry, in 1851 in Syracuse, N.Y., in which a group of around 30 Black and white abolitionists freed Henry and helped him to effect his self-liberation to Canada.

199 *Mrs. M.W. Chapman*: Maria Weston Chapman (1806–85), white U.S. leading member of the Massachusetts Anti-Slavery Society, strong advocate of Garrisonianism, and occasional editor of the *Liberator*.

*liberty party-papers*: the Liberty Party was founded in 1840 to advocate abolitionism and the view that the U.S. Constitution was an anti-slavery document.

*Isaac and Amy Post*: Isaac (1798–1872) and Amy Post (1802–89) were prominent white U.S. abolitionists and women's rights campaigners in Rochester, N.Y. They were close friends and collaborators with the Douglass family.

200 *Henry Highland Garnett*: (1815–82), born into slavery in Kent County, Maryland, Garnet escaped to the north in 1824 and went on to become a renowned activist, orator, author, intellectual, and social justice campaigner. A founder of the American and Foreign Anti-Slavery Society and

an early advocate of Black emigration to Africa, he was appointed U.S. Minister to Liberia in 1881.

*Henry Clay . . . his slaves.*: white U.S. enslaver and politician Henry Clay had been embarrassed at a political rally by a small group of local Quakers led by white U.S. campaigner, Hiram Mendenhall (1801–52), who had petitioned him to denounce slavery and colonization.

204 *corn laws*: the Corn Laws were tariffs and restrictions on imported food and cereal grains, in place between 1815 and 1846, which kept prices high and had the effect of raising food prices for the British population.

*the repeal . . . Ireland.*: a reference to the 'Repealer' movement in Ireland, led by Daniel O'Connell (1775–1847), which campaigned for the reinstitution of the Irish parliament and the repeal of the Act of Union between Great Britain and Ireland in 1800.

*Richard Cobden*: (1804–65), British member of parliament and founder of the Anti-Corn Law League.

*John Bright*: (1811–89), British member of parliament and activist, supporter of the repeal of the Corn Laws and, during the U.S. Civil War, strong advocate of the North.

205 *Sir Robert Peel*: (1788–1850), British Prime Minister (1834–5; 1841–6).

*Benjamin Disraeli*: (1804–81), British member of parliament and later Prime Minister (1868; 1874–80).

*'tide which led on to fortune'*: Douglass paraphrases Brutus's line in Shakespeare's *Julius Caesar*, 'There is a tide in the affairs of men, | Which, taken at the flood, leads on to fortune' (IV.iii.249–50).

206 *'Conciliation Hall'*: on 29 September 1845 Douglass spoke at a gathering of the Loyal National Repeal Association at its headquarters, Conciliation Hall.

207 *O. A. Brownson*: Orestes Brownson (1803–76), white U.S. clergyman, editor, and author, had converted to Catholicism in 1844. In July 1845 his *Quarterly Review* had published an article critical of O'Connell. Douglass paraphrases O'Connell's response.

*Lord Brougham*: Henry Peter Brougham (1778–1868), politician, lawyer, and founder of the *Edinburgh Review*. He was a strong supporter of the Slavery Abolition Act of 1833, which abolished slavery throughout the British Empire.

208 *William and Mary Howitt*: William (1792–1879) and Mary Howitt (1799–1888) were prolific writers and translators, as well as advocates of women's rights and abolition.

*Sir John Bowring*: John Bowring (1792–1872), economist, travel writer, and future governor of Hong Kong.

*Hans Christian Andersen*: (1805–75), celebrated Danish writer of, among other things, 'The Little Mermaid'.

209 *George Combe*: (1788–1858), Scottish lawyer and phrenologist. His book, *The Constitution of Man Considered in Relation to External Objects* (1828), argued for 'Natural Law' as the basis of morality, rather than divine sanction.

*Thomas Clarkson*: (1760–1846), a leading campaigner for the abolition of the Slave Trade in the British Empire, which was successfully achieved with the passage of the Slave Trade Act of 1807.

211 *Brev. Digest*: *An Alphabetical Digest of the Public Statute Law of South Carolina* (1814), compiled by Joseph Brevard.

213 *'the land . . . the brave.'*: the last line of the first stanza of Francis Scott Key's poem 'The Star-Spangled Banner' (1814).

*Samuel Hanson Cox*: (1793–1880), white New York Presbyterian clergyman whose early strong abolitionist views had weakened by the time of the London Temperance Convention.

216 *Free Church of Scotland,*: a Protestant denomination formed in 1843 after a break-away movement by evangelical members of the established Church of Scotland.

217 *George Thompson*: (1804–78), British politician and abolitionist, and ally of William Lloyd Garrison.

*Dr. Cunningham*: William Cunningham (1805–61), Scottish clergyman and academic.

220 *Ellen Richardson . . . Henry Richardson*: Ellen (1808–96) and her sister-in-law Anna Richardson (1806–92) were British reformers who raised the £150 price put on purchasing Douglass' legal freedom from his white enslaver Hugh Auld.

*the fugitive slave . . . that of 1850*: the Fugitive Slave Act of 1793 sought to enforce the return of enslaved people, who had fought to make their escape and effect their liberation, back to their white enslavers. The 1850 Fugitive Slave Law, passed as part of the Compromise of 1850, strengthened the force of the original Act. As a result, the northern states were legally obliged to return escaping enslaved people back to their white southern enslavers.

223 *stern rebuke from the British press*: Douglass' letter to the *Times* appeared on 6 April 1847.

225 *'THE NORTH STAR'*: Douglass' four-page newspaper was published weekly, beginning on 3 December 1847. It ceased publication in June 1851, after merging with the *Liberty Party Paper* to become *Frederick Douglass' Paper*.

227 *Russell Lant Carpenter* (1816–92), British Unitarian minister, who met Douglass while preaching in North America in 1849–50.

*Julia Griffiths Crofts*: (1811–95), British abolitionist, author, editor, essayist, and radical reformer who worked with Frederick Douglass as the business manager, contributor, and occasional editor of the *North Star* and *Frederick Douglass' Paper*.

229 *Free-Soil Convention at Buffalo*: held on 9 and 10 August 1848, the convention in Buffalo, N.Y., established the short-lived Free Soil Party, which opposed the expansion of slavery into the Western territories of the United States.

*Martin Van Buren*: (1782–1862), eighth president of the U.S. (1837–41), Van Buren was a white U.S. politician who was nominated as the Free Soil party's candidate for president in the 1848 election.

*7th of March . . . Daniel Webster*: known as 'The Constitution and the Union', Webster's address to the U.S. Senate supported the Compromise of 1850, including the provisions of the Fugitive Slave Act.

*Dred Scott decision*: Dred Scott *v.* Sandford, a landmark U.S. Supreme Court case in 1857, which judged that citizenship under the U.S. Constitution did not include Black people, enslaved, self-liberated or free. Frederick Douglass delivered a blistering protest against the 'Dred Scott Decision' in his oration published in the pamphlet *Two Speeches, By Frederick Douglass; one on West Indian Emancipation, Delivered at Canandaigua, Aug. 4th, and the other on the Dred Scott Decision, Delivered in New York, on the occasion of the Anniversary of the American Abolition Society, May, 1857* (Rochester, N.Y.: C. P. Dewey, 1857).

*the repeal of . . . Kansas Nebraska bill*: the Missouri Compromise (1820) prohibited slavery north of the 36°30′ parallel, excluding Missouri. The Compromise was effectively repealed by the passage into law of the Kansas–Nebraska Act of 1854, in which the status of slavery in any new state or territory would be decided by the popular sovereignty of its citizens rather than the U.S. Congress.

*Border war in Kansas*: the conflict between anti-slavery and pro-slavery settlers in Kansas erupted into violence between 1854 and 1861.

*John Brown . . . Harper's Ferry*: John Brown (1800–59), a radical white abolitionist, led an unsuccessful revolutionary attack on the federal arsenal at Harpers Ferry, Virginia, on 16–18 October 1859.

234 *J. W. Loguen*: Jermain Wesley Loguen (1813–72) was a world-renowned antislavery campaigner and political leader who was born into slavery in Davidson county, Tennessee. He effected his self-liberation and went onto become an inspirational teacher, religious minister, author, orator, anti-slavery campaigner, and social justice activist. He played a leading role in the 'Jerry rescue' (see note to p. 246) and aided John Brown in the recruitment of men for his Harpers Ferry revolutionary raid. He was widely celebrated as the 'Underground Railroad King' for his own and his family's heroic labors in running their home in Syracuse, N.Y., as a safe house for enslaved people on the run from slavery and on their way to freedom in the northern states and Canada. His daughter, Helen Amelia Loguen (1843–1936), an educator and social justice campaigner in her own right, married the Douglass' eldest son, Lewis Henry Douglass.

237 *Sojourner Truth*: (1797–1883), was born into slavery as Isabella Baumfree in Ulster County, New York. As a young adult, she secured her self-liberation

and went on to become a world renowned antislavery campaigner, author, orator, equal rights activist, and campaigner for Black soldiers during the Civil War.

238 *Free-Soil Convention . . . New York*: see note to p. 289.

*Liberty party,*: the Liberty Party was founded in 1840, its members having broken away from the American Anti-Slavery Society to support the view that the Constitution was an anti-slavery document, in opposition to Garrison's fierce denunciation of it.

*James G. Birney*: (1792–1857), white U.S. abolitionist and Kentucky politician, he stood for the Liberty Party as the presidential candidate in the 1840 and 1844 elections, receiving 0.3% and 2.3%, respectively, of the popular vote.

*Conscience-Whigs*: by the late 1840s, the Whig party was divided between pro-South 'Cotton Whigs' and anti-slavery 'Conscience Whigs'.

*Barn-burners*: the name given to the anti-slavery faction of the Democratic Party in New York State in the 1840s. At the 1848 presidential election, most left the Democratic Party to form the Free Soil Party, which nominated Martin Van Buren for president.

239 *Mr. Ward*: Samuel Ringgold Ward (1817–*c.*1866) escaped from slavery on the Eastern Shore of Maryland and went on to become a world-renowned antislavery campaigner, religious leader, newspaper editor, orator, freedom-fighter, political thinker, intellectual, and author of *Autobiography of a Fugitive Negro* (1855). Ward died in Jamaica.

*General Lewis Cass*: Lewis Cass (1782–1866), white U.S. enslaver and Democratic politician nominated to run in the 1848 presidential election on a conservative platform that accepted slavery and the principle of popular sovereignty to decide whether a territory should permit slavery. Cass was defeated by white U.S. Whig Zachary Taylor.

*Mr. Calhoun*: John Caldwell Calhoun (1782–1850), white South Carolina enslaver, politician, prominent anti-abolitionist, and vice-president of the U.S. (1825–32).

240 *In order to . . . assent of both.*: Calhoun's *A Discourse on the Constitution and Government of the United States* (1851) advocated for the right of veto by minority interests as a way of nullifying legislation regarded as objectionable.

242 *Shadrack*: the celebrated case of Frederick Wilkins (*c.*1814–75), widely known as Shadrach Minkins, an enslaved man who, with the support of Black radical activists and freedom-fighters, escaped a Boston courthouse in 1851 and effected his self-liberation by reaching Canada.

*Simms and Anthony Burns*: Thomas Sims (1834–1902), an enslaved man who was living a new life as a fugitive from slavery, was arrested in Boston 1851 under the Fugitive Slave Law and forcibly returned to his enslavement. Anthony Burns (1834–62), another enslaved man who was living a new life as a fugitive from slavery, was captured in Boston in 1853 and tried under the Fugitive Slave Act. His case attracted widespread publicity and outrage, with Federal troops deployed to transport him to a ship sailing back to Virginia and enslavement. Burns' freedom was eventually purchased, in 1855, with money raised by Boston abolitionists.

243 *Uncle Tom's Cabin*: the anti-slavery novel by Harriet Beecher Stowe (1811–96), published first in instalments in *The National Era*, a weekly abolitionist newspaper, between June 1851 and April 1852. It appeared in book form in 1852.

248 *colored convention*: Douglass refers here to the Colored National Convention, in Rochester, 6–8 July 1853.

249 *Henry Ward Beecher*: (1813–87), white U.S. clergyman, reformer and abolitionist, brother of Harriet Beecher Stowe.

*New York Independent*: a weekly magazine founded in 1848 to promote the principles of Congregationalism, it also advocated for abolitionism and women's rights. Beecher's letter appeared on 2 June 1853; he did not take over the editorship of the magazine until 1861.

250 *said he 'never . . . Bunker Hill monument'*: Douglass quotes remarks attributed to, but denied by, the white Georgia pro-slavery senator Robert Toombs (1810–85). The Bunker Hill Monument in Boston, completed in 1843, commemorates the Battle of Bunker Hill, fought on 17 June 1775, between American and British forces in the American Revolutionary War.

*annexation of Texas*: the Republic of Texas had declared independence from Mexico in 1836. In 1845 it was annexed into the U.S. and admitted to the Union as the 28th state in December of that year.

*war with Mexico*: the Mexican–American War (1846–8) followed in the aftermath of the annexation of Texas.

*Dred Scott case*: see note to p. 289.

*the perfidious repeal . . . the North*: see note to p. 289.

251 *the armed . . . soil of Kansas*: see note to p. 289.

*'in the deep . . . ocean buried'*: *Richard III* I.i.4.

*John C. Fremont . . . the United States*: Fremont (1813–90), opposed to the expansion of slavery, was the white U.S. Republican candidate in the presidential election of 1856, winning 11 states. William Dayton (1807–64) was the white U.S. vice-presidential nominee.

252 *'rule or ruin'*: Douglass would have been familiar with Lincoln's use of this phrase in his Cooper Union Address on 27 February 1860, where he accused white Southern Democrats of wanting to 'destroy the Government, unless you be allowed to construe and enforce the Constitution as you please, on all points in dispute between you and us. You will rule or ruin in all events.'

*the cowardly and brutal assault . . . from South Carolina.*: white U.S. civil rights campaigner Charles Sumner was caned in the Senate chamber by white U.S. politician Preston Brooks of South Carolina on 22 May 1856, after listening to Sumner's antislavery 'Crime against Kansas' speech.

252 *Stephen A. Douglas*: (1813–61), white U.S. senator for Illinois and a key architect of the 1850 compromise measures.

'*Union could not long endure . . . extinction of slavery.*': Douglass paraphrases Abraham Lincoln's 'House Divided Speech', delivered on 16 June 1858.

253 *Pilate . . . made friends*: Luke 23:12.

"*shot . . . distilment*": *Hamlet* I.v.63–4.

256 "*There can be . . . to the wicked*": Isaiah 57:21.

"*thou art . . . thy brother*": Genesis 42:21.

*President Pierce*: Franklin Pierce (1804–69), white U.S. politician and fourteenth president of the U.S. (1853–7).

*James Buchanan*: (1791–1868), white U.S. politician and fifteenth president of the U.S. (1857–61).

258 *Henry Clay Pate*: (1832–64), white U.S. marshal and captain in the Missouri militia.

259 *General Read*: John W. Reid (1821–81), white U.S. soldier in the Missouri militia.

*John C. Breckenridge*: (1821–75), white U.S. Democratic politician and vice-president of the U.S. (1857–61), he advocated for the protection of slavery in new territories. White U.S. politician Stephen Douglas insisted upon the 'popular vote' principle.

260 *William H. Seward*: (1801–72), white U.S. senator for New York and later Lincoln's Secretary of State. Douglass refers here to Seward's speech to the U.S. Senate on 29 February 1860 in which he advocated for a compromise between antislavery and pro-slavery factions.

261 *Robert E. Lee*: (1807–70), later commander of the Confederate States Army during the Civil War.

*Governor Wise*: Henry Alexander Wise (1806–76), white U.S. governor of Virginia from 1856 to 1860.

*Samuel G. Howe*: (1801–76), Boston-based white U.S. abolitionist, physician, and leader of the New England Asylum for the Blind in Watertown, Massachusetts. One of the 'Secret Six' who funded Brown's raid on Harpers Ferry (the others being white U.S. supporters Thomas Wentworth Higginson, Theodore Parker, Franklin Sanborn, Gerrit Smith, and George Stearns).

*Frank P. Sanborn*: (1831–1917), white U.S. journalist and social reformer.

262 *Thomas J. Dorsey*: (1810–75), born into slavery in Maryland, Thomas Joshua Dorsey effected his self-liberation and went on to live a new life in Philadelphia as a renowned chef, activist, and social justice campaigner.

*Ottilia Assing*: (1819–84), a German-born philosopher, journalist, and activist who emigrated to the U.S. in 1852 and became Douglass' long-term collaborator and friend.

264 *Mr. Cook*: John Edwin Cook (1830–59), white U.S. participant in the Harpers Ferry raid, was arrested and implicated several of Brown's supporters, including Douglass.

269 *Colonel Forbes*: Hugh Forbes (1808–92), British-born soldier and mercenary.

*Horace Greeley*: (1811–72), white U.S. journalist, reformer, and politician, Greeley was the founder and editor of the New York *Tribune* newspaper.

270 *'Shields Green'*: born into slavery as Esau Brown (*c.*1834–59), Green secured his self-liberation in 1856, meeting Douglass and Brown in 1858. Green joined the Harpers Ferry revolutionary campaign led by Brown and was subsequently captured and executed.

272 *Jeremiah Anderson*: (1833–59), a white U.S. abolitionist who was killed during the raid on Harpers Ferry. Douglass is in fact referring to Osborne Perry Anderson (1830–72), a Black activist and author who survived the raid and wrote an account of his experience, *A Voice from Harpers Ferry* (1861).

274 *attempt . . . Napoleon III*: Napoleon III survived an assassination attempt in Paris by the Italian revolutionary Felice Orsini on 14 January 1858.

*Annie*: Annie Douglass (1849–60), the Douglass' youngest daughter.

275 *Brown's gallows . . . being fulfilled*: in his speech 'Courage', delivered on 7 November 1859, Emerson asserted that Brown 'will make the gallows glorious like the cross'.

*the John Brown song*: 'John Brown's Body', first published in 1861.

*'principalities nor . . . things to come'*: Romans 8:38.

278 *the triumphant election of Abraham Lincoln*: Lincoln was elected president on 6 November 1860.

280 *The old pro-slavery . . . was revived*: at an anti-slavery rally in Boston's Faneuil Hall, on 26 September 1835, Garrison's printing press was destroyed and he was attacked.

281 *Mr. Ireson of Georgia*: Alfred Iverson (1798–1873), white U.S. senator from Georgia.

284 *"Erring sisters, depart in peace"*: in a letter on 3 March 1861 to white U.S. politician, William Seward, soon to be Lincoln's Secretary of State, white U.S. General Winfield Scott (1786–1866) laid out Lincoln's options for dealing with the secessionist South: one of which was 'wayward sisters, depart in peace!'

*General McClellan*: George Brinton McClellan (1826–85), white U.S. commander of the Army of the Potomac from July 1861 to November 1862, when Lincoln dismissed him from his post. McClellan would unsuccessfully run against Lincoln for the presidency in the 1864 election.

*General Butler*: Benjamin Franklin Butler (1818–93), white U.S. Union army general and, later, politician and governor of Massachusetts.

285 *the emancipation proclamation . . . was withdrawn*: in August 1861 John Charles Frémont (1813–90), white U.S. military commander in the Union

army, had issued an emancipation proclamation liberating the enslaved people living in Missouri without consulting Lincoln.

287 *the 54th and 55th*: the 54th Massachusetts Volunteer Infantry, a Black combat regiment, was founded in January 1863, and would eventually number over 1,000 Black men in its ranks. The 55th was founded in June 1863.

288 *Denmark Vessey*: Denmark Vesey (*c.*1767–1822), a self-liberated leader of a planned revolution of enslaved people in Charleston, South Carolina. Vesey was captured and executed by a white U.S. government in June 1822.

*Copeland*: John Anthony Copeland, Jr (1836–59), a free-born freedom-fighter, social justice campaigner, and a leading figure in John Brown's revolutionary attack on Harpers Ferry for which he was executed on 16 December 1859.

289 *Charles and Lewis*: Lewis Henry Douglass (1840–1908) and Charles Remond Douglass (1844–1920).

*Col. Shaw*: Robert Gould Shaw (1837–63), white U.S. commander of the 54th Massachusetts Volunteer Infantry. Shaw was killed at the Battle of Fort Wagner in July 1863.

291 *Jefferson Davis*: (1808–89), white U.S. president of the Confederate States of America (1861–5).

292 '*Hold, enough!*': *Macbeth* V.viii.34.

THE BLACK MAN . . . WHITE HOUSE: Douglass' meeting with Lincoln at the White House was on 10 August 1863.

294 '*the bubble . . . cannon's mouth*': *As You Like It* II.vii.151–2.

*Secretary Stanton*: Edwin M. Stanton (1814–69), white U.S. Secretary of War.

295 *Assistant Secretary Dana . . . New York*: Tribune: white U.S. author Charles A. Dana (1819–97) met Douglass in 1843, when Dana was a member of the utopian Brook Farm community in West Roxbury, Massachusetts. Dana would go on to be the managing editor of the New York *Tribune* newspaper, and then assistant Secretary of War in Lincoln's administration.

*Frederick*: Frederick Douglass, Jr (1842–92).

298 *Anna E. Dickinson*: (1842–1932), white U.S. abolitionist, lecturer, and social reformer.

*J. Sella Martin*: (1832–76), a self-liberated radical abolitionist, freedom-fighter, social justice campaigner, author, editor, orator, preacher, and a close Douglass family friend and collaborator in the freedom struggle.

*William Wells Brown*: (1814–84), born into slavery in Kentucky, he went on to become a leading antislavery campaigner, social justice reformer, autobiographer, historian, dramatist, essayist, travel-writer, and orator.

*Remembering those . . . with them*: Hebrews 13:3.

'*Sound the loud . . . people are free.*': Douglass quotes the first two lines of 'Sound the loud timbrel', by the Irish poet Thomas Moore (1779–1852).

'*liberty throughout . . . all the inhabitants thereof*': Leviticus 25:10. The words are also inscribed on the Liberty Bell, symbol of U.S. independence, in Philadelphia.

300 *this cowardly . . . in July, 1863*: the New York draft riots of 13–16 July, in which white working-class men's anger at laws to draft them into the Civil War as soldiers had unimaginably traumatizing and murderous consequences. During this period, white inhumane and barbaric mobs committed illegal acts of violence, murder, torture, abuse, and atrocity against hundreds of Black women, men, and children of all ages living in the city.

301 *Gen. U. S. Grant*: Ulysses S. Grant (1822–85), white U.S. commander of the Union Army from 1864, and later elected eighteenth president of the U.S. (1869–77).

*President Lincoln . . . on the situation.*: Douglass' second meeting with Lincoln at the White House took place on 19 August 1864.

305 *William the Silent*: William I of Orange (1533–84), the Protestant leader of the Dutch revolt in 1568 against the Spanish Habsburg empire. Douglass had first delivered a lengthy lecture on this figure in 1869.

*Chief Justice Chase*: Salmon P. Chase (1808–73), white Chief Justice of the U.S. (1864–73).

306 '*The judgements . . . righteous altogether.*': Psalm 19:9. Also cited by Lincoln in his second inaugural address on 4 March 1865. Douglass in turn quotes from Lincoln's address in the next paragraph.

307 *Andrew Johnson*: (1808–75), white U.S. vice-president of the U.S. and subsequently the seventeenth president (1865–9) following the assassination of Lincoln.

308 '*they all . . . to make excuse*': Luke 14:18.

310 *murder of Elijah P. Lovejoy*: Elijah Parish Lovejoy (1802–37) was a white U.S. abolitionist killed in Alton, Illinois, while defending his printing press from an anti-abolitionist mob. On 7 December 1837 white U.S. politician Wendell Phillips spoke in defense on Lovejoy's actions at a meeting in Faneuil Hall.

*Henry Wilson*: (1812–75), white U.S. senator for Massachusetts and later vice-president of the U.S. (1873–5).

*Robert C. Winthrop*: (1809–94), white U.S. politician, lawyer, and philanthropist, president of the Massachusetts Historical Society from 1855 to 1885.

311 '*gates . . . night and day*': paraphrase of Isaiah 60:11.

312 *The recently-attempted . . . James Abraham Garfield*: Garfield (1831–81), white twentieth president of the U.S. from March to September 1881, was shot by white U.S. assassin Charles J. Guiteau on 2 July 1881, dying on 19 September 1881.

313 '*touch of nature made us*': paraphrase of *Troilus and Cressida* III.iii.175.

314 *the organic law of the land*: with the ratification of the Thirteenth Amendment to the U.S. Constitution in December 1865, slavery was legally abolished.

*'Othello's occupation was gone.'*: *Othello* III.iii.357.

*John Tyler's cabinet*: John Tyler (1790–1862), tenth, white president of the U.S. (1841–5) and strong supporter of states' rights.

316 *Doctor Prichard's 'Natural History of Man'*: James Cowles Prichard (1786–1848) was a British doctor and ethnologist whose multi-volume work, *Researches into the Physical History of Man* (1813–47), argues for the initial unity of the human species that had subsequently become permanently divided.

*Dr. R. G. Latham*: Robert Gordon Latham (1812–88), British ethnologist, whose *Man and His Migrations* (1851) explored the source of African languages.

*Dr. Morton, the famous archæologist*: Samuel George Morton (1799–1851), U.S. ethnologist whose book *Crania Americana; or, A Comparative View of the Skulls of Various Aboriginal Nations of North and South America* (1839) proposed a polygenesis theory of human emergence; i.e. each race was created separately and were therefore distinct species.

*Messrs. Nott and Glidden*: Josiah Nott (1804–73), white southern U.S. surgeon, and George R. Gliddon (1809–57), white U.S. Egyptologist, whose co-authored book *Types of Mankind* (1854) argued for polygenism and endorsed white racist arguments arguing for Black inferiority.

*'Self-made Men'*: Douglass' popular lecture 'The Trials and Triumphs of Self-Made Men', first delivered in 1859.

321 *Doctor Godwin . . . baptize a negro*: Morgan Godwyn (1640–c.1686), Anglican minister and missionary in Virginia and Barbados, whose *The Negro's & Indian's Advocate* (1680) advocated for the spiritual instruction of enslaved people.

325 *Thomas H. Hendricks*: Thomas Andrew Hendricks (1819–85), white U.S. senator for Indiana (and later vice-president of the U.S.).

*Senators Revels and Bruce*: Hiram Rhodes Revels (1822–1901) was the first Black U.S. senator, representing Mississippi from 1870 to 1871; and Blanche Kelso Bruce (1841–98) was the first Black U.S. senator to serve a full term, representing Mississippi from 1875 to 1881.

326 *Oliver P. Morton* (1823–77), white U.S. Republican politician, Indiana senator and governor.

328 *Theodore Tilton*: (1835–1907), white U.S. journalist, poet, abolitionist, and reformer, Tilton was editor of the New York *Independent* newspaper from 1862 to 1871. In 1895 Tilton published *Sonnets to the Memory of Frederick Douglass*. Tilton was one of Douglass' close personal friends and supporters.

329 *Mrs. Amanda Sears*: Arianna Amanda Auld Sears (1826–78).

333 *the great amendment to the Constitution*: the Fourteenth Amendment to the U.S. Constitution declared that 'All persons born or naturalized in the United States, and subject to the jurisdiction thereof, are citizens of the United States and of the State wherein they reside'. It was adopted on 9 July 1868. The Fifteenth Amendment stated that 'The right of citizens of the United States to vote shall not be denied or abridged by the United States or by any State on account of race, color, or previous condition of servitude'. It was ratified on 3 February 1870.

334 *'could tear a passion . . . ear of groundlings'*: *Hamlet* III.ii.9–10.

335 *a large weekly newspaper*: the *New Era*, with Douglass as its corresponding editor, began weekly publication on 13 January 1870.

*New National Era*: the newspaper, managed by Douglass' sons Lewis Henry and Frederick Douglass Jr, went out of business on 22 October 1874.

336 *'Freedmen's Savings and Trust Company'*: a bank established in 1865 to assist the economic development of recently emancipated Black communities. Following the economic panic of 1873, Douglass agreed to become the bank's president, loaning it $10,000. The bank closed the following year.

337 *'the half had not been told me'*: Douglass paraphrases 1 Kings 10:7.

340 *'some drugs . . . some mighty magic'*: *Othello* I.iii.94–5.

*'to restore fourfold . . . taken aught'*: Douglass paraphrases Luke 19:8.

342 *Those who knew . . . that question*: Douglass was appointed by white U.S. President Ulysses S. Grant in 1871 as assistant secretary to a commission to the Dominican Republic charged with reporting on the likelihood of annexation to the United States. White U.S. Senator Charles Sumner was vehemently opposed to such a move.

*filibustering expeditions*: Douglass refers to white U.S. soldier and politician John Quitman (1790–858), who planned to invade Cuba in 1853–4, and white U.S. lawyer and journalist William Walker (1824–60), who attempted the same in Nicaragua.

344 *Messrs. Wade, Howe and White*: Benjamin F. Wade (1800–78), former white U.S. senator for Ohio; Samuel Gridley Howe (1801–76), white U.S. physician and social reformer; and Andrew Dickson White (1832–1918), white U.S. educator and first president of Cornell University.

345 *upper house . . . District of Columbia*: in April 1871 President Ulysses S. Grant appointed Douglass to the Council of the District of Columbia. He resigned from the post in July of that year.

347 *but may my "right hand . . . the roof of my mouth"*: a paraphrase of Psalms 137: 5–6.

*agony of blood, like France*: Douglass refers to the defeat of the French army during the Franco-Prussian War (1870–1).

*In the month . . . in New Orleans*: Douglass was appointed president of the National Convention of the Colored People, meeting in New Orleans from 10 to 13 April 1872.

347 *Mr. Schurz*: Carl Schurz (1829–1906), a German-born white emigrant to the U.S., soldier, U.S. senator from Missouri, and a key figure in the emergence of the Liberal Republican Party. This party opposed President Grant and his policies of Reconstruction and called for an amnesty for ex-Confederate states.

*Horace Greeley*: Greeley won the nomination of the Liberal Republican Party for the 1872 presidential election. At the Democratic Party national convention, white U.S. newspaper editor and political leader Greeley was also nominated, rather than risk splitting the anti-Grant vote. Grant was comfortably re-elected in the November poll.

349 *'triple steel'*: Douglass quotes John Milton, *Paradise Lost*, Book 2, line 569.

*Ebenezer Bassett*: (1833–1908), a renowned Black educator, civil rights campaigner, radical abolitionist, and social justice campaigner. He served as Principal of the Institute for Colored Youth in Philadelphia after which he was appointed as U.S. Ambassador to Haiti between 1869 and 1877.

*John Mercer Langston*: (1829–97), born free in Virginia and who was an attorney, theologian, and civil rights campaigner appointed by white U.S. President Hayes as U.S. Minister to Haiti in 1877, he would later become the first Black person elected to Congress from his home state of Virginia.

350 *Lincoln monument*: the Emancipation Memorial, also known as the Freedman's Memorial, was a public sculpture created in 1876 by white U.S. artist Thomas Ball. In this public monument, Ball depicts the bent over figure of an unnamed enslaved man whom he represents on one knee and shackled at the feet of the erect figure of Abraham Lincoln. Frederick Douglass was bitterly opposed to Ball's white racist reimagining of an enslaved man. He indignantly called for a more 'manly' memorialization not only of this figure but of all Black male subjects in fine art as an urgent and necessary antidote to any and all such white racist derogatory images which he despised and denounced all his life.

351 *United States Marshal of the District of Columbia*: Douglass was appointed to this office in March 1877, serving until 1881. The role involved supporting the federal judiciary process.

*Roscoe Conkling*: (1829–88), Republican politician and supporter of Reconstruction.

352 *its ridiculous features*: Douglass' lecture 'Our National Capital' included his searing and incisive criticisms of the white racist and white supremacist attitudes that were dominant within Washington, D.C.'s white population and which he held morally and politically responsible for the ongoing injustices and inequalities committed against all African American U.S. citizens.

*International Exhibition in Philadelphia*: Douglass attended the dedication of the site of the former Centennial exhibition as a new, permanent international exhibition space. Financial difficulties forced it to close in 1881.

353 *Under the shadow . . . all at home there.*: Douglass paraphrases white U.S. politician Daniel Webster's 17 June 1843 speech to celebrate the completion of the Bunker Hill Monument in Boston.

356 *Charles B. Purvis*: (1842–1929), physician, author, social activist and radical reformer who was the first Black doctor to head a hospital under civilian control, the Freedmen's Hospital in Washington, D.C.

   *'worthy of stripes or of bonds'*: Luke 12:47.

357 *the effort . . . the Northern States*: Douglass opposed the large number of Black people who left the Southern states in 1879 for the Midwest, as a response to ongoing acts of white racist persecution, lynchlaw, disenfranchisement, annihilation, discrimination, and murder. In an address delivered in Baltimore on 4 May 1879, 'The South Knows Us', Douglass argued that leaving the South signalled capitulation to a white U.S. nation.

358 *'milk and honey'*: Exodus 3:8.

   *Elizabeth Thompson*: Elizabeth Rowell Thompson (1821–99), white U.S. philanthropist and temperance reformer.

   *Carpenter's . . . Emancipation Proclamation'*: an 1864 painting by white U.S. artist Francis Bicknell Carpenter (1830–1900), now on display in the U.S. Capitol building.

   *Social Science Congress at Saratoga*: Douglass' paper 'The Negro Exodus from the Gulf States' was read at the meeting by his friend, white U.S. educator, and religious leader Francis Wayland, and published the following year in the *Journal of Social Science*.

359 *some bloodthirsty Legree*: a reference to Simon Legree, a white enslaver in Harriet Beecher Stowe's novel *Uncle Tom's Cabin* (1852).

   *"the Star of Empire takes its way"*: Douglass misquotes the often-cited phrase 'the course of empire takes its way', first found in Irish author George Berkeley's poem 'On the Prospect of Planting Arts and Learning in America' (1752).

366 *to come to the side of his dying bed*: Douglass made this visit on 17 June 1877.

367 *four different languages*: Douglass' *Narrative* was translated into Dutch in 1846 and into French in 1848. *My Bondage and My Freedom* appeared in German in 1860.

368 *not that I loved Caesar less, but Rome more*: *Julius Caesar* III.ii.21–2.

369 *the Spring of 1825*: in fact Douglass left for Baltimore in March the following year.

   *James Beacham built a large frigate*: the ship-building firm of J. S. Beacham and Brothers built the frigate *Baltimore* for the Brazilian navy in 1826.

   *His death . . . announced in the papers*: in fact Auld did not die until 8 February 1880.

370 *12th of June*: Douglass revisited the Wye homestead and site that had been the location of the labour camp of enslaved people on 12 June 1881.

574 *Explanatory Notes*

374 *Mrs. Buchanan, the widow of Admiral Buchanan*: Ann Catherine Lloyd Buchanan (1808–92), daughter of Edward Lloyd V and wife of Franklin Buchanan (1800–74), white U.S. confederate navy admiral.

375 *Storer College*: a school established in 1865 to train Black teachers, it closed in 1955.

*Andrew J. Hunter*: Andrew H. Hunter (1804–88), white U.S. district attorney for Jefferson County, Virginia, who drafted the indictment against John Brown.

379 *Herald of Freedom*: abolitionist bi-weekly newspaper published in Concord, New Hampshire, between 1835 and 1846.

381 *'The foxes have holes . . . lay His head'*: Matthew 8:20.

*'Moses Norris'*: (1799–1855), white U.S. Democratic politician representing New Hampshire in the House and Senate.

*George Storrs*: (1796–1879), white U.S. Methodist minister and abolitionist prosecuted by Moses Norris in 1836 for preaching against slavery.

383 *Sarah Jane Clark*: Sara Jane Lippincott (née Clarke) (1823–1904), a white U.S. author, journalist, and reformer who wrote under the pseudonym Grace Greenwood. She copyedited the first serialized version of *Uncle Tom's Cabin* for the *National Era* newspaper.

*John P. Hale*: (1806–73), white U.S. congressman from New Hampshire who helped found the anti-slavery Free Soil Party.

384 *Robert G. Ingersoll*: Robert Green Ingersoll (1833–99), white U.S. lawyer, writer, and reformer who served in the Union army and became one of the most popular orators of his time. He was a celebrated advocate of atheism.

388 *'Tide at its flood'*: paraphrase of *Julius Caesar* IV.iii.249–50.

389 *James McCune Smith*: (1813–65), a Black physician, essayist, author, philosopher, political reformer, and radical abolitionist. He attended the Free African School in New York city and, after he was denied admission to medical schools in New York state, he gained his medical degree from the University of Glasgow, Scotland. He was one of Douglass' close collaborators and friends and he authored an introduction to his second autobiography, *My Bondage and My Freedom*, published in 1855.

391 *Lucretia Mott*: (1793–1880), white U.S. Quaker, women's rights campaigner, and abolitionist.

*Lydia Maria Child*: (1802–80), white U.S. abolitionist, social reformer, novelist, and journalist, whose 1833 book *An Appeal in Favor of that Class of Americans Called Africans* argued for immediate emancipation.

392 *Sarah and Angelina Grimke*: Sarah Moore Grimké (1792–1873) and Angelina Grimké (1805–79), white U.S. abolitionists and political activists. Sarah's 'An Appeal to the Christian Women of the South' (1836) and Angelina's 'An Epistle to the Clergy of the Southern States' (1836) were powerful appeals by Southern women against slavery.

393 *the daughter of . . . Myron Holly*: Sallie Holly (1818–93), white U.S. abolitionist and teacher, founder of the Holley School in Virginia in 1869 for
the purpose of teaching African American students who had been newly
emancipated and were now legally free.

*Lucy Stone*: (1818–93), white U.S. abolitionist, social reformer, and
orator.

*Antoinette Brown*: (1825–1921), white U.S. women's rights activist,
minister, and contributor to Douglass' *The North Star* newspaper.

*Elizabeth Cady Stanton*: (1815–1902), white U.S. abolitionist and women's
rights activist, whose refusal to support the passage of the Fourteenth and
Fifteenth Amendments to the U.S. Constitution, which gave voting rights
and legal protection to Black men while white U.S. women continued to be
denied those same rights, caused a schism in the white U.S. women's
rights movement that was for the amelioration of the rights of white
U.S. women only.

398 *Professor Greener*: Richard Theodore Greener (1844–1922), free born lawyer, social justice campaigner, author, newspaper editor, and first Black
graduate of Harvard, later to become dean of Howard University School
of Law.

*President Arthur*: Chester A. Arthur (1829–86), white 21st president of the
U.S. (1881–5).

400 *'fault is not . . . we are underlings'*: *Julius Caesar* I.ii.239–40.

*'who would be free . . . strike the blow'*: George Gordon, Lord Byron, *Childe
Harold's Pilgrimage* (1812), canto II, stanza 76.

*'faith is . . . not seen'*: Hebrews 11:1.

405 *'divinity which . . . we will'*: *Hamlet* V.ii.10–11.

409 *A spade . . . you will*: Thomas Hood (1799–1845), 'The Lay of the Laborer'
(1844), ll.1–4.

410 *'Let the Union slide.'*: in a letter to president-elect Lincoln in December
1860, white U.S. journalist Horace Greeley wrote: 'Let the Union slide—it
may be reconstructed.'

*fourteenth day of April, 1866*: Douglass means 1865.

412 *Six-and-forty years ago*: the Slavery Abolition Act came into force across
the British Empire (with the exception of territories overseen by the East
India Company, Ceylon/Sri Lanka, and Saint Helena) on 1 August 1834.

413 *'When a deed is done . . . from East to West.'*: first lines of James Russell
Lowell's poem 'The Present Crisis' (1845).

416 *William Edward Forster*: (1818–86), British industrialist, philanthropist,
and politician.

*permitted Alabamas to escape from British ports*: the *Alabama*, a confederate
raider ship, built in Birkenhead, England, attacked Union naval and
merchant shipping during the Civil War.

426 *Ten years ago*: the first U.S. edition of *Life and Times* was published in 1881. The additional third part was published in 1892.

*Dickens*: Charles Dickens (1812–70), British fiction writer and journalist.

*Carlyle*: Thomas Carlyle (1795–1881), Scottish historian and philosopher.

427 *Humboldt*: Alexander Von Humboldt (1769–1859), Prussian geographer, naturalist, and explorer.

*Cuvier*: Georges Cuvier (1769–1832), French anatomist and biologist.

*Darwin*: Charles Darwin (1809–82), British naturalist, famous for his contribution to the theory of evolution.

428 *Why did I marry . . . my mother's complexion?*: Douglass married Helen Pitts (1838–1903), a white activist and author, in 1884.

*No man liveth . . . unto himself.*: Romans 14:7.

430 *Frederick May Holland*: Fredric May Holland (1836–1908), Unitarian minister and author, who wrote the seminal biography, *Frederick Douglass: The Colored Orator* (1891). This biography received Douglass' personal commendation for its accuracy.

437 *Randolph Tucker*: John Randolph Tucker (1823–97), white Virginian lawyer and politician, and staunch defender in Congress of Southern states rights.

*Owen Lovejoy*: (1811–64), white U.S. lawyer, abolitionist and congressman, conductor on the underground railroad, and brother of the murdered abolitionist Elijah Parish Lovejoy.

438 *Mr. Blaine*: James G. Blaine (1830–93), two-times white U.S. Secretary of State and unsuccessful Republican nominee for the presidency, narrowly defeated by white U.S. politician Grover Cleveland in 1884.

439 *Recorder of Deeds for the District of Columbia*: the agent responsible for tax collection in the District of Columbia. Douglass held this post from 1881 to 1886.

443 *Grover Cleveland*: (1837–1908), 22nd and 24th president of the U.S. (1885–9 and 1893–7).

446 *The dawn . . . rapine and murder.*: a reference to 'the force bill of 1875', introduced into the House of Representatives by Republicans and designed to protect Black voting rights. The bill passed in the House but was defeated in the Senate through the combined votes of Democrats and moderate Republicans.

447 *'Rum, Romanism, and Rebellion'*: a political slogan, first used at a campaign meeting of Protestant clergy in New York City in October 1884, at which James Blaine was present. It was directed at supporters of the Democratic party who were painted as drinkers, Catholic, and Irish-American.

449 *Civil Rights law of 1875*: the Civil Rights Act of 1875, designed to ensure equal treatment for all Black U.S. citizens on public transport and in public accommodations, was signed into law on 1 March 1875. In 1883 the Supreme Court, by a vote of 8–1, judged it to be unconstitutional, arguing

that Congress had no right to prevent discrimination by private individuals or organizations.

*'shake hands over the bloody chasm'*: a reference to white U.S. journalist Horace Greeley's May 1872 letter accepting the Liberal Republican party's nomination for the presidency, in which he asserted that 'the masses of our countrymen . . . are eager to clasp hands across the bloody chasm which has too long divided them'.

450 *Judge Harlan*: John Marshall Harlan (1833–1911), white U.S. Supreme Court judge (1877–1911), who gave the only dissenting vote in the Civil Rights Act of 1875 decision.

451 *'When a deed is done . . . from east to west.'*: the opening lines of James Russell Lowell's 'The Present Crisis' (1844).

457 *When we came to the clause of the Constitution*: Douglass refers to, and goes on to quote from, Article 1 Section 9 of Constitution of the United States.

462 *'waving the bloody shirt'*: a slogan used during election campaigns against political opponents deemed responsible for the bloodshed of the Civil War.

466 *William E. Gladstone*: (1809–98), British politician, four-times Prime Minister (1868–74; 1880–5; 1886; 1892–4).

*Mr. Balfour*: Arthur James Balfour (1848–1930), Conservative politician and Prime Minister (1902–5), at this time Chief Secretary for Ireland.

*Irish Force Bill*: the Criminal Law and Procedure (Ireland) Act, passed in July 1887, giving the authorities greater powers against agrarian violence that sought to secure fair rent and tenure for tenant farmers.

*Richard Webb*: Richard Davis Webb (1805–72), Irish publisher, abolitionist, and co-founder of the Hibernian Antislavery Association. Webb helped to organize Douglass' speaking engagements in Ireland at the end of 1845, and published a Dublin edition of his *Narrative of the Life of Frederick Douglass, An American Slave* in 1846.

*Richard Allen*: (1803–86), Irish abolitionist and philanthropist, co-founder of the Hibernian Antislavery Association.

*James Haughton*: (1795–1873), Irish reformer and temperance activist, co-founder of the Hibernian Antislavery Association.

467 *'Train up . . . depart from it.'*: Proverbs 22:6.

469 *Fontainebleau*: the Château de Fontainebleau, 34 miles south-east of Paris, the building of which was begun under the reign of French monarch Francis I in *c.*1528.

*the Republic*: French Third Republic (1870–1940).

470 *Bossuet*: Jacques-Benigne Bossuet (1627–1704), French theologian, orator, and bishop.

*St. Bernard*: Saint Bernard of Clairvaux (*c.*1090–1153), French abbot influential in the development of the Cistercian order of monks and nuns.

473 *Château D'If*: French fortress situated on an island in the Mediterranean sea, made famous as a setting in Alexandre Dumas's novel *The Count of Monte Cristo* (1844).

475 *Paganini*: Niccolò Paganini (1782–1840), celebrated violinist and composer.

*'It is not the thing said . . . that is important.'*: Douglass paraphrases white U.S. author and philosopher Ralph Waldo Emerson's essay 'Goethe, or the Writer' (1850): 'It makes a great difference to the force of any sentence whether there be a man behind it or no.'

476 *the spacious Forum*: location of important government buildings at the centre of ancient Rome. Much of the excavation and clearing of the Forum took place in the nineteenth century.

*Cicero poured out . . . and against Antony*: the Roman orator and statesman Cicero (106–43 BCE) delivered speeches against the insurrection led by Lucius Sergius Catalina in 63 BCE, and later spoke in opposition to Mark Antony, leading to Antony ordering his death.

*Palatine*: one of the seven hills of Rome.

477 *Pantheon*: a Roman temple, built in 113–25.

*'Simple, erect . . . Pride of Rome!'*: Douglass quotes Lord Byron's poem *Childe Harold's Pilgrimage* (1818), canto 4, stanza 146.

*Gibbon*: Edward Gibbon (1737–94), British historian and politician, author of *The History of the Decline and Fall of the Roman Empire* (1776–88).

*Titus*: the Arch of Titus (*c*.81), built to commemorate the victory of Emperor Titus against rebellions in Roman-controlled Judea.

*Column of Trajan*: completed in 113, the column celebrates Emperor Trajan's victory in the Dacian Wars in the what are now the Balkans. Napoleon I's column was erected in 1810, in imitation, in the Place Vendôme in Paris. The original column was taken down in 1871, before being rebuilt three years later.

478 *'It looks, it speaks, it acts.'*: Douglass quotes from white U.S. politician Daniel Webster's speech at the dedication of the Bunker Hill monument in Charlestown, Massachusetts, in 1843.

*indulgences*: offered or sold to Catholics to reduce the level of punishment for the committing of sins.

*Luther*: Martin Luther (1483–1546), German theologian, key figure in the Reformation that rejected many of the practices and teachings of the Catholic church.

479 *Pincian Hill*: one of the seven hills of Rome.

*Janiculum*: second-tallest hill in Rome, but not one of the seven hills.

*Campagna*: extensive area of countryside surrounding Rome, used for farming in the nineteenth century and the frequent subject of landscape paintings during the period.

*St. Peter's*: St. Peter's Basilica in the Vatican, completed in 1626, with a dome designed by Michelangelo.

483 *We find here . . . of English policy.*: British colonization of Egypt began in 1882, at the conclusion of the Anglo-Egyptian War of that year.

484 *'Backsheesh! Backsheesh! Backsheesh!'*: a request for a tip.

    *Khedive*: Persian term for the viceroy of Egypt.

486 *the shâdûf and the sâkiyeh*: Egyptian irrigation devices.

489 *Elizabeth Barrett Browning*: (1806–61), British poet who, with her husband Robert Browning, moved to Italy in 1846.

492 *John Sherman*: (1823–1900), white U.S. politician and younger brother of the white U.S. Civil War Union general William Tecumseh Sherman.

493 *Mugwump party*: political term to describe those who declined to support the Republican presidential candidacy of white U.S. politician James G. Blaine in 1884.

494 *'What doth it . . . lose one's soul?'*: paraphrase of Mark 8:36.

496 *President Harrison*: Benjamin Harrison (1833–1901), white twenty-third president of the U.S. (1889–93).

497 *President Hyppolite*: Louis Mondestin Florvil Hyppolite (1827–96), president of Haiti from 1889 to 1896.

    *Môle St. Nicolas*: a geographical region located on the north-west coast of Haiti that the U.S. government sought to lease as a 'naval station'.

    *Rear-Admiral Gherardi*: Bancroft Gherardi (1832–1903), white U.S. commander of the North Atlantic Station of the U.S. navy from 1889 to 1892.

499 *the following articles . . . October, 1891*: the articles are 'Haïti and the United States I' and 'Haïti and the United States II'.

504 *Mr. Firmin*: Anténor Joseph Firmin (1850–1911), Haitian Minister of Finance, Commerce, and Foreign Affairs.

516 *World's Columbian Exposition*: Chicago exposition, from May to October 1893, celebrating the 400th anniversary of Columbus' arrival in the Americas.

## APPENDIX: LESSONS OF THE HOUR

524 *the pestilence . . . the darkness*: Psalms 91:6.

526 *Bishop Haygood*: Atticus Greene Haygood (1839–96), a white U.S. bishop of the Methodist Episcopal Church, South and author of Our Brother in Black (1881). Douglass quotes from Haygood's article 'The Black Shadow in the South', published in *Forum* in October 1893.

    *ex-Governor Chamberlain*: Daniel Henry Chamberlain (1837–1907), white U.S. captain in the Fifth Massachusetts Regiment, the Black combat unit in which Douglass' son Charles Remond Douglass also served, and subsequently governor of South Carolina (1874–6).

    *an article of mine . . . 'North American Review'*: Douglass' 'Lynch Law in the South', published in the July 1892 number of the *North American Review*.

    *Miss Frances Willard, of the W.C.T.U.*: Frances Elizabeth Caroline Willard (1839–98), white U.S. educator, temperance reformer, and women's suffragist, became national president of the Woman's Christian Temperance Union in 1879.

526  *'I pity the Southerner . . . their own roof tree.'*: published in the *New York Voice*, a weekly pro-prohibition newspaper, on 23 October 1890.

527  *Bishop Fitzgerald*: Oscar Penn Fitzgerald (1829–1911), a white U.S. bishop of the Methodist Episcopal Church, South.

   *'Let no guilty man escape.'*: white U.S. President Ulysses S. Grant's 1875 response to the uncovering of financial corruption in the collection of federal tax revenue from numerous whiskey distilleries.

528  *'False in one, false in all.'*: the Latin legal phrase *Falsus in uno, falsus in omnibus.*

   *Prof. Weeks*: Stephen Beauregard Weeks (1865–1918), white U.S. North Carolina historian who spoke on 9 August 1893 on Black suffrage in the South at the World's Columbian Exposition, supporting efforts by southern states to disenfranchise Black U.S. citizens.

530  *condign*: deserved, worthy.

533  *Hamburg*: the Hamburg Massacre, in South Carolina in July 1876, saw white armed men besiege and overcome a Black militia company in Hamburg, a town populated largely by free Black citizens. Twenty-five of the company were captured and five were killed. The white perpetrators were never prosecuted.

   *Yazoo*: on 1 September 1875 a largely Black Republican meeting in Yazoo City, Mississippi, was broken up by white armed Democrats, causing the death of one participant and injuries to three others.

   *New Orleans*: the New Orleans massacre of 30 July 1866, at which a group of armed white men, including police officers, attacked Black Republican marchers at the Louisiana Constitutional Convention, protesting against the state's measures to prevent Black suffrage. Approximately 40 people were killed.

   *Copiah*: Douglass refers to a number of attacks against the Black community and white reformers by white armed Democrat supporters in 1883 in Copiah County, Mississippi.

534  *Chief Justice Taney . . . bound to respect*: Roger B. Taney (1777–1864), white U.S. enslaver and fifth Chief Justice of the U.S., author of the majority opinion in the Dred Scott decision (1857) denying Blacks citizenship rights under the Constitution. Douglass quotes from the opinion.

536  *While I join . . . the negro.*: Douglass' attack on the white racist discriminatory practices in evidence at the Chicago World's fair is set out in his essay 'Inauguration of the World's Columbian Exposition' (1893).

537  *The great measure . . . a failure.*: Douglass refers to the Fifteenth Amendment, ratified in 1870, which enshrined the right to vote for all citizens—defined at this time as men—regardless of 'race, color, or previous condition of servitude'.

*John J. Ingalls*: John James Ingalls (1833–1900), white U.S. senator from Kansas.

*government of the people . . . for all the people*: the final line of Lincoln's Gettysburg Address (1863).

*Much learning . . . them mad.*: Acts 26:24.

538 *John Sherman*: (1823–1900), white U.S. founder of the Republican party in Ohio and later its U.S. senator.

*General Harrison*: Benjamin Harrison (1833–1901), white twenty-third president of the U.S. (1889–93).

*Senator Hoar*: George Frisbie Hoar (1826–1904), white U.S. senator from Massachusetts.

*Henry Cabot Lodge*: (1850–1924), white U.S. Republican congressman from Massachusetts and co-author of the Federal Elections Bill (1890), guaranteeing federal protection for Black voting rights.

*Governor McKinley*: William McKinley (1843–1901), white U.S. governor of Ohio and later twenty-fifth president of the U.S. (1897–1901).

539 *The pit of hell . . . bottomless.*: Revelation 9:2.

540 *The late election . . . to its first born.*: the defeat of Benjamin Harrison, white U.S. candidate, in the presidential election of 1892 was nevertheless accompanied by slight Republican gains in congressional seats. Even so Republicans were in the minority in both the Senate and House.

542 *Lady Macbeth's hand*: Macbeth V.i.26–40.

543 *new wine . . . of slavery*: Luke 5:33–9.

544 *Words are things.*: Douglass quotes from George Gordon, Lord Byron's poem 'Don Juan' (1819–24), canto 3, stanza 88.

545 *In the great city . . . cause of the war*: Douglass refers to the New York City draft riots of 13–16 July 1863. See note to p. 384.

*Even the noble . . . cause of the war*: on 14 August 1862 Lincoln met with a delegation of Black ministers to discuss the colonization of Africa at which he read from a prepared statement, including the following: 'But for your race among us there could not be war, although many men engaged on either side do not care for you one way or another' ('Address on Colonization to a Deputation of Negroes').

546 *'As we sow, we shall reap'*: Galatians 6:7.

547 *Dr. Godwin . . . baptize a negro*: Douglass refers to Morgan Godwyn (1640–c.1686), an Anglican clergyman whose advocacy of baptism for enslaved people provoked much controversy and resulted in his exile from Virginia to Barbados. His book, *The Negro's and Indian's Advocate*, was published in 1680.

*fourteenth*: the Fourteenth Amendment to the U.S. Constitution, adopted in 1868, granted citizenship rights to 'all persons born or naturalized in the United States'.

*The Oxford World's Classics Website*

**www.worldsclassics.co.uk**

- Browse the full range of Oxford World's Classics online

- Sign up for our monthly e-alert to receive information on new titles

- Read extracts from the Introductions

- Listen to our editors and translators talk about the world's greatest literature with our Oxford World's Classics audio guides

- Join the conversation, follow us on Twitter at OWC_Oxford

- Teachers and lecturers can order inspection copies quickly and simply via our website

**www.worldsclassics.co.uk**